Becoming the Beach Boys,
1961–1963

D1595946

Becoming the Beach Boys, 1961–1963

James B. Murphy

McFarland & Company, Inc., Publishers

Jefferson, North Carolina

LIBRARY OF CONGRESS CATALOGUING-IN-PUBLICATION DATA

Murphy, James B., 1956– author.
Becoming the Beach Boys, 1961–1963 / James B. Murphy.
p.   cm.
Includes bibliographical references and index.

ISBN 978-0-7864-7365-6 (softcover : acid free paper) ∞
ISBN 978-1-4766-1853-1 (ebook)

1. Beach Boys.   2. Rock musicians—United States—Biography.   I. Title.

ML421.B38M87 2015   782.42166092'2—dc23   [B]   2015013949

BRITISH LIBRARY CATALOGUING DATA ARE AVAILABLE

Cover graphics: Limited edition replica of a Pendleton
shirt as worn by the group when they were the Pendletones;
"Surfin'" on Candix 331, the Beach Boys' first 45 rpm record;
yearbook photograph, March 1962 (Torrance,
California, High School 1962 *Torch*)

Printed in the United States of America

McFarland & Company, Inc., Publishers
Box 611, Jefferson, North Carolina 28640
www.mcfarlandpub.com

For Bernadette
Only God knows what I'd be without you

Table of Contents

Acknowledgments

My goal with *Becoming the Beach Boys, 1961–1963*, was to further our understanding of the early history and recording career of the Beach Boys.

A debt of gratitude is owed to the many writers and historians who have researched and documented the Beach Boys story, contributing immeasurably to our understanding of the band. This book would not be possible without their invaluable, and often groundbreaking, work. I wish to thank: Kingsley Abbott, Eric Aniversario, Keith Badman, David Beard, Alan Boyd, Dave Burke, Peter Ames Carlin, Brian Chidester, Mark Dillon, Andrew G. Doe, Brad Elliott, Steven Gaines, Christian Haschke, Steve Hoffman, David Leaf, Mark Linett, Stephen J. McParland, Tom Nolan, Jerry Osborne, Byron Preiss, Domenic Priore, Peter Reum, Ian Rusten, Manfred Schmidt, Gene Sculati, Ken Sharp, Craig Slowinski, Jon Stebbins, Alan Taylor, John Tobler, Paul Urbahns, Timothy White, and Paul Williams.

You Need a Mess of Help

I am appreciative and humbled by the kindness of the many people willing to assist with this project. Many of the women interviewed for this book have married or changed their surnames. To avoid confusion, and with all due respect, I refer to them by the names they used during the time period of this book.

For their generous contributions I would like to extend a warm thank you to: Neil Anson (East Bakersfield High School, '63), Patrick E. Auerbach (Alumni Relations, University of Southern California), Robina Aziz (Stanislaus County Library, Modesto, California), Tony Bacon (Jawbone Press/Backbeat UK), John Baker (Hawthorne High School alumni website cougartown.com), Charles Bates (Allen County, Ohio, Historical Society), Jolie Bergman, Derek Bill, Paula Biondi-Springer, Jed Birmingham, Jeanette Berard (special collections librarian, Thousand Oaks, California, Library), Mike Bricker, Michael Browning, Neal Burdick (St. Lawrence University, Canton, New York), Sue Burin (El Camino Community College, Torrance, California), Janie Campbell (Brigham Young University), Gordon Carmadelle (American Federation of Musicians, Local 47), Karen Caruso (Prince George's County, Maryland, inter-library loan officer), Les Chan, Drew Cherven (Petoskey, Michigan, Library), Peter J. Chinnici (archivist, Marlborough School), Don Conder, Paul Coombe (Mahanoy, Pennsylvania, Area Historical Society), Jill Cox (Modesto, California, Public Library), Perry D. Cox, Karl Crawford (Greenwood Cemetery, genealogical research, Petoskey, Michigan), Eileen Crosby (Holyoke History Room and Archives, Holyoke, Massachusetts, Public Library), Dominick Jabbia (Ohio County Public Library, Wheeling,

West Virginia), Vivian Darakjian (Glendale, California, Community College), Dave Dietmeyer (1957 Ford Fairlane research), Erin Dinolfo (archivist, Rochester Institute of Technology, Rochester, New York), Walt Dixon, Andrew G. Doe, Pat Duffy (KFWB), Miranda Eggleston (National Association of Recording Arts and Sciences), Chris Fabian (New Castle, Pennsylvania, Public Library), Edward Allan Faine, Sean Fanning, Louis Farace, David Flynn (for demystifying delta numbers and record pressing plants), Mark Galloway, Michael Federspiel (Little Traverse History Museum, Petoskey, Michigan), Michael George (Torrance, California, Public Library), Michael Gillman (Sacramento Public Library), Barbara Gossett (Garden Grove, California, Historical Society), Cathy Griffith, Peg Guinan Grigalonis (Lakewood Park, Pennsylvania), Thomas B. Ham, Ken Hamm (North Bakersfield High School, '63), Jeffrey Hammett (East Bakersfield High School, '65), R. Lee Hammett (East Bakersfield High School, '63), Raymond M. "Duke" Hammett, Luke Herbst (Nashville Public Library), Paula Hill (Librarian, Christian Science Reading Room, Annapolis, Maryland), Chris Hogard (Greenwood Cemetery, Genealogical Research, Petoskey, Michigan), Randy Holmes (Kay guitar and silvertone.com), Pete Howard (postercentral.com), the estate of Robert and Regina Jensen, Gary and Wayne Johnson (Rockaway.com), Terry Johnson (East Bakersfield High School, '63), Ulf Johnsson, Jennifer Joseph (New Castle, Pennsylvania, Public Library), Noel Kalenian (Western History and Genealogy Department, Denver, Colorado, Public Library), Mark Kennedy, Susan Kersten (Bert-Co), Phil Kimball, Paul Knapp (Hawthorne Cable Television), Ellen Knight (and the document delivery team at the University of Arizona, Tucson, Arizona), Lou Kousouris (Camp Puh'Tok, Monkton, Maryland), Howard Kramer (former curatorial director, Rock and Roll Hall of Fame and Museum), Jim Kurtz, Joy Lampe (East Bakersfield High School, '63), Dani Lassetter, David Leaf, Alice Lillie (BBFUN), Jean Lythgoe (Local History and Genealogy Room, Rockford, Illinois, Public Library), Ed Martinez (El Camino Community College, Torrance, California), Terry Martinez (Redondo Union High School, Redondo Beach, California), Jimi Mastronardi (The Fame Bureau), Stephen D. McClure, Mike McIntire, Don McKeon, Susan Mester (Bowie Public Library, Maryland), Andrew Morris (American Federation of Musicians, Local 47), Kerry A. Mullaney, Bob Noguera (Strider Records, New York City, for putting it all in motion), Brian O'Beirne, Steven O'Brien, James Osborne, Cathy J. Palmer (Burbank High School alumni website), Scott Paton, Dave Peckett (*New Gandy Dancer*), Bill Petersen (La Crosse, Wisconsin, Public Library), Petoskey Museum and Historical Society, Alice Plaster (Bowie Public Library, Maryland), Norm Reeder (Torrance, California, Public Library), Peter Reum, Patrick Reynolds, Ian Rusten, Diane Sambrano (Historical Society of Centinela Valley, Westchester, California), Kathryn Santos (archivist, California State Railroad Museum Library), Dina Sheets-Roth (Four Freshmen Management, International Ventures Incorporated), Kathleen Sheppard (William Howard Taft High School, Woodland Hills, California), Craig Silsbee, Richard Silvers, Doug Simmons, Brian Stafford, Bill Ste. Marie (Bellflower High School, '63), Jon Stebbins, Gary Steelburg (William Howard Taft High School, '64), David Swain, Jeanne Teague (William Howard Taft High School, '63), Terry Thomas (Garden Grove Historical Society), Diane Thrower (Pacific High School Library, San Bernardino), Dave Towers, Robert Treff, Rebecca Troy-Horton (New Hampshire State Library), Barbara Vasquez (Los Angeles City College), Ines Walloch, Bri Webber (Inglewood Public Library), "Wolf," Chris Woods, and Claude B. Zachary (University of Southern California).

Interviews

The following people graciously granted interviews. Without their contributions, the story could not have been told and I am sincerely grateful for their assistance: Don Allen (Hawthorne High School [HHS] '63), Steve Andersen (HHS '60), Jack Andrews, Kevin Antrobus, Theresa Kara Armijo (HHS '60), Ross Barbour (the Four Freshmen), Don Barrett, Bob Barrow (HHS '60), Chuck Block, Chuck Blore, Mike Borchetta, Judy Bowles, Don Brann (HHS '63), Jerry Calkins (HHS '58), Milton Calkins (HHS '62), Vickie Amott Calkins (HHS '60), Barret H. Collins, Stephen Curtin (HHS '64), Gerry Diez, Albert Dix, Karl Engemann, Irene Callahan Fernandez (HHS '60), Bob Flanigan (the Four Freshmen), Jodi Gable, Michael Z. Gordon (the Marketts), Bill Griggs (Buddy Holly historian), Eric Groves (Roller Gardens, Wagon Wheel Junction, 1961–1963), John Hagethorn (HHS '60), Jim Hess (HHS '65), Richard Hoffman (the Vibrants), Steve Hoffman, Randy Holmes, Paul Johnson (the Belairs), Vickie Kocher (aka Victoria Hale), Dino Lappas, Bob Levey, Steve Love, Mandi Martin, Wink Martindale, David McClellan, Dick McGrane, Jackie McKnight Saner, Hessie McKnight, Richard Miailovich (USC, Class of '62), Bruce Morgan, Randy Nauert (the Challengers), Pat O'Day, Jimmy O'Neill, Cathy Palmer, Gary Peeler (the Dartells), Lana Abbey Peterson, Val Poliuto, Randy Ray (the Dartells), Russ Regan, Faye Reis, Jim Roberts (the Belairs), Joe Saraceno, Al Schlesinger, Harriet Schock, Bruce Snoap (the Kingtones), David Stadler (the Vibrants), Robert Stafford, Helen Stillman, John Tefteller, Louis Thouvenin, Paul Urbahns, Fred Vail, Patricia Valdivia, Lyn Vandegrift, Jane Veeder, Nik Venet, Jr., Ted Venetoulis, Bill Wagner, Don Winfrey (HHS '64), and Gary Winfrey (HHS '59).

A Note About the Images

The images in the book were digitally scanned by Dave Smith of U-Photo in Beltsville, Maryland (uphoto.com). Dave, Fran, his wife, and their colleague Robin Wright made a daunting task cheerful and enjoyable. On a personal note, speaking as a veterinarian, Dave and Fran are exceptionally kind and generous people. They routinely open their hearts to stray kittens and cats, shouldering their medical costs, and working tirelessly to find them a loving home, which, on more than one occasion, has been their own. Perhaps it was kismet that a veterinarian and first-time author should find his way to their pleasant little shop.

In Memoriam

I had the great privilege of speaking with Ross Barbour and Bob Flanigan of the Four Freshmen. These gentlemen were kind and humble, and generous with their time and recollections. Ross and Bob passed away while I was working on the manuscript. There can be no doubt the heavenly choir is a little stronger now in its four-part harmony.

While this book was being written, Bob Hanes, Les Chan, and Derek Bill, friends and long-time Beach Boys enthusiasts, each passed away. They contributed immeasurably to our collective understanding and appreciation of the Beach Boys recording career. Their untimely loss is grieved by everyone in the Beach Boys community. I had hoped Bob, Les, and Derek would have enjoyed this book. Let's hope they still will.

And on a Personal Note...

Every book owes a personal debt to the author's family for the years spent researching and writing the manuscript. This book could not have been possible without the cheery encouragement, first-defense proofreading, and skilled editing of my lovely wife, Bernadette. That she can still listen to the Beach Boys is testament to her love and support. Whenever I hear "God Only Knows," especially that angelic choral ending, it is her I see.

To Natalie and Bernard Murphy, the finest parents anyone could hope for, thanks for filling our home with love, laughter, and music. Mario Lanza, Marty Robbins, Frank Sinatra, Cole Porter, and Rodgers and Hammerstein are still among my favorites. Right behind, well, you know who.

To my sister Eileen, a reluctant believer in the Beach Boys, and my brother Richard who, at its very heart, is responsible for this book, a lifetime of love and gratitude. It is said one cannot choose one's family. Well, then, I hit the jackpot, didn't I?

To my nephews, Brian and Kevin, who still accuse me of trying to sell them in exchange for tickets to a Beach Boys concert (an apocryphal story that is, at best, only partially true), thanks for never failing to make me smile and laugh. To my niece Kerry, thanks for all your work converting the manuscript, at a time when it was just slightly shorter than *Atlas Shrugged*, from Word Perfect to Word, an unenviable task even on Record Store Day. Somewhere there's a pile of mulch waiting for you. Bernadette and I are exceptionally proud of all three of you.

To my friends Jed Birmingham, Mike Browning, Mike Doyle, Don McKeon, John Mulligan, Rich and Cathy Silvers, and Jim Wise, thank you for your encouragement, support, and enthusiasm for this project. But, most of all, your friendship.

To Dr. Daniel J. Murphy and Lynn Murphy, and everyone at Capitol Hill Animal Clinic in Washington, D.C., thank you for your support, professional camaraderie, and friendship.

To My Faithful Writing Companions

Writing is a solitary endeavor and my three terriers—Wendy and Tinker, adopted as strays, and Gabby, gifted to me by a client, provided me with steadfast canine company. An untold number of problems in the manuscript were resolved in the solitude and serenity of our daily walks through the woods. My life as a veterinarian is interwoven with so many marvelous, often mystical, dog stories, convincing me dogs are the finest animals on Earth. Perhaps a gift from God, providing a roadmap that will one day lead us back to Paradise. Although I suppose they had no choice, I believe they took a measure of joy and comfort in listening to the Beach Boys musical canon. Pet Sounds, indeed.

Preface

Books are born out of many admirable intentions. A desire to educate, explore, entertain, agitate, and inspire. This one was born out of frustration.

Perhaps no other American rock 'n' roll band has been the subject of more books than the Beach Boys. Several career-spanning works have chronicled them at various points along a musical journey now in its sixth decade. Three band members have been the subject of individual biographies. Two of the group's landmark albums have received in-depth treatises. Writers have tackled the band's intimidating discography, documenting every recording session, song released, and what treasures may remain in the vault. Others have undertaken their unrelenting schedule of personal appearances. One ambitious tome dissected Brian Wilson's songs note by note, probing their harmonic structure for clues to his musical education and inspiration. Another traced the Wilson family genealogy in exhaustive detail. Still others have tilled the rather rich soil of their human foibles and missteps.

The Beach Boys have sold more than 100 million records, including thirty-seven Top 40 hits, fifty-eight Top 100 hits, and four number-one singles ("I Get Around," "Help Me Rhonda," "Good Vibrations," and "Kokomo"). *Rolling Stone* ranked them twelfth on their list of the 100 Greatest Artists of All Time. They are in the Rock and Roll Hall of Fame, the Vocal Group Hall of Fame, and received a Grammy Lifetime Achievement Award. They celebrated their 50th anniversary in 2012 with their twenty-ninth studio album, the critically acclaimed *That's Why God Made the Radio*, and embarked on a seventy-three date tour performing to sell-out crowds over four continents. In August 2013, Capitol/Universal Music Group released *Made in California*, a six compact disc box set chronicling their unparalleled musical legacy.

So, how did five young guys with little musical training form a group, write a song, rent instruments, make a record, release it on an indie label, watch it climb the charts, sign with a major record company, and go on to become one of the most creative and successful groups of all time?

I have always been fascinated with that question. But every account of how the Beach Boys got started, the origin story of America's seminal band, left me with more questions than answers. Their early history is a convoluted, contradictory puzzle, obfuscated by marketing, sophomoric journalism, revisionism, and the ravages time exacts on memory. The situation was exacerbated by writers content to accept the status quo, regurgitating what had already been written, regardless of how utterly nonsensical it was when you actually studied it.

I decided to write the book I wanted to read. I hope it will stimulate robust debate, peeling back additional layers, revealing hidden truths, and further illuminating the intricacies of the band's early history.

I also wrote this book as a thank you to the Beach Boys—Brian Wilson, Mike Love, Dennis Wilson, Carl Wilson, Al Jardine, David Marks, and Bruce Johnston—for sharing a good part of their souls through the music they created. Music that continues to provide me, and so many others, a generous measure of happiness and wonderment.

Carl Wilson, perhaps, said it best when he recalled, "I asked Brian one time why he thought we succeeded in such a big way. He said, 'I think the music celebrated the joy of life in a real simple way. It was a real direct experience of joyfulness.'"[1]

A Request

If you would like to share memories, stories, recollections, photographs—anything at all—about the early history of the Beach Boys, please visit the author's website at becomingthebeachboys.com. You'll also find supplemental reading, additional photographs, questions and answers and a reader's feedback forum.

Introduction

On a brisk Saturday in October 1966, my sixteen-year-old brother Richie raced home from a neighborhood basketball game dripping with perspiration and excitement. He burst into our second-floor apartment on Gun Hill Road in the Bronx and demanded, "C'mon, grab your coat. We're going out. I don't know what I just heard on the radio, but I've never heard anything like it. We've got to find that record. We've got to find it right now." I slipped my jacket on and asked, "What's it called?" He shook his head. "I don't know. The deejay didn't say. All I know is that some of the words are 'good, good, good vibrations.'" Then, with a mix of surprise and skepticism washing over his face like a wave at Orchard Beach, he added, "I think he said it's by the Beach Boys."

We bounded down a flight of stairs and headed up White Plains Road, under the shadow of the Third Avenue El, an elevated subway, in search of this mysterious record. We walked past Babbins Hardware, Regina's Pizzeria, Pappantonio's Laundromat, and the A&P. At Frank's Record Shop, our go-to spot for records, Richie recited what he knew of the lyrics. Frank, a stocky man in his forties, stood with his hands outstretched on the counter. Behind him a wall of 45s, each nestled in its own horizontal cubbyhole, arranged in chart order, waiting to be taken home. Frank knew the song immediately, but he was sold out. But now we had a title. We headed further north to Melody Music, but struck out there, too. We trekked a mile east to MusicRama on Boston Post Road, but had no better luck. We zigzagged back through a residential neighborhood without a record store in sight. Venturing farther north, we crossed the border into Mount Vernon and found a little Jamaican record store, but the owner didn't know the song. By now it was getting dark, and we were starting to get cold and hungry. We headed home dejected. Then Richie remembered the radio and appliance store. Didn't they carry a few records? It was still open so we figured we had nothing to lose. We strode up the center aisle anxious to cross the store off our list and head home. At the back of the store, beyond the rows of Admiral, RCA, and Zenith television sets, was a bin in front of the cash register with maybe fifty forty-fives. I watched as my brother flipped through them, pausing just long enough to read the title. Then he stopped. And there it was. "Good Vibrations." With a picture sleeve no less. He had heard right. It was the Beach Boys. Seventy-four cents later it was ours. We left the store and raced home. Suddenly, we weren't cold or hungry.

When we reached our building, we climbed the stairs two at a time, unlocked the blue metal door to the apartment, and headed for our room. We slid the record from its sleeve, snapped a yellow plastic adaptor into its large center hole, and placed it on our cream-colored Zenith phonograph with a fold-down turntable and removable speakers.

For the next three minutes and thirty-nine seconds we listened, staring at the revolving black disc with the familiar yellow and orange Capitol swirl spinning at a hypnotizing 45 revolutions per minute. I never heard the word "I" sung quite that beautifully before or since. Whose was that angelic voice? And what instrument made that deep, stuttering staccato sound that reverberated through you, conjuring the song's title, making you nervous and exhilarated at the same time? What was that otherworldly sound on the chorus? Oscillating up and down like something from a science fiction movie. We didn't speak. It was like a sacred experience. As if we were alone in St. Ann's Church and it would have been a sin to shatter the silence. If someone had recorded Heaven this is what it would sound like. The song's creator once said music was God's voice. This record seemed to prove it.

As the song finished and the needle spun wildly into the run-out grooves Richie lifted the phonograph arm, steadied it over the edge of the spinning disc, and let it drop like the water balloons we launched from the roof of our building. We listened again. And again. And again. We played that single so many times I'm surprised the vinyl didn't spontaneously combust, melting into a sticky, black glob fused onto the turntable.

Eventually, we flipped it over and listened to the other side. Something called "Let's Go Away for Awhile." What's this? There are no words to this song. We didn't like instrumentals. They seemed lazy, like someone gave up on them too soon. This was something our parents would like. It would be many years before I could appreciate that song. We tolerated one listen before flipping it over.

We must have played "Good Vibrations" fifty times in a row. We passed the picture sleeve back and forth, studying the individual photos of the band members, trying to discern the leader. We didn't know any of their names and weren't sure if the songwriters, some guys named Brian Wilson and Mike Love, were even in the group. We deduced the leader by his photo and agreed it was the clean shaven guy in the hat. He looked confident and self-assured. We were certain it wasn't the guy looking down, averting his eyes from the camera.

Every day after school we'd sit in our bedroom and listen to "Good Vibrations." One day, Mrs. Dorsey, our widowed neighbor across the street, waylaid our Dad, asking, "Who the hell is playing that song over and over again?"

Well, my father should have been a diplomat. "Maureen," he replied, "I have no idea."

Richie told a classmate about the record and how we weren't sure who these guys were.

Proud of his superior musical knowledge, the friend volunteered to identify the band members. Richie brought the picture sleeve to school and his buddy identified the five Beach Boys. The confident guy in the hat wasn't the leader. He was rhythm guitarist Al Jardine. The guy looking down was the creative force in the group, Brian Wilson, the composer of the music. It was from his fertile mind this magical sound had been born. The guy with a beard was Mike Love who penned the words. The other members were Brian's younger brothers, Dennis and Carl.

A lot of time has passed since that autumn day in 1966. But that day changed my life. It began a life-long enjoyment of the music of Brian Douglas Wilson, one of the twentieth century's most gifted composers. A man whose rare talent has brought joy and comfort, serenity and solace, earthly pleasure and spiritual transcendence, to millions of people.

Between June 1962 and December 1966, Brian Wilson wrote, arranged, produced, sang, or played on more than fifty singles, twelve albums, and guested on dozens of other artists' songs. He earned unprecedented creative control in the recording studio and the respect and admiration of veteran Los Angeles studio musicians. He crafted the exquisite *Pet Sounds*, arguably the most important album produced in the rock 'n' roll era. The groundbreaking single "Good Vibrations," a self-described "teenage symphony to God," was number one on the charts. Crafted in four studios over six months at a reported cost, unheard of at the time, of $50,000, Brian's modular production wove a mosaic tapestry of sound. His innovative use of bass, cello, harpsichord, and electro-theremin gave "Good Vibrations" its ethereal sound. Brian was already at work on his next album, an innovative song cycle dubbed *Dumb Angel*, then *Smile*, which would include "Good Vibrations," "Heroes and Villains," "Cabin Essence," "Fire," "Wonderful," and the majestic "Surf's Up." In Britain, music lovers voted the Beach Boys above the Beatles as their favorite musical group. On a nationally broadcast television special, Leonard Bernstein spoke of Brian in hushed tones, calling him one of the most important musicians of the time. Brian was twenty-four years old.

Five years earlier, in summer 1961, a lanky, awkward, nineteen-year-old Brian walked into a storefront recording studio in East LA and told the owner, in an apologetic tone, "You may not remember me. I'm Brian Wilson. Murry Wilson's son." With Brian that day were his younger brothers, Dennis and Carl, his cousin, Mike Love, and his high school classmate Al Jardine. They wanted to make a record. A few months later, these five guys had the #3 hit on LA's top radio station. Their name? Well, if they had gotten their way, the Pendletones. Then someone suggested the Surfers. But fate intervened and we know them as the Beach Boys. The song? A primitive, two minute, ten second, three chord tune called "Surfin'."

"Surfin'" was recorded by Hite and Dorinda Morgan, a middle-aged songwriting couple and long-time friends of the Wilson family. Carl strummed a cheap acoustic guitar, Al plucked a rented stand-up bass, and Brian used an index finger to tap out the beat on a snare drum draped with a shirt to dampen the sound. Apocryphal stories had the percussion played on a pie tin or garbage can lid. But buried in the grooves of that first record was the spirit of youthful exuberance and the possibility of things to come. "Surfin'" was the raw expression of adolescent nirvana. A crude, exciting, musical and lyrical melding of surf, sun-drenched beaches, and the freedom of summer, where the only care in the world was how big were the waves rolling off the Pacific Ocean. Propelled by 50,000 watts on KFWB, "Surfin'" exploded out of the South Bay like a tidal wave, creating a cultural phenomenon that ignited teenage imaginations from Southern California to Northern Maine.

How Brian Wilson took the embryonic Beach Boys from a raw garage band to the lush sophistication of *Pet Sounds* and revolutionary radicalism of "Good Vibrations" is one of rock 'n' roll's most satisfying journeys. The Beach Boys created a musical legacy unparalleled in American popular culture.

This is a tale of talent, teenage dreams, youthful innocence, and musical genius. It is also a story of parental ambition, business mismanagement, diverted corporate funds, employee conflict of interest, and the betrayal of a decade-long friendship. How such jubilant music emerged from these classic struggles is a quintessential American story. Now, for the first time, the true story of how five teenage boys formed America's greatest rock 'n' roll band and the obstacles they overcame on the way to becoming the Beach Boys.

A Note about Record Charts

In the 1950s and 1960s, *Billboard* and *Cash Box*, the two most important weekly music industry publications, were printed ten days before the date on the issue. For instance, *Billboard* for the week ending Saturday, December 30, 1961, was printed by Wednesday, December 20, and on newsstands Saturday, December 23. The Hot 100 singles chart in that issue was compiled from sales and airplay information from the preceding week, December 13–20. This becomes important when dating a record's release.

KFWB and KRLA were the two largest radio stations in Los Angeles in the early 1960s. Their local charts followed a similar schedule. For instance, the KFWB Fabulous Forty Survey for the week ending Friday, December 29, 1961, was compiled Thursday, December 21, printed Friday, December 22, and delivered to local record stores Saturday, December 23.

When referencing a record's national or local chart appearance, I have opted to use the date that chart was on newsstands or in record stores.

1

Hawthorne High and Graduation Day

A chance encounter between Brian Douglas Wilson and Alan Charles Jardine, some fifteen months after their high school graduation, would lead to the formation of the greatest rock 'n' roll band America has ever produced—the Beach Boys.

The Seventh Annual Graduation Exercises for the Class of 1960 of Hawthorne High School began at 6:30 p.m. on June 16, 1960. Neither Brian nor Al, two of the 403 graduates queued to proceed onto HalCap Field and toward their futures, realized that day the profound impact they would have on each other's lives. The outdoor ceremony was held on the field named in honor of the school's two founding football coaches. The night was clear and balmy, the kind of summer evening for which Southern California was known.

The ceremony was the usual mix of stirring music and inspiring speeches, including those by Wallace Nyman, the school's founding principal, and class president George Steven Andersen, an affable student who lettered in varsity baseball and football, and was the starting quarterback for the Hawthorne Cougars.

Brian's parents, Audree and Murry Wilson, both forty-two, watched from the stands as his name was finally called and he marched across the stage to receive his diploma. His younger brothers suffered through his interminably dull rite of passage. Fifteen-year-old Dennis had just completed his freshman year at Hawthorne and thirteen-year-old Carl would enroll that September. Ironically, Brian would never have to reciprocate as neither Dennis nor Carl would graduate Hawthorne High. In May 1962, near the end of their respective junior and sophomore years, with Murry's signature making it legal, Dennis, Carl, and Brian—along with their cousin, Mike Love, and thirteen-year-old neighbor, David Marks—would sign an ambitious seven-year contract as recording artists with Capitol Records. Although founded largely through his persistence, Al Jardine was no longer in the group when they signed with Capitol. He had decided there was no future in the music business and quit to pursue an undergraduate degree so he could apply to dental school. In September 1962, as he struggled with organic chemistry in his third year of college, the band he helped form had the number one record in Los Angeles.

At Hawthorne High, Al and Brian moved in different social circles that overlapped in two quintessential teenage pursuits—sports and music. They each played on the varsity football and the track and field teams. Although their musical tastes varied, they shared a love of vocal harmony. Brian was drawn to the intricate jazz harmonies of the Four Freshmen, the vocal quartet popular in the 1950s. As a young teen, he taught himself their songbook during five years of intense self-study with just his record collection, phonograph player, and upright piano. At Hawthorne High, he formed various vocal groups with friends and family, teaching them harmonies modeled on the Four Freshmen and performing at numerous school assemblies. Al was often in the audience and enjoyed Brian's singing, impressed with his knack for vocal arrangements. Al enjoyed the Four Freshmen, but was especially keen on the acoustic folk harmony of the Kingston Trio, exploding onto the music scene at the start of his junior year in fall 1958. He played guitar and formed a folk trio with two other Hawthorne students and performed selections from the Kingston Trio songbook for friends and family.

After graduation, Al and Brian went their separate ways and didn't see each other over the summer. Brian lived at home with his parents and brothers and that fall attended a local two-year community college with thoughts of majoring in psychology. Al and his mother moved a thousand miles away to Big Rapids, Michigan, where his father had accepted a teaching position at Ferris Institute, and Al enrolled in a pre-dental curriculum with an emphasis on science and mathematics.

Hawthorne High School was built in the early 1950s on a tract of land that once sprouted lima beans at Inglewood Avenue and West El Segundo Boulevard. The school opened for the 1951–1952 academic year and the first class graduated in 1954. Wallace Nyman, a 1931 graduate of nearby Inglewood High who was assistant principal at Leuzinger High, became Hawthorne's first principal. In the early years, the campus was a construction site with classrooms being built, parking lots littered with tar machines, new faculty members added yearly, and students searching for their next class while contending with plumbing strikes and construction delays. It was not uncommon for new students to get lost on the sprawling twenty-four acre campus.

As Al and Brian began their

SEVENTH ANNUAL

Graduation Exercises

CLASS OF 1960

HAWTHORNE HIGH SCHOOL

Centinela Valley Union High School District

HAWTHORNE, CALIFORNIA

Alan Charles Jardine (top) and Brian Douglas Wilson graduated Hawthorne High School on June 16, 1960. Fifteen months later, after a chance encounter, their actions led to the formation of the Beach Boys (author's collection).

first semester in September 1956, the student senate received approval to install sign posts to minimize the confusion. Amidst this temporary chaos arose a feeling among the faculty and students that they were all in this grand experiment together. That camaraderie, coupled with the peace and prosperity of the post-war era, had a profound effect on students during the school's first decade.

Wally Nyman recruited Hal Chauncey, director of the City of Hawthorne's Gunga Din Youth Center (later named the Hawthorne Recreation Center), as one of Hawthorne High's first faculty members and its first football coach. "Wally told me he wanted to put Hawthorne High on the map through education and athletics," Chauncey recalled. "He knew football season was the first activity of the school year and that school spirit, tradition, and community support started there."[1] Chauncey, along with Dave Capelouto, soon assembled a winning football team and led the Cougars to four Pioneer League championships.

In the 1950s, high school kids fell into broad categories still recognizable today. The jocks played sports and for them football reigned supreme. The socials, or "soshes," were popular with the opposite sex, wore the right clothes, had good hair, and socialized gracefully. The academic achievers drew an odd mixture of praise, envy, and derision. The troublemakers, hoods or greasers, hated school, conformity, and most of the other students. The large middle group defied categorization and moved comfortably among several groups. And, finally, there were the kids considered odd and seldom treated kindly.

Al and Brian were in the vast middle group of boys at Hawthorne High—popular, likable, athletic, and creative. Al kept a fairly low profile. He didn't date much and poured his energy into sports and music. Brian was known for his wry humor, an over-the-top guffaw, and enjoying either end of a practical joke. Brian always managed to get a date for some of the school's larger social functions, but he did not have a steady girlfriend. The girls he longed for breathed the rarefied air in the social strata above him. They were beautiful, idealized, and unattainable. When Brian grew into his musical gift, he wrote beautiful, introspective songs, aching with romantic longing for relationships gone astray.

Brian was the only Wilson brother whose high school experience was not impacted by the celebrity of the Beach Boys. From 1956 through 1960, ages fourteen to eighteen, years that paralleled the birth of rock 'n' roll, Brian's experiences helped create a soundtrack to the hopes, fears, and dreams we all experience as we navigate our way through the perilous sea of our high school years. Decades after graduation and the Beach Boys' success, Brian's high school friends received late-night telephone calls from him. Many hadn't spoken with him since graduation. After exchanging pleasant but awkward chit chat, it seemed Brian simply wanted to reminisce about the old days at Hawthorne High. The years before the fame, before the money, before the problems. Hawthorne represented something pure, hopeful, romantic. A happy, innocent time brimming with possibility.

———◦◦◦———

Brian took classmate Irene Callahan to their junior prom at the Hollywood Park Racetrack clubhouse on March 28, 1959. The evening was not without a few adolescent mishaps. When Brian arrived at her home, he drove into the back of her father's car. Although she told him she would wear a strapless dress, he bought a corsage which then had to be pinned to her waist. He kept knocking it off accidentally during the evening. After the prom, he insisted on retrieving his own car rather than wait for the valet. He hit a car in the garage on his way out and confessed it took several attempts to get his driver's license. Later, during dinner at the Cocoanut Grove night club at the Ambassador Hotel, he spilled Irene's hot tea on the table while listening to singer Tony Martin accompanied by Freddy Martin and His Orchestra.[2] Tony Martin had introduced "It's a Blue World," a #2 hit nominated for an Academy Award for Best Original Song in 1940,[3] which launched the Four Freshmen in summer 1952, reaching #30 on the pop chart. Brian loved the song, admitting it made him cry.[4] Irene recalled, "When we were dancing Brian started singing on the dance floor. I was embarrassed because it was loud and other people could hear him."[5] "It's a Blue World" was likely the song Brian sang to Irene on the dance floor.

Irene later told her girlfriends about prom night and Brian's eratic driving before attending Sports Night, a school-sponsored program of music, volleyball, badminton, and dancing. Afterward, they cruised to Foster's Freeze to get something to eat and hang out. "We saw Brian pulling in and, when he saw us, he drove into the building. He didn't hit it hard or anything, but my girlfriends and I started laughing. The guy he was with came up to us and said, 'You shouldn't laugh because you make him nervous.' Brian was always sweet. I'll never forget how excited he was the day his dad got him the organ. He called me and played music over the phone."[6]

For his seventeenth birthday on June 20, 1959, as the Four Freshmen headlined the Palladium in Hollywood, Audree and Murry bought Brian a two-door 1957 Ford Fairlane 500 Club Sedan so he could drive to school his senior year. No longer would he have to drive his mother's maroon 1951 Mercury.[7] His new used car had a two-tone exterior with colonial white on top, Inca gold on bottom, and gold anodized aluminum side molding. The interior was red silver shadow fabric panels trimmed in colonial white vinyl. Americans had embraced the '57 Ford and the company outsold rival Chevrolet for the first time since 1935. The car opened up a new world for Brian, providing a measure of independence from his parents and social approval among his peers. It also opened up new avenues for his sense of humor and penchant for practical jokes.

"He was a prankster," recalled Dennis. "He used to pull the most outrageous stunts. Like driving down the street going to school when we were kids. We'd be rushing to school and Brian would be drinking a carton of milk, and he'd stop and open the door and pretend he was throwing up by emptying out the whole milk carton. Or he'd stop and wait for a hitchhiker to run up to the car and then he'd take off. He'd totally let go and whatever could happen he'd let happen. The group started that way, setting up a stage in the garage to have funny performances. He was out in front almost in an embarrassing way."[8]

On September 8, 1959, Al and Brian began their senior year at Hawthorne High. That fall, the music on KFWB and KRLA, the dominant LA radio stations, included Bobby Darin's "Mack the Knife," "Poison Ivy" by the Coasters, "Till I Kissed You" by the Everly Brothers, "What'd I Say" by Ray Charles, and "Baby Talk" by Jan & Dean.

Ten days later, and the night before sixty-five-year-old Soviet Premier Nikita Khrushchev landed in LA on his historic visit to the United States, Hawthorne High held its Kick-Off Dance in the boys' gymnasium. As the first social event of the school year, the dance pumped students up for the first football game of the season the following week.

Football wasn't the only sport played at Hawthorne High, but it might as well have been. "The first day you walked into Hawthorne High, they stamped a cougar on your fore-

Inspired by the Kingston Trio's "Tom Dooley" in fall 1958, Al (center) formed the Tikis at Hawthorne High with upper classman Gary Winfrey (left) and Bob Barrow (courtesy Gary Winfrey).

head," recalled Rich Sloan, Brian's friend and classmate. "You weren't just a student. You were a Hawthorne Cougar, because football was the dominant force."[9]

Hawthorne High had B, C, Junior Varsity, and Varsity football teams. "In those days, teams went by exponents that were a combination of your age, height, and weight," recalled Bob Barrow, Al's friend and classmate. "They'd calculate your number and assign you to a specific team. I was about five-eight and 165 pounds, and started out on the B team which was kind of like a feeder program to the varsity."[10]

Foregoing sports freshman year, Al and Brian both played on the B football team as sophomores. Brian was 6'2" and 165 pounds with a strong throwing arm. He played third-string quarterback behind Mike Wood and starter Steve Andersen. At 5'8" and 165 pounds, Al was slotted into fullback, but he was one of several available running backs. On the football team, Al became good friends with Bob Barrow and Gary Winfrey, a junior, with whom he would later form a folk music trio called the Tikis.

On November 8, 1957, the Cougar B team played the Culver City Centaurs. Late in the game, with a comfortable 39–7 lead, Coach Otto Plum rested his starters and sent Brian in as quarterback and Al as fullback. A play called for Brian to pitch the ball to Al, but the players got their signals crossed and, in the chaos that ensued, Al was tackled and either injured or broke his leg.

Seven years later, during a vocal session for "Our Prayer," Brian recounted the event. "Yeah, I went like this—Whoa! And Al was running. Al's like this, you know, waiting for the ball, and about four guys (makes a smacking sound) his leg up. Right? Isn't that how it went?" Not amused, Al replied in a dour tone, "That's right, Brian." "Well, if you could have seen you, man," Brian responded. Al laughed incredulously and began, "Imagine—" before someone interjected "C'mon, Jardine," to lighten the mood.

"They placed Al on a stretcher and put him on the side of the field," recalled Barrow. "He laid there until the game was over and he came back with us on the bus. It was a traumatic fracture of his femur. I think today they would have hauled him off in an ambulance."[11]

John Hagethorn, Al's friend and classmate, recalled, "I was on the junior varsity team at the time and was unaware of it. And, because the *Inglewood Daily News* did not cover B team sports, there was no mention of it in the paper. But when I met Al in Las Vegas a few years back, he told me about it. He said he was hobbling out to the bus after the game and Coach Plum said something like 'Suck it up.' Al didn't care much for Plum after that. But if he was walking on the leg, it was probably not that serious of a fracture."[12] The Cougars beat the Centaurs 45–13.

"I had seen Al on the B football team, but it was when we were juniors that I got to know him," recalled Hagethorn. "We never had any classes together, but when we were juniors and seniors we were just about inseparable after school. There was a little park halfway between our houses and we used to go there and play hand ball after school just about every day in spring and summer. The summer of 1959, before our senior year, we did a lot of stuff together and went to the beach. He was a busboy at one of the restaurants on Hawthorne Boulevard and there was a record store on the Boulevard where he used to hang out a lot. Al taught me how to play 'Honky Tonk' on the guitar."[13]

Hal Chauncey led the Cougars to four Pioneer League championships between 1953 and 1957. In 1958, Al again played for the B team while Brian moved up to varsity. But after losing fourteen senior lettermen, the '58 Cougars went 1–6–1, their first losing season. An especially difficult loss was a 33–7 tarring from league rivals the Morningside Monarchs. The 1959 Hawthorne High yearbook, *El Molino* (the name means "The Mill," reflecting the area's agricultural and Spanish roots), included a photograph from that game of quarterbacks Steve Andersen and "Bryan [*sic*] Wilson" sitting alone on the sideline hanging their heads in defeat.

As seniors in fall 1959, Al and Brian both played varsity football. Trying out for the C football team was fourteen-year-old freshman Dennis Wilson. "Dennis's locker was next to mine," recalled his friend John Rout. "One Friday I came in from practice and Dennis was sitting there crying. Coach Bruce Halladay had cut him. I told him to talk to the coach to see where he was weak and to give him another chance. He did, Halladay did, and the next Friday Dennis was clearing out his locker again, but this time he was okay with it. Considering the kind of guy Dennis was, seeing him crying was the most shocking thing I had seen up to that time."[14]

That season, Hawthorne was moved into the stronger, more competitive, Bay League dominated by the 1958 league champion Santa Monica Vikings. Forty-two players began the '59 season including third-string quarterback Brian Wilson and fullback Al Jardine. Chauncey recalled, "Al Jardine was my hard driving fullback. Big Al Jardine, all 145 pounds of him. I'm lucky we didn't get him killed. But he didn't realize he was 145. He thought he was 200 pounds and played like it."[15] When Al attended his class's fortieth reunion, Chauncey ribbed him, "I can't believe I made you my fullback."[16]

Football games were an important social event for teenagers in 1959. Girls showed their school spirit by wearing Shu-Poms, a small pom-pom in school colors that slipped onto their shoes. Wearing a Cougar Rooter hat entitled you to sit in the special roped-off section in the stands where student behavior was monitored by league officials. Unsportsmanlike conduct in the stands tarnished the school's reputation and was discouraged through peer pressure. What constituted poor behavior? Well, for starters, throwing confetti. It was considered inconsiderate to the maintenance personnel responsible for cleaning the stands.

The varsity Cougars began their '59 season against the Lynwood Knights at 8:00 p.m. on September 25 on Murdock Field at El Camino Community College. Murdock became the team's home field that year when installation of outdoor lights on HalCap Field was delayed when it was determined the new lights were not earthquake resistant. The players ran onto the field through a pep squad corridor that included song queens Pat Bell, Carol Hess, and Carol Mountain. Chauncey started Mike Wood at quarterback. Brian had a powerful arm, but was considered less reliable. "He could throw the ball a long way, probably farther than anyone else, but Brian was flaky on the field and couldn't hit the guy he was throwing at," said teammate and friend Bruce Griffin.[17]

In early October, as the team enjoyed an early bye week, and the LA Dodgers became the first West Coast team to win a World Series, Brian quit the team. Despite encouragement from his teammates to stay, he was not dissuaded. "That was the first time I'd ever seen him get so emotional about something," recalled Griffin.[18] Sloan recalled, "Brian didn't really like people running into him when they would tackle him."[19] Hagethorn remembered, "I heard Brian knew he wasn't going to get any playing time, so he stopped going out."[20]

"I was quarterback on the second-string team," Brian said, "but the punishment and competition were too much and I quit the squad. Then I tried baseball, which I loved, because I used to stand out there in center field and kinda sing to myself in between pitches."[21] It is unknown if Brian's partial deafness played a role in his decision to quit football. He added, "I was a good thrower, but I wasn't a very good runner. I got knocked over a couple of times."[22] Carl Wilson added a new perspective, "Brian quit the football team because he wanted to do music, and the coach got so pissed off at him he wouldn't talk to him for the rest of the year."[23]

Brian was four years into his self-study of the Four Freshmen and was already planning for a career in music. In "My Philosophy," a two-page essay he submitted October 26 for his Senior Problems course, he wrote, "I don't want to settle with a mediocre life, but make a name for myself in my life's work, which I hope will be in music."[24] As Sloan noted, "Brian's way of communicating with people was through his humor and his music. His biggest gift to someone was to get them to laugh or to play them a song on the piano."[25]

When Brian quit the football team, he first joined the track and field team as a cross-country runner. Perhaps he left football for a sport in which he could participate more fully. Two of his best friends, Keith Lent and Robin Hood, also ran track. In a meet against North High, Brian was one of three runners who beat the school's previous record of 9 minutes and 12 seconds in the 1.7 mile race. At another meet, Brian and Lent dropped behind, grabbed a bite to eat, and rejoined the race just before the finish line. School officials were none the wiser.

But while Brian ran cross-country, he missed participating in the most thrilling football season in the school's history. The undefeated 1959 Hawthorne Cougars captured the Bay League Championship their first year in the league and won both the quarter-final and semi-final play-off games. On December 11, they squared off against the Long Beach Poly Jackrabbits in front of 15,000 at the LA Coliseum. For much of the contest they held their own, but the powerful running game of the aptly nicknamed Hares proved too much and the Cougars fell 42–20. Al carried the ball just once in the championship game for a five-yard gain.

The Cougars' 1959 Cinderella season is still talked about by students and alumni after more than fifty years. Al finished the season with twenty-five carries, 133 yards, one touchdown, and the award for the most improved player. A picture of Al making a defensive play appeared in the November 7 *Inglewood Daily News*. In the semi-final game against the Glendale Dynamiters, the paper noted, "The Cougars got a good performance from reserve back Al Jardine who uncorked a fine 30 yard run from fullback post."[26] But Al's elation was undermined by the *Cougar* which noted the team missed scoring opportunities by inches and seconds. "Al Jardine's fine power running wasn't enough to spring him out of the reach of Glendale's safety men when he found a big hole up the middle. If he had just a wee more spirit he could have gone all the way for six more points."[27] Al remembered that comment more than forty-five years later. "I made a draw play to go right up the middle and I had a wide open field and this kid caught me from behind. It's one of those editorial remarks that devastate a young man when he's trying to do his best. It wasn't very encouraging, but it makes me laugh now."[28]

"Carol Hess, Carol Mountain, Pat Bell, and Tracy Kara were some of the prettiest girls in our class," recalled Hagethorn. "They were nice girls too, you could talk to them."[29] Carol Mountain had large expressive eyes, a perfect smile, and dark brown hair. Her short bangs and long curls framed her face and fell just below her shoulders. She was active in student government, a former class president, and head song queen that year. She was the girl with whom Brian was secretly in love.[30] He spoke with her in Spanish class, reminded her of homework assignments, played boogie-woogie piano over at her house, but never mustered the courage to tell her his true feelings. "I really had no idea until twenty-five years later," Mountain recalled.[31]

"Brian just adored her," recalled Vickie Amott, Brian's classmate and neighbor. "He just pined away. She was put on a pedestal. If she would have just looked at him he would have melted. Brian wasn't in that group. Brian was the type of guy most girls looked upon as a brother. He was good looking, tall, thin, sandy blonde hair, and freckles. And when you got to know him he was very sweet, had a neat personality, and a sense of humor. I don't think Brian would have had the confidence to approach Carol Mountain. But he was popular within his own group."[32]

"Pom Pom Playgirl," Brian's and Mike Love's ninety-second ode to cheerleaders on the

Beach Boys *Shut Down Volume 2* in March 1964, offered a new perspective on the cliquish nature of song queens and how some parlayed their looks into elevated social status. "Caroline, No," a deeply personal song about lost love that closes *Pet Sounds* was inspired, in part, by Brian's idealized memory of Carol Mountain and a yearning for a simpler, happier time. Marilyn Wilson Rutherford, Brian's first wife, recalled, "One thing about Brian, he constantly remembers his past and still relates to it and everybody in it."[33]

After competing in the cross-country finals against eight schools in the Bay League, Brian attended the semi-annual Backwards Dance on November 20. The *Cougar* hinted at Brian's antics. "Most of the couples that had their pictures taken at the Backwards Dance have gotten them back by now. The results are pretty good, but none can compare to the ones that were taken at Charlene Haskell's house before and after the dance. Just ask Brian Wilson."[34]

December was a busy month for the Wilsons as Dennis celebrated his fifteenth birthday December 4 and Carl turned thirteen December 21. The Hawthorne High Christmas assembly was December 18, the last day of class as progress reports were sent home to parents. Students were off the next two weeks and many young guys, especially the car enthusiasts, flocked to the 1960 International Motor Sports Show at the Great Western Exhibit Center on Eastern Avenue at the Santa Ana Freeway.

On the morning of January 27, 1960, the students of Hawthorne High attended a campaign assembly prior to electing new student body officers for the spring semester. Brian volunteered to help Carol Hess in her bid for commissioner of assemblies against Karen Anderson. He crafted a campaign song for her by writing new lyrics to the Olympics' "(Baby) Hully Gully," which had just debuted on KFWB after languishing six months as a B side. He enlisted his friends Keith Lent, Robin Hood, and Bruce Griffin, assigned each their vocal parts, and rehearsed a version faithful to the original arrangement.

Brian's vocal quartet took the stage and huddled around a microphone on the podium on which they placed a handwritten lyric sheet. Guys in the audience laughed and jeered as they launched into the song: "We need a new commissioner, and what is her name? / Carol, Carol Hess / Ask the student body and they'll tell you the same / Carol, Carol Hess / She's ready and she's willing and she's able, too / Seniors vote for Carol, juniors vote for Carol / Sophomores and freshmen, too."[35] Students cheered. It was funny, catchy, and a welcome relief from tedious campaign speeches. Even the cynics agreed it took courage to pull it off. When the votes were tallied later that day, Carol had won. Under the direction of a faculty advisor, she would plan and schedule all student body assemblies for the spring semester.

Although this later became Brian's most celebrated appearance at a school assembly, it may not have been his first. He recalled, "My first time singing publicly was at a high school assembly. Mike Love came over and we sang 'Bermuda Shorts.'" The Delroys' "Bermuda Shorts" (b/w "Time," Apollo 514) was released in June 1957 and, although it never charted nationally, it was popular in LA. Al Jardine recalled that assembly. "One day we were entertained by a group of kids from the school. And I thought, 'What a great sound. What a wonderful, youthful sound.' But I didn't know the short, twelve-year-old kid playing guitar. So they sang this beautiful 'Bermuda Shorts' and I'm thinking, 'That's pretty cute. That's really neat, but who's that kid on guitar?' Turned out it was Carl Wilson. And that was my introduction to Brian's beautiful falsetto voice."[36] If these recollections are accurate, then Brian, Mike, and Carl—three-fifths of the future Beach Boys—performed "Bermuda Shorts" at a Hawthorne High assembly most likely during the fall 1959 semester.

The applause at these assemblies bolstered Brian's confidence in his singing and musical ability. It was exhilarating to be cheered by your peers while winning the affection of one of the most popular and attractive girls in the school. The experience drove him to keep practicing with his vocal group and tackle the more ambitious "That's My Desire" with its intricate doo wop harmonies interwoven with a soaring background falsetto. Written in 1931, the song was a #2 hit for bandleader Sammy Kaye and singer Frankie Laine in 1947. Brian may have been familiar with R&B versions by the Channels (September 1957), Chuck Berry (January 1959), and Dion and the Belmonts (November 1959).

With the football season over, Al moved over to varsity track and field, and tossed shot put with his buddy Hagethorn. Brian played varsity baseball and registered for courses in English, Government, Physical Education, Spanish III, Senior Problems, and Piano and Harmony.[37]

"Brian was an open-hearted, likable guy," recalled Roberta "Bobbie' Burket, a classmate in Brian's third-year Spanish class. "He was sort of a class clown, but not in a negative, disruptive way. It was like having Tom Sawyer in your class. He was an open, innocent, wide-eyed kid. But that was true of many kids in our generation. The world was an easier place back then. Brian had a magnetic personality, people were drawn to him. But he wasn't the type of boy that was going to attract the girls sexually. He was more like your younger brother."[38] Burket recalled an amusing repercussion of Brian's love of music. "In Mr. [Larry] Kirkpatrick's English class, Brian was always beating on his desk and singing to himself. One day the vibrations had worked the screws loose and the whole desk came apart with a crash."[39]

The varsity baseball team began its season with an exhibition game against the Aviation High Falcons on March 2. Brian played outfield as he had sure hands and a strong throwing arm. The Horsehiders, as the *Cougar* referred to them, a term from the sport's early history when horsehide was the covering of choice for baseballs because it was less prone to stretching than cowhide, beat the Falcons 3–0. The *Cougar* highlighted Rich Sloan and Brian as stand-out sluggers.

"We were coming home from a baseball game and I was in the lead car," recalled Sloan. "One of my guys said, 'Hey, let's do a Chinese Fire Drill!' We got out and ran around my car. Steve Andersen's car was second and Brian's was third. So visualize: You've got my car, a '49 Chevy, two-door deluxe coupe; then you have Steve's four-door, blue '52 Chevy; and then you have Brian's '57 Ford Fairlane. Brian gets out and runs up the trunk of Steve's car and jumps on the top." Just then, Coach Duff Means pulled alongside them. Everyone retreated to their cars. Brian slid down the windshield and hood and slunk back to his car. The coach told them to report to his home room the following day.[40]

The next morning, Bobbie Burket was walking alone to school when Brian stopped and offered her a ride. "I was kind of shy and I really didn't know him. I was shocked when he offered me a lift. Naturally, I accepted. It seems the baseball coach caught Brian in a Chinese Fire Drill the day before. He was going in early to apologize and plead his case. He told me 'It wasn't a very smart thing to do.' But Brian was smart enough to approach the coach in a dignified, respectful way."[41]

On March 11, Hawthorne High held its Club Charter assembly at which school clubs presented their charters for the upcoming semester and recruited new members. After the student government elections on January 27, Brian's informal vocal group had become known around school as the "Kingston Quartet," a nickname inspired by the Kingston Trio. They were invited by the student government to perform at the assembly.

As he prepared for the assembly, Brian made a personnel change. He replaced Robin Hood, who did not enjoy performing and whose epilepsy may have made him too anxious

On March 11, 1960, Brian assembled a vocal quartet to perform "The Wreck of the John B." for Hawthorne High's Club Charter assembly. From left to right, Bob Barrow, Brian, Keith Lent, and Bruce Griffin. To better project in the auditorium, Barrow borrowed Carl Wilson's acoustic-electric Kay Swingmaster guitar and amplifier (author's collection).

to be on-stage, with guitarist Bob Barrow from the Tikis, the school's popular folk trio that included Al Jardine and Gary Winfrey, who had graduated in 1959. The *Cougar* teased Brian's group: "Good luck to the Kingston Quartet on their tour of the boys' locker room, everybody really enjoys their music—to dress by."[42]

Brian chose to perform "The Wreck of the John B.," the traditional English folk song recorded by the Weavers (1950), the Kingston Trio (1958), and Johnny Cash (as "I Want to Go Home," 1959). In the days leading up to the assembly, Brian, Lent, Griffin, and Barrow got together a few times to rehearse. "We went over to Keith Lent's house and listened to Kingston Trio records," Barrow recalled. "Brian liked 'The Wreck of the John B.' and it was his gig, he was running the show." Barrow also recalled a rehearsal session at the Wilson home. "Al was more connected to Brian musically and it was through Al that I ended up over at Brian's house and met Carl. Brian was playing the piano and Carl was playing the guitar. I was real impressed at how well Carl could play the guitar because at the time I was just strumming chords. He could play rock 'n' roll lead guitar already. I remember quite a discussion from Brian about how he wanted the harmony to sound. He was somewhat deaf in one ear. He'd have to turn his head to hear what the other people were singing. Brian had us doing four-part harmony with him singing the high voice on top that later became the signature of the Beach Boys. Brian arranged 'The Wreck of the John B.' and we practiced it and did it at the assembly."[43]

Barrow provided the only musical accompaniment for the quartet during the assembly. But, because his acoustic guitar would not have projected very well, he borrowed Carl's acoustic-electric guitar and amp, which Brian lugged to school. A photograph of them performing appeared in the 1960 *El Molino* with a humorous caption: "At this time the famous quartette [*sic*] of Barrows [*sic*], Wilson, Lent, and Griffin made its first and last public appearance!"[44] It is the only known photo (except, perhaps, those owned by the Wilson family) of the guitar on which Carl received his rock 'n' roll education.

Brian attended the Spring Backwards Dance on April 1 in the boys' gymnasium. His date was Sonja Laird, a sophomore who sang, played piano, and was a member of the Modern Dance club. A photograph of them arm-in-arm appeared in the 1960 *El Molino*.

While the Four Freshmen's influence on Brian's early teen years is well-documented, the impact of the Four Preps on his late teen years is largely underappreciated. There are a number of similarities between the Four Preps (five, counting Lincoln Mayorga, their arranger and so-called "fifth Prep") and the Beach Boys: five friends inspired by the Four Freshmen begin singing in high school, sign a long-term recording contract with Capitol Records, write their own songs, and become one of America's most beloved vocal harmony groups. The Four Preps embraced the Four Freshmen style and gave it a modern spin, bridging the early '50s vocal groups with the music of Brian's high school years.

On April 8, as the school prepared for spring break, the Four Preps performed at a special assembly in the boy's gymnasium at Hawthorne High. With Mayorga accompanying them on the school's upright piano, they demonstrated their crisp vocal harmonies on a string of hits since signing with Capitol in fall 1956. "They played for about forty-five minutes," recalled Hagethorn. "It was good show. Those assemblies were mandatory. Everyone went because you got out of class for an hour."[45]

Brian kept busy during spring break as Hawthorne High hosted its first annual Invitational Baseball Tournament. The high point for Brian was driving in three runs on three hits to help the Cougars beat Redondo High 7–2. The Cougars took second-place behind El Segundo, but finished their season a disappointing 5–13.

During spring break, Dion and the Belmonts released "When You Wish Upon a Star" and it reached #30 that May. With their modern interpretation of standards like "Where or When," "That's My Desire," and "In the Still of the Night," Dion and the Belmonts bridged Brian's affection for Four Freshmen harmonies with the rhythm and blues his brother Carl loved.

Fred Morgan instructed the students in his Piano and Harmony course to write a sonata as a final examination. "Brian was the quietest one in class," Morgan recalled. "He was a nice boy and a good student and was fairly popular with his classmates because he had a good laugh. There was a portion of each class during which I would sit at the piano and play something, and everyone had to write down the notes. I remember Brian was very good at that. He had a quick mind."[46]

But that didn't stop Morgan from giving Brian an F when the piano sonata he submitted for his final examination didn't meet his approval. "Brian was asked to write a one hundred and twenty measure sonata for the piano. And he wrote thirty-two measures of music with chords in it. It wasn't one hundred and twenty measures, it didn't change key five times, and it was full of parallelism, which he's made and capitalized on, and backward progres-

On June 3, 1960, the Hawthorne High Class of 1960 celebrated Senior Ditch Day with a trip to Disneyland. Lorraine Churik (kneeling) and (front row, left to right) Glenda Cook, Theresa Kara, Karen Darnell, Janet Haynes, Linda Crow, Carol Hess, and Brian. (Back row, left to right) Carol Mountain, Patsy Bell, David Hoel, Pat Oravetz, and Robin Hood. Rich Sloan had squirted Brian with disappearing ink (courtesy Theresa Kara Armijo).

sions. And Brian knows that. And so we kind of laugh about it."[47] The failing grade lowered Brian's final grade in the course to a C. But years later, that failing grade was referred to as the "Golden F" in the halls of Hawthorne High. Although the music Brian submitted has been reported to be an early version of "Surfin'," Audree Wilson recalled it was definitely not "Surfin'."[48]

There were many events for seniors to close out the academic year. Some alumni recalled Brian, with some version of his vocal group, performed at a school assembly shortly before graduation. This may have been the Variety Show, a late substitution for two one-act plays planned by the drama club, held in Nyman Hall at 8:00 p.m. on May 27. This may have been the evening program for which Audree recalled Brian recruited a reluctant Carl and kiddingly named his quartet Carl and the Passions.

On June 3, seniors boarded busses and drove thirty miles east to Anaheim for the Eighth Annual Senior Ditch Day trip to Disneyland. A photograph of students standing in front of the busses shows Brian and the "disappearing ink" Rich Sloan squirted on his shirt as a prank. Another photograph of the group included Al Jardine strumming a ukulele. Seniors had four hours at the park and were chaperoned by a dozen faculty members who reminded them they represented Hawthorne High and not to spend all their money in the first half-hour.

—◦◦◦—

As the commencement ceremony drew to a close, the graduates disbanded in raucous anarchy as the last glint of sun slipped behind the horizon. They flitted about, streaks of charcoal and mint green, trying to drink it all in. Girls hugged and cried, mascara streaking their faces. Guys shook hands a bit too firmly and slapped each other's backs, overwhelmed by the arrival of a moment they longed for, but thought would never come. They waved good-bye and shouted best wishes for summer and whatever lay ahead.

They had shared four years together, discovering life, love, and their place in the world. Now they were saying good-bye to friends and an institution—a unique convergence of teachers, sports, education, and discipline—at once detested and beloved, that had tried its best to prepare them for the world. Perhaps more than most graduates, they were also leaving behind their carefree innocence. They had grown up in the relative peace and prosperity of the Eisenhower years. But the world was changing. The relationship between the United States and the Soviet Union had chilled since Khrushchev's historic visit to America at the start of their senior year. A month before graduation, Eisenhower was caught lying in an attempt to cover up the mission of the U2 spy plane piloted by Francis Gary Powers and shot down over Soviet airspace. The incident scuttled the Four Powers Summit in Paris and was a humiliating disappointment for Ike in the final months of his presidency. That fall, Americans would elect a young new president who would confront Soviet aggression and lead the country into a decade that would transform the world.

They began the ceremony as high school kids. Now, they were adults, ready to make their own decisions. Like most generations, their journeys were filled with college, careers, marriages, and mortgages, lives buoyed by achievement and tempered with disappointment. Any residual naiveté they carried from Hawthorne High was vanquished by the Cold War threat of nuclear annihilation, the brutal assassination of a young president caught on film, and an unending war in Southeast Asia delivered into their homes every night by the evening news. This wasn't high school anymore. And despite the earnest promises made that summer night, most graduates never saw one another again.

But they still had that night. Most seniors headed to the Palladium at 6215 Sunset Boulevard in Hollywood for an all-night graduation party. Built in 1940, the Palladium's 11,000 square foot ballroom could accommodate 4,000 dancers. The dress code for the night was dresses or formals for girls and dark suits or sports jackets for boys. Graduates of five high schools—Lennox, Leuzinger, Inglewood, Morningside, and Hawthorne—had pooled their money and rented the Palladium for their school-sanctioned celebration. Tickets were three dollars and fifty-cents. The master of ceremonies was KHJ disc jockey Wink Martindale who had just released his fifth Dot Records single, a dramatic reading of the Gettysburg Address backed by a chorus singing "The Battle Hymn of the Republic." Music was provided by Gus Bivona's band and the entertainers included Dodie Stevens, the Untouchables, and the Surfaris. Tape recorders, matched luggage, and clock radios were raffled off as door prizes. The students were warned to stay away from alcoholic beverages and to act responsibly now that they were high school graduates. The event lasted well into the morning and breakfast was served between 3:00 a.m. and 4:00 a.m.

John Hagethorn recalled, "There was a lot of drinking going on and it lasted all night long. It was fun. You were done with high school, you just graduated that day, you were out of your cap and gown, seeing all kinds of new people, the music was playing, you were drinking and having a good old time." Some thought the Palladium was a stuffy affair and left early to hang out in familiar haunts. "It was very boring," recalled Vickie Amott. "We went, but we didn't stay. We left fairly early actually."[49]

For many, the real party happened along Hawthorne Boulevard, cruising its built-in signposts of Foster's Freeze, A&W Root Beer, and the Wich Stand drive-in restaurant, with its space-age architecture and fabled thirty-five foot spire, anchoring the northern end of the loop in Inglewood.

Al cruised the Boulevard with his friend and fellow Tiki Gary Winfrey. They pulled into Foster's Freeze and there, parked in his car with a friend, was Brian Wilson. "He was sitting there in his car with one of his buddies. I said, 'Hey Brian, if you ever want to get together and play some music, it sure would be great.' He said, 'Sure, I'd love to.' I didn't expect for us to really do anything together. It was more like saying, 'Sure, okay.'"[50]

The exchange was more polite banter than serious attempt at collaboration and neither made plans to follow through. It was, perhaps, a goodwill gesture between classmates who wished they'd taken the time to know each other better. It would be fifteen months before they saw each other again.

2

Hawthorne, California

"Have you ever seen *American Graffiti*?"

"That's what it was like growing up in Hawthorne and why it's such a popular movie with people from that era," said John Hagethorn about growing up in Southern California in the 1950s.[1]

Hagethorn was eight years old when his family moved from LA to Hawthorne. By 1956 he was a freshman at Hawthorne High where he and Al became friends playing football, lifting weights, and tossing shot put. "If you had a car back in those days you cruised up and down Hawthorne Boulevard. You pulled into an all-night place like Foster's Freeze, the A&W or the Wich Stand. The girls drove their fathers' cars. There was always a party Friday or Saturday night at somebody's house and the parents were usually not home. Someone would always give you a beer, but there were no drugs. After football games, you'd go to the Gunga Din and there would be a big crowd of kids and they'd play records and you'd dance or stand around and talk. It closed around midnight. If there was any crime, it didn't have any impact on us."[2]

Of course, the 1950s were not quite as idyllic as *American Graffiti* would have us believe. For those raised in the 1960s, a decade marked by an unpopular war, campus unrest, urban riots, and the assassination of three prominent Americans, the 1950s were perceived to be a simpler, happier time. But for adults who had endured the Depression and the Second World War, the 1950s brought new worries of nuclear proliferation, fall-out shelters, and the Korean War. Kids are generally immune to their parents' concerns, and the generation born circa World War II, including all of the Beach Boys, grew up in relative peace and prosperity. They were too young, and their fathers too old, to be conscripted in the Korean War.

At the end of the Second World War, millions of GIs returned home ready to settle down, marry their sweetheart, raise a family and enjoy a slice of the American dream they had earned by their sacrifice. From 1945 to 1960, America enjoyed unprecedented growth in automobile sales and home ownership. The newly mobile population migrated from decaying urban centers into safe, affordable suburbs and the infrastructure that followed— hospitals, schools, libraries, utilities, swimming pools, recreation centers, and transportation networks. As more and more Americans lived in sprawling suburbs, cars, once a luxury, now became a necessity. Mom and pop stores suddenly had to compete with the one-stop convenience offered by shopping centers, department stores, and fast-food restaurants. Technological developments paid for by unfettered wartime research and development filtered into civilian life. Americans enjoyed a flood of new home appliances Madison Avenue promised would make life better. Soon every modern home was equipped with spacious refrigerators, convenient washer/dryers, and time-saving dishwashing machines.

In 1950, only twenty percent of homes in the United States owned a television set. By the end of the decade, it was ninety percent. The television had a significant impact on American life and in the 1950s became the primary source of entertainment as families tuned in weekly to live vicariously through *I Love Lucy, Ozzie and Harriet, Leave It to Beaver, Make Room for Daddy,* and *Father Knows Best,* absorbing a dose of conformity and consumerism in the process. Teenagers across America began racing home from school to watch Dick Clark count down the top songs on *American Bandstand.*

This was the Hawthorne in which the Beach Boys grew up. Quite a change from the rural community that became a city just forty years earlier and whose earliest inhabitants were four-legged, even-toed ungulates—sheep and cows.

Spurred by railroad expansion from LA, the Hawthorne Land Company, founded in 1887 by Benjamin Harding and Harry Dana Lombard, was one of several investors who purchased land from Robert Freeman, a Canadian rancher and farmer who purchased it from Scotsman Sir Robert Burnett in 1885. Burnett had purchased the land from Spanish nobleman Don Antonio Avila in 1868 at $1.28 per acre, expanding the livestock business and planting thousands of eucalyptus and fruit trees.

The name Hawthorne was chosen by Benjamin Harding's daughter, Laurine Harding Woolwine, who shared a birthday with author Nathaniel Hawthorne. In 1905, Harding and Lombard bought eighty acres from the company, formed the Hawthorne Improvement Company, and began advertising lots starting at eighty-five dollars in the town "Between City and Sea," a reference to Hawthorne's proximity to LA and the Pacific Ocean. Hawthorne sprouted along the Redondo Electric Car Line on what had once been fields of waving barley.

By 1907, more than one hundred families called Hawthorne home. A twenty-foot wide dirt road, that ran north and south along the western boundary, became Hawthorne Boulevard. Some of the earliest industry included factories for the manufacturing of furniture, overalls, gloves, and leather. The lone grocer received meat shipments by wagon from Inglewood three times a week. One structure served as church and school with sixteen pupils. Mail delivery began in October 1908. The population had grown to two thousand when Hawthorne voted to incorporate as LA County's thirty-eighth city in 1922.

In 1939, Northrop Aircraft, Incorporated (later Northrop Grumman) moved to Hawthorne with fifty employees and government contracts to build the P-61 Black Widow and the Flying Wing airplanes for the war effort. Aviation subcontractors flocked to the city. For the next two decades Hawthorne enjoyed an economic boom fueled by the Second World War and the prosperity of the 1950s.

By 1962, as the Beach Boys had their first success on Capitol Records, Hawthorne had 37,500 residents, three modern hospitals, LA County's first modern regional library, twenty-five churches, a parks and recreation program, and the only local airport devoted to privately owned aircraft. When Hawthorne adopted the "City of Good Neighbors" motto in summer 1961 for its fortieth anniversary, the winning entry earning Hawthorne High junior Judi Liber a twenty-five dollar U.S. Savings Bond, it was no idle boast. A local newspaper noted, "Hawthorne has Lions, Elks, Eagles, and Oddfellows; women's organizations, youth groups, senior citizen clubs, organizations of teachers, policemen, firemen, and realtors; Friends of the Library, home gardeners and rock hounds, a symphony association, Toastmasters, veterans groups, civic improvement associations and political clubs. Hawthorne has Kiwanians, Rotarians and Optimists. It lacks only pessimists."[3]

Among those optimistic migrants who now called Southern California home were two families—the Wilsons and the Korthofs. They didn't know each other, but two of their children—Murry Gage Wilson and Audree Neva Korthof—would meet, marry, and have three sons who would form the nucleus of the Beach Boys.

Murry Gage Wilson was born July 2, 1917, in Hutchinson, Kansas, the third of eight children of William "Buddy" Coral Wilson and Edith Sophia Sthole. His middle name was a tribute to Dr. G.P. Gage, the physician who delivered him.

Buddy was of English/Irish/Scottish heritage and worked alongside his father as a plumber. Edith, a short, heavyset woman, was of Swedish descent. Three months before Murry was born, the United States declared war on Germany and entered the conflict in Europe. Within days of Murry's birth, Buddy sought plumbing work in the military bases sprouting up throughout the Southwest to handle the influx of new recruits. Since the birth of his first child in 1914, Buddy had spent long stretches away from home, making the 1,400 mile trek in his Model T Ford to Escondido, California, in hope of securing a parcel of land on which to build a new life for his family and sever his ties with Kansas and his father.

By 1918 and the end of the First World War, Buddy was employed as a plumber in San Antonio, Texas. But the rough economy in fall 1920 necessitated sending three-year-old Murry and his one-year-old sister, Emily, to live temporarily with Edith's second cousin. By July 1921, Buddy had saved $200 in train fare for his family to join him in Cardiff-by-the-Sea, near San Diego. After an arduous three-day train ride with five children under the age of eight, Edith was dismayed to learn the housing Buddy secured was an eight-foot square canvas Army tent pitched in the sand on the beach. The next morning, as Edith stirred oatmeal in a tin pot over a fire dug into the sand, the children marveled at their first look at the Pacific Ocean. When work dried up in Cardiff-by-the-Sea, Buddy spent the week seventy-five miles north toiling under harsh conditions as a pipefitter for the Standard Oil Company at Huntington Beach, California. They scraped by and a year later could afford to rent a small apartment in Pasadena. In the mid–1920s, Buddy worked as a journeyman repairing portions of the two-hundred mile Los Angeles aqueduct sabotaged by area farmers whose crops were ruined by the corrupt diversion of water to the burgeoning LA metropolis.

The family moved to 605 West 99th Street near Inglewood in 1929 and, a year later, rented a farmhouse around the corner at 9722 South Figueroa for twenty-four dollars a month. Edith worked as a steam press operator for a clothing manufacturer. Buddy struggled to provide for his four sons and four daughters. But economic hardship and debilitating headaches worsened his appetite for alcohol, unmasking an underly-

Murry Wilson around the time he recorded *The Many Moods of Murry Wilson* in 1967.

ing bitterness which erupted in familial abuse. On more than one occasion Murry defended his mother and younger brother, Charles, from Buddy's alcoholic rage.

Audree Neva Korthof was born September 28, 1917, at 3301 Grand Avenue South in Minneapolis, Minnesota, the second child of Carl Arie Korthof and Ruth "Betty" Finney. Carl changed jobs and addresses thirteen times in the decade following Audree's birth. In spring 1928, the Korthofs moved to California and settled at 1420½ West 52nd Street in LA. In the mid–1930s, they moved to 1829 West 84th Street near Inglewood. Carl and his brother, Chester, along with Carl's son, Carl, Jr., opened the Mary Jane Bakery in LA.

In 1931, amidst the Great Depression, Murry and Audree enrolled in George Washington High School in LA where they met through a shared love of music. She played piano and sang in the girls' glee club. She formed the Girls Trio with classmates Lurline Uller and June Poole, and they sang popular hits of the day at school functions and community events. Earnest and ambitious, Murry lent his booming voice to the boys' glee club and ran varsity track. The 1935 *Continental* yearbook noted he was "a consistent point earner."

They graduated in June 1935 and Murry secured an entry-level job as a clerk with the Southern California Gas Company. They married March 26, 1938, and rented a small apartment at 613½ West 8th Street. Audree earned extra money giving piano lessons to neighborhood children in her home. Their first few years of marriage were spent working, saving for a home, and enjoying music in the evenings.

In 1941, Audree and Murry moved eight miles southwest to a small bungalow at 8012 South Harvard Boulevard and by Thanksgiving she was pregnant with their first child. On June 20, 1942, after nine hours of labor, Audree gave birth at 3:45 a.m. to Brian Douglas Wilson at Centinela Hospital, 555 East Hardy Street, in nearby Inglewood.

"When Brian was born," Murry remembered, "I was one of those young, frightened fathers, you know? But I just fell in love with him and in three weeks he cooed back at me. I would carry Brian on my shoulders with his little hands up above and I would sing 'Caissons Go Rolling Along' and he could hum the whole song. He was very clever and quick."[4]

Twenty-five years old and a new father, Murry had grown disenchanted with a job that offered little opportunity for advancement. Shortly after Brian's birth, Murry took a job as a supervisor at the Goodyear Tire and Rubber Company which occupied an entire city block in central LA on land that had once been cauliflower fields.

Brian grew up in a home filled with music. Audree had a beautiful singing voice and accompanied herself on piano and organ. She enjoyed the boogie woogie piano of Freddie Slack and Chicago blues pianist Clarence "Pinetop" Smith. Tommy Dorsey recorded "Pinetop's Boogie Woogie" in 1938 and it became a popular tune during World War II. Many artists recorded versions and it later inspired Ray Charles's "What'd I Say" (#1 R&B, #6 Pop, 1959). Audree taught "Boogie Woogie" to Brian and its pounding rhythmic breaks would influence his early songwriting efforts. Although Murry did not have a pleasant singing voice, it did not deter him from joining Audree at the piano and belting out a song in a deep gruff baritone. He dabbled in songwriting, plunking out melodies, and by 1950 had composed a handful of songs.

"I've been writing songs for as long as I can remember," Murry recalled. "My family has always had a great appreciation for the value of music. Many an evening my wife and I used to gather our songs and sing around our organ. Those were pretty lean days for us. We couldn't afford to go to a show, so we entertained ourselves with music."[5]

Brian recalled, "My mom was an organist and my dad was a pianist. My dad taught my mom how to play and then he would write songs and she would play along with him. It was like a husband and wife team. They were really great. He was an inspiration to melody. His melodies were real pretty. They really got to me very deeply."[6]

When Brian was very young, he took six weeks of accordion lessons. "Brian really excelled," Audree recalled. "The teacher told me, 'I don't think he's reading. He hears it once and plays the whole thing perfectly.'"[7] Brian loved to listen to his mother play piano, imploring her to play certain chords again. He began playing piano and singing with the church choir and at school functions. "By the time he was eight years old, he had a beautiful boy soprano voice and wasn't bashful about it."[8]

On June 20, 1944, Audree and Murry celebrated Brian's second birthday. They also had another reason to celebrate. She was pregnant again. At 10:56 p.m. at South Van Ness Hospital on December 4, Audree gave birth to Dennis Carl. On the birth certificate, Murry listed his profession as tread designer at the Goodyear Tire and Rubber Company.

In spring 1945, just months before the war ended, Audree and Murry finally had saved enough money for a down payment on a house. On March 7, they put $2,300 toward a new two-bedroom home at 3701 West 119th Street at the corner of Kornblum Avenue in Hawthorne just north of Hawthorne Municipal Airport. But the joy of home owner-ship was short-lived when Murry was involved in an industrial accident that summer at Goodyear.

Murry was supervising a new employee charged with using a metal pole to swab an acidic conditioning solution on the sides of newly molded tires as they spun on a circular rotating rack. But the worker was timid and the caustic solution was splashing everywhere. Exasperated with the trainee's timidity, Murry cut the power to the apparatus. The pole flew out of control, struck Murry in the face, shattered his eyeglasses, and pierced his left eye. He was rushed to Avalon Hospital across the street where it was determined the eye could not be salvaged. Murry was sedated and underwent an enucleation whereby the sur-geon ligated and transected ocular muscles, blood vessels, and optic nerve, and removed the ruined eye from its bony socket. Murry was fitted with a temporary space-occupying device to prevent a sunken appearance until he could be fitted with a prosthetic glass eye at Centinela Hospital where Brian had been born. He could only insert the prosthesis for brief periods until the tender tissues of his ocular socket became calloused. In the meantime, he wore a black eye patch. He was understandably despondent about the loss of his eye. In time, however, he turned this adversity into personal motivation. "When I was twenty-five I thought the world owed me a living," Murry recalled. "When I lost my eye, I tried harder, drove harder, and did the work of two men and got more raises."[9]

He returned to Goodyear after his injury, but soon left for a job at Garrett AiResearch, one of many local aeronautic companies that included Northrup, Lockheed, Boeing, Doug-las, Hughes Aircraft, and North American Aviation. Founded by John Garrett in 1936, AiResearch expanded five years later into a new facility built on a former bean field at Sepul-veda and Century Boulevards near the future Los Angeles International Airport. Dennis recalled, "He worked at AiResearch and on Friday nights he'd get his paycheck. The three of us would be in the back seat of the car singing away. Actually, that's the birth of the three brothers singing together at that early age."[10] "We grew up in an atmosphere where your father is a songwriter and music was a very important emotional factor. My father used to cry over beautiful music or if we three sang something pretty, you could see tears in his eyes. It's a form of support to know your father really loves something."[11]

Murry worked at AiResearch from 1945 to 1950, during which time he and Audree welcomed a third son, Carl Dean, on December 21, 1946. In the years following the war, AiResearch hired scores of returning veterans. Not having served in the military, Murry couldn't share in their camaraderie and it created a gulf between him and the younger men he supervised. Murry left AiResearch on his fifth anniversary and began working for his younger brother, Douglas, at Admiral Machinery Company at 7601 South Santa Fe Avenue in Huntington Park, an industrial area south of LA and twelve miles northeast of Hawthorne. Admiral was a heavy machinery leasing business which thrived in the post-war building boom.

—◦◦◦—

Psychologists and social scientists have long debated what effect, if any, the order in which children are born into a family affects their development, relationships with their siblings and parents, and other relationships in adulthood. Although there are many variables and researchers do not all agree, birth order does appear to play a role in a child's development.

In general, firstborn children receive the most time, attention, and emotional nourishment from parents. Firstborns are generally responsible, conscientious, detail-oriented, and good at following through. First-time parents are often nervous and overprotective, heaping praise on their firstborn's every achievement. This can produce a smarter, more confident child. It can also motivate a child to overachieve and demand perfection.

Middle children are affected by whatever role the firstborn child plays in the family. Rather than compete with the firstborn, a middle child may take an opposite track. Because they don't get their way easily, they learn to deal, negotiate, and compromise, which makes them pragmatic and independent. They may feel they don't fit in and seek friendships outside the family. But struggling for a unique identity may leave them feeling alone and adrift. "We didn't get along as well as we should have when we were children," Dennis recalled. "Even in our teens, we weren't exactly united."[12] "We were very competitive because Brian was the oldest and most important. I spent more time with Carl because I could beat Carl up."[13]

By the time the lastborn comes along, parents tend to relax the rules. The youngest child tends to get away with more than their siblings. This can make a child more easygoing, carefree and able to get along with others. With something to prove to their siblings, they may try to distinguish themselves by succeeding through a more rebellious route. "When you're the youngest one in the family," recalled Carl, "you tend to be the observer because the show is already going on. That pattern had been established for years before the group got going."[14]

Siblings play many roles in our lives: playmate, friend, tormentor, rival, role model, co-conspirator, and confidante. They are among our earliest teachers from whom we learn social interaction, how to conduct friendships, problem solve, and resolve conflicts. In dysfunctional families, siblings help insulate each other against chaos and upheaval. In the case of a physically abusive parent, the oldest child often becomes the protector of the younger children, sacrificing a once-close relationship with the parent. The Wilson brothers, close in age and sharing one bedroom, had an indelible effect on one another that informed who they were and who they became. When they began singing together, the timbre and intonation of their voices, nurtured by their close upbringing and shared experiences, created a unique vocal blend.

—◦◦◦—

By summer 1951, Murry was thirty-four years old, had three young children, and worked for his brother Douglas. He began to devote more time toward nurturing his dream of being a songwriter. He admired songwriters like Irving Berlin, Richard Rodgers, Cole Porter, and the Gershwins. But Murry only tinkered at the ivories and songwriting never came easy. Some writers have only one song in them. Some have five hundred. Murry had twenty-eight. At least that's how many he registered with Broadcast Music, Incorporated (BMI) in two creative bursts, one in the early 1950s and another in the mid–1960s after the success of the Beach Boys. Only a handful of his 1950s compositions were ever recorded. BMI and the American Society of Composers and Producers (ASCAP) are the major performing rights organizations that collect licensing fees on behalf of songwriters and music publishers.

Two of Murry's earliest songs were "Whistle Head" and "Tabarin," a term synonymous with a cabaret or nightclub. "Tabarin" caught the attention of Sherman Williams, an LA sax player who owned the Unique record label and was friends with Art Rupe, owner of the LA–based Specialty Records. Williams had the R&B group the Four Flames record "Tabarin" and, instead of releasing it on Unique, arranged for Rupe to release it on Fidelity (3001), Specialty's new subsidiary, in November 1951. "Tabarin" was a sentimental R&B ballad in which the singer reminisces about a love he lost at the nightclub. The reviews for "Tabarin" were not kind. *Billboard* noted, "A new male quartet specializing in the wobbly-note bending style, gives out with a rather feeble ballad."[15] "Tabarin" saw another release that month when Bob Williams with the Red Callender Sextette recorded it as "Tabor Inn" on the B side of "September in the Rain" on Federal 12049.

In January 1952, the Four Flames, now called Hollywood's Four Flames, decided to give "Tabarin" another chance (b/w "Cryin' for My Baby," Unique 005). Although none of these versions of "Tabarin" charted or received much airplay, Murry had the satisfaction of having one of his songs recorded three separate times and having the 78 rpm records he could play at home. On February 29, 1952, a song called "Shamrock" was registered with BMI for which Murry was credited as the third writer.

"My favorite song my dad wrote was one called 'His Little Darlin' and You,'" recalled Brian. "It was a ballad (sings 'When a bee loses his queen bee, his days are numbered it's true.'). Great. My dad had talent, he sure did. He was a talented man. He had some music in him."[16] Although Murry never achieved fame as a songwriter, he provided an environment for his sons that fostered a love of music and an appreciation for the creative process of songwriting.

Around summer 1952, Murry converted his attached garage into usable living space. He purchased an electric Hammond organ on credit and, along with their upright piano and Wurlitzer jukebox, moved them into the new music room. Now that he was beginning to have some minor success as a songwriter, this sanctuary, insulated from the rest of the house, allowed him to concentrate on his music.

Although he could be a strict disciplinarian, Murry also had a tender side and often surprised his sons with thrill-seeking gifts like the BB gun and motorized go-kart he bought for Dennis. On December 4, 1954, Murry hosted an all-boys celebration for Dennis's tenth birthday. Don Allen, Dennis's third grade classmate at York Elementary School, recalled, "It was very sweet when I think back on it. They converted the whole house to a jungle gym for the kids to tear around in. They took the furniture out of all the rooms and put big mattresses on the floor for these wild, rambunctious little boys. We used the whole house as a playground, jumped up and down, wrestled, fought, and threw things. Dennis's dad was very much in the spirit of the whole enterprise. He was having a great time. He'd give kids horseback rides, wrestle with them, and squirt them with water guns. Just all kinds of crazy things like that, sort of a little boy's heaven. I remember him being outgoing, friendly, jovial, enthusiastic, and quite in the spirit of being a ten-year-old boy."[17]

After four years working for his brother, Murry saw a market niche for the rental of smaller machines and tools. He borrowed $20,000, and on March 7, 1955, incorporated ABLE (Always Better Lasting Equipment) Machinery Company in a one-story rented store-front at 6825 South Santa Fe Avenue in Huntington Park, a half mile north from Douglas's Admiral Machinery. Murry imported a line of lathes and drills from the British firm Binns & Berry, Ltd. He flooded local aeronautics firms with flyers touting the ability of the imported lathes to exceed the most stringent engineering specifications. Murry later moved ABLE four miles southeast to a one-story two-room 3,000 square foot storefront at 4969 Firestone Boulevard in Southgate where he often recruited his sons on Saturday afternoons to clean the machinery.

Murry's younger sister, Emily, who everyone called Glee, was born in 1919, and attended George Washington High School two years after Murry. She grew into a beautiful young woman active in the Girls' League, the Tri-Y Club, and the Ladies, the counterpart to the Knights. She delighted in performing in many of the drama club's stage productions and starred her senior year in *The Red Mill*, Victor Herbert's 1906 operetta of two American vaudevillians stranded in Europe. She also sang in the glee club with her future sister-in-law, Audree Korthoff. Emily caught the eye of upperclassman Milton Love, a handsome athletic fellow of English-Irish heritage and older brother of her classmate and fellow thespian, Stanley. Milt was a Knight, All-City end on the Generals varsity football team, ran varsity track with her brother, Murry, and was treasurer of the Hi-Y, a group allied with the YMCA and dedicated to the "high standards of Christian character."

Milt and Emily dated throughout their high school years. After he graduated in 1936 and she a year later, they married September 10, 1938, in a civil ceremony in Ventura, California. Milt briefly attended the University of California, Los Angeles (UCLA), before working full-time at Love Sheet Metal Service Company at 1882 West Washington Boulevard, the company founded by his father, Edward, in 1909. Milt joined the Sheet Workers International Association and installed galleys for the United States Navy during the war years. The family business enjoyed two decades of prosperity fueled first by the war effort and later the post-war economic boom. In flush times, Edward purchased a Cadillac every year for Milt and his younger son, Stanley, who also worked for the company. In the mid–1940s, they expanded into cabinetry and woodworking. "They were sheet metal workers,"

Mike recalled. "My dad would get up at five in the morning to take a shower and be out the door by six. He'd work six days a week, sometimes seven. That was hard work."[18]

The sheet metal business afforded Milt and Glee a very comfortable lifestyle and, in the late 1940s, they built a three-level, fourteen room Mediterranean-style home at the sloping intersection of W. Mount Vernon Drive and Fairway Boulevard in the affluent View Park—Windsor Hills section of Los Angeles. He built a darkroom where he could pursue his passion for photography. They filled the home's seven bedrooms with six children—Michael (1941), Maureen (1943), Stephen (1947), Stanley (1949), Stephanie (1951), and Marjorie (1960). There was little the Love kids went without, including a wide array of sports, music, and artistic adventures. Brian later described the Love residence as 'a mansion on a hill' when he immortalized it in "Mt. Vernon and Fairway (A Fairytale)," a special seven-inch record packaged with the Beach Boys *Holland* in 1973.

In late 1950, Glee held a concert at her home to celebrate Murry's songwriting efforts. She hired a musical trio to perform his songs and invited her friends. One of the highlights of the evening was eight-year-old Brian's performance of "Bugle Memories," a song his cousin Mike wrote in fall 1950. Murry wrote a musical score for Brian to use. "Mike wrote a song about a soldier who died in the war," Murry explained. "I heard it over at my sister's house and I thought it was just darling. But I heard it as a hymn. I went home and composed other lyrics to it."[19] On the handwritten score, Murry credited Mike with words and music, and added the notation "Murry Wilson lyrics." In 1951, Murry filed the requisite paperwork with the U.S. Copyright Office in Washington, D.C., making Mike the first member of the future Beach Boys to have a song copyrighted.

Glee had come a long way from her humble beginnings living in a tent on the beach. But her memories of economic deprivation and her father's alcohol-driven tantrums made her a high-strung, protective mother. It also made her fiercely protective of Murry whom she idolized for bearing the brunt of their father's two-fisted abuse sustained while defending their mother. As she eased into her mid-thirties, Glee had a secure life—a beautiful home, a busy calendar with other socially conscious wives, appreciation of the fine arts, and healthy children.

For most of the 1950s, even as the Love Sheet Metal Service Company experienced hard financial times in the latter part of the decade, Glee hosted a traditional Christmas holiday dinner to bring her and Murry's families together. The secular comforts of plentiful food and modest gifts reaffirmed that they had, each in their own way, forged better lives for themselves. At the heart of their holiday gatherings was music—a chance to renew and sustain themselves in something beautiful. As in Murry's and Glee's childhood, music could stir their hearts, lift their souls, and heal their psychic wounds. After dinner, the families exchanged presents and gathered around the piano to sing Christmas carols. The festive mood often spilled outside and the singing troupe went caroling around the neighborhood. As the Love and Wilson cousins got older, they participated in the obligatory Christmas carols before breaking off on their own to sing the rock 'n' roll and R&B hits of the day.

"Music goes way back for all of us," recalled Mike Love. "My mother used to have fantastic Christmas parties and we'd all sing together. And Brian would always have to sing 'Danny Boy' for our grandmother because he had such a nice voice. He didn't particularly *like* singing this song every Christmas, but he did it."[20] Mike later recalled Brian singing on their grandfather Wilson's lap. "Even at nine or ten years old, Brian sang, oh my God, it was so special, like an angel. He was channeling something from another realm."[21]

Glee kept a fastidious home and took certain precautions before her nephews arrived. Mike recalled, "My parents would rope off the upstairs of the house when the Wilsons came to visit. They were such wild kids!"[22] But she was also quick to offer encouragement. After Brian sang at one of her Saturday evening programs, she wrote him, "You surely have a nice clear high voice and everyone said if you take care of it and practice singing later—you may be a really great singer."[23]

Murry only lived ten miles from Glee, but his life stood in sharp contrast to hers. His single story, five-room house was cramped, and his three growing sons were forced to share one bedroom. His salary was modest and he grew increasingly frustrated as Audree began to undermine his discipline whenever the boys sought her refuge to avoid his punishments.

Glee had acquired a comfortable life by marrying into a family who attained the American dream by hard work, individualism, and faith in themselves. Perhaps driven by Milton Love's achievement, Murry had formed his own business, investing any future success in his own self-determination. Ironically, as he drove his 1950 Henry J automobile north along Crenshaw Boulevard to Glee's Christmas parties, Murry could not have known that his future was behind him, literally sitting in the back seat. Murry would soon pin his dreams, his need for self-actualization, on the musical aspirations of his three sons.

3

Headed for Hollywood
Dorinda and Hite Morgan

Hite and Dorinda Morgan are familiar names to most Beach Boys fans. The husband and wife songwriting team owned a music publishing company, operated a recording studio in their home, nurtured struggling artists, recorded demonstration records, and shopped these demos to record companies. Murry Wilson befriended the Morgans in 1952, and they published several of his songs and arranged for a few to be recorded. In fall 1961, when Murry's sons, nephew, and their friend, wanted to make a record, they turned to Hite and Dorinda. Over the next six months, the Morgans recorded nine songs by the fledgling Beach Boys who could barely play their instruments. Raw recordings hinted at the harmonic genius that lay ahead. The Morgans were essential in launching America's most beloved band on a musical journey now in its sixth decade. And yet, embarrassingly little is known about the Morgans as most books about the band pay scant attention to them. Most Beach Boys fans do not even know what they looked like.

Here is their story.

In 1952, Murry met forty-six-year-old Hite Morgan, who, with his wife, Dorinda, owned Guild Music Company, a music publishing firm, and operated a recording studio from their home. The Morgans also owned Mastaflor, an industrial flooring company, and Bruce Morgan, their son, believes Murry met Hite at one of his father's commercial flooring job sites.

Dorinda Morgan was a songwriter with seventy-nine songs registered with BMI and sixteen with ASCAP. Dorinda and Hite made demo recordings in their living room studio for struggling artists trying to interest record companies in signing them to recording contracts. Hite enjoyed meeting songwriters and was intrigued to learn Murry had written "Tabarin" for the Four Flames. The two men struck up a mutually beneficial friendship. Morgan was always on the lookout for songwriters whose tunes he could publish and copyright. He had connections with record companies and radio stations all over town and could place Murry's songs with aspiring singers and have them released on local record labels.

Hite Bowman Morgan was born April 29, 1906, in New York City, the only child of Jesse Canby Morgan, a Scotch-Welshman from Oregon, and Mary "Mamie" Pauline Bowman from Louisville, Kentucky. Although Mamie had sung opera in Paris, she did not pursue a professional singing career in New York. Her creativity found an outlet in the movie posters she painted that were displayed beneath the marquees of New York's finest theaters.

Between 1924 and 1926, Hite enrolled for three semesters at the University of Pennsylvania. In New York, he met Dorothy Brickwedde, a beautiful woman of German heritage

dog owned at one time by then–Secretary of the Treasury Henry Morgenthau, Jr. How he wound up in the middle of the road is a mystery, but he spent his remaining years living happily with the Morgans. He sired a litter of red Dobies for which Dorinda found good homes, keeping a little red female they named Rhoda.

In summer 1943, with the war in Europe raging and the resultant upswing in the American economy, California's military and aviation industries experienced unprecedented growth. Hite reasoned LA presented a tremendous opportunity for the specialized flooring he manufactured. Furthermore, the warm climate would be good for their health, and Dorinda would enjoy living in the heart of the West Coast music scene. They decided Jonathan and Bruce would start their new school year as California boys. To celebrate this milestone in their lives, Dorinda composed "Heading for Hollywood" as a playful tribute to their cross-country adventure and published it through their Melody Music company. The Morgans made many good friends during their eight years in Brookhaven and leaving was not easy. "I didn't want to move," recalled Bruce. "We had just gotten glass in our windows and indoor plumbing."[3]

Everything Hite and Dorinda owned squeezed into two vehicles—a 1937 Dodge truck that had once been a bakery truck and a 1939 Chevrolet that had been a taxi. Hite and Jonathan pulled away from their home in the Dodge, followed by Dorinda, Bruce, and Rhoda in the Chevrolet. The long, steamy trek to LA had its share of adventures. They got separated along the way, the steering wheel of the Chevy came off in Dorinda's hands, and then there was the great marble mishap. As they crossed the Mississippi River, Bruce's prized marble collection, hard won from numerous competitions on the streets of Brookhaven, jarred loose and soon the air was filled with an ominous "ping, ping, ping, ping" as hundreds of marbles dropped and scattered across the steel grating of the roadway. Naturally, ten-year-old Bruce was upset over losing his collection, but he tried to focus on the excitement ahead. He had discovered the Los Angeles River on a map and was anxious to explore an unchartered waterway. "You can imagine my disappointment when I realized the Los Angeles River was a trickle at the bottom of a concrete aqueduct."[4]

The Morgans arrived in California in late summer 1943 and, on September 21, Hite and Dorinda bought a two-bedroom, single-family, 2,000 square foot home at 2511 Mayberry Street, a tranquil quarter-mile stretch tucked away in the Silver Lake area east of Hollywood and three miles northwest of downtown LA. The single level stucco home had a detached cottage in the back yard. (See Appendix 6.) The Morgans purchased the home from James and Evelyn Martin, becoming its seventh owner since it was built in 1914.

Bruce enrolled in seventh grade and showed up for his first day of school with a southern accent and short pants. Now, shorts may have been the norm in Georgia, but they were odd in 1943 LA. And nothing coaxes cruelty out of children more than odd. Bruce was ridiculed unmercifully. The next day, he showed up at school in long pants.

As Dorinda settled the boys into school and their new life, Hite drove a taxi to pay the bills and learn how to navigate the city. The smog in LA was abysmal at the time, stinging eyes and searing lungs. It was an unsettling change of environment for Hite and Dorinda who were both developing asthma from residual pulmonary scarring secondary to their bouts of pneumonia in New York. In 1944, Hite landed a job as a lighting grip in the movie industry. On the sets and studio back lots, he befriended many stars and had the sheet music for Dorinda's "Heading for Hollywood" autographed by more than fifty celebrities including

Groucho Marx, Harry James, the Andrews Sisters, and Bing Crosby. In his free time, Hite began purchasing cement mixers and other specialized equipment to resume his flooring company.

A year before the Morgans moved to California, in part because of the music business, life for professional musicians changed drastically. On August 1, 1942, James C. Petrillo, the president of the American Federation of Musicians (AFM), called for a national strike that prohibited union musicians from playing at sessions for phonograph recordings, except those produced for the war effort, and from performing live on the radio. Petrillo argued the most pressing concern was the threat phonograph records posed on the livelihood of professional musicians. AFM members were paid a flat hourly rate for their work on a recording. They did not receive any royalties on the sale of that recording. Petrillo also reasoned that radio posed a threat to working musicians. When record companies refused Petrillo's demands for royalties, he called for the strike. The "Petrillo Ban" lasted until November 11, 1944. Ironically, the ban may have contributed to the birth of doo wop as background singers who, inspired by vocal groups like the Mills Brothers and the Ink Spots, supported the lead vocalist by using their voices to emulate the musical sounds of absent instruments. The ban also provided opportunities for musicians not in the union.

By 1945, Hite had Mastaflor back in operation and began bidding on government and commercial flooring jobs. Never the low bidder, he knew he delivered a quality product and was one of the few contractors, if not the only, to guarantee his work. He installed floors to withstand the acidic effects of blood at meat packing facilities, the crushing weight of industrial vats of cheese, and the corrosive impact of battery acids at railroad roundhouses where trains turned around. He secured contracts to manufacture and install a spark-proof floor at an ammunition depot and, at Northrop Aircraft, a shock-resistant floor capable of withstanding the powerful drop hammers used to forge sheet metal into airplane fuselages.

Hite's proprietary formula for his floor included such eclectic materials as camel hair, steel, milk, and some sort of stone that was close to being categorized as a precious gem. It was very difficult work, often requiring several weeks to complete a job. Bruce began working with his father in the late 1940s, often toiling sixteen-hour days, beginning at 4:00 a.m. and working until sundown. In the morning, Bruce picked up materials and supplies, drove to the job site, and began making the mix. The crew consisted of six to twelve well-trained finishers and laborers. The heavy mix was extracted from the mixer by muscled workers using steel hoes. It was then transported to the job site on a special motor-driven buggy. Competing contractors would try to plant their own employees on Hite's projects to learn his formula. But they never succeeded. "It was hard, grueling work," recalled Bruce. "Some years my dad would only do two major jobs. But after collecting a check or two for $60,000, he paid his expenses and workers, and took some time off while he worked with my mother on the music business. In that sense, the flooring business supported my mom's musical interests."[5]

Dorinda was constantly humming melodies, jotting down lyrics, and working out new songs on her upright blonde-wood spinet piano. Although Dorinda did not read music, she devised a graph-like system to chart her compositions. She then asked her musician friends to transcribe a lead sheet that professional musicians and singers could read. In exchange for the transcription, Dorinda often gave the friend a co-writing credit. But lead sheets had their limitations. Many producers, record company owners, radio program directors, and disc jockeys could not read music. To circumvent this problem, many songwriters pitched their compositions with recordings called dubs, lacquers, or, most commonly, acetates.

An acetate was a thick aluminum disc, eight, ten, or twelve inches in diameter, sprayed with a thin layer of ultra-high-grade methylcellulose, a substance that resembled nail polish and why records are sometimes referred to as "wax." The original audio tape recording was placed on a reel-to-reel tape deck connected to a lathe, a sophisticated recorder that operated like a phonograph player but, instead of a stylus to amplify the music in a record's grooves, it was equipped with a cutting head to create the grooves. A blank acetate was placed on the lathe's turntable, the tape queued, and the process started. While the acetate spun at 45 rpm (or other speeds), the cutting head moved across it radially in an inward direction, cutting grooves into the methylcellulose in a continuous circular fashion, and transferring the electronic signal of the music. Acetates were often used as a reference recording to ensure the finished record would sound like the original master tape.

An acetate could be played on a phonograph player, but if it was played too many times the phonograph stylus eroded the methylcellulose, exposing the underlying metal and rendering the acetate useless. Hence, acetates were short-lived recordings meant primarily to be used in the first step of the process of manufacturing records.

An acetate was taken to a metal works plant where it was submerged in a tank filled with a silver or nickel solution that plated it completely. When the solution hardened, the methylcellulose acetate was manually separated from the metal disc, now called a converted metal stamper, or "father," with raised ridges corresponding to the grooves of the acetate. The acetate was usually destroyed during this process and could not be used again. The "father" then went through the plating process again, separated, and yielded a "mother"— a metal duplicate of the acetate, complete with grooves that could be played on a phonograph as a test pressing before the record was mass produced. In this two-step process, the "mother" was safely stored and the "father" was used as a metal stamper to press, or "stamp" out, about 1,000 records. The "father" usually chipped or wore out after that and had to be discarded.

To produce a larger quantity of records, pressing plants used a three-step process by which the "father" was plated many separate times and yielded, for example, twelve "mothers" that were plated and separated to yield twelve stampers which could press about 12,000 records in an eight-hour shift.

By the mid–1940s, Hite decided Dorinda needed the competitive edge of acetates to promote her songs. He purchased some electronic equipment and built a simple recording facility in their home on Mayberry Street. The spacious 15' × 25' living room, the first room after the enclosed front porch, had hardwood floors, plaster walls, and Dorinda's upright piano. When the Morgans held a recording session, they moved their furniture to the room's perimeter to accommodate musicians, vocalists, and background singers. In the porch, Hite set up his "control booth" and "mastering facility." Here he arranged his recording and disc-cutting equipment—Presto and Universal lathes equipped with diamond-cutting stylus and cutter heads, turntable, microphones, mixer, work bench, and a supply of blank acetates. From the porch, Hite ran as many as five microphones into the living room studio where he would mic the lead singer, background singers, and instruments, usually piano, guitar, and bass.

One of Hite's and Dorinda's musical ideas was to produce instrumental versions of popular songs over which people could record their own vocal—an early form of karaoke. They named their innovative venture Vocompany, but never introduced it commercially. Over the next twenty years, Hite and Dorinda's living room studio became a magnet for local singers, musicians, producers, promoters, and record company owners—a musical Grand Central Station providing a welcoming home to anyone who shared a passion for music and were trying to make it in the fiercely competitive music business. "The living room was like a coffee shop," recalled Bruce. "There were people in it at all times. You could always hear some new song being worked out or my dad getting ready for a recording."

Many of the singers and songwriters Hite and Dorinda worked with became their closest friends. The Morgans recorded folks like Jack Holmes, Jack Carrington, and Lee Penny, who along with Louise Massey, wrote the 1941 hit "My Adobe Hacienda," which scored on the pop and country charts making it perhaps the first crossover hit. They also recorded Betty Hall Jones, a pianist/singer/songwriter, whose "Ain't That Fine" was published by Guild Music and recorded by nineteen-year-old Ray Charles for Jack Lauderdale's Down Beat Records in 1948. The flip side, "Don't Put All Your Dreams in One Basket," was written by Dorinda and Jones. Lauderdale was one of the first black entrepreneurs to own an independent record company.

Some of the people who walked through the Morgans' door were a virtual Who's Who in West Coast Rhythm and Blues, including John Dolphin, Sam Cooke, and Richard "Bumps" Blackwell, who produced Little Richard's "Tutti Frutti" for Art Rupe's Specialty Records in November 1955. Bruce recalled Hite and Bumps discussing a song Cooke was set to record called "You Send Me." With its lush orchestration, smooth female background vocals, and Cooke's unique phrasing, "You Send Me" was the perfect blending of pop and R&B. It sold 1.7 million copies and reached #1 on the R&B and pop charts in fall 1957. It was a harbinger of an important change in the music industry—the extraordinary power of a crossover hit.

As an artist played or sang live in the Morgans' living room, Hite recorded them directly onto an acetate disc. He worked on the fly, adjusting the knobs on his mixer for volume, equalization, and the single monaural sound level meter. After the session, Hite gave the 78 rpm acetate to the artist, a wax coated metal calling card of his or her ability. The acetates could be eight, ten, or twelve inches in diameter, depending on how many songs were recorded. When Hite wanted to produce a more fully developed demo, he would visit his friend Henry Schelb, an accomplished keyboard player who owned Crystal Studios on Santa Monica Boulevard.

Over the years, Hite formed several record companies including Maestro, Dice, Deck, and Randy. Most were short-lived and only Deck saw more than a handful of releases. Hite and Dorinda also formed several music publishing companies. Melody Music operated for most of the 1940s before they formed Guild Music with BMI in the late 1940s. In the mid–1950s, they formed Prestige Publishing Company with ASCAP. By affiliating with both performing rights organizations, the Morgans maximized their publishing opportunities with both BMI and ASCAP songwriters.

To give his recordings a competitive edge, or at least level the playing field, Hite used the two-step process at the A&M pressing plant at 1107 N. El Centro Avenue near Santa Monica Boulevard to press upwards of 1,000 records. These trial records were used to get feedback from disc jockeys and program directors and had the potential to act as a springboard in launching a new artist. Morgan printed the El Centro address on his Deck Records label.

But manufacturing the records was easy compared to getting them played on the radio. Although Hite's recordings were useful demonstrations, most radio stations were reluctant to play an acetate by an unknown artist on an independent label. In such a competitive business, program directors had too many legitimate releases to consider. There were times, however, when a program director heard an acetate he felt was destined to be a hit record. Those dubs were typically brought in by a record promoter or an artist and repertoire (A&R) man whom the program director knew professionally, if not personally. The song was often produced by an established record company and thousands of copies were already in production. A shrewd program director, eager to point out a hit song was heard first on his station, would seize the opportunity to get that all-important jump on the competition. The appearance of having a finger on the pulse of popular taste translated into marketing dollars from corporate sponsors.

Hite was his own record promoter. He visited local radio stations and met with station managers, program directors, and disc jockeys. He would play them his record and solicit their opinions. What did they like about the song? Was it commercial? What could be done to improve it? As Hite made his rounds, Dorinda remained in the car. "She was actually quite shy," recalled Bruce. "She didn't enjoy visiting radio stations and meeting program directors and disc jockeys. She left that to my dad. But while she was waiting for him, she'd compose two or three songs in her head."[6]

While Hite's asthma attacks could be controlled with an inhaler, Dorinda required intramuscular injections of adrenaline. She needed up to sixteen injections a day, rotating around both shoulders and thighs. "My mother struggled to breathe every day of her life," remembered Bruce.

Bruce's own musical inclinations began to emerge in his teenage years. Encouraged by his mother, Bruce wrote his first song, a cautionary tale called "Proverb Boogie." After Bruce graduated from John Marshall High School in June 1949, Hite and Dorinda arranged for him to stay with their friend Syd Nathan, owner of King Records in Cincinnati, and learn the music business. Bruce hopped in his 1949 Nash and headed east. Nathan was the quintessential cigar-smoking, coffee-drinking, fast-talking record company president. He was short, overweight, wore thick eyeglasses, and had chronic bad breath. Bruce found him brash and uncouth, and was pleased to finally return to LA.

In 1950, while backstage at the Orpheum in LA, Hite showed Bruce's "Proverb Boogie" to R&B singer Louis Jordan, who liked the song, renamed it "Heed My Warning" (claiming a co-writing credit in the process), and recorded it. "Heed My Warning" (b/w "Baby's Gonna Go Bye Bye," Decca 24981) was released in April 1950. It was a local hit, but failed to crack the national charts. Meanwhile, Hite and Dorinda's "Turn Your Head Sweetheart (I Can Still See Your Face)" was recorded by radio personality Jim Hawthorne on RCA Victor and received local play for its comic play on words.

When Hite met Murry Wilson, their friendship was forged in music. He offered to publish two of Murry's new songs and work on getting them recorded through his contacts in the LA music world. On October 3, 1952, Murry signed a Standard Songwriter's Contract with the Morgans' Guild Music for "Two Step, Side Step" about a dance that originated in the Arthur Murray Studio in Santa Monica, California, and later introduced in Murry's three hundred dance studios across the country. Dance instructors Claude Sims and Juanita Raye, accompanied by the Lawrence Welk Orchestra, taught the dance at the Aragon Ballroom on the Lick Pier in the Ocean Park district of Santa Monica. Dorinda wrote Murry a check for fifty dollars as an advance on any future royalty and Murry registered "Two Step, Side Step" with BMI November 21. He also signed a songwriting contract with Guild for "I'll Hide My Tears" and registered it with BMI December 19.

In early 1953, Hite learned of a new local record company called Palace Records whose owner, twenty-five-year-old Alfred W. Schlesinger, was looking for songs for his artists to record. Schlesinger had befriended a trio called the Bachelors after seeing them perform at the Hotel Long Beach.[7] Hite invited Schlesinger to his home to observe a recording session and showed him Murry's "Two Step, Side Step." Schlesinger liked it and brought it to the Bachelors. "We recorded 'Two Step, Side Step' at Gold Star," Schlesinger recalled. "Hite was there and so was Murry. I didn't invite him, but he came. Recording is fairly intense and, as I produced the recording, I didn't

On October 3, 1952, Murry Wilson signed a Standard Songwriter's Contract for "Two Step, Side Step" with Guild Music Publishing, owned by husband and wife Hite and Dorinda Morgan, who arranged to have it recorded by the Bachelors on Al Schlesinger's Palace Records in early 1953. The Lawrence Welk Orchestra performed "Two Step, Side Step" during a live broadcast from the Aragon Ballroom on the Santa Monica pier in spring 1953. Johnnie Lee Wills and His Boys recorded a version on RCA Victor in September 1953 (author's collection).

have much interaction with Murry. We said hello, he made a comment or two during the recording, and we said good-bye. I don't think I saw him again until I became the Beach Boys' attorney in late 1962."[8]

In spring 1953, to help promote the Bachelors' new record, group member Jimmie Haskell arranged to have "Two Step, Side Step" performed by the Lawrence Welk Orchestra and broadcast live on his "On the Air From the Aragon" ABC radio program or his one-hour television show telecast 9:00 p.m. on Friday night on KTLA-TV channel 5. Since its debut May 18, 1951, Welk's television show had become one of the top ten shows in Southern California. *Billboard* reported, "During the band's stand, an estimated 1,700,000 patrons have passed through the Aragon's turnstiles. The gross hit an all-time high of $1,486,000 for the ocean front ballroom which previously was in the economic doldrums."[9] On July 2, 1955, forty million viewers tuned in as ABC-TV began broadcasting *The Lawrence Welk Show* nationally in prime time on Saturday evening (6:00 p.m. on the West Coast) and the show moved from the Aragon Ballroom to Studio E at the ABC Television Center in Hollywood. On June 4, 1960, Welk moved his show back to the Aragon Ballroom.

Morgan called Murry with the good news and Murry gathered Audree and the kids around the radio or television for one of the highlights of his musical career. Less than a year after they met, Murry's friendship with Hite Morgan had paid off handsomely. Here was Lawrence Welk, one of the country's most beloved orchestra leaders, performing Murry's original composition on one of LA's top-rated programs. Although Welk never recorded "Two Step, Side Step," Morgan printed sheet music with a cover photograph of Welk playing the accordion and the notation "Featured by Lawrence Welk, Coral Recording Artist." On the back were instructions on how to do the dance. Murry's songwriting career was off to a good start.

In summer 1953, Schlesinger had the Bachelors record Murry's sentimental ballad "I'll Hide My Tears" on Palace. Morgan arranged to have two of Murry's songs recorded by country singer Johnny Hall—"Painting with Teardrops (of Blue)" backed with "Two Step, Side Step." The A side was a medium-paced song about a dissolution of a marriage in which the singer muses that although their home will be sold, his heart will remain there for her. The record was released on Recorded in Hollywood, one of the labels John Dolphin operated out of his Dolphin's of Hollywood record store in South Central LA. It failed to chart.[10]

On June 11, 1953, the Texas Swing band Johnnie Lee Wills and His Boys recorded "Two Step, Side Step" in the studio of radio station KVOO in Tulsa, Oklahoma. Johnnie Lee was the younger brother of Bob Wills, the King of Western Swing. When "Two Step, Side Step" was released that summer as the B side to "Sold Out Doc" (RCA Victor 5449), *Billboard* called Murry's tune "A bouncy novelty and a real toe tapper. A good dance number that should keep the jukes humming in the Southwest."[11] Although Texas Swing remained popular regionally, it was fading nationally and the song never charted.

Murry finally registered "Painting with Teardrops (of Blue)" with BMI on January 29, 1954. He signed songwriting contracts with Hite Morgan for "Back to Texas" and "Don't Be Down Hearted" and registered them with BMI April 9. Murry registered "I'm All Thru Pretending," co-written with Milo Townes, with BMI September 5. Murry registered "Ippsi Ippsi Oh" (August 31, 1953) and "Lov 1 Another" (May 19, 1955) by mailing them to himself via Registered Mail. It is unclear if these last five songs were ever recorded.

In May 1954, Morgan placed Murry's "I'll Hide My Tears" with the Jets, a reconfiguration of the Hollywood Flames, and had it first released on 7–11 Records (b/w "Got a Little Shadow," 2110) and then Aladdin Records (3247). Mor-

Murry Wilson's "I'll Hide My Tears," published by Guild Music, was recorded by the Jets on Aladdin in May 1954 (author's collection).

gan knew Aladdin's owners, brothers Eddie and Leo Mesner, who had operated a record company in LA since 1945 and recorded legendary R&B artists Amos Milburn, Charles Brown, and the Five Keys. But now the label struggled to place records on the national chart. None of the fifty-five singles Aladdin released in 1954 charted. "I'll Hide My Tears" is a sentimental R&B ballad in keeping with Murry's preference for songs about lost love and unhappy relationships. It is highly sought after by R&B and vocal group collectors.

In August 1954, Bonnie Lou, one of the first female rock 'n' roll singers whose genre-bending records often crossed over to country and rockabilly, released "Two Step, Side Step" (b/w "Please Don't Laugh When I Cry," King 1373). *Billboard* called the A side "A cute bouncy tune with some of the ingratiating qualities of 'Tennessee Waltz.' Ought to grab juke box loot with little trouble as well as scores of spins."[12] That November, "Two Step, Side Step" was also released by Suzi Miller and the Johnston Brothers with Johnny Douglas and His Orchestra (b/w "I'll Hang My Heart on a Christmas Tree," Decca 45-F10423). In late August, the Tangiers, yet another reconfiguration of the Four Flames, recorded Murry's "Tabarin" (b/w "I Won't Be Around," Decca 29603), but it failed to chart. This release of "Tabarin" was co-credited to William York, a pseudonym for thirty-one-year-old Don Pierce, the LA sales representative for the Houston-based Starday Records, which he co-owned, and a record promoter for John Dolphin's Hollywood label, of which he owned fifty percent. The music publishing was now assigned to Golden States Songs, which Pierce had acquired from Dolphin. Murry must have been livid his song was now co-credited to "William York." It made him distrustful of music industry people. He finally registered "Tabarin" with BMI on October 14, 1955.

In April 1955, the Bachelors recorded "Te-e-e-ex-as" (b/w "I'm Lost," Excel 106) written by Murry with George Wilson. It's a fast-paced country hoedown with accordion and clip-clop horse's hoof percussion about a fellow who longs to leave the big city and return to the heart of Texas. Both songs were published by American Music, a Hollywood company affiliated with BMI whose writers supplied songs to West Coast labels including majors like Capitol. In 1957, Audree and Murry published their "Chinese Waltz" with Guild Music. Ten years later, Murry renamed it "Betty's Waltz" and recorded it for *The Many Moods of Murry Wilson*, a solo album released October 1967. Murry struck a deal with Hite Morgan in which the Beach Boys' publishing company, Sea of Tunes, paid Guild fifty percent of the song's mechanical royalty.

Record companies were required under copyright law to obtain a license from a song's publisher granting permission to mechanically reproduce the song onto records. This mechanical license specified the amount, or mechanical royalty, the record company would pay the publisher for every record sold. The statutory rate was two cents, which the publisher typically split with the songwriter. The record company paid the publisher quarterly and the publisher then paid the songwriter.

Dorinda scored her first major chart success with "The Man Upstairs" by Kay Starr in March 1954 (Capitol 2769, #7 Pop). She took home a BMI award that December and the song was covered by many artists despite being banned by the British Broadcasting Corporation because it was "likely to offend large numbers of listeners."

Bumps Blackwell put struggling singer-songwriter Sonny Knight (real name Joseph C. Smith) in touch with Dorinda and he recorded her "Confidential" for Pasadena-based Vita Records in August 1956. Dot Records bought the master that fall and it hit #8 R&B

and #17 Pop. Dorinda wrote Knight's next three Dot singles, "End of a Dream," "Insha Allah," and "Dedicated to You," all in 1957, and "So Wonderful" on Starla in 1958.

The Morgans continued writing, producing, and publishing songs for a variety of artists. Although they failed to chart at the time, many are now highly sought after. Bruce Morgan's "Rock It, Davy, Rock It," a parody of "The Ballad of Davy Crockett," was recorded by the Jaguars, a racially integrated doo wop quartet that included Morgan family friend Val Poliuto (Aardell 003, June 1955). Hite recorded "Always Forever" by the Sabers in his living room studio (Cal-West 847, November 1955) and published "Bongo Washie Wado" by Gene Morris and His King Trotters (Cal-West 108, fall 1956). Cal-West was owned by Hite and Jack Arbuckle and based in Arbuckle's electronics store in Fresno.

In spring 1958, Hite called Murry and arranged for Brian to audition for the Original Sound Record Company, a new label owned by Hite's friend Art Laboe, a disc jockey on KPOP he had met in 1949. Laboe, a thirty-two-year-old Armenian-American whose real name was Arthur Egnoian, borrowed his new surname from a secretary at his first radio job. He often played Sonny Knight's "Dedicated to You" on his live dedication broadcasts from the parking lot of Scrivner's Drive-In restaurant at Sunset Boulevard and Cahuenga Avenue, just down the street from Hollywood High School.

For his inaugural Original Sound release, Laboe chose Dorinda's "Chapel of Love," which had been released that March by Bobby Williams on Deck 142.[13] Laboe assembled a new R&B group made up with members of other groups and called them Hitmakers. They were Lorenzo "Bobby" Adams, an admirer of the Four Freshmen who sang lead with the Calvanes, Valerio "Val" Poliuto, who played keyboards and sang tenor with the Jaguars, a second tenor named Don and a baritone named Duke, whose last names history has forgotten. When Hite learned Laboe wanted to find a new, undiscovered singer for the group, he called Murry and suggested Brian audition.

Murry accompanied fifteen-year-old Brian to the Morgans' home on Mayberry Street to audition "Chapel of Love," a spiritual ballad about the inner peace a man finds when he enters a chapel and encounters an angel. It is an allegory for a man on his wedding day.[14] Dorinda thought Brian's performance was terrific, but Laboe selected a young tenor named Rodney Gooden.

"Chapel of Love" was recorded June 11 and released later that month, but failed to chart.[15] Dorinda recalled, "I had been very impressed with Brian's voice, a high, clear tenor. He sang with a lot of feeling, but I think Mr. Laboe thought he was too young. Art turned him down, a mistake he might have regretted a few years later."[16] "I think it would have been a big hit if they had used Brian."[17]

4

On Our Way to Sunny California
Virginia and Donald Jardine

A pivotal event in summer 1955 for the future Beach Boys was the arrival in Southern California of Donald and Virginia Jardine, and their two sons, sixteen-year-old Neal and twelve-year-old Alan.

Donald Charles Jardine was born October 24, 1912, in Toledo, Ohio, to Charles Jardine and Ella Mary Tildesley, whose mother, Charlotte Thomas, had been an actress in her native England. Charles was an electrical engineer for the Willys-Overland Motor Company and the family lived in a modest home on Wildwood Road in south Toledo. Charles had worked with Thomas Edison on developing an electric automobile and helped sell them at the 1900 Paris Exposition Universelle.

As a teenager, Don attended nearby Edward Drummond Libbey High School and grew into a serious young man. He played clarinet, which he affectionately called his "gob stick." He was tall and thin with thick black hair worn short on the sides. His wire-framed eyeglasses gave him a studious appearance. Friends found him a personable, outgoing, no-nonsense guy. To some he was gruff and somewhat intense. In 1930, he enrolled at the University of Toledo and volunteered as staff photographer for the *Campus Collegian*, the school's weekly newspaper, and the *Blockhouse*, the annual yearbook. He played clarinet in the university's orchestra and also served as the orchestra's manager-librarian. On Sunday mornings, he played with the school orchestra at the Washington Congregational Church at Lawrence and Woodruff Avenues in Toledo. "I'll never forget the fun I had singing the 'Hallelujah Chorus' with the church choir," he recalled.[1]

In September 1933, the start of his senior year, Don was busy checking musical instruments in a storage room at the base of University Tower on campus. He stepped out of the elevator onto a lower corridor and into a sea of freshmen students registering for fall semester. As he gazed out over the crowd, his attention was captured by a petite co-ed with short dark hair. Eighteen-year-old Virginia Louise Loxley was the most beautiful girl he had ever seen.

"It was like that song in *South Pacific*," Don recalled, "but it was daylight and not evening. I looked across the crowded room and I saw a stranger. Our eyes met and something clicked. I don't think we said anything to each other. She was with her father and I guess I was afraid."[2] But the attraction was mutual. "I remember so well how I saw this boy and I liked him immediately," Virginia recalled. "And I knew he liked me. You hear people tell about love at first sight. This was really it."[3]

A few days later, the orchestra met for its first rehearsal. Virginia was there with her violin and Don with his clarinet. "I'm not sure how long it was before we had our first date," she recalled, "but neither of us was going with anyone in particular, so we started going together."[4] She became the orchestra's assistant librarian and soon they were seen holding hands as they rode the trolley to and from school.

Virginia was born May 21, 1915, in Versailles, Ohio, the oldest of four children of Frances Caroline Hile and Jeremiah Miller Loxley. Her father was a railway mail clerk and the family lived on Island Avenue near Walbridge Park, less than a mile from Don Jardine in south Toledo. They were both at Libbey High School for one year, but never met. "Libbey was a big school, and he was three years ahead of me, so that's understandable," Virginia recalled.[5] Virginia was an ardent member of the Philalethean Literary Society whose motto was "Literature is the garden of wisdom." The club sponsored discussions of literary works and social teas and dances.

Don graduated from the University of Toledo in June 1934 with a degree in business administration in economics and a minor in Spanish. His first job kept him near the university and close to Virginia. He worked as a photographer recording the progress of local construction projects for the Works Progress Administration and Public Works Administration, FDR's most ambitious New Deal programs.

Don and Virginia dated throughout her college years. Virginia sang with the university chorus and with the choir at Collingwood Presbyterian Church in Toledo. As part of her curriculum, she took night classes at the Toledo Museum of Art. Don drove her to and from the museum and sat in on her classes. They developed a lifelong love of art. Don recalled, "We've been crazy about art ever since. It is something we enjoy doing together and we often visit museums and special displays and exhibits."[6]

In June 1937, Virginia graduated with a bachelor of arts degree, and they married shortly thereafter. Don wrapped up his projects for the government and, before the end of the year, they moved an hour northeast to Detroit where he managed a photography studio. On December 15, 1938, Virginia gave birth to a son, Neal Jay. In mid–1939, Don accepted a position as a photographer at the Lima Photo Engraving Company in Lima, Ohio. They packed their modest belongings, trekked 125 miles southwest, and settled into a home at 915 Brice Avenue in the small town in rural northwestern Ohio. One of the company's largest clients was the Lima Locomotive Works where Don was assigned to take builders' photographs of new steam locomotives on a contract basis. Like most industrial firms of the era, the Locomotive Works used photography for advertising and recordkeeping. By 1940, the workload had become so great the company decided to establish its own photography department. On January 1, 1941, Don became the first full-time photographer at the Lima Locomotive Works.

The Lima Machine Works built its first steam locomotive in 1880 based on a design by lumberman Ephraim Shay for hauling logs in the lumber industry. The company was renamed Lima Locomotive Works in 1916. Don worked for both the Locomotive Division and the Shovel & Crane Division. He began as a one-man shop, but soon supervised a staff of two or three men. The photography department and chemical lab were located on the second floor of the Scale House where the locomotives were weighed. Don reported to O. B. "Ben" Schultz, Engineer of Tests, within the company's quality control section.

In his new position, Don used several types of large format cameras mounted on tripods for the requisite lengthy exposures. He used 4" × 5", 5" × 7", 8" × 10", and 7" × 17" black-and-white film, and favored a 4" × 5" camera over the bulkier 8" × 10" camera. "A Speed Graphic press camera with an f4.7 Ektar lens became Don's constant companion around the plant," wrote Eric Hirsimaki in *Trains* magazine.[7] Don is credited with introducing several innovative techniques for creating beautifully detailed images of the locomotives. "Donald realized the best way to way to depict the locomotives was to use an orthochromatic film because it was sensitive to blue light," wrote Hirsimaki in *Lima: The History*. "Since a black locomotive reflects blue light, he obtained more natural shades of grey than he could with the more common panchromatic films."[8]

Photography was never a by-the-numbers proposition for Don. He was an artist with a camera, experimenting with different films, f stops, exposure times, paper, and darkroom techniques to achieve optimal results for whatever the job required. Long before software programs like Photoshop, Don was skilled in "opaquing"—removing the extraneous background in a photograph. The painstaking process took hours to complete, but the quality of his finished work was unparalleled. He experimented with various chemical formulas to make a developer that produced negatives with separation of tones which he then used in the darkroom to create images with exquisite shades of grey. His developer was never available commercially. At Lima, he introduced the seven-eighths view of locomotives which gave them a more three-dimensional feel. When he wasn't photographing the company's latest steam locomotive, Don spent a considerable amount of time doing less glamorous work such as x-raying welds, safety pictures, tests, and assorted tasks for the Shovel & Crane Division.

Don was a perfectionist and bristled at the often inane suggestions upper management made concerning how he should do his job. So, to ingratiate himself with the upper echelon, he occasionally left a blemish in his prints so management could point it out and feel important about having a role in the process.

As a twenty-nine-year-old father of a three-year-old son, and a wife pregnant with their second child, Don was granted a deferment from military service when America entered World War II in December 1941. The Locomotive Works soon began manufacturing tanks for the war effort and employee rolls swelled from 2,500 to more than 3,500.

Virginia gave birth to their second son, Alan Charles, on September 3, 1942. With two musical parents, Neal and Alan grew up in a home filled with music. "We had a beautiful Magnavox," Virginia recalled. "We'd play symphonies, the great pianists, orchestras, Beethoven and all the hits on the radio."[9] "We sang nursery rhymes such as 'Farmer in the Dell' and 'Loopy Lou' and things like that. Alan also got a big kick out of singing along with children's records like 'Little Toot.'"[10] When he was six years old, Al sang and played "Old Dan Tucker" on a four-string toy ukulele. In fourth grade, he picked up his grandfather's clarinet, but the instrument's poor quality made playing difficult and he soon abandoned it. Although Alan showed musical aptitude at a young age, Virginia opted not to give him lessons. "I thought it was a hardship on a kid to make him sit still and practice. I didn't think it was good for you."[11] Al later recalled, "My brother never went professional, although he and my dad had great voices, which is probably where I get my singing voice from. We were similar in that we both played clarinet in school."[12]

In 1945, as the war in Europe ended, the Jardine family moved to 1225 North Union in Lima and the following year to 962 West Wayne Street. Louis Thouvenin was a twenty-five-year-old GI returning home to Canton, Ohio, and looking for work. He had studied photography in school and the Air Force had utilized his skills throughout his thirty-nine-month enlistment. In March 1946, he fired off a letter to the Lima Locomotive Works and received a response from Don Jardine who explained he had an opening and, in a handwritten postscript, added if Thouvenin was ever in the area he should stop in and introduce himself. The following Monday, eager for employment, Thouvenin was on the train to Lima. The two men hit it off, and Don offered him a job in the photo shop.

"I was so overwhelmed when I first met Don Jardine and saw the quality of the work he did there at the lab," recalled Thouvenin. "When he asked me 'How would you like to go to work here?,' I told him 'You've got to be kidding! I'm no more qualified to work in your lab than to sweep the floors.' He assured me I would work out okay with his training. And that was true. He was a master photographer if there ever was one. Don had a personality you automatically respected because of his knowledge of photography. He had a real forceful voice. When he said something, his voice carried over all the noise of the shop. I was new to the area and he treated me like a member of his family. He wanted me to pursue the right path and not get involved with the wrong element."[13]

When the company was interested in purchasing the government-owned building where tanks had been manufactured, they asked Don to obtain aerial photographs of the site. Well, that caused a slight problem. Don didn't like to fly. He asked Thouvenin 'How would you feel about going up and taking a picture? I don't leave the ground.' Thouvenin went up with the pilot and got the needed images.

Don and Thouvenin became close friends and colleagues. Don trusted him implicitly and soon Thouvenin began babysitting Neal and Alan. It gave Don and Virginia a much-needed night out. But babysitting your boss's eight and four-year-old sons can be a nerve wracking experience. "The first time I babysat them I put the boys to bed according to my instructions from Virginia. All at once, I heard this crying, piercing sound. The boys came downstairs from their bedroom and little Alan had tears streaming down his cheeks. I couldn't figure out what was the problem. Neal told me Alan couldn't find his toy rabbit Oswald. But Alan couldn't pronounce it. To him it was 'Oswas.' After searching all over the house, the floor was strewn with toys, we finally found 'Oswas' under a piece of furniture. And with that the tears stopped and once again we had peace and quiet in the house." Thouvenin babysat the boys many times over the next three years. When Don traveled to photography conventions, Thouvenin helped Virginia with the boys and grocery shopping. Thouvenin recalled Neal as a quiet and serious young boy, and not as assertive or quick to apply himself as Alan. Once, when Don bought the boys new bicycles, he inadvertently caused an adolescent crisis for Neal. Don could only afford a smaller children's bike. But the neighborhood boys all rode full-sized bicycles. They teased Neal mercilessly for riding a child's bike. To spare his son the emotional turmoil, Don went out and bought him a full-sized bicycle.

In his rare free time at work, Don enjoyed a pipe (although he never smoked at home) and delighted in finding printing errors in the local newspaper. At noon, he and Thouvenin hopped in Don's 1938 Ford Coupe and drove to a cafeteria in downtown Lima for lunch.

For many years, Don was the secretary of the Lima Camera Club which met monthly at the local YMCA. He was also a member of the Professional Photographers Society of Ohio and won several awards for his work. His commercial print of a locomotive entitled "Power" was displayed at the Photographers Association of America's convention in Chicago in 1948. He also lent his expertise to conferences on industrial safety sponsored by the State of Ohio. Each December Don and Virginia enjoyed the holiday dinner party hosted by the engineering department of the Locomotive Works with entertainment provided by the company's very own Locomotive Quartet.

Although he did not have a model railroad at home, he joined the Lima Southern Model Railroad Club and attended club meetings Tuesday and Thursday evenings. He built model train kits and donated them to the club and, in June 1945, was elected the club's president.

In September 1948, Al enrolled in first grade at Horace Mann Elementary School in Lima. On Sundays, the family attended local church services and enjoyed outings in their car. Don, Virginia, and Neal rode in the front seat and young Alan, because there was no back seat, squeezed into the ledge beneath the rear window. At home, Don enjoyed listening to his 78 rpm records. "My dad loved Gilbert and Sullivan, and Gershwin, but he also enjoyed rock and roll," recalled Al. "He actually appreciated Elvis Presley and all the early influences that made it possible for me to start my own band and hook up with the Beach Boys."[14]

In October 1947, Lima Locomotive Works merged with the General Machinery Corporation of Hamilton, Ohio. On May 13, 1949, Don photographed the last steam locomotive produced by the Lima-Hamilton Company. For the next few months, he photographed the company's new diesel-electric locomotives. But, as is often the case with corporate mergers, the new management had a different approach and did not place the same value on the photography department. "Don and I were always pretty frank with each other," recalled Thouvenin, "and I told him I thought somebody was asleep at the switch when they made that deal." Shortly after the merger, Don was invited to a company dinner at a nearby hotel and took souvenir photos of the event. That did not go over well with the new management. They saw no need for such extravagance. "Don thought the company would eliminate the photography department," recalled Thouvenin. "He put in a call with the Eastman Company in Rochester, New York, and went up for an interview and came back with a position. If something didn't suit him and there was nothing he could do about it, he would just pack up and leave."[15]

In spring 1949, after photographing more than 1,500 locomotives and countless shovels and cranes, Don said good-bye to the Lima Locomotive Works and moved his family to upstate New York. During his tenure, he had grown a mustache while his thick black hair thinned. In December 1949, while working at the Eastman Company, Don had a series of photographs displayed at the Hall of Contemporary Photography in the Eastman Museum, also known as the George Eastman House after the company's founder. The photographs had been taken at the Lima-Hamilton plant and illustrated the construction progress of a diesel engine.

As the family settled into life in upstate New York, Al transferred into a public elementary school in Rochester where he completed first grade, second grade, and the first half of third grade. In early 1950, Don accepted a position at the nearby Rochester Institute of Technology (RIT) as an instructor in the Printing Department. He taught courses in industrial photography and business. He was also one of fifteen instructors in the General Education Department providing a well-rounded liberal arts education to students who attended RIT primarily for the technical education.

The Jardine family in front of their home in Lima, Ohio, circa 1950. From left to right, Alan, Neal, Virginia, and Donald (courtesy Lou Thouvenin).

In September 1950, Don created and taught a new course in industrial photography in the Photographic Technology Department. The *RIT Reporter*, the school's bi-weekly newsletter, reported he had spearheaded the construction and installation of a combination darkroom-cameraroom and that his students were "taking another step in progressive technical training."[16]

Thouvenin kept in touch with his former boss and Don invited him to study at RIT during the 1950–1951 academic year. Because Thouvenin was still eligible under the GI bill he took Don up on the offer, although he did not take any courses Don taught. But Don grew disillusioned with teaching. "I don't think he felt he was cut out to be a teacher," recalled Thouvenin. "These were all adult students at RIT and when they wouldn't go along with him, he resented it. He felt the average student didn't appreciate the knowledge he wanted to impart to them. He felt there was so much he could teach them, but they didn't appreciate his expertise. He wasn't content for things to remain that way. I never knew him to have any feelings about staying put."[17]

In early 1951, the family moved north of Rochester to Summerville near Lake Ontario where Al completed third and fourth grade at an elementary school in the West Irondequoit School District. Inspired by his father, Al began playing his grandfather's old clarinet and joined the school orchestra. He became discouraged, however, because the instrument leaked air and required lots of maintenance. After the completion of the school year in June 1952, Don accepted a job at the Royal Blueprint Company in San Francisco. Neal was thirteen and Alan was almost ten. "My dad traveled a lot," Al recalled. "He was in lithography. It was something that extended itself to military applications and he would help make the plans and printouts for the bases all around the world, so we moved around a lot."[18] More than fifty-five years after the cross-country move, Al wrote about the experience in the title track of *A Postcard from California*, his 2010 debut solo album. "This is a song I wrote in a reflective mood about my family's migration from upper New York State to California. My dad had the wanderlust. He was typing away late at night [sending out job applications]. He was never quite happy where he was, in the teaching profession or industry or whatever. So he got a letter back from California."[19] "He got a job at the Royal Blueprint Company and had to leave right away. We stayed behind, sold the house, packed up our things, and moved out west. The song is about parting from one another, and their hopes and dreams. It is a lyrical description of the Jardine family trip, or migration I'd guess you'd call it, from the eastern United States to the West Coast of California. In that time of prosperity in the early 1950s, people were moving around quite a bit and looking for new jobs and my father was one of those many looking for new hopes and a new purpose, and he found that here in California."[20]

Don's new job was managing the Royal Blueprint plant in San Francisco. Virginia and their two young boys flew aboard an American Airlines DC-6 from Rochester to San Francisco. "Man, it was the longest trip I ever took," Al recalled. "Sixteen hours with a long stopover in Dallas."[21] The family settled into life in San Francisco where Al attended fifth, sixth, and seventh grades, and joined Boy Scout Troop number 250.

Meanwhile, Don kept his former colleagues at RIT apprised of his new endeavors. Under the headline "Choo Choo Jardine Working in London," the *RIT Reporter* noted, "Don Jardine is in London at present doing some technical trouble shooting for an affiliated British company. In letters received by friends at the Institute, Don writes enthusiastically about his work, the historical piles, and compares the merits of London and San Francisco fogs."[22] Don traveled quite a bit while he worked for Royal including an extended trip to Spain where he helped set up a blueprint facility.

In 1955, after living in San Francisco for three years, the Royal Blueprint Company reassigned Don to Los Angeles where he was charged with replicating the success he had in San Francisco. They rented a residence on 117th Street in Hawthorne and, over the next five years, moved to 12111 Grevillea Boulevard and then to an apartment on El Segundo Boulevard.

Alan attended eighth grade at a local intermediate school and Neal transferred into Hawthorne High School for his junior year. An outgoing and popular student, Neal was active in the Boys League and the golf team. In May 1956, he represented Hawthorne High in a foreign language speaking contest at the University of Southern California (USC) and delivered an eight minute speech in Spanish. He had a beautiful singing voice and starred in many of the drama club's productions, including Egeus in *A Midsummer Night's Dream*, the school's first Shakespearean play. Of his role as Gramps in *On Borrowed Time*, the 1957 *El Molino* praised him: "veteran performer Neal Jardine gave his usual smooth performance."

Al recalled, "My brother helped inspire me by paving the way for me to succeed in my secondary education. He set an example for me simply by being there. It's always nice to have a senior classman brother to look out after you in the proving grounds of high school. His friends were my friends and I took great comfort in that."[23] John Hagethorn recalled, "I only saw Neal a couple of times when I went over to Al's house. Neal was more like their father physically, tall and thin, whereas Al was short and stocky."[24]

Neal graduated Hawthorne High in June 1957 and attended El Camino Community College and studied theater arts. There he met future author and artist Susan Alcott, but they lost touch after Neal transferred to UCLA and moved to London to continue his studies. Neal later earned a law degree from the University of West Los Angeles and was admitted to the California Bar in June 1985. In 1995, in a bit of fairytale romance, he was reintroduced to Alcott who was working as a legal secretary for an entertainment attorney. They married in March 1996 and he is now retired from the practice of law.

Virginia recalled her sons were quite different. "They're friendly now, but they always used to fight because they were so different. Alan was the shy one. Really shy. Cutest little thing, but not outgoing. And Neal would say hello to anybody all his life."[25]

On September 8, 1958, as Al and Brian began their junior year at Hawthorne High, the Kingston Trio—Bob Shane, Dave Guard, and Nick Reynolds—released "Tom Dooley." It sold more than six million copies, charted five months, reached #1 Pop and #9 R&B, and was the Trio's only gold single. The Kingston Trio revitalized American popular music, paved the way for the folk music revival, and set the stage for the protest music era of the early sixties. Their phenomenal popularity prompted the Martin guitar company to build a new factory in Nazareth, Pennsylvania, to keep up with demand.

"Al had all the Kingston Trio records," recalled Virginia Jardine. "He had a friend [Gary Winfrey] who'd come over, and they'd try to copy what they heard. They weren't singing as much then, but they would try to copy the music, the chords, work them out. Al had a gorgeous record collection, everything in the world. I gave him an allowance and he spent it mostly on records. We played them and had so much fun. His friends would come over after school and play the records."[26]

Al played football that fall along with Bob Barrow and Gary Winfrey. Inspired by their collective admiration of the Kingston Trio, they sang "Tom Dooley" in the locker room after practice and talked about forming a group. "Our group didn't have a name at the time," recalled Winfrey. "We just liked singing Kingston Trio stuff and tried to learn all their songs. I don't remember how we got the name the Tikis."[27]

By June 1959, as Winfrey graduated Hawthorne High and enrolled at El Camino Community College, the Tikis were singing tunes from the Kingston Trio's first four albums including "Tom Dooley," "The Wreck of the John B.," "Scotch and Soda," "Raspberries, Strawberries," and "All My Sorrows."

The Tikis rehearsed on the back porch of Winfrey's home. Before Winfrey bought a Wollensak reel-to-reel tape recorder to chart their progress, they rehearsed at his Aunt Verna's house and recorded their sessions on a tape player in her stereo console.[28] "When we first started, I didn't play anything," Winfrey recalled. "But Al and Bob played guitar, and I wanted to learn. So, in between songs, I'd pick up a guitar and stab at it and gradually I started playing. Al taught me some things and my dad played so he showed me some stuff. I couldn't play the guitar and sing at the same time. I believe Al had a Stella guitar."[29]

Bob Barrow, a popular student lettering in football and wrestling, took one guitar lesson at Hogan's House of Music before he broke his thumb playing football. He then bought an instruction book and Al showed him some basic chords. "The Tikis were nothing more than Al, Gary, and me playing guitars over at Gary's house," Barow recalled. "I think Al came up with the idea of the name for the group." In summer 1959, after playing touch football at Richard Henry Dana Middle School most Saturday mornings, they would buy a few gallons of root beer at the A&W on Hawthorne Boulevard and go to Winfrey's house to play guitars and sing. Song ideas came in common things like Al's "Steam from the Washing Machine," a bluesy riff inspired by the dryer vent. Al was the most serious about music, but he planned on attending college and pursuing a more traditional career path.[30]

"My mom and dad just loved Al," Barrow recalled. "They called him 'Hungry' because the first thing he would do was ask if there was anything in the fridge. Al is a really sincere, good-hearted person. He has a sweet spirit and a real charm about him. The Beach Boys had some tumultuous lives and, as they were having their issues and their problems, Al was always stable, dependable. He wasn't going out doing a bunch of stuff that would make him incapable of performing. Al was always able to step up and be under control."[31]

In summer 1959, Al put music to "The Wreck of the Hesperus," the Henry Wadsworth Longfellow poem he and Barrow had just studied in third-year English at Hawthorne High. Written in 1842, Longfellow's twenty-two stanza poem is a dark tale of a sea captain who ignores the advice of his crew about an impending nor'easter off the coast of Gloucester, Massachusetts. His decision to lash his young daughter to the mast to prevent her from being swept overboard ends with tragic consequences when the ship hits a reef and sinks. *Mad* magazine spoofed the maudlin poem with a seven-page parody in its October 1954 issue. But Al's inspiration to set Longfellow's nautical tale to music came from the Kingston Trio's version of "The Wreck of the John B." on their eponymous debut album in June 1958.

Winfrey recalled, "After we got into folk music, we decided we should write some music. Putting the poem to music was an early attempt at writing. After that we wrote some songs and found it to be a lot of fun. We figured we could do it, so we did it. We rotated leads on most of the recordings."[32]

The three-minute and seven-second Wollensak-recorded "The Wreck of the Hesperus" began with a simple circular melody on the banjo with a faint rhythm accompaniment on acoustic guitar. All three guys sang the first stanza as a chorus ("Twas the schooner Hesperus / That sailed the wintry sea / And the captain had taken his daughter along / To bear him company") which they repeated after singing the third, fifth, and fourth stanzas, and again after the tenth, eleventh, and twelfth stanzas. They made slight edits to conform the words to the melody. On his first ever recording, sixteen-year-old Al sang lead on the verses in a strong, clear, pleasant voice. However, the somber nature of the poem gave the song a plodding, dirge-like quality, with none of the buoyant calypso fun of "The Wreck of the John B." But they were happy with their efforts and wondered how much better they might sound if they were able to record it in a professional studio.

The Tikis also recorded Al's "Steam from the Washing Machine," a simple call-and-response blues number that ran a minute and thirty-nine seconds ("Say man / Yeah? / What's that over there? / Steam from the washing machine / Well now my momma does the clothes / And I dig it the most / Steam from the washing machine"). They also recorded Leiber and Stoller's "I'm a Hog for You," the B side to the Coasters' "Poison Ivy" in summer 1959.

As if embarrassed by the suggestive lyrics, the song broke down in boyish laughter after only twenty-four seconds. A slightly more realized Barrow song idea, although only thirty-seven seconds, was "Banana Boat," which evolved into "Lonely Islander" ("It's morning when I go / Evening when I return to my shack / I never see the sun / Without banana on my back / But I'll go, I'll go / Down and load the banana boats / Yes, I will go today / But soon I'll be on my way").

The Tikis kept playing and singing together throughout Al's and Bob's senior year at Hawthorne High. The musical spark that drove Al to help form the Tikis would soon play a key role in the formation of the Beach Boys. But in June 1960, as Al and Bob graduated, the *Cougar* ribbed the Tikis by voting them "most likely to ruin American music."

5

A Musical Education

As young children, the Beach Boys grew up listening to the music of their parents' generation. The Wilson home was typical. Murry was a teenager during the golden era of Big Bands and male vocalists in the 1930s. When LA began to rival New York and Chicago as an artistic mecca, nightclubs and dance halls sprung up throughout the Southland, attracting the orchestras of Bob Crosby, Tommy Dorsey, Duke Ellington, Jan Garber, Horace Heidt, Stan Kenton, Glenn Miller, and others. That was the music Murry loved and—when he began writing songs at age thirty-four, late for most creative types—the music he emulated. As he ran headlong into his dream of being a songwriter, he reasoned there would always be a demand for his style of "good music," a belief validated by Lawrence Welk's performance of "Two Step, Side Step."

But the music industry was changing and the narrowing market for Murry's old-fashioned sentimental ballads would soon disappear. By the early 1950s, the dance halls began experiencing a decline in attendance. In June 1952, Tommy Dorsey closed his Casino Gardens and the beachfront Rendezvous Ballroom was shuttered and auctioned in October 1953. A number of factors contributed to eroding attendance including a change in musical tastes, television, phonographs, and the demands the G.I. Generation felt from raising their own families. The tireless youngsters who once burned up the dance floor were now in their thirties with kids of their own. By the end of the work week, they looked forward to a quiet evening at home listening to music or watching their favorite television program. Bandleader Stan Kenton, whose orchestra packed the Rendezvous in its heyday, reopened it in 1957, but couldn't make a profit and it closed again.

What really changed music is the force that has renewed and refreshed society for eons—the younger generation. Millions of kids born around the war years, the so-called baby boomers like the Beach Boys, were entering their teens. Kids born in 1940 became teenagers in 1953 and the numbers increased exponentially as the decade wore on. Most of these teens were raised in suburbs with conveniences their parents never imagined—single family homes, automobiles, televisions, modern home appliances, and allowances. It sounds quaint today, but it shaped that decade profoundly. These teens did what every generation does—reject the old and embrace the new. Eager to toss off their parents' boring parlor music, they yearned for something radical and rebellious. Music they could call their own. And what set this generation apart was their relative prosperity and the sheer number in which they, and their allowances, entered the marketplace. They represented a vast new demographic to which radio, television, and record companies could market all sorts of things.

Rhythm and blues was exciting. White kids who loved R&B helped tear down the rope that literally divided audiences into white and colored. They fooled record company executives by seeking out and purchasing the original recordings by black artists. They tuned into R&B radio stations to hear songs they couldn't hear elsewhere. None of this was lost on white artists, many from rural America and raised on country and hillbilly music, who interpreted and assimilated R&B in a way that defied definition.

Technology was also changing the musical landscape. The fragile, cumbersome 78 rpm gave way to the 33⅓ long-play album which remained, for the time being, the domain of adults listening to music on furniture consoles in their living rooms. On March 31, 1949, RCA Victor introduced the first 45 rpm, which revolutionized the music industry and made jukeboxes possible. On June 8, 1954, record companies began supplying radio stations with 45 rpm records instead of 78 rpm records. The affordable forty-five, embraced by teenagers, could be listened to on portable record players in the privacy of their bedrooms. Radio underwent a similar transformation with the advent of transistor radios and car radios. As more and more teens secured their drivers' licenses, radio station managers had a new demographic for which to program. The once homogenous radio market became segmented into different musical tastes.

Meanwhile, American cinema tackled the subject of juvenile delinquency as *The Blackboard Jungle* fused images of alienated youth and teenage rebellion with the unbridled abandon and freedom of "(We're Gonna) Rock Around the Clock." Teens reveled at the on-screen confrontation, seething with violent unpredictability, between high school students and their teacher, an archetypal figure of authority. After the film opened March 25, 1955, scattered reports of fighting and vandalism caused some to wonder which came first—delinquency or rock 'n' roll—and which was worse.

Whether or not "Rock Around the Clock" was the first rock 'n' roll record, it had a profound impact on teenagers and hurtled Bill Haley and His Comets to the top of the chart for eight weeks. For the first time since they were introduced, 45 rpm records outsold 78 rpm records.[1] "When Haley was happening was about the time I first got involved in music," Al recalled. "I think I must have bought every record Bill Haley ever made"[2] Brian remembered, "I had a radio I listened to at home and I thought 'Rock Around the Clock' was a great record."[3]

In 1955, R&B fused with country, hillbilly, and pop, and emerged as something both familiar and different. The Beach Boys' junior high and high school years paralleled the birth, growing pains, and setbacks of this first wave of rock 'n' roll. They heard it all. Every new record, every new sound, every new twist on an old theme, ushered in by artists with singular identities—Fats, Chuck, Richard, Elvis, Jerry Lee, and Buddy.

In April 1955, "Ain't That a Shame," became Fats Domino's first single to crack the Top Ten on the pop chart. In July, Chuck Berry debuted with "Maybellene," an R&B update of the Appalachian folk tune "Ida Red." In November, Little Richard shocked and confused with "Tutti Frutti." Elvis ("Heartbreak Hotel") and Carl Perkins ("Blue Suede Shoes") owned 1956 as Capitol Records, late to the rock 'n' roll party, scurried to release Gene Vincent's "Be-Bop-a-Lula." In 1957, Jerry Lee Lewis electrified television audiences with his incendiary performance of "Whole Lotta Shakin' Goin' On" on *The Steve Allen Show*. Buddy Holly and the Crickets showed teenagers on both sides of the Atlantic what a self-contained rock 'n' roll band looked like, and the Everly Brothers put vocal harmony in the spotlight with "Bye Bye Love" and "Wake Up Little Susie." In 1958, Eddie Cochran gave voice to teen angst with "Summertime Blues" while Jan & Dean, with their California cool, hit with "Jennie Lee," written and first recorded in their garage.

On a musical foundation dominated by Chuck Berry's chugging rhythm guitar, the Beach Boys added an eclectic mix of white and black vocal groups—the jazz harmonies of the Four Freshmen, the pop of the Four Preps, the folk of the Kingston Trio, the R&B of groups like the Coasters and the Five Satins, and the doo wop of Dion and the Belmonts. The fusion of such diverse musical influences, coupled with the lyrical concerns of white suburban teenagers, expressed in stunning block harmonies, made the Beach Boys unique in American popular music.

⎯⎯◦◦◦⎯⎯

One of Brian's earliest musical memories, perhaps as young as two, was hearing Glenn Miller's 1943 recording of George Gershwin's "Rhapsody in Blue" on his grandmother's phonograph. The music had a profound impact on him and he has always cited it as a pivotal influence in his development as a composer. "'Rhapsody in Blue' was a revelation to me. I was just a little kid when I heard it, but it's a great piece of music. I loved it."[4]

Brian recalled, "Around our house, when I was a child, I heard things from my parents' record collection like Les Paul and Mary Ford, Tennessee Ernie Ford, Rosemary Clooney, and the Four Freshmen. Those were my first inspirations. To try to describe exactly what each influence was is hard to explain because it's very subtle, but it can be felt when you listen to my music. I don't think people realize just how much Rosemary Clooney affected my singing. She taught me to sing with love in my heart, she's got to be the greatest. I loved the way she sang (sings) 'Hey there, you with the stars in your eyes.' I practiced to that. I would play it and I would sing along with it, studying her phrasing, and that's how I learned to sing with feeling. I got a whole education from that."[5] Clooney's "Hey There" began a six-week stay at #1 in September 1954 as Brian began seventh grade at Hawthorne Intermediate. He already had a beautiful singing voice.

Audree recalled, "One time, a lady heard him sing and asked if he could sing with the choir at her church for Christmas. He was just a little guy and it was really a thrill to see him with this choir behind him. They did 'We Three Kings of Orient Are' and Brian did a solo."[6]

It was at this Christmas recital when Brian's hearing loss was first detected as he tilted his head to better hear the choir. "When Brian was eleven," Murry recalled, "Mrs. Wilson discovered he kept turning his head. And she found out that he couldn't hear very well out of that ear. Then it got worse and he became deaf in that ear. He was injured in some football game or some injury of some kind. Or it just happened, who knows?"[7]

Audree was uncertain whether Brian's deafness was congenital. "We don't really know," she said. "Brian thinks it happened when he was around ten. Some kid down the street really whacked him in the ear. However, it's a damaged ninth nerve, so he could have been born that way and there's nothing they can do about that. I think it makes him more incredible."[8] It seems unlikely Brian's hearing loss was congenital as such defects generally manifest at an early age.

It took personal fortitude to sing in public and Brian endured an occasional taunt for singing "like a girl." Dennis recalled, "In the sixth grade, he used to sing so beautiful and very high. All his buddies laughed at him. He ran home from school and I chased after him. It broke my heart to see him emotionally involved in the music at such an early age and have his friends laugh at him."[9]

In spring 1956, Brian taught a vocal arrangement of "Ivory Tower" to Dennis and Carl as they lay in bed at night in the bedroom they shared. After Cathy Carr released "Ivory Tower" that March (#2 Pop), it was covered by Otis Williams and His Charms (#5 Pop, #11 R&B) and Gale Storm (#6 Pop). Brian recalled, "We used to do 'Ivory Tower.' That was the special one we'd sing. We developed a little blend for that."[10] Brian's bedtime vocal sessions often ended in horseplay as Carl recalled, "All of us slept in the same room and, after we had to go to bed, Brian would sit there just trying to make us laugh. So my mother would come in and warn us to be quiet. If our father came in, it was curtains. So we'd be really trying not to laugh, covering our mouths, hiding underneath the bed sheets, but Brian would still keep cracking us up."[11]

The bedtime vocal sessions and a rash of rock 'n' roll movies in December 1956 inspired Dennis's entry for a talent show at Hawthorne Intermediate. In spring 1957, twelve-year-old Dennis organized a group of sixth-grade classmates to pretend they were a rock 'n' roll band and lip synced the Dell-Vikings' "Come Go with Me." Don Allen was one of the kids Dennis recruited. "Dennis organized it and picked 'Come Go with Me' because he knew the song and the group. He said, 'Hey you guys, we could do this and it would be really cool.' He got four or five of us together and had us all wear white shirts and black pants. We drew fake sideburns on our faces. It was so innocent and amateurish. I don't think we even rehearsed. We just got up on stage, played the record, and cavorted around, acting out what we thought rock stars would do. But to me, though, it's interesting because Dennis had his eye on being a rock star quite early in the game."[12]

On June 13, 1955, a week before Brian turned thirteen, the Four Freshmen released their twelfth single, "Day By Day" (b/w "How Can I Tell Her," Capitol 3154). "My Mom turned me on to them. She turned the radio on and goes, 'Hear that song? This is called "Day By Day" by the Four Freshmen.' And I listened and I went, 'Oh, I love it, Mommy! I love it!'"[13] "She took me to Lishon's Records. We went in and she said you can take records into these little booths and play them to see if you wanted to buy them. So I took a Four Freshmen album in and I absolutely—something magical happened to my head. I instantly transcended. Whew! It gave me so much spiritual strength. It came out of me. You know how you sit in a sauna bath and your pores open and the sweat will come out? That's what that whole experience in that room started to be. I purged all kinds of bullshit and picked up the Freshmen. It was magic. Total magic."[14] "I listened to the whole album in the booth. I walked out and went, 'Oh please, can I please have it, Mommy? Please buy it.' So she bought it for me."[15]

The Four Freshmen met and formed during their first year at the Arthur Jordan Conservatory of Music at Butler University in Indianapolis. They were brothers Don and Ross Barbour, their cousin, Bob Flanigan, and friend Hal Kratsch for whom the group was first named Hal's Harmonizers, and then the Toppers.

"We all grew up singing harmony parts with our families," recalled Flanigan. "Don and Ross were singing barbershop. I wasn't involved in that. When they decided to do something else, I went in with the group. I had a high tenor voice."[16] Flanigan explained, "The Barbour brothers set the unison sound in the group because they both had the same timbre in their voices. I had a similar timbre, but not quite the same. I never had a vibrato, so that's why we never used it."[17]

The four studied in college to be music teachers and began singing together. Flanigan recalled, "We envisioned ourselves just singing in college, having a good time doing it. We then decided we had something worthwhile and decided to go on the road. We started off singing a cappella, but all of us also played instruments, so on the road we started playing as well as singing. We were only going to go on the road for a year, and then go back to school, but we started doing some business and said, 'Okay, one more year.'"[18] In Chicago, they signed agent Bill Shelton who renamed them the Freshmen Four, which they reversed to the more melodic Four Freshmen.

On March 3, 1950, bandleader Stan Kenton caught their act at the Esquire Lounge in Dayton, Ohio, and admired how beautifully they sang five-part jazz harmonies with only four voices. Kenton, a Capitol Records recording artist and shareholder in the company, arranged an audition, and Capitol president Glenn Wallichs signed them. *Billboard* noted "A spirited new group makes a promising disk debut,"[19] but their first two singles failed to chart.

Flanigan recalled, "Then we had a thing called 'It's a Blue World.' We were going to Detroit for an engagement and we had a friend who was a dee jay there. He said 'Give me something I can play.' So we gave him 'Blue World.' It got forty plays in one day. That record launched our career."[20] "It's a Blue World" (b/w "Tuxedo Junction," Capitol 2152), only their third single in nearly two years, was released in July 1952 and reached #30 on the pop chart.

Although the Ink Spots and the Mills Brothers were still going strong, fewer orchestras were featuring vocal groups. "It's a Blue World" proved vocal harmony groups could still sell. "We let the bass note of the chord, the tonic note, be played by the bass instrument and that freed us up to sing five-part harmony with four voices," recalled Ross Barbour. "And one of those four voices would sing a 'color note'—an unexpected note, a note that wasn't logical, a note that would surprise the listener and make the song sound more interesting. We were interested in doing music, not just having hits."[21]

Captivated by their harmonies, Brian listened to his Four Freshmen records over and over, isolating each voice, trying to solve the sonic mystery of how four voices blended into one beautiful sound. "I learned them bar by bar. I'd go to my hi-fi set and I'd play a little bit. Then I'd stop and try to figure it out, back and forth, back and forth, until I figured the whole song out."[22] By late 1958, in a rite of independence from his brothers, Brian had commandeered the family music room as his bedroom. "I would get home from high school in my eleventh year and go to the kitchen, usually get a glass of milk or orange juice. Then I'd go downstairs to my bedroom where I had my hi-fi set, piano, and Hammond organ, and I would throw on a Four Freshmen record. And I'd pick up where I left off the day before. The point was that I never quit until I got the whole arrangement down. And that's how I did rock and roll when the Beach Boys got going."[23]

Brian had a difficult time figuring out the Freshmen harmonies for one song on *Voices in Love* released in fall 1958. "The toughest one to figure out was 'I'm Always Chasing Rainbows.'"[24] Ironically, the Freshmen had recorded it in one take. "When we finished singing 'Rainbows,'" Flanigan recalled, "we all held our breaths waiting for the studio light to go off signaling it was okay to talk. The musicians broke into appreciative applause, tapping their instruments. It was one of the proudest and most memorable moments in my career."[25]

Brian recalled, "I could identify with Bob Flanigan's high voice. He taught me how to sing high."[26] Flanigan noted, "Brian sings a lot higher than I do. The highest note I could hit comfortably was about a C. I imagine Brian could sing the E flat above that, or the F above that, very comfortably. But we had pretty much the same sound, and the same approach to lead singing. His intonation was really marvelous. Better than mine, I think. When they first started there was an obvious Four Freshmen influence. But as Brian wrote more and more, he took the influence we had on him and applied it to what he was thinking. He made the Beach Boys sound like he wanted them to sound, rather than a Four Freshmen copy."[27]

Ross Barbour noted, "I feel certain what intrigued Brian about our sound, in addition to the long tones and sustained harmonics, was that we were singing overtones. An overtone is when a note is sung true by one singer and a little bit different, just a little flat or a little sharp, by another singer. The resulting overlap, or overtone, creates an interesting sound that tricks the listener's ear into hearing a note that is not actually in the chord. Pop vocal groups had not done that before. We also opened up the chord by singing one of the middle notes a full octave lower. That stretches the chord and makes it sound fuller and richer."[28]

Brian spent years in disciplined self-study listening to the Four Freshmen, dissecting their melodies, deconstructing complex jazz harmonies, and discovering how component voices made up an overall sound. It was a rigorous musical education that paralleled, and eventually surpassed, his formal education at Hawthorne High. Teenage interpersonal relationships can be difficult to navigate. Music was pure and non-judgmental. It assuaged fears and insecurities and never disappointed. And when music began to bring him love and admiration, he channeled it, like a gift, and offered it back to millions of people worldwide.

A pivotal event in Brian's life occurred when Murry took him to see the Four Freshmen at the Crescendo night club at 8572 Sunset Boulevard on May 18, 1958, the third night of a multiple night engagement. The May 17 *Los Angeles Times* reported, "The Four Freshmen have returned to the Crescendo with vocal and instrumental harmonies. The boys sing and play together, offer solos, and mix ballads with fast numbers to advantage. This group is a heavy favorite with the younger set and it seemed most of them were on hand opening night."[29]

Audree recalled, "We couldn't afford to take Murry, Brian, and me. We really didn't have very much money. So Murry took Brian this one Sunday night in the hope he could meet them because he was so thrilled with their music. He was already writing vocal arrangements even though he hadn't had any musical training. And he did get to meet them."[30]

"Bob Flanigan and the Freshmen were my harmonic education," Brian recalled. "My dad took me to see them in 1958. I was blown away by their sound. It inspired me to create the music I did with the Beach Boys."[31] "They had the most unique harmony, the best arrangements, and a fantastic blend of voices. But they didn't reach the teenagers. They played and sang for the adult market."[32] After the show Murry took Brian backstage to meet his musical idols.

"I know Brian very well," recalled Flanigan. "His father brought him down to the Crescendo. He told me that once he heard us he knew that was how he wanted to write music. He's a very, very talented man. And he alone was the sound of the Beach Boys."[33]

The concert and that meeting had a profound effect on Brian. "My voice was shivering as I was talking to them. I was shaking, I was so scared. I was so in awe of them. It was one of the biggest moments in my life."[34]

Brian may have been anxious about meeting the Freshmen, but that's not what Flanigan remembered. "I'm sure he was a little nervous. What teenage kid wouldn't be? But the thing I remember most was that he looked me straight in the eye when he spoke. You could tell he was sincere about his appreciation for our music and very clear and set on what he wanted to do with music. Even at that young age, an absolute sincerity shone through."[35]

Bill Wagner, the Four Freshmen's personal manager, recalled Brian visited him in his second-floor office at 6047 Hollywood Boulevard in summer 1958. He had gotten their address from the telephone book and told Wagner's secretary he wanted to talk to someone about the Freshmen. Wagner recalled, "He told me he was the group's biggest fan and knew every note of every record, and challenged me to test him. I played him 'The Day Isn't Long Enough,' which the Freshmen had difficulty recording. Brian listened to the song four times and then sang each of the harmony parts perfectly. I told him he should have a group and he replied, 'Well, that's why I'm here. You're going to show me how to start a group.' He knew exactly why he was there."[36]

On June 20, 1958, Brian's sixteenth birthday, Audree and Murry gave him a Wollensak 1500 two-track reel-to-reel tape recorder, which opened up a world of sonic possibility and played a key role in Brian's development as a record producer. It enabled him to make the leap from picking out melodies on the piano to recording his own four-part vocal arrangements on tape. He experimented with overdubbing—recording one vocal part on top of another—lining them up in effect, to structure his layered harmonies.

Brian enlisted Audree, Murry, and Carl for the additional voices he was now capable of recording. Too restless and impatient to learn vocal parts, Dennis was seldom interested in these family recording sessions. Audree recalled, "He loved the Four Freshmen and he would make these incredible arrangements, sort of like them, but he'd add what he wanted. And we'd sing the first two parts on the tape recorder, then play it back and sing the other two parts with it. That was great fun."[37]

Brian worked out the harmonies for his brothers and Mike Love using major seventh and minor seventh chords. "You can hear those Four Freshmen harmonies throughout my career. It's there in 'Surfer Girl' and it's there in the a cappella 'One for the Boys' on my 1988 solo album."[38]

Carl remembered, "When I was eight years old, Brian was teaching me arrangements. It was literally, 'Mom, make Carl sing.' I learned to do very complex harmonies and voicings, and I learned how to do them quickly so I could go out and play. He would sing the third part, record the three of us singing together, and then he would sing to the playback to hear the fourth part."[39] "The thing about that kind of modern jazz is the parts are very strange. It's not like singing Christmas carols. They weren't your regular three chord tunes. If I made a mistake, Brian would say, 'No, it goes like this.' And I'd have to do it again until I got it right. It was great training. By the time I was fifteen, I could hear a part once and have it."[40]

Mike recalled, "Brian would memorize songs and deal out parts to us. It never ceased to amaze me. It would be hard to grasp one part, yet he'd have all four parts in his head."[41] "Brian, me, and Carl were the only ones who could sing the intricate harmonies. We didn't know anybody who had the ear to tune in to those things. So, his mother, my aunt Audree, would sometimes sing the top part of the melody and we'd sing three parts, well not on our records, but this is how we actually got together the first time singing."[42]

Like many musicians, radio played a major influence on Brian's musical education. "My favorite was KFWB in Hollywood," he recalled. "I used to listen to them all the time. Every record had something you could listen to. Every record had some kind of twist that gave you a feeling. You'd go to the piano and say, 'Now, how did they do that?' You'd start learning about it. It's an education. Anybody with a good ear is going to pick up on those records. And they're going to go to the piano and they're going to say, 'Oh, this is it, yeah that makes it, that doesn't make it.' It's a great education to hear the radio."[43]

After he obtained his driver's license in summer 1958, Brian occasionally drove to Mike's house to listen to the radio, debate the merits of their favorite songs, and harmonize. "I can remember around 1957 or 1958," recalled Mike, "Brian had an old Rambler, and he used to come over my house a lot to hang out and sing. We had knotty pine bunk beds built into the wall and we had a sun porch outside where we could sit out and look all over the city. We used to sleep in the bunks and I'd have a transistor radio on under the covers so we could listen to the late-night R&B on KGFJ and KDAY."[44] "And then, about eleven o'clock, my dad would yell at us, 'If you're going to play that music and make a racket, get outside.' We'd go outside and stay in the car, play the radio and sing songs, and sometimes spend the night in his car."[45]

On many Wednesday nights, Mike, Brian, and Maureen, Mike's younger sister, went to Youth Night at Angeles Mesa Presbyterian Church, a short walk from the Love home. After a program of activities that included religious hymns, they walked home harmonizing popular tunes on the radio. Although they each had their preferences, they could always agree on songs by the Everly Brothers like "Bye Bye Love," "Wake Up Little Susie," "All I Have to Do Is Dream," "Bird Dog," and "Devoted to You."

In December 1958, the Loves and Wilsons gathered for Glee's traditional Christmas dinner and caroling. Mike recalled, "We'd get together and sing, and then break up into groups—the parents doing their kind of music and the kids doing their kind of music. Their music was boring for us, so we'd listen to our records in the play room and do our R&B. That was the origin of the Beach Boys."[46] Maureen Love recalled, "Brian was so kind-hearted, talented, and cute. When he came over, he'd barely say hi, just go right to the piano. He'd start banging out songs, give Mike his bass part, give my mom an alto part, and we'd all sing together, harmonizing. Those are some of my favorite memories."[47]

Mike's appreciation for R&B like "Bermuda Shorts," "One Kiss Led to Another," "In the Still of the Night," and "Smokey Joe's Café," was rooted in his years at Susan Miller Dorsey High School, an ethnically and racially diverse school in South Central LA. As Carl recalled, "Most of Mike's classmates were black. He was the only white guy on his track team. He was really immersed in doo wop and R&B music and I think he influenced Brian to listen to it."[48] Mike graduated in June 1959 and attended LA City College, where he ran track and played basketball. In 2007, the unauthorized *Garage Tapes* included two takes of Mike singing "Bermuda Shorts," which Brian recorded on his Wollensak perhaps during a rehearsal for their performance of the song at a Hawthorne High assembly in fall 1959.

Brian and Mike shared an appreciation for Chuck Berry. Mike was inspired by Berry's lyrics, how his guitar licks moved those along, and the real-life vignettes he created.[49]

The first Chuck Berry song Brian heard was "Johnny B. Goode" (b/w "Around &

Around," Chess 1691, #2 R&B, #8 Pop), which Berry performed on *The Dick Clark Show* May 28, 1958. "I was in my car and when that came on I flipped out. I pulled over and stopped. It got me. I liked the electricity of it. I just had to pull over and I went through this little process I do when I get my mind blown."[50] "Chuck Berry taught me how to write songs. I learned from listening to him about his melodic thoughts and his ability to make lyrics. At the same time, my brother Carl was very influenced by Chuck's guitar playing, and he brought that style into the Beach Boys as well."[51]

Carl recalled, "I remember growing up always loving the guitar. I used to love watching people play on the country and western shows on television [Spade Cooley]. My folks told me that when I was just a toddler, I used to pretend I was playing a guitar on a toothpick. A family friend [Dean Brownel] came over when I was about twelve and left his guitar at our house for me to play. I got really interested in it and learned how to play a few barre chords."[52] "Dean was a very technical musician. He used to say of a chord, 'Oh that's a G flat third, augmented fifth.' We were amused by that, but I was very impressed with his playing. From that point on, I'd get a real thrill seeing a Fender guitar in the music store window."[53]

For Christmas 1958, Audree and Murry gave Carl a gift that changed his life—a six-string, acoustic-electric Kay Swingmaster guitar. Just as Brian had dissected the Freshmen harmonies, Carl began studying his guitar idols, picking out iconic riffs, and learning rhythm and lead guitar. Carl's Swingmaster was model number K6960, a thin-line guitar with a single rounded cutaway for easier access to the lower frets. Its slim neck, reinforced with a steel truss rod, was glued into the body and the triple-humped headstock bore a silkscreened Kay logo. It had nickel frets, bound rosewood fingerboard with single and double dot inlay position markers, a single humped metal-covered pick-up (called a "Speed Bump"), separate tone and volume controls with white ribbed Bakelite knobs, and a trapeze tail piece with two cross bars. The top of the guitar was spruce and the back and sides were curly maple. The hand rubbed walnut finish with golden highlights was protected from errant strumming by a white Bakelite winged pick guard. It boasted an exclusive crack-proof laminated body with a heavy celluloid binding on the body and fingerboard. It sold for a suggested price of $99.95 and the case was an additional $16. This is the guitar Bob Barrow borrowed from Carl and played at the Club Charter assembly at Hawthorne High on March 11, 1960.

The Kay Musical Instrument Company was based in Chicago and owned by Henry Kuhrmeyer, whose fraternity brothers nicknamed him Kay. The name on the Kay guitar you purchased depended on where you bought it. For instance, Sears sold Kay guitars branded on the headstock with a Silvertone logo, either an ornate laminated panel or a simple silkscreen. The 1958 holiday season capped a banner year for Kay. With the rising popularity of rock 'n' roll and the chart success of the Kingston Trio's "Tom Dooley" it seemed every teenager in America wanted a guitar. And Kay filled an affordable market niche for parents who wanted to encourage their children's musical inclinations without spending three hundred dollars for a Fender, Gibson, Gretsch, or Rickenbacker.

Carl recalled, "My folks got a single cut-away Kay for me. It was an acoustic, but it had a pickup, and that's the guitar I learned to play on. I took guitar lessons at an accordion studio. There was a guitar teacher there, and I took lessons from him for a couple of months, but it was boring because I was just reading notes—stuff like 'Yankee Doodle Dandy.'"[54] Once, while Carl was practicing an old standard at home, Brian heard him play a wrong chord and chided their mother, "How can you let him take lessons when he's learning the wrong chords?"[55] Carl added, "The lessons got very boring and I wanted to boogie. It was no fun playing the notes."[56]

Across the street from the Wilsons that Christmas, a similar scenario played out in the living room of Josephine Ann and Elmer Lee Marks, as their ten-year-old son, David, unwrapped a Kentucky Blue Silvertone acoustic guitar. In 1955, the family had moved to California from New Castle, Pennsylvania. In summer 1956, they bought a three-bedroom house at 11901 Almertens Place on the Inglewood side of Kornblum Avenue. Dennis and Carl welcomed David to the neighborhood by taunting him and tossing trash onto his yard. David enrolled in third grade that September at Andrew Bennett Elementary School in Inglewood and soon became good friends with his former tormentors, exploring the neighborhood and getting into trouble typical of boys their age.

"I didn't play the guitar until I had it in my hands," Marks recalled. "I saw it under the Christmas tree. So I pestered my parents to open my gift early because it was obviously a guitar. It was wrapped in paper and it was shaped like a guitar. I went nuts. I had to open it."[57]

Introduced in fall/winter 1955, the model 0653L Kentucky Blue guitar was manufactured by Kay, marketed under the Silvertone name, and retailed at Sears for $18.95. It came with a guitar pick and home study book. A hardshell case cost another six dollars and an extra set of strings a buck. With the Kentucky Blue, Kay boasted "color styling has come to the arched guitar" and noted that it was "keyed to the latest in automobile design."[58] The three-ply, lacquered, arched maple body had two ornate f-sound holes carved symmetrically on either side of the top. The hardwood neck may have been rosewood and celluloid dot inlays marked the fifth, seventh, ninth, and twelfth frets. It had an adjustable rosewood bridge, nickel-plated trapezoid tailpiece, and an ivory-colored celluloid pick guard that floated on rubber washers. The back, sides, and headstock were painted a deep metallic blue. The upper half of the top was also painted blue and shaped like a heart, the apex of which ended at the bridge. The lower half of the top was painted ivory. A white stripe was painted to appear like binding joining the top and bottom to the sides. The chromed Kluson deluxe tuning pegs worked well and the guitar was surprisingly easy to play, although steel strings were painful until the novice musician developed calloused fingertips.

Marks had been enthralled by the guitar since he was a young boy growing up in Pennsylvania listening to his grandfather and two uncles sing and play mandolin and guitar. In summer 1958, David tagged along with his mother, Jo Ann, to one of her book club meetings at the Hermosa Biltmore Hotel in Hermosa Beach. The hotel, originally the Surf and Sand Beach Club when it opened in 1929 as an exclusive professional men's club, had recently undergone an extensive renovation. During intermission, a sister and brother act billed as John and Judy sang and played a few songs. Their mother, Regina Maus, a friend of Jo Ann, occasionally babysat David. "I knew I had to play guitar when I saw John play that day," Marks recalled. "All I wanted was to be John Maus and play guitar all day. From then on, I constantly bugged my parents for a guitar."[59]

Jo Ann Marks recalled, "That guitar became his whole life. I used to come into his bedroom at night and he'd be asleep with the guitar in his bed next to him."[60]

In early 1959, David began taking guitar lessons from fifteen-year-old John Maus, recommended for the job by his eighteen-year-old sister, Judy. After his fifth grade classes,

David trekked three and one-half miles north to John's house at 637 South Inglewood Avenue in Inglewood.

John Maus was born November 12, 1943, in New York City. The family moved to California in 1947, settling in Redondo Beach and later Hermosa Beach, as his father worked as a machinist at North American Aviation. By 1954, John showed a flair for acting and Regina helped him land bit roles in television and films. In 1956, while in eighth grade at Pier Avenue Junior High, he injured his knee playing football and his parents bought him an Epiphone acoustic guitar for the long recuperation at home. Two years later, he bought a Carvin electric guitar for $139 and his father bought him a Fender Bassman amplifier. John formed a musical duo with his older sister, Judy, and they competed in local talent shows like *Rocket to Stardom*. John and Judy recorded "Who's to Say" (b/w "Bother Me Baby," Aladdin 3420) and in fall 1958 befriended Ritchie Valens who helped John with his guitar playing.

Marks later bought the Carvin electric guitar from Maus. "John Maus was responsible for introducing electric guitar to the Beach Boys," Marks recalled. "I remember one time we set up in his garage and his dad came out and threw us out because we sounded so bad. We learned a lot of Duane Eddy instrumentals. John was acquainted with Ritchie Valens, so he taught us how to do that strum which you can hear on our ballads like 'Surfer Girl' and 'In My Room.' He also taught us how to do the Chuck Berry boogie and single string leads. He was a tremendous influence on our playing."[61]

By spring 1959, Carl also began taking lessons with Maus. "Dave told me about a kid he knew who played guitar pretty well, but couldn't play any lead," Maus recalled. "He brought Carl over to meet me and I began teaching him how to play some lead riffs. It's all unrelated stuff that, when put together, forms a kind of rock 'n' roll vocabulary."[62] In summer 1959, while living briefly with the Marks family and tutoring David and Carl, Maus and his sister scored a local hit with "Hideout" (b/w "Love Bug," Doré 530), recorded at Western Recorders, and written by John, but credited to Regina Maus for contractual reasons.

Marks recalled, "Carl and I would play our guitars after school every day practically. One day he came over with an album called *Chuck Berry Is on Top*. We learned to play all the songs. And that's what perked Brian's ears up, when we were playing those rhythm parts."[63] Berry's third album in five years, *On Top* was a compilation of singles including "Maybellene," "Roll Over Beethoven," and "Johnny B. Goode."

While Murry encouraged Brian's admiration for the Four Freshmen, he was not so inclined with rock 'n' roll. In 1970, Carl recalled how disappointed he was when a rock 'n' roll revue starring Chuck Berry, Jerry Lee Lewis, and Duane Eddy came to LA, but he could not go because his parents could not afford a ticket.[64] "Of course, when rock and roll started and the boys became interested in it, my wife and I had the natural objection to it that parents had then," Murry recalled. "To me it was not pretty music. It was a retrogressive step. I thought a minor craze for minors. Even when Brian and his brothers were caught up in it and I could see it was exciting music, I still had this mental block against it. A minor craze, I still thought. Well, I was wrong."[65]

David's and Carl's lessons with John Maus continued into summer 1959. "Carl sat in with John's band for a few bar gigs," Marks recalled. "Carl and I started doing Ventures tunes, sitting around the living room learning them off the records for our own amusement."[66] Maus taught the budding guitarists signature riffs of many popular songs including the infectious opening of "What'd I Say" released that June by Ray Charles. It charted 15 weeks, hit #1 R&B, and became Charles's first song to reach Top Ten on the pop chart where it hit #6.

—◦◦◦—

By 1959, after years of studying and recording songs with his family on his Wollensak, Brian's musical gift had begun to be appreciated by his friends and classmates. Vickie Amott lived at 3748 West 119th Street, diagonally across the street from the Wilsons. She and Brian were classmates from third grade at York Elementary through senior year at Hawthorne High.

As youngsters, Amott, Brian, Mary Lou Manriquez, and Dennis Morris, had spent much of their time outdoors playing kick the can, kick ball, football, riding bikes, and sliding on cardboard boxes down a nearby drainage ditch. They'd play until it got dark and their parents called them inside. In the mid–1950s, they'd walk up to Imperial Highway for a Saturday matinee at the Imperial movie theater. Their parents took turns driving them to and from the Gunga Din Youth Center on Friday and Saturday nights to listen to records and dance. Birthdays were celebrated with parties at home, and Melody Music gift certificates were always welcomed and soon redeemed for the latest records.[67]

"We would go over to Brian's music room and he would play some of the music he created," Amott recalled. "He was always writing music and putting sounds together. He'd find two or three notes to put together that really sounded different than what you would normally hear. That thrilled him to death. 'Oh, listen to this! Do you hear that? You have to hear this!'"[68]

But when Murry came home, Audree shooed the kids out the front door. After a long day at work, Murry had little patience for a house full of neighborhood kids. Amott recalled, "Murry had the attitude they were better than the rest of the people on the block. I think he felt he was an entrepreneur and someday he would do very well. But the boys and Audree weren't that way. Audree was a wonderful, warm person and a loving mother. She always had a smile and a good word. We all loved Audree. But if we saw Murry coming we went the other way. He could be very intimidating when he wanted."[69]

Amott attended many of Brian's baseball games. Brian was very competitive with himself and took it personally if he dropped the ball, didn't throw it straight, or struck out. It hurt him to let the team down.[70]

"I met Mike at a couple of parties the Wilsons had at their house," Amott recalled. "Brian and Mike weren't buddies growing up. They were family, you have cousins, but that doesn't mean you're close. I think how your parents feel about people rubs off on you. There was no love lost between Brian and Mike. Brian was never excited about going over to Mike's house. When they started the band, I felt Mike just came in and took over. Brian was so laid back and Mike had such a dominant personality. Brian was kind of in the clouds. He was one of the kindest people you'd ever want to meet, but it was like he was always thinking and sometimes you had to bring him back to the present."[71]

6

Life After High School
(July 1960–July 1961)

Had Al and Brian gotten together to sing after graduating Hawthorne High in June 1960 as Al suggested, the Beach Boys may have formed a year earlier than they did. But had it gone badly, they may never have tried again and the band, as we came to know them, may never have formed. Because neither Al nor Brian pursued the idea, it evaporated like so many empty promises between high school acquaintances.

Four days after graduation, Brian turned eighteen while the Kingston Trio began a two-week stay at the Cocoanut Grove. Brian spent the summer doing things eighteen-year-old guys still love doing—playing baseball for a community team, listening to music, going to parties, hanging out with friends, and cruising the boulevard at night. Baseball, with its rigorous schedule of games and practices, demanded most of his time. Music was a constant presence and his car radio delivered new and exciting sounds.

<hr>

In early 1960, after working nearly eight years for Royal Blueprint, the last five in LA, Don Jardine accepted a teaching position in the Trade and Industrial Division of the College of Technology at Ferris Institute, and moved 2,200 miles east to Big Rapids, Michigan, where he began teaching March 1. Al's mother, Virginia, packed the family's belongings and joined her husband there that August.

Al completed an admission application to Ferris shortly after graduation from Hawthorne High. After his mother relinquished their apartment on El Segundo Boulevard, Al moved in with Gary Winfrey and spent August and early September with the Winfreys in their home on 130th Street in Hawthorne.

It was a tumultuous time for Al. After moving to the West Coast in 1955, just before he turned thirteen, he spent the next five years—virtually all his teenage years—living a rather peaceful, idyllic life in Southern California. Hawthorne High was the first school he started and finished without his education and social network being interrupted by a move. He had done well at Hawthorne High—a well-liked, affable student and varsity football player. His modest musical ambitions were realized with his own folk combo. Now, just shy of eighteen, he was facing the most disruptive move of his life. With his parents gone and his twenty-two-year-old brother, Neal, out on his own, he was without family for the first time in his life.

That summer, Al bussed tables at Stacks, a family-style restaurant where he earned a dollar an hour, the minimum wage at a time when gasoline was twenty-five cents a gallon. Because he didn't have a girlfriend, he spent most of his time with buddies like John Hagethorn, lifting weights, playing handball, and sharpening his card skills at late-night poker games. "Al was a big poker player in those days," recalled Hagethorn. "Somehow he'd find out where these garage games were going on and he would go there and play poker for a couple of hours. And then he'd tell me to come and pick him up. That was his excuse. He'd always tell me, 'Tell them something so I can get out of here.' There was a book out about poker based on the *Maverick* television show. Al had that book in his bedroom. We always joked around and kidded each other. He was fun to be with."[1]

Al shopped for the latest Kingston Trio records at Melody Music and, with Winfrey and Barrow, continued playing music as the Tikis, including "The Wreck of the John B.," repopularized that summer by Jimmie Rodgers. The Tikis faced their first personnel change when Barrow, awarded a football scholarship to Brigham Young University, moved to Salt Lake City in late July to begin practicing with the team. "After Bob left," recalled Winfrey, "my brother, Don, because he had been listening to us, joined the group. He didn't play an instrument at the time, but he learned to play guitar."[2]

Impressed with Brian's vocal and musical talents displayed at various Hawthorne High assemblies, Al decided to ask Brian's help with the Tikis' recording of "The Wreck of the Hesperus." Barrow remembered Al saying that "Brian's dad had some contacts that might open doors to the music business."[3] Winfrey thought of asking Brian to join their group. That August, with Barrow in Utah, Al and Winfrey went over to visit Brian. "The first time I went over to Brian's house with Gary, Audree Wilson answered the door," Al recalled. "We went to see if Brian was home. I think he was at baseball practice. But I got a wonderful feeling from Audree. I thought she was the most perfect person in the world to be Brian, Carl, and Dennis's mom. I remember that very clearly. Because I was kind of bulky I gave Audree all my theories about dieting. She loved it. She stocked their fridge with apples because my theory was that we should all eat apples. Soy was the new super food so I was eating all these soybean products and it was just cracking her up. It was working. I was losing weight. Whenever I went over there I would raid their fridge and grab an apple."[4]

Winfrey recalled, "Brian's mom knew us so she invited us in. Al and I sat with her in the living room and talked. She showed us some of her husband's published music and said he was a songwriter and knew somebody called Hite Morgan who had a recording studio. She suggested we contact Morgan and gave us the information. So Al and I made a copy of our demo, 'The Wreck of the Hesperus,' that we had recorded on my aunt's tape deck and placed it on a three-inch tape reel. Al and I then went over to Hite Morgan's studio on Melrose Avenue."[5]

The Morgans were in the process of establishing Stereo Masters, a record mastering facility in a rented storefront at 5434–5438 Melrose Avenue in Hollywood. (See Appendix 10.) Bruce Morgan recalled, "Al Jardine called my father at home and introduced himself. He was a very polite young man, very respectful. He told my dad about his group and that they wanted to record themselves. My dad and Al arranged to meet at Stereo Masters."[6]

Winfrey recalled that "The Wreck of the Hesperus" sounded pretty good on his Wollensak, but terrible on Morgan's Ampex 400 tape machine and studio speakers. "My recollection was that they were just starting up their recording studio. And we got this kind of 'Don't call us, we'll call you' type of response. They said something like 'Okay, if anything comes up we'll give you a call. We're trying to get our studio up and running, and we'll give you a call if we find anything for you.' So we left the tape with them. They wrote down my name and phone number, put it with the tape, placed it in a manila envelope, and stuck it in a file cabinet. We left and just kind of said, 'Oh well, that was our big shot.' We kind of forgot about it."[7]

In the wake of the Kingston Trio's success, there was no shortage of amateur folk groups. "Alan had come to us with another group first," recalled Dorinda Morgan. "They were older, very good. They had a much slicker sound, but they didn't have any original material. They were doing the Kingston Trio sort of thing. Professional, but not original. We turned them down."[8] Dorinda added, "They were imitators, not innovators. It's hard enough to get a new group off the ground, impossible if they don't have something different to set them apart."[9] Although it is likely Audree told Brian that Al and Winfrey stopped by, Brian did not contact Al that summer.

At summer's end, with their dream of making a record dashed, Winfrey prepared for his second year at El Camino Community College while Al got ready to leave for Michigan. On the KFWB chart out September 3, Al's eighteenth birthday, "It's Now or Never" by Elvis continued its reign at #1 for the sixth consecutive week. With Barrow in Utah and Al headed to Michigan, the Tikis disbanded like so many other high school groups.

Al did not arrive in Big Rapids, Michigan, in time for the start of the school year on September 12. Instead, he registered September 16 and moved in with his parents in the small apartment they rented at 620 Linden Street near the school. The move to Michigan was Don's and Virginia's tenth move in twenty-three years of marriage. Ferris Institute was the seventh school at which Al enrolled in the last twelve years.

The Trade and Industrial Division at Ferris included departments for heavy equipment, body shop, automotive repair, visual reproduction, and graphic arts. The faculty was amicably referred to as the "Tink Tinks" because of the experimental, tinkering nature of their work. Don taught classes in visual reproduction, training students to become visual reproduction technicians.

Virginia recalled, "We wanted Al to come with us. He didn't want to leave. He was very happy where he was."[10] John Hagethorn took him to the airport. "He was going east to go to school to be a dentist. In those days going to the airport was a big deal. I dropped him off, saw him get on the plane, and thought 'Well, that's it, I'll probably never see him again.'"[11]

In Big Rapids, Al settled into his new life and applied himself to his first-year courses. "After I left high school," he recalled, "it was very difficult for me because I felt very alienated from just about everything. I felt no satisfaction for years."[12] He was living in a new town, adjusting to college, forging new friendships, and living with his parents. In Big Rapids, his musical aspirations found a new outlet. He formed another folk combo and sang during lunch hours.[13]

Al was a serious and industrious student, the embodiment of the sturdy midwestern work ethic. As soon as he was old enough, he had a job. "I don't think any of the Wilson children had a real job," Al recalled. "I'm probably the only one who did. Mike pumped gas for a while, but I wouldn't call that a real job. I actually worked in a chemist's lab as a paint chemist for a summer job. We just mixed paint, but I had to go to work every day. I was not real thrilled with it. It wasn't what I wanted to do. It was very boring."[14]

Perhaps the mundane work of mixing paint convinced Al he needed a profession. At Ferris, he planned on being a dentist and enrolled in pre-professional courses including biology, chemistry, and calculus. It was a demanding curriculum designed to separate the serious from the curious. "I was in pre-dentistry," he recalled. "I had no idea why, but I was. I should have studied music. Actually, I did take music for a semester and I flunked. All those damn chords."[15] "My undergraduate work involved a lot of science. Biology was enjoyable, but I didn't enjoy botany very much."[16] To earn his doctor of dental surgery degree, Al would have to complete four years of college and four years of dental school. The work was respected, lucrative, not physically difficult and, compared to other health professionals, dentists rarely had their personal lives disrupted by emergencies. A young man could build a comfortable life for himself as a dentist, and Al's even-keeled personality seemed well-suited for such a steady profession.

Big Rapids is a quiet university town along the Muskegon River, two hours northwest of Detroit, founded in 1894 by Woodbridge Nathan Ferris who later served Michigan as a United States Senator. As with all university towns, Ferris was the lifeblood of Big Rapids. The faculty was comprised of dedicated academicians, the townspeople were warm and friendly, and life was simple and pleasant. The quaint campus was dominated by a quadrangle with academic buildings arranged nearby. Students were never without an ice cream fix as the dairy bar inside the Student Union served up daily ice cream concoctions. There were men's and women's dormitories, but most students rented rooms in private homes in town, close to the usual establishments essential to college life—a movie theater, a pizza place, and a club featuring live music. From December through March, the temperature dipped below zero and heavy snow blocked access to roads. On more temperate weekends, local bands played Top 40 rock 'n' roll on the flat roof of a local garage. The town had a police department, although there was hardly any crime, a firehouse, and a post office from which students received essential care packages from home.

The first academic session at Ferris finished December 3 and the second session began two days later.[17] Al remained in Big Rapids over the Christmas recess December 17 through January 3.

In fall 1960, life at the Wilson home settled into the routine of another school year. Dennis started his second year and Carl his first at Hawthorne High. Brian lived at home and commuted to El Camino Community College where classes began September 13.

El Camino was a two-year junior college built in the late 1940s on eighty acres of Alondra Park. The first class had fewer than 500 students and early classrooms were surplus military barracks trucked north from the Santa Ana army base in Orange County. The college was named for California's first road, El Camino Real—the King's Road or the Royal Road, along which Father Junipero Serra, a Spanish Franciscan priest, founded a network of nine missions between 1769 and 1782. An additional twelve missions were built after Father Serra's death in 1784. The twenty-one missions are each about thirty miles apart, roughly a day's walk. The college's symbol of a bell on a hooked staff is in tribute to California's mission history. Although the college had grown considerably in its first decade, it was still a relatively young institution when Brian enrolled.

Brian was a full-time student registered for first-year classes including psychology and music appreciation. "I was going to be a psychologist," Brian recalled. "I wanted to be able to teach people about the first two years of life. The very delicate years of life."[18] Music was a constant and he continued to work out intricate vocal arrangements, teaching them to anyone he could enlist. His favorite and most accessible vocalists were still Carl and Audree. Dennis was seldom around and his frenetic personality and limited attention span made him a poor candidate for Brian's painstaking instructions. Murry joined in occasionally, but Brian often had to dodge his suggestions to sing one of Murry's songs.

As Al and Brian started college that fall, three guys, who each had attempted a singing career, accepted new jobs in the LA music industry. In September, twenty-eight-year-old Joe Saraceno was hired as A&R director for a newly formed record label called Candix Enterprises. On October 16, Capitol Records, desperate for younger blood in its A&R department, lured twenty-two-year-old Nick Venet away from World Pacific Records as a talent scout and staff producer. On November 12, thirty-year-old Russ Regan started working as a record promoter at Buckeye Record Distributors in LA.

Within eighteen months, each of these three men would play a crucial role in launching the career of the Beach Boys.

———❦———

As the Wilson boys anticipated the end of the year and the Christmas vacation, their Love cousins grappled with some startling news. In the midst of preparing for her annual holiday party, Glee Love learned that Mike's eighteen-year-old girlfriend, Frances Emily St. Martin, was pregnant. And, to make matters worse, he planned on driving Franny two hours south across the Mexican border to Tijuana to seek an abortion.[19]

When Franny told Mike she was pregnant, they hid the news from both sets of parents. They had not yet planned on getting married and were unprepared for a baby. The couple pooled their meager savings and planned for an abortion. If everything went well, they'd be back the same day and no one would be the wiser. But somehow Franny's parents learned of the plan, confronted Mike's parents, and demanded their son "do the right thing" and marry their daughter. Glee was appalled at Mike's behavior and the social stigma it brought her family. A wedding date was hastily arranged for early January. In the meantime, Mike was no longer welcome in her home. In a fit of maternal rage, she tossed his clothing and possessions out of his second floor bedroom window onto the front lawn. She was determined to teach him a lesson and face the adult consequences of his teenage indiscretion. It's unclear whether the Wilson-Love holiday get-together went on as scheduled that year.

Mike was born March 15, 1941, the oldest of Glee and Milton Love's six children. He attended Susan Miller Dorsey High School, two miles north of his View Park home, and ran long distance on the track team. Although his senior portrait appears in the school's 1959 *Circle* yearbook, he is also mentioned in several spring 1959 issues of *The Collegian*, the weekly newspaper for LA City College, as a member of the college's track team. When Mike ran a four-minute, thirty-second mile at an April 25, 1959, track meet, *The Collegian* wrote, "Mike Love continued to surpass expectations as he came away with third places in both the mile and two mile. The cocky redhead has shown amazing improvement since he turned out for the team two weeks after the start of the season."[20] A few weeks later, the paper called him "an outstanding dark horse in the mile and two mile."[21] For the fall 1959 semester, he ran track and played on the college's basketball team. The December 11 *Collegian* noted, "Mike Love led the scoring for the Cubs with 13 points, hitting for six baskets and one free throw."[22] Mike's athleticism had a positive effect on his later musical career. "I want it [a song] to be successful," he recalled. "I have a competive streak. It comes from my days of running track and cross country. And hating to get beat."[23]

After completing two semesters, Mike did not enroll for the spring 1960 semester. That left him with an eclectic mix of college credits, but without an associate degree. He took an entry-level job at the Love Sheet Metal Service Company at 3301 East 14th Street scraping rust off large pieces of sheet metal. He spent 1960 working, dating, playing sports, listening to music, and hanging out with friends. That November, Franny delivered the news she was pregnant and, after the foiled abortion scheme, a wedding was hastily arranged. With a child on the way, Mike took a second part-time job pumping gas at the Standard Oil gas station on the northwest corner of South La Brea Avenue and West Washington Boulevard, but quit after being held up at gunpoint. Life had certainly changed for the former high school and college athlete.

1961

On January 4, 1961, Mike and Franny married in a low-key civil ceremony and moved into 5404 Eighth Avenue in South LA, about a mile southeast from his childhood home. The teenage newlyweds were off to a rough start. Any emotional support the young couple could have used from their families lay scattered in the stigma of a shotgun wedding.

Seven months after his graduation from Hawthorne High, Brian and a few other alumni returned to their alma mater on January 13 and performed "Bermuda Shorts" at an assembly to elect new student government officers. The February 17, 1961, *Cougar*, referencing "Bermuda Shorts" as "that a la Brian Wilson and other alumni tune," reported the student government house and senate took note of the performance and encouraged students attending the varsity basketball game that night against Morningside High to wear Bermuda shorts to promote team spirit.[24] Despite Hawthorne's 58–50 loss, the Bermuda shorts theme carried over to the dance that night at the Eucalyptus Park building on Inglewood Avenue.

On March 15, as Mike turned twenty, pondering imminent fatherhood and an uncertain future, a new musical genre emerged on the West Coast that would change his life forever. While California music may have been a more apt description, the term that stuck was far more colorful and imaginative—surf music.

Although the Beach Boys would become one of the first bands to sing about surfing,[25] the groundswell of surf music began with instrumentals by artists like Duane Eddy, the Fireballs, and Johnny and the Hurricanes. Influential surf progenitors like "Bulldog" (the Fireballs, 1959), "Moon Dawg!" (the Gamblers, 1960), "Church Key" (the Revels, 1960), "Underwater" (the Frogmen, spring 1961), and "Mr. Moto" (the Belairs, spring 1961) gave the genre some historical depth when it was embraced by a bohemian sub-culture of nomadic surfers in search of the perfect wave.

Surfing surged in popularity after *Gidget* opened in theaters nationwide in April 1959. America embraced this romanticized depiction of California beach culture, but hard-core surfers detested the film for its trivialization of their sport and the resultant overcrowding of prime surf spots by hoards of gremmies, or novice surfers. They preferred legitimate surf films by auteurs Bud Browne (*Surf Happy*), John Severson (*Surf Fever*), and Bruce Brown (*Surf Crazy*), shown in recreation centers and school auditoriums like the Pier Avenue Junior High School in Hermosa Beach. "It wasn't like going to a movie," recalled Mike Purpus. "It was a giant surfer party with the sound of beer bottles rolling down the aisles and enough licorice and sunflower seeds to make you sick. It was like going to the best party of your life."[26] Early surf film screenings were low-budget affairs with the film-maker narrating live and playing records cued to the action. Raucous guitar and sax-driven instrumentals best captured the freedom and exhilaration of the coastal sport.

California had a rich history of surfing ever since George Douglas Freeth, Jr., a Hawaiian of Irish extraction considered the Father of California Surfing, gave a surfing exhibition in a cove near Hermosa Beach in 1907. Over the next half century, the sport rose in popularity with surfers forming clubs named for their favorite surfing spots. "The South Bay surfers were really ripping at that time," recalled legendary surfer Mike Doyle. "They had their own style of talking and dressing. They wore faded jeans, blue T-shirts, blue tennis shoes, and St. Christopher medals around their necks. They surfed together in the morning and drank together every night."[27]

One of the most prestigious clubs was the Manhattan Beach Surf Club whose members obtained permission from local authorities to build a 15' × 40' clubhouse among the pilings under the Manhattan Beach pier. City officials hoped the clubhouse would help contain the unkempt surfers. Club members wore a distinctive leather thong tied in a square knot around their left ankles and woe to the non-member gremmie who dared wear one. One such foolhardy soul was stripped naked and tied to a stop sign.

In a sort of musical kismet, the gear which gave life to the spirit of surf music originated from a shop just thirty miles from the Pacific Ocean. In a small factory located in a former orange grove in Fullerton, California, thirty minutes east of Hawthorne, Clarence Leonidas Fender began building electric guitars and amplifiers in the mid–1940s. The fifty-three-year-old inventor and native Californian revolutionized the electric guitar and the entire music industry.

The Belairs were a surf quintet formed by Paul Johnson and Eddie Bertrand while students at Bishop Montgomery High School in Torrance. After being introduced to the electric guitar by his sister's friend, John Maus, Johnson bought a Fender Stratocaster from Chuck Block, a country bluegrass musician who worked at Hogan's House of Music on Hawthorne Boulevard in Lawndale. Johnson penned "Mr. Moto," whose title was inspired by a Japanese wrestler in LA who took his name from the motion pictures starring Peter Lorre as the polite, mild-mannered detective I.A. Moto, a secret agent of Imperial Japan, based on the books by John P. Marquand.

The Belairs recorded a demo of "Mr. Moto" and four other original songs at Conway Recorders on Sunset Boulevard and shopped them to independent record labels. They visited Candix Enterprises because the Frogmen's "Underwater" was on that label. "We went into Candix and there were two real slick East Coast kind of guys—Joe Saraceno and Russ Regan," recalled Johnson. "It was the classic deal where you walk into a little record company and they were sitting on the desks and go, 'Okay, let's hear what you got.' We were just young kids, all excited, just like in the movie *That Thing You Do*. So we played the demo and one of them said, 'Your bass man's weak.' And we said, 'Well, we don't have a bass.' They looked at each other like they both had the same idea and said, 'We don't have a band to tour as the Frogmen, so would you guys like to be the Frogmen?' We said, 'No, we want to be the Belairs.' So, we said no thanks."[28]

Art Laboe at Original Sound offered the Belairs a one-half cent royalty, but they opted instead for Richard Vaughn's offer of three cents with Arvee Records. "Mr. Moto" (b/w "Little Brown Jug," Arvee 5034) was released in March 1961. A local civic-minded businessman opened a club for teenagers at 312 South Catalina Avenue in Redondo Beach, named it Club Bel Air, and hired the Belairs as the house band. Johnson recalled, "Dave Marks told me he and Carl Wilson came down there."[29] "The rhythm guitar was really prominent in a surf band. I played these barre chords with an emphasis, kind of a thump, on the bottom string, and then a percussive snap on the chord. It was a bottomy, yet full chordal rhythm sound. It was just Eddie and me at first, so I developed that to cover for the absence of bass and drums. It became identified as the classic surf rhythm guitar style. I know Carl Wilson picked up on it."[30]

As Brian finished his first year of college in early May, baseball season in Hawthorne got underway. Cities throughout the South Bay sponsored baseball leagues tailored to specific age groups. Hawthorne's Middle League, for boys thirteen, fourteen, and fifteen, consisted of the American League and its cross-town rival National League. Brian volunteered as the assistant coach for the American League Pirates, whose manager and head coach was his Hawthorne High buddy Steve Andersen. As the former starting quarterback and student body president, Andersen excelled at leadership. He would later attain the rank of captain in the Army, become an attorney, serve on the Hawthorne City Council, and be elected Hawthorne mayor in the early 1990s. Although Brian was well-liked and respected by the team, Andersen was its clear leader and strategist. The Pirates played a twenty-game season, fielding two contests a week and alternating between Prairie Field and Cordary Field.

Brian's involvement with the Pirates amounted to a five-month commitment. Tryouts began mid–March and the season ran May 14 to July 28. Steve Curtin, then fifteen, pitched for the Pirates and occasionally played third base where Brian coached. "Brian was a really nice guy," recalled Curtin. "He wasn't full of himself. He was down-to-earth. You could tell he loved baseball and was a good athlete himself."[31]

Early in the season, Bill Hollon, one of the Pirates' best players, suffered a nasty compound fracture sliding into second base. The team rallied around his injury to win the 1961 American Middle League championship. In the team photo, bookended by Andersen and Wilson, Hollon is the player on crutches. An interesting footnote to the photo involves the one player not shown—Bob Levey, the son of legendary jazz drummer Stan Levey. After his parents divorced, Levey moved from Brooklyn, New York, to Hawthorne in the late 1950s. Levey pitched, played third base, and was a strong pinch hitter. "Brian was a fabulous guy," Levey recalled. "Just a real good person. He was always out there cracking jokes."[32]

Two brothers on the Pirates would have a direct effect on Brian's personal life and musical career. Jimmy and Jerry Bowles, fifteen and fourteen, were good athletes and their mother and stepfather attended their games. Tagging along was their fourteen-year-old sister, Judy, who was Jerry's fraternal twin. She was pretty and petite, with short blonde hair, big brown eyes, and a lovely smile.

Judy Bowles was born October 31, 1946, and lived at West 115th Street and Imperial Highway in Hawthorne. She had a happy childhood and, with two brothers, became a good athlete and a bit of a tom boy. "In summer 1961, there was a fair in Hawthorne," she recalled. "I was there with my parents and Brian was about four feet away from us. He attempted a few times to come over to talk with me, but didn't because of my parents."[33]

A short time later, Judy was at a Pirates game when Brian spied her in the grandstands and fell in love. "He was real bold," Judy remembered. "He wanted to kiss me right away."[34] Curtin recalled a running gag that season in which Andersen, knowing Brian was in the stands with Judy, bellowed, "Has anyone seen Brian? Brian, get your ass down here and your head in the game."[35]

Judy added, "Brian started coming over to my house. I know he was a little bit older, but it wasn't an issue back then. My parents were fine with the age difference. They liked Brian and he liked them." Although they were dating, the relationship was not exclusive. Another guy once took Judy for an ice cream sundae and accompanied her back home. "When we got to my house, Brian was there and he was not very happy."[36]

Although he disapproved of her seeing other guys, Brian persevered in his pursuit of Judy. She didn't have much money for new clothes so he bought her gifts, including a new pair of red shoes and cinnamon nylons. Intent on having their mothers meet, he dragged Audree over one night before she could change out of her house dress and pink slippers. Judy recalled, "If he had an idea to do something, he did it."[37]

Brian and Judy became inseparable. Most nights he'd pick her up and drive to a coffee shop in Inglewood where they talked over Brian's favorite meal—a sirloin steak, baked potato with butter, and a salad with Thousand Island dressing. Sometimes they cruised to the A&W for cherry cokes and fries. "After our dates, he'd say 'I'll call you.' My parents would be asleep so I'd have to pick up the phone real fast so as not to wake them. He was a fun guy to be with. He'd make you laugh so hard. Just giggle for hours on end once he got on a roll. He could have been a stand-up comedian. He was so smart and witty. Totally out of the box and so much energy. He was just enjoying life. He'd act on any instinct he had."[38]

Judy Bowles, sister of Jimmy and Jerry Bowles, and Jerry's fraternal twin, attended her brothers' baseball games in summer 1961. Brian spotted her in the grandstands and they soon began dating. Judy was the inspiration for "Surfer Girl," "Judy," and, after a painful break-up in fall 1963, "The Warmth of the Sun" (author's collection).

Don Jardine finished the winter 1961 session at Ferris Institute March 10 and resigned his teaching position. He and Virginia moved back to Southern California and rented apartment F at 16636 Yukon Street in Torrance near El Camino Community College. Don resumed working in private industry. Al remained in Big Rapids, registered for the spring session, and started classes March 16. During the spring session, Al notified the school his permanent home address had changed to the Yukon Street address in Torrance.

Al finished the year at Ferris Institute and final examinations were Monday, June 5, through Thursday, June 8. Once his exams were over, Al hitchhiked his way back to Southern California.[39] "Someone told me Al was back in town and we got together," recalled John Hagethorn. "I don't know if it just wasn't working out or if he decided he didn't want to be a dentist."[40]

During the week of June 12, Al registered at El Camino Community College for the summer session which ran June 21 to August 2. Although he registered, he never enrolled in any courses. That summer, Al lived with his parents and resumed his folk combo with Winfrey. Because Bob Barrow did not return to Southern California after his freshman year at Brigham Young, they recruited Winfrey's younger brother, Don, to complete their trio. Winfrey recalled, "We told someone we were the Tikis and they said there was another group by that name, so we changed our name to the Islanders. There was probably another group called the Islanders, but no one ever said anything."[41]

The Islanders rehearsed three times a week at the Winfrey home. On Gary's Wollensak, they recorded a rollicking version of "Molly Dee" with Gary singing lead, and Al and Don handling background vocals, and a ninety-second take of "The Wreck of the John B." with Gary singing lead. The recordings were solid efforts, but there was no commercial market for Kingston Trio imitators.

Two weeks after Al returned to the West Coast, a new $70 million terminal opened at Los Angeles International Airport a few miles northwest of Hawthorne. On June 25, Vice President Lyndon Johnson delivered the keynote address at the culmination of a three-day celebration dedicating the new space-age terminal whose centerpiece was the Theme Building, which resembled a flying saucer on four legs.[42] On the terminal's opening day, Al and Gary Winfrey, dressed in suits, drove over to seek employment. When they told a security guard they were looking for a job, he spotted a guitar in the back seat and assumed they were the entertainment for the event. "We went in and ate at this big buffet lunch," recalled Winfrey. "We walked around and never did find the employment office."[43]

Al resumed working as a busboy at Stacks and for fifty dollars bought a blue 1950 Ford truck prone to breaking down and the source of much laughter and frustration that summer. Once, he pulled up to Winfrey's house and one of the headlights fell out and smashed on the asphalt. He later abandoned the truck on the side on the road. When they weren't working or going on an occasional double date, Al and Winfrey spent time at Chips coffee shop on Hawthorne Boulevard brainstorming ideas for new inventions. Although they never came up with a marketable scheme, it was a fun, creative outlet.

As Al settled back into life in Southern California, Brian was two months into his first serious romantic relationship and it consumed nearly all his time. "We saw each other every day and talked on the phone every night," Judy recalled. But as the relationship progressed, Brian began to witness things about Judy's mother that troubled him. "Brian started to not like my mother so much. She was something else. He couldn't feel any sense of family. One time, my parents weren't home and Brian wanted to take me out. So we got in his car and went to leave. And we saw them coming home and we waved at them. And my mom said, 'Get back here!' So I went back and she said, 'What is it you think you're doing leaving without permission?' And she slapped me across the face because the dishes weren't done." Judy retreated to her room and Brian left. Her mother called Brian later and he returned. He told Judy, "I cannot believe she slapped you in front of me." Although he was angry about such harsh discipline, Brian never discussed his own home life. "He didn't speak a lot about his father. I think he kept that hidden. I remember Murry was a volatile guy. He would get real mad, real quick."[44]

Judy recalled another incident that elicited Brian's empathy. "I bleached my hair blonde and my mom went ballistic. She marched me down to the beauty salon and had them dye my hair dark brown. It was very traumatic. I ran home, burst into tears, ran into my bedroom, and called Brian. I asked him not to look at me when he picked me up the next day and to bring black flowers. He couldn't find black, but he found dark red. As I slid into the passenger seat he handed me the flowers. He drove a few blocks keeping his head turned away. Finally, he looked at me and said, 'It doesn't look that bad.'"[45]

⸻

By summer 1961, as the Belairs played Club Bel Air in Redondo Beach in Orange County, Dick Dale and the Del-Tones were drawing loyal legions to his electrifying shows at the Rendezvous Ballroom on the Balboa peninsula, a narrow five-mile stretch jutting south from Newport Beach. Dale's breakthrough song originated as an untitled instrumental he told kids at the Rendezvous was a work-in-progress. When they shouted back "Let's Go Trippin'," referencing a surfer's journey, Dale had his title. He recorded the song August 23 at the storefront studio of Rendezvous Records, the label on which it was first pressed before being released on Del-Tone Records, owned by Jim Monsour, his father and manager.

Dale had a tremendous influence on fourteen-year-old Carl Wilson who had been playing guitar then for nearly three years. "Surf music was a real simple, hokey guitar style," Carl recalled. "They'd play the melody down in a lower register. These kids would buy these huge Marshall amps, crank them up, and those simple little melodies would just roar. But Dick Dale was different from the rest because he had more control and more bite. Dick Dale is who you wanted to sound like if you were a guitarist in LA in those years."[46]

Dennis Wilson was sixteen in summer 1961. Rugged and handsome, his short brown hair lightened by long days in the sun. Of the three Wilson boys, he was the most like Murry—intense, physical, a bit of a loner. He was adventurous, athletic, and daring, prowling side streets, exploring back alleys, rummaging through dumpsters, and crawling under piers, all with insatiable curiosity. He also could be volatile and combative, and neighborhood boys learned it was better to be his friend than risk an unprovoked punch. Girls were charmed by his chiseled good looks, fun-loving nature, and precocious sexuality.

The popular CBS television show *Dennis the Menace*, two years into its four-year run, made Dennis an easy, albeit fitting, target for that nickname. But much of the neighborhood mischief Dennis caused was fueled simply by teenage curiosity. He once chopped down a tree because his friend, David Marks, fell from it and broke his arm. He set a brush fire with a Bunsen burner from Marks's chemistry set, high-tailing it when the fire department arrived to quell the blaze. A favorite pastime was shooting out street lights with his BB gun or rumbling down the street in his go-kart. He once devised a homemade firearm with firecrackers and a CO_2 canister packed into a steel pipe. He fooled Marks into believing a jar of ashes was all that remained of Brian after their water heater exploded.[47] Another stunt left Murry stranded at home when Dennis took his glass eye to school for show and tell.[48] "I'd sit on the curb with Louis Marrotta and let farts go and light 'em," Dennis recalled. "Skateboard all night. 'Let's go over to Margo's house and look in her window.' Play volleyball at the church."[49] One exploit was emblematic of his approach to life. Neighborhood boys dared each other to see who could ride their bikes the furthest into a pitch-black drainage pipe. Fearless, Dennis left the others in his wake, pedaling headlong into the unknown.[50]

Tales of Dennis's exploits invariably whispered their way back to Murry. Although Murry's parenting approach is often assailed, few would disagree that raising three boys, two years apart from each other, required a firm hand. Dennis was the middle son between first born Brian, sensitive and creative, and baby Carl, peaceful and pudgy, their mother's favorite. At sixteen, Dennis showed neither Brian's musical promise nor Carl's domestic tranquility.

As he sought to find and express his identity, Dennis often took the brunt of Murry's discipline. Described by Brian as the most anxious person he ever knew, Dennis's nervous energy found release outside the Wilson home where he could dodge Murry and tedious suburban chores like mowing the lawn. Hawthorne's tract homes and neat lawns may have been suburban bliss for Murry, but for Dennis it was restrictive and claustrophobic with only one saving grace—the Pacific Ocean. A thrill-seeking teenager could be romanced there by a care-free culture governed only by the sun, moon, and tide. "When I started getting a little bit of freedom out of the house, when I could stay out until midnight and sneak a beer, that's when the group happened," Dennis recalled.[51] "I was *completely* behind it. All the way. I was into carburetors, cars, peeling out, cruising, A&W root beer, I was into *root* beer. I was into tit, nipples, dirty pictures. I loved dirty pictures, magazines, Tijuana, surfboards on top of the car. Even if I wasn't going surfing on that day, I'd put 'em up there anyway. Anything to do with having fun."[52]

One of Dennis's favorite pastimes was sneaking out to go fishing Saturday morning, sometimes accompanied by his cousin Mike. Dennis's carefree life was in stark contrast to the restrictive turn Mike's had taken. On July 15, Mike and Frances had a baby girl they named Melinda. Mike toiled at a soul-deadening job at Love Sheet Metal, returning home to a small apartment and the responsibilities of marriage and fatherhood. He had little time or money for the things he used to enjoy. That frustration would spark a dramatic change in both Dennis's and Mike's lives.

"Dennis and I used to go fishing together and that's when we first talked about doing a surfing song," Mike recalled. "We were on Redondo Beach pier breakwater fishing. We'd talk about girls and how we ought to do a surfing record."[53] "Dennis had been telling Brian and me about this group of people in Southern California who were dressing a certain way, acting a certain way, and talking a certain way, and they called themselves surfers."[54]

Whenever Dennis visited Mike in his apartment on Eighth Avenue, they talked about surfing and how there were no songs about the sport. "There were thousands of kids out there at the beach every day, but there was no music to go with it," Mike recalled. "No identifying sound."[55] "There were surf instrumental bands, but no one had done a song about surfing."[56]

Carl recalled, "I remember Dennis and Michael going to the beach and when they came back they were talking about making a song about surfing and going to the beach. That's the first thing I remember as far as the reality of a group actually forming."[57]

"Dennis was the only real surfer in the group," Carl conceded. "I tried it, but I was never any good, so I gave it up. Dennis was really living it; that was his life. I remember everyone was bleaching their hair; Brian tried it and it turned out a very unnatural orange, very funny. But Brian drew on Dennis's experiences. I remember Brian would drill Dennis on what was going on, really pump him for the terminology and the newest thing. Dennis was the embodiment of the group; he lived what we were singing about. If it hadn't been for Dennis, the group wouldn't have happened in the same way. I mean, we could have gotten it from magazines like everyone else did, but Dennis was out there doing it. He made it true."[58]

Although Brian was a good athlete, surfing eluded him. "Yeah, I tried it once," he confessed. "I had a board. It wasn't my board, it was Dennis's. I went out in the ocean a ways and then turned around. The board flipped through the wave and hit me on the head. I swear my head was bleeding. I will never try that again."[59]

Brian added, "Dennis came home from school one day and said surfing looked like it was going to be the next big craze, and we should write a song about it."[60]

—∞∞∞—

As summer chugged along, Al and Brian registered sometime between June 26 and September 1 as full-time students for the fall 1961 semester at El Camino Community College. They had to apply in person at the college's counseling office for a weekday appointment for testing, counseling, and registration. Brian signed up for an eclectic mix of humanities while Al registered for his second-year pre-dental curriculum including a year of organic chemistry, the academic hurdle that thwarts many pre-professional students.

Once the school year began September 11, Al and Brian would be on the El Camino campus several days a week, providing many opportunities for them to cross each other's paths.

7

Someone Should
Write a Song About Surfing
(August–October 1961)

In late summer and fall 1961, a series of events led to the formation of the Beach Boys and the writing, recording, and release of their debut single, "Surfin'." Determining what actually occurred and the chronology of those events has frustrated music historians and writers for more than fifty years.

The conventional origin story entrenched in Beach Boys folklore is addled with errors and incongruities. The first press biography of the band, written by a Capitol Records' staff producer with input from Murry Wilson, spun a wholesome, media-friendly tale for easy consumption by the teeny bopper pulp that passed for music journalism at the time but obfuscated their true history. This was later compounded when the principal players involved, in a sort of musical *Rashomon*, recalled divergent and conflicting accounts that could never be woven into one cohesive narrative. Enthusiasts of the band were left to ferret out clues, piecing together arcane bits of evidence from interviews, books, and documentaries. But the true picture of what really happened never emerged. It was like assembling a jigsaw puzzle with pieces from two or more puzzles. Some of the pieces simply did not fit. The present challenge is determining which pieces belong and which should be placed aside, unencumbered by preconception.

Ten people had direct knowledge of the events that led to the formation of the Beach Boys—Audree, Murry, Brian, Dennis, and Carl Wilson; Mike Love; Al Jardine; Hite and Dorinda Morgan, and their son, Bruce. Two others, David Marks and Gary Winfrey, had peripheral knowledge of some events. Bear in mind these events happened more than fifty years ago. Memories fade, conflate, distort, and disappear. Some may confuse their memories with something they once read. Some recall an event, but not when it happened. Others recall an event the way they wish it had happened. Then there is the intriguing phenomenon of a myth so often repeated it becomes truth and even those involved, however unwittingly, can no longer differentiate fact from fiction. Even more troublesome is interview fatigue. Over the years, the band members, Brian most famously, developed rote responses to the same tiresome questions. Regurgitating the media-friendly origin tale promulgated by Murry and the Capitol Records marketing machine, became an easy way to dispense with yet another interminable interview. Perhaps it became too difficult, or simply not worth the effort, to extricate themselves from the myth.

The following narrative is what I believe happened. It is a working theory subject to modification as new information is uncovered. I hope it will spark discussion, perhaps with input from the surviving band members, into demystifying the most baffling four months of the Beach Boys musical journey.

August 1961

As he had promised he would if something came up, Hite Morgan called Gary Winfrey and asked him to audition a song written by his twenty-year-old son, Bruce, called "Down by the Rio Grande." Bruce recalled, "I loved 'El Paso' by Marty Robbins and tried to write a song in that style."[1] Released in October 1959, "El Paso" reached #1 on both the *Billboard* Hot 100 and country charts. Although not a proficient guitarist, Bruce roughed out chords for a three-minute tale evoking the cowboy tradition. The young lovers fall asleep under the stars, but when a stampede occurs suddenly she is trampled and killed.

Winfrey remembered two sessions at Morgan's Stereo Masters with Al and Keith Lent, who they enlisted when Don Winfrey was unavailable. Lent was a 1960 Hawthorne High alum who had sung in some of Brian's vocal groups. Winfrey recalled, "I remember singing the song and listening to the playback. But we ran out of time and had to come back. The second session was a week or two later."[2]

After a second unsuccessful attempt at "Down by the Rio Grande," Al decided to ask Brian for his help. He was keenly aware of how beautifully Brian sang and his talent for vocal arrangement. "We needed more depth, more voices," Winfrey recalled. "I think that's why we brought Brian in and he came down and messed around with it for a while. I don't know why, but the whole project stopped. Maybe we couldn't make it happen or we just couldn't get it right."[3] None of these attempts at "Down by the Rio Grande" were recorded.

After he returned from Michigan, Al got together with Brian at least this one time *before* the start of the school year on September 11, 1961. "My dad decided to go back to LA and I went with him," Al recalled. "That's where Brian and I hooked up over the summer and then later we hooked up at El Camino the following semester."[4]

When Al enlisted Brian's help with the Islanders' third attempt at "Down by the Rio Grande," it gave Dorinda and Hite Morgan an opportunity to become reacquainted with Brian. The Morgans had known Audree and Murry for nearly a decade, and had watched the Wilson brothers grow from young boys into teenagers. But they had not seen Brian in several years, perhaps since May 1958 when he auditioned Dorinda's "Chapel of Love" for Art Laboe's Original Sound label. Now, more than three years later, Brian's voice had matured into a beautiful, clear tenor.

When "Down by the Rio Grande" fizzled out, Al contacted Brian again and suggested they revisit Stereo Masters to record "The Wreck of the John B." After Al returned from Michigan, the Islanders recorded a version on Winfrey's tape deck. Al recalled Brian's vocal arrangement of the song at a Hawthorne High assembly and wanted to enlist his help. Mike, Carl, and Dennis decided to accompany Al and Brian to Stereo Masters. "That was the pretense in which we went down to the studio," Al recalled. "I called Brian and suggested to him we record some folk music."[5] "We were supposed to record "Sloop John B.," but the folks at the publishers wanted us to record one of their son's songs, which never made it to tape."[6]

Bruce Morgan recalled, "'Down by the Rio Grande' wasn't an appropriate number for them. It was a country song and they were a pop group."[7] Hite Morgan recalled a scenario in which Murry played a role. "Murry called me and said, 'Hite, the boys won't record my songs and I know you're recording a lot of rock and roll, so see what you can do with them.' He wanted me to coach them and help them make a decent record. But they were in no position to make a record. We had many, many rehearsals. Dorinda helped them and guided them with it."[8]

Dorinda picks up the story. "Alan came over with the Beach Boys. Of course, they weren't called that then. Brian said, 'I bet you don't remember me' and, honestly, I didn't. He had grown so much since he was a little boy. Brian was very engaging, over-tall, ambitious, but at the same time diffident, a little belligerent toward Dennis. Dennis was the surfer, very physical. Carl was the peacemaker. Mike and Alan seemed older, more mature. Mike was already married and the father of a baby. They weren't as smooth as the other group Alan had brought. They did several Top Ten numbers for us and were very good with a smooth vocal blend and catchy arrangements. We asked them if they had any original material and they said they did not. They were doing Top Ten, I think, 'Duke of Earl.'"[9] "We told them that what they needed was an original idea, something that hadn't been done to death. Brian and Michael looked at each other and nodded."[10]

Dorinda continued, "To our surprise, Dennis broke in excitedly and said, 'No one has ever written a song about surfing!' We all looked at him in amazement. Surfing didn't mean a thing to us, but I said, 'We have nothing to lose.' Undaunted, Dennis continued, 'But all the kids listen to the surfing reports on the radio. It's new, but it's bigger than you think.' I was intrigued. It might work. I asked Dennis to write down a list of surfing terms. He did, and Brian and Michael started writing immediately. It came quite quickly. They picked up the harmony on it. I think Alan brought a guitar. They had a rough draft of 'Surfin'' before they left our office. They took what they had home and improved it. After just a couple of days they came back all excited. They had it in good shape."[11] Dorinda related a similar story in a brief memoir published posthumously in the liner notes for *The Beach Boys, Lost & Found, 1961–1962* in 1991.

Mike recalled that he and the Wilson brothers "manufactured an instant surfing song after having spoken to the guy Al put us in touch with, Hite Morgan."[12] "We prevailed upon him saying, 'Give us some time to come up with a song.'"[13]

Dorinda encouraged young groups doing cover versions to write their own material. "My mother's love of music was contagious," Bruce Morgan recalled.[14] During the 1950s, Murry and Audree would visit the Morgans, and Murry would pitch his songs for hours on their upright piano. But the Morgans viewed his songs as old-fashioned, sentimental tunes with little commercial appeal.[15]

"When my mother learned Dennis was a surfer, she decided, as a way of diverting attention away from Murry, to involve Dennis in a surfing-theme project," Bruce recalled. "She sat down with him at the house and they listed surfing terms as an informal glossary which she later used to write 'Luau.' Dennis went on to pester Brian and Mike to write a song about surfing, but the genesis of the project came from my mother working with Dennis. She thought Murry would be thrilled to have his sons involved in songwriting. But Murry wasn't thrilled. He was resentful. He didn't like losing the spotlight and no longer being the center of attention."[16]

Bolstered by Dorinda's encouragement to write an original song, the guys left Stereo Masters, returned to Hawthorne, and began working on a song about surfing. Brian, Mike, and Carl, inspired by Dennis's exploits of life at the beach, gathered in the Wilsons' music room and wrote "Surfin'," extolling the joy of a day spent surfing. It was a simple two-minute, three-chord tune influenced by many songs the boys heard growing up including the Delroys' "Bermuda Shorts," the Six Teens' "A Casual Look," the Silhouettes' "Get a Job," and Jan & Dean's "Baby Talk," a Top 10 hit from summer 1959 from which Mike developed the "bom-bom-dip-di-dip" for "Surfin'." They were probably unaware of two earlier songs that touched on similar turf. "Surfin' Man" (b/w "Jailbreak," Dot 16068, March 1960) by the Talismen was a romantic look at the surfing lifestyle in which the mythical title character is killed by a mighty wave and immortalized in folklore. The Pentagons' "Down at the Beach" (b/w "To Be Loved (Forever)," Donna 1337, January 1961) served up a sax-driven R&B stomper with a shout and response chorus in which the singer raves about how good his girl looks in her shorts down at the beach.

Mike recalled, "Within a few short minutes we came up with 'Surfin'.' I did the 'bom-bom-dip-di-dip' thing and then came up with just about all of the words, and Brian did a little bit of primitive harmonies."[17]

Brian added, "I began noodling around the piano singing 'surfin', surfin', surfin'.' It sounded stupid. But then Mike sang 'bom-bom-dip-di-dip.' He was fooling around trying to spark a new idea with the same bass sounds he'd sung countless times before. A couple of hours later, I finished the song and called it "Surfin'."[18]

It is unclear the extent, if any, of Al's involvement in writing the song. He recalled, "In the meantime, they had written a song called 'Surfin'' and I kind of went into that thing with them."[19] "Brian had come up with this tune shortly before going down to the studio. The surfing idea was actually Dennis' idea."[20]

The Wilson brothers and Love returned to Stereo Masters and previewed an early version of "Surfin'" for the Morgans. Although it still needed work, the Morgans were anxious to record it and Dorinda began thinking of potential songs for the single's requisite B side. As had been their informal agreement with artists for more than two decades, the Morgans preferred the guys record one of their songs for the flip side. That way if "Surfin'" was a hit, their song would tag along and enjoy the same ride up the chart. It would also enjoy the same sales as you couldn't buy one song without the other.

Dorinda showed them "Lavender," a moody ballad she had written several years earlier about a woman who yearns for her lover long after their relationship has ended. The title was inspired by her favorite scent. Hite recorded a version of "Lavender" by the Calvanes, an R&B quintet, on August 9, 1958, but it remained unreleased. Dorinda also began writing a new song using the surfing lingo Dennis had supplied.

As Brian, Carl, Mike, and Dennis refined "Surfin'" in the Wilsons' music room, Brian recorded a few rehearsals on his Wollensak. One of these rehearsals was released on *Good Vibrations: Thirty Years of the Beach Boys* box set in 1993 and a second one on *Hawthorne, CA* in 2001. But most revealing are the nineteen minutes of unedited rehearsals, from which these two takes were selected and edited, on the unauthorized *Garage Tapes* in 2007.

There is no audible evidence of Al being present at these rehearsals. Mike recalled, "I remember writing and rehearsing 'Surfin'' in the Wilsons' music room with my cousins Brian and Carl. And, at some point, Alan."[21] Keep in mind Brian's template for his vocal group was the Four Freshmen, a quartet of two brothers, a cousin, and a friend. Brian may have envisioned the group as a foursome comprised of his two brothers, their cousin, Mike, and himself.

The earliest taped rehearsal of "Surfin'" opens with a minute of Brian adjusting microphone levels on the Wollensak and Mike warming up vocally. The first full take of "Surfin'" is a sluggish, three-minute a cappella version with Brian providing occasional finger snap percussion. Unlike the released version, with its snappy snare drum opening and instant mantra proclaiming surfing as the only life, the song starts with the bloated chorus. Brian and Carl chant "Surfin'" eight times over Mike's "bom-bom-dip-di-dip" counterpoint, culminating in the mantra sung by Dennis alone. The song then follows a standard verse/chorus structure. In this earliest take the first two verses are transposed with the second appearing first, the first verse is then repeated, this time with the fourth line from the eventual third verse, followed by a closing chorus. The third verse, which details the conclusion of a day spent at the beach, had either not been finished or they simply made a mistake by repeating the first verse. The recording is raw and crude, but with enough charm and talent to hint at the promise to come.

September 1961

As August drew to a close, Americans prepared for the Labor Day holiday, the three-day weekend that marked the unofficial end of summer. Many adults spent it relaxing with friends and family, firing up a charcoal grill, and enjoying a backyard barbecue. For kids, it signaled freedom's death knell, drawing them inexorably closer to the start of another school year.

The September 1 issue of *Life* magazine entertained landlocked Americans with a seven-page photo essay on a nutty craze gripping the West Coast. Entitled "The Mad Happy Surfers: A Way of Life on the Wavetops," the article featured photos of men and women, one dressed in a tuxedo, riding surfboards in the frothy Pacific at Malibu and Doheny Beach. The article announced, "Surfing, just beginning to catch on in the rest of the U.S., has become an established craze in California. A new vocabulary has sprung up with such words as 'kook' (a beginner) and 'ho-daddy' (intruding wise guy). 'If you're not a surfer,' explained one high school surfer, 'you're not in.'"[22]

During the Labor Day weekend, Al celebrated his nineteenth birthday on September 3. It had been a tumultuous year for him. The Islanders, in one form or another, had been together for nearly three years, but had not written any new songs, played any live gigs, or realized their dream of making a record.

Meanwhile, the Wilson brothers and Love continued to rehearse "Surfin'." During another rehearsal, Brian's Wollensak captured an exchange that offers a glimpse of the friction "Surfin'," and its potential for financial reward, had already begun to cause within the family. An unidentified boy present at the rehearsal who, based on the audio evidence, sounds like a young teen, asks incredulously, "You guys wrote that song by yourselves? Who wrote it, all of you?" Dennis responds, "I did." Brian clarifies, "We all did. Dennis and Carl got the great idea. Mike and I just got a few ideas." Mike counters sardonically, "Yeah, well, we got a few ideas like the music and most of the words." When they continue to argue about writing credits, Dennis offers, "We all wrote a tremendous amount of words." Mike says, "You shouldn't even sweat it because it's all going to be a big flop the way we're going now." They discuss an argument from the night before, ostensibly between Brian and Dennis. The inference is Dennis did not receive credit for his lyrical contribution to "Surfin'." When Carl prods Brian to tell Mike about "that argument last night," Mike shoots back, "Yeah, he told me. Don't sweat it. It's not worth arguing about until the coins start coming in because there won't be any coins at this rate."[23]

In light of the legal battles the band endured years later over songwriting credits, it's interesting to note that before their first song was even recorded they argued over writing credit and how the money would be divided. "There was turmoil in the band from the very first day and it continued every day," recalled Jodi Gable, their friend and first president of their fan club. "It was always there. When you put a bunch of very creative people together, you're going to have conflict."[24] Although Dennis has always been credited as the inspiration for "Surfin'," the songwriter's credit and royalty were shared by Brian and Mike. Dennis later downplayed his role in the song's creation. "I think lyrically there was an influence, an idea. That's about it. I didn't participate in the writing at that time at all."[25]

At another rehearsal captured on tape, Brian coached his brothers and cousin to "sing out natural, sing it with your voices and don't hold back. Sing loud if you have to. Stand up like this. Stand with your hands on your hips you get a lot more breathing."[26] This more polished rehearsal was released on *Good Vibrations, Thirty Years of the Beach Boys* in 1993. "Surfin'" still opened with the chorus, but now the first verse claimed its rightful place and Mike made a slight lyric adjustment, replacing "listenin' for" with the smoother "checkin' on" to describe the surfing scene. Dennis was still prominent vocally, but now the entire group declared surfing as the only life. It still did not contain a third verse.

On Monday, September 11, one week after Labor Day, the new school year began for thousands of kids in Southern California. Al and Brian started their second year at El Camino Community College, Dennis and Carl began their junior and sophomore years at Hawthorne High, and Mike worked for his father and uncle at Love Sheet Metal. They continued meeting in the Wilsons' music room to work on "Surfin'."

Around this time, they decided to call themselves the Pendletones, a name inspired by the plaid wool shirts made by the Oregon-based Pendleton Woolen Mills and favored by surfers on chilly nights at the beach, and by groups with names like the Del-Tones and Surf-Tones. Crafted from versatile, medium-weight 100 percent wool sheared from sheep in Umatilla County, Oregon, Pendleton's Board Shirt could also be worn as a light jacket. It sported a straight bottom, sport collar, two flap pockets and sold for about fourteen dollars. In their youthful naiveté, the boys reasoned the Pendleton Company would send them free shirts in exchange for whatever meager publicity they could muster for the company. In 2002, the Pendleton Company reintroduced its Board Shirt and manufactured a limited edition of 800 shirts in Beach Boys blue plaid. The marketing campaign included a three-foot promotional surfboard featuring a photograph of the band and print advertisements with Mike sporting the shirt.

As they refined and improved "Surfin'," Brian continued to record an occasional rehearsal. On one such recording Brian asks, "What's wrong?" Murry responds, "Nothing, I just want to hear it." Their vocals are more confident and assured, the take appreciably more polished. It also features a significant musical advancement. Although it still opened with the lumbering chorus and a third verse was nowhere in sight, "Surfin'" was no longer a cappella. Carl now accompanied their vocals with a guitar rhythm inspired by John and Judy's "Hideout." Carl strummed a few simple chords on his unplugged acoustic-electric Kay Swingmaster. This two and one-half minute rehearsal was released on *Hawthorne, CA* in 2001.

As work progressed on the song, fourteen-year-old Carl focused on his guitar playing and stepped up his practices. Coach Jim Bunyard, Carl's physical education instructor at Hawthorne High, experienced Carl's determination first hand. "On those rare occasions he did dress for class," Bunyard recalled, "he would come out wearing cowboy boots and carrying his guitar. He would sit on the bench and play his guitar and never took part in any class activity. So, one day I decided to have a man-to-man talk with Carl. I sat down beside him and told him he was probably going to fail PE." Carl responded, "Coach, that's okay, I really don't like PE." Bunyard inquired, "Well, what do you want to do with your life?" Carl answered, "Coach, all I want to do is learn how to play this guitar and join a band." Bunyard advised, "Carl, you are never going to make a living playing that guitar. You would be smart to put that guitar in a closet someplace and go find a real job. Ten years from now, I will probably see you on Hawthorne Boulevard selling pencils or something. Boy, that was some advice. By the way, I did give him an 'F' in PE."[27]

Campus Rage

by Lauretta Cleaver

Hawthorne's campus has been overtaken by a new wool sensation—the Pendleton.

The Pendleton Company has made wearing apparel such as shirts, skirts, jackets and capris from a fine wool for many years. People have spent good amounts of money for items made of this wool. But never before have guys wanted this wool so much as they do this year.

All colors and sizes hang on "frosh" to senior guys. Some guys wear their Pendletons as shirts, others as jackets worn with a white, dress shirt. Some tuck them in, others leave them loose. However they wear them, the guys are happy and feel well dressed.

It's very good to see the Pendleton on campus, it adds flash to the scene, and it adds another fashion to the list at HHS.

The boys called themselves the Pendletones, inspired by the woolen shirts made by the Pendleton Company and favored by some surfers on chilly nights at the beach. The Cougar, Hawthorne High's weekly newspaper, reported that Pendleton shirts were the campus rage (author's collection).

When the boys had "Surfin'" in good shape, Murry and Hite arranged to have it published by Morgan's Guild Music. On September 15, Mike and Brian signed a two-page Standard Songwriter's Contract for "Surfin'" with Guild. (See Appendix 5.) Because Brian was under twenty-one years of age and a minor, Murry countersigned at the bottom of page two as "Murry G. Wilson, Legal Guardian for Brian Wilson." Murry also corrected the spelling of Brian's name from "Bryan" and initialed the correction "MGW."[28] The contract stipulated Brian and Mike, as the songwriters, would receive fifty percent of Morgan's mechanical royalty. They would also receive five cents for every copy of sheet music sold domestically at the wholesale price of twenty-eight cents per copy and fifty percent of all sheet music sold in any foreign country.

Around this time, Dorinda showed them "Luau," a new song she wrote with a beach theme to complement "Surfin'." Inspired by Dennis's surfing glossary and perhaps "Luau Cha-Cha-Cha," the flip side of Annette Funicello's current hit "Pineapple Princess," Dorinda composed "Luau" on piano. Although her son, Bruce, only contributed minor lyric changes, she credited the song to him to encourage him to keep writing. "My mother would purposefully put mistakes in songs just to test me, to see if I was paying attention," recalled Bruce. "I'd say what I liked and what I didn't like. I think that's what she did with 'Luau.' But my input was very slight. She was an ASCAP writer and I was BMI, and when it came time to establishing credit for the B side to 'Surfin'' she thought it would be easier to list me as the sole writer."[29] "Luau" was a slight, ninety-second song, strictly B side material, celebrating the universal appeal of beach parties that, with a little imagination, could be held on your patio. Now, in addition to "Surfin'," they had "Lavender" and "Luau" to rehearse.

While walking across the El Camino campus between classes one day, around mid to late September, Al ran into Brian and suggested they get together and sing. Al and Brian met on campus the following day and Al invited Gary Winfrey to join them. The three of them went to the music-theatre arts building on the south end of campus, found an empty classroom with a piano, and sang their favorite Kingston Trio, Four Freshmen, and Top 40 hits.

"He wanted to show me his stuff," Al recalled. "Brian wanted someone to sing with, too. He was showing me some Four Freshmen things when, all of a sudden, the teacher comes in with his class. It was scary because all of these people suddenly came in and shouted, 'What are you doing here? You don't belong in here. You're not allowed to be on that piano, scram!' So we high tailed it out of there."[30]

After they were gently evicted from the classroom, they reconvened in the nearby Health Center which adjoined the physical education department and the heated indoor swimming pools. At the Health Center, Al, Gary, and Brian met a stocky Warrior football player who had sprained his ankle during a practice scrimmage. He had been treated and was resting on a cot. This football player, whose name history has forgotten, had a deep voice and the guys recruited him to anchor their harmonies. But they soon discovered he couldn't carry a tune. This impromptu quartet didn't make much progress and the vocal session ran its course. Al recalled, "Brian invited me over his house. That was the first inkling of the Beach Boys right there at that moment."[31]

Al, accompanied occasionally by Winfrey, soon began going over to Brian's house to sing with Brian, Carl, Mike, and Dennis. "Brian wrote a couple of songs about a girl he was going with," Al recalled. "One was called 'Judy' and one was called 'Surfer Girl.'"[32] In the Wilsons' music room, the guys explored their eclectic musical tastes. Brian had a clear preference for vocal harmony groups, Al had a folk sensibility, Mike brought an appreciation for doo-wop and R&B, Carl loved rock 'n' roll, and Dennis had a soft spot for romantic ballads like Ritchie Valens's "Donna," #1 on KFWB when he turned fourteen in 1958. With such a broad range of tastes, there was no limit to the songs they could play and sing.

Brian had been experimenting for years with various combinations of family and friends, forming vocal combos modeled on the Four Freshmen. High school assemblies provided the opportunity to test these groups in front of live audiences. Some friends had decent voices, but none had quite the timbre, tone, and range Brian needed. Besides, most viewed singing as a pastime and never dreamt of singing in a band or making a career of it. Brian's most successful combo, and certainly the most stable and accessible, included his two brothers and cousin. In Carl, Mike, and himself, Brian had three strong voices with which to stack his harmonies. Brian sang the high part, emulating Bob Flanigan of the Four

Freshmen, Carl sang the mid-range, and Mike handled the low part. Dennis had a warm, plaintive voice with an earnestness that gave "Surfin'" street credibility, but it was not the ideal fourth voice Brian needed. And Dennis was not easy to work with during rehearsal. His nervous energy and outside interests made it difficult for him to concentrate on singing. He simply did not have the patience to submit to Brian's rigorous rehearsals. As they practiced "Surfin'," Brian became frustrated with Dennis's clowning. Although Brian may not have realized it at the time, running into Al at El Camino could not have been more opportune.

"One of the biggest quests was the search to find a person who could sing a second or third part in between Brian's high part and my low part," Mike recalled. "Al Jardine popped up after three or four people came through that would go sharp or flat. But Al could sing right on and he could learn quickly. And his voice blended in very well."[33]

Al recalled, "The music room might have been an old garage at one time, but it was a music room as long as I went over there. It was like a little sanctuary. As soon as you came in the front door, then immediately on the left was a door with two steps down. Brian had an upright spinet piano. Brian played the piano and Audree played organ. We always rehearsed in the music room."[34]

One of the first songs Brian taught his new vocal group was "Their Hearts Were Full of Spring," the Bobby Troup tune the Four Freshmen included on *The Freshman Year* released in January 1961. Brian acted as choirmaster, assigning vocal parts according to each individual's range. Al recalled, "He taught me the Four Freshmen style of singing which I had not really appreciated very much until I hooked up with Brian. Then he imparted that to the rest of us. So that was the first music we ever sang together. I would take the tenor under Brian's falsetto, Carl would be a low tenor and Mike would be a baritone. Dennis would just fit in pretty much between Carl and Mike."[35]

Al's voice blended beautifully between Brian's and Carl's. Although their voices were still untrained, it was clear this combination had something special. These were the voices Brian needed. "Al's voice just worked," recalled Jodi Gable. "You had to be there sitting in their den when they hit those harmonies and their voices blended together. It was magical."[36]

By late September, Al was singing with both groups—the Islanders with the Winfrey brothers, and the Pendletones with the Wilson brothers and Mike. After Al learned Brian's arrangement of "Their Hearts Were Full of Spring," he taught it to Gary and Don Winfrey, and a fourth vocalist, who Gary thought may have been Keith Lent. The Islanders rehearsed it and recorded a ninety second version on Gary's Wollensak. Their take is a solid effort, but illustrates just how difficult the song is to sing.

Al was at a musical crossroads. The Islanders first gave expression to his folk music aspirations and had achieved some modest success. But Al and Gary were neither prolific songwriters nor proficient live performers. They had taken the Islanders as far as they could.

With the Wilsons and Mike, Al had a new opportunity to explore his musical future and fulfill his dream to make a record. But it would require a little musical compromise. Although they appreciated the Kingston Trio's vocals, Brian and Mike were not as fond of folk music as was Al. But for Al, the positives outweighed this minor concession. For starters, all three Wilsons and Mike could sing. Carl played guitar and Mike had a fertile imagination for lyrics. But what really set this group apart was Brian. Talented and versatile, Brian composed music, wrote lyrics, played keyboards, sang, and created intricate vocal arrangements. And he was a natural leader capable of shaping this inexperienced ensemble into a disciplined vocal group. If Al had a future in music, it was no longer with the Islanders.

"When my parents were working with the boys, they were very embryonic," Bruce Morgan recalled. "They were poor musicians and their equipment was crude. They were playing Silvertone guitars made by Sears. My mother rehearsed them several times in our home on Mayberry. Their rehearsals seemed to go on forever. I thought my folks were knocking themselves out over a lost cause. They sounded pretty terrible at the time. Murry hated 'Surfin'' and was ashamed of it. He told my father he didn't want anyone in the music business to know they were his boys. He didn't like 'Surfin'' until it began to sell. And it wasn't until after the success of 'Surfin'' that we saw the other side of Murry. My father was too trusting. He was a man of his word and he assumed Murry was too. I don't think he ever met someone like Murry Wilson."[37]

A four and one-half minute rehearsal on the unauthorized *Garage Tapes* provided a glimpse into some of the internal growing pains the band experienced in its infancy. On this tape, a rehearsal breaks down when Dennis develops hiccups. Brian and Mike voice their frustration and Dennis promises, "I can get rid them, watch." Brian, frustration evident in his voice, responds, "Now look, it isn't so drastically hard. Just apply yourself. Apply yourself." Dennis counters, "They're going away. I can suffer through it. If I hiccup in the song (he then hiccuped) it's natural." When he continues to hiccup and laugh, Brian threatens, "You keep laughing, Dennis. I'm not kidding, I'll get Al Jardine." Dennis protests, "I can't help it. You will not get Alan. I get the hiccups and you kick me out?" Mike adds, "You get the hiccups and you don't sing the words all the time and you geek us out." Brian deadpans, "You know, he's more experienced." That is met with laughter. Brian continues, "I'll get him. I swear to God I can get him. I can, Dennis. He's willing. He's got a *pretty* guitar." More laughter. Mike says, "Yeah, I know, but he's always saying—(two pounding noises are heard, like a fist being banged on a hard surface, as if to illustrate Al's take-charge attitude)." Dennis then refers to Al as "Napoleon" and Mike adds "Napoleon and a half, besides Hitler, too." As they discuss kicking Dennis out of the band, Brian suggests he and Mike could quit this band and form their own. Brian later reasons they could tolerate "a little Napoleon" instead of putting up with Dennis's disruptive antics.[38]

Most of this discussion was typical adolescent bickering, but the discussion of Al indicates that, although he was singing with them, he was clearly not considered a member. Brian poked fun at Al for claiming to be "more experienced," something Al must have said or conveyed during an earlier meeting at the Wilsons. Al did have a fair amount of experience and had been singing off-and-on for nearly three years with his own group and had made home recordings of half a dozen songs. Al was a serious young man determined to make a professional sounding record. But the recorded rehearsal indicates Brian, Mike, and Dennis found his approach a little overbearing.

The band was a family enterprise at this point and some of Mike's siblings may have been considered. Eighteen-year-old Maureen played harp, and sang with Brian and Mike at the Wilson-Love Christmas get-togethers, Wednesday youth night at Angeles Mesa Presbyterian Church, and a Hawthorne High School assembly. Stanley Love, one of Mike's two younger brothers, recalled, "I was obviously interested in becoming a Beach Boy when the group got started. But I was in seventh grade and there was no way my parents were going to let me get into a rock group. Michael was already out of the house when the group got going, but in the case of my brother Steve and me, they thought we were much too young."[39]

—◦◦◦—

There are two significant dates that surfaced after music enthusiast/historian Paul Urbahns tracked down Bruce Morgan in 1990 and unearthed the original tapes of the Beach Boys earliest recordings produced by Hite Morgan. The tapes were subsequently remastered by audio engineer Steve Hoffman and representative tracks were released on *Lost & Found*. Based on information Bruce Morgan provided Hoffman, Urbahns wrote the liner notes that included a brief memoir of the band written by Dorinda Morgan that Bruce discovered among her personal papers after she passed away in 1986. The Coda discusses the tapes in greater detail, but two dates in the liner notes are critical to the discussion of these recordings.

Here are the dates and their significance:

• **Friday, September 15, 1961**, was listed as the date of a recording session at the Morgans' home studio at 2511 Mayberry Street which produced demos of "Surfin'," "Luau," and "Lavender." This became known as the demo session.

• **Tuesday, October 3, 1961**, was listed as the date of a recording session at World Pacific Studio at 8715 West Third Street in LA which produced more polished versions of "Surfin'," "Luau," and "Lavender." From this session, master takes of "Surfin'" and "Luau" were paired and released on a 45 rpm single. This became known as the recording session.

The release of *Lost & Found* was a landmark event in the recording history of the Beach Boys and garnered Urbahns and Hoffman much-deserved praise and appreciation from music fans worldwide. It was the first time the source tapes of these seminal recordings had been used in thirty years and the remastered sound was impeccable. A judicious selection of tracks and studio chatter offered rare insight into the workings of the band and Brian's emerging musical talent and leadership. The two dates were hailed as finally bringing some coherent structure to the Beach Boys early recording career. Because the project used the original tapes owned by Hite Morgan, the dates were considered unassailable. In the years since *Lost & Found* was released, every reference to the band's origin has used these dates as the cornerstone and attempted to construct the rest of the chronology around them.

In the course of re-examining the band's origin story, it was imperative to verify the documentation for these two dates. I communicated with Urbahns, Hoffman, and Bruce Morgan and was surprised to learn that each believed the dates had been provided by one of the others. Urbahns recalled he got the dates from Hoffman who recalled he got them from Morgan. But Morgan did not recall giving them to Hoffman and believed the published dates were inaccurate. However, Hoffman advised he has a slip of paper with the dates written on it which he believed he received from Morgan. Because the tapes have been in the Morgan family's possession since 1961, it seems logical Hoffman received that information from Morgan and passed it along to Urbahns to write the liner notes.

So, what documentation exists for September 15 and October 3, 1961?

The demo and studio versions of "Surfin'," "Luau," and "Lavender" were recorded at non-union sessions. Therefore, an AFM contract was not required to be filed with the musician's union. Perhaps there was some other documentation—a contract, letter, journal, or the legends on the original tape boxes. A legend is a blank form attached to the cover of an audio tape box on which detailed information about the recordings therein is written. Along the top of the legend are places to write the name of the artist, studio, producer, engineer, tape speed, and date of the session. The rest of the form is where song titles are written along with notations describing the take as partial, false start, complete, or master.

The legends on the tape boxes of the Beach Boy's historic 1961 recordings of "Surfin'," "Luau," and "Lavender" do not have any dates on them at all. On the legend of the tape box for the demo session is written "Pendeltons surfing song" in Dorinda Morgan's handwriting. Note the misspelling of the band's name—neither "Pendletons," like the shirt, nor "Pendle-tones" like the band's play on words. On the legend of the tape box for the recording session are written the three song titles and notations for each of the various takes.

In litigation concerning the tapes spanning more than four decades, the Morgan family never produced documentation for when "Surfin'," "Luau," and "Lavender" were recorded. They never mentioned September 15 or October 3 in any legal document or proceeding related to the recordings, but rather stated the songs were recorded sometime in fall 1961.

So, where did the dates come from?

There are some clues. Most likely the date of September 15, 1961, assigned to the demo session, was taken from the Standard Songwriter's Contract that Mike and Brian, with Murry co-signing for Brian, signed with Hite Morgan's Guild Music. That document bears a handwritten date of September 15, 1961. Hence, it appears the theory was advanced that the band recorded demos of all three songs on the same day Brian and Mike signed the songwriter's contract. But keep in mind that Al didn't reconnect with Brian until sometime after school began September 11 and the demo is considerably more polished than the home recording on which Al is mentioned. Hence, even if Al ran into Brian on the first day of school, it seems unlikely there was enough time for him to go over to the Wilson house, begin singing with them, be mentioned at a rehearsal for which he was not present, and then be included in a demo on September 15, just four days after running into Brian. There is also the intriguing possibility that Al was not present at the demo session.

I reasoned the date of the demo session might be narrowed down if it could be deter-mined when "Luau" was written.[40] "Luau" was written specifically for them as a potential B side to "Surfin'," and they would have needed some time to practice it before the demo session as the recording shows some evidence of rehearsal. However, Bruce does not recall when his mother wrote "Luau" and its copyright and BMI registration both post-date its release.

The October 3, 1961, date may have been derived from Dorinda's memoir in which she recalled, "At the beginning of October 1961, the boys re-recorded 'Surfin'' and 'Luau.'" Of course, "the beginning of October" is not the same as October 3. Furthermore, there are a number of errors in Dorinda's memoir concerning the release of "Surfin'." For instance, she indicated she and Hite owned X Records and Candix was owned by Herb Newman.[41] Both statements are incorrect and further obfuscated the band's early history.

Finally, and this cannot be proven, but I always found it odd that if the recording ses-sion that yielded master takes of "Surfin'" and "Luau" was truly held October 3 then why did it take another eight weeks for the single to be released? It is unlikely it took Hite Morgan that long to find an independent record label to release it. When Morgan had a potential hit record, he wasted no time shopping it around and getting it released. Morgan was friends with Bill Angel, then the record librarian at KFWB, and Angel knew someone at every record company in the city. Morgan routinely visited Angel and played him dubs of his new records. If Angel liked the record, Morgan felt it had a chance of being a hit. And, as we shall see, Morgan had to look no further than Candix Enterprises, an indie record company a few doors down from KFWB in the Stanley-Warner Building at 6419 Hollywood Boulevard.

In summary, there is no documentation or other verifiable proof for the dates of September 15 and October 3, 1961. I examined several potential scenarios incorporating both dates and concluded that, unless documentation for them can be produced and authenticated, they are not reliable in a study of the Beach Boys early recording history.

October 1961

By early October, Hite Morgan decided the Pendletones were sufficiently rehearsed to record demos of "Surfin'," "Luau," and "Lavender" in his living room studio. It gave Hite a chance to assess their progress and introduce them to the recording process, singing into professional microphones, breathing techniques, and performing songs in their entirety without mistake. However, the demo session in the Morgans' home may not have been the band's first experience in a recording studio. One of the enduring mysteries of the band's early history involves anecdotes from two producers who owned two different LA recording studios.

David Gold and Stan Ross owned Gold Star, derived from their names, at 6259 Santa Monica Boulevard, where Brian would record many of the Beach Boys most celebrated recordings. Ross recalled, "The first time the family came in was before they were even called the Beach Boys. Murry and Audree were in with the boys to do some demos. Brian was the leader of the group. He had the ideas and would tell them what to do."[42]

Richie Podolor, co-owner with his brother, Don, of American Recording Company on Sunset Boulevard next to the Palladium, recalled a session there around August 1961 with some combination of the Wilson family that included Brian and Murry. "This was before they had done any recording with anyone else. All I remember about that early session with them is that it was not surf."[43]

Unfortunately, Ross and Podolor could not recall the material Brian worked on, and, unless acetates were kept by the Wilsons, the recordings were not preserved. Brian has never publicly confirmed these early recording attempts. It appears by summer 1961, before "Surfin'" was written, Brian may have taken a crucial step toward employing the capabilities of a professional studio to more fully produce the music he was creating with family and friends and recording on his Wollensak at home.

Gathered around a microphone in the Morgans' living room studio, the Pendletones recorded three takes of "Luau," four takes of "Lavender," and one take of "Surfin'." The first take of "Luau," a composite of take three and take four of "Lavender," and the sole attempt at "Surfin'" were released on *Lost & Found* in 1991.

The demo recording of "Surfin'" is considerably more polished than the final existing rehearsal Brian recorded at which he threatened to replace Dennis with Al. It is apparent that some time had passed since that rehearsal. It does not appear that Brian taped any rehearsals of "Luau" or "Lavender." Yet the Morgan demos of these two songs are fairly polished. It is likely the guys practiced them at home or at the Morgans' home prior to the session.

"Luau" is a simple song with an undemanding arrangement. Because Brian had mastered complex Four Freshmen arrangements, it is doubtful "Luau" posed much of a challenge as he prepared them for the recording. Before they launched into "Luau," Brian snapped, "Look at your paper, look at your paper like this, just look at your paper" and Mike instructed, "And look at the words when I sing it." Their frustration is evident. Carl strummed simple chords on his guitar and Brian sang a high non-verbal line over Mike's low "loop-de-loop luau" part. Mike and Brian doubled the lead on the verses and after each line the others chanted "loop-de-loop luau." There are no drums and Brian snapped his fingers for occasional percussion. Despite their admonition to the others, Brian and Mike flubbed a line resulting in a muddied vocal and a botched take. Dennis sang the first two lines of the third verse. Brian sang the first three lines of the bridge and everyone joined in on the fourth line. It was a pleasant, but unremarkable song.

Before they launched into their only take of "Surfin'," Brian urged, "Keep rolling Hite." And then, much lower to the others, "Here we go. Let's do it." "Surfin'" now had a third verse, never evident on the rehearsal tapes, in which our hero wraps up his day at the beach as dawn breaks, but he promises to be back. The song still opened with the chorus, Carl strummed his guitar, Mike sang his bass vocal riff ("bom-bom-dip-di-dip"), Brian provided percussive finger snaps, and the guys harmonized "surfin'" eight times before breaking into a group vocal on the anthemic line. It's a solid take with no obvious mistakes, but the tempo is much too fast and sounds rushed.

"Surfin'" owed much of its simple charm and success to Mike, who penned most of the words and ably handled the lead vocal. He also showed considerable skill with a bass part steeped in California doo wop, confirming his appreciation of R&B and Jan & Dean.

As the vocal harmonies on "Lavender" were more complex it would seem it required a bit of rehearsal. But that's not what Bruce Morgan recalled. "'Lavender' was sort of an afterthought. There was some leftover time at the session and very little rehearsal. But 'Lavender' really suited them. Of those early recordings, I always thought it was the best example of their talent."[44] They recorded four a cappella takes of "Lavender" at the demo session. Brian instructed, "Okay Hite, we're ready to roll" and then, in a lower voice, urged the others, "Hey, go slower you guys, okay, make it slow." It is a near flawless take and a prime example of the beauty of Brian's untrained voice. Even more remarkable if they indeed rehearsed so little.

When the guys finished recording the demos, Morgan advised them to keep rehearsing at home and he would soon schedule a studio session to record more professional versions of all three songs. The guys piled into their cars and drove back to Hawthorne, excited by the prospect of their first session in an actual recording studio.

In summer 2007, an exhibit at the Rock and Roll Hall of Fame and Museum in Cleveland entitled "Catch a Wave: The Beach Boys, the Early Years," featured memorabilia from Audree Wilson's collection. Howard Kramer, then the Hall's curatorial director, recalled, "One of the most interesting things I found was the original hand-written lyrics to 'Surfin'.' It is written on an 8" × 11½" lined paper, like you'd find in any sort of notebook, and at the top it says 'The Pendletones.' It's all drawn by Brian. It has everybody's names with their ages underneath and says: Mike 20, Carl 15, Dennis 17, and Brian 19. It doesn't say Al Jardine and it doesn't say David Marks."[45] The handwritten lyrics are dated October 12, 1961, the day the nation commemorated the annual Christopher Columbus holiday.

Sometime, probably in mid–October, Audree and Murry Wilson took a three-day trip to Mexico City with Barry Haven, a business associate, and his wife. Haven was a British citizen who worked for Binns & Berry, Ltd., the British manufacturer of lathes that Murry imported for ABLE. Haven was the company's sales representative in the United States and, in fall 1961, while he and his wife were in the process of relocating to Southern California, they visited Murry and Audree, and accompanied them on the trip.

Everything about this trip is controversial—when they went, where they went, how long they stayed, and how much money Murry left with the boys while they were gone.

Murry recalled, "It all started when my wife and I went to Mexico City and left the boys with $80 emergency cash for food. We returned and found that our sons, along with Mike Love and Al Jardine, had spent all the money on instruments and amplifying equipment because they had decided to become a musical group."[46]

Over the years, group members recounted so many conflicting stories about the trip and the money, this story came to exemplify why the band's early history was so murky. Dennis once told an interviewer his parents went to Europe for a few weeks. Carl repeated a similar story. Mike and Al simply recalled the Wilsons were out of the country entertaining a business associate. Jo Ann Marks, David's mother, thought the Wilsons may have gone to England. The amount of money was reported to be $80, $90, $100, $300, and an unlikely $800.

Murry Wilson's United States Passport records provide some answers about the trip. Murry first applied for a passport August 20, 1959, for a business trip to England and Paris for which he departed September 4 and returned September 19. The trip began at the start of Labor Day weekend and may be the source of the oft-repeated myth the boys rented their gear over the 1961 Labor Day weekend. Murry's next travel outside the United States that required a passport was in November 1962. However, this does not preclude a trip to Mexico in fall 1961 as passports were not required at that time for U.S. citizens traveling to Mexico. Hence, Murry's passport records would not have indicated any travel to Mexico. But his passport records do rule out any travel to England or elsewhere in Europe in 1961.

In preparation for the trip, Audree stocked the refrigerator with food the boys could easily prepare while she and Murry were away. Because food would have been the major expense for a three-day trip, $80 seems a reasonable amount for Murry to have left them in case of an emergency. The Wilsons and Havens drove to Los Angeles International Airport and boarded a plane for the 1,500 mile flight to Mexico's capital city.

With the Wilson parents out of town and the house to themselves, Al suggested to Brian they rent musical equipment, specifically a bass and drums, to elevate their musical enterprise to another level.[47] Murry later promulgated the story his sons used their food money to rent the gear, but most, if not all, of that $80 may have been gone before the plane left the runway. Al recalled, "The story that we used the grocery money, which is a great story, really sounds great in print, [but] it's not true, cause we all ate the damn grocery money long before we rented the equipment."[48]

Because the food money was either spent or depleted, Mike asked Al to ask his mother,

Virginia, to loan them money to rent the equipment. Virginia was a shrewd investor and she wanted to hear them sing before she backed them financially. "We auditioned for my mother to get the money to rent the instruments to make the first record," Al recalled. "She said, 'Well, okay, why don't you come over and sing for me.' Well, that made sense. If you want to invest in something you should hear the product."[49]

Brian, Mike, and Carl drove together, and Dennis rode with Al, to see Virginia. "We sat around in a circle on her living room floor because we didn't have enough chairs. We sang 'Surfin'' and 'Their Hearts Were Full of Spring.' We always pulled that one out when we wanted to impress someone. It just knocked her out. She loved it. She went to the bank to borrow three hundred dollars. That was a lot of money in '61. That was a hell of a lot of money."[50]

Louis Thouvenin, Don Jardine's friend and colleague at Lima Locomotive Works, recalled, "Al didn't want to lose that opportunity so he asked his mother to stake him. If it hadn't been for his mother they would never have gotten started. I thought that was rather interesting because she must have had some money which I know Don didn't have. Don was always, shall we say, not very flush. But Don was very enthusiastic about the first record. He thought that was just wonderful. He always approved of Al's musical career, but cautioned him not to get into drugs. Al respected what his father had accomplished even though he bounced around a lot."[51]

The guys drove to Hogan's House of Music on Hawthorne Boulevard, and Virginia accompanied them to sign the guarantor's slip ensuring the safe return of the equipment. "I went over to Hogan's House of Music and rented a large double bass for myself," Al recalled. "I knew how it sounded because I played it in the Islanders. Then I rented a snare drum and some drum sticks for Dennis because by that time Dennis was in the band."[52] Al later reflected on the subtle influence the snare drum had on the band. "I added one little ingredient, a snare drum. One little thing that began to evolve from the pure acoustic nature of what would have been folk music to the beginnings of a rock band."[53]

Although he was family and had suggested the surfing theme, Dennis's role in the band was tentative. "We were originally reluctant to have Dennis," recalled Mike. "He didn't play an instrument and didn't particularly show much interest in singing."[54] Dennis's antics often disrupted rehearsals and, when Brian became frustrated with his lack of commitment, he kicked Dennis out of the band. "Audree just cried and cried," Al recalled. "She just broke down and couldn't stand it. She gave her heartfelt feelings on how she wanted Dennis to be involved and that it was really important to her. So, Brian took him back into the group."[55] Because no one else knew how to play drums, Dennis became the drummer by default.

Dennis's disruptive behavior may have facilitated Al's tacit admission to the group. Al played rhythm guitar, bass, and sang beautifully. But there was a time, perhaps prior to renting instruments and motivated by a preference for a family venture, Murry moved to exclude Al. In a display of personal fortitude, Brian stood up to his father, argued he needed Al's voice to complete his group harmony, and demanded Al be allowed in the group. Years later, when he acknowledged this story, Brian noted that he had won that battle. Al, however, was surprised to learn Murry had tried to exclude him, apparently never knowing he was *not* a member.

"When it came to singing, we had a pecking order," Al recalled. "Brian would sing the highest part, I would sing the next highest part, then came Carl, and Mike would always sing the bottom. We kind of had it all figured out. Dennis just plugged in wherever he could. That's when renting the drums came up. We all had to have a role."[56] In 1979, on the television show *Midnight Special*, Al revealed his mother was concerned something might happen to the stand-up bass and would not get her deposit back. In 1972, the group thanked Virginia on the back cover of *So Tough*: "Thanks to Alan's mom for renting the bass fiddle on the first session."

Carl recalled, "Well, I was going to play guitar, but we didn't know who was going to play the other instruments. Alan could play stand-up bass, Brian could play keyboards and had been hammering out arrangements since he was twelve. Dennis just chose the drums. And Brian said, 'Well look, I'm going to play the bass, and you play guitar, and then it will be like a rock sound, it'll be rock and roll.' Michael didn't play anything, but he got a saxophone. He thought he'd play sax, but Mike never practiced. The group really learned how to play after we made records."[57]

David Marks, who had turned thirteen August 22 and had been playing guitar with Carl for two and one-half years, recalled being part of those early rehearsals. "I wasn't really in the group then. I was practicing with them, but Al was playing upright bass with the group. I was just their kid friend from across the street going, 'Hey guys, can I play too? Can I, huh, huh?'"[58]

Because Al and Carl owned guitars, it would appear there was no need to rent one. But keep in mind both their guitars were beginner's models and they were entering a music store filled with upscale electric guitars. Carl recalled he "played a six-string Rickenbacker for a few weeks"[59] around this time, but whether he rented it then or sometime later is unclear. There is no audible evidence of electric guitar on any of the 1961 demo or studio recordings. But Hogan's was an authorized Rickenbacker dealer and it is not difficult to imagine fourteen-year-old Carl being enticed by a Rickenbacker with its sleek maple neck, rosewood fingerboard, and cutaway horns.

Hogan's House of Music was located at 14704 Hawthorne Boulevard in Lawndale, California. Frank Hogan, a professional musician, was fifty-four years old when he and Jim Laverty opened their music store in 1947. Hogan and Laverty sold instruments for orchestras and school bands. The one-story, square building was less than 1,000 square feet. There was a small house behind the store where private

Frank Hogan helped bring numerous civic improvements to the City of Lawndale. He served on the first elected city council and as its fourth mayor from 1964 to 1965. He owned Hogan's House of Music at 14704 Hawthorne Boulevard in Lawndale where the Pendletones rented musical gear for their first recording session at World Pacific Studio at 8715 West Third Street in Los Angeles in October 1961 (courtesy James Osborne).

music lessons were given. A second house behind that was where Hogan, his older, widowed sister, Grace, and Laverty lived. In the early 1950s, Laverty sold his interest in the store to Hogan and contented himself with his primary work in the aerospace industry. In 1955, sixteen-year-old Chuck Block began working at the store and learning how to repair stringed instruments.[60]

The centrally located front door of Hogan's was bracketed by two large plate glass windows displaying sleek new guitars on bleacher-like shelves. As you entered, the sales counter ran along the left side of the store perpendicular to the street. In the back left corner was an instrument service area fully partitioned off from the rest of the store except for a service window. There was a small bathroom in the back right corner. The store was small and cramped. Every day felt like Christmas as the concrete floor was painted in a red and green checkerboard. For Hogan, it was a constant challenge on how best to display his merchandise—acoustic guitars, electric guitars, drum kits, marching band instruments, public address systems, amplifiers, sheet music, and instructional music books. Hogan's was an authorized dealer for Fender, Gretsch, Martin, and Rickenbacker guitars. But if you wanted to check out a new Gibson Les Paul or an SG with its seductive twin horn cutaways you had to drive five miles north on Hawthorne Boulevard to Melody Music in Inglewood.

In addition to being the local Gibson dealer, Melody Music carried records and is where Brian bought many of his Four Freshmen and Al his Kingston Trio albums. Melody Music catered to home entertainment, things like record players and pianos, rather than to professional musicians and bands. For a bunch of teenagers wanting to start a band, Hogan's had at least one advantage over Melody Music—you could rent instruments by the day. Unlike the one month minimum at Melody Music, Hogan's had no minimal rental period.

Frank Hogan and Chuck Block were working at the store when the Pendletones came in to rent some gear. To rent an instrument a customer had to complete a rental agreement, pass a TRW credit check and, for minors without a credit history, obtain a signature from an adult who guaranteed the equipment would be returned in the same shape it left the store. Hence, the lion's share of Virginia Jardine's $300, the cost of a new Fender Telecaster at the time, went toward the guarantor's deposit for the return of the gear, primarily the stand-up bass. Hogan's did not retain their rental agreements. "They were discarded as soon as the instruments were returned," Block recalled.[61] The boys placed the stand-up bass and snare drum in the back of Al's truck, piled into their vehicles, and headed over to the Wilsons' house and began refining "Surfin'." Al created a bass line and Brian a simple drum beat to complement Carl's rhythm guitar.

"When we finished 'Surfin'" we decided to have a little party for the whole neighborhood," Al recalled. "Murry and Audree were still in Mexico. We held this little, audition I guess you'd call it. We wanted to see how it would go over. We had 'Their Hearts Were Full of Spring' and we played a whole bunch of Chubby Checker songs. A lot of kids poured into the music room. I guess that was the official first performance of the Beach Boys."[62]

Judy Bowles recalled the musical equipment was already set up when she arrived. "I was over Brian's house a lot when we were dating. His parents were away and they had a jam session in their den. They had a party and maybe ten or so people from the neighborhood were over. Everyone was having fun and laughing and then Carl piped up and said, 'Hi Mom' and everything stopped. But he was only kidding. They played 'Surfin'" over and over.

It was the only song they played. I met Al at that session. He had kind of a quirky smile like Brian."[63]

Audree, Murry, and the Havens returned from Mexico City, their flight landing at Los Angeles International Airport, and drove home to Hawthorne. Audree recalled, "We came back and here they had gone out and rented a bass, a big stand-up, as tall as Al for sure, and drums and a microphone. They had used every bit of their food money. And they said, 'We want to play something for you.' They were very excited about it and I thought the song was darling, never dreaming anything would happen."[64]

"Murry was furious when he first saw what the boys had bought with the food money," Barry Haven remembered. "But his attitude changed pretty fast after he heard the songs. They had the teen beat and all that, but also pretty melodies. He went into a huddle with his boys about getting the songs published and recorded."[65]

Murry recalled, "They had written a song called 'Surfin', which I never did like and still don't like, it was so rude and crude. And so they kept saying to Hite Morgan, 'We've written a song about the surfing sport and we'd like to sing it for you.' Finally, he agreed to hear it, and Mrs. Morgan said, 'Drop everything, we're going to record your song. I think it's good.' And she's the one responsible."[66]

Al recalled, "We kept the instruments for about a month, did a couple of local shows, and then went down and recorded 'Surfin'.' We had to audition the song for the Wilsons before Murry got the idea 'Hey, these guys are pretty good, after all' because he didn't believe in us."[67] This is the only time a group member recalled doing "a couple of local shows" before "Surfin'" was recorded. Nothing is known of these appearances. Around this time Al and Brian went to J.C. Penney at the Del Amo Mall on Hawthorne Boulevard in Torrance and bought five blue plaid Pendleton Board Shirts at the cost of $13.95 per shirt.

For the rest of October they rehearsed with their rented gear while Morgan booked time in early November at a professional studio with the hope of recording two usable masters for the group's first single. Al was deposed in a legal proceeding in 2001 and was asked if he recalled Murry mentioning the Morgans. He stated, "Only in so much they were publisher friends of his and they had a recording studio and offered to let us use the studio. And then Murry called my mother to get permission for me to go and record. That's how I got involved."[68]

On October 20, Brian, Mike, Dennis, and Carl attended the Four Freshmen concert in the women's gymnasium at El Camino Community College.[69] In late October, as Judy turned fifteen, Brian finally agreed to let her drive his car. He coached her around an empty parking lot, but when she ventured tentatively onto busy Imperial Highway, they were stopped three blocks later by the police and ticketed. Another time, while Brian was driving, a cop pulled them over, asked for Brian's license, and demanded his can of Coke to check for the smell of alcohol. "Brian was livid for being treated that way," Judy recalled. When they cruised around, Brian often worked on new songs. "I joined in once and he leaned over to listen to me as we sang and said, 'That's incredible! How can you know the words when I just wrote the song last night?' I just shrugged. I don't know if the lyrics were so simple you could just guess them or what?"[70]

8

Pendletones Become Surfers
(November 1961)

In early November 1961, Hite Morgan took the Pendletones into World Pacific Studio in LA and recorded eight takes of "Surfin'," four takes of "Lavender," and twelve takes of "Luau."

The squat, brick building at 8715 West Third Street has a fascinating musical history. Built in 1952, the 6,500 square foot building was first owned by Ida and Abe Klein who sold it to Edith and Michael Mermel in November 1955. The Mermels rented it as a sound stage for film and television work.

In spring 1957, Greek-American brothers Alex and John Siamas, owners of Randall Engineering, an aviation industry contractor, formed Rex Productions, named for Randall's chief engineer, Rex Oberstock. John Siamas soon convinced Bob Keane, a thirty-five-year-old clarinet player who worked for them during the day and fronted his own eighteen piece orchestra at night, to help them form Keen Records to record traditional Greek music. Keane convinced Siamas that R&B was more lucrative and signed Sam Cooke, who released "You Send Me" that September.

Hite and Dorinda Morgan were friends with Cooke's producer, Richard "Bumps" Blackwell, who was looking for material to record for the new label. The Morgans placed two songs published by Guild Music on Keen's first two releases—"Hey Team" by Jack Rogers and "Desire Me" on the flip of Cooke's "(I Love You) for Sentimental Reasons" (#5 R&B, #17 Pop, 1957). They later placed "Never Want for More" by Rogers and "Full House" by the T-Birds on Andex, a Keen subsidiary. Dorinda also wrote "Lolita" for the Salmas Brothers on Keen.

Bolstered by his immediate success, John Siamas decided to build his own recording studio. In late 1957, George Floor, a production manager at Randall, ran into an acquaintance named Dino Lappas in a camera shop. Floor mentioned Siamas was interested in establishing his own studio. Lappas was Greek-American and had two older brothers who were audiophiles and proficient with electronic equipment. He had recently been discharged from the service and jobs were scarce, so he told Floor he and his brothers could build the studio.

In spring 1958, Siamas rented 8715 West Third Street from the Mermels, moved Rex Productions into the space, and hired the Lappas brothers to build the studio. When the studio was completed, Siamas hired Dino Lappas as a recording engineer. "I grew up surrounded by sound," recalled Lappas. "My older brothers, Anthony and Thomas, had always been fascinated with high fidelity. They were always buying sound equipment and public

100

A rare view of World Pacific Studio, 8715 West Third Street, Los Angeles, where the Pendletones recorded "Surfin," "Luau," and "Lavender" in early November 1961. Seen here are the Challengers recording *Surfbeat*, their debut album on Vault Records. (From left to right) Glen Grey (guitar), Randy Nauert (maracas), Richard Delvy (drums), Richard Bock, owner/producer, World Pacific Records (in booth and wearing glasses), John Marscalco, songwriter (in booth wearing a white shirt), Jimmy Roberts (piano), Jack Lewerke, owner of Vault Records (in booth and with goatee). In the foreground, first row, with their backs toward the camera, Skip and Terry Hand. In the foreground, second row, with his back toward the camera, Don Landis (guitar) (©Ray Avery/CTSIMAGES).

address systems, and playing records at all the local dances. We bought all the equipment and made the board ourselves."[1]

The studio became home to Richard Bock, who used it for his Pacific Jazz imprint, which became World Pacific Records, the preeminent West Coast jazz label. On April 18, 1959, Bock produced the soundtrack to Bruce Brown's first surf film *Slippery When Wet* with music composed and performed by the Bud Shank Quartet. In October 1959, Bock hired twenty-three-year-old Nick Venet as A&R man and charged him with boosting World Pacific's profile in the singles market. Venet worked with monologist Lord Buckley, the Les McCann Trio, Don Sargent ("St. James Infirmary"), Stan Ross ("Please Don't Tease"), the Starlings ("That's Me"), and the Gamblers ("Moon Dawg!"). On October 16, 1960, Venet joined Capitol Records. In 1965, the studio was rented to Liberty Records and, in June 1995, sold to Neil Diamond's Archangel Recording Studio.

Hite scheduled a three-hour session at World Pacific with the goal of recording two masters for a single—"Surfin'" as the A side and either "Luau" or "Lavender" as the B side. There is no AFM contract for this session because none of the Pendletones were union members at the time and, therefore, there was no requirement to submit a contract.[2] Accompanying the Pendletones to World Pacific that night were Murry, Hite, and Bruce Morgan. They unloaded their cars and carried their gear into the studio. Carl later recalled the studio still had soundproofing panels on the walls from the time it was used as a sound stage.

Hite introduced them to Dino Lappas, the twenty-seven-year-old recording engineer who had been working at the studio for nearly four years. "I first met Hite around 1960," Lappas recalled. "But the Beach Boys session was the first and only time I ever worked with him as producer and me as engineer. I also knew him from the record promotion he did with artists he recorded. He was a real gentleman. If he told you something, if he gave you his word, you could bank on it. He wasn't one of those 'Hollywood types.' I never heard a bad thing about him."[3]

"Hite called and was interested in booking a session for a group of kids he wanted to record. Our rates were inexpensive and, when the studio wasn't being used by Pacific Jazz artists, we rented it to other artists, usually at off-times like in the evening. I was able to schedule him within a few days. On the night of the session, Hite, Bruce, and Murry showed up with these five young kids. Dorinda wasn't with them. The boys carried their equipment into the studio while I chatted with Hite and Bruce. The boys were very nice, very clean-cut and polite. While they were setting up and tuning their guitars, Hite, Bruce, and I set up the microphones. Hite was an experienced producer and knew the set-up he wanted. We miked the lead and background vocals separately. Hite coached the boys on where to stand so they wouldn't be too close or too far from the mikes."[4]

After a brief rehearsal, they began recording. Morgan stayed in the studio and joined Lappas in the control booth for the playback. "They were very well rehearsed," Lappas recalled. "They knew exactly what they wanted to do. There were very few mistakes or retakes."[5]

"I recorded them on three-track, half-inch tape. We used a very high quality, state-of-the-art audio tape. With some of the cheaper brands, the tape was wound too tight and began to stretch and warp. Lesser quality tapes could develop a problem called 'print through' where the tape picks up extraneous noise. From that half-inch tape, I dubbed it down to mono, mixing and balancing the vocals, guitar, and drums, and put it on quarter-inch tape. Hite used the mixed down quarter-inch tape to make his acetates."[6]

Bruce Morgan, however, recalled the World Pacific songs were recorded monaurally in the first place—that is, instruments and vocals recorded all at the same time onto one track. In either case, whether the songs were mixed down to mono or recorded monaurally, the surviving tapes are monaural. Hence, the instruments cannot be separated from the vocals, allowing no possibility of a rudimentary stereo mix with instruments on one channel and vocals on a second channel.

Al recalled, "We worked on 'Surfin'' for a while before we went down there."[7] "The first time we went down, we recorded their stuff. The second time we recorded 'Surfin'.' I guess the Morgans thought we were going to record all this folk music, but it just wasn't us. 'Surfin'' really clicked. That was a lot of fun, really exciting. That first session was great."[8]

Al added, "We cut 'Surfin'' real quickly. We sang and played all at one time. We just stood up in front of the microphone and played the song for Murry and the publisher. The next time we heard it was on the radio and that was the exciting part."[9]

They recorded twelve takes of "Luau," five being complete, from which Hite selected number twelve as the master. They recorded eight takes of "Surfin," five being complete, from which Hite selected number eight as the master, editing out Mike whispering to Brian, "This is a complete take? From the beginning?"

Carl strummed an authentic sounding surf rhythm on his acoustic guitar.[10] He recalled, "I would mute the strings a bit to get that clipped surf sound. I'd just hit the strings lightly with the palm of my picking hand to give it more of a percussive sound. It was a style that became popular in Southern California with a lot of surf bands. Most of them were guitar bands and we surfaced because we had the vocals. I combined that surf style with a white approach to the Chuck Berry style."[11]

Instead of beginning with the chorus like the demo had a month earlier, "Surfin'" now kicked off with a sharp drum beat and right into the theme of surfing being the only life. "Brian ended up playing the snare drum with his right index finger because I forgot to rent sticks," Al recalled. "It just bled into the mike. We had one microphone hanging above us, and we all gathered around and tried to get as close to the center as possible. And this big bass fiddle that I was playing was kind of taking up a lot of room, so Brian had to reach back to where the drum was with his finger. Carl had his guitar on the other side of Brian. We were trying to get as close together as possible."[12] "Dennis sang on that, too. I thought he sounded great. His voice had a very raw tone to it."[13]

They recorded four takes of "Lavender" with only take four being complete. The only instrumentation was Al's stand-up bass. He recalled, "I remember being totally amazed I could play it because it was kind of a jazz tune. Brian arranged it in a Four Freshmen style. It surprised everyone. I was really impressed."[14] Al later remarked he could not discern the bass on a version of "Lavender" he had recently heard. That version must have been the composite of the four a cappella takes from the demo session released on *Lost & Found* in 1991. The studio version with Al's stand-up bass remains unreleased. This raises the question whether Al was present at the demo session at the Morgan's home or simply did not recall the a cappella demo of "Lavender."

"We were five green idiots the first time we went into a recording studio," Brian recalled. "We had a song and a dream, that's all. We sang and played our song once through, paid the guy for the use of the hall and walked out with the demo record clutched in our hot fist."[15] Brian added, "We did it at a movie editing studio. It was all mono, so we recorded it all at once, backing tracks, everything. We practiced until we got it to the point where we knew we had a hit."[16]

The recording session showed considerable improvement, instrumentally and vocally, over the demo session. Carl's guitar intro for "Luau" is much more intricate. Who paid for the recording session has been the source of some controversy. Bruce Morgan maintained his parents arranged for the session and paid for it. However, Al recalled, "We had to pay one hundred dollars of our own money to make the record." In 1966, *Movie Teen Illustrated* reported, "The five young rookie artists waxed it at an obscure recording studio at their own expense and the rest is history."[17]

It was around this time Hite Morgan changed their name from the Pendletones to the Surfers and advised Brian, Al, Dennis, and Carl they should join the musicians' union, Local 47 of the AFM. According to author Steven Gaines, when the session was over the Morgans took them to a local hamburger joint. When they finished eating their burgers and fries, Brian, Mike, Carl, and Al piled into Brian's car and split, leaving Dennis with the Morgans.

Before driving him home, the Morgans treated Dennis to a slice of apple pie a la mode. He confided to them that he didn't have high expectations for the band's musical career and that he really wanted to be a screenwriter or short story writer.[18]

The Morgans decided to back "Surfin'" with "Luau" because the songs fit thematically. For the time being, "Lavender" would remain unreleased. Hite made a two-sided acetate at Stereo Masters with "Surfin'" on one side and "Luau" on the other. On a blank Stereo Masters label he typed "(Wilson-Love)" / "The Surfers" in two lines of type at the six o'clock position. He then checked boxes on the label to indicate the recordings were mono and 45 rpm, and affixed it to the "Surfin'" side of the acetate.

Carl recalled, "We didn't know anything about the sounds or how a record was made. We just lucked out. My dad knew a publisher and we went to a studio and we made a record. And the way it sounded was the way it sounded."[19] "We did a bunch of things. We did a couple of folk songs Hite Morgan published ['Down By the Rio Grande,' 'Luau'], a Four Freshmen–type thing ['Lavender'], and then we did 'Surfin'.' It was sort of like if we did his tunes, he'd let us do ours. I guess he played it for the labels he was trying to get a deal with on his own, and Candix liked it in a big way. That sort of got us started."[20]

Al was proud of the recording. He stopped by John Hagethorn's house to play it for him, but John was at work. Hagethorn recalled, "My mother said, 'He wanted you to be one of the first to hear it.' He hadn't even gone home yet. He just came from the studio where they did it. He played it for her and she said he was so excited."[21] Because Al must have played her an acetate, it seems likely Hite Morgan also made acetates for the Wilson brothers and Mike.

After the session, the guys continued going to school, working, and writing new songs. Hite shopped the acetate around to his usual contacts at record companies and radio stations. In mid–November, he visited his friend Bill Angel, the forty-two-year-old record librarian at KFWB, to get his opinion on "Surfin'."

Born Angelo Fiorvanti in Conway, Pennsylvania, in 1919, Angel got his start in radio on WJS in Pittsburgh. After serving four years during World War II, he moved to Southern California, worked at KIEV in Culver City, and attended the Pasadena Institute for Radio for two years. After working in radio in New Mexico and Texas, he returned to LA in 1955 at KWKW.[22] Since joining KFWB in 1956, he had worked as a newsman, a traffic reporter behind the wheel of Mobile Unit 98, and assistant station manager.

KFWB, 98 on the dial, was launched in 1925 by Sam Warner, the founder of Warner Brothers (the K was used for all stations west of the Mississippi River, and the FWB stood for Four Warner Brothers). In 1957, KFWB General Manager Robert Purcell hired Chuck Blore, the legendary program director who had the idea that if there could be color TV, why not color radio? On January 1, 1958, KFWB launched Color Radio, a high-energy, fast-paced format, filled with jingles, promotional spots, weather, and news that left little time for the disc jockeys to wander too far from the script. It was embraced by teenagers and young adults, and KFWB garnered a phenomenal forty-percent of the crowded LA radio market. "Here was top forty music played twenty-four-seven by 'the Seven Swingin' Gentlemen' a group of disc jockeys who seemed to be genuinely enjoying what they were doing and didn't make you feel like a cretin for tuning in," recalled Neil Ross who, as a high school student, was inspired by KFWB to become a disc jockey.[23]

Now, as record librarian, Angel was in charge of the station's vast record collection.

His duties included pulling records for disc jockeys to play on air and keeping track of the many new records received each week. He also sat in on the weekly meeting Blore held with the station's seven disc jockeys to select the new Fabulous Forty Survey and which records would be added to the play list for the coming week.

In order for a record to be a hit, it had to be played on the radio. Hence, program directors wielded tremendous power and were sometimes offered bribes in various forms of cash, gifts, and personal services. Blore was once offered, and declined, unrestricted use of a yacht and its crew. The question of whether disc jockeys could create a hit record simply by playing it frequently was discussed by the 850 jocks meeting in Kansas City at their first annual convention in March 1958. Blore told the group, "I believe you can spot a trend. We contact music stores and others in the business. We discover a hit before it becomes a hit—and we play it."[24] To prevent unethical practices, Blore instituted specific guidelines by which a new record could be played on KFWB.

Local record promoters (called promo men) were invited to bring their label's new releases to Angel every Wednesday. He received fifty to sixty new records each week and whittled them down to a manageable ten or fifteen before playing them for Blore. The next morning, Angel and Blore played them for the station's seven disc jockeys. A record needed a thumb's up from at least five jocks to be added to the station's play list. If it didn't make the cut, the promo man was welcome to resubmit the record for three more weeks. If the record sold well during those three weeks, the station added it to their play list. If it didn't, it was rejected. But the system had a built-in override. If Angel heard a record he thought was a smash hit, he played it for Blore and, if Blore agreed, the record was added to the play list immediately as their "Pick to Click" (later names were "Pick Hit" and "Disc/overy"). Once the disc jockeys voted Thursday morning, Blore distributed a memo the next day with the results of the meeting and what songs would be added to the play list. If he and Angel had selected a "Pick to Click," it would debut Saturday night immediately following the countdown of the station's new Fabulous Forty Survey distributed to record stores earlier that day. A "Pick to Click" record was played hourly for the next week. If there was adequate audience reaction, it was added to the station's play list.[25]

Morgan played the "Surfin'" acetate for Angel, who liked it and thought it could be a hit. Angel called his friend Joe Saraceno, the A&R director at Candix Enterprises, a few doors west on Hollywood Boulevard in the Stanley-Warner Building. Saraceno told Angel to send Morgan over to see him. Morgan slipped the acetate back into its protective sleeve, thanked Angel for his time and referral, and headed over to Candix. The Surfers' future would now depend on what Saraceno thought of "Surfin'."

Joseph Frank Saraceno was born in 1932 in Utica, New York, an industrial city along the Erie Canal known initially for textiles and later as "the radio capital of the world" when General Electric's manufacturing plant provided employment for nearly 8,000 workers. He attended Proctor High School where he played football, ran track, and formed a vaudeville act with upperclassman Richard Mancini. "We both loved Al Jolson. We imitated him and knew the words to every one of his songs."[26]

In 1950, Saraceno received an athletic scholarship to St. Lawrence University in nearby Canton, New York, where he played football, basketball, track, and volunteered at KSLU, the university's radio station. He sang with the Laurentian Singers, a choral group that performed at university functions, and enjoyed the vocal harmony of the Four Aces, who charted forty-four Decca records between 1951 and 1959 including the #1 title songs from the films "Three Coins in the Fountain" and "Love Is a Many-Splendored Thing." He matured into a handsome young man whose brown eyes and thick black hair earned him the nickname "Joe Black."

An injury derailed a sports career and his dream of being an FBI agent vanished when he learned he needed an accounting or law degree. After graduation, he worked for Permanent Stainless Steel, a local company that manufactured stainless steel pots and pans. He saved his money, bought a baby blue 1954 Oldsmobile Starfire convertible, and met Gail Houseman, a showgirl whose dance troupe was performing at one of the elegant nightclubs in New York's Finger Lakes resort region.

In late 1955, Saraceno was selling kitchenware, missing Gail, who was traveling with her dance troupe, and dreading the approaching winter in upstate New York where the mercury could dip to a bone-chilling fifty degrees below zero. A family friend who had moved from Utica to LA sent him the employment section from the *Los Angeles Times*. He fired off a resume to the Secco Insurance Company and, after a flight to the coast for an interview, was offered a job as an underwriter inspecting homes and determining their eligibility for fire insurance.

In January 1956, Saraceno packed his Starfire, drove to LA, rented an apartment near La Cienega Boulevard and Willoughby Avenue, and started working for Secco at Wilshire Boulevard and South La Brea Avenue. Saraceno arranged for his brother to buy a diamond engagement ring in Utica and mail it to Gail in Detroit. "To this day, I tell people I got married through the mail," she recalled.[27] In an amusing, foreshadowing twist, the nightclub she was working at was Club 409. They married in April 1956 and lived in his LA apartment. He left Secco and

Hite Morgan played an acetate of "Surfin'" by the Surfers for Bill Angel, left, record librarian at KFWB, the number one radio station in Los Angeles, shown with an unidentified co-worker. Angel liked "Surfin'" and suggested Morgan visit his friend Joseph Saraceno a few doors down at CANDIX Enterprises, an independent record company (author's collection).

began working as an auditor for Axelson's Manufacturing Company, a division of U.S. Steel, with contracts with the Navy. "But don't confuse auditor with high finance," Saraceno admitted wryly. "I was counting nuts and bolts. And I hated it."[28]

They bought a new home in La Puente, California. A son, Marc Edward, was born in September 1956. In early 1957, Saraceno accepted a job at another insurance company auditing companies' employee payroll records. One day at Schwab's Pharmacy on Sunset Boulevard, he heard a familiar voice calling, "Hey, Joe Black." He turned to see Giovanni Ventura, a high school friend who had moved to Hollywood to pursue an acting career. As they rekindled their friendship, Ventura introduced Saraceno to record and movie people like Max Baer, Jr., Mike Connors, Burt Reynolds, Robert Mitchum's son, Jim, and Marc Cavell, an aspiring actor and singer.

Saraceno also met a singer/songwriter named Robert Plaisted who went by the name Bobby Please and thought himself the next Elvis. Saraceno and Please began writing songs together. Although not a

Joseph Saraceno (right) had been half of the duo Tony and Joe who scored a hit with "The Freeze" in summer 1958. He was now artist and repertoire director for CANDIX Enterprises. After Hite Morgan played him "Surfin'," Saraceno called CANDIX owner Bob Dix and recommended he release it (courtesy Joseph Saraceno).

musician, Saraceno found he had a knack for writing lyrics. They cobbled together enough money to record two of their songs for Herb Newman's and Lew Bedell's Era Records. Saraceno occasionally tended bar at a club Bedell owned. "Your Driver's License, Please" (b/w "Heartache Street," Era Records 1044) by Bobby Please was released in September 1957. The novelty A side detailed a frustrating evening for a young couple whose amorous intentions are continually interrupted by an overzealous police officer. The baritone voice of the patrolman booming "May I have your driver's license please" is purportedly Eddie Cochran. The flip is a close cousin to "Heartbreak Hotel." The single got some local radio play but failed to chart.

Arranger and pianist Ernie Freeman ("Raunchy," #1 R&B, 1957) introduced Saraceno to the world of professional musicians, arrangers, producers, and recording studios. Saraceno began working with songwriter/pianist Tony Savonne (real name Henry Imel) on a song Savonne called "The Pause," inspired by the dancers on *American Bandstand*. Savonne thought it would be intriguing if the dancers suddenly stopped, or paused. Saraceno suggested a better title, "The Freeze." They showed the song to Freeman who, although he detested it, arranged to cut a demo in Ted Brinson's garage with Plas Johnson on sax and Ed "Sharky" Hall on drums. Unable to afford professional singers, Saraceno and Savonne sang it themselves, hoping to pitch it to Jan and Arnie on Arwin Records. But after they played it for Herb Newman, he suggested they release the demo under their first names, Tony and Joe. "The Freeze" (b/w "Gonna Get a Little Kissin' Tonight," Era 1075) was released in June 1958. The silly song struck a chord with the record-buying public and, propelled by an appearance on *American Bandstand*, reached #33 on August 4, the date *Billboard* renamed its singles chart the Hot 100. A follow-up single on Era, written by Phil Spector ("Where Can You Be?"), and one each on Flyte and Gardena, failed to chart, but Saraceno was undeterred. Over the next year, he co-wrote a dozen songs recorded by various artists on indie labels, all with minor success.

In summer 1959, Saraceno became an independent record promoter and shared the monthly rent for an office at 1107 North El Centro with colleagues Russ Regan and Jack Andrews, and Ernie Freeman. As an independent promoter, Saraceno brokered deals for artists. He found a song, or someone brought him a song, and he would set up the elements of the deal—musicians, singers, arranger, producer, studio, publisher, record company, and promotion.

Naturally, the more elements in the deal you owned, the more lucrative the deal. The most accessible elements for an independent promoter were songwriting credit, producer credit, and, by far the most lucrative, music publishing. Saraceno has seventy songs registered with BMI, thirty-two registered with ASCAP, and owned or co-owned several music publishing companies including Lock, Strat, Free-Sac, Aut, and Jo-Go (ASCAP), and Wrist, Drink, Saracen, and Go-Jo (BMI). By owning publishing companies affiliated with both BMI and ASCAP, a publisher could maximize his negotiations with new songwriters.

Saraceno and Freeman scratched together $3,000 to record three songs in one session and released them over the next several months. First up was "(There Was a) Tall Oak Tree" by Dorsey Burnette (January 1960, #23 Pop), "Beautiful Obsession" by Sir Chauncey, a pseudonym for Freeman (April 1960, #89 Pop), and "National City" by the fictitious Joiner, Arkansas Junior High School Band (May 1960, #53 Pop).

In spring 1960, Saraceno worked briefly for Fred Astaire's Ava Records (named for his daughter). "I didn't stay there long," Saraceno recalled. "It was very disorganized." He met Bob Field at Aldo's, a restaurant at 6413 Hollywood Boulevard, just east of the entrance to KFWB. Singers, songwriters, producers, A&R men, and hangers-on looking to hustle a deal, would meet at Aldo's, pour over the trades, and swap the latest industry gossip. Saraceno accepted a job at Field's Pacific Record Distributors at 2663 West Pico Boulevard, which handled Jamie, Laurie, Era, Doré, Roulette, and others. In August 1960, he and Gail had a second son, Dana Francis.

In September 1960, Saraceno was hired as A&R director for Candix Enterprises and began scouting songs and artists for the new indie label. Over the next fourteen months, Candix released thirty singles, scoring their biggest hit in spring 1961 with the Frogmen's "Underwater" (Candix 314, #44 Pop) put together by Saraceno and Jack Andrews. But Saraceno also had his share of potential hits wither due to the lack of money to promote them and keep them stocked in record stores. By November 1961, Saraceno had had enough of the management of Candix Enterprises. "I thought Candix could become as big as Dot, Liberty or Laurie," Saraceno recalled. "We had all the right ingredients. We were a bunch of young, eager guys starting to have some success. But the Dix brothers bullshitted me. They never had any money. They couldn't come up with the money to have enough records pressed for the distributor."[29]

Saraceno's frustration with Candix came to a head with a song called "Surfer's Stomp," written by twenty-year-old Michael Zane Gordon, an insurance salesman and self-taught guitarist. One weekend in early fall 1961, Saraceno and Gordon went to see Dick Dale and the Del-Tones at the Rendezvous Ballroom in Balboa. They witnessed a tribal ritual of three thousand surfers pounding out a primitive dance called the surfer's stomp—stomping their right feet twice, their left feet twice, in orgiastic unison, their leather huarache or tire-tread sandals detonating thunderous waves across the hardwood floor. Gordon went home and wrote a guitar instrumental for the dance. Saraceno assembled his trusted studio musicians, booked time at Conway Recorders, named the group the Mar-kets, inspired by a name on a delivery truck, and copyrighted the song to John Blore, a record promoter at Candix. As A&R director, Saraceno was obligated to release "Surfer's Stomp" on Candix, but feared if the song was a hit, the company would be incapable of pressing a sufficient quantity of records. "I was going to bring the Mar-kets and 'Surfer's Stomp' to Candix," Saraceno recalled, "but I asked Bob Field to put the money up and we formed Union Records."[30]

Gordon recalled, "In the early sixties you could make a record for about one hundred dollars, have it pressed up, give a deejay fifty dollars, and you had a record on the air. That's how we broke 'Surfer's Stomp.' Saraceno didn't think my band was good enough to record in a studio, so he used studio guys to play with us. Joe put his name on 'Surfer's Stomp' as a co-writer and, to add insult to injury, I had to change my name because Saraceno was with ASCAP and I was with BMI.[31] He also took my name off as producer of 'Surfer's Stomp,' but left it on the flip side, 'Start.'"[32]

Paul Johnson of the Belairs explained, "That's the way it was done back then. Producers were always angling how to structure the deal so they could share in the various income streams. If you didn't want to do it, they'd find someone else to write the song. But if you wanted to be in on the project, you'd have to give up half your writer's credit. Rene Hall told me the Mar-kets session was another Saraceno production where he'd hire studio guys and jump on a trend. And then he'd hire a bunch of college-looking guys to go on tour as the Mar-kets. You have to dismiss 'Surfer's Stomp' as having anything to do with genuine surf music."[33]

"Surfer's Stomp" (b/w "Start," Union 501) was released in late November 1961. The music publishing for "Surfer's Stomp" was credited to Strat Music–E.D.M. Music (ASCAP). Strat Music was owned by Saraceno and E.D.M. Music was owned by Edward D. Marmor. "Start" was credited to Drink Music (BMI) co-owned by Saraceno and Marmor. "Start" is currently credited by BMI to Go-Jo Music, owned by Saraceno, and Marmor Music.

"Surfer's Stomp" was picked up by Liberty Records (F-55401) within a few weeks. An interim pressing on Union bore the notation "Distributed by Liberty Records Sales Corp.," which provided ordering continuity and signaled that a major label was getting behind the record.

While he was employed by Candix, Saraceno began promoting "Surfer's Stomp" from an office at Liberty Records at 6920 Sunset Boulevard, helping it reach #31 in *Billboard* and *Cash Box* by early March 1962. "When Bob [Dix] found out Joe was working at Liberty Records, he was furious," recalled Al Dix. "He walked into their offices, marched right up to Saraceno's desk, and told him 'Next time you double-cross me like this, I'll introduce you to my two attorneys—Smith and Wesson.' Joe was shocked."[34]

With co-credit for writing, publishing, and producing "Surfer's Stomp," and releasing it on Union, a new record label he co-owned, Saraceno positioned himself to maximize his revenue stream. His success in the music industry would no longer be dependent on Candix.

"There were some local surfing records happening, but most of them were instrumentals," Saraceno recalled. "There was no big hit. Bill Angel knew me from 'Your Driver's License, Please' and 'The Freeze.' He trusted my instincts. He called me and said 'I have this song called 'Surfin'' and I want to get your opinion on it.' So he sent Hite Morgan over to see me with the 'Surfin'' dub. Hite was a very nice man, very down-to-earth, not a pushy guy at all. After the song finished, Hite asked, 'What do you think of it?' Well, as soon as I heard it, I loved it. I always loved group harmonies."[35]

Morgan told Saraceno the band was composed of five teenagers, three of whom were brothers and whose parents were his friends. When Saraceno asked the name of the group, Morgan told him the boys had wanted to call themselves the Pendletones, but he didn't think most people would make the connection between surfing and a Pendleton shirt. So Morgan renamed them the Surfers, a direct, but unimaginative derivation of the song's title. Although that was a common practice, it was also the best way to ensure they'd never have another hit. Saraceno told Morgan he would run the song by Bob Dix and get back to him. Morgan thanked him and left the acetate with him.

Saraceno called Bob Dix and told him, "I have a record here by these kids I want you to hear."[36] Richard Dix recalled he and his brothers, Bob and Al, his son, Richard Jr., and John Blore, were present in Candix's office when Saraceno played them "Surfin'."

When the song finished, Bob remarked, "Well, it's a little weak in the bridge, but we'll put it out immediately."[37]

9

CANDIX Enterprises, Inc.

On August 26, 1960, identical twin brothers made the four and one-half-hour drive from their homes in Fresno to Los Angeles to make their own mark on the music and entertainment business. They looked so much alike friends had a difficult time telling them apart. But Richard had a stockier build and a wider face than Robert. In the race to greet the world, he edged across the finish line just minutes before his twin. That was something he always liked to tease his "younger" brother about. The brothers were professional musicians with a home construction business to supplement their income. Now they were about to try their hand at starting their own record company. Their names were Richard and Robert Dix, and their new company was called CANDIX Enterprises, Incorporated, which they insisted be spelled in capital letters. But their southern trek along Highway 99 from Fresno to LA had its roots in the small gulf community of Taft, Texas, along U.S. Highway 181 and the Southern Pacific Railroad, just north of Corpus Christi on the Gulf of Mexico.

In this city of 4,000, Sherman Strong Dix met Nancy Catherine Groh, a large Pennsylvania Dutch woman with blonde hair and a sweet round face. They married in 1913 and had a baby girl they named Sarita Mae, Spanish for "little Sarah." Their first son, Theodore Samuel, was born October 21, 1914. Identical twins, Richard Kenneth and Robert Edwin, came kicking and screaming December 4, 1915. Sherman Irwin came along February 21, 1918, and Albert Franklin completed the family April 2, 1922.

After Sherman senior found himself embroiled in a town scandal involving the mayor's daughter, he and Nancy left Taft and moved to Calexico, California, near the Mexican border. They later moved to the western end of the Southern Pacific Railroad and settled in Fresno, the geographical center of California about an hour south of Yosemite National Park. Sherman worked construction and as a refrigeration mechanic, a skill very much in demand.

The Dix boys were close in age, often accompanying each other to school and about town. Adolescent years are tough and their last name brought its share of teasing. Upon seeing them approach, some kids would taunt "Here come the Dix brothers—red, raw and hairy," recalled Al. "But we didn't care what they called us, as long as they spelled it right."[1] Growing up in the Depression was hard, but made infinitely more enjoyable by the constant presence of music. Their mother had a beautiful singing voice and accompanied herself on violin. Their father was quite the artist with pen and ink, and may have turned professional had it not been for the financial realities of raising six children. The twins, Richard and Robert, began playing violin at an early age. Richard played second violin and cello in the Fresno High School orchestra. Robert, who went by Bob, studied music theory and composition, and business management, at Fresno State College. He continued management

The Dix brothers (left to right), Al, Richard, and Bob, formed CANDIX Enterprises, an independent record company, on August 26, 1960. The "CAN-" came from William Silva Canaday, whom they hired as president of the company for his connections in the LA music industry. A fourth Dix brother, Sherman, agreed to channel the profits from their Fresno-based real estate business into the record company (courtesy Al Dix).

courses with LaSalle Business Institute by correspondence. Younger brothers, Sherman and Albert, also showed early musical talent. When he was very young, the oldest brother, Ted, had a serious accident on the park swings that left him a little slower than the other boys, and he never learned to play a musical instrument.

By 1936, the four musical brothers had formed the Dix Brothers Orchestra. Bob played third alto sax, Richard played tenor sax, Sherman played lead alto, fourteen-year-old Albert played baritone, and they each alternated on clarinet. The orchestra was rounded out with several other musicians, including a pianist, drummer, and vocalists. Bob and Richard also played first and second violins, respectively, in the local symphony. The Dix Brothers Orchestra played big band jazz and swing for a generation learning to enjoy itself in the wake of the Great Depression and not yet thrust into the chaos of the Second World War. Soon they were packing them in every Friday and Saturday night at the Rainbow Ballroom in Fresno. That led to a national tour with members of the famed Jan Garber Orchestra.

The Second World War disrupted their lives as professional musicians. Richard and Bob, both certified welders, along with Al, worked at the Kaiser Shipyards in Richmond, California, repairing vessels for the Navy's Pacific fleet. Bob later served in a military band. Sherman landed an accountant's desk job at the Presidio in San Francisco. He processed paperwork for soldiers heading off to war and joked, "If I do my job right, everyone else will ship out except me."

When the war ended, the Dix brothers settled down, got married, and began raising families. Longevity in marriage eluded them and, in 1953, Richard, Bob, and Al were each divorced from their first wives. They recognized the growing real estate market in post-war California and Bob became a real estate broker and a B-1 building contractor. In 1958, Bob and Al loaned Sherman $1,000 to purchase plots in the eighty acre Country Villa Estates subdivision in Fresno. The plan was to build and sell triplex homes on the lots. Richard managed the real estate holdings, Sherman handled the accounting, and Al helped with the designs of the homes. Although he had no formal education as an architect, Al had trained with a civil engineer and worked in the construction industry. He had impressed local drafts-men with his ideas and designs, and eventually became a member of the American Institute of Building Designers.

In spring 1960, the drama coach and motion picture director Patrick Michael Cunning, who had worked with Edgar Bergen, came to Fresno to build a movie studio. As local real estate developers, Richard and Bob met Cunning and they talked about their mutual love of music. During one conversation, Cunning suggested Richard start a record company. Richard mentioned that idea to his brothers and they began exploring the idea in earnest. They agreed Sherman would run the real estate business in Fresno and channel most of the profits into the record company. Cunning advised them that, if they were serious, they needed to go to Los Angeles and contact his friend, Bill Silva, who knew the record business inside and out. Bob followed up, drove down to Los Angeles, and met with Silva.

Born of Portugese and Hawaiian heritage, Silva was 5'10"tall, 165 pounds, with jet black hair, brown eyes, a light brown complexion, and two protruding front teeth that gave him a slight lisp. He wore dark-rimmed eyeglasses and walked with a pronounced limp in his right leg, a reminder of the polio he contracted as a child. Bob hired him as president of his new company and put him in charge of its day-to-day operations.

The first order of business was selecting a name for the fledgling record label. A com-mon practice was to forge a clever new name from the owner's names. Where the "Dix" in Candix came from is pretty clear. But where the "Can" came from puzzled Beach Boys writ-ers and historians for years. Silva's mother had remarried and, although most people knew him as Bill Silva, he preferred his stepfather's name, Canaday. Bob and Richard took the "Can" from Canaday, paired it with their last name, and came up with "CANDIX."

Bob hired Harold A. Parichan, the senior partner of Parichan, Krebs & Levy, whose law offices were located in the Security Bank Building in downtown Fresno, to draft the eight-page Articles of Incorporation for his new record company. On August 26, 1960, Parichan filed the papers with the State of California, and Richard and Bob Dix became the proud owners of Candix Enterprises, Incorporated. Soon after, they formed Candix Music with BMI to handle their music publishing. The corporate structure for Candix Enterprises was Richard and Bob Dix, co-owners; Bill Silva (Canaday), president; Bob Dix, also served as vice-president; and Al Dix, treasurer-secretary.

They rented suite 207 on the second floor of the Stanley-Warner Building at 6425 Hollywood Boulevard. (See Appendix 7.) For a start-up record company it was an impressive address that communicated prestige and success. From the roof of the building one could see the iconic Hollywood sign in the Hollywood Hills area of the Santa Monica Mountains. Many of the building's tenants were in the music business—publishers, record companies, promotion firms. Down the hall from Candix was James W. Alexander, Sam Cooke's man-ager, and Imperial Records, whose roster included Fats Domino and Ricky Nelson, two of the most successful recording artists of the 1950s. KFWB, the #1 radio station in LA, broadcast from the second floor of 6419 Hollywood Boulevard.

The lobby of the building was clean and professional, but not extravagant. It had a high ceiling, an elevator, and a staircase that wrapped around the elevator bank to the second floor. Stepping out of the elevator, suite 207 was the first office on the left. The front door had frosted glass and lettering that announced "Candix Enterprises." Once inside, the 20' × 20' space was almost spartan in its decor. Bare wood floor, no artwork on the walls, and a lone desk and chair where a secretary worked, answering a smattering of phone calls and handling a small amount of correspondence on a manual typewriter. To the right of the receptionist was a small storage area where advance copies of Candix records were kept when received from the pressing plant. Beyond the secretary's desk were two offices, one shared by Bob and Richard when they were in town, and one for Bill Silva. Each office had a desk, two chairs, and a door with a glass panel, and windows overlooking Hollywood Boulevard.

Around September 1, 1960, shortly after the label's first release, Silva received permission from Bob to hire Joe Saraceno as A&R director at $125 a week. It was an oral agreement and Saraceno was not required to sign a contract with his new employer. Around that time Silva also hired John Blore as promotion manager. Although it was doubtful the new label could justify Blore's $125 a week salary, Silva had a specific reason for hiring Blore. His older brother, Chuck Blore, was the Program Director at KFWB, the number one radio station with forty percent of the LA market and several million daily listeners. Chuck Blore won the Gavin Award for "Radio Man of the Year" for 1961.

Al Dix recalled, "Silva suggested we hire Blore because his brother controlled which records got played on KFWB, and he figured we'd have a direct in at the station. I guess it was an early attempt at payola without a direct exchange of money. But that's what you did in those days. Chuck was a real straight arrow and his kid brother working here never meant a thing to him. In fact, it may have hurt us. Hiring John may have been a detriment."[2] "Underwater" by the Frogmen and "Surfin'" by the Beach Boys were the only two of forty-one Candix singles to make the KFWB Fabulous Forty Survey. That's a five-percent success rate and not a very good return on their "investment." They hired a woman in her early 30s as their secretary and Sidney Stern, a certified public accountant, to handle their financial ledgers and modest payroll.

Al designed the record label and drew the word "Candix" with a bamboo and Polynesian feel as a nod to Silva's Hawaiian heritage. He wrapped a stylish, curving box around the letters and topped it with a patriotic outline of the map of the United States. There would be no mistaking this was an American record company. Candix contracted with Record Labels, Incorporated, at 6201 Santa Monica Boulevard in Hollywood, for the printing of burgundy labels with silver lettering.

Candix used a 300 series to number its 45 rpm single releases beginning in September 1960 with Candix 301, pairing two instrumentals written by Jack N. Stern (misspelled Stearn on the label) called "Undertow" and "Magnifique," released by the fictitious Ethan Du Veaux. Candix was destined to be associated with the ocean as "Undertow" presaged two saltwater-themed hits, "Underwater" and "Surfin'." But, unlike them, "Undertow" sank like a stone.

Beginning with Candix 303, "The Waterboy"—Saraceno's good-natured jab at Russ

Regan billed as Russ Regan and the Rowdies, but voiced by Lou Rawls—Candix began manufacturing about 1,000 white-label promotional copies of each of its singles to distribute to radio stations. These records bore the notation "Promotion Copy, Not For Sale."

Like most record companies, Candix identified their releases by assigning each an alphanumeric code called the matrix number. It was printed on the record label and etched into the run-out grooves of the vinyl. Beginning with Candix 326, "Beware Below" by the Frogmen in October 1961, Candix began a new matrix numbering system that incorporated the artist's initials. For instance, "CD-F-1" in which "CD" stood for Candix, "F" stood for the Frogmen, and "1" for the A side. The B side was designated "2." This new matrix numbering system is crucial in unraveling the mystery of when the Surfers were renamed the Beach Boys.

To compete with the majors, indie labels like Candix signed struggling artists, bought masters from smaller indies, and purchased songs outright. On November 2, 1960, Silva purchased "It Wouldn't Be the Same (Without You)" from Charles "Chaw" Mank, owner of Blue Ribbon Music Company in Staunton, Illinois. The song was written by Murray Wilson and Chaw Mank and registered with ASCAP in May 1944. It is unclear whether this is the Wilson patriarch, Murry. In summer 1961, Candix released a single by the Sensationals, a female vocal group with a sound similar to the Fleetwoods, of a song with the same title, but written by Fred Rose and Jimmy Wakely. It is unclear whether there is any relationship between the two songs. For an indie label, Candix had its share of talent including Lou Rawls, Faye Reis, Theola Kilgore, Lanny Duncan, the Kelly Four (with Eddie Cochran), the Moongooners (with Scott Engel and John Maus), and David Box.

In July 1961, Silva and Blore accompanied Jim Mitchum, actor Robert Mitchum's twenty-year-old son, on an East Coast radio tour to promote "Lonely Birthday" (Candix 324) which Saraceno produced at Gold Star. Al Dix recalled, "Saraceno was a real wheeler dealer. He worked every angle of every deal with only his own interests in mind. A lot of our other records suffered from poor promotion because Silva and Blore were preoccupied with promoting Jim Mitchum as a way to impress his father. It was a waste of time and money."[3]

Meanwhile, Sidney Stern, Candix's certified public accountant, had conducted an audit and advised Bob Dix there were serious financial irregularities with Candix's books. Stern had discovered nearly $10,000 in money orders purchased by Candix and that nearly $5,000 in corporate checks had been cashed by Silva and the reasons could not be substantiated. In mid–June, Stern confronted Silva and asked him to explain nearly $15,000 in unaccounted expenses. Silva responded he had no substantiating documentation and the money should be treated as loans charged against his share of corporate profits. But there were no profits. In fact, Stern estimated Candix had lost between $30,000 and $40,000 in its first year. Bob Dix was enraged. He accused Silva, the record man he trusted to run the label, of financial irregularities and initiated a lawsuit. Bob maintained Silva used the money to pay his rent and purchase a new car.[4]

On July 14, Bob sent a telegram to Silva at the Park Sheraton Hotel in New York, where he was staying with Jim Mitchum, requesting his presence at an emergency meeting of the Candix board of directors on July 17. Silva requested the meeting be postponed to July 21. Bob agreed, but when the board—Bob, Richard, and Al—met in Candix's office, Silva didn't show. They voted to remove Silva as president and appointed Bob president.

On July 25, Silva was served with a summons to appear in LA County Superior Court. When he did not answer the complaint, the Court entered a default judgment against him in the amount of $14,157.40 plus interest and costs on October 20.

During its first year of operation it was not uncommon for small record companies to struggle financially. Candix was no exception, but it was further hampered when Bob discovered that, rather than channel their real estate profits to the record company as agreed, Sherman spent the money on a lavish personal lifestyle. Bob was so angry he actually contemplated going to Sherman's house and shooting him. Al talked him out of it, reasoning that Sherman wasn't worth spending the rest of his life in jail.[5]

In the weeks following Silva's departure, Candix tightened its belt and prevailed upon their pressing plant to extend their credit so they could continue releasing their next six records (Candix 325–330). Bob renewed the Candix copyright on October 16, 1961, but the company's finances were in shambles due to the diversion of $15,000, the concurrent legal fees, loss of an experienced employee, the betrayal by Sherman and loss of financial support from their real estate business, and, as Bob would soon discover, the diversion of "Surfer's Stomp" from Candix to Union Records that Saraceno, his A&R director, had formed with Bob Field.

This financial crisis and personnel chaos consumed Bob's time, distracting him from managing the company. It could not have happened at a worse time. He had just agreed to release the first record by five guys called the Surfers.

10

"Call Them the Beach Boys"—Russ Regan

Once Bob Dix gave the green light, "Surfin'" by the Surfers was assigned record number 331, the next sequential number in the company's catalogue, and matrix number "CD-TS-1" which stood for "Candix, the Surfers, side 1." Because Morgan's original acetate had been played several times and the sound quality had been degraded, he provided Candix with a new acetate of "Surfin'" and an acetate of "Luau."

The acetates were then brought to a facility that made the metal works (converted metal masters, mothers, and stampers), where the matrix numbers, "CD-TS-1" for "Surfin'" and "CD-TS-2" for "Luau," were hand etched into the acetate's run-out grooves, the so-called dead wax at the end of the recording. The three-step process was used to produce twelve sets of stampers, in which one "Surfin'" stamper and one "Luau" stamper comprised a set. The entire process from acetate to stampers could be completed in one or two days.[1]

Saraceno called his friend Russ Regan at Buckeye Record Distributors, who handled Candix's account to give him a heads up on the next Candix release. He played the "Surfin'" acetate over the phone for Regan. "I called Russ and asked him if he thought surfing was going to happen nationally," Saraceno recalled. After it finished, and with a clear reference to the bom-bom-dip-di-dip, Regan remarked, "It sounds like a Jan & Dean record. Who are they?" Saraceno replied, "It's a new group we're signing over here at Candix. They call themselves the Pendletones, but we're thinking of changing it to the Surfers." Regan reminded him, "Joe, you can't call them the Surfers. There's a Hawaiian act on Hi Fi Records called the Surfers." Saraceno replied, "You know, you're right. I forgot about that. Well, give me a name." Regan offered surf-related names like the Hang Tens and the Woodies, which Saraceno vetoed. Finally, Regan said, "Then call them the Beach Boys." Saraceno replied, "That's it!"[2]

Russ Regan was born Albert Harold Rustigian on June 15, 1929, in Sanger, California, fourteen miles east of Fresno, in the heart of California farmland. He was the first of four children born to Albert A. Rustigian and Grace A. Nahigian, both of Armenian heritage. Albert Sr. played violin and enjoyed entertaining friends and family. He wanted his oldest son to learn the violin, but young Albert preferred the drums.

After graduating Modesto High school in June 1946, Albert Jr., worked a number of different jobs including sales, gold prospecting in Mexico, and filling orders at a Gallo Wine distributor. By 1956, he had moved to LA where he met and befriended aspiring singer songwriter Salvatore "Sonny" Bono. They cobbled together enough money to record a new version of "Hey Mrs. Jones," a #7 R&B hit for Jimmy Forrest in November 1952. They called themselves the Checkmates and convinced Richard Vaughn to release it on Arvee Records in spring 1958, but it failed to chart.

Around this time, Rustigian changed his name to the decidedly more Hollywood-sounding Russ Regan. He wrote and recorded "I Never Knew" for Corvette Records in August 1958. The single generated sufficient buzz to be picked up by ABC-Paramount that September.

In early 1959, he wrote a romantic ballad called "Joan of Love" that caught the attention of Buck Stapleton, a producer at Capitol Records who signed him to a two-plus-two deal, two sides with an option for two additional sides. "Joan of Love" backed with "That's When I Ran" was released on Capitol 4169. Of the B side, the March 23, 1959, *Billboard* said, "Regan has a frantic rockabilly sound much in the Presley tradition on this good rocker." Despite the solid review, it failed to chart. When his follow-up, "Just the Two of Us" (b/w "Adults Only," Capitol 4280), failed to chart in September 1959, Capitol did not renew his contract.

While discussing the music business with Joe Saraceno one day in their office on North El Centro, Regan noted how Rostom ("Ross") Bagdasarian, a fellow Armenian from Fresno, had scored a #1 hit with the 1958 Christmas novelty "The Chipmunk Song (Christmas Don't Be Late)." Regan reasoned if chipmunks could sing, why not reindeer? He wrote "The Happy Reindeer" with Bobby Please, whom he met through Saraceno. He played the master for Buck Stapleton, and "The Happy Reindeer" (b/w "Dancer's Waltz," Capitol 4300) by Dancer, Prancer, and Nervous, the Singing Reindeer, was released late October 1959. The November 19 *Billboard* reported it was "currently the label's top selling single with orders totaling 500,000 since its release." Americans embraced the singing quadrapeds and they scampered to #34, selling a staggering 800,000 copies.

As 1960 got under way, Regan formed Algrace Music Publishing, named for his parents, Al and Grace. Regan and Please followed "The Happy Reindeer" with "The Happy Birthday Song" (b/w "I Wanna Be an Easter Bunny," Capitol 4353) by the Singing Reindeer in spring 1960. It garnered a brief notice in *Billboard*, but didn't chart.

Regan continued writing songs and placing them with other artists. He co-wrote "Lost and Found" with Nick Venet, which Venet recorded for Jack Hoffman's Enith International label in May 1960. Frustrated with his stalled singing career and not having much success with songwriting, Regan acted on a job referral from Sonny Bono. On November 12, 1960, he began working as a record promoter for Dorothy Freeman's newly formed Buckeye Record Distributors on West Pico Boulevard, the Record Row of LA distributors.

Dorothy Freeman was born Colleen Googe on a farm in Baxley, Georgia, in 1928. After high school, she moved to St. Simons Island, off the coast of Brunswick, Georgia, where she worked as a waitress at a restaurant whose owner mistakenly called her Dorothy and the name stuck. In 1947, she and her twin sister, Novadeen, traveled by bus to New York City and stayed at the Waldorf Astoria, the lavish accommodations paid for with the fifty dollar cash-on-the-spot settlement the bus company offered each passenger in lieu of a potential lawsuit following an accident near Richmond, Virginia. Dorothy then moved into the Roosevelt, a residential hotel in midtown, and began working as a bookkeeper for Mercury Records Distributor.

In 1952, Mercury sent her to Cleveland to start their distributorship there. After a few years, she left Mercury and began working for Concord Distributor in Cleveland owned by Art Freeman who, with Ben Herman, a distributor in Pittsburgh, also owned BenArt Distributor in Cleveland. When Dorothy and Art married in May 1958, Randy Wood, owner of Dot Records, held their reception at his home in Beverly Hills. But the marriage was short-lived and Dorothy moved with her two young children to LA and, in October 1960, opened Buckeye Record Distributors on West Pico Boulevard. In deference to her years in Ohio, and her new landlord who hailed from Ohio, she named her new distributorship after the state nickname. Six months later, Buckeye moved into a larger space across the street at 2583 West Pico Boulevard. She hired Janet Devaney from Hi Fi Records as a salesperson, and Bobby Singer left Concord in Cleveland to work for her as a record promoter. Then she hired Russ Regan as a record promoter.

"The first six months were the hardest because we didn't have any labels to work on," Regan recalled. "Gradually we got more companies and it became a pretty good distributorship. Record promotion is not a nine-to-five job. You talk to your manufacturers. The product comes in. You listen to records and select whatever is right. That's called 'using your ears.' If you guess right, you're a genius. If you guess wrong, you're nothing. I'd take a record to a radio station. If you believe in it, that's where the selling came in."[3]

The first records Regan successfully promoted at Buckeye were Linda Scott's "I've Told Every Little Star" on Canadian-American (April 1961), the Marvelette's "Please Mr. Postman" on Tamla (August 1961), and Sue Thompson's "Sad Movies (Make Me Cry)" on Hickory (October 1961). Buckeye also handled Caprice, Disneyland, Dot, Nomar, Riverside, and Shasta.

While working at Buckeye, Regan continued writing songs and in April 1961 collaborated with Sonny Bono on "Tight Sweater" by the Marathons on Arvee, their follow-up to "Peanut Butter," a parody of the Olympics' 1959 hit "(Baby) Hully Gully," whose melody Brian used for Carol Hess's campaign song in January 1960.

Regan was very successful at record promotion. His extroverted, gregarious personality was well suited for the work and he had a knack for picking hit records. Program directors began to trust his instincts. He was friends with all the local disc jockeys and record promoters, and had a modest expense account of $60 to $80 per week for business-related meals. A standing Wednesday night poker game with music business friends, including Saraceno, A&R director at Candix, enabled him to develop lasting friendships in the industry and keep his eyes and ears tuned to what was selling and what was coming down the pike. At night, he visited clubs, record hops, and Dolphin's of Hollywood, the legendary R&B record store at Western and Vernon.

Regan spent most mornings on the road visiting program directors and disc jockeys in the greater LA and San Diego areas. He traveled with a stack of Buckeye's current records and did his best to convince stations to add them to their play list. "When Russ got on your back about a hit, you'd better play it or he didn't get off your back," recalled Dorothy Freeman. "Russ was a great record promoter and he brought the Candix account to Buckeye."[4]

In 1974, when he was president of 20th Century Records, Regan shared his record promotion philosophy. "If you've got a hit record, you've got to supply it to the radio stations and if they wear that copy out, then you've got to give them another one. I got a kick every time I broke a record. I would try harder than the next guy, I would say to myself: I'm going to go out and do something he isn't."[5]

One of Regan's key responsibilities at Buckeye was to deliver new releases to local radio stations. And, with a forty percent market share, no station was more important in LA than KFWB. And no day of the week was more important than Wednesday—Record Day at KFWB—the day you played your new releases for Bill Angel. This meeting at KFWB was so crucial many record companies scheduled their new releases for Monday to give their promoters a day to prepare for their Wednesday meeting with Angel. As a promoter, much was riding on that meeting. If you got your record on KFWB, other stations followed and the record had a good chance of being a hit.

"I liked to have my new releases several days before my Wednesday meeting with Bill," recalled Regan. "I played them repeatedly until I knew them inside and out. Then I would concentrate on the ones I wanted to play for Bill. I would bring him six to ten new records, but I would only play him maybe three. I learned not to overwhelm him by pitching too many records. But I had done my homework. I knew which ones had a chance of being a hit."[6]

So how did the Surfers, formerly the Pendletones, find out they were now the Beach Boys? The entrenched story is they only learned of the name after "Surfin'" was released. Brian recalled, "We were given the name the Beach Boys by Russ Regan. Our group was called the Pendletones and Russ said, 'Why don't you call them the Beach Boys and tell them after you release it. Just say, 'Hey, your new name is the Beach Boys.' They told us over the phone and we went 'What?' But, later on, we accepted it."[7]

Judy Bowles recalled Brian was not always pleased with the name. "He wanted to be called the Pendletones with the plaid shirts. He was mad because now they were the Beach Boys because some public relations guy named them that and they had to go with it."[8]

Mike recalled, "We got the name the Beach Boys handed to us by Russ Regan who was working as an independent promotion man and heard the record."[9] "We didn't even know we were the Beach Boys until the song came out. It was that kind of thing. We could have said, 'No, we're not going to be the Beach Boys,' but it sounded pretty far out."[10] In 2011, Mike recalled they were consulted about the name. "They asked us 'Since the record is called "Surfin'," what do you think about the name the Beach Boys?' Well, that's better than what we have. It wasn't underhanded. It was just from outside the group."[11]

John Maus recalled Carl visited him at the music store where he worked and expressed concern about the name. "He didn't like it, thought it was embarrassing." Maus told Carl that having a hit record was more important than worrying about the name.[12] The name was not particularly unique as there had been several groups called the Beach Boys, including an instrumental and vocal trio in the late 1940s specializing in Hawaiian and Latin favorites.

Further complicating things is that not everyone agreed Regan suggested the name. Bruce Morgan maintained his mother suggested the name during a "Surfin'" rehearsal at their home on Mayberry Street. "They were all gathered in the living room and she said something like 'Well, isn't this nice. We're going to have a little beach party. We'll have our beach girls on this side of the room and our beach boys over here.' The name stuck. My mother decided they should be called the Beach Boys because they were doing beach and surf music. It just made sense. My dad went to Joe Saraceno at Candix to build consensus for the name."[13]

Dorinda, however, never claimed credit and offered two slightly varying accounts. She told author Byron Preiss the name came out of a meeting of Hite, Saraceno, and Herb Newman, owner of Era Records, in Newman's office.[14] But, in a brief account found posthumously in her papers, she wrote, "Herb, along with Joe Saraceno and Russ Regan, were in our office when the name 'The Beach Boys' was decided upon."[15]

Richard Dix was adamant his son, Richard Dix, Jr., came up with the name "Beach Boys." According to Richard Sr., he was present with his brothers, Al and Bob, Blore, Saraceno, and Richard, Jr., when Bob played the "Surfin'" acetate in the Candix office. Bob commented the name "The Pendletons" didn't fit the theme of the song and they should rename them.[16] When they couldn't come up with a name, Richard suggested that he, his son, and Blore go to Aldo's and discuss it over coffee. Richard recalled, "Blore suggested we call them 'The Surfers' and my son said, 'That name is too general because I'm a surfer and anyone that uses a surf board is a surfer, and they go to the beach to surf, so they should be called "The Beach Boys" and the three of us agreed.'"[17] As Richard paid for the coffee, Blore ran ahead, burst into the Candix office, and announced they had the name for the group— the Beach Boys. This account suggests the name the Surfers was never a serious contender despite the matrix numbers indicating otherwise.

Theoretically, when the band's name was changed from the Surfers to the Beach Boys, "Surfin'" and "Luau" should have been assigned new matrix numbers "CD-BB-1" and "CD-BB-2." But, because the metal works were either made or in the process of being made, Candix was in no financial position to have new sets made. Matrix numbers were for internal accounting and had no impact on the actual record. The same, however, could not be said for the record label.

Because record labels were applied to the record as it was being pressed, they had to be delivered to the pressing plant *before* the record went into production. Therefore, record labels were generally ordered at the same time metal works were ordered. Because the name change from the Surfers to the Beach Boys happened after the metal works were ordered, it raises the question whether record labels with "Surfin'" by the Surfers on Candix 331 were ordered or printed.

When Candix was formed in August 1960, Al Dix submitted his original label artwork to Record Labels, Incorporated, which then printed thousands of Candix labels with stock information that never changed from one release to another—the Candix logo at the twelve o'clock position, two horizontal parallel lines, a half inch apart, from the nine o'clock to the three o'clock position, and "45 RPM" above the top line. These labels were stockpiled at the printer.

Whenever Candix prepared a new record for release, someone, most likely Saraceno or Blore, completed a label copy work order and submitted it to the printer. The work order contained specific information pertaining to that release—artist, song titles, writers, publishers, times, master numbers, and record number. Pre-printed stockpiled labels were then sent through the printing press and the new information was printed onto them. A typical print run was 12,000 each of the A and B side labels. Another 1,000 of each were printed using white labels with black type with the added notation the record was for promotional use only and not for sale.

It is unknown whether record labels had already been printed when the name of the band was changed from the Surfers to the Beach Boys. Copies of Candix 331 with the band listed as the Surfers are not known to exist. Perhaps someone at Candix was able to modify the work order before the labels were printed. Furthermore, if labels had been printed, most likely they were subsequently discarded or destroyed.

There are no white label promotional copies of "Surfin'" on Candix 331 despite the company having done so for each of its preceding twenty-eight releases (Candix 303–330). Perhaps when the band's name was changed to the Beach Boys, the labels had been printed as the Surfers and had to be discarded. In the confusion, or as a minor cost-cutting measure, perhaps Candix opted not to reprint white promotional labels. Of course, the lack of white promotional labels simply may have been an oversight.

The record labels for "Surfin'" and "Luau" were printed with matrix numbers CD-TS-1 and CD-TS-2, respectively. "Surfin'" was spelled in all capital letters and without an apostrophe. The artist was "Beach Boys" and the songwriting credited to B. Wilson—M. Love and timed at 2:15. "Luau" was credited to Bruce Morgan, although it was written by Dorinda, and timed at 2:00, although it was actually 1:43.

The music publishing for "Surfin'" was co-credited to Drink-Guild Music (BMI), but should have been Guild Music alone as was done for "Luau." Drink Music was owned by Joe Saraceno and Edward D. Marmor. It is unclear, however, how they expected to split the mechanical royalty with Guild Music.

The printed labels were delivered to the pressing plant, but it is unclear what plant was used. Large record companies like Capitol, Columbia, Decca, and RCA Victor, had their own pressing plants in LA dedicated to manufacturing their own records. These plants used a distinctive alpha-numeric code that was either machine-stamped or hand-etched into the run-out grooves to identify the recording and which plant produced it. If scheduling permitted, these larger companies would occasionally press records for smaller labels.

Generally, independent record companies in LA pressed their records at one of three dozen plants. The larger plants included Monarch Records, Alco Research and Engineering, Allied Record Company, and H.V. Waddell. In 1954, Monarch began identifying their work by having a five-digit number preceded by a small triangle (Δ, the Greek letter delta) etched into the run-out grooves of their records. These are called delta numbers. A five-digit delta number followed by a lower case "x" designated the B side. Other pressing plants, as well as firms that made metal works, but did not necessarily press records, shared in the delta numbering system. Hence, the presence of a delta number on a record does not mean a record was pressed at Monarch. As with the matrix numbers, delta numbers were transferred from the acetate to the metal works and subsequently pressed into the run-out grooves of every record. The delta numbers can be used to approximate the month and year a record was manufactured.

Alco Research and Engineering was founded by Al Levine and L.A. Cottrell (Alco was an amalgam of their names) in a one-story brick building at 1107 North El Centro Avenue in 1942. After a catastrophic fire June 9, 1950, fueled by the flammable shellac of a quarter million 78 rpm records, they relocated around the corner to 6201 Santa Monica Boulevard, one-half block east of Gold Star. Alco participated in the delta system and, although primarily a pressing plant, also did limited metal work such as manufacturing stampers from mothers.

These pressing plants identified their work by stamping a distinctive logo into the dead wax. Monarch machine-stamped MR within a circle, Alco machine-stamped a stylized AL[C] within an "O," Allied hand-etched a small "x" followed by a four-digit number, and H.V. Waddell machine-stamped a "W." Years later, bootleggers steered clear of these trademarked logos and their presence on a record often distinguished an original from a counterfeit.

Candix singles 301 through 331 ("Surfin'") bear either machine-stamped or hand-etched matrix numbers, but none of the alpha-numeric codes of the major label's pressing plants or the delta numbers and logo inscriptions used by Monarch, Alco, Allied, or H.V. Waddell. There were, however, many other pressing plants in LA that did not use delta numbers or identifying logos. Hence, it is likely Candix used one of these smaller plants.

The twelve sets of metal stampers were delivered to the pressing plant (unless the metal works' facility also pressed the records) where each set was placed into its own station on a hydraulic press. A small rectangular block of solid black vinyl called a "biscuit" was positioned between the stampers. The record label for "Surfin'" was placed between the "Surfin'" stamper and the biscuit, and the record label for "Luau" was placed between the "Luau" stamper and the biscuit. This entire unit was then compressed at a temperature of 300 degrees Fahrenheit, squeezing the biscuit between a set of stampers and affixing the labels onto each side of the hot, soft vinyl. The resulting disc was rapidly cooled, trimmed of excess vinyl, a large center hole punched out, and slid into a brown paper sleeve. In an eight hour shift, a press with twelve sets of stampers could produce 12,000 records.

The Beach Boys' first record, "Surfin'," backed with "Luau" on Candix 331, sold 12,000 copies in little more than a week and sent CANDIX owner Bob Dix scurrying to finance a repressing (author's collection).

"Surfin'" (b/w "Luau," Candix 331) was released Monday, November 27, 1961, in a plain brown paper sleeve. An initial run of 12,000 copies were manufactured and packed in boxes of twenty-five. A few boxes were delivered to Candix and the rest to Buckeye Record Distributors. Russ Regan listened to it and put a copy in his short stack of records for his meeting at KFWB.

On November 29, Regan played "Surfin'" for Bill Angel who remembered it from the acetate Hite Morgan had played for him a few weeks earlier. Angel liked the song and it made the cut. The next morning Angel and Chuck Blore met with the station's disc jockeys to vote on that week's new releases and determine the new Fabulous Forty Survey. Angel played "Surfin'" and the response was enthusiastic.

Blore recalled, "'Surfin'' was one which Bill Angel and I put on immediately upon first hearing. It was our 'Pick to Click.' No contest. It was played immediately following the Saturday night countdown of the new Fabulous Forty Survey. Then it was played once an hour for a week after which, if there was adequate audience reaction, we added it to our regular play list rotation."[18]

11

A Month of Firsts
(December 1961)

A clue as to when "Surfin'" was first heard on the radio can be found in the unlikeliest of places—the National Oceanic and Atmospheric Administration (NOAA), the government agency that records hourly weather reports throughout the country. Those archived reports, along with Dennis's recollection of rain, reveal the day, date, and time the Beach Boys first graced American radio.

Friday, December 1, was a dreary day in greater LA with only a forty-one percent possibility of sunshine peering through the clouds. Scattered thunderstorms began at 4:00 p.m. dropping 0.22 inches of rain between 10:00 p.m. and midnight. The bleak weather spilled over into Saturday, December 2, with the precipitation becoming markedly heavier. One and one-tenth inches of rain fell throughout the day with the heaviest period occurring between 6:00 p.m. and 11:00 p.m. It only rained two other days that December in the LA area, and both days only a very small amount—Wednesday, December 13 (0.03 inches) and Thursday, December 14 (0.09 inches).[1]

On Saturday, December 2, during the 3:00 p.m. to 6:00 p.m. time slot, KFWB played its new Fabulous Forty Survey for the week ahead. The records were played in descending chronological order from #40 to the much-anticipated #1 as the Tokens' "The Lion Sleeps Tonight" ended Henry Mancini's one week reign with "Moon River."

It was raining as the survey concluded and the station played its new 'Pick to Click' for the week. Sitting in Brian's 1957 Ford Fairlane in the parking lot of Foster's Freeze on Hawthorne Boulevard were Brian, Carl, Dennis, and David Marks. They were devouring burgers, fries, and shakes, and listening to KFWB. As the Fabulous Forty Survey concluded, the disc jockey announced, "Now here's a group from Hawthorne called the Beach Boys with their song, 'Surfin'.'" Suddenly, blasting through the AM radio speakers was "Surfin'."

"We were all on Hawthorne Boulevard in Brian's 1957 Ford," Dennis recalled. "It was raining, I think. And they played "Surfin'" on the radio. That was the biggest high ever. Nothing will ever top the expression on Brian's face. Ever. That is the all-time moment."[2]

For thirteen-year-old David, the occasion was less momentous. He had just smoked a cigarette and was feeling nauseous. The thrill of hearing "Surfin'" and the pandemonium in the car, caused him to vomit.[3]

After morning classes at El Camino Community College, Al and Brian went to Al's parents' apartment and listened to KFWB. "We kept listening and hoping, and finally it came on the radio," Al recalled. "It was the most unbelievable feeling."[4] Al took his mother to a hamburger place on campus and listened to "Surfin'" on a jukebox. "We thought it was so marvelous," she recalled.[5] "The boys were so excited. They'd call each other up on the telephone and say, 'Listen to this! It's on so and so station.' They'd listen to it together on the phone. It was sweet. Like little kids."[6]

On Monday, December 4, Dennis's seventeenth birthday, KFWB began playing "Surfin'" every hour. By the end of the week, orders were pouring into Buckeye Record Distributors and the record was flying out of record stores. "Dennis was so thrilled because he was living it," Carl remembered. "He went to school and his friends said, 'We were on our way home from the beach, totally exhausted from riding the waves all day. We heard your record come on, and it turned us on so much that we went back to the beach.'"[7]

There is a handwritten document dated December 5, 1961, described as a Lease Contract between Hite Morgan, as Lessor, and Bob Dix of Candix Records, as Lessee. It appears to be a draft as it contains instructions for the number of spaces a typist should leave between sections of the document. There are signatures on the bottom of the document purported to be those of Hite Morgan and Robert E. Dix. Apparently a final, typewritten version of the document, signed by Hite and Bob, either does not exist or has never been found. The document states Morgan agreed to transfer the masters and all takes of "Surfin'" and "Luau" to Candix Records. For each record sold, Candix agreed to pay Morgan six cents which included the artist royalty due the Beach Boys. Because the terms of the document benefit Candix—all previous contracts Morgan may have had with the Beach Boys were to be terminated and the name "Beach Boys" was to be "owned now and forever" by Candix—it would appear the document may have been drafted by Bob Dix or someone associated with Candix.

The earliest known document acknowledging the existence of this Lease Contract is a letter dated June 18, 1962, from Alfred Schlesinger, Morgan's attorney at the time, to Schlesinger's colleague, Averill C. Pasarow, a skilled litigator with the Beverly Hills law firm Pasarow and Spiegel, and the Beach Boys' attorney at the time. Since recording Murry's "Two Step, Side Step" by the Bachelors on Palace Records in 1953, Schlesinger had become an attorney specializing in the music industry. Schlesinger advised Pasarow "it is highly questionable as to whether any part of this agreement, particularly the portion dealing with a 'term' agreement, is enforceable" and doubted the agreement would hold up in court due to the minor status of some of the boys. Bruce Morgan maintained the signature purported to be his father's was fraudulent and that Hite never entered into any such agreement with Candix.

Hite Morgan's copyright of "Surfin'" to his Guild Music publishing company with the Library of Congress in Washington, D.C., is dated December 7, 1961. Allowing for mailing and processing time, Morgan certainly mailed the application well before then.[8]

"Surfin'" has been cited incorrectly as being released December 8 because Murry told Tom Nolan in a 1971 *Rolling Stone* article that "eight months before the record 'Surfin'' of December 8, 1961, is when the Beach Boys really started."[9]

That would place the band's origin around April 1961, perhaps when his boys and his nephew began singing together in earnest. But that would exclude Al Jardine, who was attending Ferris Institute in Big Rapids, Michigan, at the time. Furthermore, December 8 was a Friday and it is extremely unlikely any new record, including "Surfin'," was released on a Friday.

Radio stations paid close attention to the competition and KDAY, serving LA and

San Diego, noticed the buzz "Surfin'" was getting on KFWB. Between 8:30 a.m. and 10:00 a.m. on Saturday, December 9, "Surfin'" competed against two other songs in KDAY's weekly "Best of the Batch" contest in which listeners phoned in (HO 1–9981) and voted for their favorite song. Disc jockeys Sam Babcock and Dan Baxter announced the winning song that afternoon. It was added to the play list the following week and on the weekly survey under the heading KDAY Listener Pick. If it continued to do well in sales and requests it would be added to the KDAY Top 50 Survey.

Brian remembered, "We stood around the phone and called and we'd go (in a deep voice) 'I vote for "Surfin'."' And then (in a high voice) 'I vote for "Surfin'."' We did that ten or fifteen times, me and my brothers. They said, 'The winner this week is "Surfin'."' We went, 'We won, we won!'"[10] Dennis was so excited he ran down the street screaming, knocking on doors and telling everyone they had a record on the radio.[11] Audree was astonished the radio was playing their song.[12]

"My whole family, my dad, mom, Jim, and Jerry, we must have voted thirty times," Judy remembered. "My mother showed Brian the telephone bill with all the calls to the radio station. It won the contest and for a week they played it every hour. I took my radio to school and I heard it so many times."[13]

But not everyone was thrilled with "Surfin'," especially those for whom it should have been an anthem. For surfers, genuine surf music was instrumental. The Beach Boys were ridiculed as gremmie or wanna-be surfers cashing in on their sport. "I remember a bunch of guys saying, 'Let's go beat up the Beach Boys,'" recalled Paul Johnson of the Belairs. "They were really down on it. They thought the Beach Boys were trying to move in on their personal territory. The disdain surfers had for the Beach Boys lasted as long as the Beach Boys continued to sing about surfing."[14]

Legendary surfer Greg Noll recalled, "When I had my shop, the Beach Boys would send their music to us. We'd say 'Thank you very much' and the minute they'd leave, the records would go right in the trash."[15] But Jim Roberts, the Belairs' keyboardist, reasoned, "They were the first group to add vocals to surf music. It really set them apart."[16]

By December 11, "Surfin'" was being played heavily on LA's three major stations—KFWB, KRLA, and KDAY. Although snubbed by serious surfers, "Surfin'" reached #5 mid–February on KFXM in San Bernardino and Riverside, the Inland Empire where Dick Dale ruled supreme.

By December 13, stock of "Surfin'" at Buckeye Record Distributors was getting low and would soon be sold out. Bob Dix tried to order a second pressing, but the owner of the pressing plant refused to manufacture any more records or extend his credit until Bob paid his outstanding balance. Bob didn't have the money to pay the pressing plant. Saraceno had an idea.

Saraceno arranged for Candix to lease the "Surfin'" master to Bob Field, his former boss at Pacific Record Distributors, who would finance a second pressing of "Surfin'" on Candix 331. Bob Dix and Bob Field signed a standard three-page lease agreement on Friday, December 15. Unbeknownst to Bob Dix, Saraceno and Field were co-owners of Union Records, and "Surfer's Stomp" by the Mar-kets, the label's inaugural release which Saraceno diverted from Candix and now a *Billboard* spotlight single, was about to break wide open. It is unclear whether Saraceno and Field intended to release "Surfin'" on Union Records.

But over the weekend Bob Field changed his mind. On Monday, December 18, he decided not to finance a second pressing of "Surfin'." "Bob Field never wanted to be in the business of making records," recalled Michael Gordon of the Mar-kets. "Pacific was strictly a distributor."[17]

By now, "Surfin'" was almost sold out and Bob Dix was desperate. This was his biggest hit since "Underwater." But unlike the Frogmen, which broke over several months, the Beach Boys sold out in about two weeks. If "Surfin'" broke nationally, he would not be able to meet demand and the record would die. Of course, a hit record would help alleviate some of Bob's financial problems, but it would require a cash infusion now in order to make money down the road. He had to come up with a way to manufacture more copies of "Surfin'" on Candix. And then it hit him. Who said it had to be on Candix? If the pressing plant wouldn't extend credit to Candix, then he'd form a new label, open a new account with a different pressing plant, and release "Surfin'" on the new label.

Bob named his new label X Records, a Candix subsidiary also derived from his last name. He asked Saraceno where they could get "Surfin'" repressed and Saraceno suggested Alco Research and Engineering, where "Surfer's Stomp" had been pressed.

On December 19, from near his home in Fresno, Bob fired off three Western Union telegrams in quick succession. At 12:43 p.m. he wired Al Levine at Alco, "This is to confirm our ('our' was crossed out) conversation and pending written contracts. X Records, a subsidiary of Candix Enterprises Inc., agrees to be distributed by Alco Research and Engineer-

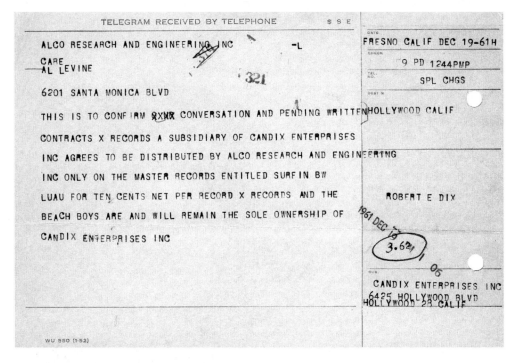

When the pressing plant denied his order for a second pressing of "Surfin'" on Candix 331 because of an unpaid balance on his account, Bob Dix formed X Records. On December 19, 1961, Dix sent a telegram to Al Levine of Alco Research and Engineering, a record pressing plant, and authorized a one-time pressing of "Surfin'" on X Records. Dix selected number 301 since it was the inaugural release on this new subsidiary, just as he had done with "Undertow" backed with "Magnifique," the inaugural Candix release in September 1960 (author's collection with appreciation to Al Dix).

ing Inc. only on the master records entitled Surfin b/w Luau for ten cents net per record. X Records and the Beach Boys are and will remain the sole ownership of Candix Enterprises Inc." At 12:44 p.m. he sent the same telegram, without the word "our," to himself at the apartment he and his brother, Richard, shared at 1261 North Laurel in Hollywood. At 12:45 p.m. he sent the same telegram to himself at Candix Enterprises.

Bob crossed out the word "our" in the telegram to Levine because he had not spoken with him personally. The deal had been brokered by Saraceno. Bob needed the press run of "Surfin'" on X Records to be ready as soon as possible. The coming weekend was Christmas Eve and he wanted to have it available in stores for last-minute holiday shopping.

Because Bob did not have physical possession of the metal stampers that produced Candix 331 (they were at the original pressing plant), he had to have new acetates and metal works made. "Surfin'" and "Luau" were assigned new matrix numbers, "CD-TS-1-R" and "CD-TS-2-R," modified from the original matrix numbers by the addition of "R," which stood for re-release or reissue. These new matrix numbers were hand etched into the run-out grooves of the acetates, which were then delivered to Alco so new metal works could be made. At least one entire business day was needed to create new metal works and press 12,000 records.

Meanwhile, a simple black label was designed for X Records and labels ordered from Record Labels, Incorporated. The record should have been given catalog number 331 to be consistent with Candix 331. But, because X Records was a new record company, a decision was made to assign it number 301, just like Candix's inaugural release in September 1960.

"Surfin'" backed with "Luau" was released on X Records 301 on December 20, the day before Carl's fifteenth birthday. The group was again listed as "Beach Boys," but there were some changes in the information printed on the record labels. It now bore the notation "Producer H. Morgan" at the six o'clock position on both labels. It was unusual for Candix to print the name of the producer on the label. Of its previous thirty records, only five listed producer credit and two of those involved Saraceno. The music publishing for both songs was now incorrectly credited to Drink-Guild Music, instead of Guild alone. "Surfin'" was again listed at 2:15, but somehow "Luau" picked up an extra ten seconds and was now 2:10, although it was still actually 1:43. The writing credit for "Luau" was shortened from Bruce Morgan to B. Morgan.

In the run-out grooves on X Records 301, there were three markings—hand-etched matrix

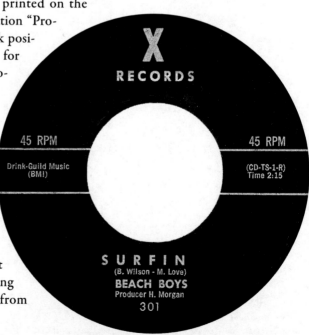

"Surfin'" on X Records 301, the sole release on the Candix subsidiary (author's collection).

numbers, CD-TS-1-R and CD-TS-R-2, a machine-stamped Alco logo, and hand-etched delta numbers, Δ41389 for "Surfin'" and Δ41389x for "Luau." Warren Cook, a record collector, devised a record dating chart based on delta numbers. Although the method is approximate, it is consistent with "Surfin'" on X Records 301 being released on or about December 20, 1961.[18]

When Bob Dix wired Al Levine December 19, it is possible "Surfin'" on X Records 301 had already been manufactured or was in the process of being manufactured. Everything moved so quickly the telegram may have been an after-the-fact effort to communicate the salient points to be included in the "pending written contracts."[19] The written contracts do not survive.

So how many copies of "Surfin'" on X Records were made? John Tefteller, a record collector and dealer, shed light on the subject. "I don't believe "Surfin'" on X 301 is that rare a record. In the early 1970s, I would go to the record swap in Paramount, California, every morning. That was held seven days a week. I also scoured all the local thrift shops and flea markets. I could buy one to three copies of "Surfin'" on X every week. At one point, I had a metal filing cabinet and in one drawer I had approximately 500 copies of "Surfin'" on X. By 1975, I could only find one copy every six months. Most of them are in private collections. The Beach Boys have always been very popular in Europe and Japan. The X record may be scarce now, but ten or twelve years after its release, it was very plentiful in the second-hand market."[20]

Gerry Diez, another record collector and dealer, worked at Pal's Records in Canoga Park when he was a sixteen-year-old high school student in 1961. Pal's was your quintessential mom and pop record store. It was owned by husband and wife Paul and Pauline Levy who had moved to California from Brooklyn, New York. They could sell 600 to 800 copies of a hit record and Record Merchandiser, a large record distributor owned by Syd Talmadge, kept them well stocked. "We got a one hundred count box of 'Surfin'" on X in a plain sleeve and it sold really fast. I reordered it on the X label, but when the box came in the record was now on the Candix label. When that happened, I had a hunch that X Records might be a rare label so I put aside a few copies of 'Surfin'" on X for myself."[21] As noted in Chapter 12, Diez is most likely referring to a pressing of "Surfin'" on Candix released after X Records 301.

A story about X Records 301 that wormed its way into Beach Boys mythology over the years was speculation that a second pressing on X Records was not forthcoming because RCA Victor owned a subsidiary label by that name and threatened legal action unless Bob Dix ceased and desisted. This is not the case. On April 20, 1953, RCA Victor announced the formation of X Records, a wholly owned subsidiary with its own independent distribution network. The name for the new label was derived from the secrecy RCA maintained with the recording industry trade press in the late 1940s over the company's development of the 45 rpm which it named "Project Madam X." In two and one-half years, there were a number of releases on X Records, including, in a bit of ironic foreshadowing, a song called "Kokomo" by Bill Darnell on X 0087.[22] On September 10, 1955, RCA replaced X Records with Vik Records. It is unlikely RCA executives or lawyers even knew or cared about Bob Dix releasing a regional record like "Surfin'" on a label with a name they abandoned six years earlier.

With "Surfer's Stomp" and "Surfin'" breaking loose, Saraceno was on a roll. To capitalize on the craze created by the re-release of Chubby Checker's "The Twist," Lew Bedell had Saraceno and Tony Savonne rework their 1958 hit "The Freeze" as "Twist and Freeze" (Doré 619), but it failed to chart.

On December 21, Chuck Blore, Bill Angel, and the KFWB disc jockeys held their weekly meeting to vote on new records, discuss the station's play list, and determine the new Fabulous Forty Survey for the coming week. Based on listener requests and sales reports from the preceding week, "Surfin'" would debut at #33 on the survey printed Friday, December 22, and delivered to local record stores by Saturday, December 23, for the week ending Friday, December 29. Although the record label stated the group as "Beach Boys," they were listed on the chart as "The Beachboys." On the KRLA Tunedex Survey out that same day, "Surfin'" fared slightly better, debuting at #32 and they were listed as "The Beach Boys."

Judy recalled, "I remember Brian taking me to Wallichs Music City on Sunset Boulevard. They had small booths and you could listen to a record before buying it. I remember someone told Brian that Melody Music on Hawthorne Boulevard refused to carry 'Surfin'"

KFWB *Fabulous Forty Survey*

FOR WEEK ENDING DECEMBER 29, 1961

#	Title	Artist—Label	LAST WEEK		#	Title	Artist—Label	LAST WEEK
1.	*CAN'T HELP FALLING IN LOVE	ELVIS PRESLEY—RCA VICTOR	2		21.	YOUR MA SAID YOU CRIED	Kenny Dino—Musicor	20
2.	THE LION SLEEPS TONIGHT	The Tokens—RCA Victor	1		22.	TOWN WITHOUT PITY	Gene Pitney—Musicor	18
3.	THE TWIST	Chubby Checker—Parkway	3		23.	UNCHAIN MY HEART	Ray Charles—ABC/Par	24
4.	*MOON RIVER	Henry Mancini—RCA Victor	4		24.	MOMENTS TO REMEMBER	Jennell Hawkins—Amazon	26
5.	LET THERE BE DRUMS	Sandy Nelson—Imperial	8		25.	*JINGLE BELL ROCK	Bobby Rydell-Chubby Checker—Cameo	35
6.	IF YOU GOTTA MAKE A FOOL OF SOMEBODY	James Ray—Caprice	13		26.	I DON'T KNOW WHY	Linda Scott—Can-Am	19
7.	I KNOW	Barbara George—A.F.O.	12		27.	*SURFERS STOMP	The Mar-Kets—Liberty	Debut
8.	*HAPPY BIRTHDAY SWEET 16	Neil Sedaka—RCA Victor	6		28.	*WHEN THE BOY IN YOUR ARMS	Connie Francis—MGM	23
9.	PEPPERMINT TWIST	Joey Dee & Starliters—Roulette	22		29.	*SMALL SAD SAM	Phil McLean—Versatile	36
10.	*WHEN I FALL IN LOVE	The Lettermen—Capitol	17		30.	*POCKETFUL OF MIRACLES	Frank Sinatra—Reprise	34
11.	DUKE OF EARL	Gene Chandler—Veejay	38		31.	JUST OUT OF REACH	Solomon Burke—Atlantic	31
12.	WALK ON BY	Leroy Van Dyke—Mercury	11		32.	*BIG BAD JOHN	Jimmy Dean—Columbia	30
13.	*GOODBYE CRUEL WORLD	James Darren—Col-Pix	9		33.	*SURFIN'	The Beachboys—Candix	Debut
14.	*LITTLE BITTY TEAR	Burl Ives—Decca	7		34.	*AND THEN CAME LOVE	Ed Townsend—Challenge	32
15.	*RUN TO HIM	Bobby Vee—Liberty	5		35.	*JAMBALAYA	Fats Domino—Imperial	Debut
16.	THERE'S NO OTHER LIKE MY BABY	The Crystals—Philles	10		36.	TONIGHT	Ferrante & Teicher—United Artists	28
17.	LET'S GO TRIPPIN'	Dick Dale—Deltone	15		37.	THE WANDERER	Dion—Laurie	Debut
18.	*BABY IT'S YOU	The Shirelles—Secpter	21		38.	CRAZY	Patsy Cline—Decca	33
19.	*PLEASE MR. POSTMAN	The Marvelettes—Tamla	16		39.	REVENGE	Brook Benton—Mercury	29
20.	YOU'RE THE REASON	Bobby Edwards—Crest	14		40.	*DEAR IVAN	Jimmy Dean—Columbia	Debut

*RECORDS FIRST HEARD ON KFWB

98 IS GREAT!

FAVORITE ALBUMS

1.	KING OF KINGS	Frank Chacksfield—London
2.	BLUE HAWAII	Elvis Presley—RCA Victor
3.	YOUR TWIST PARTY	Chubby Checker—Parkway
4.	BREAKFAST AT TIFFANY'S	Henry Mancini—RCA Victor
5.	OLDIES BUT GOODIES VOL. III	Various Artists—Original Sound

This survey is compiled each week by radio station KFWB, Los Angeles, California. It is a true, accurate and unbiased account of record popularity, based upon sales reports, distributor accounts and all information available to the music staff of KFWB.

"Surfin'" on Candix 331 debuted at #33 on the KFWB Fabulous Forty Survey in record stores December 23, 1961, for the week ending December 29. The group was listed as the Beachboys (author's collection).

because it was 'only a one-hit wonder.' Brian grimaced and, I believe, told himself he was not going to be a one-hit wonder."[23]

On December 23, as "Surfin'" debuted on the new KFWB chart, the Beach Boys made their first live public appearance performing a short set during intermission at Dick Dale and the Del-Tones' final appearance at the Rendezvous Ballroom in Balboa. (See Appendix 1, the Beach Boys Personal Appearances, 1961–1963.) The December 22 *Newport Beach Daily Pilot* reported, after nearly two years at the Rendezvous, Dale had quit and would forego a $1,500 bonus. A recent rash of problems inside and outside the ballroom involving rowdy behavior, often secondary to public intoxication, drew an outcry from local residents who urged police and city officials to close the hall. Dale placed the blame on the ballroom's manager, Ralph Morris, whom he claimed was more interested in profit than the kids. The news that it would be Dale's last show drew a crowd of 3,000.

Writer Timothy White reported that prior to the show the Beach Boys visited Gene Ronald's clothing store in Santa Ana and bought matching navy blue Gant popover short-sleeved shirts to set off their white chino pants.[24] These three-buttoned dress shirts, worn outside your pants and slipped, or "popped over," your head, were a popular Ivy League fashion. The Boys loaded their gear into their cars and drove thirty miles south to Newport Beach. After some opening acts and a brief intermission, the Beach Boys ambled out on stage and set up their equipment. With Carl on guitar, either his Kay or a rental from Hogan's, Al on the rented stand-up bass, Dennis on drums, perhaps just a snare, and Brian and Mike huddled around a microphone, the group sang and played "Surfin'" and one other song, perhaps "Johnny B. Goode" or "Bermuda Shorts."

"They were delighted with the record, but they were scared stiff of performing live," recalled Dorinda Morgan. "The only boys who weren't were Mike and Alan, and probably Carl because Carl is basically a musician. He gets so involved in his music he forgets about the crowd. Brian and Dennis had a little stage fright. Brian was a little perturbed by the crowd. The Beach Boys were not a smash there, but they weren't badly accepted. But they thought they were, especially Brian. Brian had thought this first shot was going to be big."[25]

The week after Christmas, the Boys rehearsed for their first local television appearance scheduled for December 30 on *Dance Party*, a local program modeled after *American Bandstand*. The booking may have been arranged by Murry or the Morgans, or perhaps the show's producer contacted them. On the KFWB chart out December 30, "Surfin'" jumped fourteen spots from #33 to #19.

Before they could appear on *Dance Party*, the guys had to join the American Federation of Television and Radio Artists (AFTRA) union. On December 29, Murry accompanied them to the AFTRA office at 6331 Hollywood Boulevard, Suite 714, in Hollywood. On their individual membership applications, they each wrote their address and telephone number, and signed their name. Brian, Mike, and Al wrote their social security numbers in the space provided. For the question "Agent's Name," Al and the Wilson brothers each wrote "Manager, Murry Wilson," with Al misspelling Murry's name with an "a." The question "Commitment and Date" corresponded to the date which an artist had a commitment to appear on radio or television thereby making them eligible to join AFTRA. Applicants were required to have a "bona fide offer of employment for compensation." Instead of writing *Dance Party* and December 30, 1961, they each wrote, with minor variations, "Dec. Candix

12/1/61." A union official corrected the error by writing "POP dance party 12–30–61" along the bottom of the applications.

Brian's and Al's applications were assigned numbers 58900 and 58901, respectively. For some reason, Mike's, Carl's, and Dennis's applications received higher numbers—58967, 58968, and 58969, respectively. Inexplicably, Mike's application appears to be dated "2–1" with the last digit in the year overwritten and obscured. It appears to be "1" or "2." Obviously, "February 1, 1961" seems unlikely, but "February 1, 1962" doesn't make better sense.

In addition to their applications, they each signed a separate document on AFTRA stationery with the handprinted date "12–29–61" and the typewritten statement: "It is understood $25 will be deducted from my compensation for the Wink Martindale Show [*Note*: "Wink Martindale Show" was crossed out and "POP Dance Party" handwritten above it], date of (12–30–61 was handprinted), to be applied toward my Initiation Fee to AFTRA."

The Beach Boys made their first television appearance lip-syncing "Surfin'" on *Dance Party* telecast live from the Aragon Ballroom from 6:00 p.m. to 7:00 p.m. on KTLA-TV channel 5. The ballroom was just south of Pacific Ocean Park, the twenty-eight acre outdoor amusement park on the Santa Monica pier jutting out over the Pacific Ocean. On July 28, 1958, 57,000 people attended the opening weekend of the nautical theme park, known colloquially as P.O.P. Admission was ninety cents, less for kids, and was a reasonable alternative to budget-minded parents who couldn't afford to take their tikes to Disneyland every weekend.

There is, however, conflicting and incorrect information about *Dance Party* and the Beach Boys' appearance. Here is the story.

Winston "Wink" Conrad Martindale began his radio career in 1952 at age seventeen on WPLI in Jackson, Tennessee. In April 1953, he moved to the morning show on WHBQ, an RKO radio station in Memphis where he soon began hosting a local television show called *Top Ten Dance Party*, on which Elvis guested July 16, 1955. Martindale requested a transfer to an RKO station in LA in January 1959 and by mid–March was the morning jock on KHJ, working a split shift of 5:30 a.m. to 9:00 a.m. and noon to 1:00 p.m. On July 18, in addition to his radio show, Martindale began hosting *Dance Party*, a one-hour Saturday television show produced by Al Burton and broadcast 6:30 p.m. to 7:30 p.m. on KHJ-TV channel 9 from the KHJ studios at 5515 Melrose Avenue next to Nickodell's restaurant (5511) and down the street from Paramount Pictures (5555). Among Martindale's first guests were Jan & Dean, whose "Baby Talk" was #3 on KFWB. The KHJ studio had once housed the headquarters of the National Broadcasting Company, and Capitol Records had used it before moving to the Tower in April 1956. In 1961, Hite Morgan opened Stereo Masters across the street at 5534–5538 Melrose Avenue.

In May 1960, Al Burton convinced the owners of P.O.P. to telecast *Dance Party* live from the amusement park on KHJ-TV channel 9 Monday through Friday in the after-school time slot of 4:00 p.m. to 5:00 p.m. and Saturday 6:30 p.m. to 7:30 p.m. The show debuted June 20, Brian's eighteenth birthday and four days after Martindale emceed Hawthorne High's graduation party at the Palladium. The guests again included Jan & Dean. At P.O.P., *Dance Party* telecast from the Super Sea Circus, an outdoor marine mammal pavilion with three large tanks housing trained dolphins, seals, and sea lions, and viewing stands that held about 2,000 people. Amidst the tanks was a stage where guest artists performed among the show's dancers. One ticket, marketed as a "Wink Martindale Ticket," allowed admission to the park and the *Dance Party* broadcast. The June 26 *Los Angeles Times* ran an article about the popular new show entitled "Martindale Tames Rock 'n' Roll Tiger."

On October 1, 1960, Martindale moved to KRLA in the 6:00 a.m. to 9:00 a.m. slot following Bob Eubanks's midnight to 6:00 a.m. shift. *Dance Party* then moved to KCOP-TV channel 13 Monday through Friday 4:00 p.m. to 5:00 p.m. and Saturday 8:00 p.m. to 9:00 p.m.

During the colder months of early 1961, Martindale moved the show indoors. From January 7 through March 18, he hosted *Dance Party* on Saturdays from 8:00 p.m. to 11:00 p.m. at the Long Beach Municipal Auditorium where, on June 7, 1956, Elvis had electrified 4,000 fans in his first LA area appearance. *Dance Party* may have been less frequent than weekly at this time. For the $1.50 admission, attendees watched the one-hour *Dance Party* live telecast followed by a two-hour show featuring additional artists. For instance, on January 7, Sam Cooke and Dodie Stevens were on the telecast, followed by Cooke and Buddy Knox headlining a six-act show.

On July 21, 1961, Lawrence Welk moved his television show from the Aragon Ballroom to the newly redecorated Palladium on Sunset Boulevard next to American Recording Company, which soon moved to Studio City after a dispute with Welk about noise. Meanwhile, Freddy Martin and His Orchestra ended its twenty-year residency at the Cocoanut Grove in the Ambassador Hotel and moved to the Aragon Ballroom, which became alternately known as Pacific Ocean Park Pavilion, P.O.P. Pavilion, or P.O.P. Aragon Pavilion.

On July 22, Martindale's *Dance Party* moved to KTLA-TV channel 5. On September 16, P.O.P. began its fall/winter schedule of weekends only, except for the Thanksgiving and Christmas school holidays, and *Dance Party* began telecasting live from the P.O.P. Pavilion Saturday 6:00 p.m. to 7:00 p.m. Guests included the Castells and the Paris Sisters (September 9), Dick and Dee Dee, and Jan & Dean (September 23), and the Ventures and the Lettermen (September 30). After the telecast, the audience had to clear out immediately to make way for an older crowd and a night of dancing to Freddy Martin and His Orchestra. The younger set wandered over to the nearby 76 Pavilion to listen and dance to live bands like the Mixtures and the Red Jackets.

Martindale last hosted *Dance Party* September 30 before leaving KRLA to accept Randy Wood's offer of director of national promotion and assistant A&R for Dot Records. KRLA had become embroiled in controversy when, in July 1960, the Federal Communications Commission (FCC) began investigating allegations that programming promises were not met, on-air contests were rigged, station logs were falsified, and a non-citizen was involved in managing the station (Canadian Jack Kent Cooke, brother of station owner Donald Cooke). In 1962, the FCC did not renew KRLA's license and, two years later, the non-profit Oak Knoll Broadcasting was selected as interim owner and licensee.[26]

When Martindale left KRLA, Bob Eubanks moved into his 6:00 a.m. to 9:00 a.m. slot and began hosting *Dance Party* October 7, welcoming Dick Dale and the Del-Tones (October 21), the Lettermen (November 18), Dick and Dee Dee (December 9), and the Beach Boys (December 30) at the P.O.P. Pavilion from 6:00 p.m. to 7:00 p.m. on KTLA-TV channel 5. However, Jolene "Jodi" Gable, president of the Beach Boys first fan club, recalled a December 30 appearance by the band that might suggest an alternative venue.

Jodi loved watching *American Bandstand* and parlayed her love of rock 'n' roll into doing on-air dedications at KBLA which broadcast from a log cabin on the grounds of McCambridge Park Community Center near her home in Burbank. She spent many Friday and Saturday nights at the Olive Recreation Center in Burbank. Jodi recalled a concert there on December 30, 1961, with the Platters, the Olympics, Dick and Dee Dee, and a local group she never heard of called the Beach Boys. "When the Beach Boys came on I was totally fascinated," she recalled. "Their harmonies were so different. I was talking with this man next to me and he was so much fun, and we were laughing, and he finally told me he was the Wilson brothers' father, Murry. After the show, I told Al I really wanted to hear them play again. I gave him my phone number and he wrote it on a matchbook. A few days later, Al called and put Murry on the phone. Murry said they talked it over and wanted me to head up their fan club. Then my parents got on the phone with Murry. My parents took me over to meet the Wilsons at their home in Hawthorne. And our parents really hit it off."[27]

As the first president of the Beach Boys fan club, Jodi began thinking of ways to promote the band's personal appearances. She gave a copy of "Surfin'" to the KBLA program director and convinced him to play it on the air. In time, the fan club grew in members and organization, with stationery, membership cards, news sheets, and promotional photographs.

So, perhaps the December 30 *Dance Party* was telecast from the Olive Recreation Center. It is also possible the Beach Boys played the Olive Recreation Center that afternoon and then appeared on *Dance Party* at the P.O.P. Pavilion later that evening.

This Certifies That

IS AN OFFICIAL MEMBER
of

The Beach Boys Fan Club

AUTHORIZED SIGNATURE

A membership card to the Beach Boys Fan Club.

On New Year's Eve, the Beach Boys were on the bill for a Ritchie Valens Memorial Dance and Show at the Long Beach Municipal Auditorium. Also on the bill were the Rivingtons, the Carlos Brothers, and the Ike and Tina Turner Revue, who had just released "I'm Blue (The Gong-Gong Song)" as by the Ikettes, the duo's background singers, for contractual reasons because they were signed to Sue Records and "I'm Blue" was on Atco (6212).

When the Ikettes finished, the Beach Boys performed "Surfin'" and two other songs. Years later, group members could not agree which two songs they performed, collectively suggesting "Johnny B. Goode," "The Twist, "What'd I Say," and "Bermuda Shorts." A strong case can be made for each song.

Carl had mastered many Chuck Berry songs so it's possible they did "Johnny B. Goode." "The Twist," currently #2 on KFWB, was an easy crowd pleaser, and Al recalled they performed many Chubby Checker songs around this time. That move toward Pop disheartened folk purist Jardine. The interactive call-and-response of Ray Charles's "What'd I Say" made it a live favorite for the band. And Brian, Mike, and Carl had performed "Bermuda Shorts" at a Hawthorne High assembly.

For Mike, with a wife and five-month-old daughter at home, the New Year's Eve concert had a profound effect. After their set, they each received sixty dollars at the box office. "I can still remember it because we got paid for something besides working," Mike recalled. "We got paid for playing music. We earned $300 and we sang three songs, so we picked up $100 a song, which wasn't bad when you remember that I was a sheet metal apprentice. I don't think we were very good. We certainly didn't look great. We wore ochre-colored sport coats which cost us $30 each. But the thing then was for groups to wear a uniform, so uniforms we wore. I was so nervous that I decided never to be nervous again and I never have. It was quite easy. I just said 'I won't be nervous. Who needs it?'"[28]

Curiously, there is very little known about the Ritchie Valens Memorial Dance and Show. Although Valens had been dead nearly three years, he was still popular in the LA area especially within the Chicano community. And Bob Keane had kept his memory alive with posthumous releases on Del-Fi. There seems to have been no coverage of the concert in local newspapers. The earliest mention of this Beach Boys appearance was in Capitol press materials and a 1964 concert program. "Five really scared guys made their stage debut on New Year's Eve, 1961, at the Municipal Auditorium in Long Beach, California, with a galaxy of established entertainers. They fumbled through their entire repertoire of three songs and received, if not a thundering ovation, at least a fair share of the applause."[29]

Brian recalled that on the way home they realized they had forgotten Dennis's rented drum kit and Al was worried they'd lose his mother's deposit.[30]

Sometime before the end of the year, while driving along La Brea Avenue, Brian wrote the melody to "Surfer Girl," one of his most beloved and enduring love songs. In 1976, Brian said, "'Surfer Girl' is my favorite Beach Boys song. It was the first ballad we ever did. We actually recorded it before 'Surfin',' though we didn't release it until much later. It was an innocent try, our first innocent recording experience."[31]

In 1990, Brian recalled, "Back in 1961, I'd never written a song in my life. I was nineteen years old. And I put myself to the test in my car one day. I was driving to a hot dog stand and I created a melody in my head without being able to hear it on a piano. I sang it to myself. I didn't even sing it out loud in the car. When I got home, I finished the song, wrote the bridge, put the harmonies together, and called it 'Surfer Girl.'"[32]

But in 1989, he recalled its inception a bit differently. "I was in my '57 Ford, cruising around, and I started humming along to a song that was on the radio. I turned the radio off and I kept humming it, but I went into my own little composition. Then I got home, went to my piano, and doctored it up a little bit."[33]

Brian's insistence that "Surfer Girl" was his first song puzzled his closest high school friends who recalled his earlier compositions. It is unclear if any of those songs are extant. If "Surfer Girl" was indeed written first, then it preceded "Surfin'" as the group's entry into surf music. Perhaps Brian bestowed such import on "Surfer Girl" because it was the first song for which he wrote both melody and lyrics, or simply because it holds a special place in his heart.

Another mystery about "Surfer Girl" concerns its inspiration. "At the time, I thought 'Surfer Girl' was written about me," recalled Judy Bowles. "But I've read what Brian said in his book that he didn't write it with anyone in mind. I remember my girlfriend, Diana, she was real little, she begged Brian, literally begged him, if she could be the 'little one' at the end of the song. And Brian kind of laughed and said okay."[34]

In 1964, Brian said, "'Surfer Girl,' a hit for us and a song I'm proud of, was directly inspired by a girl I was dating at the time."[35] And Mike, when asked if the inspiration for "Surfer Girl" was more mythical than real, responded, "No, she was definitely the existing person. Her name is Judy and she lived somewhere near Brian's house. We just started doing records then and it was one of the first songs he wrote."[36] When Mike, Al, and Carl appeared on *Today* March 19, 1979, Mike told host Jane Pauley that Brian wrote "Surfer Girl" for Judy while driving to his orthodontist.

During one of the campfire sequences for the *Endless Summer* television show in 1989, Mike asked Brian, "So, let's hear the story of the original surfer girl, Judy Bowles." Brian responded, "No, she was not 'Surfer Girl.' There is no 'Surfer Girl.'" Mike countered, "You told me a long time ago it was her." After some bantering and laughter, Brian admitted, "Oh, I know which girl you're talking about. Yeah, it was about her."[37] Judy was Brian's first serious girlfriend and they dated for two and one-half years. It's unlikely he would have forgotten her.

While the sentiment in "Surfer Girl" was inspired by Judy, the melody owed a debt to "When You Wish Upon a Star," the 1940 Oscar winner for Best Original Song from *Pinocchio*. Brian may have been familiar with versions by Glenn Miller, Guy Lombardo, Rosemary Clooney, and Eddie Fischer. It was the first song he sang in front of his family.[38] He also may have been familiar with versions by Joni James (April 1955), Little Anthony and the Imperials (January 1959), and Dion and the Belmonts (April 1960).

So perhaps Brian was driving around Hawthorne one day in his '57 Ford and Dion's "When You Wish Upon a Star" came on the radio and he began humming the melody. And his thoughts turned to Judy, the girl he loved, and the image of her sitting atop a surfboard, rising and rolling under each warm wave, beckoning to him along the shore. Blonde, suntanned, and eternally beautiful. Could he make her dreams come true? And did she love him as much as he loved her?

"Brian gave me a picture of himself which I had on my vanity for years," Judy recalled. "He had a butch haircut, practically shaved it was so short. In those days that was the clean cut collegiate haircut. He had written, 'To Judy, love forever, Brian.'"

Then she added, somewhat wistfully, "I don't know what happened to that."[39]

12

Number 3 in LA
(January–February 1962)

January 1962

When "Surfin'" began to climb the local charts, Brian decided to concentrate on his music career and drop out of El Camino Community College. He had completed three semesters. "In college, I took a music appreciation course, but the teachers were one-hundred percent against anything except operas, symphonies, cantatas, chamber, and classical," he recalled. "Well, I wasn't going to sit there and let any guy tell me that pop music is bad. I love both."[1]

The music course Brian took at El Camino was given by Dr. Robert Haag. In his mid-forties and often sporting a bow tie, Dr. Haag made his music appreciation and basic harmony courses interesting. Paul Johnson also took Dr. Haag's courses. "I remember listening to Brian's stuff and thinking, 'Yeah, it sounds like Brian is taking the basic stuff he learned from Dr. Haag and applying it to his arrangements and productions. It was all about voicing and chords. Dr. Haag gave him the tools he needed to translate the ideas he got from the Four Freshmen into his own musical compositions.'"[2]

With his college career over, Brian concentrated on songwriting. He was working on a follow-up single with Mike called "Surfin' Safari," inspired in part by John Severson's 1959 surf film *Surf Safari*, and refining "Judy" and "Surfer Girl." Fifteen-year-old Carl, a sophomore at Hawthorne High, was working on a guitar instrumental called "Karate."

Al was a full-time student at El Camino working toward his undergraduate degree. Seventeen-year-old Dennis, a junior at Hawthorne High, was practicing to become more proficient on the drums. "Right after I started the fan club, Denny called me up," recalled Jodi Gable. "He was my very first date. I asked a girlfriend of mine and he asked a friend of his, and we went to the 7 Seas Restaurant on Hollywood Boulevard across from Grauman's Chinese Theater. There was a floor show with Tahitian dancers and I was so nervous I could hardly eat. They came around to the tables and took our picture. Denny and the other guy had to pool their money and we almost didn't have enough to pay the bill."[3]

Around this time, the Morgans arranged for the guys to join Local 47 of the AFM. Mike didn't have to join because he wasn't a musician. "Al had to get one hundred dollars to join the union," Virginia Jardine recalled. "Al just had little jobs. That was a sacrifice for those kids."[4]

A week after the Beach Boys played the Ritchie Valens Memorial Dance and Show, "Surfin'" was listed as a regional break-out in LA in *Billboard* on newsstands January 6. It also debuted at #118 on the Bubbling Under the Hot 100 chart, the first time the Beach Boys appeared on the *Billboard* chart. Locally, it moved from #32 to #29 on KRLA and #19 to #11 on KFWB. The Belairs' "Mr. Moto" debuted at #33 on KFWB, belying its popularity as Dot had already rushed out a cover by Vaughn Monroe in December (Dot 16308).

On January 9, Soupy Sales played "Surfin'" on his daily noontime comedy show on KABC-TV. Murry Wilson fired off a Western Union telegram that night and wrote, "Bless your heart for playing our song "Surfin'." We appreciate it very much. The Beach Boys, all five of us."[5]

On January 13, "Surfin'" jumped from #11 to #6 on KFWB and from #29 to #6 on KRLA. It moved up from #118 to #112 in *Billboard* and made its first appearance in *Cash Box* at #17 on their Looking Ahead chart. But it was about to run into a major problem. Hite Morgan, Murry Wilson, and the Beach Boys were unaware of Candix's personnel and financial problems, and its inability to press more records.

The original press run of 12,000 on Candix 331 was sold out and X 301 was selling in larger stores like Pal's and Wallichs Music City, but many smaller stores were unable to get sufficient copies from Alco Research and Engineering. And with "Surfin'" breaking on *Billboard* and *Cash Box*, there would not be enough copies to support national distribution. Without records to sell in stores, a song's ranking on the charts fell precipitously.

Candix needed a third pressing of "Surfin'," but Bob Dix didn't have the money to pay for it. By mid–January, Saraceno no longer worked at Candix, after Bob Dix confronted him for diverting "Surfer's Stomp" from Candix. The January 20 *Cash Box* reported, "Joe Saraceno has resigned as A&R director of the Candix Record Company and plans to produce records for various companies on an independent basis."[6]

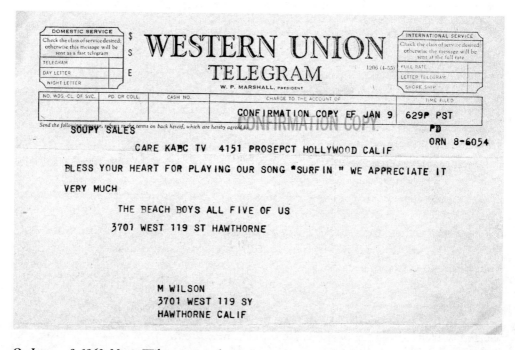

On January 9, 1962, Murry Wilson sent a telegram to Soupy Sales to thank him for playing "Surfin'" on his weekday television show (author's collection).

"Surfer's Stomp" was #2 on KFWB and had been picked up for national distribution by Liberty Records. It was a Pick of the Week in *Cash Box*, reached #31 in *Billboard*, and drove the sales of a successful Liberty album by the same name. If "Surfer's Stomp" had been released on Candix, it may have alleviated the company's financial problems and enabled Bob Dix to pay for subsequent pressings of "Surfin'" on Candix 331.

With the lease to Pacific Record Distributors still in effect, Saraceno still had a financial interest in "Surfin'." Rather than let it wither on the chart, he brokered a deal with his friend Herb Newman of Era Records, which had been in business since March 1955 and, like Candix, was located in the Stanley-Warner Building on Hollywood Boulevard. Newman had a proven track record of leasing hit records from smaller indies and using his national distribution network to get them into every major market. Newman agreed to finance a new pressing of "Surfin'," release it on Candix for continuity, and distribute it on his Era Records.

Once Newman got behind "Surfin'," there were two issues that had to be addressed—

the manufacture of the records and the printing of the record labels. For some reason, perhaps because they were worn, damaged, or incapable of producing a larger press run, the metal stampers used to press "Surfin'" on X Records 301 could no longer be used. Hence, new acetates and metal works had to be manufactured before the record could be pressed again at Alco. The work order is long gone, but as Newman intended to meet national demand he most likely would have ordered at least 40,000 to 50,000 records.

Because "Surfin'" was listed in *Billboard* and *Cash Box* as Candix 331 (X 301 never appeared in either publication), for continuity Newman decided to release it on the Candix label rather than X or Era. "I got a call from Herb asking permission to use the Candix label," Al Dix recalled. "I told him that would be fine."[7]

But when the labels

Herb Newman produced promotional copies of "Surfin'" on his Era-distributed Candix 301 with the notation "Audition Copy" (courtesy Thomas B. Ham).

were reordered at Record Labels, Incorporated, instead of reverting back to catalog number 331, the number 301 from the X Records release was used. This may have been an oversight or done purposely to keep the ordering number consistent with the X Records release. Whatever the reason, the Newman-funded re-release of "Surfin'" was on Candix 301 despite the company having already used number 301 on their inaugural release of "Undertow" in September 1960.

Most of the information printed on the Candix 301 label was identical to that of X 301—the song titles ("Surfin'" and "Luau"), the artist's name ("Beach Boys"), the credit "Producer: H. Morgan" (but now with the addition of the colon), the matrix numbers (CD-TS-1-R and CD-TS-2-R), and the times (2:15 for "Surfin'" and 2:10 for "Luau"). There was, however, one key change. The publishing for both "Surfin'" and "Luau" was now correctly credited solely to Guild Music.

Sometime early during the press run, the record labels were revised to reflect that Newman's Era Record Sales was now behind the record and arranging for its distribution. The new labels moved "Guild Music (BMI)" from the nine o'clock to the three o'clock position and added the notation "Dist by ERA RECORD SALES INC." in three lines of type at the nine o'clock position. This fourth version of "Surfin'" is referred to as "Candix 301 Era."

Because Candix 301 was pressed from different metal stampers than X 301, the actual vinyl records differ as do the three markings in the run-out grooves and their relative positions to one another—hand-etched matrix numbers (CD-TS-1-R for "Surfin'" and CD-TS-2-R for "Luau"), hand-etched delta numbers (Δ41389 for "Surfin'" and Δ41389x for "Luau"), and Alco's distinctive machine-stamped logo, ALc within a circle. On the other hand, because Candix 301 and Candix 301 Era were pressed from the same metal stampers, the

---

Pick of the Week

Newcomers

In an effort to call D.J. attention to Pick records by "Newcomers" (artists never before on the Top 100) the editorial staff of Cash Box will list such records under this special heading.

"SURFIN' " (2:15) [Guild BMI—Wilson, Love]
"LUAU" (2:10) [Guild BMI—Morgan]
BEACH BOYS (Candix 301)

There's enough vocal and instrumental tricks in this deck to put it into hitsville in no time flat. Side, simply tagged "Surfin'" (on the Era-handled Candix label) has the Beach Boys happily joining in on the stomp craze. It's already a sales-sizzler so get with it. Coupler, "Luau," takes an intriguing cha-cha-like ride.

"Surfin'" on the Era-distributed Candix 301 was a Pick of the Week in the January 27, 1962, *Cash Box* (author's collection).

three markings in the run-out grooves (matrix number, delta number, Alco logo), and their relative positions to one another, are identical.

Newman also ordered about 1,000 sets of record labels that included the words "AUDITION" at the nine o'clock position and "COPY" at the three o'clock position. But instead of the white promotional labels Candix had used previously for releases 303 through 330, the stock black Candix label was used.

"Surfin'" on Candix 301 Era was released Monday, January 15, 1962. In *Cash Box* on newsstands January 20, "Surfin'" moved from #17 to #14 on the Looking Ahead chart and was a Pick of the Week. "There's enough vocal and instrumental tricks in this deck to put it into hitsville in no time. Side, simply tagged 'Surfin'' (on the Era-handled Candix label) has the Beach Boys happily joining in on the stomp craze. It's already a sales-sizzler so get with it. Coupler, 'Luau,' takes an intriguing cha-cha-like ride."[8]

In *Billboard* that week, after moving from #118 to #112 on the Bubbling Under the Hot 100 the previous week, "Surfin'" disappeared from the chart. It was, however, noted on the front cover, misprinted as "Sue Surfin'," as a Break Out in San Francisco. On KFWB, "Surfin'" stalled at #6, but moved from #6 to #4 on KRLA. Meanwhile, Newman arranged for "Surfin'" (b/w "Luau") to be released in Canada on London Records (M.17224) with "Candix 301" noted on the label in parentheses. (See Appendix 2, Timeline of "Surfin'" Releases.)

———

On a Sunday afternoon in early January 1962, twenty-three-year-old singer songwriter Gary Lee Usher, to appease his uncle, knocked on the door of the Wilsons' home and met Brian Wilson. The two hit it off immediately, wrote a song within an hour, and went on to collaborate on some of the Beach Boys most famous songs.

A few weeks earlier, while visiting his cousin Greg Jones and his uncle Benny at their home at West 118th Place and Kornblum Avenue, Usher heard a rock 'n' roll band rehearsing in the neighborhood. Benny told him it was the Wilson brothers down the street who had just released their first record. Usher had released two singles in spring 1961, and Benny suggested he go over and introduce himself.

"I was reluctant because they were younger, but I went over and Brian came to the door," Usher recalled. "Brian and I hit it off very well. He brought me into his den where they were practicing. He had incredible pitch and refresh-

Twenty-three-year-old bank teller Gary Lee Usher, an aspiring singer-songwriter, was visiting his uncle Benny Jones, who suggested Usher go over and meet the Wilson boys, who had a song on the radio. Usher and Brian hit it off immediately and within an hour wrote "Lonely Sea." This is Usher's senior portrait from Westborough High School in Westborough, Massachusetts, in 1957.

ing musical concepts, but they weren't Top 40 oriented. Brian was attuned with the pure, creative soul aspect of his music. I was able to introduce him to the business aspect of music."[9] "He knew all about the Four Freshmen, but needed someone to help him break it down into contemporary forms and apply that vast knowledge to rock and roll. We started exchanging stories and an hour later we wrote 'Lonely Sea.'"[10]

Usher showed Brian the chords to "Lonely Sea" and Brian penned the words. There is a songwriter's contract for "Lonely Sea" dated January 15, 1962, between Brian and Usher, and Sea of Tunes on which Usher listed his address as 134 East 135th Street in Hawthorne. However, as Sea of Tunes was not in existence in January 1962, this contract may have been backdated.

Brian recalled, "He kind of showed me the spirit of competition, how to write songs."[11] "The feel of a song is a big part of writing for me, more important than getting things exactly right musically."[12]

Usher added, "Brian was like a piece of clay waiting to be molded. He looked for leadership, for someone to share ideas with and for someone he could relate to. And he was looking for a friend. He wasn't that close to any of his brothers on a social level and, to my knowledge, did not have any close personal friends except his girlfriend, Judy Bowles."[13]

Gary Lee Usher was born December 14, 1938, in San Gabriel, California. His parents divorced when he was young and his mother remarried and moved the family to Westborough, Massachusetts, a Boston suburb. Usher grew up enthralled with Elvis, country, and rockabilly. In June 1957, he graduated Westborough High School and drove to California in his 1957 Ford Skyliner. He lived with his grandmother in Hawthorne and worked as a laborer for his uncle Benny. "I spent all summer across the street from a family named Wilson, yet never meeting them," Usher recalled. "Even then the name Dennis Wilson was on everyone's lips because he had a reputation of being one of the craziest kids around. My uncle always talked about the crazy kid who lived across the street."[14]

Usher took a night job in the cash vault at a bank where a musician co-worker showed him some chords on guitar. During a stint in the Army, he improved as a rhythm guitarist and began writing songs. After an honorable discharge, he returned to Southern California and began making demo recordings. What he lacked in singing and song composition, he made up for in drive and perseverance. In March 1961, "Driven Insane" b/w "You're the Girl" was released on George Brown's Titan Records (1717). Brown arranged a few personal appearances to promote the record and paired him with a Titan artist named Ginger who had just released "Dry Tears" (b/w "Spare Time," Titan 1716). Ginger (real name Saundra Glantz), a pretty sixteen-year-old aspiring singer songwriter, had released "Love Me the Way I Love You" (b/w "Truly," Tore 1008) as Ginger and the Snaps in October 1960. She recently penned "You Are My Answer" (b/w "My Diary," Columbia 41976) for Carol Connors (real name Annette Kleinbard), who sang "To Know Him Is to Love Him" with Phil Spector's Teddy Bears in 1958.

In March 1961, Usher, Ginger, and Connors performed at the National Orange Show at San Bernardino hosted by KRLA disc jockey Roger Christian. "After the show, Roger and I struck up a friendship that centered around his customized 1955 Corvette," Usher recalled. "I drove to Hollywood and met Roger after he got off the air at midnight. There was a coffee shop below KFWB [Aldo's, 6413 Hollywood Boulevard] where we sat and talked about cars until dawn."[15] Although he was twenty-two and she was sixteen, Usher and Ginger began dating and he soon met her cousins, sisters Marilyn and Diane Rovell.

In May 1961, Usher released "Tomorrow" (b/w "Lies," Lan-Cet 144), but the label only pressed 300 promotional copies and Russ Regan, who handled the account at Buckeye Record Distributors, couldn't fill an order even if he had one. By late 1961, Usher was working in construction, dating, and writing songs. Then, in early January 1962, he strolled over to the Wilsons' house and knocked on the door.

—⁓⁓—

The January 19, 1962, *Cougar* confirmed the Beach Boys were on the leading edge of a new fashion trend. "Hawthorne's campus has been taken over by a new wool sensation—the Pendleton. Never before have guys wanted this wool as much as they do this year."[16]

In a local newspaper article, Don Morgan of San Bernardino High School and Carole Baldwin of Pacific High School reported they spent Sunday, January 21, 1962, "listening to the Beach Boys." It is unclear whether they listened to them in person at an undocumented early appearance or simply listened to their record "Surfin'."[17]

On January 25, a school night for Al, Dennis, and Carl, the guys headlined an 8:00 p.m. "Surf Nite" at the Angeles Mesa Presbyterian Church, 3751 West 54th Street at Mullen Avenue in View Park-Windsor Hills, where Brian, Mike, and Maureen had sung on many Wednesday evening youth nights in the late 1950s. The band's instrumentation was still quite rudimentary with Al playing the rented stand-up bass and becoming weary of lugging the cumbersome instrument around. The church printed 3" × 6" individually numbered, one-dollar tickets on blue card stock, which could be torn along a printed dotted line to enter to win the door prize, a surfboard. A few mint tickets survive and are the earliest known tickets to a Beach Boys concert. They most likely performed "Surfin'," "Johnny B. Goode," "The Twist," "Bermuda Shorts," and perhaps instrumentals like "Mr. Moto" and "Let's Go Trippin'." There is anecdotal evidence the band sold copies of "Surfin'" on X Records at their personal appearances in early 1962. With "Surfin'" now available on Candix 301 Era, the Boys may have earned some extra cash by selling leftover copies of X 301.

$1.00	№ 127	№ 127
SURF NITE *Featuring* The BEACHBOY'S Presbyterian Church 54 st. & Mullen (w. of crenshaw) Door Prize: Surfboard Thurs. January 25 Time: 8:00		Name Phone

This ticket to Surf Nite at the Presbyterian Church in Hawthorne, California, on January 25, 1962, is an example of the earliest known Beach Boys' concert ticket (author's collection).

After Surf Nite at the Presbyterian Church, the guys had to be up early the next morning to play a 7:00 a.m. breakfast in the Hawthorne High School cafeteria. The event kicked off Black Friday, the fifth and final event of the second annual Pep Week, celebrating the end of the first semester and mourning the day report cards were sent home. An alumnus who attended the breakfast recalled the Beach Boys played "Surfin," but that "it was so slow it almost sounded dead. It was dreadful. The record was much better."[18] Also performing at the breakfast were the Mellow-Teens and singer Chris Montez, Brian's classmate from the Class of 1960, who scored a #4 hit with "Let's Dance" in fall 1962. The proceeds from the breakfast helped buy a permanent crown, robe, and scepter for the school's Victory Queen.

The Boys had some good news with the charts for the weekend of January 27. After stalling at #6, "Surfin'" moved to #4 on KFWB and advanced one spot to #3 on KRLA. But the real good news was that "Surfin'" reappeared in *Billboard*, bubbling under the Hot 100 at #105.

On January 29, Murry and Brian copyrighted a song they wrote called "Heartbreak Lane" published by Mills Music. But when it was recorded by the John Buzon Trio on *My Great Sin* and by Murry on *The Many Moods of Murry Wilson*, it was credited to Murry alone and published by Sea of Tunes. The John Buzon Trio also recorded Murry's "Young Love Is Everywhere."

Also on January 29, Brian and Mike signed a Standard Songwriter's Contract for "Surfin' Safari," and Brian for "Surfer Girl" with Hite Morgan's Guild Music. Murry co-signed for the underage Brian and added the handwritten notation "Father, for Brian Wilson." A similar contract was completed for Carl's "Karate," but has since been lost. It is unclear whether such a contract was executed for Brian's "Judy."

As "Surfin'" enjoyed its stay on the charts, "Surfin' Safari" and "Surfer Girl," both future Top 20 hits, were ready to be recorded as a follow-up single.

February 1962

The 1962 Winternational Rod and Custom Car Show, the largest show of its kind in Los Angeles, ran February 1 through 4 at the Great Western Exhibit Center off the Santa Ana Freeway. Dick Dale and the Del-Tones and Sandy Nelson provided entertainment nightly. Gary Usher, a hot rod enthusiast, enjoyed sharing his car knowledge with Brian. In September 1961, shortly after Usher returned to California, he bought a 1959 white four-speed Chevy Impala with a 348 cubic inch engine.[19] But what he really wanted was at the car show, the first true muscle car—the new Chevrolet SS Impala with a 409 cubic inch V8 engine.

By late 1961, the big three American auto makers were in a war of cubic inches. For most of the year, Ford's new 390 cubic inch engine had been leading the pack and outperforming Chevrolet on drag strips across the country. In mid–1961, Chevrolet responded by introducing the 409 cubic inch V8. Ford answered with a 406 cubic inch engine. *Car and Driver* said, "In those days, 409 cubic inches was an awesome quantity and only Ford's 406 cubic inch version was capable of doing serious battle with the Chevy at the nation's drag strips, stock car races, and stop lights."[20] Increasing the appeal of the Chevy 409 was its rarity—only 142 Impala Super Sport 409s were built in 1961. To procure one would take a lot more than saving your pennies and dimes.

The third song Brian and Usher wrote captured every young guy's dream of owning a Chevy 409. "I had a '59 Chevy that was a four-speed 348, but I wanted a 409," Usher told Roger Christian. "We wrote the song '409' about the car we wanted. We were on the way to a speed shop to buy some equipment for my car and we were talking about the new 409 which had just come out. We made some comments about 'giddy-up, giddy-up' in reference to horsepower, and Brian started humming a little song and I threw some more lines out."[21]

They rushed back to Brian's house, finished the song, and recorded a demo. To lend some automotive authenticity, Usher suggested they record some engine sounds. David Marks, the Wilsons' thirteen-year-old neighbor, remembered the late-night session. "It was around 11:00 p.m. and Brian was using my Roberts reel-to-reel tape machine, with a seven and a half-inch reel, to record Gary Usher in his white Chevy Impala. Brian had it hooked up to an extension cord that came out through his front door to the corner of 119th Street and Kornblum Avenue. Gary started at 120th Street and sped down Kornblum Avenue about five or six times. They recorded it late so there would be no traffic."[22]

With Brian checking the sound meters on the reel-to-reel tape deck, Gary revved up his Chevy Impala and peeled down the street in front of the Wilson home. He was able to make a few passes before waking the neighborhood. Usher recalled, "Dennis later told me the police were roaming the neighborhood for the remainder of the night looking for my car."[23]

After filing a lawsuit in 1993, Mike Love was awarded co-writing credit for contributing lyrics to "409" and thirty-four other Beach Boys songs. Mike recalled, "I came up with 'She's real fine my 409' and 'Giddy-up, giddy-up, 409' and was not credited, but Brian Wilson did give credit to Gary Usher for his contribution. So it was weird. It was like directly against me. He wouldn't fuck with anybody else, but he screwed me over royally."[24]

Usher recalled, "Brian was constantly being badgered by Mike for songwriting credits to songs he claimed he made contributions to. If Mike was in the house, he wanted a song-writing credit on the song Brian was working on at the time. There was many a night when I would come over to the Wilson home and find Brian sitting in the music room sobbing. I'd ask him what the problem was, and he would say, 'It's Mike, he's driving me crazy!'"[25]

Brian's friendship with Usher had a profound impact on the success of the Beach Boys. Usher's music industry experience, determination, and perseverance proved invaluable. In addition to their shared passion for music, Brian and Usher were simply good friends.

For the weekend of February 3, "Surfin'" held at #4 on KFWB and slipped from #3 to #4 on KRLA. It crept up to #101 in *Billboard* and debuted at #96 in *Cash Box*.

—◦◦◦—

In early 1962, *Dance Party* again moved indoors to the Long Beach Municipal Auditorium where, between January 6 and late March, Bob Eubanks hosted five Saturday evening shows that were taped and broadcast the following Saturday. Producer Al Burton recalled the Beach Boys appeared on *Dance Party* several times in 1962. There are no advertisements or television listings documenting these appearances and, unfortunately, episodes of *Dance Party* were not preserved. Martindale recalled, "Tape was expensive and no one realized how much of a treasure those recordings would become. If I had realized it, I would have paid for the tape myself."[26]

There are, however, some clues about the Beach Boys 1962 *Dance Party* appearances from members of two surf bands who recalled appearing with them.

Ray Hunt, the Surfmen's lead guitarist who wrote their then-current single "Paradise Cove" (Titan 1723), recalled appearing with the Beach Boys at the Long Beach Municipal Auditorium along with James Darren, Gene McDaniels, Frankie Avalon, Della Reese, and Bobby Rydell. Although Hunt recalled it was late 1961, an advertisement in the February 8 *Long Beach Press-Telegram* noted the Surfmen and James Darren were among the guests on Bob Eubanks's *Dance Party* at the Long Beach Municipal Auditorium from 8:00 p.m. to 11:00 p.m. on February 10. The show was taped before a live audience and telecast February 17 on KRLA-TV channel 5. This may have been the show Hunt recalled. He also remembered something unusual about the Beach Boys performance. "What I really remember about the Beach Boys at that time was that they were only an instrumental group. They didn't sing a lick that night."[27] While the Boys may have played some instrumentals that night, it seems likely they would have taken advantage of another appearance on local television to play and promote "Surfin'."

Paul Johnson of the Belairs recalled he first met the Beach Boys when both groups appeared on *Dance Party* telecast from the Long Beach Municipal Auditorium. The January 6 *Long Beach Press-Telegram* reported the guests that night included the Four Cal Quettes, Don Julian and the Meadowlarks, Vince Howard, the Bel Aires, and Johnny Burnette. It is likely "Bel Aires" is a misspelling of "Belairs," whose "Mr. Moto" would debut on KFWB the following week. However, Johnson does not recall appearing on *Dance Party* with the other artists listed.

"The show was a one-hour live broadcast hosted by Wink Martindale from the Long Beach Municipal Auditorium," Johnson recalled. "It was our first TV appearance and it was the Beach Boys' first as well. Also on the show were the Lettermen, Ketty Lester, and a couple of other acts I can't recall. At the end of the evening the Boys said, 'Hey, why don't you ride home with us.' I think Brian was driving. And they really poured it on saying, 'Yeah, we got all these songs we're writing and we're going in and recording and this is just the beginning. We're actually a vocal band and Brian does these arrangements with Four Freshmen harmonies. We're going in next week to record this song called "Surfer Girl," which they sang for me a cappella in the car.'"[28]

Johnson's recollection that "Surfer Girl" would be recorded "next week" places this show on February 3, 1962. However, some of what he recalled does not fit with what is known. For instance, the Beach Boys' first TV appearance was actually December 30, 1961, and Wink Martindale had not hosted *Dance Party* since September 30, 1961. It is possible, however, Martindale had returned to guest host a show in February 1962.

If these dates are correct, the Beach Boys may have appeared on *Dance Party* February 3 and 10. While unusual, it is not entirely impossible. "Surfin'" was #4 and #3 those two Saturdays and, because they were local, the Beach Boys were easy to book.

Johnson continued, "After that night, I started going to their home and hanging out with them. Their parents, especially their mom, seemed intensely protective of Brian. They singled Brian out as the one the whole thing was about. 'Oh, you can play with Dennis and Carl, but you can't disturb Brian. He's in his room composing.' He was being sealed off from life because they regarded him as some sort of genius. I felt it was destructive for Dennis and Carl because they were treated like pawns in their brother's stardom scenario."[29]

Johnson became close friends with Dennis, drawn to his dominant personality and confidence to say whatever was on his mind. "One night we went to the movie theater in downtown Inglewood. We sat in the balcony and two girls sat down in front of us. Dennis started talking so the girls could hear. 'Yeah Paul, we're going into the recording studio to cut our follow-up to "Surfin.'" They looked at each other and giggled, but wouldn't turn around. So he leaned over and tapped them on the shoulder, 'You know that song "Surfin"' by the Beach Boys?' And they said, 'We don't really like that record.' 'Well, what about "Mr. Moto" by the Belairs?' 'Oh, we really like that record.' 'Well, he's one of the Belairs.' When they started singing about girls and cars and cruising, their credibility went way up. They were singing about their life."[30]

Vickie Amott, Brian's childhood friend, recalled Murry and Audree protected Brian from outside distractions and never allowed anyone to attend rehearsals. When she and other friends knocked on the door they were told Brian was unavailable.[31] Vickie credits the band's early success to their innate talent and Murry's aggressiveness, but believed Murry's motive was less than altruistic. "Murry was interested in them being successful for Murry, not for Brian," she said. She also thought Murry impacted the group dynamic. "Because of Murry's parenting, Brian, Dennis, and Carl did not have the confidence or stage presence to get out there like Mike did. Al didn't have that kind of personality either. When Mike came on the scene, he took over because he had a strong personality. In the beginning, Murry and Mike got along because Mike had the stage presence that was needed."[32]

On February 4, the *Los Angeles Times* reported "Surfin'" was #3 of the Top Ten best-selling singles at Wallichs Music City behind Dion's "The Wanderer" and Chubby Checker's "The Twist." On February 8, the Beach Boys returned to World Pacific Studio at 7:00 p.m. for a three-hour recording session. With Dino Lappas engineering, the Boys planned to record four new songs—Brian's and Mike's "Surfin' Safari," Brian's "Surfer Girl" and "Judy," and Carl's guitar instrumental "Karate." Brian recalled, "I remember it was raining the night we cut 'Surfer Girl.' I looked out the door and it was pouring down rain and it was just a mood."[33] NOAA records verify Brian's recollection as the weather was overcast, fifty-nine degrees, and a torrential 3.91 inches of rain fell throughout the day.[34]

Accompanying them to their second recording session were Murry, Hite and Dorinda Morgan, Bruce Morgan, and a drummer Brian enlisted who he saw play at The Shed House, a local country music club. As the drummer set up his kit, Dennis, angry about being sidelined, stormed out of the studio. But the drummer didn't really mesh with the band. He chewed tobacco, overplayed, insisted on a solo, and was obnoxious. Dorinda recalled "He was a hillbilly Gene Krupa. We paid him union scale and sent him away."[35] Dennis was cajoled into coming back into the studio.

Another musician present at the session was twenty-four-year-old Val Poliuto of the Jaguars who Hite had known for years and who had helped Brian audition Dorinda's "Chapel of Love" for Art Laboe in May 1958. "I had played some of the songs previously with Brian at the Morgans' home," Poliuto recalled. "I was asked to play piano and, if necessary, back up on the drums if the members of the group were going to sing up front at the microphones."[36]

"Surfin' Safari," written by Brian and Mike as a follow-up to "Surfin,'" explored the treks dedicated surfers embarked on in pursuit of bigger waves. Its structure was similar to "Surfin'" and was influenced by Brian's appreciation for Chuck Berry.[37] Author Philip Lambert noted, "It's not hard to hear a connection between 'Surfin' Safari' and a Chuck Berry song such as 'Brown-Eyed Handsome Man' which uses exactly the same chord pattern."[38]

They recorded ten takes of "Surfin' Safari" with takes one, two, three, five, seven, and eight breaking down early and being abandoned. They recorded one overdub each on takes six and ten. Morgan considered takes nine and ten to be the best versions and noted them as "hold" for possible release.[39]

They recorded six complete takes of "Surfer Girl" and one overdub on take four which Morgan noted "hold." The guys were still learning how to sing and play their instruments at the same time. Brian preferred to concentrate on his vocals and asked Morgan if he could overdub his bass later. When Brian did not hear Morgan's response, Mike whispered sheepishly, "He said, 'No.'"[40]

Don Cunningham, editor of the Beach Boys fanzine *Add Some Music* (1978–1984), described the group's first attempt at "Surfer Girl." "In the early recording, somewhat loose harmonies and a too-slowed 4/4 rhythm simply cannot belie the song's melodic greatness. 'Almost a cappella' might describe the production, as the boys are accompanied by only a steady, 'skipping' triplet beat, which seems to emanate from the likes of a trash can lid, and throbbing bass, which does little more than cue each chord. To round out this garage production, a faint electric guitar picks crude arpeggios, audible about a quarter of the time. Again, the harmonic mix of voices is uneven. Yet the careful listener will detect the promise of the Beach Boys' harmonic sound that would be polished over the next two years."[41]

"The chord progressions in 'Surfer Girl' are straight out of doo-wop," said Lambert. "It seems only natural that a young songwriter well-schooled in the music of the late 1950s would use this progression in one of his earliest efforts."[42] "Its simplicity is deceptive. The three-note melodic pattern occurs five times over the doo-wop progression and the chords that follow: taken to this extreme, the repetition takes on an artful purity and elegance that's hard to dismiss."[43]

Lambert noted "Surfer Girl" is sung largely in a choral style, meaning all the voices sing the words together, a style Brian knew from his study of the Four Freshmen and songs such as the Delroys' "Bermuda Shorts" (1957), the Mystics' "Hushabye" (1959), and the Jaguars' "Don't Go Home" (1960). Val Poliuto was a frequent visitor to the Morgan's home, played on many of their recordings, and may have helped coach the Beach Boys a cappella recording of Dorinda's "Lavender," a beautiful illustration of how Brian had mastered the choral approach.

"I think 'Surfer Girl' is my best song," Brian recalled. "I believe it in my heart. It may not be the best 'record' we ever made, but if you think of it as just a song, it's so simple and the bridge is so lilting. It tells a story about love. Something that will be forever."[44]

Lambert pointed out Brian deviates from the choral style in the bridge as he sings the first three lines by himself. "But then, with dramatic impact, and in direct imitation of a Four Freshmen trick, the choral texture returns for 'Everywhere I go.' The Boys further emphasize this point by shifting the key up a half step on the word 'go,' and the rest of the song remains in this higher key while stating its last bit of text. The most notable precedent for a key change prior to completion of the lyric is the Four Freshmen's 'Their Hearts Were Full of Spring,' which shifts up a half step at the end of the bridge and remains in that key, exactly as in 'Surfer Girl.'"[45] "Indeed, 'Surfer Girl' is the first example of one of Brian's most celebrated achievements: the adaptation of Four Freshmen style into the pop idiom."[46]

Carl remembered, "'Surfer Girl' has a real spiritual quality to it. The chords are just so filling. The way our voices sounded on that, the melody Brian wrote, the way he put the arrangement together, that might be the perfect melding of all the elements. Our vocals were voiced like horn parts. The way those R&B records made background vocals sound like a sax section. They're all within the same octave, that's really the secret to it. We didn't just duplicate parts; we used a lot of counterpoint, a lot of layered sound. We're big oooh-ers; we love to oooh. It's a big full sound, that's very pleasing to us. It opens up the heart."[47]

Brian recalled, "I think we were always spiritually minded. We wrote music to give strength to people. I always feel holy when it comes to recording. Even during 'Surfer Girl,' I felt a bit spiritual."[48]

"Judy" is a fast paced song with Mike singing the bass line "Judy, Judy, Judy bop-a-Judy" beneath Brian's falsetto on the verses. The group was well rehearsed and they needed only two takes and two overdubs onto take two. Brian and Judy had been dating about eight months and she had turned fifteen the previous October. "Judy" offers a glimpse into Brian's first serious relationship as he questions whether she returns his affections." Judy recalled the incident behind the lyrics. "I went to the beach with another guy. I was a young teenager and I was interested in other guys, too. When Brian found out he was upset and angry."[49] Lambert noted the background vocals in the bridge of "Judy" echo what Brian sings and that he would use this echo-dialogue technique "with increasing frequency and sophistication in the coming years."[50]

"Karate" was the Beach Boys first recorded attempt at the musical genre their detractors accused them of imitating—a surf guitar instrumental. Lambert noted, "'Karate' is a series of twelve-bar blues choruses with strong roots in familiar instrumentals from the recent past by Link Wray, the Fireballs, and the Revels."[51] They recorded two takes of "Karate" and two overdubs onto take one. A slightly longer version of "Karate," with a section duplicated and spliced onto the end, later became known as "Beach Boy Stomp."

Because Brian, Al, Dennis, and Val Poliuto were in Local 47 of the AFM, the February 8 session at World Pacific was a union session and a contract had to be completed and submitted within fourteen days. (See Appendix 8.) The AFM contract for the Beach Boys second recording session was for the personal services of musicians between the employer, Hite Morgan's Deck Record Company, with Morgan's authorizing signature, and four employees, Brian, as session leader, Alan, Dennis, and Poliuto. Murry co-signed the contract as Brian's and Dennis's legal guardian. Although Carl played electric guitar on the session, he is not listed on the contract because he was too young to join the union. Although Poliuto maintained he played keyboards, there is no aural evidence of keyboards on any of the recordings.

The song titles were listed as "Karote," "Surfin' Safari," "Little Surfin' Girl," and "Judy." Morgan wrote the song titles as he heard them, hence "Karote" instead of "Karate" and "Little Surfin' Girl" instead of "Surfer Girl." The contract also lists "Surfin'" and "Luau," but obviously they were not recorded that night as they had been released two months earlier. They were simply added to the contract because they had not been recorded at a union session and now that both songs were paired on a hit single, they had to be "made legal with the union."

The legends on the two original tape boxes were the standard form used at World Pacific Studio. The writing is that of Dino Lappas and the significant information included the client listed as "Hight (*sic*) Morgan," the program as "The Surfers," the mixer and recorder as "Dino," and "Karate" is misspelled "Karatta." Both legends are stamped "Monoaural." The listing of the group as "The Surfers" is a mistake carried over from the first session at which "Surfin'" was recorded and may indicate Lappas was unaware the group was now called the Beach Boys.

On February 9, the day after the Beach Boys recorded a potential follow-up single to "Surfin'," Hite Morgan met with attorney Al Schlesinger to straighten out Morgan's mechanical royalty for the sales of "Surfin'." When Herb Newman agreed in early January to finance a new pressing of "Surfin'" and distribute it by his Era Record Sales, he agreed to abide by the terms of the original lease Saraceno, on behalf of Candix, brokered with Bob Field of Pacific Record Distributors on December 15, 1961. But neither Candix nor Pacific had obtained a mechanical license from Morgan. Hence, the lease failed to ensure Morgan was paid properly for the copyright to "Surfin'." Morgan had straightened out the publishing credit on the record label for "Surfin'" on Candix 301 but, without a mechanical license, what was printed on the label had little bearing on royalty payments.

Morgan met with Schlesinger at his law office at 1619 North Cherokee Avenue in Hollywood. Representing Candix was Bruce L. Wolfson of the law firm Shiffman and Wolfson. Representing Pacific Record Distributors was its owner Bob Field, fresh from his February 7 appearance at the payola trial of Hunter Hancock at which Field testified he paid the LA disc jockey twenty-five to fifty dollars a month to play records distributed by Pacific. Herb Newman of Era Records did not attend the meeting.

The original lease stipulated Pacific Record Distributors would pay Candix sixteen cents for every copy of "Surfin'" sold. Schlesinger got all parties present to agree to an amended contract that stipulated Era Distributors was to pay Candix ten cents per record and the remaining six cents to Morgan. It was also agreed that Bob Field would obtain a mechanical license from Morgan for "Surfin'." Four months later, Field had still not obtained the mechanical license.

Schlesinger recalled, "Bob Field was a nice guy, quiet, quite thin, about late 30s. He was never my distributor, but it's a small business and everybody knew everybody. Joe Saraceno was a major player and I ran into him from time to time. There's an old proverb, if you can't say something nice about somebody, don't say anything at all."[52]

For the weekend of February 10, after stalling the prior week at #4, "Surfin'" moved to #3 on KFWB and finally broke into the *Billboard* Hot 100 at #93. On KRLA, however, it slipped from #4 to #8. In *Cash Box* it was #94. But the chart news was tempered with Al Jardine's announcement that he was quitting the band.

"Al's parents thought the band was a flash in the pan and they wanted him to stay in college, work on his studies, and have a stable career," recalled Jodi Gable.[53]

Al recalled, "Brian was pissed. Boy was he mad. I was too bull-headed. I just wanted to finish school."[54] "I was taking my organic chemistry to concerts with me. I always thought I'd be a professional person, and sing as a hobby or have fun being in a band."[55] "We were travelling around a lot and it just got to be a little hard on me physically. Murry had us doing a lot of promotions. I told Brian I had to take a break and finish my courses. While I was finishing school they were playing supermarkets and shopping centers for free. They were paying off disc jockeys for airplay. Murry still didn't understand. He didn't believe in the music."[56]

Usher recalled, "Al and I actually talked about forming our own group, just the two of us singing. I even remember going over to his house one day and practicing some Kingston Trio songs on guitar. Al was a nice guy, very sincere, and a little older than the other kids. I always thought of him as being rather ambiguous in nature because he would never commit himself. He also had two distinct sides—the side he'd let you see and a side seldom seen."[57]

A myth that persisted for decades was that Al quit the band to attend dental school. He contributed, however inadvertently, to that misconception. In 1976, for a six-hour radio special on the band, he recalled, "I left the group right at the point they went to Capitol. I made a decision, I didn't want to really put a big investment into equipment and at the same time I wanted to finish dental school." When Al quit in February 1962, the band was three and one-half months away from signing with Capitol and Al was two years away from even applying to dental school. There may have been other reasons that influenced his decision to leave. Al was dissatisfied with "Surfin' Safari" being groomed as the follow-up single and unhappy with the group's musical direction. To fill out their meager live repertoire, they were playing songs like "The Twist," "Bermuda Shorts," and "Johnny B. Goode." But Top 40 was not Al's main musical interest. He never imagined they would become a pop quintet much less a rock 'n' roll band.

Gary Winfrey offered a unique perspective on why Al left. "He quit the Beach Boys to continue his education, thinking the record 'Surfin'' would be a one-time thing. It cost them $100 to record 'Surfin'' and 'Luau,' and they didn't make their money back, so there wasn't any money to be made being a Beach Boy. And he hated the concerts. He said he got tired of being hassled by jealous boyfriends every time they came off stage. Girls would swoon and some guy would want to take a punch at them as they came down. He didn't like it."[58]

When Al left, Murry wasted little time in calling Harry Klusmeyer, a producer with Promotional Productions whom he hired to book the Boys' personal appearances, and advised him the group now consisted of four members. Klusmeyer was not a talent agent. He was an independent broker who assembled a number of acts for a show, paid them, and then sold the entire show to the venue at a higher cost. This was common practice at the time, but also points out how naive Murry was about that aspect of the music business. Klusmeyer responded to Murry February 11 and inquired if dropping to four members would require a change in instrumentation for the band's personal appearances. Klusmeyer expressed interest in Murry coordinating all future appearances through him and sought to assuage Murry's concern over how little money the group was commanding for personal appearances, including two upcoming shows in San Diego. Klusmeyer hoped their fee could be increased to $400 to $500 per engagement depending on their next single and television appearances.[59] Clearly, the band's financial success depended on a follow-up single.

After Al left the group, someone inexplicably crossed out his name on the AFM contract for the February 8, 1962, session at World Pacific Studio. Although he was no longer in the group, Al was still entitled to the $53.50 union scale wages he earned that night. But when the contract was received by the union, Al's wages appear to not have been paid and the allotted $4.28 not contributed to his pension fund.

For the weekend of February 17, "Surfin'" slid to #9 on KFWB and #11 on KRLA. It was #90 in *Billboard* and #95 in *Cash Box*. The Beach Boys are believed to have played their first show without Al Jardine on February 16 at the Rainbow Gardens, a nightclub in Pomona owned by Eddie Davis, who managed the Mixtures, an ethnically diverse R&B septet from Oxnard who played there Friday nights and may have provided instrumental support for the Beach Boys. There are anecdotal reports that Brian, Mike, and Carl sang without playing instruments while Dennis stood playing just a snare drum and hi-hat.

"When I was a disc jockey at KRLA, I would hire the Beach Boys," Bob Eubanks recalled. "I would pay them a hundred and fifty dollars to come out on Friday night and play Rainbow Gardens. I had a good relationship with the guys. It was obvious the father was the true boss of what was going on. I always thought Murry was a bit of a bullshitter, but he was in there plugging for his boys. For that, I admired him. I tried to get them to change their name because I felt their name was so regional they wouldn't have much success out of a coastal area."[60]

Eubanks asked Murry if any of the boys surfed. "Denny is the only one who surfs," Murry replied. "They know a lot of kids who surf. It's all image, the whole beach thing. You don't have to surf to sing about it, do you?" When Eubanks expressed doubts about the group's name, Murry said, "We tried some others, like the Pendletones, but changed it. Russ Regan over at Era Records came up with the name. I think the Beach Boys is fine. We're sticking with it."[61]

Mike Love recalled, "Murry Wilson was very good at promoting, getting radio stations to play our records. He was very smart and clever about it. He would have us go out and do hops and events where a DJ would make a couple of hundred bucks and we could make a couple of hundred bucks. And the DJ, since he made some money, he'd be playing our records for the next six months until we did it again. So we built a real good foundation doing that kind of thing not only in Southern California, but all around the country until we got a momentum going."[62]

On February 19, the Beach Boys headed 100 miles south to play the first of two consecutive nights during intermission of Bruce Brown's film *Surf Crazy* at the Academy Fine Arts Theatre at 3721 University Avenue in San Diego. It was Brown's follow-up to his 1958 *Slippery When Wet*. It was the band's first show outside LA and Al accompanied them because it was booked by Klusmeyer prior to Al's decision to leave. A small ad for the film and the band's appearance ran in the February 16 *San Diego Union*. Admission was $1.50 and kids were advised to come early for seats. Shown at 7:00 p.m. and 9:00 p.m. the seventy-two minute film had an intermission after forty-two minutes. The guys came out, set up their equipment, and played a short set to the surf-friendly audience. Then the second half of the film played. They repeated their set during the 9:00 p.m. showing.

Bruce Brown produced a 9.5" × 12.5" handbill to promote the screening that was displayed in various stores and on utility poles throughout the neighborhood surrounding the theatre. Brown had a stock poster on which he printed additional information specific to the venue. Beneath the heading Bruce Brown Presents "Surf Crazy," the handbill shows a bluish-toned photograph of three surfers—Byron Kough, Pat Curren, and Pete Cole—in Waimea Bay, Hawaii, on January 17, 1960. It is described as the largest wave to hit Hawaii in five years. Printed over the photograph in several lines of red type was "Also See Here In Person, The Beach Boys Singing Their Hit Tune 'Surfin'"And Other Hit Tunes." This is the earliest known handbill promoting a Beach Boys concert.

The Beach Boys played during intermission of the 7:00 p.m. and 9:00 p.m. showings of the film *Surf Crazy* at the Fine Arts Theatre in San Diego on February 19 and 20, 1962 (author's collection).

During one of the campfire sequences on the *Endless Summer* television show, Al reminisced about these shows, "We sang 'Surfer Girl' for the first time in San Diego." Mike interjected, "It was after a surf movie, wasn't it?" Al continued, "On the way back from San Diego, we dropped by somebody's beach party. And they laughed at that one line, 'Standing by the ocean's roar.' They thought that was really funny and we went home kind of dejected because we hadn't released it yet."[63] For the weekend of February 24, "Surfin'" stalled at #9 on KFWB and slid to #15 on KRLA. It jumped to #83 in *Billboard* and #86 in *Cash Box*.

After the chaos of "Surfin'" being leased to Pacific, pressed on the hastily created X Records, and then picked up by Era Records, Candix had no chance of releasing another Beach Boys single. The band never signed a contract with Candix and was under no obligation to provide another record. And with the difficulty he was having with the convoluted royalty agreements, it was unlikely Hite Morgan would bring a follow-up single to Candix. Bob Dix was unaware the Beach Boys had even recorded a potential second single.

Although his brothers Richard and Al helped out occasionally, Bob was effectively running Candix by himself. He stayed at his LA apartment during the week and made the four-hour drive to his home in Fresno on weekends. On April 13, Richard, against Bob's wishes, agreed to execute a satisfaction of judgment in exchange for the return of former Candix president Bill Silva's twenty-four shares of Candix stock on which the Sheriff of Los Angeles County had filed a notice of levy December 21, 1961, just three days after the Candix stock book and minute book, which Silva had retained after Bob fired him, were returned to Bob from Silva's lawyers. Because Bob hadn't released a new record in nearly three months, John Blore and John Fisher, Candix's record promoters, were seldom in the office. In fact, after receiving the copyright to "Surfer's Stomp," Blore probably no longer worked for Candix.

On February 12, Bob directed attorney Sidney Shiffman of Shiffman and Wolfson to file a lawsuit against Joe Saraceno. The suit alleged that on or about February 1, 1961, songwriter Leona Wenz brought to Candix a tape of a song she wrote called "Shy, Shy Boy" and negotiated a written agreement with Bill Silva by which Candix would represent the song and attempt to have it recorded and released. Three weeks later, Saraceno released Wenz from her contract without Bob's or Silva's knowledge. Two weeks later, Wenz leased "Shy, Shy Boy" to Corsair Records, owned by Mabel Lafferty and Al Furth, who had it recorded by Lafferty's daughter, Claire Terese, backed with Terese's "You Told a Lie."

In his suit, Bob claimed Saraceno misappropriated "Shy, Shy Boy" and "You Told a Lie," converted them into "Surfer's Stomp" and "Start," re-recorded them with studio musicians, released them as a single by the Mar-kets on Union Records, leased it to Liberty Records, and it became a Top 40 hit. Bob named Saraceno, John Blore, Bob Field, Union Records, and Liberty Records in the lawsuit. Candix, joined in the lawsuit by Leona Wenz and Corsair Records, retained attorney Averill Pasarow.

In the meantime, with these legal proceedings whirling about him, Bob secured an extended line of credit with Alco to release "Red River Valley," the third Candix single by Faye Reis, written by Reis's friend Pat Johns, Miss California in 1953, to the tune of "Red River Valley" (Candix 332). Bob arranged an in-store autograph session for Reis at Wallichs Music City and booked her on *Dance Party*.

Before driving to the *Dance Party* appearance, Reis and Bob met at the Candix office where he introduced her to the Beach Boys. "I remember telling them I was going to appear on *Dance Party*," Reis recalled. "One of them, the tall one with blond hair, came over and said something like 'Oh, so you're going to be on *Dance Party*, that's great.' And then, out of nowhere, he punched me real hard on my upper arm. I was wearing a dress with spaghetti straps and a huge black-and-blue mark appeared almost instantly. Bob was annoyed. He used a make-up kit to cover the bruise. Other than that, they were real nice. They were just kids."[64]

Roger Christian recalled, "Candix had a hard time following up a hit with another hit. A small label is not going to get paid on their first hit until they come along with a second one. The way you get your money is once you've had a hit and the stores are calling you for the follow-up record, then you get paid on the original one or you don't give them the follow-up."[65]

Meanwhile, less than three months after their first release, the Beach Boys were faced with their first personnel change. Paul Johnson of the Belairs recalled, "I got a call from either Brian or Carl saying, 'Al's going away and we need a guitarist. Do you want to join the Beach Boys?'" Johnson declined, preferring to work on a follow-up to "Mr. Moto," and was surprised when thirteen-year-old David Marks joined.

"Marks was this skinny kid with stars in his eyes who liked to hang out with them. I thought Al was an integral part of the group and never thought Marks had any serious musical connection. I thought, 'Good grief, why would he be in the band?' They could have had their pick of some great guitar players. But the rhythm guitars on early Beach Boys records sounded good. That's a credit to the producer, doubling guitars to get that chunky rhythm sound."[66]

Marks, an eighth grader at Albert F. Monroe Middle School, recalled, "I was sitting at home with mommy and daddy watching TV and getting ready for school the next day when the Wilsons came over and said, 'Do you want to be in the group? We begged my mom and dad to let me join. For my first gig we wore these ugly mustard-colored coats that were way too big."[67] Because he no longer had any use for it, Al gave David his blue plaid Pendleton shirt.

Usher recalled, "Even when I first met David, his days as a Beach Boy were also numbered. He was an average rhythm guitarist who knew about a dozen songs. Mr. and Mrs. Marks were very protective parents, just like Murry."[68]

13

One Hit Wonders
(March 1962)

The Beach Boys played during a screening of Don Brown's film *Surf's Up* at Millikan High School in Long Beach at 8:00 p.m. on March 2. This was David Marks's first appearance with the band and he rented a solid body Rickenbacker electric guitar before later buying a sunburst Fender Stratocaster. It was Brown's first surf film and he printed a 9" × 12" handbill for the event promoting the Beach Boys "singing their big hit Surfing." But "Surfin'" was running out of steam. That weekend it dropped to #19 on KFWB and fell ten spots to #25 on KRLA. In *Cash Box* it peaked at #85 and was gone the following week. It hung tough in *Billboard* where it remained at #83 for a second week.

Bruce Morgan recalled his father was interested in recording a full-length album with the Beach Boys at World Pacific Studio. He had seven songs recorded—"Surfin'," "Luau," "Lavender," "Surfin' Safari," "Surfer Girl," "Judy," and "Karate" (aka, "Beach Boy Stomp")—and would have needed three to five more to fill out an album.

Sometime in early March, Morgan called Murry and asked if the Boys would come down to Stereo Masters to record vocals on two songs written by Dorinda, but credited to Bruce. The instrumental tracks for "Barbie" and "What Is a Young Girl Made Of?" had already been recorded with another singer in mind, but Dorinda thought Brian's voice suited the material better. "They had him record this song that was real high," recalled Judy Bowles. "It really stretched his vocal cords and was just so beautiful."[1] Which other members of the group sang on the songs has been the subject of some debate.

Dorinda recalled, "Mike and Dennis didn't come to the session, but Alan, Carl, and Audree did. Audree is singing on those."[2] Brian recalled, "My mother and I and a friend of mine did this demo. I was Kenny and the other guys were the Cadets."[3] In 1978, Audree expressed some doubt about her participation. "I was there. I don't know if I'm on the record."[4] She also stated she did not think Carl was on the record.

The lead vocal on "Barbie" is sung by Brian and the background vocals are most likely Carl, Audree, Al, and possibly Val Poliuto singing bass. Audree's mid-range vocal can best be heard during the chorus beginning with "This is the year we have prayed for."

The lead vocal on "What Is a Young Girl Made Of?" is sung by Brian and the pre-recorded background vocals were supplied by a female chorus. The stereo mix of "What Is a Young Girl Made Of?" on 1991's *Lost & Found* ended with studio chatter in which Carl apologized, "I, I started to laugh, but I didn't" and Brian reprimanded him, "You did laugh though; you didn't have to."[5] Al has never said whether he was there and it's difficult to determine aurally if he is on the record. It seems odd Brian didn't mention Carl and Al, and it's unclear who he meant by "a friend of mine," perhaps Val Poliuto. It is generally agreed Mike and Dennis did not attend and there is no aural evidence of them on the recordings.

The legend on the original tape box sheds no light on who attended or the actual date of the session. Taped to the legend is a piece of Stereo Masters stationery with notes in Hite Morgan's handwriting: "Barbee #6 & #7 / MAE 422-A / Barbee Take #6 (punches in bridge on 'prayed') use insert from take #7 * / Young Girl take #5 (second take #5) / * Note: Build up piano base on 'Barbee.'"[6] When he remastered "Barbie" and "What Is a Young Girl Made Of?" in 1990, audio engineer Steve Hoffman confirmed the instrumental tracks had been pre-recorded.[7]

"Barbie" backed with "What Is a Young Girl Made Of?" was released in March 1962 on Randy 422, a new

The Beach Boys played during the showing of *Surf's Up* at Millikan High School in Long Beach, California, on March 2, 1962. This is believed to be the first show with David Marks in the band (author's collection).

label Morgan named as a nod to his friend Randy Wood of Dot Records. The number 422 was randomly selected to make it appear Randy had many prior releases. Indie label owners like Morgan did this routinely to give disc jockeys the impression the label was successful.

Dorinda wrote "Barbie" for the Barbie doll manufactured in Hawthorne by the Mattel Toy Company owned by Ruth and Elliot Handler. Named for the Handlers' daughter, Barbara, the doll revolutionized the toy industry when it was introduced at a toy fair in New York City on March 9, 1959. Mattel sold 351,000 dolls the first year and, at the height of her popularity, three dolls were sold every second. The Handlers soon created a boyfriend for Barbie and named him after their son, Ken. Mattel pressed a promotional 45 rpm record called *Barbie Sings!* featuring "Nobody Taught Me" and "Ken" voiced by Charlotte Austin and Bill Cunningham.

For Dorinda's "Barbie," she named her fictitious group Kenny and the Cadets. It has been reported Dorinda chose the name Cadets because one of the costumes for Ken was a military uniform. Mattel eventually made a military costume for him, but it was not available in spring 1962.

Two versions of "Barbie" on Randy 422 were pressed—a standard black vinyl copy and a multi-colored copy in which half the record is translucent red and half is translucent yellow. This so-called "splash wax" record, also known as the red and yellow Barbie, was made by Morgan as a promotional item. It was pressed using two vinyl biscuits, one red and one yellow, resulting in a random "splash" pattern much like a Jackson Pollock canvas. Each color covers about half the record, the dividing line is usually not finely demarcated, and the position of the label relative to the demarcation differs on each. In short, no two records are identical.

Most copies of "Barbie," on black vinyl or splash wax, that have surfaced are in mint condition, giving rise to speculation it was never released commercially. There are, however, anecdotal stories of a handful of copies that were purchased in record stores. Despite a pleasant and memorable melody, and Brian's soaring falsetto, "Barbie" didn't chart and Morgan forgot about it, finally copyrighting it to his Guild Music on August 17, 1963. A decade later, it was rediscovered and became one of the most sought-after records ever made.

"Barbie" records are primarily sought after by Beach Boys collectors, but many copies of the splash wax are owned by rare record collectors not necessarily interested in the band. One collector, who wished to remain anonymous, called it a "stunningly beautiful record to behold." The rediscovery of "Barbie" is a fascinating story in the world of rare records.

In 1973, Gerry Diez, a California record collector and dealer, received a phone call from his friend Murray Gershenz, owner of the LA record store Music Man Murray. As he had often done with rock 'n' roll and R&B records with which he was unfamiliar, Murray asked Diez to appraise several boxes of records Murray had purchased. The boxes were those used by pressing plants to ship records to distributors and some of them were still sealed.

There was a 100-count box each of "Dreamworld" by the Calvanes (Deck 579), "Horror Pictures" by the Calvanes (Deck 580), and "Everyword of the Song" by Billy Jones and the Squires (Deck 478), and a 50-count box of "Di-Di" by the Dell Rays with the Spades (Dice 479). All four of these records were produced by Hite Morgan. There were eight or nine copies of "Sunday Kind of Love" by the Highlanders on the Rays label. There was also a 100-count box of the black vinyl "Barbie" by Kenny and the Cadets, a group Diez had never heard of, on Randy Records, a label he had never seen.

Diez never met the man who brought the records in and Murray didn't recall his name. Diez priced the other records, but could not find any information about "Barbie," Kenny and the Cadets, or the record's estimated worth. In partnership with Murray, Diez began selling copies of "Barbie" to dealers and collectors. Within a few weeks, he sold eight copies to Rockaway Records in LA and another seven to collectors on the East Coast. He sold the record for $250 and kept $50 commission on each sale. Initially, Diez kept five copies for himself, but once he realized how much interest there was in the record he negotiated an additional ten copies to use as trade for rare records he wanted for his own collection. Murray kept five copies for himself to sell through his store. That accounted for about thirty-five copies of the original 100 count. According to Diez, Murray later sold the remaining copies, perhaps as many as sixty-five, to record collectors Jeff and Daryl Stolper.

About a year later, sometime in late 1974, Diez received a phone call from his friend Dave Antrell (real name Dave Antrobus), an avid R&B vocal group collector. Antrell had recently returned to LA from a record buying excursion in Nevada where he had gone to find Hite Morgan, whom he knew produced black vocal groups in the late 1950s. Antrell wanted Diez to come over and check out his latest acquisitions. Antrell had a minor career as a singer songwriter and was now a medical student at USC. He was a highly intelligent, hyperkinetic man with a keen ability to ferret out rare records. He searched for people who had worked in the record industry as record pressers, distributors, rack jobbers, or in promotion and A&R. These individuals often put aside records for themselves and traded with colleagues at other record companies, distributors, and pressing plants. Most of these folks were now retired and willing to sell their records, which were often in mint condition.

"Barbie" backed with "What Is a Young Girl Made Of?," written by Dorinda Morgan, but credited to her son, Bruce, were recorded by Brian, Carl, and Audree, at Stereo Masters in spring 1962, and released on Randy 422 as by Kenny and the Cadets. Dennis and Mike did not attend the vocals-only session, and Al was enlisted for his vocal support. Hite Morgan pressed one hundred copies on black vinyl and twenty-five (one seen here) on red and yellow "splash wax" as a novelty for promotional purposes. A red, yellow, and green copy is known to exist, and a blue and yellow copy may also exist (author's collection).

When Diez arrived at his friend's house, Antrell showed him fifteen copies of "Barbie" by Kenny and the Cadets on red and yellow splash wax. A few copies had splashes of green intermingled with the red and yellow. Antrell had found Dorinda in Nevada (Hite had passed away) and she offered to let him "take a look around and see if anything interests you." Antrell came across an opened box with fifteen copies of "Barbie" on splash wax and was intrigued. Given Morgan's history of recording black artists, Antrell reasoned Kenny and the Cadets was an obscure LA black vocal group. He bought all fifteen copies.

When Antrell returned home, he played the record repeatedly, searching for aural clues as to the identity of Kenny and the Cadets. Vocal groups in the 1950s changed names and members so often you never knew who might turn up on a recording. Antrell was surprised that "Barbie" and "What Is a Young Girl Made Of?" were pop songs and Kenny and the Cadets didn't sound like a black vocal group at all. In fact, the more he listened, the more he thought the record sounded like a young Brian Wilson. Antrell knew Morgan had produced the Beach Boys early recordings so he reasoned Kenny and the Cadets may have been an earlier name of the group and "Barbie" an early Beach Boys recording time had forgotten.

Diez traded Antrell a black vinyl "Barbie" and bought three red and yellow copies for

$300 each. It is unclear what Antrell paid Dorinda Morgan for the fifteen red and yellow copies, but Diez believed it was "pretty reasonable." Although he could not be certain, Bruce Morgan thought his father may have produced 100 black vinyl copies and perhaps twenty-five red and yellow copies. Today, a red and yellow "Barbie" is valued at approximately $3,000.

Twenty-five years later, the Beach Boys came full circle with the Barbie doll when Brian wrote, sang, and produced "Living Doll" for the Mattel Company, which pressed it on a blue, flexible, five-inch sound sheet and included it in its California Dream Barbie in December 1987. Although credited to the Beach Boys, the record was all Brian. "Living Doll" was first recorded as "Christine" in June 1986 as Brian rekindled his friendship with Gary Usher and began work on his first solo album.

On March 10, as "Surfin'" dropped to #25 on KFWB, climbed six spots to #77 in *Billboard*, and disappeared from KRLA and *Cash Box*, the Boys piled their gear into their cars and drove fifteen miles northwest from Hawthorne to the exclusive Pacific Palisades where they were part of the entertainment for an 8:00 p.m. Mardi Gras Costume Ball at the Bel-

The Beach Boys, now with David Marks on rhythm guitar, perform at the Bel-Air Bay Club in Pacific Palisades, California, on March 10, 1962. From left to right, Carl, Dennis, Mike, David, and Brian. For this upscale engagement, they traded their Pendleton shirts for mustard-colored sports jackets.

Air Bay Club at 16800 Pacific Coast Highway. Built in 1927 by LA developer Alphonzo Bell, the Bel-Air Bay Club still offers a spectacular view of Santa Monica Bay and Catalina Island. The Beach Boys were not mentioned on the ticket or show program. The upscale club called for stage clothes dressier than Pendletons and Levis.

Two black-and-white photographs from this event are the earliest known of the band. Although cameras were not as ubiquitous as today, it seems odd there are no photos of them taken during the five months Al was an original member. Bruce Morgan recalled a photograph of the group with Al, but it has not surfaced. The band's 50th anniversary celebration, during which friends, family, and fans scoured their attics, did not uncover such a photo.

In the Bel-Air Bay Club photographs, they are wearing white dress shirts, dark ties, dark pants, and what appear to be the mustard-colored sport jackets Marks recalled. By this time they had upgraded to Fender instruments and amplifiers. Brian played a sunburst Precision bass, and Carl and David each played a sunburst Stratocaster. They plugged into a late 1950s Fender Bassman amplifier and a 1961 Fender Showman, the company's first amplifier with the electronics in a separate compartment atop the speaker cabinet. The Showman had a fifteen-inch speaker manufactured by the LA-based James B. Lansing Sound, Incorporated (JBL D130) and was covered with cream-colored Tolex, a flexible vinyl Fender began using in 1960, replacing the tweed covering in use since 1948. "When the group really got going," recalled Carl, "we bought a Stratocaster, a Precision bass, some drums, and some other guitars. I played that Stratocaster for a couple of years. We learned how to play by listening to the records."[8] The investment in quality gear improved their live sound, but the expenditure at this early stage in their career was not without some risk. Donald Conder, a classmate of Brian's at Hawthorne High, recalled cruising down Hawthorne Boulevard with Dennis Wilson and another friend when "Surfin'" came on the radio. Dennis, without a hint of bragging, remarked, "I hope we make enough money to pay for our new instruments."[9]

Shortly after their Bel-Air Bay Club appearance, a local newspaper ran a photograph of them at the club with an article that noted, "There's no shocking ducktails or Fabian type hairstyles in this group. The boys present a neat appearance. Their mothers see to that." The article stated they had "appeared in Long Beach, San Diego, Balboa, and Riverside."[10] Little is known about the appearance in Riverside, but Brian may have referred to it when he recalled, "After we did 'Surfin',' I wrote 'Surfin' Safari' and '409,' and Mike wrote the lyrics, and we took a little tour around California, went to Riverside and San Bernardino. Quite a memory."[11]

On March 7, Steve Love, one of Mike's two younger brothers, arranged for the Beach Boys to play Morningside High School. He was making good on a campaign pledge after being elected president of his freshman class in January and sworn in February 9. "I asked my mom to telephone her brother Murry to ask if I could safely make that pledge," Steve recalled. "Murry agreed and wished me luck with the election. Murry looked at the gig as a paid rehearsal and some useful practice before a live audience. It made for a persuasive campaign speech and I was elected. It was decided that two thirty-minute concerts would be held during lunch hour, one for the freshman and sophomore classes, and one for the juniors and seniors. I charged twenty-five cents and nearly 700 kids showed up for a gate of $172, split equally with the band and the freshman class treasury."[12]

The Beach Boys played one show during Prom Week, March 12–16, 1962, at Torrance High School in Torrance, California. Prom Week was a week-long fundraiser sponsored by the junior class to raise funds for the prom later that spring (author's collection).

During the school week of March 12–16, the Beach Boys played a thirty-minute show at Torrance High School as part of Prom Week activities sponsored by the junior class to raise funds for the prom later that spring. A photograph of the band from the event appeared in the school's 1962 *Torch* yearbook.

They were hardly getting rich playing these high school gigs, but Murry knew the value of promotion and exposure. Brian's friend Rich Sloan recalled, "One afternoon in early 1962, my wife and I picked up Dennis hitchhiking on El Segundo Boulevard. Dennis said, 'My dad doesn't charge enough. He only charges a hundred dollars a night.' I told him the exposure was more valuable than the money."[13] Murry recalled, "The kids could see the Beach Boys for two dollars, whereas they paid three dollars and fifty-cents to four dollars for other groups. That way, we always had a full house."[14]

The Beach Boys played the 47th Annual National Orange Show "Citrus Centennial" at the fairgrounds in San Bernardino sometime during its eleven-day run from March 15, Mike's twenty-first birthday, to March 25. The show may have been March 23 at 4:00 p.m. as a local newspaper reported it was Kids Day and a teen hop was held.[15] Usher recalled, "In early '62, we were in San Bernardino for a Beach Boys show at a fair. Brian and I liked the happy scene of the county fairs. We picked up on the spirit of the rides and the girls, and at one of our daily writing sessions, with Brian at the piano and me sitting there, we wrote 'County Fair' in ten minutes."[16] Usher recalled it was the second song he wrote with Brian, which places the writing of "409," which Usher recalled was their third collaboration, sometime after the National Orange Show.

A photograph of the Boys wearing their Pendletons and performing in the Orange Blossom Room of the Orange Show Restaurant beneath a Gay Paree banner with a backdrop of the Eiffel Tower appeared in *Made in California*, a 6-CD box set released in August 2013. A clue to this appearance is in the 1962 *Pacificana* yearbook for Pacific High School in San Bernardino. The yearbook included a photograph of the school's basketball homecoming held February 2, 1962, at the Orange Show Cafeteria, also known as the Orange Blossom Room, with the identical backdrop of the Eiffel Tower. This photograph of the Beach Boys

appeared in the 2008 U.K. documentary *Dennis Wilson: The Real Beach Boy* in what seemed to be a mockup of "Surfin'" sheet music. There are, however, no known copies of "Surfin'" sheet music.

On March 16, the Beach Boys played the first of three days with the Belairs and the Vibrants at the Monica Hotel in Santa Monica. Billed as teenage dance parties, the Friday and Saturday evening shows ran 8:00 p.m. to midnight, while the Sunday afternoon show was 1:00 p.m. to 5:00 p.m. A handbill for the dances promised surprise Hollywood guest stars each night, as well as dance contests, trophies, refreshments, and door prizes. All you had to do was "follow the search lights to the beach." That weekend "Surfin'" disappeared from the KFWB chart and peaked at #75 in *Billboard*. (See Appendix 3, "Surfin'" Chart Position History.)

"These shows were jammed with kids," recalled

The Beach Boys shared the bill with the Belairs and the Vibrants at the Monica Hotel in Santa Monica, California, on March 16, 17, and 18, 1962 (courtesy David Stadler).

Vibrants' bassist David Stadler, "We played two forty-five minute sets each day, but the times we played varied each day. I spent a few minutes talking with Carl and Dennis. They were the two I knew best and I always found them to be really nice guys. Mike was pretty arrogant in my view. Never mixed or tried to talk to us that I can remember. David Marks was playing with them during these shows."

On March 23, the Beach Boys played a variety revue at the Mira Costa High School auditorium co-sponsored by the school's student body and the Manhattan Beach Police Officers Benefit Association. Proceeds from the show were donated to the memorial fund established for the widow and two young sons of twenty-nine-year-old Officer Timothy Giles, a three-year veteran of the force, who died from injuries sustained when his motorcycle was struck by a car while pursuing a speeding motorist on Sepulveda Boulevard on February 13, 1962. Listed in the 6" × 9" six-page program as pop recording artists, the Beach Boys shared the bill with Spencer and Allred, the Twin Tones, and Tommy Terry. The City of Manhattan Beach holds a Peace Officer Memorial Ceremony each May to honor Giles and two other city police officers killed in the line of duty. "Surfin'" disappeared from the Hot 100 in *Billboard* on newsstands March 24.

William F. Williams, a disc jockey on KMEN covering the Inland Empire cities of Riverside and San Bernardino, recalled the Beach Boys played a teen fashion show sponsored by the Harris Company, an upscale department store whose flagship store occupied an entire city block in downtown San Bernardino. Williams recalled, "KMEN was one of the first stations to play the Beach Boys and San Bernardino was a big Beach Boys' town. Harris Department Store had a Deb-Teens department and the girls at the area high schools who bought their clothes there became members of a club. Harris had a fashion show/concert each year for the girls who were members. KMEN was in charge of putting together the talent for the concert. Murry Wilson came to us and literally begged us to let the Beach Boys be the opening act. As I recall, they barely knew which end of the guitar case was up. They looked very badly, played very badly, and sang very badly."[17]

The Harris Company sponsored two teen fashion events in spring 1962 and it is unclear at which the Beach Boys appeared. The Hi-Teen Easter Fashion Show was held in the fourth floor auditorium of the Harris Department Store at West 3rd and North E Streets in downtown San Bernardino at 1:30 p.m. on March 24. A similar event was held that day at 2:00 p.m. at the Harris store in nearby Redlands. Seven weeks later, on May 12, Harris sponsored a Campus Deb Jamboree billed as "Fantasy in Fashion" at the California Theater at 562 West 4th Street in San Bernardino. An advertisement in the *San Bernardino County Sun* promised "surprise guest stars with an autograph session afterwards in Harris' new Record Shop."[18] The March 24 show seems more likely because securing an appearance then, as "Surfin'" slipped off the charts, would have been more urgent.

Surf-O-Rama, a surfing industry trade show, was held 1:00 p.m. to 10:30 p.m. on March 23 and 24 at the Santa Monica Civic Auditorium. The Beach Boys most likely played late afternoon on March 24 after the teen fashion show at The Harris Company in San Bernardino. In his February 11 memo, Harry Klusmeyer wrote Murry, "Except for Surf-O-Rama, I would appreciate you calling me on all other surf film situations that are offered at present."[19] Surf-O-Rama featured five surf films, twenty-five exhibits, a surf wagon contest, a bathing suit contest, a raffle for a roundtrip to Hawaii, and door prizes including a surf board.

At 8:00 p.m. on March 24, the band appeared at an outdoor dance headlined by the Vibrants on the athletic field of Newport Harbor High School in Newport Beach. "Bill Meecham, our manager, arranged to have the Beach Boys appear," recalled David Stadler. "On the night of the event, we set up our equipment on a small riser on the fifty-yard line adjacent to the track. Just three members of the Beach Boys showed up—Mike, Carl, and Dennis, along with Murry Wilson. There was another guy who played bass for them. They didn't bring their instruments because Meecham told Murry they could use ours. Meecham never told us, but we were okay with it. Murry was upset about the small stage and he didn't like our Shure sound system. They played three or four songs and left. We played for an hour. Less than 100 kids showed up and it wasn't a great event. Meecham was supposed to distribute flyers to schools and local hang-outs, but he didn't do a good job at it."[20]

On March 29, Murry sent Hite Morgan a one-page Letter of Intent and Agreement, outlining what he wanted Morgan to accomplish for the Beach Boys now that "Surfin'" was gone from the local and national charts, and the Beach Boys were no closer to a follow-up single. (See Appendix 9.)

"Murry was so ecstatic," Dorinda recalled, "He just handed them to us on a silver platter."[21] Murry typed the letter on new Beach Boys stationery that proclaimed along the top "Teenage Dances/Recording Artists/Television, Radio and Stage Appearances." Brian was listed as the group's leader and Murry their manager.

The letter reads like it was written by a lay person trying to sound like an attorney. But, of course, Murry was not an attorney and had not consulted one. The stilted language, random capitalization, and rambling structure give the letter a clumsy, amateurish tone that revealed how little Murry understood about the music business. But the Morgans were his best contact with the industry and he needed their help in furthering the group's career. Murry sought to secure Morgan's commitment as the group's producer and obtain for them a recording contract with a major record company. In exchange, Murry promised the Morgans would share equally in such a contract and receive fifty percent of the group's earnings for one year.

Murry asked Morgan to ensure any future contracts "will be in writing, and in favor of Hite & Dorinda Morgan and the Beach Boys," a reference to Murry's perception of what happened to "Surfin'" because there was no written contract with Candix. Murry also asked Morgan to prevent "other firms forcing the group to record songs that may not be beneficial to them" or "which might conflict with the type of music or songs the Beach Boys do best." It is unclear what Murry meant because, at the time, the group had only recorded for the Morgans. In a curious passage at the end of the letter, Murry tells Morgan that Brian has the right to "hire or fire any one of the Beach Boys from time to time at his discretion" or to improve the group by "adding a new member or reducing the number of persons known as the Beach Boys." It's interesting whether Murry intended this authority to rest solely with Brian or, after the shake-up with Jardine and Marks, felt he needed to control who was a member of the group. Morgan signed the agreement and began working to secure them a recording contract with a major record label. How much work the Morgans did to promote the band is the subject of some debate. Russ Regan stated he had personal knowledge that most of the effort to get "Surfin'" played in the LA area was done by Murry. Regan also believed "Surfin'" was produced by Murry and Brian, and that Morgan served as a sound engineer.[22]

The March 30 issue of *The Warwhoop*, El Camino Community College's weekly newspaper, contained an article about "Surfin'" based on an interview with Al. Although the article is dated seven weeks after he quit the band, Al indicates he is a current member and there is no mention of David Marks. Al said he "enjoyed working with the group, but it just takes too much of his time" and that he "does not foresee any long range recording career unless we make it really big." He stated "Surfin'" could possibly net more than "$25,000 by the end of the year in personal appearances and royalties, has already paid handsomely, and they were planning to release another record in the near future."[23] The same day the *Warwhoop* article appeared, "Surfin'" disappeared from the KFWB chart after a thirteen-week run.

On March 31, the Beach Boys played a dance headlined by the Vibrants at the National Guard Armory at John Galvin Park in Ontario, California. Murry contacted Bill Meecham and arranged for the Beach Boys to play a fifteen-minute set and again borrow the Vibrants' equipment. Meecham printed 5.5" × 8.5" handbills and advertised on the radio that the Beach Boys would be there. They showed up during the Vibrants' second set with Murry leading the way like they were royalty. "Murry was rather pushy, like 'We're the Beach Boys and you're whoever you are,'" recalled David Stadler. "He had a couple of people reposition the guitar amps and Dennis liked the drums set up a certain way. I remember Carl watching our lead guitarist and picking up a lot of his riffs."[24] Richard Hoffman, the Vibrants' rhythm guitarist, recalled, "We thought of ourselves in competition with them until the thing turned upside down. It was like a football rivalry in those days with the bands. You know, this was our territory."[25]

In addition to the show in Riverside mentioned in an early newspaper article, it seems likely the Beach Boys made other personal appearances during the first three months of 1962. Shane Wilder recalled they played at his record store in Thousand Oaks shortly after "Surfin'" was released.[26] Judy Bowles recalled, "The first Beach Boys concert I attended was at a local high school. They didn't have much of a repertoire. They only knew about three songs. They played them and then they had to leave. Audree and Murry were there. A guy asked me to dance and I danced with him. Brian wasn't too happy, but I wanted to dance."[27] They may have also played additional shows with the Mixtures at the Rainbow Gardens and at Lueders Park Community Center in Compton.

Audree and Murry often talked about the fifty freebies, shows the Boys played for little or no pay as they worked to build a name for themselves. Audree recalled, "It was very hectic. Telephones never ever stopped ringing. I was doing all of the book work, the forms for the musician's union, going to the bank, and being careful all five of them got exactly the same amount to the penny."[28] "Sometimes I would make dinner and nobody would eat it. I would have a roast ready and all of a sudden we would have to tear out and leave everything there. They went to about fifty or sixty so-called 'freebies.' Disc jockey hops. They were called freebies because there was no admission charge and there was no pay for the performers, a hot dog maybe. So we went everyplace. If my husband didn't go, I would go. I traveled a great deal with them. It's a heck of a hard job. For me it was only getting ready and being there and I would get a little tired. For them it was much worse. But I loved it, because I loved being with them."[29]

One of the reasons Al cited for quitting the group was the strain personal appearances put on his school work. Hence, it is likely they made more personal appearances in early 1962 than are currently documented.

With "Surfin'" gone from the local and national charts, no follow-up single in sight, and no record company anxious for another single, Murry worried their music career might be over. "The boys were off the air and they couldn't get back on the air," Murry recalled. "No one wanted them. They thought they were a one-shot record."[30]

The boys looked to Murry for career guidance and Murry looked to Hite Morgan. The Letter of Intent and Agreement Murry sent Morgan on March 29, 1962, was designed to secure Morgan's commitment to get the Boys a recording contract with a major record company.

In less than three weeks, Murry would regret asking Morgan to sign that agreement.

14

Making Tracks ... to the Tower
(April 1962)

Sometime in the first half of April, Gary Usher booked two separate sessions at Western Recorders at 6000 Sunset Boulevard. At the first session, the plan was to record four songs Usher could shop as demos to advance his own career. At the second session, they would record three songs the Beach Boys would use to land a deal with a larger, more successful record company. Murry agreed to finance the sessions. Although Audree Wilson maintained the Morgans knew about these sessions, Dorinda disagreed. "We found out through the grapevine. We were a little angry, but we weren't surprised. This is a dog-eat-dog business. They started to make it. It was very simple."[1] The dates of the sessions have been reported to be April 16 and 19, but there is no documentation for them and there is reason to believe they were held earlier in the month.

"I kept telling Brian you can't just sit around and wait for a company to come to you," Usher recalled. "We should go in and cut some masters ourselves."[2] Usher recommended Western as the best studio he had ever been to.[3]

Usher's insistence that Brian record his own demos played an important role in the Beach Boys' career. At Western, Brian met thirty-four-year-old Chuck Britz, a talented and intuitive recording engineer with whom he would forge a creative partnership that produced many of the Beach Boys' most memorable recordings. Brian came to trust and respect Britz and valued his opinion in the studio. "Chuck Britz was great for Brian," recalled Usher. "Chuck understood Brian's strengths and weaknesses more than anybody else. He was a great engineer and a very sensitive human being."[4]

Britz had been at Western for less than two years when he met Brian, but had already earned the reputation as an exceptional recording engineer. "When I first started working with Brian in 1962, he was very precise," recalled Britz. "There were no questions in his mind. He never changed how he wanted a record to sound."[5]

At the first session, Usher introduced Britz to Brian, Carl, Dennis, and Mike (David was not present) and they got down to work recording four songs. Usher's "One Way Road to Love" is a saccharine boy-loves-girl song on which Usher sang over a monotonous track of rhythm guitar, piano, bass, and drums. Brian and Carl sang background vocals, and Brian added falsetto during the bridge. When Carl and Brian argued about how close they should stand around the microphone, Britz barked, "All right Carl, back it off. Now!"[6]

"The Beginning of the End," written by Usher and Roger Christian, is about the dissolution of a relationship and had a pleasant track of rhythm guitar, bass, drums, and organ, with a simple lead guitar solo of the melody. The first three takes broke down early and before take four, Britz said, "That cymbal is still banging the devil out of this. Are you doing anything on the snare?"[7] The "No" response sounds like Brian, although the drums were most likely played by a studio musician. Before take six, Britz asked Brian, "Can we get any more out of the organ? Let me hear some more. Hit it pretty hard. I don't want to bring the mike up and pick up everything else in the room." A simple organ line is prominent in the middle of the take and then drops out. On a vocal overdub, Britz cautioned, "This is it boys, take nine. Don't cough, you're on mike." Brian asked, "Did I cough, I'm sorry." Brian sang lead and a beautiful soaring falsetto fade repeating "of the end" five times.[8]

"Visions," written by Usher and Brian, begins with a loping old West sounding piano and guitar. The song has a catchy melody and the subject matter is once again romantic yearning. The song is light on lyrics and repeats verses to fill out two and one-half minutes. Brian delivered a sweet lead vocal and after take two Britz commented, "Best take, best take."[9]

Usher's "My Only Alibi" covers the familiar ground of young love anguish. Usher sang the lead in a droning monotone that soon becomes tedious. Brian and Carl sang background vocals echoing the lyrics and sang the word "human" airily behind the chorus.

A few days later, Usher, Brian, and the Beach Boys, returned to Western and recorded "Lonely Sea," "409," and a new version of "Surfin' Safari," which had first been recorded by Hite Morgan at the February 8, 1962, session at World Pacific Studio. Since then, the song's third verse had been rewritten with active verbs and exotic-sounding locales like Cerro Azul in Peru to ratchet up the safari excitement.

Brian's and Usher's most sophisticated composition at the time was "Lonely Sea." It was another relationship song. But rather than being spot-on about their feelings, they used a more mature, albeit time-honored, metaphor of the sea with its mysterious depths and endless swells to conjure up a complicated love. "What most people don't know is that Gary wrote the music including the guitar intro to 'Lonely Sea,'" recalled Marks. "Brian helped with the melody, but his main contribution was the great lyrics. Carl and I helped them work out the arrangements on our guitars."[10] The spoken bridge, which some believe ruins the song by devolving into teenage melodrama, may reveal Brian's feelings about his relationship with Judy.

Usher recalled, "That first session was me tolerating a lot of Brian and Murry because neither of them knew anything about the studio. Murry pretended he knew things he didn't. He wanted to put the vocal up front like they did in the '40s and '50s. I was hearing things altogether differently and I'm sure Brian was also. Murry had been trying for years to get something going in the music business yet hadn't succeeded. Then here we come, young kids, and all of a sudden everything is happening. He had to prove to his boys they couldn't do it without him, that he was instrumental in their success, that it was his contacts, his experiences."[11]

Britz recalled, "They had done a thing called "Surfin'" at Hite Morgan's place and they weren't too happy with Hite. They wanted to use studio three, but only the booth was finished so I put them in studio A across the hall and ran lines to studio three's booth. Murry, Audree, and I stayed in the booth and spoke to them on the intercom."[12] Britz recorded the guys on a three track tape machine, placing all the instruments on one track and using the other two tracks for vocals. He used a thirty-five dollar 545 microphone for Brian because he sounded great on it. He got an intimate, deep bass sound from Mike by having him sing very close into a U47 microphone. The others recorded background vocals on a U47.[13]

"The reason I got along with the guys is that I was like a father to them," Britz continued. "Murry was a father, but they didn't get along. Next to Brian, Dennis was my favorite because he was a very loving person. He loved his dad, even though they fought. Dennis sounded rough and nasty, but he was like a little baby, because that was just the way he did things. Carl was so young at the time, but he was a great man. I think Mike was an essential part of the Beach Boys, but without Brian I don't think he would have ever been that great for anybody."[14]

"Brian was the guiding light, producing everything even at that early stage. He knew what he wanted and was the only guy who could put all the parts together. I made the mistake once of saying, 'Gosh, Brian, that sounds terrible.' So he comes in the booth and says, 'Charlie, wait until you hear the second part.' And once you put that second part on it, it was great."[15]

Murry had his own take on how "409" was produced. "Truthfully, I'm not beating myself on the back, but knowing them as a father, I knew their voices, right? And I'm musical, my wife is, we knew how to sing on key and when they were flat and sharp and how they should sound good in a song. And we put the echo on and we got the balance. We used Telefunken mikes and we surged on their power here and there to make them sound better. When they'd run out of wind at the end of the sentence, we'd surge on the power to keep the level of their musical tone the same. Or if they were singing a phrase weak, when Mike was singing 'She's real fine, my '409' we'd surge on the part. Without their knowledge at first."[16]

Britz recalled, "I know Murry said things like 'surge, surge, surge' to me all the time. And I just turned the monitor up to make him think I was surging. His idea was to pin those needles right up on the board and I kept saying, 'Murry, you can't do that, you're not going to get anything worthwhile.' I finally just started lowering everything way down on the machines so he could look up and see those needles pegging and then I just turned the monitor up to full bore and he'd think I was surging like crazy."[17]

"I was one of the few people who liked Murry," Britz said. "I always did. Without Murry they would never have made it. He forced those kids to rehearse and sing and sing and sing. I admired him for the way he got the kids mad at him and made them conscious of what they were trying to achieve. I realize maybe he did it the wrong way, but he made them work as a team which was the way it should be."[18]

Thanks in large part to Gary Usher and Chuck Britz, the Beach Boys now had a three-song demo tape of "Surfin' Safari," "409," and "Lonely Sea," which they could shop around to record companies. They later spliced a take of "Judy" and "Surfin' Safari" from the February 8 Hite Morgan session at World Pacific onto the demo reel. The song titles on the tape box legend were written as "Surf + Safari," "Judy," "Lonely Sea," and "Four-Oh-Nine."

Usher sought advice about publishing the songs from Don Podolor at American Recording, who had published Usher's "Tomorrow" backed with "Lies" on Lan-Cet in May 1961. When Podolor declined, Usher suggested he and Brian form their own company to copyright their songs. But Brian was reluctant, concerned with what Murry would think if he formed a company with Usher and not his family, and they didn't move forward on the idea.

With the exception of "409," Usher's and Brian's songs were about being in love and the rigors of personal relationships. Usher had recently ended a strained long-distance relationship with his girlfriend in Massachusetts and was involved with Ginger who, in addition to being 3,000 miles closer, shared his love of music and making records. Brian and Judy had been dating for ten months. "He was your normal, healthy American guy," Judy recalled. "He just had a lot of energy. A lot of energy. It was like a discovery. We were treading unknown waters."[19] Like many young couples, they sought a place where they could be together without being discovered. With their homes off limits, that sanctuary was Brian's new 1960 red Chevy Impala. And perhaps the best place to park for several hours at night without raising suspicion was the drive-in, a popular Friday or Saturday night destination, although they didn't always get to see the movie. In spring 1964, Brian immortalized the youthful appeal of outdoor theaters in "Drive In," in which he recalled the danger of attendants dressed in white scouring the parking lot for couples in the throes of passion.

"Brian was the athletic, collegiate type," Judy recalled. "He never drank or smoked. I started smoking in my junior year. I had one cigarette in the morning before school. When Brian picked me up he would kiss me and tell me he could still smell the cigarette on my breath. He was disappointed in me."[20]

As inseparable as Brian and Judy were, she still enjoyed the attention of other boys and, if a boy she liked asked her out, she'd go out with him. Invariably, Brian found out and became upset and jealous. But Judy recalled that while they were dating Brian kept in touch with a girl he had known, and perhaps dated occasionally, in high school. "One day he came over to the house and he had bleached hair. In the front it was kind of red or orange. And I asked him, 'What did you do?' And he said he went over to her house and she bleached his hair. He always went back to her for a visit. I was real jealous."[21] While this uncertainty made for a roller coaster relationship, it was fertile material for a young songwriter.

The first annual Teen-Age Fair, produced by Al Burton April 13–23 at P.O.P., was billed as the world's first major exposition for youth. Network television carried live broadcasts from the park. The thirty-five cent program featured a surf lingo glossary and boasted 200 exhibits including record displays, judo and karate expositions, hot rods and racing cars, and a Miss Teen USA contest. It is likely most of the Beach Boys attended at some point, perhaps catching scheduled performances by Jan & Dean, Bobby Vee, Paul Petersen, Shelly Fabares, and Johnny Mathis.

With "Surfin'" gone from the charts, the Beach Boys personal appearances steadily declined in April and May. As Murry and Hite Morgan struggled to find them a new record deal, Brian and Usher worked on new songs, and Carl, Dennis, and David, hardly skilled live performers at this point, spent many hours practicing. "When they started out, the Beach Boys were terrible," recalled Dick Burns, Usher's friend and collaborator. "Dennis was awful on drums, Brian was awkward on stage, and only Carl was halfway decent as a musician. The thing that impressed me was their vocal ability. But they were not commercial. The only things they could sing were Four Freshmen tunes. Gary worked with them and convinced them to use today's lyrics and combine them with that sound. He nurtured them and rehearsed them. He would bring them over to my house in Burbank and tell them, 'Listen to these guys play because this is what you'll have to compete with out there.' They would sit there like little kids and say, 'Gee Gary, will we ever be like those guys?'"[22]

Around this time, Dennis was expelled for two weeks from his junior year at

Hawthorne High for punching a boy in Coach Plum's sixth period class who made a joke about his mother.[23] Dennis's high school days were already numbered and he dropped out before his senior year began in September 1962.

Driven to find the boys a recording contract on his own and ease Hite Morgan out of the picture, Murry began contacting the few people he knew in the music industry—Russ Regan at Buckeye Record Distributors and Don Podolor at American Recording.

"Murry was a great guy and we got along real well," Regan recalled. "He trusted me more than anybody. He said, 'Russ, you know everybody, get me with a major.' I sent him over to Dot Records because Buckeye was distributing Dot and I wanted it to be one of 'our' companies. I sent them 'Surfin' Safari' and Wink Martindale called me up and said, 'I love this record Russ, but Randy Wood thinks surfing music is a fad so he's taking a pass.'" In March 1962, six months after leaving *Dance Party*, Wink Martindale accepted Wood's offer of national promotion director at Dot Records, a position he held until that September when he returned to radio on KFWB. Regan continued, "And then Murry said, 'Well, what am I going to do next? What do you think of Capitol Records?' Someone had recommended Capitol to him, whether it was Richie Podolor or his brother, Don. I said, 'Capitol's a great company. I know Nick Venet there and I think this is something Nick will really go for.' And he said, 'Well, set it up.' So I set it up and Nick heard them and signed them."[24]

Don Podolor recalled, "Murry Wilson, who was my friend and called me five times a day, was shopping a demo of the Beach Boys' next record. He asked me to help him and I did my best for him and the boys. I went to all of the record companies and finally got one of the labels really interested—Dot Records. Then I was told that Randy Wood, president of Dot, had turned it down. I looked across the street, and there was the Capitol Records building. One of my friends, Nick Venet, was working at Capitol, and he was using our studio a lot."[25] According to Podolor, Venet had run up a tab with him that exceeded $1,000, a debt he would forgive if Venet agreed to meet with Murry. "I called Nick and basically forced him to take a meeting with Murry. And from that meeting the Beach Boys got signed."[26]

Murry recalled, "Mr. Morgan and I went to Dot Records and cooled our heels in the foyer, nobody would talk to us. We went to Liberty and the big shots there were too busy to see us. Finally, I asked Morgan 'What'll we do? He says, 'I don't know Murry, you're their dad and manager, rots of ruck to you.' And he says good-bye. And that cost him $2,700,000, that statement. It cost him $2,700,000."[27]

But Bruce Morgan questions the infamous "rots of ruck" quote. "As far as I know, that conversation never took place. My father would never have said that. He was not that kind of man. Furthermore, he was fully intent on producing the Beach Boys and was working very hard to advance their career. Remember, my dad and Murry had been friends. And it was common practice then to accept the signature of a parent on behalf of their juvenile children. My dad was a trusting man and after all the work he put into launching their career, it was very upsetting the way Murry treated him. My mother didn't internalize it. She was more concerned about Hite, his health, his state of mind. But I don't think my father ever got over the way Murry betrayed him."[28]

Hite and Dorinda Morgan were very good friends with Randy Wood, president of Dot Records.[29] While Wood may have passed on the Beach Boys, it is unlikely Hite and Murry sat in the foyer cooling their heels while no one would speak to them. Morgan also offered the Beach Boys to Art Laboe of Original Sound, but, according to Bruce, Laboe declined.[30] In his twenty-five year career in the music industry, none of the artists with whom Morgan worked ever accused him of turning his back on them or releasing them. Morgan walking away from the Beach Boys with a sarcastic "rots of ruck" would have been out of character. Furthermore, Murry did little over the years to foster credibility. In interviews, he used his celebrity as the Wilson patriarch to take public jabs at Morgan and Venet, and leveraged his paternity into coercing Capitol to release *The Many Moods of Murry Wilson* in 1967. He was not above revising history to suit his needs. After he was famously fired by his sons in spring 1964, Murry explained, "After their second hit, I realized the business I had built up was going to fail unless I went back to it. So I told the boys I would have to give up their management and go back to my business, otherwise I could lose our home. They begged me not to do it."[31]

For his part, Murry maintained he made first contact with Capitol Records. "I went into Capitol's offices and fortunately a man there remembered my name from a song I had written eight years before."[32] In the midst of Elvis hysteria, Ken Nelson brought rock 'n' roll to Capitol when he signed Gene Vincent and the Bluecaps in summer 1956. But Capitol was reluctant to embrace rock 'n' roll, preferring original soundtrack recordings and country artists like Sonny James, Wanda Jackson, and Buck Owens, all of whom Nelson produced during his distinguished career with Capitol. Nelson served as president of the Country Music Association for many years and was known as a modest, no-nonsense, straight-shooter.

"I received a phone call from Murry Wilson," Nelson recalled. "He said, 'Ken, you did me a favor and now I want to do one for you. My sons have formed a sensational group called the Beach Boys, and I want you to sign them.' I asked Murry what favor I had done for him and he replied, 'You recorded one of my songs.' I had no recollection of him or the song, but I asked him what kind of group it was. Murry said it was pop rock. I told Murry I ordinarily didn't produce this type of artist, but if he gave me his phone number, I would have Nick Venet, our rock 'n' roll producer, call him."[33]

"I gave Nick his phone number and told him I promised Mr. Wilson he would call him. Two weeks later, Murry called me and said Venet hadn't called. I told him I would remind him again to call. Another two weeks went by and Murry phoned again to say Venet hadn't called. I was embarrassed and assured him Venet would call."[34]

"I confronted Nick and angrily said, 'Damn it Nick. This is the third time I promised this man you would call him. Please do it!' He finally did and when Murry sent him a tape, he excitedly ran to A&R director Voyle Gilmore. He, too, was impressed and met with Murry and signed the Beach Boys."[35] In another account Nelson indicated Murry dropped off the tapes with Venet. "Nick had the stuff lying on his desk for maybe a few weeks and every so often I'd say 'When are you going to do something about that Murry Wilson thing?'"[36]

Clearly, Nelson had not recalled Murry. It is also unclear which of Murry's songs, if any, Nelson had recorded. Murry placed their meeting in 1954, the year "Two Step, Side Step" was recorded by Johnnie Lee Wills (RCA Victor), Bonnie Lou (King Records), and Suzi Miller (Decca). Although Nelson worked for Capitol, perhaps he had a hand in one of these recordings. Author Steven Gaines reported Murry had submitted a few of his songs to Nelson some years earlier, but Nelson had passed.[37]

Armed with the demo reel, Murry now realized it had been a mistake to sign an agreement with Hite Morgan in which he agreed to give the Morgans fifty percent of the Beach Boys' earnings for the next year. Murry hired attorney Averill Pasarow. The forty-three-year-old UCLA Law School graduate was a contract law expert. On April 6, he spoke about record industry contracts at the 8th Annual Institute on Legal Aspects of the Entertainment Industry co-sponsored by the USC Law School and the Beverly Hills Bar Association.[38] Ironically, Pasarow was also representing Candix in its lawsuit against Saraceno and others.

Pasarow recalled, "In April 1962, Murry Wilson hired me to represent the Beach Boys in order to dissolve any dealings, agreements, or understandings the Beach Boys had with Hite Morgan. I became aware that all of the Beach Boys were minors at the time of the recordings, and that any deal had never been approved by the Superior Court."[39]

On April 17, 1962, Pasarow sent a letter to Candix attorney Bruce Wolfson, and copied Al Schlesinger, attorney for Hite Morgan, in which he advised that Murry Wilson's March 29 Letter of Intent and Agreement was not a legally binding contract because, at the time of the recordings, the Boys were minors. He further advised that Candix still had not obtained a mechanical license for "Surfin'" and the purported December 5, 1961, lease agreement between Candix and Morgan was invalid and not binding on the Beach Boys.[40]

Pasarow later claimed he obtained an order from the Los Angeles Superior Court terminating any agreement the Beach Boys had with the Morgans. However, the Court had no record that a petition for such an order was ever filed, served, or adjudicated.[41]

Murry received a letter from Averill Pasarow, dated April 18, 1962, conveying a check from Hite Morgan for $990 drawn on Morgan's account with United California Bank on Sunset Boulevard in Los Angeles. Pasarow wrote, "This represents payment of three cents per record on 33,000 sold from Candix No. 301." On the check, Morgan tabulated a total of 39,790 copies from which 6,790 copies were withheld, leaving a balance of 33,000 copies on which he paid three cents per copy ($0.03 × 33,000) or $990.

But to Murry, already distrustful of the record industry, $990 seemed low. Audree recalled, "He always said they got cheated because the record went to number seventy-five nationally and was a big hit on the West Coast."[42]

Al echoed that sentiment. "The single was on two labels, X and Candix Records, which must have been the same label when you think about it, just two different ways to steal money. They only paid us $900 in royalties for the whole thing, so they definitely buried a little money. They probably paid us on the one label, the one that sold the $900 worth, and kept the other label's worth somewhere else in a vault. Murry added $100 to the check to make it an even $1,000 so we could each get $200. That was very nice of him."[43] Actually, Murry added ten dollars to bring the check up to $1,000. This is the only known or acknowledged payment the band received for "Surfin'."

But were they cheated? Should they have received more money? To answer these questions, let's examine how the revenue stream from the sale of a 45 rpm record worked. (See Appendix 4, "Surfin'" Revenue and Expense Stream, and Production Flow.)

In late 1961, the suggested retail list price (SRLP) of a 45 rpm record was ninety-eight cents. The price a customer actually paid, however, depended on where it was purchased. In general, mom and pop stores charged the SRLP, but larger retailers and department stores flexed their purchasing power to wage price wars and charged sixty-six to seventy-four cents. Sam Goody, a New York music retailer, stunned the industry and pressured competitors by lowering its price to fifty-six cents, a loss leader at four cents lower than cost.

AVERILL C. PASAROW
ATTORNEY AT LAW
EQUITABLE BUILDING
6253 HOLLYWOOD BOULEVARD
HOLLYWOOD 28
HOLLYWOOD 4 2165

April 18, 1962

Mr. Murry Wilson
3701 West 119th Street
Hawthorne, California

Dear Mr. Wilson:

I am enclosing your check which was received from
Mr. Hite Morgan in the sum of $990.00.

This represents payment of three cents per record
on 33,000 sold from Candix No. 301.

Sincerely yours,

[signature]
Averill C. Pasarow

ACP:cl
Enclosure

[handwritten: "SURFIN" BEACH BOYS FIRST ROYALTY CHECK]

[check image: United California Bank, Sunset and Alvarado Office, 2035 Sunset Boulevard, Los Angeles, California. Pay to the order of Murry Wilson, Mgr. $990.00. Nine Hundred Ninty & no/100 Dollars. Hite B. Morgan, 2511 Mayberry Street, Los Angeles 26, Calif. Signed Hite B. Morgan]

On April 18, 1962, Averill C. Pasarow, the Beach Boys' recently hired attorney, sent Murry Wilson a check for $990 which Pasarow had received from Hite B. Morgan as payment for the songwriters' royalty on the sale of 33,000 copies of "Surfin'" on Candix 301. This is the Beach Boys' first royalty check (with appreciation to Ted Owen, the Fame Bureau, Jim Mastronardi, and Kerry A. Mullaney).

Based on radio play, chart position, and customer requests, a store owner ordered copies of a new record on credit from the distributor handling the record company releasing the song. The distributor, in turn, ordered records on consignment from the pressing plant with which the record company had contracted. To encourage a distributor to stock a record by a new artist, many independent record companies offered free copies with each order as an incentive or rebate. For instance, for every 100 copies ordered a distributor might receive 110 copies, allowing the distributor to sell the ten free copies and keep the proceeds. The distributor had ninety days to pay the record company or return any unsold records. Most store owners, however, could not return unsold records and continued to sell them, often at a reduced price. The distributor sent copies of their orders to the record company, but the company often did not receive an accurate accounting of how many records were actually sold.

A customer purchased the record and paid the store owner between sixty-six and ninety-eight cents. After about three months, when the record was off the charts and sales had trickled, the store owner squared up with the distributor, paying sixty cents for each record ordered. The distributor made nine cents, its standard fifteen percent fee, and kept one additional cent to cover postage as a box of twenty-five records costs twenty-five cents to mail to a store. The distributor paid the record company the remaining fifty cents from which the record company paid its expenses, including the cost for an original recording or the lease/purchase of a master recording, acetates and metal works, pressing plant, artist royalty (from which the artist paid the producer), publisher's mechanical royalty (from which the publisher paid the songwriter), and promotion.

Hence, Candix should have been paid sixty cents by Buckeye Record Distributors for each record sold. Candix should have paid Hite Morgan for the lease/purchase of the "Surfin'" master, the Beach Boys an artist royalty from which they should have paid Morgan a producer fee, and Morgan a mechanical royalty which he should have split with Brian and Mike for their songwriter royalty. Brian and Mike (songwriters) and Morgan (publisher) should have eventually received performance royalties from BMI, the performing rights organization, for the song being played (performed) on radio.

That is how Candix, Morgan, and the Beach Boys should have been paid. And it would have been straightforward if "Surfin'" had been released only on Candix 331 and distributed only by Buckeye Record Distributors. But the accounting became obfuscated by the song's subsequent lease to Pacific Record Distributors, its pressing on the X Records subsidiary, its pressing on the Era-distributed Candix 301, and the involvement of four different distributors—Buckeye Record Distributors, Pacific Record Distributors, Alco Research and Engineering, and Era Record Sales. The situation was further complicated because neither Bob Dix nor Bob Field had obtained a mechanical license from Morgan.

In a business in which the product was sold on credit, it took three months or more before the record company received its first quarterly sales report and payment. The distributor was often blamed for lagging behind with payments, but the distributor had to wait for store owners to settle their accounts. This delay trickled down to the artist, songwriter, and publisher, who were not paid until the distributor paid the record company.

Morgan had convened a meeting February 9, 1962, with all interested parties, at which it was agreed to amend the December 15, 1961, lease between Candix and Pacific, whose terms were still in effect in early January 1962 when Herb Newman agreed to finance a pressing of "Surfin'" for release on Candix 301 and distribution by his Era Record Sales.

The original lease stipulated that Candix receive sixteen cents for every record sold. The amended lease reduced it to ten cents with the remaining six cents going to Morgan. Curiously, six cents was the figure specified in the purported lease between Morgan and Candix dated December 5, 1961, which Bruce Morgan later disputed. It would appear Candix considered the six cents to cover everything—lease/purchase of the master, artist royalty, and mechanical royalty.[44]

As to how much the Beach Boys should have been paid, well, that depends on how many copies of "Surfin'" were sold.

Documents pertaining to sales figures for "Surfin'" on Candix 331 and X Records 301 have not survived. But their sales can be reasonably estimated based on standard press runs and the song's chart success. Bob Dix pressed about 12,000 copies on Candix 331 and most likely a comparable number on X Records 301, let's say 10,000 copies. A document exists referencing the sale of 33,000 copies of "Surfin'" on the Era-distributed Candix 301.[45] Hence, "Surfin'" sold an estimated 55,000 copies initially.

The initial pressing on Candix 331 and subsequent pressing on X Records 301 were most likely never properly accounted. And, without a mechanical license, Morgan would not have received his publisher royalty, and Brian and Mike would not have received their songwriter royalty. It is unclear what happened to the money Candix should have received from Buckeye Record Distributors for sales of "Surfin'" on Candix 331 and from Alco Research and Engineering for sales of "Surfin'" on X Records 301. Only the 33,000 copies of "Surfin'" on Candix 301 distributed by Era Record Sales figured into the royalty calculations.

Candix should have received ten cents for each of the 33,000 records sold ($.10 × 33,000) or $3,300. But on June 12, 1962, Bob Dix directed his attorney, Bruce Wolfson, to write Bob Field of Pacific Record Distributors advising that Candix had thus far only received six cents per record ($1,980) and was still owed four cents per record ($1,320), which Bob Dix later maintained he never received.

In accordance with the terms of the amended lease, whose terms may have been derived from the purported lease of December 5, 1961, Morgan received six cents for each of the 33,000 records, or $1,980, which he split with the band, sending Murry a check for $990. Morgan's statutory mechanical royalty of two cents was split with Brian and Mike for their songwriter royalty (0.02 × 33,000 ÷ 2) or $330. The band's artist royalty was four percent of the SRLP of ninety percent of all records sold (0.04 × $0.98 × 0.90 × 33,000) or $1,164.24. [*Note*: The ninety percent figure was based on an expected ten percent breakage rate for which record companies did not pay recording artists.]

Murry was correct. The band was owed more than $990. On the sale of 33,000 copies, they should have been paid an artist royalty of $1,164.24 plus a songwriter royalty of $330, or $1,494.24. On the sale of the estimated 55,000 copies, they should have been paid an artist royalty of $1,940.40 plus a songwriter royalty of $550, or $2,490.40. The Beach Boys' lost revenue came from unaccounted sales of Candix 331 and X Records 301. It is unknown, however, whether Candix ever received the appropriate funds from the record distributors (Buckeye and Alco) from which to pay the artist royalty.

Given the circumstances, Morgan appears to have paid the Beach Boys fairly. He struck a balance paying Brian and Mike their songwriter royalty and the band an artist royalty, while trying to recoup some of the money owed him for the lease/purchase of the master, his producer fee, and the mechanical royalty he should have received for Candix 331 and X Records 301. Morgan paid the Beach Boys based on the only accounting he could obtain from Candix, Buckeye, Pacific, Alco, and Era.

The Beach Boys played Newport Harbor High School stadium in Newport Beach at

7:00 p.m. on April 18 as part of the annual Bal-Week celebration during which thousands of teenagers descended on nearby Balboa for Easter week vacation. The handbill for the show beckoned teenagers to the "Come as you are—Stomp," and listed the Belairs, the Beach Boys, the Vibrants, the Fabulous Biscaines, and Dodie and Dee Dee. Paul Johnson recalled, "I believe that was the night we were on our way to the gig and got into a car accident. I'm pretty sure the Belairs had to bail on that gig."[46]

The celebration continued as the band played Easter Week Stomp at Redondo Union High School auditorium April 20 and 21. The stomp also featured the Belairs, the Vibrants, and Dodie and Dee Dee. Originally scheduled at Mira Costa High School, a poster for the shows has the word "Redondo" pasted over "Mira Costa." The poster and a corrected 4" × 5" handbill printed after the venue change noted the Beach Boys' latest hits were "Surfin'" and "Surfer Girl," which they had added to their live set and were considering as a follow-up single.

Nick Venet told the story of how he met Murry Wilson many times, including five accounts given under oath during thirty-two years of various legal proceedings. Each of the five accounts Venet gave under oath differed:

• February 1965. Murry called Ken Nelson. Nelson asked Venet to call Murry. Venet couldn't recall whether he called Murry or Murry called him but, when they spoke, Murry told him he could not meet for two weeks.[47]

• January 1992. Hite Morgan called Venet and asked him to call Brian. Venet called Brian, left a message, and Murry called him back.[48]

• March 1992. Russ Regan called Venet and suggested he call Morgan and buy the "Surfin'" master for release on Capitol. Venet called Morgan, who told him he was trying to get the Beach Boys a deal on his own and that, if he decided to sell the master, he would call Ken Nelson whom he knew. A short time later, Nelson called Venet and told him Morgan had called and Venet should call Morgan back. As in the January 1992 account, Venet called Morgan and Morgan asked him to call Brian. Venet called Brian, left a message, and Murry called him back.[49]

• July 1995. Murry called Venet directly.

• October 1997. Regan arranged for Venet to meet Murry.

When they finally spoke, Venet told Murry he couldn't meet with him for two weeks because he was going to Nashville on business. Contrary to Venet's February 1965 account, it is unlikely it was Murry who couldn't meet for two weeks. Venet likely adjusted the story to avoid mentioning he procrastinated and had not called Murry for several weeks. There were two pieces of Capitol business that could have taken Venet out of town or, specifically, to Nashville in late April and early May 1962. First, the Lettermen were on a two-week tour of eight Eastern markets to promote their new album *Once Upon a Time* and Venet may have accompanied them on these dates. Second, Capitol held a gala party at the Executive Club in Nashville on May 10 to celebrate the groundbreaking ceremonies for the new Capitol Records Building to be constructed there on 16th Avenue South.[50] Venet may have flown to Nashville to make advance arrangements for Joe Csida, Capitol's Eastern division vice president in charge of singles, who presided at the event.

In anticipation of his meeting with Venet, Murry had the Beach Boys record an a cappella version of Bobby Troup's "Their Hearts Were Full of Spring," opting to omit the wordless choral introduction. This beautiful ballad about the eternal nature of love had been recorded by Jimmie Rodgers (1957), the Lettermen (1960), and the Four Freshmen (1961). "They sang Four Freshmen songs almost like the Four Freshmen, except they had a sweeter, younger sound," Murry boasted.[51] The Beach Boys version was a prime example of Brian's emerging talent as a vocal arranger.

Mike recalled, "When we were learning an arrangement of a song, first of all Brian had lived with it for a while, and he'd sit at the piano and he would deal all the different parts. He would teach me a bass part. He would sing the melody or else the high falsetto part. But he would have all the parts in his mind. I mean intricate parts, too. Like when we learned 'Their Hearts Were Full of Spring' by the Four Freshmen, that was their arrangement. And he had all the parts in his head. And they were hard parts. They were moving all over the place. It was all you could do to learn your one part, but he'd have four of them in his head. That always kind of blew my mind that Brian had that ability to hear all those parts simultaneously and be able to deal them to the different individuals who could handle that range."[52]

Lambert noted the recording was "understandably rough, here and there, plagued by imperfections in pitch accuracy, tuning, and blend. But the simple fact that this group of mostly teenagers would even attempt such a performance shows remarkable skill and ambition."[53] Murry spliced "Hearts" onto the April demo tape and added a personal message: "That was a sample of the Beach Boys, Nick." And then, as if to dispel any doubt for whom the message was intended, added "Venet." Murry drove to the Capitol Tower and dropped off a box containing the April demos recorded by Chuck Britz at Western and the February 8 demos recorded by Hite Morgan at World Pacific. He arranged to have the box placed on Venet's desk for him to listen to when he returned from Nashville.

Nikolas Kostantinos Zahahoulai Demetrius Venetoulis was born December 3, 1937, in Baltimore, Maryland. He was the second of four children born to Flora Baouris and Kostantinos Venetoulis—who had emigrated from Rhodes, Greece, married in June 1931, and settled in the Highlandtown section of East Baltimore, a working-class neighborhood with a large Greek population. After decades of European immigration, American cities were ethnic enclaves linked together by their dream for a better life. One generation fought to retain its cultural heritage as the next generation struggled for assimilation. For Kostantinos and Flora, three sons and a daughter came in quick succession—Theodore, Nikolas, Seva, and Kathleen. Although their parents only spoke Greek at home, the children learned English in school and desperately wanted to be American.

During the Second World War, Kostantinos bought a little restaurant called Nick's on the corner of Newkirk and Eastern Avenue, and moved his family into the apartment on the second floor. In the late 1940s, he bought Gustav's Sandwich Shop on Lombard Street and adopted the nickname Gus. Ten-year-old Nick was tasked with picking records for the jukebox that would garner the most plays and, hence, the most profit. Soon he was reading *Billboard* every week and advising other jukebox operators which records they should buy.

In 1952, Nick entered Towson High School near Baltimore and worked summers at Camp Puh'Tok (an Indian word for "in the pines") in Monkton, Maryland, north of Baltimore, that hosted five hundred boys ages five to sixteen every summer, teaching them leadership, teamwork, spirituality, American heritage, and an appreciation of Nature. Founded in 1942 by Brigadier Douglas G. Eldredge, a Salvation Army officer, the 400-acre camp had an American Indian and Old West theme. Nick tended the horses and loved to entertain, staging shows dressed as an Indian, playing banjo, making people laugh, and acting the clown.

At Towson High he was active in student government and the drama club. He graduated in June 1956 and beneath his senior portrait in the yearbook was noted: "Greek— talent for the dramatic and artistic; makes the banjo hum; crazy about sports, cars, and pony tails."

Friends at Camp Puh'Tok recalled that after graduation Nick packed his Indian costume and headed to Hollywood in search of an acting career. He landed minor roles that year in the television series *Broken Arrow* and *Telephone Time*.

Venet later claimed a number of accomplishments in the mid to late 1950s, but it is a challenge to make the timetable work. He worked his entire adult life in the youth-oriented music industry in which people often changed their age, altered their biography, and inflated their achievements. In a sworn deposition, he evaded answering how old he was and said he dropped out of school in eighth grade. He said he worked with Lou Rawls, Sam Cooke, and the Pilgrim Travelers, staging gospel music tent revivals throughout the South when he was sixteen. He said he was in Shreveport, Louisiana, when he was sixteen and organized the recording session for "Susie-Q" by Dale Hawkins, for which he did not receive credit. He recalled the drive to Chicago in which the master was sold to Leonard Chess for $500. However, when "Susie-Q" (b/w "Don't Treat Me This Way," Checker 863, #7 R&B, #27 Pop) was released in May 1957, Venet was nineteen.[54] Around this time, he said he shared a small office with Bobby Darin in the famed Brill Building on Broadway in New York. "We met on the elevator and just hit it off," he recalled. "We rented a broom closet and turned it into an office just so we could put our name on the door. Bobby was writing songs and the term producer wasn't really being used yet."[55]

To the people who knew him best, Venet was charming, charismatic, energetic, talented, and gregarious. He loved to laugh and was a loyal friend. In a career spanning forty years in the music industry, the list of artists he worked with reads like a Who's Who in Music. He collected more than his share of stories that he freely, and comically, built upon. To his friends and family it was just Nick being Nick. The stories were so entertaining that, even if you suspected they were embellished, you enjoyed them all the same. Perhaps more so.

In spring 1957, Venet began working in and around the LA music scene. With his extroverted personality, he had no problems making friends with lots of people in the industry including songwriter and music publisher Jack Hoffman who was always recording demos and shopping them around to record companies. Hoffman had written "Dreamy Eyes," the Four Preps' debut (Capitol 3576, October 1956), and "Ooh-Whee Marie," Dick Dale's debut (Del-Tone 5012, May 1958). Once, when a scheduled vocalist didn't show, Hoffman persuaded Venet to sing on the tracks and later sold the demos to RCA Victor for $500.[56]

The June 24, 1957, *Billboard* reported RCA Victor had signed rockabilly artist Nick Venet and in November the label released "Flippin'," a four-song extended play (EP) single with "Oh Baby," "Kinda Slow," "Readin', Writin', N' 'Rithmetic," and "Stop (What You're Doin' to Me)." Venet wrote "Kinda Slow" and on "Oh Baby" teamed with his brother Seva, who had Americanized his name to Steve Venet and followed Nick to LA to pursue a career in the music industry. The picture sleeve showed him surrounded by seven young women playing guitars and noted, "Nick sings with unrestrained vitality of the joys and wonders of this remarkable teen-age world."

"Flippin'" debuted on WCAO in Baltimore at #38 on November 18, 1957, and RCA Victor placed a half-page ad for it in *Billboard*, December 2, 1957. That Christmas, Venet returned home to Baltimore where Mayor Tommy D'Alesandro, Jr., proclaimed it Nick Venet Day. His career took a hit when the February 8, 1958, *Los Angeles Times* panned "Flippin'."[57] Later that month, Lew Chudd, president of Imperial Records, purchased his RCA contract. He was in good company as Imperial was then home to Fats Domino for eight years and Chudd had recently bought Ricky Nelson's contract from Verve Records. In June 1958, Venet released "Love in Be-Bop Time" (Imperial 5522), co-written by Jimmie Haskell and best known for its rockabilly guitar solo by Joe Maphis. Despite a solid effort, sales were poor and Chudd passed on a follow-up. "Baby Doll" and "Darlin' Sue," recorded at his Imperial session, remain unreleased.

In summer 1958, Venet played an uncredited delinquent in the 20th Century–Fox film *Rally 'Round the Flag, Boys*, a satirical comedy starring Paul Newman, Joanne Woodward,

Nikolas Kostantinos Zahahoulai Demetrius Venetoulis became Nick Venet (standing, left) when he launched a singing career in LA in 1957. He returned home to Baltimore in November 1957 where Mayor Thomas D'Alesandro, Jr. (seated) proclaimed it Nick Venet Day in recognition of his first record, a four-song extended play single called "Flippin'," a copy of which the young lady holds. (Left to right, Major Douglas Eldredge, Nick Venet, unidentified man, Tom Kuhl, unidentified man, football queen) (courtesy Ted Venetoulis and Nik Venet, Jr.).

Joan Collins, and Tuesday Weld. With his singing career stalled, he began writing songs and placing them with other artists. In July 1958, he wrote "Love Is a Funny Little Game" for the Vogues on Randy Wood's Dot Records (Dot 15798).

In June 1959, he wrote two songs for the soundtrack of American International Pictures' *Ghost of Dragstrip Hollow*. "Charge" (b/w "Geronimo," American International 536) were produced by Kim Fowley and performed by the Renegades, a studio band that consisted of Richie Podolor, Kim Fowley, Bruce Johnston, Sandy Nelson, and Venet. Both tunes, perhaps inspired by his days at Camp Puh'Tok, were frantic instrumentals enhanced with war-whoops, gunshots, and horse's hoof beats. Podolor later took exception to Venet's writing credits. "I wrote 'Geronimo' and 'Charge,' but they were taken away from me. It was all my stuff, but between Nick Venet, Kim Fowley, and Bruce Johnston, I had no chance. It was cut in my studio, I did all the guitars. I wrote it and Nick Venet walked away with the credit."[58]

In early October 1959, Venet began working for Richard Bock, a respected producer of West Coast jazz, at World Pacific Records, and charged with "building new singles artists" and "buy[ing] masters for World Pacific release."[59] Venet recorded monologuist Lord Buckley, Don Sargent ("St. James Infirmary"), the Starlings ("That's Me"), and Stan Ross ("Please Don't Tease"), and signed the Les McCann Trio. He also formed his own music publishing firms, Ridge Music (ASCAP) and Niven Music (BMI).

In late 1959, Venet was involved in what became one of the most interesting records of the era, "Moon Dawg!" (b/w "LSD-25," World Pacific X815) recorded by the Gamblers, a group of LA musicians Venet assembled, at American Recording and Radio Recorders. The title was inspired by Alan Freed's on-air nickname 'Moondog' and the character 'Moon-doggie' from *Gidget*. Venet arranged for its release on World Pacific Records and received label credit for arranging and directing the session, and the publishing went to his Niven Music. He also did the distinctive wolf howl on the record. "Moon Dawg!" was written by Derrick J. ("Derry") Weaver, a nineteen-year-old Canadian working in LA as a session guitarist. Weaver recalled, "Nicky didn't arrange anything except the deal with World Pacific in exchange for the publishing. We'll let him have that one. He also did the dog howl. Great job! We were all gathered around the mike singing and Nick howled. Great overdub. One take."[60] "Moon Dawg!" was released in February 1960. It failed to chart nationally, but reached #12 on KFWB that July.

In June 1960, Venet wrote "Lost and Found" with Russ Regan and recorded it for Jack Hoffman's Enith International label, but it failed to chart. In August, while still employed at World Pacific, Venet signed a non-exclusive arrangement as a producer for Liberty Records and placed his "Dream Girl" on the flip of "Wishing Well" by Garry Miles and the Statues.

On October 16, 1960, Venet joined Capitol Records as staff producer and talent scout. Capitol hoped the addition of the twenty-two-year-old Venet to its aging A&R department would help the label capture a larger share of the lucrative youth segment of the pop market. The Four Freshmen, the Four Preps, and the Kingston Trio, were all experiencing a downturn in sales and Capitol needed artists that could appeal to teens and young adults. "Most of Capitol's acts were middle-of-the-road," recalled Roger Christian. "There was a lot of Sue Rainey, Nancy Wilson, Nat King Cole, Stan Kenton, the Four Freshmen, Billy May. There wasn't a lot of youth product there until 1961 when the Lettermen came in."[61]

In February 1961, the Lettermen signed with Capitol and Venet was assigned as their staff producer. Over the years it became a central part of Venet's professional biography that he found the Lettermen and signed them to Capitol. But the story is more involved than that. The Lettermen were Tony Butala, Jim Pike, and Bob Engemann. Bob's brother, Karl Engemann, had been at Warner Brothers when the trio signed with that label in late 1959. But after two failed singles in 1960, Warner Brothers dropped them. When Karl joined Capitol in late 1960, he facilitated the Lettermen signing with the label.

On February 23, 1961, Venet accompanied the Lettermen into the Tower for their first recording session and that June released "The Way You Look Tonight" (b/w "That's My Desire," Capitol 4586), which reached #13 on the Hot 100 and #3 on the Adult Contemporary chart. Capitol had found a new group to assume the vocal harmony mantle and the Lettermen became a key part of the company's effort to garner a larger share of the youth market.

In spring 1961, Capitol divided its A&R department into albums and singles, and Venet began reporting to singles director Voyle Gilmore. Meanwhile, Venet produced sessions for the Mavricks, the Derringers, and the Four Coquettes, and instrumental covers by the Hollyridge Strings, but had very little chart success. He spent many evenings in night clubs socializing with music industry friends and keeping an ear out for new talent. Kim Fowley helped him gauge the interests of white suburban teens. "He took me out to a soda fountain place in Pacific Palisades and said we were going to watch the kids who came in and listen to the records they played on the jukebox," Venet recalled.[62]

In early July, Venet heard a singer at Pandora's Box, a coffee house at 8118 Sunset Boulevard on an island in the middle of an intersection diagonal from the legendary Schwab's Pharmacy and across from where the notorious Garden of Allah had been. Lou Rawls was working for $10 a night and all the pizza he could eat. Venet signed him and "That Lucky Old Sun" (b/w "In My Heart," Capitol 4622) was released that September. On October 18, Venet produced Gene Vincent's last Capitol session as the Dave Burgess band backed him up on "Lucky Star" (b/w "Baby Don't Believe Him," Capitol 4665).

In the first four months of 1962, Venet produced follow-up singles for the Lettermen, Lou Rawls, the 4 Cal-Quettes, and northern soul singles for "Good Rockin'" Sam Taylor, Jr. and Carl "Little Rev" Lattimore. He capitalized on the stomp craze by writing "Bug Stompin' (Stomp That Roach)" (b/w "The Big Stomp," Capitol 4692) with arranger Jimmie Haskell, credited to a fictional group called the Barnstormers. He wrote and produced "Song of Greece," credited as Nickolas Venetoulis, which Haskell recorded with the Hollywridge Strings as the flip to "It Happened in Athens," the title track of the 20th Century–Fox film that June. He was charged with revitalizing the career of twenty-two-year-old Kathy Linden, known for her "little girl" vocals on love songs like "Billy," her last Top Ten from 1958. Venet produced four singles for Linden, but they failed to generate much excitement and Capitol dropped her. He jumped on the surf craze, copyrighting "Easy Surf," "Rhodes Surfer," "Earl's Shore Break," and "Three Surfer Boys."

On April 7, the Lettermen taped their first appearance on *The Ed Sullivan Show* for an episode that aired June 10. They sang "How Is Julie?," their fourth Capitol single from their sophomore album *Once Upon a Time* produced by Venet and released April 23. The single's B side, "Turn Around, Look at Me," was a #62 hit in October 1961 for its writer, Glen Campbell, who had just signed with Capitol and whose first session would be produced by Venet on May 9. With a new single and album, the Lettermen embarked on a two-week promotional tour of eight East Coast cities.

When Venet finally called Murry, they arranged to meet after Venet returned from a two-week business trip. While Venet was out of town, Murry delivered a box of tapes to the Capitol Tower.

Venet recalled the box contained multiple reels of tapes with a total of twelve to sixteen songs. If this is true, it would have included the band's entire recorded output to this point—"Surfin'," "Luau," "Lavender," "Surfin' Safari" (World Pacific), "Surfer Girl," "Judy," "Karate," "Barbie," "What Is a Young Girl Made Of?," "Surfin' Safari" (Western), "409," "Lonely Sea," "Their Hearts Were Full of Spring," and possibly the four songs Brian and Usher recorded at the first Western session that April.

The boys' chance at signing with a major record company now sat in a box on Nick Venet's desk. The tapes were about to change their lives.

They would also transform, more than once, Venet's future with Capitol Records.

15

A Capitol Contract
(May–June 1962)

The Beach Boys played a stomp from 8:00 p.m. to midnight on May 4 at the Inglewood Women's Club at 325 North Hillcrest Boulevard in Inglewood. Gary Hallmark, a neighbor of the Wilsons, remembered, "When I went into the Service in 1961, I heard about a group in Southern California called the Beach Boys. I was in Fort Riley, Kansas, until April 1962. I came home on leave before going to Germany and the boys were playing a local women's club. Jo Ann Marks and Audree Wilson were taking money at the door. They told me that because I was a soldier at home on leave I could go in for free. When I heard them I thought it was a good thing I got in free. Mike Love was playing the saxophone and something seemed wrong. I played clarinet and told him if he wanted to look right, and have it appear he knew what he was doing, to turn it around and cover his bottom teeth with his lip and play it. The first few times he was just making a tooting sound to go with the music, but he learned to play it."[1]

A 5" × 8" handbill for the event proclaimed "Let's Stomp All Nite with the Beach Boys, Popular Recording Artists" and offered "free soft drinks for thirsty stompers." The handbill mentioned "Surfin'" as their "latest hit record" although it had dropped off the chart six weeks earlier. And even though they were without a record label and several record companies had already turned them down, the handbill, in a bit of foreshadowing, promised "Newest Hit to Come."

Murry, Brian, and Usher met with Venet in his office on the twelfth floor of the Capitol Tower on or about May 7, 1962. Venet often reported he heard "Surfin' Safari" for the first time at this meeting, decided within seconds it was a number one record, started jumping up and down unable to contain his enthusiasm, and wanted to buy it immediately. Usher, who, perhaps, remained the most objective about what transpired, recalled it differently.

"Murry gave the masters to Ken [Nelson] who suggested he give them to Nick Venet and that's where the positive response came from," Usher recalled. "Nick called and said Capitol wanted to see us and so we went up to see him. Nick did not hear the records and decide to buy them on the spot. He listened to them, slept on it, and then waited a few days before calling back with the news he liked them. I remember those three or four days after we left the masters with him because we were sitting on pins and needles the entire time. Then the phone call came and we went crazy. That's when Murry stepped in and wanted to run the whole show. It was Murry, Brian, and I who went up to meet with Nick, who was really 'Mr. Hollywood' with the stylized hair, the fancy shirts, the French cuffs, the whole shot. He looked quite impressive. This was Capitol Records, the big time."[2]

Venet's retelling of what transpired at the meeting may have been best recalled in February 1965, three years after the event. "Murry came to Capitol with a tape containing '409,' 'Lonely Sea,' and 'Surfin' Safari.' He brought along some of his own songs, but I wasn't interested in hearing them. He showed me $1,000 in cash which he stated was all he had received from Candix as an advance against royalties. He complained about the treatment he received from Candix and said he wanted the boys to be in good hands with a good company. He did not care what they were paid. He stated he was only the parent of the boys, or some of them, was not their manager, and that he was bowing out of the picture."[3]

"I told them I wanted to play the recordings for Voyle Gilmore, the A&R director to whom I reported. I played the masters for Voyle, who said Capitol should purchase them and authorized me to offer the group $300. [*Note*: In his other accounts, Venet said Murry wanted $300 to break even with his investment in the group and that Gilmore authorized the unlikely sum of $50,000.[4]] I told the group they had a deal. Murry said he did not want any-

An 8" × 5" handbill for the Beach Boys appearance at the Inglewood Women's Club on May 4, 1962.

thing for himself, but we agreed to pay him a five-percent royalty for the master. This verbal agreement is what is typically known as a 'master purchase deal.' It is Capitol's custom to obtain an artist contract with the recording group where there is a 'master purchase deal.' I explained this to Murry and that it would be necessary to have court approval of Capitol's contract with the Beach Boys because they were minors. I also explained that certain monies would be impounded and set up in a trust fund. We discussed the songs, who wrote them, who produced them, how many people were in the group, and their ages. I was trying to find out if Brian and Murry owned the copyrights and were the publishers."[5]

Although Venet later claimed that he recommended Brian retain the music publishing of his songs, Usher maintained Venet was intent on acquiring those rights for Capitol's Beechwood Music and that Murry was willing to sign them over. Usher interjected that he and Brian had their own music publishing company. They had discussed doing this but hadn't gotten around to it. A few tense seconds elapsed as Venet pondered his next move. Finally, he accepted those terms, shook hands, and said he'd be back in touch after Capitol's legal department drew up the contract. Usher's critical preemptive strike for the music publishing resulted in millions of dollars for the Wilson family.[6]

"We left Nick's office and got into the elevator and to my surprise I thought Murry was going to crucify me on the spot," Usher recalled. "He put his nose about an inch from mine and thundered, 'Do you realize Gary, do you realize what you just did? Do you realize that you just told a lie! Son, we don't have a publishing company.' I replied, or at least I tried to, 'But you don't understand, Brian and I are going to form our own publishing company.' At that point Murry exploded, 'You are going to do what? Do you mean you and Brian are going to cut out Carl and Dennis, not give them a cent, and forget about me! You lie to Capitol Records, put us in a position of perjury. We should have given them the publishing. They might not have signed us.' He just went on and on and on. I thought Brian was going to die of humiliation (we were still in the elevator). I didn't know what to say. I was only looking out for our benefit."[7]

Joe Saraceno recalled Karl Engemann called him about signing the Beach Boys to Capitol and that Saraceno released them from Candix. "The group went on, but never knew what I had done for them," Saraceno recalled. "Brian knew later on, but the rest of them always had sort of a bad feeling toward me. If I had just stayed put, they would have been tied to a contract for five years."[8] By May 1962, Saraceno had been gone from Candix for nearly five months. Candix did not have the Beach Boys under contract. If Bob Dix had the foresight to sign a contract with the group and have it approved by the Los Angeles Superior Court, Candix would have been able to negotiate a lucrative deal for the sale of the Beach Boys to Capitol.

Al Coury, Capitol's national promotion manager at the time, recalled it wasn't "Surfin' Safari" that caught Venet's attention. "Nick was very interested in '409,' the hot rod side. He didn't care too much about the surfing stuff or the other music that was in the content. He played the four sides for Voyle Gilmore and said to him, 'I want to buy these records because I want '409.' The price was very reasonable and Gilmore authorized him to buy the records."[9]

Venet was left with four boxes of tapes that had somewhere between twelve and sixteen songs. "I had to edit the tapes and re-master them, making enhanced copies of all of the recordings to determine which, if any, could be brought up to a level of quality sufficient to be utilized by Capitol. Some were master quality and some were clearly demos."[10] According to Venet, he called Hite Morgan and was told that some of the reels might have been mislabeled. Venet further recalled Morgan said he was only interested in the music publishing under his Guild Music and expressed the opinion the group would never be successful. Venet said that Morgan told him he was glad to "get rid of the clutter" that the Beach Boys' tapes had been to him and was pleased with the prospect of not having to deal with Murry Wilson any further. Venet later maintained Murry neglected to tell him Morgan owned the copyright on "Surfin' Safari," "Surfer Girl," "Judy," and "Karate."[11]

In October 1965, Murry recalled an intriguing scenario. "After turn downs from four companies, Morgan released them and I called Ken Nelson at Capitol and set up an audition. We played a couple of tapes and although there was nothing they wanted, they were interested to hear more. So we went back to Western Recording where the boys do all their recording, and recorded 'Surfin' Safari,' 'Lonely Sea,' and '409' in three hours and twenty minutes."[12] The May 22, 1962, *Inglewood Daily News* ran a brief article about the band noting they had been "turned down by most of the recording companies who said they liked them, but to come back when they had better material."[13] Essentially, Murry indicated Nelson passed on the four demos recorded February 8 at World Pacific, but left the door open for them to "come back when they had better material," which they did after the Western session. But none of the other principals involved, Nelson, Venet, Usher, or Brian, ever hinted at that scenario. Murry's comment in 1965 appeared two months after Morgan filed a lawsuit against Capitol for copyright infringement for the improper use of "Surfin'," "Surfin' Safari," and "Surfer Girl."

On May 8, 1962, Venet sent a memorandum to F.M Scott III, director of business affairs, requesting a contract be prepared for the Beach Boys. After graduating Stanford University, Scott worked in Capitol's A&R department for thirteen years and was promoted to this newly created position the previous January. That same day, Murry, Audree, and all five guys came to Capitol. Venet recalled, "Murry took pictures and we posed with blank pieces of paper simulating contracts."[14] Five photographs are known to exist from this occasion.

Murry Wilson staged a contract signing with blank pieces of paper. Gathered around a table in a conference room at the Capitol Records Tower are (left to right) David, Brian, Dennis (signing), Nick Venet (standing), Carl, and Mike (courtesy David Marks and Jon Stebbins).

Venet and Murry discussed which two songs would be on the single. Venet recalled, "The customary practice was to make a single with an A side with what we believed would be a hit and a less favored B recording. I wanted to break with tradition and release a record with what I believed were the two strongest potential hits—'Surfin' Safari' and '409.' Murry wanted to include a B recording, 'Lonely Sea,' and hold back '409' for a later release. Eventually I prevailed and the first Beach Boys 45 rpm single on the Capitol label was 'Surfin' Safari' backed with '409.'"[15]

On May 9, Venet was in the studio producing a session that yielded "Too Late to Worry—Too Blue to Cry" and "How Do I Tell My Heart Not to Break" for a new artist he had recently signed, twenty-six year-old singer songwriter Glen Campbell. Two and one-half years later, Campbell joined the touring Beach Boys to fill in for Brian in a move that enabled Brian to create some of his most celebrated music, including *Pet Sounds*.

Because they told Venet they had a music publishing company, Brian and Usher now had to form one. Murry wanted to be involved in forming the company. Usher and Brian reasoned if Murry was occupied with running the publishing company it might keep him away from the recording studio and be less intrusive on their creative process. Usher recalled, "I just said, 'All right, let Murry run it.' Naturally, I assumed I would be part of it, but I was still a little naive. I was confident Murry would draw up the appropriate papers, but of course he didn't and it didn't take him too long to get me out of the scene altogether."[16]

On May 10, Capitol assigned matrix numbers to "Surfin' Safari" (37735) and "409" (37736). Matrix number 37737, ostensibly intended for "Lonely Sea," is blank in Capitol's files, and the song later received matrix number 37865.

Murry recalled, "Nick called me up one day after we handed him the tapes on 'Surfin' Safari,' and said 'Now, we can't have two producers. You're over the hill old man and I'm young and I know the tempo and I sold $50 million worth of records for Capitol last year. So move over and let me take your sons and make big stars out of them.' That's what he told me in a nice way. And I said, 'Okay, well, do a good job with them Nick, they're your babies.' And I was kinda' glad because it was a lot of pressure. You can work with strangers easier than you can with your own goddamn kids, you know."[17]

Venet recalled, "I don't think the father really knew where his son was at. Murry once told me that his son was the next Elvis Presley. I said, 'Mr. Wilson, I think Brian might be as big as Presley in sales, but I don't think he wants to be Presley.' He said, 'No, he's doing everything Presley does, but he's doing it better.' I said, 'Mr. Wilson, I think Brian's doing a different kind of music which is really Brian Wilson music.' He kind of shook his head, looked at me, and walked away."[18]

Usher was more blunt with his assessment of Venet. "The only influence Nick Venet had upon Brian and I—and Brian and I used to talk about this—Nick taught us both how *not* to act and how *not* to be. He never taught us what to do or how to be. We both knew we definitely didn't want to be like him. We both knew we wanted to have nothing to do with his production technique or sound."[19]

On May 11, motivated by the sale of the masters to Capitol, Usher and Brian copyrighted "409" and "Lonely Sea." That same day, Capitol prepared Form 4319, Label Copy and Notice of Coupling, for the printing of 45 rpm record labels for release number 841 and record number 4777—"Surfin' Safari'" backed with "409." The label copy included the

LABEL COPY AND NOTICE OF COUPLING

LABEL CUT: 45 STANDARD

LABEL COLOR: PURPLE

COLOR INK: SILVER

45 RPM

RECORD SIZE: 7 INCH

USUAL PRICE: $ .94

COMPOUND: FLEXIBLE

RECORD NO. 4777

RELEASE NO. ___841___

DATE ___June 4, 1962___

THE FOLLOWING INFORMATION IS TO APPEAR ON LABEL AS LAID OUT:

SURFIN' SAFARI
(B. Wilson–M. Love)

Guild Music Company
BMI–2:05
4777
(45–37735)

BEACH BOYS

THE FOLLOWING INFORMATION IS THE STATUS OF THIS SELECTION AND IS NOT TO APPEAR ON LABEL:

U. S. MECH: LICENSOR: GUILD MUSIC COMPANY
ADDRESS: 2511 MAYBERRY
LOS ANGELES 26, CALIFORNIA

U. S. PERFORMANCE RIGHTS: BMI
ROYALTY:

REMARKS: _____

TRUST FEE PER THIS MASTER — ½ BASIC RATE
TRUST REPORT CLASS _____

COPYRIGHT INFORMATION HAS BEEN COMPILED FROM SOURCES BELIEVED TO BE RELIABLE; HOWEVER, NO REPRESENTATION OR WARRANTY IS MADE

THE FOLLOWING INFORMATION IS TO APPEAR ON LABEL AS LAID OUT:

409
(B. Wilson–G. Usher)

Sea of Tunes
BMI–1:58
4777
(45–37736)

BEACH BOYS

THE FOLLOWING INFORMATION IS THE STATUS OF THIS SELECTION AND IS NOT TO APPEAR ON LABEL:

U. S. MECH. LICENSOR: SEA OF TUNES
ADDRESS: 3701 WEST 119TH STREET
HAWTHORNE, CALIFORNIA

U. S. PERFORMANCE RIGHTS: BMI
ROYALTY:

REMARKS: _____

TRUST FEE PER THIS MASTER — ½ BASIC RATE
TRUST REPORT CLASS _____

COPYRIGHT INFORMATION HAS BEEN COMPILED FROM SOURCES BELIEVED TO BE RELIABLE; HOWEVER, NO REPRESENTATION OR WARRANTY IS MADE

11May62

TRUST FEE RATES

RETAIL SELLING PRICE EQUIVALENT	BASIC RATE PER RECORD CLASSES A-E	CLASS F
$ .00 THROUGH $1.00 USA	1.00%	1.20%
$1.01 THROUGH $1.25 USA	1.50%	1.80%
$1.26 THROUGH $1.50 USA	U. S. $.025	U. S. $.029
$1.51 THROUGH $2.00 USA	U. S. $.050	U. S. $.058
$2.01 AND ABOVE	5.00%	2.90%

FORM 4319 REV. 5 2/61 RET. (P)

Capitol Records' "Label Copy and Notice of Coupling" for the Beach Boys' first Capitol 45 rpm single, "Surfin' Safari" backed with "409" (author's collection).

artist's name, song titles, songwriters, times, producers, arrangers, and music publishers. It was an old form Capitol had used for years as it indicated the single would be printed on a purple label with silver ink, which the company began phasing out in January 1962 when it introduced its distinctive yellow and orange swirl label with black ink.

Venet recalled, "My secretary called Murry to ask for the label credits. Murry said either Guild Music or Hite Morgan should be credited as the copyright proprietor for 'Surfin' Safari.' My secretary called Morgan and was told the credit should be Guild Music instead of Hite Morgan. Up to this time I had never talked with Morgan directly, although he occasionally called my secretary and asked for free copies of the record, which we sent to him in due course. At one point Morgan did call me directly to ask me how the record was doing and I told him it was a big hit, and he said, in effect, 'You're kidding.' In fact, he said he would call various disc jockeys himself to confirm this because he was quite surprised the record was doing so well."[20]

At 8:00 p.m. on May 11, as newly minted Capitol recording artists, the Beach Boys played a dance at the Community Fair on the tennis courts of El Camino Community College. The two-day fair, which continued noon to midnight the next day, was held in conjunction with the annual Camino Welfare Week during which funds collected from various club-sponsored games and activities were donated to charities.

Sometime during the next week, Venet called Murry and told him the group was to report to the Capitol Tower that afternoon for promotional photographs. Marks was not at home so Brian scratched out a note and left it on his door—"Dave: Get Dessed [*sic*] right away, Pendletone, white shirt, T-shirt—Black pants, Jeans + Coat, We all have to go to Capitol Records to have pictures taken with surf boards, Don't forget any clothes (both Pendleton + dress outfits), Wait at our house by 4:00 or earlier = Brian."[21]

Brian's note infers Capitol had already secured one or more surfboards to be used as a prop. The one board they had was red with a wide white stripe down the middle with a

The Beach Boys in Nick Venet's office on the day their first Capitol Records promotional photographs were taken.

thinner central red stripe. Dressed in white T-shirts, blue plaid Pendleton shirts, and dark blue jeans, the guys lined up roughly in height order, holding the surfboard under their left arms. In a second pose, Brian and Mike held the surfboard vertically between them while the others kneeled in front. Reportedly, the photographer noticed a hole in the right knee of Marks's jeans and asked him to cover it with his right hand. But before the photo was snapped, Marks spread his fingers to reveal the hole in his jeans. These two photos became their first promotional photographs as Capitol recording artists. Two other photos taken that day show them sitting in Venet's office.

On May 18, Capitol's printing department reviewed 45 rpm record label proofs for Capitol 4777 to ensure there were no typographical errors before millions of labels were printed. Noticeably absent from the label copy was the producer credit. Venet was remarkably vigilant about ensuring he received producer credit on every record for which he could stake that claim. But "Surfin' Safari" and "409" had been produced at Western without his involvement. Assigning production credit for the songs, however, would have been tricky because it was likely shared among Brian, Usher, Murry, and Chuck Britz.

On the label proofs, the music publishing for "Surfin' Safari" was correctly credited to Hite Morgan's Guild Music Company. However, the music publishing for "409" was credited to "Murray [sic] Wilson Music" and had to be corrected to Sea of Tunes. Because the label copy for "409" was most likely relayed over the telephone by Murry to Venet's secretary, it would appear Murry had briefly considered naming the publishing company after himself.

As Capitol readied the Beach Boys' debut single, its legal department prepared the group's contract. In order to meet a summer release date, Capitol entered into two contracts with Murry Wilson (doing business as "The Beach Boys") as an interim measure pending a court-approved contract with the group, necessary because of the minor status of all but Mike Love.[22]

On May 24, with the guidance and approval of attorney Averill Pasarow, Murry signed Capitol Contract Number 3347, Master Purchase Agreement, and Capitol Contract Number 3348, Master Royalty Agreement, on behalf of the group. On page one of the Master Purchase Agreement is a clause that states Murry, as owner of the three masters, represents and warrants they were recorded under the 1959 Phonograph and Record Labor contract with AFM and the 1959–1962 Code of Fair Practices for Phonograph Recordings with AFTRA. Capitol must have overlooked this language as the three masters were not recorded under AFM or AFTRA rules governing payments to musicians, vocalists, and the Pension Welfare Fund.

On page two of the Master Purchase Agreement, section four states, in part, "Capitol agrees to pay Owner within fourteen (14) days after the masters are delivered, the sum of One hundred and sixty-six and 67/100 ($166.67) dollars for each of the masters which Capitol finds to be technically satisfactory. Capitol agrees to return to Owner any of the masters found to be technically unsatisfactory." The contract was prepared with the originally agreed-upon sum of one hundred dollars per master typed in this section. It was then typed over with a line of "X's" ending with an asterisk linked to the typewritten sum $166.67 initialed by Murry. Apparently, between May 10 and May 24, Murry either renegotiated the sale of the three masters or Capitol decided to pay him $500.01 ($166.67 × 3) rather than the original offer of $300.

The Master Royalty Agreement stated royalties would not be payable unless records manufactured from the masters sold more than the number for which the royalty would have been $520 (the $500.01 paid for the masters plus four percent). The contract was prepared with $312 typed in this section (the $300 originally offered plus four percent). It was then typed over with a line of "X's" ending with an asterisk linked to the typewritten sum of $520 initialed by Murry.

On page three of Capitol Contracts 3347 and 3348 was an addendum that listed (a) Titles of Selections embodied in the masters: "409 (Four-O-Nine)," "Surfin' Safari," "Lonely Sea," (b) Recording Artists: Brian D. Wilson, Dennis C. Wilson, Karl D. Wilson, David L. Marks, Michael E. Love. Group Performing as "The Beach Boys." Murry signed the contract and corrected his first name by crossing out the erroneous "a" Capitol had inserted. There was, however, no similar effort to correct Carl's first name.

On the day the Beach Boys signed their interim contract with Capitol Records, Jan & Dean performed as part of an all-star show at El Camino High School in Sacramento organized by eighteen-year-old senior Fred Vail, who would later play a pivotal role in the Beach Boys' live shows and their development as a successful touring band.[23]

In late May, Murry published "Bye Baby Bye," co-written with Brian and Audree, with Sea of Tunes. He asked his sons to record it, but they declined.[24] He later recorded it with the Sunrays for the B side to "I Live for the Sun" in June 1965.

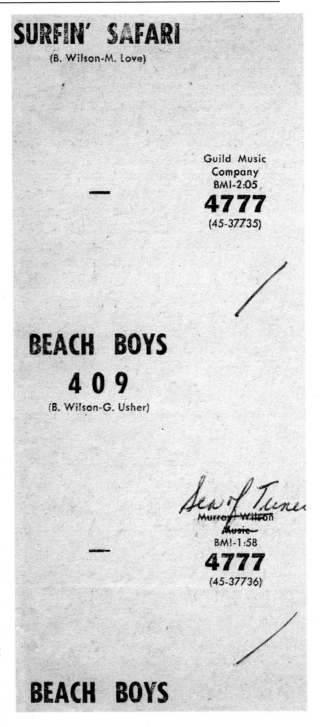

The handwritten correction to the music publishing credit for "409" on this record label proof indicates the Beach Boys' music publishing company was called "Murray [sic] Wilson Music" before being named Sea of Tunes (author's collection).

June 1962

On June 1, Hite Morgan copyrighted "Surfin' Safari" and "Judy." The *Billboard* and *Cash Box* that hit newsstands the next day contained the first mention of the Beach Boys' debut single on Capitol. *Billboard* gave "Surfin' Safari" four stars and commented, "The beach scene gets a rolling, rocking treatment on this side by the boys. Tune swings along neatly on lead singer's talent and support of the rest of the group." "409" received three stars. *Cash Box*, apparently a stricter grader, conferred a B+ on "Surfin' Safari" and a B on "409."

Also on June 2, the Beach Boys played their first concert at the Azusa Teen Club in Azusa, California, thirty miles northeast of Hawthorne along the southern edge of the San Gabriel Mountains, and would return there several times that summer. They performed for about one hundred kids. They were steadily improving as a live band and their song selection reflected an expanding repertoire with more depth. In addition to originals like "Surfin' Safari," "409," and "Surfer Girl," they sang covers of "Runaway," "Louie, Louie," "Johnny B. Goode," and "What'd I Say." They also played instrumentals like Dick Dale's "Let's Go Trippin'" and "Misirlou," and Duane Eddy's "Ramrod" and "Movin' N' Groovin'."

The Azusa Teen Club, physically located in the gymnasium at the Azusa Recreation Center, was a community-sponsored meeting place where teens could socialize, dance, and listen to records and live entertainment. It kept them off the streets and out of trouble most Friday and Saturday nights. It was formed that spring by Richard Adler to address the community's growing concern about the national problem of teenage delinquency.

Nineteen-year-old David McClellan was a Washington state transplant who had lived in Southern California since 1950. After graduating Azusa High School in 1961, he attended a local college and pursued an interest in journalism by writing an entertainment column called *Teen Beat* for the *Azusa Herald*. Adler asked him to write publicity for the club and McClellan joined the staff of the Azusa Teen Club. Adler knew KFWB disc jockeys Gene Weed and Roger Christian, and enlisted their help in bringing top-name talent to the club including Jan & Dean, Johnny Crawford, Dorsey Burnette, Dick and Dee Dee, Paul Petersen, Little Eva, Connie Stevens, Ann-Margret, and the Beach Boys.

McClellan met Murry and the Beach Boys as they arrived at the club June 2 and began unloading gear from their cars. Brian was so focused on the music it seemed like he had little time for anything else. Carl was reserved, Mike was aloof, and he found David a little hostile as if McClellan's presence was an intrusion. But Dennis was warm and engaging, and they had an instant rapport. "When Dennis learned I was a surfer, he suggested we go surfing sometime," McClellan recalled. "Later that summer, we hung out and went surfing at El Segundo because Dennis felt it was less crowded there."[25]

Murry took a liking to McClellan and invited him to attend a rehearsal session at the Wilson home in Hawthorne where the band practiced three nights a week—Sunday, Tuesday, and Thursday. On June 21, the day after Brian's twentieth birthday, McClellan drove down to Hawthorne and listened as they rehearsed. He chatted with Audree and interviewed Murry on his thoughts on the music industry and managing the group. McClellan recalled, "Audree and Murry were gracious hosts and always made me feel welcome in their home. Audree talked about the musical career and aspirations she and Murry once had. Murry enjoyed giving me fatherly advice. He always had an air of authority about him, letting you

David McClellan, seen here with his then-girlfriend, Becky, met Murry and the Beach Boys when they first played the Azusa Teen Club on June 2, 1962. Murry invited McClellan to the band's rehearsals at the Wilsons' Hawthorne home and appointed him director of publicity (courtesy David McClellan).

know who was in charge. Later, when I flew to Europe to cover the 1964 Olympics, he told me about his experiences in Europe and recounted how beautiful it was flying into Copenhagen at night. I recall, and I'm still amused by this, Murry told me 'We realize the life span of a rock group is probably three to four years.' And here we are, fifty years later."[26]

Murry realized McClellan's writing ability could help the band and asked him to do promotion. With his new title "Director of Publicity," McClellan began writing press releases, contacting the music press, drafting biographical information about the band, visiting radio stations with free singles, answering fan letters, travelling with the band, and helping out at local gigs. At Murry's suggestion, McClellan occasionally wore the same Pendleton shirt as the band.

On June 4, Capitol Records released their first Beach Boys single— "Surfin' Safari" (b/w "409," Capitol 4777) with a picture sleeve featuring a color photograph of the guys

Above and following page: "Surfin' Safari" backed with "409," the first 45 rpm single by the Beach Boys on Capitol Records, was released June 4, 1962. Whether by mistake or intention, the band was called Beach Boys, not The Beach Boys. When the band made local promotional appearances, they often played a short set and then autographed copies of the picture sleeve for fans (author's collection).

holding a surfboard under their arms that was taken at Capitol a few weeks earlier. The fade on each song was ten seconds shorter than the original demos recorded at Western in April. Capitol restored the original fades when both songs were included on the *Good Vibrations* box set in 1993.

There is lingering controversy about whether "Surfin' Safari" or "409" was the intended A side. Murry recalled, "We told Nick right at the outset we thought 'Surfin' Safari' was the A side. He says, no, '409.' So Capitol put all the push on '409' and had to turn the damn record over in about three weeks. 'Surfin' Safari' was the song that made them surfing kings, vocally and lyrically, around the United States."[27]

Venet disputed that he wanted "409" as the A side and noted, rather convincingly, "If it was '409' I was interested in, why did I have the group take pictures at the ocean with a surfboard?"[28] Capitol's work order for the single indicates "Surfin' Safari" was the A side. And, because they are printed and folded in a way that results in a clear front and back, the picture sleeve also indicates "Surfin' Safari" was the A side. Most likely, Murry and Venet simply disagreed as to which was the stronger song.

"We released the record and in the period of one day the company knew it was a hit," recalled Venet. "I mean they don't happen that fast. We were getting reports from spots like Phoenix, Arizona, where you couldn't go surfing if you tried. I think the biggest order Capitol had that year had been on the Beach Boy record in New York City. The Beach Boys became very important. And it sold close to eight or nine hundred thousand records. Within days after the release of 'Surfin' Safari,' agents called and asked me for an introduction to the Beach Boys in order to represent them. I also received calls from producers who wanted to put the Beach Boys in movies. Promoters and disc jockeys called and wanted to book the Beach Boys in concerts and on-air interviews."[29]

"Surf music was a shot in the arm to the entire industry," Venet continued. "It was a pure California phenomenon. The Beach Boys represented to the rest of the country that California was something. Some sort of fantasy got triggered by the Beach Boys' records."[30]

Rene Wexler grew up in Southern California in the early sixties. "The Beach Boys put those feelings and times into words and music. Most high schools were divided between the surfers and the greasers, which were the car clubs, the James Dean types. But kids that were surfers became interested in cars and, at the same time, the Beach Boys won over the car boys. They really got the whole audience."[31]

In summer 1962, "Surfin' Safari" had a profound influence on twelve-year-old Lindsay Buckingham, future Fleetwood Mac guitarist, growing up in Atherton, California, twenty miles southeast of San Francisco. "I remember first hearing 'Surfin' Safari' when I was in sixth grade. It had the beat, the sense of joy, that explosion rock 'n' roll gave to a lot of us. But it also had this incredible lift, this amazing kind of chemical reaction that seemed to happen inside of you when you heard it."[32]

The Beach Boys played a concert at the Roller Gardens in Wagon Wheel Junction, a forty-acre Western-themed complex built in the 1940s at the intersection of Highway 101 and Pacific Coast Highway, five miles north of Oxnard. It was likely June 9 or 16. Lydia Lee (then Lydia Sexty) was finishing seventh grade in her hometown of Camarillo, eight miles west of Oxnard. She celebrated her thirteenth birthday on June 5, the day after "Surfin' Safari" was released. "I just loved the Beach Boys from the first time I heard 'Surfin' Safari' on KRLA," she recalled. "My friends and I would meet after school, listen to the radio, and talk about the latest groups. Shortly after my birthday, I heard the Beach Boys were coming to the Roller Gardens and I begged my mother to let me go to the concert. She knew how much I wanted to see them so it was the perfect birthday present."[33]

Lydia recalled watching the band members arrive, rolling their equipment across the floor, and setting up on a small riser at one end of the rink. They played one hour for about 200 teens. "All the kids thought they played a really good show. I remember thinking they sounded very good, very professional, but they didn't have a lot of stage personality. But it was a great night. A lot of fun."[34]

On June 20, Brian said good-bye to his teenage years and celebrated his twentieth birthday. So much had happened in the last year. He had a hit single climbing the charts, started a music publishing company, and was a recording artist for one of the largest record companies in the world. In *Billboard* out June 23, the Beach Boys were mentioned for the first time in a Capitol full-page ad as "Surfin' Safari" b/w "409" was included under the heading "Bright New Sparklers from Hit-makers New to Capitol." Although the single had not yet charted, it was getting lots of radio play and Capitol had high hopes for their new youthful sound. The *Cash Box* out June 30 contained a full-page ad with the heading "Capitol's Hot 11" that included "Surfin' Safari" b/w "409."

Within a month of "Surfin' Safari" and "409" being released, Brian met twenty-eight-year-old KFWB disc jockey Roger Christian, a hot rod enthusiast who kept a notebook of original poems about cars. Christian grew up in Buffalo, New York, a blue collar steel mill town. In 1948, at fourteen, he hitchhiked to California in search of his perfect car—a 1932 Ford Coupe, called a Deuce Coupe after the "2" in 1932. He worked cleaning dishes in a Chinese restaurant in Long Beach and saved his money for his dream car. An ad in the *Los Angeles Times* caught his eye and he hitched a ride with a passing trucker sixty-five miles north to the old Southern Pacific Railroad town of Lancaster, California. He paid $375 cash for a beautiful Deuce Coupe. Incredibly, without a license or insurance, the fourteen-year-old Christian drove his cherry coupe back to Buffalo. A few years later, he got his start in radio on WSAY in Syracuse and then moved to WWOL in Buffalo. But the upstate New York winters were harsh and the call of California too strong.

In summer 1960, Christian moved to LA and landed the noon to 3:00 p.m. spot on

KRLA. In late March 1961, he left KRLA and went to KDEO in San Diego. On July 11, contract negotiations broke down between AFTRA and KFWB over the union's demands for higher wages for announcers and newscasters, and AFTRA called for a walkout against the station, the first strike in LA by the twenty-year-old union. Some KFWB disc jockeys walked out in solidarity with the announcers while others, including program director Chuck Blore, remained on-air and were fined $5,000 before resigning from the union. Meanwhile, KFWB recruited jocks from other stations and enlisted management to man the microphones. Record librarian Bill Angel covered Sunday morning 6:00 a.m. to 10:00 a.m. and Blore, using the name Charlie Brown, did a noon to 3:00 p.m. shift for one week in mid–August.

On October 6, Christian began working for KFWB from midnight to 6:00 a.m. The station was a twenty-minute drive east from his new 1,500 square foot, three-bedroom home at 22470 Cass Avenue in Woodland Hills. The strike ended November 12 and Crowell-Collier Broadcasting Company, owners of KFWB, agreed to a pay announcers and newscasters an increase of $32.50 a week.

Both Usher and Murry recounted stories of how they each introduced Brian to Christian. Usher first met Christian while promoting "Driven Insane" at the National Orange Show in San Bernardino in March 1961.[35] Usher had written "The Beginning of the End" with Christian, but had not generally kept in touch with him. So it was a bit risky when Usher took Brian to KFWB one night to introduce him to an old friend. "When he came up that night he looked different," recalled Christian. "Gary said, 'Do you remember me, Gary Usher?' and I replied, 'Gary who?' Brian laughed and then I said, 'Oh yeah, now I remember. It hurt Gary I didn't recognize him because he had told Brian he knew me."[36]

One night, as Murry listened to KFWB, Christian played "409" and explained the song's car lingo like dual quad and posi-traction. Murry, always looking for ways to promote the band, called Christian, complimented him on his automotive knowledge, and asked if he ever wrote any songs. "I got together with Brian and we started writing," Christian recalled. "I came up with a story lyric and a rough idea for a melody, which Brian would promptly dismiss! Brian's melodies were so unique, original, imaginative, and melodic that I would just write a lyric and he would put a melody to it. Sometimes, he would improve on a lyric, which is hard for a lyricist. But Brian was phrasing them so they'd sing better."[37] In Christian's notebook, Brian found a wealth of inspiration. Together, they would solidify the Beach Boys' reputation as America's premier hot rod vocal group.

Little Eva's "The Locomotion," a major influence on Brian, debuted at #40 on the KFWB chart out June 29. The

THE BEACH BOYS
CAPITOL RECORDING ARTISTS
For Your Entertainment Pleasure

BRIAN WILSON, LEADER	TEENAGE HOPS
BUS. OR 8-6054	TV, RADIO AND
RES. OS 5-6566	STAGE APPEARANCES

Murry Wilson had business cards printed for the band noting they were Capitol recording artists and available "For Your Entertainment Pleasure." Brian was identified as the group's leader (author's collection).

June 9 *Billboard* noted, "It's a new dance with a rhythm close to the Twist and the gal belts it in fine style over a solid arrangement. Watch it." After her performance on *American Bandstand* July 5 and a full-page ad in *Billboard* July 21, it was the #1 record in the country by mid–August.

"The Loco-motion" was written by husband and wife songwriters Gerry Goffin and Carole King under contract to Aldon Music, a publishing firm owned by forty-seven-year-old Al Nevins and twenty-eight-year-old Don Kirshner since May 1958. It was the inaugural release on their Dimension Records. At the 1961 BMI Awards, Aldon won a record-setting twelve awards, four more than any other company had ever received, including song of the year for Goffin's and King's "Will You Love Me Tomorrow" by the Shirelles. By 1962, Aldon had eighteen young songwriters on staff all tuned in to the emotions of the teenage market, including the teams of Goffin and King, Neil Sedaka and Howard Greenfield, and Barry Mann and Cynthia Weil. At the 1962 BMI Awards, Aldon took home ten awards and King and Greenfield tied at four apiece.

"The Loco-Motion" challenged Brian's and Usher's competitive natures and raised the songwriting bar. It was the kind of song they needed to aim for—a melodic hook, direct lyrics, soulful vocal, and a great production. A sonic assault on the senses. A song that demanded you listen to it. It was a lesson in song construction, record production, and the elusive commercial appeal needed to have a number one record. Brian and Usher were up for the challenge and set about making their own Loco-motion.

For the fiscal year ending June 30, 1962, Capitol Records took a major financial hit with annual sales down $6.5 million from the previous year. For stockholders, that translated into a precipitous drop in earnings per share from $3.93 to seventy-six cents. Capitol president Glenn Wallichs allayed investor jitters by writing stockholders and assuring them Capitol was "strongly geared for the competitive period ahead and that the record market was expanding with the teenage population."[38]

Wallichs could not have known that the vocal quintet Capitol had signed just a month earlier would play a major role in the company's future creative and financial success.

16

Safari, California Style (July 1962)

If Jimmy O'Neill had excelled in Latin, his mother might have gotten her wish that he become a physician. But the world would have been denied one of the great LA radio and television personalities in the 1950s and 1960s. When O'Neill failed Latin, a high school classmate suggested radio class because it was an easy credit. That led to a series of radio jobs in his hometown of Enid, Oklahoma, before moving to larger markets in Oklahoma City and Pittsburgh. He moved to LA and on September 1, 1959, launched KRLA's format change from country to Top 40 rock 'n' roll. Within a year he was the top disc jockey in LA. He soon hosted *The Jimmy O'Neill Show,* a Saturday television show at midnight on KCOP-TV channel 13, and, in summer 1960, the weekly *Teenage Jamboree* at the Super Sea Circus at P.O.P.

While driving down Sunset Boulevard in spring 1962, O'Neill noticed Pandora's Box. "It didn't look like a night club," he recalled. "It looked like a private residence. It was two stories and had a big wall and I thought, 'I've got the TV show, I've got the radio show, it would really be nice to have my name on that wall on Sunset Strip and own a teenage nightclub.'"[1]

O'Neill struck a deal with club owner Bill Tilden and began hosting rock 'n' roll acts at Pandora's Box. "I had fifty-percent of the net," O'Neill recalled. "People thought I owned it, but I didn't. I had total creative control and the authority to make changes and decide who to hire."[2] Leon Russell and David Gates played in the house band. On a small stage equipped with a piano, they backed regular performers like Shelley Fabares, Paul Petersen, Bobby Rydell, and Jackie DeShannon, often accompanied by her friend and co-songwriter Sharon Sheeley.

"I knew the Beach Boys before Pandora's Box because I played 'Surfin' Safari' once an hour on KRLA and on my television show," O'Neill continued. "Now and then Murry called and thanked me for the support. I appeared every week at venues like El Monte Legion Stadium, Anaheim Ballroom, Balboa Ballroom, and Santa Ana Auditorium, and I'm sure the Beach Boys made some personal appearances with me. When they signed with Capitol, Nick Venet called, thanked me for my previous support, and wanted to make sure I would continue to support them. I liked Nick. He was a real extrovert and promoter. An entertainment industry politician."[3] In a sense, Pandora's Box was to the Beach Boys what the Cavern Club was to the Beatles. Both clubs gave these little-known bands a residency in which to hone their live skills and garner a local following.

The Beach Boys began appearing at Pandora's Box on August 26. They played three shows a night (9:00 p.m. 10:30 p.m. and midnight) for five consecutive evenings. Admission was two dollars (there were no actual tickets) and the club held about 200 people. The crowd was cleared out between each show and a line of kids snaked around the block.

201

"They refused payment, but I gave them gas money to commute from Hawthorne," O'Neill continued. "Murry was calling the shots and got more involved when they signed with Capitol. In a good way, Audree was kind of a stage mother and tagged along with them everywhere they went. They were still driving second-hand cars and setting up their own equipment. It was just starting to happen for them. They received a huge ovation every night. People just adored them."[4]

O'Neill was impressed with how down-to-earth they were. "Brian was friendly and pleasant, but quiet and subdued. Not aloof, but introspective, lost in a creative cloud thinking about his next song. It never occurred to me he had any shortcomings. He was a creative genius and he could kind of get by socially. Better than John Lennon did, I think. Carl was the public relations guy. I didn't get to know David and Mike very well. They were just kind of in the background, kind of like George Harrison was with the Beatles. With Mike it was on-the-surface friendliness. I never felt I had a true relationship with Mike. He was just a front man who really didn't get involved with anyone."[5]

During the Beach Boys' late August residency, O'Neill proposed to Sharon Sheeley. "I said to Audree, 'I'm going to Las Vegas to marry my girlfriend and I'd like to leave a little early tonight. Could you ask the guys if they would be willing to do an extra set to cover my absence?' And she said, 'No problem, we'd be happy to; congratulations.' She was very sweet."[6]

"Dennis and I became drinking buddies. Every night after their shows, the Beach Boys packed their equipment into their cars and went home with their mother. Except Dennis. I lived with Sharon in a posh apartment four blocks down Sunset Boulevard and I think he had a crush on her. Dennis would come to our apartment and we'd drink vodkas until dawn."[7]

O'Neill left KRLA in October 1962 and began working at other nightclubs and hosting *Parade of Hits* on KCOP-TV.[8] In May 1963, he joined KFWB as a disc jockey.[9] O'Neill hosted shows at Pandora's Box through early November 1962. "When I left Pandora's Box, the Beach Boys left, too."

On July 2, 1962, Murry's forty-fifth birthday, David Marks joined AFTRA. For "Commitment and Date," Marks wrote "Capitol Records (May 24, 1962)." The next day the Beach Boys played a dance from 8:30 p.m. to midnight in the cafeteria of Dykstra Hall, a women's dormitory on the campus of UCLA. The concert also featured Chris Montez, and Dante and the Evergreens, and was emceed by Roger Christian. The show was the second of four summer dances sponsored by the Dykstra Hall Residents Association and booked by Edward Vandegrift, a twenty-year-old student who had transferred to UCLA from Santa Monica City College. The series kicked off in late June with Little Richard and continued with Jennell Hawkins (July 13) and the Lettermen (July 17). The house band for the summer concert series was the Renegades,[10] who later became the Sunrays when they were mentored by Murry Wilson after the Beach Boys fired him as their manager in spring 1964.

Vandegrift snapped five photographs of the Beach Boys playing, posing, and relaxing between songs. They wore their dress Pendleton outfits—white shirt, black tie, black pants, white socks, black shoes, and plaid Pendleton shirt as a jacket. David and Carl played matching sunburst Fender Stratocasters, Brian his sunburst Fender Precision Bass, and Mike, as seen in one photo, played sax. This dance is most likely the earliest show the Beach Boys did with Roger Christian. Hence, it is likely Brian's introduction to Christian, arranged by

The Beach Boys played a dance from 8:30 p.m. to midnight in the cafeteria of Dykstra Hall, a women's dormitory on the campus of UCLA, on July 3, 1962. The dance also featured Chris Montez, and Dante and the Evergreens, and was emceed by KFWB disc jockey Roger Christian. The show was the second of four summer dances sponsored by the Dykstra Hall Residents Association. Left to right, Mike, Brian, Dennis, Carl, and David (courtesy Edward Vandegrift and Peter Reum).

Murry or Usher, took place within the month following the June 4 release of "Surfin' Safari" and "409."

This may also have been the first time the Beach Boys met Dante (real name Donald Drowty) and His Friends, who had a minor hit that spring with "Miss America" (Imperial 5827). In summer 1960, as Dante and the Evergreens, the group scored a #15 hit with a cover of the Hollywood Argyles' "Alley Oop," which reigned at #1 for three weeks that June. Perhaps hearing Dante croon "Miss America" to appreciative Dykstra Hall coeds inspired Brian to give Dennis, the band's emerging sex symbol, his first lead vocal when the Beach Boys recorded it on their debut album later that summer.

On July 5, as Little Eva performed "The Loco-Motion" on *American Bandstand*, "Surfin' Safari" had been out for a month but, despite strong sales and radio play, had not charted. On July 6 Murry received a Western Union telegram from Nick Venet, "Congratulations, Beach Boys hit 91 in Cash Box. Regards, Nick Venet."[11] [*Note*: It debuted the following day at #92.] But the group's elation was short-lived as it disappeared from *Cash Box* for the next two weeks. On the front cover of *Billboard* out July 7, "Surfin' Safari" was listed as a regional break-out in Detroit, where there was no surfing on the Detroit River, but the Motor City was the perfect town to embrace "409."

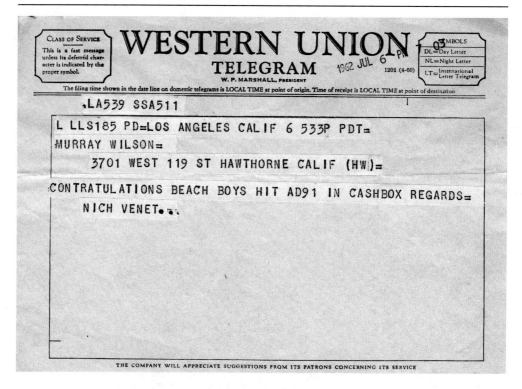

Nick Venet sent a telegram to Murry Wilson on July 6, 1962, assuring him "Surfin' Safari" would finally enter the *Cash Box* chart out the following day for the week ending July 14 (author's collection).

Venet later boasted "Surfin' Safari" took off immediately, but that was not the case. On July 9, a month after its release, Venet wrote Murry, "We are putting the full weight of Capitol behind 'Surfin' Safari' and we are getting some reaction. Capitol will stay on this record until they get it into the Top 10. Tell the boys to work very hard because we will be recording within a week or two; and tell them, too, that they are doing a very good job at the record hops."[12] At the bottom of the letter is the handwritten notation 'Request group photos to be made soon,' perhaps an indication Murry was already pressing Capitol for additional marketing attention. Although Venet complimented them on their record hop shows, there are very few documented personal appearances in the month following the single's release. At these events, they typically played a few songs and autographed the "Surfin' Safari" picture sleeve. They probably autographed hundreds of picture sleeves that summer, but very few have surfaced in the last fifty years.

On the strength of the single's sales and radio play, Capitol decided to invest in its new teen vocal group and release a full-length album. Although Venet wanted them in the studio by mid–July, Brian and the guys weren't ready and needed more time. Their success had caught them unprepared to record a full-length album. Their first session was a month after Venet's letter and two more sessions were held a month after that. "In those days, Brian and I were writing sketches," recalled Usher. "We'd demo them and I figured one day we'd go back and pick the best and polish them. When 'Surfin' Safari' hit, it was so sudden. So Brian grabbed the latest songs we'd written and recorded them."[13]

In June and July, the Beach Boys made local personal appearances and rehearsed new songs for the album. While Brian devoted himself to songwriting, Usher worked full-time at City National Bank. Between writing sessions, they relaxed by playing baseball. "One time, when all the guys got together at Griffith Park, I hit a ball at Carl who was playing first base. I hit a line drive and Carl put his glove up in self-defense and it knocked him over! Brian and I enjoyed those kinds of breaks. They were a good outlet."[14]

Usher got along great with Dennis and Carl, was indifferent to David due to their nearly ten-year age difference, and had a strained relationship with Mike because he had replaced him as Brian's main collaborator. "Gary was writing more songs with Brian than Mike," recalled Judy Bowles. "Mike and Brian weren't getting along that well, even back then."[15] After the initial success of "Surfin'" and "Surfin' Safari," it must have been a little off-putting that Brian had a new songwriting partner with whom he had developed such a deep affinity and friendship. Although he was still involved with Ginger, Usher began dating Bonnie Deleplain, a friend of his cousin Karen Jones. "When I went out to see the boys play, I would take Karen and Bonnie along. We soon started dating and the four of us— Brian, myself, Bonnie, and Judy—would go on double-dates and really have some crazy times."[16]

On July 14, the Beach Boys drove an hour north to perform in Oxnard at the Plaza Park, a patch of green in center city, for the First Annual Diaper Derby. The tongue-in-cheek event, sponsored by the Downtown Merchants Association, pitted diaper-clad infants crawling along a twelve-foot carpet toward a finish line. Paul Schneider, owner of radio stations KOXR-AM and KAAR-FM, and his eleven-year-old son, Richard, awoke early to set up the station's equipment for a live remote broadcast from 10:30 a.m. to 2:30 p.m. They set up their equipment at one end of a flatbed trailer that doubled as a makeshift stage.

KOXR disc jockey Nelson Eddy (not the singer) emceed the event and, in between rounds of derby competition, introduced the entertainment provided by the Beach Boys, the Surfmen, and a black vocal group whose name history has forgotten and who had difficulty lip syncing their one song when the wind kept blowing the phonograph needle across their 45 rpm record, a problem resolved when Paul Schneider placed a quarter on the phonograph's tone arm.

Paul Johnson of the Belairs accompanied the Beach Boys to the Derby. "I remember getting up with them to play 'Mr. Moto.' I didn't think they were one of the best bands around. They didn't sound that great. They had great vocal abilities, but as far as what they were able to do in a live setting, it wasn't real sophisticated. I always had the impression Dennis learned to play the drums just so he could be in the band. He never really took it that seriously. He was more into being a celebrity than a musician. But Dennis was clearly the one guy in the band who was the character the Beach Boys' music portrayed."[17]

Dennis impressed the younger Schneider who recalled, "I was most fascinated by Dennis. He would break a stick and pick up another one without skipping a beat. I asked how long it took him to learn how to play the drums and he said six months."[18]

Beach Boys historian Derek Bill unearthed a three-minute tape that included the final fifteen seconds of Johnson playing "Mr. Moto" with the Beach Boys, followed by Brian being interviewed by Eddy.[19] It is the earliest known radio interview with one of the band members. Although the group was at a point in their career when media exposure was critical, Brian did not take the interview seriously. For someone who later earned the reputation as a notoriously difficult interviewee, often changing responses to identical questions, his cavalier approach to interviews was evident quite early. Frustrated by Brian's antics, Eddy asked, "What's your problem?" to which Brian dead-panned, "My problem is health." Eddy later avoided being lured by Brian into the Sir Walter Raleigh tobacco gag. [*Note*: A popular joke was to ask a shop owner if he carried Sir Walter Raleigh in a can. If he answered yes, the smart aleck response was "Well, let him out for a breath of air!"] Brian endured inane questions like, "Tell us your biggest one. Is it thirty-three, forty-five, or what?" to which he responded, "Eight hundred and sixty-five, I think it was."

There are a few substantive revelations. They gave away several autographed copies of their new single and Brian hinted at another commitment that evening when he remarked, "This is going to have to be our last number. We just got the signal from the Capone wagon that we're supposed to be back in [laughs] what's the place?" They played a Canteen Dance at Hawthorne High School that evening. Brian said they had six songs in the can and revealed their next single would be "Chug-A-Lug," written by him and Usher, but not yet recorded, and for which Mike was granted co-writing credit in 1994.

Because the group had not done any recording since April, it's difficult to know which six songs Brian meant. The other contenders are "Surfer Girl," "Judy," and "Karate" from the February 8 session; "County Fair," which Usher and Brian wrote after attending the National Orange Show in San Bernardino in March; "Lonely Sea" from an April session; and "The Shift," copyrighted solely to Mike on May 1, and "Ten Little Indians," both of which the band would record in two weeks.

On July 15, Frances, five months pregnant with their second child, and Mike celebrated Melinda's first birthday. The next day the Beach Boys and Murry were back at the Capitol Tower to sign Capitol Contract Number 3374, Recording Artist Agreement, which Capitol later petitioned the Los Angeles County Superior Court to ratify because four of the five members were minors. The four-page contract covered an initial period of one year and granted Capitol six additional consecutive one-year option periods. In the first year, the Beach Boys agreed to deliver at least six masters to Capitol. That increased to eight and ten for the second and third years, and twelve for the remaining three years. The contract allowed for the three songs purchased from Murry ("409," "Surfin' Safari," and "Lonely Sea") to be applied to the six masters required during the first year. The Beach Boys agreed to a five percent royalty for the initial period and all six option periods. Capitol agreed to release at least one single during each option period and, if they failed to do so, the Beach Boys had the right to terminate the contract.

In a two-page supplement, also dated July 16, 1962, Capitol ensured the band owned the name "Beach Boys" and had them indemnify Capitol against any claim otherwise from Hite Morgan or Candix Records.[20] That same day, Morgan copyrighted "Surfer Girl" to Guild Music. But the group he helped launch would never again record for him or copyright a song with his publishing company. After nearly three decades in the music industry, Morgan watched his most promising discovery leave him behind. The financial loss was incomprehensible. But he wasn't the only one to have the Beach Boys slip away from him.

As the guys signed their Capitol contracts, Al Jardine finished his second year of predental undergraduate work at El Camino and worked that summer at Garret AiResearch. He quit the group when their prospects were bleak and college seemed the safer path. But now, just a few months later, they were on the threshold of one of the most successful careers in the music industry. And Dave Marks, not yet fourteen, had gladly taken his place.

Marks was now a Beach Boy and, thanks to Walter Hurst, the attorney his parents hired to review the Capitol contract, entitled to a twenty percent share in the group. Hurst authored *The Record Industry Book: How to Make Money in the Record Industry*, and had given a series of lectures on the record industry at UCLA in March. The contract signing was an incredible windfall for Marks and a potentially staggering loss for Jardine. "When they signed the Capitol contract, David was one of the original Beach Boys," Audree recalled. "He was at our house all the time. David was so young. I always liked him and felt sorry for him. He was a pain in the neck, he really was, he drove everybody crazy. Brian would not allow him to sing on the records, because he couldn't sing."[21] Jardine's singing voice, which blended so perfectly with Brian's plan for a vocal harmony group, would prove central in rock 'n' roll's most fascinating story of second chances.

On July 18, the group played a sweet sixteen birthday party in Burbank for Jodi Gable, president of their fan club. "They bought me a cake decorated with five beach boys and a little girl sitting on the sand with an umbrella," she recalled. "And they played a concert on the patio in my backyard. I have pictures and my next door neighbor filmed them playing. They parked their cars on the next street over because if I had seen Denny's car I would have known right away. Because it was my birthday, Dennis decided to spend the night after everyone else left. Him and my girlfriend."[22] On July 20, more than six weeks after its release, "Surfin' Safari" finally debuted at #35 on KFWB, climbing to #23 the following week.

On July 23, Murry sent a Western Union telegram to KRLA disc jockey Jimmy O'Neill thanking him for playing "Surfin' Safari." Sales were healthy, but did not enjoy a boost from

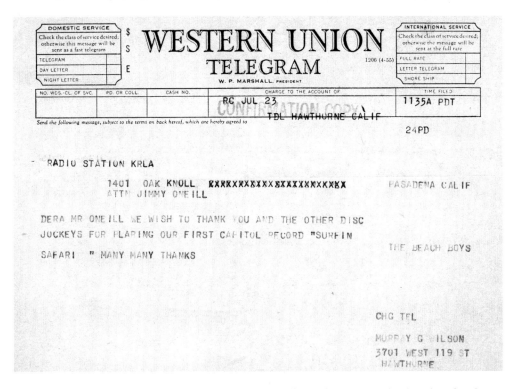

Murry sent a telegram to KRLA disc jockey Jimmy O'Neill on July 23, 1962, thanking him for playing "Surfin' Safari." A month later, "Surfin' Safari" was #1 on KRLA (author's collection).

a single national television appearance in 1962. Most significantly, the band was not invited to perform on *American Bandstand*. The Lettermen and Lou Rawls, new Capitol artists produced by Venet, had already appeared on the show.

The earliest extant film of the Beach Boys performing was taken July 27 at the Azusa Teen Club for *One Man's Challenge*, a twenty-five minute, black-and-white documentary produced by twenty-six-year-old writer-director Dale Smallin and narrated by Roger Christian. The Beach Boys' appearance was arranged by their newly appointed director of publicity, David McClellan. They spent several hours filming their two minutes of screen time, which synced live audio with video of them miming playing and singing.

Smallin hoped *One Man's Challenge* would provide a blueprint for the establishment of teen clubs in other cities. McClellan attended the taping in the gymnasium and snapped nine black-and-white photographs of the Beach Boys rehearsing. The only people present in the cavernous gym were the five band members, the six-member film crew, and three teen

The Beach Boys filmed a live version of "Surfin' Safari" on Friday, July 27, 1962, at the Azusa Teen Club in Azusa, California. This photograph shows the band rehearsing at the Azusa Recreation Center. (Left to right) David, Brian, Carl, Mike, and Dennis (author's collection with appreciation to David McClellan).

club members. The on-screen introduction by KFWB disc jockey Gene Weed and the "live" audience in the final film were added in post-production.

The rehearsal photos show two different arrangements for the audio and film recordings. For the audio track, the guys set up their instruments, amplifiers, and two microphones at one end of the gym near the overhead basketball nets. Brian, Carl, and David played their guitars huddled around one microphone. Mike stood six feet away at his own microphone. Ten feet away from Mike, isolated along an inner brick wall, was Dennis and his drum kit. Smallin and the recording equipment were at a six-foot table a few feet in front of the band. Unlike their appearance at UCLA a few weeks earlier, where they wore their dress Pendleton outfits, here they chose their casual surfer uniforms—J.C. Penney Towncraft white T-shirts, off-white Levi's, white socks, black loafers, and plaid Pendleton shirts. All of them except Carl shed the wool Pendleton while they recorded their vocals. A large dark stain is evident on the left leg of Brian's pants near his knee.

For the filming, the club's decoration committee arranged bamboo and palm for a tropical backdrop. David, Brian, Carl, Mike, and Dennis, lined up left to right between three surfboards, angled on the floor, and a seven-foot tall wooden Tiki crowned with a

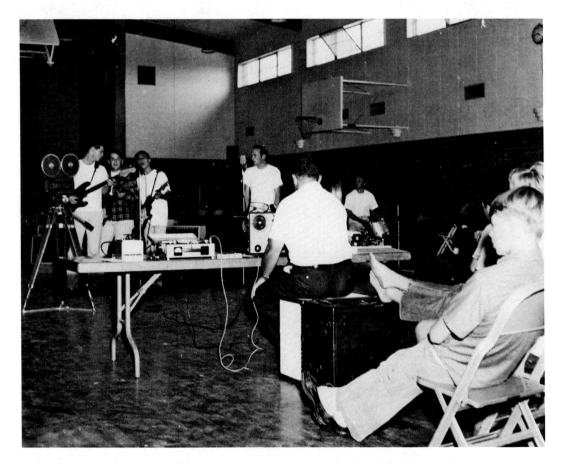

A film crew records the Beach Boys, in T-shirts except Carl, singing "Surfin' Safari" for their appearance in Dale Smallin's *One Man's Challenge*. (Left to right, Brian, Carl, David, Mike, and Dennis; far right, unidentified teen spectators (author's collection with appreciation to David McClellan).

Dennis behind his Gretsch drum kit for the band's appearance in Dale Smallin's *One Man's Challenge* (author's collection with appreciation to David McClellan).

Hawaiian lei. Smallin used three camera angles—a wide shot of all five of them, a medium shot for David, Brian, and Carl, and a close-up of Mike. Smallin made no effort to conceal the lip-syncing as there are no amplifiers, microphones, or guitar cables, evident in the film. And it is doubtful Dennis's drum sticks ever make contact with the skins. The film demonstrated Dennis's lack of formal training. Although he was left-handed, he played a right-handed drum kit, but hit the hi-hat with his left hand and the snare with his right. A properly trained drummer usually does just the opposite, crossing his hands to hit the hi-hat with his right and snare with his left. Dennis was also an unconventional surfer, placing his right foot forward on the board in a stance called "goofy-footed." Although they mime their playing, Brian, Carl, and David appear confident with their instruments and to enjoy the filming, rocking back and forth in a two-step shuffle.

"Carl played the lead on 'Surfin' Safari,'" recalled Marks. "But during that clip they zoomed in on my fingers during the lead. Carl probably thought, 'What the—.'"[23] The film, however, does not zoom in on anyone's fingers. Instead, during the guitar solo, the camera shifts to a medium shot of David, Brian, and Carl. The viewer gets the impression David and Carl both play lead, although at different positions on the fretboard.

On July 28, the Beach Boys played a concert in San Bernardino, most likely at the Swing Auditorium on the National Orange Show Fairgrounds. The following day they played a show with the Tornadoes, a surf quintet from nearby Redlands, at the Casino and Dance Pavilion at Lake Arrowhead, an exclusive Alpine resort nestled among the San Bernardino Mountains sixty miles east of LA. The Tornadoes had just released "Bustin' Surfboards," which reached #2 on KFWB in late October. George White, the Tornadoes' saxman, recalled, "The kids threw pennies at the Beach Boys. They couldn't sing worth a damn. We really smoked them that night."[24]

On July 31, the Beach Boys performed "Surfin' Safari" live on the fourth episode of *Parade of Hits*, a half hour weekly television show that premiered July 10 on KCOP-TV, channel 13. The show was sponsored by White Front Discount Department Store and emceed by KRLA disc jockey Dick Moreland. The Mixtures, with whom the Beach Boys had played at the Rainbow Gardens, were the house band. The show ran for thirty-two weeks.

Also on July 31, typed on Beach Boys stationery with the Wilsons' home address, Jo Ann Marks wrote to the advertising director of Pendleton Mills referencing their telephone conversation from earlier that day. She enclosed three copies of the "Surfin' Safari" single with the picture sleeve depicting the guys wearing their blue plaid Pendletons. "Since we cannot seem to find these same shirts we are hoping you can help us. You might say we are getting a little desperate because the Boys never do an appearance without their 'Beach Boys' shirts. I trust you will do all you can to get the Boys new shirts of the very same color and pattern as soon as possible."[25] Without referencing quantity, she added the requested sizes were three large, one medium, and one small. On August 2, the company responded that they did not sell directly to the public and that, although the shirt was not included in their fall 1962 line, stores may still have stock from the previous spring and enclosed a list of local establishments that carried Pendleton. The band may not have been able to procure blue shirts and, by fall, began performing in red plaid Pendleton shirts.

Around late July, Murry and Dennis had an argument and Murry kicked his sixteen-year-old son out of the house. It was the culmination of years of conflict, tension, and hostility. David Marks had witnessed one particular violent altercation between them. "The Wilsons' garage was directly across the street from us and they faced each other. We heard a scuffle and turned around and it was Dennis and Murry in their garage pushing each other around. We saw Dennis trying to throw some blows at Murry. My father was a very big, strong man and he ran over there and tore them apart like dogs and broke the fight up."[26]

Suddenly, in the midst of preparing to record their first album, Dennis had nowhere to stay. He slept nights in his friend and neighbor Louie Marotta's car until Gary Usher allowed him to stay with him at his apartment on Eucalyptus Street in Inglewood. "What else could I have done?" Usher recalled. "Dennis would have gotten into more trouble if he had been allowed to wander the streets. He had no money, no real friends, and no place to go. He was just a kid. I think he stayed with me for three or four months, maybe even half a year."[27]

17

Pandora's Box and
Azusa Teen Club
(August 1962)

During the first week of August, McClellan took Dennis to the film set of Stanley Kramer's *It's a Mad, Mad, Mad World* on the beach at Portuguese Bends in Rancho Palos Verdes. McClellan recalled Dennis was fascinated seeing all the movie stars and the process of filmmaking. Eight years later, Dennis became the only Beach Boy to star in a major motion picture as filming on Monte Hellman's *Two-Lane Blacktop* began August 13, 1970. Hellman recalled why he cast Dennis in the role of the Mechanic, "I think he had lived with that role. He really grew up with cars. It was almost as though he had been born with a greasy rag in his back pocket."[1] Co-starring Warren Oates, James Taylor, and Laurie Bird, the film was released July 7, 1971, and has become a cult classic.

On August 4, the Beach Boys played a dance at the Azusa Teen Club as "Surfin' Safari" jumped from #23 to #8 on KFWB, moved from #10 to #3 on KRLA, debuted at #85 in *Billboard*, and, after a two week hiatus, reappeared in *Cash Box* at #99. The following day the world was stunned when thirty-six-year-old Marilyn Monroe was found dead in the bedroom of her Brentwood, California, bungalow from an apparent overdose of barbiturate sleeping pills. On August 8, in a private ceremony arranged by her third husband, Yankee legend Joe DiMaggio, Marilyn was interred in a crypt at the newly built Westwood Village Memorial Park Cemetery in LA. That day the *Azusa Herald* ran an article about the Beach Boys under the headline "Musical Kids Hit Big Time With Surfin' Discs" written by David McClellan. In addition to their musical talents, the article claimed Dennis was a championship caliber wrestler and Carl excelled in baseball.

That night, the Beach Boys entered the studio at the Capitol Tower and began work on their first album, *Surfin' Safari*. The standard album at the time had twelve songs, preferably with a hit single leading off each side. So, with "Surfin' Safari" and "409" already recorded, and "Surfin'" and "Luau" deemed too primitive or off limits because their copyright was owned by Hite Morgan, the band needed ten songs to complete the album. None of the three remaining songs from the February 8 session at World Pacific, Usher's four songs from the April session at Western, or "Lonely Sea" from the second Western session that April, would be used.

At the August 8 session, and two more sessions a month later, the Beach Boys recorded a total of ten songs—five written by Brian and Usher, three covers, one by Brian and Mike, and one by Brian alone. They were accompanied into the studio by Murry, Usher,

SURFIN' SAFARI

By BRIAN WILSON and MIKE LOVE

As Recorded by THE BEACH BOYS on Capitol Records

The sheet music for "Surfin' Safari," published by Hite Morgan's Guild Music Publishing, is one of the rarest pieces of 1960s sheet music (author's collection).

and Venet, who recently had been released from a local hospital after treatment for a bleeding ulcer.

The musicians listed on the three AFM contracts for the sessions are the five Beach Boys and Derry Weaver, the session guitarist who composed the instrumental "Moon

Dawg!," which Venet had recorded with the Gamblers when he worked at World Pacific Records in late 1959. Venet trusted the twenty-one-year-old Weaver's musical instincts and, earlier in 1962, hired him as a union contractor to assist with Venet's rock 'n' roll productions at Capitol. Years later, Venet was the best man at Weaver's wedding.[2]

Despite Weaver's name, address, and social security number being listed on all three AFM contracts, Venet recounted conflicting stories about Weaver's presence in the studio. In 1997, eight months before Venet died, he told author Stephen McParland that Weaver was not present, claiming he listed Weaver's name only so that he, Venet, could collect an extra paycheck as a session player. But he also claimed he and Weaver were the same person, and later falsely said Weaver died in an automobile accident.[3] In the mid–1970s, Venet told noted Beach Boys historian Peter Reum that Weaver did in fact play lead guitar on "Moon Dawg!," although Reum believes it sounds like Carl's guitar work.[4] When Paul Vidal interviewed the enigmatic Weaver in 2001, there was neither confirmation nor denial of his participation, but it is unclear if the question was asked directly.[5] David Marks and writer Jon Stebbins said Venet hired Weaver as "an auxiliary guitarist to help pad the Beach Boys' sound in places."[6]

While their musicianship at the time can be debated, there is no doubt Carl and David had very little recording experience. Brian had rehearsed and prepared them, but studio time cost money and Capitol wanted the album out as soon as possible. So, perhaps Venet hired Weaver to assist or overdub some lead guitar, but it may never be known how much of Carl's playing and how much of Weaver's playing, if any, wound up on the final album.

Venet told McParland that Joe Osborn, then the bassist in Ricky Nelson's touring band, played bass guitar on half the tracks on the album, with Brian showing him what to play, freeing Brian to play keyboards.[7] But Osborn reports he did not play on the sessions, but that he "did do a few Beach Boys' sessions later in their career, but was never in a session with Brian."[8]

Steve Douglas (real name Steve Douglas Kreisman) recalled playing sax on Beach Boys recordings beginning with "Ten Little Indians."[9] But there is no aural evidence of sax on that record or any of the tracks on the first album. Douglas is not listed on the AFM contracts, but all three contracts bear the handwritten notation "bill for sax." The sax was a key instrument in many surf bands, so perhaps Venet hired Douglas anticipating some tracks could be punched up with a sax solo. Usher sang background vocals on some of the songs, but his name would not appear on the AFM contracts because those documents only listed musicians.

On August 8, from 6:00 p.m. to 9:00 p.m. at the Capitol Tower, they recorded three songs—"Ten Little Indians" and "Chug-A-Lug" written by Brian and Usher, and "The Shift," now credited to Brian and Mike.[10] "All the arrangements were done over at the Wilson house," recalled Usher. "Brian knew exactly what he wanted to do before going into the studio. He just followed the same format we used when we cut the masters at Western."[11]

David Marks recalled, "I had no say in the music at all. It was always Brian. Maybe Mike helped with the lyrics and some of the vocal arrangements, but we were essentially a vehicle for Brian's expressions. He'd get us in the den and teach us our guitar parts. Complete control from the word go. His dad tried to horn in on the producing, and Brian would get pissed off and storm out of the studio."[12]

The new songs were recorded in stereo on a three-track Ampex tape deck. Brian and the engineer set the sound levels in the control booth. But when Brian went into the studio to play bass and sing, Murry often changed the settings. "Murry preferred a really trebly sound on guitar," Marks recalled. "When you heard that first drum beat of 'Surfin' Safari' coming out of the radio, and those guitars cutting through, it was really exciting. Ironically, I think Murry was responsible for that."[13]

Venet thought the album was a good beginning, but it was a challenge working with Murry who was critical after each take. Brian was frustrated, but persevered.[14] Although Usher co-wrote five of the ten songs to be recorded, Murry resented his presence at the sessions and demanded he leave the studio. "Usher would come back when Murry was gone," Venet recalled. "He'd sit in the booth with me or go out into the studio. Then we'd get a phone call from the guard saying, 'Here comes Murry,' and Usher would leave."[15]

Usher recalled, "Murry had this close knit family band going, and I think he intuitively sensed success and was concerned about who could influence his boys. I had been around the record business for some time and he was a little leery of me. He wanted no one around who might undermine the control he had over his boys."[16]

Mike handled the lead vocal on "Ten Little Indians," inspired by the children's nursery rhyme, about nine Indian boys who fail to win an Indian girl's affection, and the tenth boy who wins her heart by being himself. Despite some dreadful lyrics, Mike does a good job with a fast-paced delivery. The highlight is the vocal harmony in the chorus which Brian arranged against pounding tom toms. "Besides 'Surfin' Safari,' Brian recalled, "'Ten Little Indians' represented the first original sounding Beach Boys' record. I had Mike singing lead and an exciting bass part in the chorus. The boys and I were singing 'woo-woos' to imitate American Indians."[17]

Usher recalled the song's inspiration was "Running Bear," written by J.P. "The Big Bopper" Richardson and recorded by his Cajun friend, Johnny Preston, who took it to #1 for three weeks in summer 1959.[18] Recording a song based on the nursery rhyme was not a new idea. Bill Haley and His Comets recorded a sax and guitar-driven "Ten Little Indians" in November 1953 that used Native American rhythms and the 'one little, two little' chorus. Ramsey Kearney released a variation called "Nine Little Teardrops" in June 1962. And there were plenty of precedents for Indian-themed records, including Chuck Berry's "Broken Arrow" (1959), the Renegades' "Geronimo (1959)," Larry Verne's "Mr. Custer" (1960), and the Revels' "Comanche" (1961).

"Chug-A-Lug," an ode to root beer that Brian mentioned would be the follow-up single, was an up-tempo, slice-of-teenage-life about cruising the root beer stand. Its clever lyrics offered insight into each band member's personality. Mike handled the lead vocal and counter bass vocals. The song was inspired by the drive-in A&W root beer stand on Hawthorne Boulevard that Brian and his friends frequented throughout high school. A popular Saturday night pastime was "Cruising the A"—turning into the A&W parking lot, exiting back onto Hawthorne Boulevard, and cruising five miles north to the Wich Stand at West Slauson Avenue and Overhill Drive in View Park-Windsor Hills, less than a mile south of Mike Love's house. Known as "The Stand" or "The Hill," this drive-in coffee shop restaurant anchored the northern end of a night of cruising for every young guy with a set of wheels to show off. And when you got hungry, a cheeseburger, fries, and milk shake set you back $1.05. Opened in 1957 by brothers Glen and Lewis Burford, the Wich Stand accommodated sixty-one people in the coffee shop and another fifty-eight in the bar/dining area. But if you were a teenager, it was cooler to use the drive-in. "Chug-A-Lug" had all the markings of a Top 40 a.m. radio hit—driving lead vocal, clever chorus, and a tasteful organ break followed by a sharp guitar solo. The song was copyrighted November 5 as "Root Beer (Chug-A-Lug)."

The third song recorded August 8, mistakenly written on the AFM contract as "The Baker," was Brian's and Mike's "The Shift," detailing Mike's appreciation for a female fashion re-popularized by First Lady Jacqueline Kennedy and actress Audrey Hepburn. The shift, a simple A-frame dress, typically sleeveless and knee-length, hung loosely from the shoulders without hugging the body's curves. By not accentuating the waistline, it allowed women greater freedom—to shift, both literally and socially. Surprisingly, despite the wholesome image Murry cultivated, the song contains sexually suggestive lyrics. It was the only song on the album that dealt, a bit obsessively, with the female form. Devoid of any lyrical sophistication, it seemed written by a pubescent boy. It did, however, feature a nice guitar solo, presumably from Carl.

These three new songs, along with their current single, gave them five songs for their debut album. It would be a month before they returned to Capitol to continue work on the album. In *Billboard* out August 11, "Surfin' Safari" moved from #85 to #79 and Capitol placed a full-page ad promoting its seven charted singles, listing "Surfin' Safari" second beneath Nat King Cole's "Ramblin' Rose." Cole was still King of the Tower, but Capitol's future would be with a younger sound.

While he was refining and rehearsing the remaining seven songs for the album, Brian turned his attention to two projects outside the group. He began working on "The Surfer Moon" with Bob Norberg and his girlfriend, Cheryl Pomeroy, who Brian befriended when the Beach Boys played a function for the Sigma Chi fraternity at USC that spring or early summer. Norberg and Pomeroy performed as Bob and Sheri between the Beach Boys sets. Before graduating USC in 1961, Norberg had been a member of Sigma Chi and played guitar in a rock 'n' roll trio with his fraternity brothers, Rich Miailovich (Class of '62) on drums and Dave Boyle (Class of '63) on piano. In fall 1959, Miailovich pledged for Sigma Chi and moved into the fraternity's house at 928 West 28th Street on The Row with his Slingerland drum kit. He soon discovered Norberg played guitar, a Silvertone 1421 hollowbody electric with two pick ups, a single cutaway, and a shaded walnut finish. They struck up a friendship and added Boyle, a freshman pledge who applied his piano skills to the baby grand donated to the fraternity. Although they never had a name, the trio practiced weekly, playing two or three events a month on campus, the Sigma Chi house, or the home of a Hollywood celebrity whose son or daughter attended USC. "We played the hits of the day, songs like 'What'd I Say,' and shared the vocals," recalled Miailovich. "We backed up Connie Stevens when she visited the school and played at the home of Phillip Bonnell, a fraternity brother whose mother was Gale Storm. We never had aspirations of a music career. But, of the three of us, Bob was the most talented."[19]

After Norberg graduated in 1961, he and Miailovich drifted apart and the trio disbanded. As Miailovich never met Pomeroy, it seems likely Norberg began dating her sometime between graduation in June 1961 and spring/summer 1962 when Brian met them. Miailovich was quite active in campus social life, but does not recall the Beach Boys playing at the school. As the Sigma Chi house was razed in early 1962 to make way for a controversial new quarter of a million dollar house that fall, any event the Beach Boys played, while perhaps sponsored by Sigma Chi, was not held at the fraternity's house. There is no mention of the band in the *Daily Trojan*, the school's newspaper, during this period. A few events at which Brian may have met Norberg and Pomeroy include the senior farewell party (April 7), alumni day (April 28), and spring formals (May 4 and 5).

Norberg worked part-time as a photocopy machine salesman and swimming instructor, and later became a commercial airline pilot. Tall, thin, and soft spoken with a warm sense of humor, Norberg lived in a second-floor one-bedroom apartment in the Crenshaw Park Apartments at 10800 Crenshaw Boulevard in nearby Inglewood. He wrote songs and had rigged up a rudimentary, but effective, recording system with a Wollensak reel-to-reel tape deck, a second tape deck, a pre-amplifier, amplifier, and other electronic gear.

"The Surfer Moon" was a pretty, two and one-half minute ballad with a sweet melody and skillful lyrics about the moon's mysterious pull on tides and hearts. Like "Surfer Girl," it was one of the earliest songs for which Brian wrote both music and lyrics. Brian, Bob, and Sheri began working on a demo in the Wilsons' music room. To evoke the stillness of the evening, Brian wanted to overdub the sound of chirping crickets. "'The Surfer Moon' was the first thing Brian ever produced in his bedroom/music room at the Wilson home in Hawthorne," recalled Jodi Gable. "He held onto my legs as I hung out the window of the music room with a microphone to record the crickets. I just thought that was so cool."[20]

Bob and Sheri's personal relationship made an interesting impression on Brian. Judy Bowles recalled, "Brian would say, 'They love each other so much. One of them will get down on their knees and cry and say, please forgive me, let's get back together. And then the other one will say the same thing. That's something I would never do.' I don't think Brian thought a relationship should be like that."[21]

While working on "The Surfer Moon," Bob suggested Brian move in with him. It would allow them to work with fewer distractions and away from Murry's dominating influence. At twenty, whatever natural pull Brian felt toward independence from his parents was compounded by his unique circumstances. He had a Top Ten hit, a seven-year recording contract with a major record company, and was the musical leader of a band that included his two younger brothers. As the group's only songwriter, the responsibility of delivering their first album, indeed their future in the music business, fell solely on him. He had a clear vision of what he wanted to achieve, but needed the freedom and physical space in which to do it without having his creative choices second-guessed by his father.

"I was in the music room with Brian and Murry was in the bedroom watching television," Audree recalled. "Murry came rushing down and criticized Brian's rhythm. Brian was furious, just furious."[22] Tensions continued and shortly after beginning work on the "The Surfer Moon," Brian moved out of the Wilson home, packed his clothes and records into his Chevy Impala, and moved in with Norberg, splitting the $150 rent on his apartment. The move was less than two miles, but an incalculable step toward becoming an individual. "Brian didn't want to be held back in his creativity," recalled Norberg. "And it was hard for Murry to allow that."[23]

The move was not without tension. Murry later recalled, "I didn't mind so terribly much when you left our home to get an apartment, but the fact that you were ready to hit me in front of Gary Usher, when my wife and I were trying to get rid of Gary and his evil influence on our family, did cause much hurt because you left fighting against your own family for the benefit of Mr. Usher, his purposes, and your own selfish purposes which you and Gary were scheming out. You may have forgotten how Gary told you I was a square and didn't know what I was doing, and that you didn't have to listen to me because of countless other derogatory remarks made by people such as Bob Nor[berg]."[24]

Dave Nowlen, a guitarist and aspiring songwriter who later moved in next door to Brian and Norberg, recalled, "I had the door open and I was playing some Ventures tunes trying to get the attention of the girls down at the pool. This guy stuck his head in and said, 'Would you mind if I come in and sit down and listen?' I played another Ventures song and he said, 'You're pretty good. Have you ever done any recording?' I said, 'Yeah, have you ever heard of Dave and the Shadows from Grand Rapids, Michigan?' He said, 'No. Have you ever heard of the Beach Boys?' I said, 'Yeah.' He said, 'I'm Brian, I'm your next door neighbor.'"[25]

Although Brian was finally living on his own, he still had to navigate dealing with his father. Murry didn't just criticize what Brian did, he criticized him personally, which can have a far more corrosive effect. "Murry told him he would never be a man," recalled Nowlen. "Brian ripped his [Murry's] eyeglasses off, threw them on the ground, broke them, and said, 'I'm more of a man than you'll ever be,' and jumped in his car. Murry was still trying to control Brian like a young kid."[26] When Murry suffered a fatal heart attack June 4, 1973, neither Dennis nor Brian attended his funeral. A few days later, Brian told *Record World* the loss of his father was "making a man of me."[27]

Typical for two young guys, the apartment Brian and Norberg shared was a sparsely furnished bachelor pad. "When you walked in the living room, there were two couches on the right side in the corner," Nowlen recalled. "They had an eight by five foot mirror encased in white wood, a Wollensak tape recorder, and barbells. Brian had a multi-function phone and they may have had a 1950s aluminum dining room table."[28] They began writing songs and recording demos. "Bob and Brian would spend hours writing, recording, and experimenting with sound," said Alan Boyd in his liner notes for *Hawthorne, CA*. "There's no doubt many of Brian's musical innovations were developed with Bob's help in that little apartment in Inglewood, particularly his techniques of doubling parts, vocals and instrumental, to get the lush swirling sound that became one of his trademarks. Bob would use a variable speed oscillator to change the pitch just enough on the second pass to create a 'dual-track audio' effect."[29]

In mid–August, "He's a Rebel," credited to the Crystals, but actually Darlene Love and the Blossoms, was released and spent two weeks at #1 that November. Produced by twenty-two-year-old Phil Spector at Gold Star with some of LA's best session musicians, the record changed Brian's world. From its infectious opening piano riff, the song exuded attitude and sexual tension unlike anything heard in a pop record.

"Bob Norberg introduced me to Phil Spector's music," Brian recalled. "I was so blown out by that sound. The drum sound was immediately special, the depth he was able to achieve through the drums."[30] "He used major seventh, minor, and minor seventh chords. That's where I learned how to produce records. I would listen to his records and pick up ideas. I'd try to work out how much echo he was using on particular instruments and how he achieved that sound."[31] "He taught me how to create a record versus how to make a record." One studio technique Brian gleaned from Spector was combining two instruments to produce a new sound.[32]

Brian now had several collaborators vying for his time. Usher, who had supplanted

Love as Brian's primary writing partner, was a little put off by Brian's friendship with Norberg. "I was probably a little envious because Brian and I were working together with some success," Usher recalled. "Perhaps I was also guilty of becoming possessive of Brian. I never had any words with Bob but, on a subconscious level, I resented him because he was a distraction from the projects Brian and I were doing. None of the group around the Wilson household thought Bob and Sheri had much going for them. I always suspected Brian might have liked the girl because she was quite attractive. They took up a lot of Brian's time because Bob would hang around for hours talking about just one little thing. The general feeling was that Brian should be putting more of his efforts into his own productions."[33]

Around midnight on August 16, Dennis and Al woke Gary Winfrey up from a sound sleep by tapping on his bedroom window. Al wanted to borrow $105, perhaps to buy a used car. At Winfrey's father's suggestion, they returned the next morning and signed a promissory note. Al reimbursed Winfrey when he got paid the following Friday.[34] With "Surfin' Safari" in the top three on KFWB and KRLA, and starting to climb the *Billboard* and *Cash Box* charts, the Beach Boys were not the same band Al left in February. Perhaps he was beginning to second-guess his decision to quit.

On August 19, the Beach Boys played the First Annual Surfer's Ball with headliner Dick Dale and the Del-Tones at the Palladium, 6215 Sunset Boulevard, from 8:00 p.m. to 1:00 a.m. The show was produced by Hal Zeigler and a 16" × 24" poster for the event listed the Beach Boys with "Surfin' Safari" beneath their name. The event was more of a dance than a concert and the Beach Boys played a forty minute set before Dale took the stage.

The following day, the Beach Boys kicked off a series of eleven appearances at The Broadway department stores throughout the LA area between August 20 and 25. The shows took place in The Terrace, the

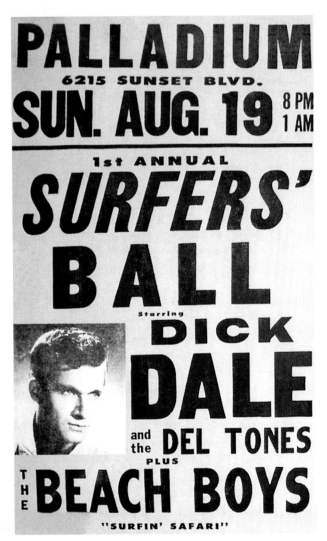

The Beach Boys played the First Annual Surfers' Ball, opening for headliner Dick Dale and the Del-Tones, on August 19, 1962, at the Palladium at 6215 Sunset Boulevard in Los Angeles (author's collection with appreciation to Stephen D. McClure).

store's rooftop restaurant, and promoted The Broadway's annual "Back-to-School Jam" and fashion show for its Teen Debutante Club. KFWB sponsored a Miss Teenage America contest and its disc jockeys emceed each event. An ad in the August 16 *Los Angeles Times* listed Kathy Linden, the Genteels, and the Beach Boys, all Capitol recording artists.[35] They each played short sets as they appeared, on average, at two stores a day. David Marks recalled, "The Broadway had a bunch of events all over Southern California and we always played on the roof."[36]

The August 23 *Hollywood Reporter* noted, "The Beach Boys, Capitol artists, have been set to record the musical score for a documentary motion picture completed by Dale Smallin of Glendora for the Azusa Teen Club. Brian Wilson, leader of the group, will do the arranging. Group also appears in the film performing 'Surfin' Safari.'"[37] The Beach Boys filmed their appearance in *One Man's Challenge* at the Azusa Teen Club on July 27, but whether they actually recorded the score for the film is the subject of some debate.

The evidence in favor of their involvement is: (1) the *Hollywood Reporter* news item was reprinted from a press release written by David McClellan based on information provided by Brian or Murry; (2) the late Dale Smallin, the film's writer and producer, was adamant when he told writer Domenic Priore the Beach Boys recorded the film's score; and (3) a song snippet in the film sounds a bit like "Surf Jam," an instrumental written by Carl and recorded February 12, 1963, for their second album.

The evidence against their involvement is: (1) David Marks recalled only recording "Surfin' Safari" for the film; (2) when Marks listened to the soundtrack with writer Jon Stebbins, he did not believe it was either Carl or him playing guitar on any other songs; (3) documentation such as a master tape, contract, or an AFM session sheet has never surfaced; (4) Marks recalled "Surf Jam" was improvised in the studio; and (5) there is some debate whether group members were skilled enough musicians at the time to record the soundtrack.

One Man's Challenge was released on DVD April 3, 2012.[38] Over the opening credits a title slide states "Music by the Beach Boys and the Raindrops." Hailing from nearby Glendora, the Raindrops were a young quartet with guitar, bass, sax, and drums. They performed an energetic two and one-half minute guitar and sax-driven instrumental onstage mid-way through the film.

Another title slide states "Opening Theme, 'The Hitchhiker' by the Genteels, courtesy of Capitol Records." The Genteels are not seen on camera and little is known of them except the lead guitarist was Lenny Angelo and the drummer was Carl Hubert. They were largely a studio creation of producer/engineer Paul Buff who ran Pal Recording Studio in Cucamonga, California, where "Wipe Out" and a demo of "Pipeline" were recorded in 1963.[39] In April 1962, the Genteels released "Take It Off," a surf instrumental cross between "Peter Gunn" and "The Stripper," paired with "The Hitchhiker" on Stag Records. When it got radio play in LA, Capitol picked it up in late June (Capitol 4798). Although the youth market was Nick Venet's domain, it was produced by Voyle Gilmore.

So, what does the audio evidence from the film reveal? The twenty-five minute film has four minutes of generic background music, three minutes where there is no music at all, and nine minutes filled by "The Hitchhiker," "Surfin' Safari," and the song by the Raindrops. The remaining nine minutes contain eight distinct musical passages—four forty-second guitar instrumentals; a twenty-second drum solo; a one-minute-and-forty-five second guitar instrumental cover of "Lonesome Town," a #7 hit for Ricky Nelson in 1958; a one-minute-and-twenty-second instrumental cover of "(Do the) Mashed Potatoes," a #8 R&B hit for James Brown and the Famous Flames, recording as Nat Kendrick and the Swans, in 1960; and a two minute-and-thirty-five second instrumental cover of "Midnight Sun," a jazz tune written by Lionel Hampton and Sonny Burke in 1947 for which Johnny Mercer wrote lyrics in 1954 and Ella Fitzgerald recorded on Verve in November 1957. One of the forty-second instrumentals sounds a bit like "Surf Jam," but it is uncertain whether this is an early version by Carl or if it inspired Carl's later composition.

It is unknown when or where the score for *One Man's Challenge* was recorded. Smallin produced the film for local television and wanted to reach teens as the new school year began, so late August or early September seems likely. The AFM Local 47 does not have a contract for it so it may have been a non-union session, which might be further evidence the Beach Boys did not participate because they may not have wanted to circumvent the union.

Carl never said anything publicly about recording the score and Marks's opinion that he and Carl do not play on the score holds considerable weight as musicians develop a personal style and recognize their own playing. The band is not known to have played "(Do the) Mashed Potatoes" or "Midnight Sun" in concert in 1962, at a time when cover songs filled out their live repertoire. It is possible the Beach Boys were set to record the score, but plans changed amidst rehearsals and recording sessions for their debut album. Unless further information is uncovered, it seems doubtful the Beach Boys recorded anything for *One Man's Challenge* except their on-screen performance of "Surfin' Safari."

On August 25, three days after David Marks turned fourteen, "Surfin' Safari" dethroned "The Loco-Motion" to become the #1 record on KRLA and KFWB. Making its debut at #22 on KFWB was a song by a vocal group that began a friendly rivalry with the Beach Boys by virtue of being from the opposite coast and featuring a lead singer with a brilliant falsetto. But that summer, as both groups launched their careers, the Four Seasons ruled the charts. The following week, "Sherry," written by group member Bob Gaudio, began a four-week run at #1 on KFWB followed by three weeks at #2. Nationally, it was #1 in *Billboard* and *Cash Box* for five and six weeks, respectively. Brian couldn't turn on the radio late summer without hearing "Sherry," and being inspired and challenged by Frankie Valli's falsetto, Gaudio's songwriting, and Bob Crewe's production.

Usher recalled that summer he and Bonnie went on a double date with Brian and Judy to a drive-in. "We were all drunk on beer singing 'Sherry' at the top of our lungs. It was Brian's favorite song at the time."[40] Marks recalled riding to the Azusa Teen Club in Audree's Ford Falcon station wagon when "Sherry" came on the radio, inspiring an impromptu singing lesson from Brian. "When we got to the gig, Brian took us into the restroom and taught us the vocal parts to 'Sherry.' We played it that night and kept it in our set for quite a while."[41]

On August 25, with the #1 record in LA, the Beach Boys played the sixth annual Reseda Jubilee, a community carnival that featured rides, games, food concessions, and entertainment. The event ran August 22 to 26 in Reseda in the San Fernando Valley twenty-two miles northwest of Hawthorne. Jodi Gable recalled, "They played in a parking lot in front of a market and to one side there was a little carnival going on. Before the show, they all came to my house and my dad made maps for them because it was in Reseda and they didn't know how to get there. My mother was in the kitchen making sandwiches. That night 'Surfin' Safari' went to #1 on KFWB. Carl, Denny, and I went over to a friend's house who had a keg of beer and we toasted 'Surfin' Safari.'"[42]

Also on the bill at the Reseda Jubilee were Jan & Dean. This may have been the first time the Beach Boys met them. "Since we weren't a self-contained band," Dean Torrence recalled, "the Beach Boys were going to back us up. So we met a couple of hours early in a house trailer and practiced. They learned our four songs and they had their six or seven. The audience was very pro–Beach Boys. It went pretty quickly. After they did their songs, we did our songs. We didn't talk very much. The total concert was maybe thirty minutes." When the audience wanted an encore, he and Jan suggested they sing "Surfin'" and "Surfin' Safari." "They kind of looked at us as if to say, 'You'd do our songs with us *and* let us stand up front?' They thought they had to stand in the back. They were really amazed. We had a lot of fun doing it."[43]

Brian and Mike found they had a lot in common with the duo and they became fast friends. Although they were only Mike's age, Jan & Dean had been recording together for more than four years and had just released their sixteenth single. Jan was a versatile singer whose range could handle low and high parts, and who had a tremendous influence on Mike. Brian and Mike soaked up stories of their experiences in the industry, how they approached songwriting, and the little pearls they learned about recording studios.

On August 26, the Beach Boys began a five-night stay at Pandora's Box. Jodi Gable recalled, "They played Pandora's Box for five days straight and I was there every night. My parents would drop me off and one of the boys would take me home. I remember Jackie DeShannon and Sharon Sheeley visiting one night while the Beach Boys played. It was a

Jodi Gable with the Beach Boys backstage at Pandora's Box in summer 1962 (courtesy Jodi Gable).

very small club and the tables were so tiny that, if you had to go to the bathroom, someone had to get up and move the table to get out. That's the first time they encountered an obsessive fan, an older guy attracted to Brian. The Wilsons sat him down, had a long talk with him, and, finally, he was banned from the club."[44]

Usher took Ginger and her cousin, Diane Rovell, to see the Beach Boys early on during their one-week stay at Pandora's Box. Impressed by the young guys in their Pendleton shirts, Diane convinced her younger sister, Marilyn, to attend the show the following night. "They were on stage singing," Marilyn recalled. "I was drinking hot chocolate. After they finished their song, Brian looked at me and said, 'Can I have a sip?' I said, 'Sure' and, as he gave it back to me, it spilled all over me and we started laughing. That's how we met."[45]

Diane, Marilyn, and Barbara Rovell were born in Chicago to Mae Gausmann and Irving Rovell (originally Rovelski). Irv owned and operated a hand laundry. Their home was filled with music and the girls spent hours gathered around Mae's piano singing their favorite songs by the Andrews Sisters and the McGuire Sisters. Ginger (real name Saundra Glantz) was also born in Chicago and grew up with show business parents—Dorothy, a ballerina, and Gene, whose vaudeville act sometimes included three-year-old Saundra and her eight-year-old sister. In 1955, both families made the westward trek to Southern California. With a $6,000 loan from his mother, Irving and Mae bought a two-bedroom white stucco house at 616 North Sierra Bonita Avenue for $16,000. He began working as a metal worker for the Lockheed Aircraft Corporation at the Burbank airport and part-time on weekends as a clothing salesman.[46] By 1958, the Rovell Sisters (Diane, 13; Marilyn, 11; and Barbara, 9) had developed a stage act and were appearing on local television shows and competing in amateur talent contests like *Rocket to Stardom* with their renditions of the McGuire Sisters' "Ding Dong" and "Sugartime," a #1 hit that March.

By 1962, Ginger was dating Usher, singing with Marilyn and Diane (Barbara had lost interest in the singing venture), and working at Pacific Bell, where she wrote "Shoot the Curl" on the back of a telephone company envelope. The title was slang for riding a surfboard inside a wave with the curl of water above your head. Diane helped her finish the song and the girls recorded a demo, but nothing came of it.

"Brian was always eccentric," Marilyn recalled. "From the day I met him I couldn't stop laughing. Just everything he did was funny. The way he lifted his fork was funny."[47] Marilyn, Diane, and Ginger began singing over at the Wilsons' house. "Brian was fascinated by women to begin with," recalled Marilyn. "He just took a liking to us and the different sounds of our voices, and was kind of infatuated. We all became real good friends. Brian was a very, very, very tender person, but to him being tender was sissiness. Brian always felt that people would laugh at him because he sang really high like a girl. That was just his voice naturally and he loved singing like that. He always wanted a low voice and he had a hang-up about it."[48]

When Ginger went to Pandora's Box, she recalled, "Gary said, 'Do not laugh at Brian if he starts to sing falsetto. He's very self-conscious about it and he's trying out this song "Surfer Girl."' So, Brian sang and somebody in the audience started to laugh. He got very upset about it. I told him, 'They're not laughing, they just never heard anything so great before.'"[49]

When Brian met fifteen-year-old Marilyn Rovell at Pandora's Box, he was smitten. There was just one problem. He was dating fifteen-year-old Judy Bowles. "I went to Pandora's Box a lot," Judy recalled. "That was one of the first steady gigs they had. But it was an unpleasant experience for me. When he became attracted to Marilyn, I think I was on my way out. He pursued Marilyn. He ran his fingers through her hair and said things like 'I like your hair.' Marilyn had a couple of sisters and he started going over to their house. One day he came to me and said, 'All I wanted was a family.' That was the reason he went there. They welcomed him with open arms."[50]

That summer, as "Surfin' Safari" worked its way up the charts, the Beach Boys played a variety of gigs, some for free, to garner a larger audience and build their reputation as a live band. They played a private party for television producer (*Topper* and *Mr. and Mrs. North*) John W. Loveton's eighteen-year-old daughter, Laurie Jean, in the back yard of their home at 440 South McCadden Place in the Hancock Park section of LA. Laurie graduated from the exclusive Marlborough School on June 7. The band ran extension cords into the home and played on the concrete terrace overlooking the lawn and in-ground swimming pool.

Murry accompanied the Boys to Fresno where, in wilting 100 plus degree heat, they hoisted their gear up a ladder to play on the tar roof of a one-story building at 2020 East McKinley Avenue that housed radio station KMAK.[51] Billed as the First Annual McKinley Avenue Festival of the Water, a tongue-in-cheek promotional stunt after street construction disrupted water service to the station and disc jockeys urged listeners to bring them water. In lieu of payment, Murry accepted a voucher for free food at Sambo's Restaurant two blocks west at the intersection with North Blackstone Avenue.

Ron Swallow, Carl's friend from Hawthorne High who often traveled with the band as a roadie, provided rehearsal space that summer in his parents' garage at West 123rd Street and Glasgow Place in Del Aire just west of Hawthorne. Occasionally, they ran extension cords from Swallow's home and practiced across the street on the athletic field adjacent to Juan de Anza Elementary School. Swallow recalled they played several times that summer at the Rendezvous Ballroom in Balboa and the Cinnamon Cinder, a night club for the younger set co-owned by KRLA disc jockey Bob Eubanks. The Cinder opened that July on Ventura Boulevard in Studio City.

During a business trip to LA that summer, twenty-nine-year-old Seattle disc jockey and concert promoter Pat O'Day (real name Paul Berg) was introduced to Murry Wilson by Jay Swint, a former Capitol Records' marketing executive who had worked for the label in Seattle. Murry was anxious for the boys to break into new markets and O'Day agreed to book them into the Spanish Castle, a dance hall on the Seattle-Tacoma Highway south of Seattle, and his Party Line club which had just opened that August at 707 1st Avenue in the historic Pioneer Square district in downtown Seattle.[52] O'Day promoted the shows on his KJR radio show, sent Murry five round-trip airfare tickets at $110 apiece, and the group, with Brian, flew into Seattle on a Friday afternoon. The Spanish Castle held 2,000, but less than 300 people showed up. Attendance the following night at the 200-seat Party Line was light. O'Day recalled, "The Beach Boys had two hits then ["Surfin'" and "Surfin' Safari"]— but it's one thing to have a hit and a whole 'nother to be a *dance* attraction. Well, we brought them up for the weekend to play the Spanish Castle and then they played my club, the Party Line. And it was a *disaster*. The Beach Boys were booed off the stage their first time in Seattle!"[53] O'Day explained, "Seattle teens were accustomed to rock 'n' roll dance bands dressed in peg pants, sports jackets, narrow ties, and leather boots. They didn't know what to make of five guys from Southern California with sun-bleached hair, denim jeans, and Pendleton shirts playing surf music."[54]

The band's initial lukewarm reception in the Pacific Northwest was not typical of how their music was received in most other regions. "Surfin' Safari" hit #1 in Buffalo, Hartford, Dallas, Minneapolis/St.Paul, Los Angeles, and San Diego. It was Top 5 in Chicago, Cincinnati, Columbus, Dayton, Nashville, New York, Phoenix, San Francisco, Springfield, and Tucson. But its fast-paced rhythm did not appeal to everyone. At a dance at the Prairie Dunes Country Club in Murry's hometown of Hutchinson, Kansas, an anonymous ninth grader commented, "Kids our age don't like to dance fast. Oh, maybe occasionally the girls like 'Surfin' Safari' by the Beach Boys; but when the crowd needs pulling together, or settling down, we play 'Tammy,' 'Together,' 'Moon River,' or 'Ramblin' Rose.' Everyone likes those pieces best."[55]

The last weekend in August, when "Surfin' Safari" hit #1 on KRLA and KFWB, it was #45 in *Cash Box* and #51 in *Billboard*. As it began to take off nationally, there was increased demand for the band's personal appearances and a need for a professional talent agency to represent them.

18

Beyond the Boys
(September 1962)

Twenty-two-year-old Mike Borchetta, in charge of promotion for Capitol Records in Southern California, Arizona, and Nevada, arranged for the Boys to audition with Al Alwhile, a talent agent at General Artists Corporation (GAC) in Beverly Hills. On the strength of "Surfin'," Borchetta had gone to see them perform at the National Orange Show Fairgrounds in San Bernardino that March. "They were the worst performing group I had ever seen," he recalled. "They were just all over the place. Their show left a lot to be desired. And now they were on Capitol. For some reason David couldn't make the audition and Al was with them. They rehearsed before the audition and Al wasn't quite with it. So I said, 'Al, sit down next to me. I don't think you're ready to work with the Beach Boys.'"

Alwhile liked what he heard and offered to sign the band with $1,800 guaranteed monthly. But after he met with Murry, Alwhile rescinded the offer and called Borchetta. "He said, 'I don't want them. I will not work with Murry Wilson.'" About a month later, Alwhile joined the William Morris Agency. Borchetta recalled, "He called and said, 'Mike, I'm cursed. They just signed the Beach Boys to William Morris and gave them to me. I can't stand this guy [Murry].'"[1]

Alwhile reassigned the Beach Boys to junior agent Marshall Berle, the twenty-four-year-old nephew of comedian Milton Berle, who had begun working at William Morris in February 1961 after serving four years in the Navy.[2] One of the first gigs Marshall booked for them was the seventeenth birthday party for Victoria Melanie Berle, the daughter his uncle and Joyce Mathews adopted as a newborn September 2, 1945, and named in honor of V-J Day, marking the Allies' victory in World War II.[3] The party was September 2 at Berle's Beverly Hills home. Berle and his new wife, Ruth Cosgrove, had just adopted an eight-month-old boy named Billy. Uncle Miltie complimented the Boys on their performance and slipped them each twenty dollars.[4]

On September 3, Labor Day, Al celebrated his twentieth birthday. He had completed two years of college, one at Ferris Institute and one at El Camino Community College. He worked that summer at Garret AiResearch, but had no engineering training to qualify for a long-term career with the company. To pursue a career as a dentist, he would have to finish another two years of college, pass the Dental Admission Test, and complete four years of dental school. His pre-dental curriculum included biology, chemistry, physics, and calculus. He registered for the fall 1962 semester at El Camino as a full-time student with a credit load that included a year of organic chemistry. For the next four months, Al concentrated on the abstract rigors of chemistry, played music, and sang with Gary and Don Winfrey.

226

Meanwhile, "Surfin' Safari," which Al had sung and played on when it was first recorded with Hite Morgan, dominated LA radio.

There is an AFM contract dated September 4 for an 11:30 a.m. to 2:30 p.m. session at Harmony Recorders, 1479 Vine Street, authorized by studio owner Bob Ross, at which Brian produced four songs for two projects outside the Beach Boys. "Humpty Dumpty," written and performed by Bob Norberg and Cheryl Pomeroy, was one hundred forgettable seconds about a fictional dance with silly references to the nursery rhyme. It became the B side to "The Surfer Moon." The couple's "Recreation," co-written with Brian and copyrighted with Sea of Tunes, clocked in at 1:55, remained unreleased, and little else is known of it.

Also recorded at this session was "The Revo-Lution," Brian's and Usher's West Coast response to Carole King's and Gerry Goffin's "The Loco-Motion," which Little Eva rode to #1 that August, inspiring a new dance craze. Brian and Usher hoped "The Revo-Lution" would spin the same magic. To create an authentic R&B record, they drove to South Central LA to find a black female singer. After asking strangers on the street, knocking on doors, fending off puzzled looks, and rejecting one hopeful singer, they reached an agreement with a young woman and began rehearsing at Brian's apartment. The woman has been reported to be Betty Willis or Betty Everett, but a case could be made it was neither.

When Brian felt she was sufficiently rehearsed, he booked time at Harmony Recorders, but who paid for the session is unclear. Usher recalled borrowing the money from a co-worker at City National Bank. Meanwhile, unknown to Usher, Brian approached an unlikely financier, Al Jardine, who loaned him the extraordinary sum of $800, rather inexplicably because Al had borrowed $105 from Gary Winfrey just two weeks earlier. Murry may have referred to this session when, in May 1965, he wrote Brian, "When you think of how you and Gary conned me out of a recording session and let me pay your bills, not only for that series of deals, but for studio time while you were experimenting with other artists."[5]

"The Revo-Lution" featured a raucous R&B vocal over a sparse instrumental track. The AFM contract listed only three musicians—Brian, presumably on bass, Larry Lennear, a twenty-four-year-old saxman who toured with Little Richard in the late 1950s, and Dennis Wilson on drums. Usher, however, recalled it was Plas Johnson on sax and perhaps Sharky Hall on drums, noting, "It was the first session I know of where Brian recorded in a studio using professional musicians."[6]

Usher further recalled, "The saxophones were playing fifths, similar to Goffin's and King's arrangement of 'The Loco-Motion.' I would try to get the same kind of feel by getting into the spirit of the movement. This is how Brian and I worked in the early days by getting into the feel of what was going on around us."[7] Lambert noted, "I would say the resemblance is very close, deeper than just sound and groove, but not quite an instance of one song providing a template for another."[8]

Brian can be heard counting off the song and he, Usher, and Carl sang background vocals. The song suffered from a muddy mix that made some of the lyrics nearly indecipherable. The singer's vocal on the chorus, in which she drags out the 'rev' in revolution interminably, becomes strident and grating.

For the B side, Brian and Usher recycled their "Visions" from the first demo session that April at Western.[9] They renamed it "Number One," derived from the lyrics, and, despite being listed on the AFM contract, Usher recalled Brian overdubbed the singer's new vocal onto the demo's original instrumental track at his apartment. "He had a fairly up-to-date tape recorder and we were able to do overdubs. It was sung in the exact same key Brian sang it on the demo, and Brian and I snapped our fingers in the background. It was Brian, the girl, and a piano. A little echo was added to doll it up as a master."[10] "Number One" may have been listed on the AFM contract to process the song through the musician's union.

Brian asked record promoter Russ Regan to help place the finished master of "The Revo-Lution" with a record company other than Capitol. Regan brought it to his friend Randy Wood at Dot Records. Perhaps after passing on the Beach Boys, Wood was receptive to a record written and produced by the creative team associated with the group. Wood agreed and, in exchange for brokering the deal, Brian and Usher gifted the music publishing for "The Revo-Lution" and "Humpty Dumpty" to Regan's Algrace Music. The publishing for "Number One" was assigned to Usher's new company, aptly named Number One.

Because the vocalist on "The Revo-Lution" was reportedly under contract with another record label, she could not use her real name on the record. Brian and Usher came up with a spin-off of the song's title and called the group Rachel and the Revolvers. "The Revo-Lution" (b/w "Number One," Dot 16392) was pressed at Monarch Records and released around September 10. It was one of seven new singles Dot Records promoted in a full-page advertisement in *Billboard* on newsstands September 15. It received scant air play in LA, most notably on KDAY, and failed to chart. King and Goffin were safe for the time being; Brian still had a few things to learn about crafting a powerhouse pop record. But it was undeniably an important step in Brian's evolution as an artist and producer. "The Revo-Lution" was Brian's first production released outside of the Beach Boys. The distinction of his first *credited* production released outside the group, meaning a label notation "Produced by Brian Wilson," would soon go to "The Surfer Moon."

Regan did not see much return on his music publishing, but perhaps the biggest financial setback was dealt to Al Jardine. In 1986, during filming for the Beach Boys' 25th anniversary television special in Hawaii, Al reminded Usher that he never repaid the $800 loan for the "The Revo-Lution" session. Usher was mystified; he had been unaware Brian borrowed the money from Al.[11]

On September 5, the Beach Boys, Murry, Venet, and Derry Weaver resumed work on the group's debut album. They recorded three songs—covers of Eddie Cochran's "Summertime Blues" and Dante and His Friends' "Miss America," and a Brian original called "Land Ahoy."

ULTRA HIGH FIDELITY

Dot

PROMOTIONAL RECORD

not for sale

Algrace Music
BMI
Time 2:10

45-16392
MB-17165

DOT RECORDS, INC., HOLLYWOOD, CALIFORNIA · A DIVISION OF PARAMOUNT PICTURES CORPORATION

THE REVO-LUTION
(B. Wilson–G. Usher)
RACHEL
and The Revolvers
8-62

Inspired by Little Eva's "The Locomotion," written by Carole King and Gerry Goffin, Brian and Gary Usher wrote and produced "The Revo-Lution" by Rachel and the Revolvers in September 1962. This is a white label promotional copy of the single (author's collection).

"Summertime Blues" (b/w "Love Again," Liberty 55144, #8 Pop, #11 R&B), written by Eddie Cochran and producer Jerry Capehart, was recorded by Cochran at Gold Star in summer 1958. Cochran performed it on *The Dick Clark Show* August 30, 1958, and it charted sixteen weeks that fall. The twelve-bar blues anthem gave voice to teenage frustration. Capehart recalled, "There had been a lot of songs about summer, but none about the hardships of summer."[12] Twenty-one-year-old Cochran died Easter Sunday, April 17, 1960, when the taxi taking him to London's Heathrow Airport slammed into a concrete lamppost. The Beach Boys' cover of "Summertime Blues," which Brian recalled was suggested by Dave,[13] was the first time the song was recorded by a major artist since Cochran's death and Capehart reportedly attended the session. Brian recalled Carl sang lead, but Dave may have doubled the vocal. Mike provided the deep authoritative voice punctuating each verse. It is a competent, but unambitious version that captured none of Cochran's rock 'n' roll angst.

The second cover they recorded was "Miss America," written by Herb Alpert, Vince Catalano, and Donald Drowty (Dante). However, when it appeared on the Beach Boys album, Drowty was gone from the credits. Capitol also had difficulty keeping the song's title straight as it appeared as "Little Miss America" on the album jacket and "Little Girl (You're My Miss America)" on the record label. Brian gave Dennis the lead and his voice imparted warmth, sincerity, and vulnerability, making it a stand-out track on the album. But getting a take that met with Brian's approval was no easy task. On October 4, 1966, as the Beach Boys recorded the vocals for "Our Prayer" and the engineer called for take thirty-two, Dennis remarked, "Thirty-two! We're almost up to 'Little Miss America.'"[14] Four years later, the challenge of his first lead vocal was still a potent memory.

"Dennis used to sing 'Little Miss America' to me all the time," Jodi Gable recalled. "Denny used to tell people I was one of his first girlfriends. Probably not true, but cute he would say that."[15]

Brian's production of "Miss America" opened with the doo-wop refrain from the original, but modified some of the lyrics and structure. As a lead vocalist, Dennis was underutilized on early Beach Boys records, but with only twelve songs per album it was difficult for Brian to exercise a perfect democracy. The group's signature sound was established early on with Mike's youthful tenor and Brian's lush falsetto. Hence, the majority of leads were handled by them. But Brian sensed when Dennis's earnest, everyman voice suited the material.

"Land Ahoy" has a fast-paced rhythm track with Mike singing about a guy at sea who spots land and anticipates reuniting with his lover. The break features hand claps and a simple guitar solo. It's another early song written by Brian alone, but one of his weakest and it is hard to fathom its inspiration.

On September 6, everyone was back to work at Capitol recording three Brian and Usher originals—"Cuckoo Clock," "Heads You Win, Tails I Lose," and "County Fair"—and a cover of the Gamblers' "Moon Dawg!"

"Cuckoo Clock," written on the AFM contract as "Cookoo Clock," is a silly tale of a how a guy's plan for an amorous evening with his girlfriend is thwarted by the inopportune appearance of the cuckoo. Brian sings a mid-range vocal over a metronome-like chorus of "tick tock" and a pretty Hammond organ break. The chorus mimics the cuckoo and implores him to go away. It was inspired by Murry's pet mynah bird and a practical joke Brian played on his father. One night, Brian and Usher hid Brian's Wollensak outside Murry's bedroom window and played a recording of the mynah bird. When Usher could no longer contain his laughter, he let out a loud shriek. "Murry came to the window and screamed, 'Usher! Is that you? I can't see you, but I can hear you. You're going to pay for this!' That episode sealed my fate around the Wilson household. I don't think Murry ever let me in the house again unless he had a good reason for me being there."[16] Another night Brian played a similar gag with a tape that repeated, "Hey, who's there?," waking Murry and prompting him to investigate. Brian persisted, but fessed up when Audree became worried.[17]

About "Heads I Win, Tails You Lose," Usher recalled, "Brian and I would always flip a coin to decide things. We were always looking for contemporary expressions to make into songs."[18] The song, whose title was a popular trick usually played on unsuspecting younger kids, was about a guy trying to level the playing field with his girlfriend. Mike sang lead and demonstrated his facility at handling rapid-fire lyrics.

"County Fair" was written after the Beach Boys played the National Orange Show in San Bernardino in March. It's a humorous tale about a young guy named Nicky, a comical wink to Venet, pressured into trying to win his girlfriend a stuffed animal at a local fair. It begins with a rolling guitar riff reminiscent of Johnny Preston's "Feel So Fine" from June 1960. Writer Don Cunningham noted, "In the first eight measures, Mike repeats a downward vocal arpeggio, truly lacking in nuance, in counterpoint with a base chord which moves up. Musically, the song never develops from there."[19] There is no refrain and the verses are punctuated with the spoken words of a carnival barker (Venet) baiting Nicky as his girlfriend pleads for him to win a stuffed koala bear. Marks told Stebbins that Andrea Carlo, his seventeen-year-old aunt and mother's younger sister (Jo Ann Marks was thirty-three at the time), was invited to observe the recording session and Murry suggested she record the part of the girlfriend. The song ends when Nicky, unable to win the prize, loses his girl to a stronger guy. A clever production touch was the organ rendition of Juventino Rosas's "Sobre las olas" ("Over the Waves") behind the spoken interludes. That 1888 waltz, a popular tune at fairs and amusement parks, created a dreamy, whirling atmosphere. Brian may have known the melody as "The Loveliest Night of the Year," a #3 hit in 1951 by Mario Lanza in MGM's *The Great Caruso*.

As the first band to cover "Moon Dawg!," the Beach Boys helped solidify its status as a surf music staple long before it was recorded by the Challengers, Ventures, Tornadoes, and Surfaris. The Beach Boys' version was even called "Surf Dawg!" on the AFM contract, but retained its original title on the album. David and Carl laid down a relentless rhythm track on their dual Stratocasters. Reportedly, Carl also played drums and lead guitar, which would have required overdubbing. The guitar licks that punctuate the rhythm track are solid, but not as blistering or frenetic as Weaver's original with the Gamblers. The continuous "aahhs" for background vocals were modeled on the original and Venet reprised his wolf howls.

In early September, in preparation for the marketing campaign to promote *Surfin' Safari*, Capitol released its first official biography of the Beach Boys and mailed it to the media, music press, and radio stations. Written by Venet to appeal to teenagers, the two-page biography tried hard to be hip. It is silly, sophomoric, and filled with hyperbole. The emphasis was on marketing, not historical accuracy, and Venet introduced a number of errors into their early history. He stated it was November 1961 when Dennis came up with the idea for "Surfin'"; Mike wrote the song by himself; Venet signed them immediately after hearing it;

bi·og′ra·phy

THE BEACH BOYS

Surfing is a comparatively recent phenomenon on the West Coast. Yet the sport has become so popular that the coast line where intrepid youths hitch hair-raising rides on high rolling waves is beginning to take on the look of a Los Angeles freeway during rush hour.

Soaring with these sturdy lads among the white caps was one Dennis Wilson, 17, who decided last November that it was high time somebody lionized the sport in song.

Somebody did, thus starting the wave of popularity which swept The Beach Boys with breath-taking speed to the front rank of hit makers.

Dennis took the song idea to his musically talented and versatile family. His cousin, Mike Love, wrote "Surfin'." His brother Brian got together a vocal group consisting of cousin Mike, Dennis, and a third brother Carl. Dad Murray Wilson, a long-time songwriter, ram-rodded a recording session.

The West Coast was soon inundated by the sound of The Beach Boys and their new hit. The saturation success in California was, in fact, sufficient to give the disk a respectable rating on nationwide best-seller lists.

With an ear ever to the ground to detect the slightest vibration of a new musical trend, young Capitol Producer Nick Venet heard the roar of The Beach Boys' first hit, immediately snagged them for an exclusive Capitol contract.

(MORE)

Capitol Record's first official Beach Boys biography, written by Nick Venet in September 1962 with input from Murry, oversimplified their origin story and contained several errors. It became the basis for virtually every story on the band through 1963, including the Artist Biography that appeared in the October 6, 1962, *Billboard* (author's collection).

and Murray (the misspelling of Murry always a red flag for careless research), a long-time songwriter and, apparently, a guitarist, ramrodded the first recording session. The bio did, however, get the group's personnel change correct. David was described as "the youngest and newest member of the group" who joined "after an original member dropped out."[20]

With recording for the album finished, Capitol art director Ed Thrasher began work on the album cover design. The band's name and album title *Surfin' Safari* pretty much dictated an outdoor surf-related theme. Thrasher and Kenneth Veeder, Capitol's in-house photographer, chose a stretch of beach in Malibu called Paradise Cove whose sheltering cliffs provided a dramatic visual backdrop. It was just a few miles south of Leo Carillo State Beach where *Gidget* was filmed. Thrasher spotted a beat-up yellow truck on Hollywood Boulevard and offered the driver, a beach character called Calypso Joe, fifty bucks for the one day use of his truck. It wasn't a woody, but with its running board, heavy tires, and open back, it looked like a vehicle surfers could use for hauling their boards to the beach. With Veeder and the band following, Calypso Joe trekked twenty miles north on Pacific Coast Highway to Paradise Cove.

Veeder directed Calypso Joe to inch his truck down to the shoreline until it was framed by the cliffs and a slice of Pacific Ocean. The vast stretch of overcast sky was the perfect backdrop for Thrasher to place the album's title, group name, and song titles. The guys piled out of their cars, milling about barefoot on the beach while Veeder prepared for the shoot. They were dressed alike—white T-shirts, blue plaid Pendleton shirts, and khaki chinos. They unloaded Dennis's 9'1" Hermosa surfboard, off-white with two blue stripes bracketing a central red stripe, sold exclusively by The Outrigger, a surf shop at 2606 Hermosa Avenue in Hermosa Beach. Although no one realized it at the time, the surfboard would become the central element of an iconic image of the band. And yet, two years later, as Murry prepared to move from Hawthorne to 9042 La Alba Drive in Whittier, he told his sons to clear out their remaining belongings including the surfboard. Dennis carried the board across the street and asked Louie Marotta to store it for him. Marotta slid it along the rafters in his garage where it remained for the next two decades until he gifted it to Robert Stafford, a close friend and life-long Beach Boys fan who named his son Brian in honor of the oldest Wilson brother. The Staffords loaned the board, yellowed with age and a bit scarred from use, to the Grammy Museum in LA for *Good Vibrations: 50 Years of the Beach Boys*, a year-long exhibit that opened September 18, 2012. When the exhibit closed, the board was offered for sale through Rockaway Records initially for $150,000.

Veeder fitted the truck with palm branches to give it a tropical island feel. He took several posed shots to ensure he had something usable for the cover, positioning them on the truck to keep the composition visually interesting. Mike and Brian perched atop the truck, clutching the surfboard under their left arms, shielding their eyes from the sun, and gazing at the Pacific. David sat on the hood and pointed, ostensibly to a breaking wave. Carl peered timidly from the back looking rather unsportsmanlike. Dennis sat in the driver's seat like he owned the truck. He gazed out the side window with his right arm draped comfortably on the wheel. The Beach Boys were not alone at Paradise Cove that day. In the background, seen through the truck's side window just above Denny's head, are two youngsters playing at the water's edge, unaware of their presence on this classic album cover.

Once he knew he had something Thrasher could use, Veeder set them free and clicked away unobtrusively. The outtakes show five young guys lounging on the beach, kicking sand at each other, checking under the hood, and leaping off the truck in unison. When the work was done, Mike, Dennis, and David raced into the breaking surf with the board. Brian stood off to the side—the quintessential observer and chronicler of the sport.

"He thought they were a bunch of goofy kids," Jane Veeder recalled of her then-forty-three-year-old father. "He was used to working with Frank Sinatra, Nat Cole, and Peggy Lee. Who were the Beach Boys? He was a jazz fan and wasn't impressed with them musically."[21] But Veeder's photograph was the perfect melding of sight and sound. At first, the music defined the image. Now the image amplified the music into bigger ideas and universal dreams. This was the West Coast. California. Carefree, dangerous, and exciting. Brimming with possibilities as vast as the Pacific itself. The dozen songs tucked inside this album jacket were things young people cared about. Honest, direct, infectious, stripped down rock 'n' roll. This image, a moment captured in time, introduced the Beach Boys to the world.

For the back cover, Thrasher divided the 12-inch square into quadrants into which he dropped the two obligatory design elements—a block of text about the Beach Boys and the surfing craze, and the list of song titles bathed in an eye-pleasing amount of white space.

With the text blocked out, Thrasher could exercise a little more creativity with the remaining two quadrants. He anchored the upper left corner with a pen and ink drawing of a woody loaded with surfboards heading down the road, capturing the escapism and freedom of a surfing safari. As the front cover showed the guys at play on the beach, Thrasher used Veeder's photographs of them at work in the studio. Once again, they were instructed to bring their white T-shirts, Pendleton plaid shirts, and casual and dress pants. There they were, right off the beach, with guitars and drums, making music. But all of them dressed uniformly made for a static image. So Veeder had Brian, Dennis, and Mike shed their Pendletons and photographed them in their T-shirts. He left David in his long-sleeve Pendleton and Carl in a short-sleeve Pendleton. To evoke a casual beach look, he had Carl in white socks, Dennis barefoot, and Mike in flip flops. He captured them playing their instruments and doing what they did best, harmonizing around a music stand. David and Carl anchored the rhythm section with Denny keeping the beat, his sun-bleached hair falling over his eyes. Brian and Carl each took turns at the bass. It gave the photos a relaxed, dynamic look. The images were as exciting as the promise of the music inside. You believed these guys worked as hard as they played. Here was staid Capitol Records, the hallowed studios where Sinatra and Nat King Cole recorded in suit and tie, overrun by teenagers in T-shirts. A clear signal, if not a complete changing of the guard, that this was the new young sound of Capitol.

Five of Veeder's photos made it onto the back cover. Outtakes include a photo of Mike on his knees honking the sax that may have been nixed because Venet can be seen playing guitar in the background. Another captured Dennis stompin' away barefoot with a blonde, reportedly the girlfriend of Venet's younger brother, Steve.

As the Beach Boys completed their first album, Brian's talent and leadership became more evident. It was clear Brian could do it all. He wrote, arranged, and played music. He was a competent lyricist, had a beautiful singing voice, taught the guys their instrumental parts, and arranged their vocal harmonies. He had earned Chuck Britz's respect at Western and was learning to use the recording studio to interpret and expand his creative vision.

Brian owed much of his progress to Usher, who introduced him to Chuck Britz, helped record the demo that landed the Capitol contract, and suggested they form their own music publishing company. It was Usher who urged him to dismiss Murry's antiquated musical ideas and pursue his own path. It was Usher who encouraged him to get competitive with his songwriting and record production. It was Usher who helped him crystallize his musical ideas, guiding him through a songwriting apprenticeship as he transitioned out of his teenage years.

On September 7, the day after the Beach Boys completed work on their first album, Hite Morgan finalized lease contracts for the tape rights of "Surfin' Safari" backed with "Luau" to five foreign record companies—Radio Record Co. of Africa Pty. Ltd. (South Africa), Arc Sound Ltd. (England), Ariola G.m.b.H. (West Germany), Editions Musicales Charles Bens (Benelux and Scandinavia), and Dick James Music Ltd. (the territories of the United Kingdom). Morgan received an advance payment of fifty dollars per contract. The New York attorney handling the transactions expressed interest in "receiving sample pressings of the additional masters you mentioned which embody the Beach Boys and three sets of tapes for 'Surfin Safari / Luau.'"[22] It is unknown whether Morgan forwarded pressings of any other recordings he produced for the Beach Boys.

"Surfin' Safari'" (b/w "Luau," RCC 736) was released in Johannesburg, South Africa, that fall in a company title sleeve, erroneously crediting "Luau" to Brian and Mike. Morgan did not receive label credit as producer and had to share the music publishing for both songs.

"Surfin' Safari" (b/w "Luau," Ariola 45 441), released in West Germany in a company title sleeve, was a mono mix of the stereo overdub attempt on take six recorded February 8, 1962, at World Pacific. Only 800 copies were pressed and it was notably different from the version the Beach Boys recorded at Western that April and released on Capitol. The guitar solo is different, the drumming less skillful, and the overall production not as crisp. It had the earlier lyrics and, in the process of making Ariola's copy, Morgan also sped the tape up. The label notation "Original X Records Recording" generated incorrect speculation Morgan owned X Records. This alternate "Surfin' Safari" was only available on the rare Ariola single until it appeared on *Lost & Found* in 1991.

On September 13, a week after the *Surfin' Safari* album sessions concluded, Brian, the other Beach Boys, and Murry, were at Western to lay down the instrumental track for "The Surfer Moon" and to record "Cindy, Oh Cindy," a Top Ten hit for both Vince Martin and the Tarriers, and Eddie Fischer, in late 1956 when Brian was a high school freshman. In June 1962, the Highwaymen recorded "Cindy" as the B side of "The Birdman" from the soundtrack to the Burt Lancaster film *The Birdman of Alcatraz.* "Cindy" was standard '50s fare about a sailor pining for his girl. Like the Highwaymen, Brian began with the first verse and not the chorus as did Martin and Fischer. Lambert noted, "They gave it their best shot, trying to give

Hite Morgan leased an alternate version of "Surfin' Safari," recorded February 8, 1962, at World Pacific, to Ariola Records in West Germany (author's collection).

it a rock beat and hip arrangement, but perhaps it was just too undeniably folkish, too square."[23]

Around September 12 or 13, Brian and Dennis were interviewed by Daryl Dry for the Armed Forces Radio & Television Service. The interview began with "Surfin' Safari," which Dry mentioned was #11 in Australia, and ended with "409." There are a number of interesting things revealed in this six-minute interview, some of which are better appreciated listening to it. For instance, Brian comes across quite humble, emphasizing their success was a group effort. When asked about the arrangements, he sheepishly admitted, "I do most of it." When Dennis discussed having finished *Surfin' Safari* a week earlier, the calm confidence and surety in his voice is not your average seventeen-year-old kid being interviewed. He spoke about the album's chances for success as if he was the group's leader. When the subject of school came up, Dennis said Carl and David were in junior and freshman year of high school, respectively, but omitted he had dropped out of school and was not attending his senior year at Hawthorne High. Although the interview does not sound scripted, it is clear the Capitol Records' marketing machine was already in full force. Dry stated, "Your dad, of course, was Murry Wilson, who was a long-time songwriter," lifted verbatim from Capitol's biography. When asked about personal appearances, Dennis replied, "We're planning on going to Las Vegas, Nevada, we hope, if we're lucky, and we've been playing Hollywood at Pandora's Box."[24]

On September 14, the Beach Boys performed a few songs in the cafeteria of Hawthorne High School to celebrate Howdy Hop, an annual event to welcome incoming freshmen by encouraging students to greet each other with "Howdy!" A photograph of Brian, Carl, and David, in matching olive-brown cardigan sweaters, appeared in the 1963 *El Molino* yearbook under the headline "Welcome Back to School." That evening they played the Surfers Ball at Morgan Hall at 835 Locust Avenue in Long Beach. For $1.50, teens stomped from 8:00 p.m. to midnight to the music of the Beach Boys, the Bonnavills ("Bonnavills Stomp"), Lonnie Belmore ("Night of Love"), Russ Starman ("Little Eva"), and Dean Long. A poster for the event advertised free records, a raffle for a free surfboard, and a stomp contest.

Edward Vandegrift, the UCLA student who booked the band at Dykstra Hall that summer, arranged for them to play at Helen Lee Stillman's sixteenth birthday party at her home at 327 Delfern Drive in the exclusive Holmby Hills section of LA. Because the party was written up in the society column in the September 16 *Los Angeles Times* and the band mentioned briefly,[25] it is presumed the event occurred the preceding day, September 15. But that might not be the case. Stillman noted her birthday is May 9 and, although she cannot be certain, does not believe her parents held the party four months later.[26] However, eighteen-year-old Barret Collins, Stillman's guest who flew in from Louisville, recalled that a day or two after the party he flew to San Francisco to begin his freshman year at Menlo College, placing the event in September.[27]

The Beach Boys arrived late at the Stillman home and were further delayed when Dennis discovered he forgot the key to the trunk of the car and could not retrieve his drums. Fortunately, a guest owned a similar vehicle whose key fit the lock. The band set up in the driveway near the garage and about seventy-five teenagers danced to their music from 8:00 p.m. to 11:00 p.m. Collins was not familiar with the Beach Boys, but the local kids all knew who they were. He remembered they were very loud and especially enjoyed hearing "409."

On September 22, the Beach Boys squared off in a battle of the bands against the

Casuals, a quintet of Oxnard teenagers formed in 1959 and managed by twenty-eight-year-old Tom Ayres, who co-owned a local record store. On September 3, the Casuals had won a battle of the bands on their home turf at the Roller Gardens skating rink in Wagon Wheel Junction. A local newspaper reported, "As a result of the victory, the Casuals will go another battle within two weeks, this time against an established Capitol Records outfit, The Beach Boys, whose record 'Surfin' Safari' is the number one hit in Southern California listings. 'They're a highly regarded group with a major agency representing them,' said Ayres. 'This will be the Casuals first big prestige show.'"[28]

Randy Ray, the Casuals' keyboard player, recalled, "They had 'Surfin' Safari' out, but our hometown crowd wanted us to be better than the Beach Boys. The first band would come on, play their set, and then break down their equipment. Then we played our set and the Beach Boys played their set. The voting was by applause and we won. But it was pretty subjective when you think about it. The song we did that would win every night was 'Shout' by the Isley Brothers. We did it with a lot of choreography and the audience response was always very good."[29]

"I didn't see the talent in the Beach Boys," Ray confessed. "I thought they were a flash in the pan. I didn't think the surf music craze was well respected. But none of us were top-notch musicians at the time. I think each of us knew about five chords. We were just young kids having fun with music. The competitiveness was popularity, not musicianship. We just wanted to be more popular than everybody. I was really impressed with Dennis because he had such energy. I remember telling our drummer, 'Man, look at him, you have to be more like him.' He was just very animated when he played, good eye contact with the audience, he was a joy to watch."[30] The Casuals later became the Dartells and scored a #11 hit with "Hot Pastrami" in summer 1963.

In *Billboard* out September 22, "409" debuted at #116 on the Bubbling Under the Hot 100 and a condensed version of the group's Capitol biography appeared in the recurring Artists' Biographies column. While surfing was limited geographically, "409" tapped into something guys everywhere wanted—freedom, power, respect, independence, and sex. It opened with the thunderous sound of a monstrous engine rumbling under a massive hood, a thrilling injection of automotive adrenalin. And when Mike's lead vocal and the group's layered harmonies entered, you had better buckle up for the ride.

"'409' was such an important song," recalled Bob Clark, disc jockey then at WHHM in landlocked Memphis. "I started playing it at night and I'd get telephone requests for it all the time. I never played 'Surfin Safari.' It was always '409' that was number one in my book. At the time, I had a '58 Ford with a big V-8. I wish I could have afforded a 409. Everybody knew what 409 meant. You have to understand the car culture in the Midsouth."

WHHM was in a ratings war with number one WDIA, and Clark was up against that station's Rufus Thomas, the popular R&B singer turned disc jockey. Around 9:00 p.m. one weeknight, Clark invited his listeners to cruise by the station with their windows open and tune in to WHHM. Over the next few hours, nearly a thousand cars converged on Poplar Avenue near the station's studio at the Hollywood Towers. Clark spun "409" for a straight hour, some thirty times in a row. "I walked outside and as far as I could see there were Chevys and people standing outside their cars waving at me," Clark recalled. "I could not believe the number of people that showed up that night or the sound of 1,000 horns honking. It was like the old days of rock 'n' roll Top 40 radio. It locked up most of downtown

Memphis. I got all kinds of complaints from the city, but the station manager called the next morning and said, 'God bless you, our ratings are going to go through the roof.' I got the record so hot and Poplar Tunes, the local distributor, had sold so many copies, I got a call from Brian Wilson thanking me for playing the record."[31] Brian was working his way down a list of radio stations Capitol Records had supplied in a promotional effort to boost sales. Whatever ratings boost "409" provided WHHM was short-lived. By the end of the year, the station went off the air after months of financial and legal struggles.

Despite its radio popularity, "409" did not enjoy much chart success. It peaked at #76 in *Billboard* out October 6, disappeared for four weeks, and resurfaced for three weeks at #102, #101, and #102. Its fate, however, was tied to "Surfin' Safari" and it may have fared better had it been released by itself as EMI/Capitol did in the Philippines with "Surfin' Safari" (b/w "Chug-A-Lug," Capitol 4-C-3036) and "409" (b/w "Cuckoo Clock," Capitol 4-C-3038). A third single from their debut album, "Summertime Blues," was also released there and reached #7.

On September 27, the Beach Boys played the Inter-Fraternity Council Street Dance on The Row, a stretch of fraternity houses at USC. The dance kicked off a weekend celebration of the reopening of the International Student House which had received a facelift by students during Help Week. For the 7:00 p.m. to 10:00 p.m. dance, the *Daily Trojan* mistakenly billed the Beach Boys as the "originators of the Surfer Stomp" instead of the Marketts who also performed.[32] That same night, surfers could also catch a free screening of *Surf Crazy* narrated by Bruce Brown in the Student Union at UCLA.

Capitol began working on the track line-up for *Surfin' Safari* shortly after the final recording session September 6. Because the standard album had twelve songs and the Beach Boys only had twelve for consideration, there wasn't much to the selection process. Capitol preferred to lead off each side of a pop album with a hit single. Because "409" had not charted yet, Capitol leased "Surfin'," a #3 hit in LA, from Hite Morgan and let it kick off side two. "Land Ahoy," the weakest of the ten new songs recorded for the album, remained in the can for now.

Hite Morgan maintained Nick Venet contacted him about leasing "Surfin'" and he granted his permission. It meant an additional two cents for Morgan for every album sold. Because he also owned the mechanical royalty for "Surfin' Safari," Morgan would now receive four cents for every album sold. But that's not how Venet recalled it. "Hite Morgan called and said he heard the Beach Boys were putting out an album and asked if Capitol would use 'Surfin'.' I said I would talk to the Beach Boys and see what they wanted to do. They were willing and Karl Engemann had the papers drawn up for the rights to the song. Morgan sent a tape over by messenger and gave us the label copy indicating the copyright should be Guild Music. He said the master was not doing him any good and he would just as soon collect the publisher royalties."[33]

By late September, with the line-up finalized, the album was mastered, metal works produced, and album jackets printed. Brian took Judy to see the album being pressed at Capitol's Los Angeles plant at 2121 North San Fernando Road. "I remember he was so excited to see the albums being made. And the little holes being punched out in the middle."[34]

On September 30, Capitol's quarterly royalty statement for "Surfin' Safari" indicated the single had sold 301,022 copies thus far and Hite Morgan received $6,020.44 in publisher royalties. The Beach Boys soon received their artist royalty and Brian, Mike, and Usher, their songwriter royalties. It was the first time they were paid a considerable sum of money for their music. Judy recalled, "After Brian received his first royalty check from Capitol, he asked my mom if he could pay for a phone in my bedroom. She said okay and the telephone man came and installed a pink Princess telephone."[35] Jodi Gable recalled that phone very well. "I was so jealous. I bugged my dad until he finally got me that same phone."[36]

Meanwhile the Beach Boys' success reaped dividends for their A&R man. The *Billboard* out September 29 reported Capitol signed Nick Venet to a long-term contract, thwarting efforts by RCA Victor and Columbia to lure him away. It made him the only A&R man at Capitol with such a commitment, advancing his reputation in the industry as a sought-after producer. Not yet twenty-five, he was at the peak of his Capitol career, turning out hits for Jimmie Haskell, Ray Anthony, the Lettermen, the Beach Boys, Bobby Darin, Lou Rawls, Glen Campbell, and a new Capitol artist, Johnny Rivers.

But less than a year later, after a bitter falling out with Murry and the Beach Boys, Nick Venet would resign from Capitol Records.

19

An Album Debut and the Pressure's On (October–December 1962)

October 1962

On October 1, on Deck Record Company stationery, Hite Morgan granted Capitol Records permission to include "Surfin'" on *Surfin' Safari* (Capitol T 1808), the Beach Boys' forthcoming debut album. He stipulated Capitol could use the song for three years, but only on *Surfin' Safari*. On October 19, he extended the grant for as long as Capitol cared to use it on that album. On November 6, Capitol sent Morgan a License Agreement for "Surfin'" and paid him one dollar, noting the master could only be used as part of an album.

In *Billboard* on newsstands October 13, the editors included *Surfin' Safari* as a Late Pop Spotlight indicating the album had just been released. *Billboard* called it "exciting wax for the teen set."[1] The *Cash Box* out the following week noted "the boys display some first-class vocal and instrumental talents." But not everyone agreed. Dave Wagner, youth editor for the *Daily Northwestern* in Oshkosh, Wisconsin, wrote, "A new album by a group of pseudo-singers who should have stayed on the beach. They have reached success by using the following formula: LITTLE TALENT plus INFERIOR MATERIAL plus TASTE-LESS DJ's equals BIG HIT. The album will follow the same equation."[2]

Clocking in just under twenty-five minutes, the album contained three hit songs—"Surfin'," "Surfin' Safari," and "409." There were six Brian and Usher songs, three by Brian and Mike, and three covers. Mike handled the lead vocal on seven songs, Brian on two, Dennis on one, Carl and David shared one ("Summertime Blues"), and one was instrumental.

Side one opened with the title track and closed with "409," while side two kicked off with "Surfin'," which Capitol's engineers sped up a semitone from the key of G to A flat. Its acoustic guitar, stand-up bass, and muffled snare drum, a stark reminder of the band's acoustic folk roots, lent the album a sense of completeness. This is where they came from. It was the only song on the album on which Al Jardine played and sang. It's interesting to wonder how the other songs on the album may have sounded if Brian had Al's voice in the mix as he mapped out the vocal arrangements.

By today's standards, *Surfin' Safari* was not a great debut album. But in 1962, it was a solid first effort, a product of its time when, on the strength of a hit single, record companies rushed out an album to capture sales while the single was hot. There was no concept yet of an album as a fully realized artistic statement. But its solid instrumentation, strong vocals, and goal-oriented production hinted at better things to come. And best of all, they did most of it, if not all, themselves. Not many bands were capable of doing that in 1962.

Surfin' Safari is invariably compared to other debut albums by major groups of the era, most notably the Beatles. In sixteen months, as the Beach Boys worked on their fifth album, *Meet the Beatles* raised the bar for debut albums. In hindsight, *Surfin' Safari* seemed amateurish by comparison. But in fairness to the Boys, the Beatles had been playing together, in one form or another, for six years before they released an album. They had matured through two personnel changes, learned how to play together as a band, perfected pop song-writing, secured a skillful manager in Brian Epstein who knew how to promote them, and, most significantly, joined forces with producer George Martin who was critical in shaping their sound. When Epstein arranged for them to audition for EMI, he sent George Martin a list of thirty-three songs to consider. In contrast, the Beach Boys had been together only nine months when "Surfin' Safari" hit, and Brian had to scramble to finish enough songs to fill an album. During that time, Brian's studio education was a handful of hours with Gary Usher and Chuck Britz at Western. But as his talent emerged, each successive Beach Boys album revealed him to be a producer of extraordinary skill and sensitivity.

In later years, the Beach Boys viewed *Surfin' Safari* as a quaint artifact, almost an embarrassment, of their beginnings. "That first album was shitty because Nick Venet was rushing us to get through with the session so he could get to New York and a session with Bobby Darin," Mike recalled. "He was saying things like, 'Come on, I have to get out of here and get to New York to cut Bobby.' I mean he was that blatantly ridiculous about it."[3] Regardless of what he may have told the Beach Boys, Venet did not produce a Darin session in New York that would have caused him to rush through any of the three sessions for the band's debut album.

"When I hear our first album I really laugh my head off," Carl recalled. "I crack up because it's a comedy album. It wasn't until after the first couple of years together that we started to appreciate what we were really doing. Now when I listen to those early albums they bring back good memories."[4]

Marks offered a reasoned perspective. "You listen to that first album today and it sounds campy, corny, but Brian was dead serious. Like 'Cuckoo Clock,' 'Chug-A-Lug,' and 'Ten Little Indians,' he was dead serious about them and that's what made them work. It wasn't like he was trying to put something over. 'Is this commercial?' There was no formulating, no plotting, no planning. He was just doing what he loved. He told me he wrote about things that turned him on—girls, cars, high school. It's hard to believe anyone could be that naive and honest, but he was. That's what made those records successful. You can feel the sincerity on them."[5]

In 1967, Dennis was asked if he was embarrassed about the surfing days. "People who called our stuff 'surfing music' didn't know anything about music. There's no such thing. Music is music. Period."[6]

Brian was a little more sentimental about his first effort. "I wasn't aware those early songs defined California so well until much later in my career. I certainly didn't set out to do it. I wasn't into surfing at all. My brother Dennis gave me all the jargon I needed to write the songs. He was the surfer and I was the songwriter."[7]

In 1962, Capitol was releasing most of its albums in both monophonic and stereophonic sound. Although *Surfin' Safari* was recorded in three track stereo, it has never been released in stereo. At the time, that was due primarily to economics. Most teenagers didn't own stereo equipment and wouldn't pay an extra dollar for a stereo album. Hence, Capitol saw no need to spend money mixing and mastering *Surfin' Safari* in stereo for a teenage market that wouldn't buy a stereo album anyway. Besides, who knew this bunch of kids called the Beach Boys would be around for fifty years and that one day these recordings would be historic.

Initially, Capitol released *Surfin' Safari* in monophonic (T 1808) and, on November 12, duophonic (DT 1808), which bore a banner across the top of the album cover noting, "Capitol Duophonic for Stereo Phonographs Only." When *Surfin' Safari* sold nearly half a million copies in three months, Capitol seized an opportunity to generate additional sales and released it in a new jacket with a banner across the top proclaiming "Capitol Full Dimensional Stereo." But rather than spend the time and money to actually produce and master a stereo mix, Capitol used the same duophonic mix and the album bore the same DT 1808 catalogue number. In fact, in some instances, new "Full Dimensional Stereo" album slicks were simply pasted over duophonic album covers. Stereophiles were not fooled and Capitol eventually discontinued the "Stereo" album covers.

Surfin' Safari is an eclectic mix when it comes to sound quality because the songs were recorded at different studios, by different engineers, and using different processes. "Surfin'" was recorded in mono by Hite Morgan and Dino Lappas at World Pacific, "Surfin' Safari" and "409" were recorded on two-track stereo by Chuck Britz at Western and mixed to mono, and the ten new songs were recorded at Capitol by Nick Venet in three-track stereo and mixed to mono. Because it is doubtful the original two-track tapes from Western survived, "Surfin' Safari" and "409" (and "Lonely Sea," recorded at the same session) can never be released in true stereo. But Beach Boys' musicologists have long pondered whether Capitol retained the original three-track tapes of the ten new songs recorded for the album. "Land Ahoy," the lone outtake from the album, was released in stereo on *Rarities* in 1983 and later included as one of three bonus tracks on the *Surfin' Safari* and *Surfin' U.S.A.* twofer compact disc in 1990. The appearance of a stereo mix of "Land Ahoy" gave rise to the hope the three-track tapes had been saved and that *Surfin' Safari*, or at least nine of its twelve songs, could someday be released in stereo.

On October 4, the Beach Boys played at a school assembly at Glendale Community College, twenty minutes north of Hawthorne. Their forty-five minute set got off to a rocky start when they had technical difficulties with their equipment. In addition to "Surfin'," "Surfin' Safari," and "409," they played "Monster Mash," "Palisades Park," and "Johnny B. Goode." They were not well received by the student body. *El Vaquero*, the college's weekly newspaper, printed a photograph of the band and a review of the show noting, "It appears the Beachboys' recording success far surpasses the success of their personal appearances. This was indicated by an unenthusiastic response toward the end of their performance. Their closing song, 'What'd I Say,' was sung to a rapidly departing audience, some muttering, 'If nothing else, they had volume.'" An unnamed band member told the reporter "Surfin'" had sold 100,000 copies, a generous estimation at best, and "Surfin' Safari" had already sold more than 500,000 copies. They added *Surfin' Safari* would be released soon and their next single would be "Ten Little Indians."[8]

On the day they played in Glendale, Milton Love filed for involuntary bankruptcy of the Love Sheet Metal Service Company. A court-ordered liquidation of the company's assets was assigned to auctioneer Jack H. Feldman and scheduled at the company's 3301 East 14th Street facility at 10:30 a.m. on November 15. As a result, Milton and Glee were forced to sell their home at Mount Vernon and Fairway. They moved into an 1,800 square foot home at 10212 South 6th Avenue in Inglewood made more affordable because it lay beneath the flight path for Los Angeles International Airport. The drone of planes overhead every few minutes was an audible reminder of how life had changed for the Love family. Although Mike was no longer living at home, this change in family circumstances must have been felt just as deeply.

In October, "Surfin' Safari" (b/w "409," Capitol CL 15273) became the Beach Boys' first release in the United Kingdom. *Disc and Music Echo*, a weekly British music paper, commented, "The Beach Boys sound like a very ordinary vocal group to me. And although they've got a fairly useful chanter in 'Surfin' Safari,' which is really doing well in the States, I can't see it reaching very high places. Routine material and presentation, which hardly seems worth the Atlantic crossing. '409' is either a motorbike or a hot-rod car. I'm not sure which, despite the sound effects gimmicks of the twister on this B side." The British did not yet embrace the Beach Boys and "Surfin' Safari" failed to chart.

It is interesting that as early as October 4, while "Surfin' Safari" was still ascending the charts, "Ten Little Indians" was already being considered for their follow-up single. But, it would be nearly eight weeks before it was released, two days after "Surfin' Safari" slipped to #52 in its final *Billboard* appearance. Most record labels released a group's follow-up just as the previous hit peaked or began to slide down the chart. But "Surfin' Safari" had begun to slip five weeks earlier, so the follow-up was late in coming. The problem may have been because Nick Venet had another song in mind entirely.

Although "Ten Little Indians" was an odd choice, there were few other eligible candidates on *Surfin' Safari*. Discounting the three songs already released and the three covers, that left only six from which to choose—"County Fair," "Ten Little Indians," "Chug-A-Lug," "Heads You Win, Tails I Lose," "Cuckoo Clock," and "The Shift."

Although Brian suggested "Chug-A-Lug" in July, Venet wanted them to record a song he found called "C.C. Cinder" about a dance popularized at Bob Eubanks's Cinnamon Cinder in Studio City. A second Cinder was set to open in Long Beach in December. Venet was hoping to recreate the success Joey Dee and the Starliters had with "The Peppermint Twist," a #1 hit in January 1962 about the Peppermint Lounge in Manhattan, where the Starliters were the house band. Russ Regan had a similar idea and wrote "The Cinnamon Cinder (It's a Very Nice Dance)" and recorded it with the Pastel Six, the Cinder's house band, for his new Zen Records distributed through Buckeye.

Venet played a demo of "C.C. Cinder" for Brian and told him he thought it could be a hit for the Beach Boys. Brian hated it. Usher recalled, "One day while over at the Wilsons, Brian said, 'You're not going to believe this. Listen to what they want us to record. I can't do this.' It was written by some guys out of New York and Nick was pressuring Brian to record it. Brian flat out refused. He felt it was bad record."9

In *Billboard* out October 6, "Surfin' Safari" peaked at #14 for the first of two weeks. It fared slightly better in *Cash Box*, where it reached #10 for one week. Down Under it reached #7 in Sydney's *Music Maker* September 29. In Sweden, it topped the national Radio 3 for three weeks during peak surfing season that November.

In early October, "The Surfer Moon" (b/w "Humpty Dumpty") was released by Bob and Sheri on Safari 101, a record company formed by Murry Wilson and bearing his home address, "3701 W. 119th St., Hawthorne, Calif.," on the record label. The record was pressed at Alco with delta number Δ45097 hand etched into the dead wax of the run-out grooves. That corresponds loosely to early November, but the delta numbering system lagged behind and the record was released early October. "The Surfer Moon" was published by Sea of Tunes and "Humpty Dumpty" by Algrace Publishing, suggesting Russ Regan's support for handling its distribution through Buckeye Record Distributors. Stock copies have a light blue label and promotional copies have a white label with the additional designations "Promotional Copy" and "Not For Sale." At the six o'clock position on both versions, beneath the names "Bob and Sheri" is the notation "Produced by Brian Wilson"—the first record to bear that credit. It seems unfortunate such a tender ballad was released just prior to the Cuban Missile Crisis and the Cold War's closest brush with nuclear war. It did not chart or receive much, if any, radio play.

Brian presented everyone that helped with "The Surfer Moon" their own copy of the record. Jodi Gable received the sixth copy on which Brian wrote the number six and circled it, and the date 8/62, perhaps indicating work began on the song in August. It is unknown how many copies of "The Surfer Moon" were made. As the rarest Brian Wilson related record, it is likely very few were made and even fewer survived.

In the seventies, a bootleg of "The Surfer Moon" was produced, but it's easy to spot from the genuine record. The counterfeit has a light pink label and the music publishing for "Humpty Dumpty" is credited to "Algrace Publishin" without the "g." In the late seventies, an enterprising fan produced a second boot as volume one of the "Beach Boys Collectors Series." This version was pressed on bright blue vinyl in a limited numbered edition of 1,000 and came in a blue cardboard title sleeve. Ironically, now even these bootlegs are collectible.

"'The Surfer Moon' is both new and familiar," notes Lambert. "It's new because it shows Brian reaching a musical milestone, making all the right decisions to perfectly capture the style and sound of a certain genre of pop ballad. But it's familiar because it's essentially 'Surfer Girl' phase two: it uses the same doo-wop-based chord progression and AABA form of his earlier masterpiece."[10]

The *Cash Box* out October 20 reported Capitol's first quarter sales of pop singles were up fifty-one per-

SAFARI
3701 W. 119th St., Hawthorne, Calif.

Sea Of Tunes
(BMI)
PROMOTIONAL
COPY

(926-A)
Time 2:25
NOT FOR SALE

THE SURFER MOON
(Brian Wilson)

BOB and SHERI
Produced by Brian Wilson
101

A white label promotional copy of "The Surfer Moon," which Brian wrote and produced for Bob and Sheri. Murry created Safari Records and listed his home address on the label. The chirping crickets heard on the record were recorded by Jodi Gable, who dangled out a window of the Wilson music room as Brian held her legs. It is the first record to bear the credit "Produced by Brian Wilson" (author's collection).

cent and noted "Surfin' Safari" contributed to that surge.[11] The music weekly also had a short review of *Surfin' Safari* noting it was a "logical candidate to score." But the album had not yet charted when "Surfin' Safari" began to fade, slipping from #14 to #21 in *Billboard*, #50 on KRLA, and disappearing from KFWB. It held at #12 for the second week in *Cash Box*.

Sometime in fall 1962, Murry had an argument with Averill Pasarow, the group's attorney, and replaced him with Al Schlesinger, who was uncertain how Murry selected him. "Whether they told Averill they were leaving and he suggested me or because Murry knew me from recording 'Two Step, Side Step' on Palace Records. Shortly afterward, I was presented with a copy of their Capitol contract to review."[12]

On October 18, Murry borrowed $10,000 as an advance against royalties provided in Capitol Contract 3348, which he had signed May 24 on behalf of the group for the sale of the three-song demo. The royalties were on the sales of the "Surfin' Safari" single. But Capitol stipulated the loan also could be repaid from royalties provided in Capitol Contract 3374, which the five members of the group signed July 16 and which covered future recordings.

As October drew to a close, the Beach Boys had a busy weekend with two appearances scheduled for October 27. In the morning, they performed at the 30th Annual Y-Day, an all-day event at the Hollywood Bowl emceed by Art Linkletter and co-sponsored by the Hollywood Branch of the Los Angeles YMCA and the Hollywood Advertising Club. The talent roster included Annette, Shelly Fabares, Paul Petersen, the Castells, Bobby Vee, the Rivingtons, and Wink Martindale.

After Y-Day, the band took a noon flight on Western Airlines from LA to San Francisco, arrived at 1:00 p.m. and checked into the Burlingame Hyatt House near the airport. They played a benefit show at the Fox Theatre for the National Cystic Fibrosis Research Foundation, sharing the bill with several other artists including Annette, Glen Campbell, Donna Loren, and Bobby Freeman, and flew home the next day. At a pre-concert dinner for the artists, Brian drank a bottle of champagne and after the band's opening number became sick. He deftly turned away, vomited toward the back of the stage, and resumed playing and singing.[13]

In *Cash Box* out that weekend,

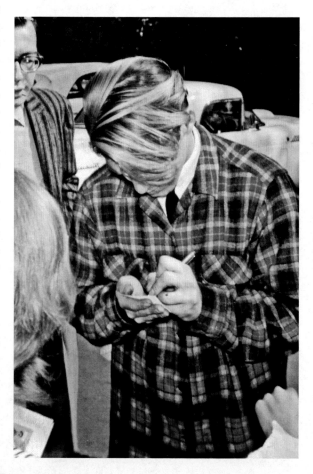

Dennis signs autographs after the group's appearance at Y-Day at the Hollywood Bowl on October 27, 1962 (courtesy Ines Walloch).

"Surfin' Safari" slipped from #12 to #15 and the top spot was held by "Monster Mash" by Bobby "Boris" Pickett and the Crypt Kickers. In LA, "Monster Mash" was kept at #2 on KFWB for three consecutive weeks by "Sherry." But it toppled the Four Seasons in *Billboard*, where it reigned for the two weeks before Halloween. Sometime that fall, Pickett performed "Monster Mash" with the Beach Boys as there is an undated photograph of him on stage beside Brian and David. The Beach Boys had been playing "Monster Mash" live and included it on their *Concert* album in October 1964.

November 1962

On November 1, the Beach Boys played at the grand opening of a new Leonard's Discount Department Store at Pacific Coast Highway and Crenshaw Boulevard in Torrance at 7:00 p.m.[14] Two days later, they appeared at Leonard's on Harbor Boulevard in Garden Grove at 2:00 p.m. They played a forty-five minute set at each store and autographed copies of *Surfin' Safari*.[15] After their set, they sat at two nearby tables where, as announced by Murry, anyone who purchased the album could have it autographed. Audree Wilson and Jo Ann Marks sold albums at the first table and the guys greeted their fans and signed albums at the adjacent table.

Patricia Valdivia, a teen at the time, recalled, "My mom paid, so I didn't take notice of the women. I remember waiting in line with about a dozen people in front of me. Albums were expensive at the time and none of my friends had one. The Beach Boys seemed kind of shy signing autographs like it was pretty new to them."[16] They also gave away 5" × 7" black and white promotional photos with their first names printed beneath their respective images. On Valdivia's photo, Audree Wilson signed her name, adding "Mother of Brian, Dennis & Carl & aunt of Mike," and Jo Ann Marks signed her name and, in parentheses, added "Dave's mom."

After leaving Leonard's on November 3, they taped an appearance on *Pickwick Dance Party* at the Pickwick Recreation Center at 921–1001 Riverside Drive in Burbank. Hosted by Bob Eubanks, kids could stomp and twist from 5:30 p.m. to 10:30 p.m. for $1.75. The handbill featured a photo of the Beach Boys and promised "See yourself on TV next Saturday afternoon" as ninety minutes were taped for *Dance Party* on KTLA-TV on November 10. Live music was provided by the Continentals and the Beach Boys shared the bill with Val Jean ("Mr. Mozart's Mash") and Maureen Arthur ("Don't Make the Angels Cry"). Kids could skate and dance, but event organizers felt the pool posed too great a liability and "swim" was blacked out on the handbill.

When Brian refused to record "C.C. Cinder," Venet went with "Ten Little Indians" (b/w "County Fair," Capitol 4880) as the group's next single. Although Usher stood to collect co-writer royalties on both songs, he knew "Ten Little Indians" had its limitations. "I never thought of it as a hit record or, for that matter, a good record. It was just something Brian and I had fun with."[17]

Mike Borchetta arranged for an advance copy of "Ten Little Indians" to be played on KMEN in San Bernardino. Borchetta recalled, "They called me back and said, 'Mike, this record has nothing. There's no response. Don't put it out.'" Borchetta passed that advice to Capitol executives, but the single was released anyway.

The *Billboard* out November 3 contained a four-star review of "Ten Little Indians"

SATURDAY NOV. 3rd.
Pickwick Dance Party

1½ HOUR TAPING SESSION - SEE YOURSELF ON TV NEXT SATURDAY AFTERNOON

STOMP and TWIST · 5:30 – 10:30

**BOB EUBANKS "KRLA",
M.C.**

Guest Stars

THE BEACH BOYS
    "Ten Little Indians"

VALJEAN
    "Mr. Mozart's Mash"

MAUREEN ARTHUR
    "Don't Make the Angels Cry"

LIVE BAND

    THE CONTINENTALS

The Beach Boys

**DANCE
~~SKATE~~
SKATE
PARTICIPATE IN SHOW**   —ALL FOR **$1.75** Admission

New Air Time
KTLA Channel 5, 2:00 – 3:30 pm
Each Saturday

PICKWICK RECREATION CENTER
921 - 1001 RIVERSIDE DRIVE
BURBANK, CALIFORNIA

For Information: TH 6-0032

On Saturday, November 3, 1962, the Beach Boys taped a performance of their upcoming new single "Ten Little Indians" at the Pickwick Recreation Center in Burbank, California, for Bob Eubanks's *Dance Party* broadcast the following Saturday on KTLA-TV (author's collection).

and noted, "The old children's melody is handed a rock treatment in medium tempo. It's a swinger which should get play following the boys' 'Surfin' Safari' hit. Side shows off good vocal and combo work." About the flip, "A fetching and interesting side in the rocking groove that features smart singing work from the lead and group. This is a teen item with much appeal."[18] The single had the minor distinction of being the first by the group to include "The" before their name. On all the Candix permutations and the Capitol debut, they were simply "Beach Boys." Now, suddenly, they were "The Beach Boys."

The new single was issued with a full-color picture sleeve with a photo from the Paradise Cove album session. It showed the group walking along the surf carrying the surfboard under their left arms. David, Carl, and Mike are laughing. Dennis looks straight ahead, his sun-bleached hair falling onto his face. Anchoring the end of the line, Brian looks amused, but serious, as he is probably dealing with the surfboard's fin poking him in the side. The blue-green colors, the Pendleton shirts, the hint of the Pacific Ocean, and the band's name printed along the surfboard, combined to make one of the most beautiful picture sleeves Capitol ever produced for the group. It is also one of the most collectible as Capitol did

The picture sleeve for "Ten Little Indians" backed with "County Fair" (above), the Beach Boys' second Capitol single, released on November 26, 1962. Capitol/EMI art directors in other countries had the latitude to design their own picture sleeves. This rare sleeve for "Ten Little Indians" (following page) was released in Denmark (author's collection).

not print anywhere near the number of sleeves for "Ten Little Indians" as they did for "Surfin' Safari." After the initial marketing launch, the company reasoned the follow-up would sell on the strength of "Surfin' Safari." The sleeve is sought by fans and music lovers in general because of its iconic image of the band.

There is, however, something odd about the sleeve. Here they are holding a surfboard beneath the words "Ten Little Indians" and "County Fair," neither of which has anything to do with surfing. But Capitol was intent on promoting them as a surfing group and that photo helped solidify the image. It didn't matter it had nothing to do with the subject of the songs. They were the Beach Boys and this was their image.

EMI/Capitol art directors in other countries had creative control over the design of their picture sleeves. The art director in Denmark designed a sleeve dominated by a drawing of a somber looking Indian chief with a full-feathered headdress. In the lower right corner was a solid outline of a kneeling brave with a single feather in his hair stoking a campfire with a stick. The sleeve, printed in mustard yellow and brown, is not especially attractive, but it is unusual, prompting the question, "What were they thinking?" As Denmark is only

two-thirds the size of West Virginia, relatively few sleeves were printed and it is one of the rarest Beach Boys picture sleeves in the world.

In Sweden, where "Surfin' Safari" was #1 for three weeks, the group's follow-up was eagerly anticipated and reached #6. Unlike his Danish counterpart, the Swedish art director used the American artwork. But there may have been some confusion over which song was the intended A side as two versions of the sleeve exist—one with "Ten Little Indians" listed first and in larger type, and one with "County Fair" more prominent. The photograph on the sleeve appears to be cut out from a U.S. sleeve and rephotographed, as the printing is dark and muddy, and only somewhat lighter on the "County Fair" version.

"Surfin' Safari" paved the way in Sweden for additional releases from *Surfin' Safari*, including an EP 45 rpm that coupled "Surfin' Safari," "409," "Ten Little Indians," and "Summertime Blues." It came in a cardboard sleeve with a photo that differed slightly from the U.S. "Surfin' Safari" sleeve. Sweden released a third single from the album, "Moon Dawg" (b/w "The Shift"), with a picture sleeve of the promotional photo in which Mike and Brian stand holding the surfboard vertically while the others kneel in front. It is extremely rare.

In Spain, an EP combined "Ten Little Indians," "County Fair," "Surfin' Safari," and "409." A French EP featured "Surfin' Safari," "409," "Surfin'," and "Moon Dawg." Both came in a cardboard sleeve with the album cover photo. France was unique in that it later included songs from *Surfin' Safari* on two EPs released the following year—"Chug-A-Lug" and "The Shift" were on the *Surfin' USA* EP and "Cuckoo Clock" appeared on the *Surfer Party* EP. A French pop singer covered "Ten Little Indians" and "Surfin'" was released in Italy by twenty-three-year-old pop singer Peppino di Capri. Some countries printed record labels in their native language, giving us "Safari Accidentado" in Chile, literally a "stormy safari."

By 1962, Capitol had discontinued manufacturing promotional copies of singles and albums. But to promote the Beach Boys' debut, Capitol manufactured a seven-inch 45 rpm EP entitled "Complete Selections from *Surfin' Safari* by the Beach Boys." The record had two selections from *Surfin' Safari* on one side and two selections from Ray Anthony's *I Almost Lost My Mind* on the other. The Ray Anthony side, numbered PRO 2185, featured "Midnight Flyer" and "Goodnight My Love." The Beach Boys side, numbered PRO

Above and following page: To help market the *Surfin' Safari* album to radio stations, Capitol produced a promotional extended play single that featured "Ten Little Indians" and "Little Miss America" on one side. The other side featured two songs from a new album by Ray Anthony. The EP came in a cardboard sleeve with a picture of the *Surfin' Safari* cover on one side and a picture of the Ray Anthony album on the other side (author's collection).

Two Great Tunes From The Great New Album T-1808

"TEN LITTLE INDIANS" AND "LITTLE MISS AMERICA"

FOR DEMONSTRATION USE ONLY... NOT FOR SALE

2186, featured "Ten Little Indians" and "Little Miss America." The red record label bore the notation "Demonstration Record For Promotional Use Only, Not For Sale." It came in a cardboard sleeve with a black and white photograph of *Surfin' Safari* on one side and a black and white photograph of *I Almost Lost My Mind* on the other side. The EP was sent to Capitol's sales representatives to play for their record store accounts to promote sales of both albums. It was pressed in Capitol's LA plant and, judging by how rare it is today, a relatively small number were manufactured and even fewer survived. A few were later found in record collections of former Capitol salesmen.

In late 1962, the Veterans Administration produced two public service announcements for veterans for which Capitol arranged Brian to record introductions of a few Beach Boys songs. Program 866 of the VA's "Here's to Veterans" series was a twelve-inch, 33⅓ disc in which veterans were informed of the importance of keeping the VA apprised of any address change. Between announcements, Brian introduced five selections from *Surfin' Safari*: "Surfin' Safari," "Ten Little Indians," "409," "Surfin'," and "Moon Dawg."[19]

The second VA public service announcement was for their "Soundtrack Five" series and used Brian's "Okay guys, let's do 'Ten Little Indians'" introduction from the "Here's to

Veterans" program. The record was a ten-inch, 33⅓ disc and the label noted "Program 10, The Beach Boys (New VA Hospital Program)." Both these VA records were manufactured in small quantities and many were tossed after they served their purpose.

At 9:00 a.m. on November 8, Brian, Dennis, and Carl, accompanied by Audree and Murry, and David, accompanied by Jo Ann and Elmer, appeared in LA County Superior Court to have their July 16 Capitol Records contract ratified. Attorney Skip Chaum, head of Capitol's Business Affairs, attended with Nick Venet's secretary. Mike and his parents did not attend as Mike was already twenty-one and did not need to be present. A photograph shows the boys and their parents sitting in an outer room of the court house. The court ordered twenty-five percent of each of their royalties set aside for trustee savings accounts.[20]

On November 10, the Beach Boys performed their upcoming single "Ten Little Indians" on *Pickwick Dance Party* from 2:00 p.m. to 3:30 p.m. on KTLA-TV channel 5. Film of their appearance has never surfaced as television stations, especially local programs like *Dance Party*, saw no need to preserve their broadcasts.

Although *Surfin' Safari* was selling well, Capitol did not place any ads in the music trades dedicated to just the Beach Boys. Instead, they leveraged their marketing dollars and grouped the band with other artists. The *Billboard* and *Cash Box* on newsstands November 10 had identical full-page ads for three new Capitol singles, including "Ten Little Indians."

In that same issue of *Cash Box*, "Ten Little Indians" was one of eight Pick of the Week singles: "The Beach Boys, who racked up tremendous sales with their 'Surfin' Safari'– '409' double-header, can make it two twin-hits in a row. They're two pounding twist'er, an up-dating of 'Ten Little Indians' and a newie, 'County Fair,' that the artists sock out with coin-catching authority."[21] The Beach Boys played their final night at Pandora's Box on November 11, following a two-night stand there by John and Judy Maus.

Surfin' Safari debuted at #114 in *Billboard* out November 17. On November 21, the Beach Boys and the Journeymen played a Thanksgiving Eve Dance and Stomp in the ballroom of the Biltmore Hotel on the Strand near 14th Street in Hermosa Beach. For $2.50 a couple, a buck less for stag, kids could dance and stomp from 8:00 p.m. to 1:00 a.m. The dance was sponsored by Alpha Omega, a professional Jewish dental fraternity founded in 1907 which had chapters on the campuses of USC and UCLA. Although it may have been lost on many of the kids, there was plenty for

The Beach Boys played a pre–Thanksgiving Day Stomp on Wednesday, November 21, 1962, at the Hermosa Biltmore Hotel in Hermosa Beach, California, for Alpha Omega, a Jewish dental fraternity at the University of Southern California (author's collection).

which to be thankful. The day before, satisfied the Soviet Union had removed their missiles, President Kennedy lifted the naval blockade of Cuba, bringing the missile crisis to an end.

Around this time, the Beach Boys played a show in the gymnasium of William Howard Taft High School in Woodland Hills, California. Only students who had purchased activity cards for the semester were allowed to attend certain school events including the Beach Boys show. Gary Steelberg, then a student and activities director, recalled Brian agreed to play the show against objections from Capitol Records.[22] A photograph of the band in matching dark pants and Pendleton shirts, with Mike honking the sax, appeared in the school's 1963 *Atinian* yearbook. Brian played his sunburst Fender Precision Bass, David his sunburst Fender Stratocaster, and Carl his new white Fender Jaguar, which the company introduced in mid–1962.

On November 23, Murry paid five dollars for his renewed passport at the LA Passport Agency on Wilshire Boulevard. On November 28, he flew Scandinavian Airlines from LA to Copenhagen. Over the next seventeen days he traveled to Stockholm (where he wrote the Morgans about his interview with Klas Burling on *Pop 62* also broadcast that evening on Swedish Radio), London, West Germany (where the stated purpose of his visit was for medical reasons), and Luxembourg for a radio interview to promote "Surfin' Safari."

In *Billboard* out November 24, *Surfin' Safari* jumped from #114 to #75 and Capitol placed a two-inch square ad—"Breaking! Ten Little Indians." That *Billboard* marked a milestone for the band. It was the first of nine times over the next three years in which they

The Beach Boys played a special concert for activity card holders at William Howard Taft High School in Woodland Hills, California, in November 1962 (author's collection with appreciation to Kathleen Sheppard and Gary Steelburg).

placed three singles on the same weekly chart—"Surfin' Safari" was #53, "Ten Little Indians" debuted at #77, and "409" was #102. But those East Coast challengers reigned supreme as the #1 record in the country for the third of five consecutive weeks was the Four Seasons' "Big Girls Don't Cry."

On November 30, the Beach Boys headlined a free dance at the Albert S. Goode Auditorium on the Kern County Fairgrounds in Bakersfield. The event was sponsored by Schick Razors, Mayfair Markets, and radio station KWAC. Joining the Boys were Kenny and the Ho-Daddies ("Surf Dance"), the Revlons ("Boy Trouble"), and Cindy Malone, whose recent Capitol single, "Little by Little," was produced by Nick Venet.

December 1962

Founded in 1927, the non-profit Pacific Lodge Boys Home in Woodland Hills, California, provided services for troubled boys ages thirteen to seventeen. The Beach Boys were one of many acts who played the Home's Fifth Annual Fund Drive at the Fox Van Nuys Theatre on December 1. KRLA disc jockey Sam Riddle emceed the first half of the show featuring Dorsey Burnette, the Lively Ones, Dobie Gray, and the Crystalettes. KRLA's Arlen Sanders kicked off the second half of the show by introducing the Beach Boys. A photograph of them on stage, with Mike clutching a saxophone, appeared in *Teen Post*, a sixteen-page weekly newspaper published in Hollywood as a "service for Teenage America."[23]

The Beach Boys were on the bill at the Van Nuys Theater on December 1, 1962, for the Fifth Annual Fund Drive for the Pacific Lodge Boys Home in Woodland Hills, California (author's collection).

On December 3, the Beach Boys played at the Rose Bowl Gala in Bovard Auditorium on the campus of USC. The gala was a pep rally for the Trojan football team as they prepared to meet the Wisconsin Badgers in the 1963 Rose Bowl. Also performing at the rally were the Countrymen and the Golden Horse Revue from Disneyland. That same day, Mike and Frances welcomed their second child, a baby girl named Teresa.

On December 6, two days after Dennis turned eighteen, the Beach Boys performed at the grand opening of the new Cinnamon Cinder at 4401 East Pacific Coast Highway in Long Beach. Also on the bill were Jan & Dean, Sandy Nelson, and two house bands, the Challengers and the Savoys. It was the second Cinnamon Cinder operated by twenty-four-year-old Bob Eubanks, who co-owned the club with Mickey Brown, a former LA cop who managed the club, and brothers Stan and Roy Bannister, who owned skating rinks in Van Nuys. A local newspaper reported, "800 youngsters danced the twist energetically and deliriously inside while 350 disappointed others lined up outside, unable to get in because the place was jammed."[24] One youthful attendee enthused, "Marvelous fun! What I like is that no liquor's served. All the kids think about is dancing and having a ball!"[25] Eubanks predicted his club would gross $200,000 its first year. It got a marketing boost when "The Cinnamon Cinder (It's a Very Nice Dance)," written by Russ Regan and recorded by the Pastel Six, reached #5 in LA and a studio group called the Cinders released a cover in mid–November.

By December, flush with royalty money from "Surfin' Safari" and "409," Dennis moved from the apartment he shared with Usher and rented an apartment one block from the ocean at 1727 Hermosa Avenue in Hermosa Beach. Mike was experiencing some marital turbulence around this time and moved in with Dennis. Mike recalled, "Dennis and I would race—I had a Jaguar XKE and he had a Corvette—around Highway 101 coming back from the Cinnamon Cinder in Long Beach. There was a big turn on the 101 and we'd be going 100 miles per hour on that thing, drifting from one lane to another. We were young guys being crazy after a show on our way back to the apartment I shared with Dennis."[26]

In *Billboard* out December 8, *Surfin' Safari* peaked at #34, but remained on the chart another three months before bottoming out at #147 March 30, 1963. The album charted thirty-seven weeks over a two-year period. Meanwhile, Murry and Brian were becoming disenchanted with Nick Venet. It was obvious to everyone involved that Brian had produced the sessions for *Surfin' Safari* and yet Capitol insisted their A&R man receive credit on the album cover. These tensions were exacerbated when "Ten Little Indians" failed to chart on KFWB or KRLA, and stalled nationally. Murry blamed Usher for the weak material and Venet for selecting it as the follow-up. But while Murry and the Beach Boys pulled away from Venet, Usher became good friends with him, perhaps sharing a mutual disdain for the Wilson patriarch.

"Murry would tell me to keep Gary away from Brian," Venet recalled. "Murry was very insecure about Gary working with Brian. Whatever great records Brian and Gary made at Capitol, they were made under duress. Murry was a disruptive factor in the studio. He would sit between you and the engineer and, if you asked him to move, he would sit someplace else or stand in front of the booth, face the kids, and wave at them and make hand signals."[27]

Usher had written some new songs but, because they weren't intended for the Beach Boys, he could not enlist Brian's help because Brian was under contract with Capitol. Through his friendship with Brian, Usher befriended Capitol's record promoter Mike

Borchetta. When Usher mentioned he had new songs to record, Borchetta agreed to finance the venture in exchange for full partnership. But first Venet convinced Usher to record "C.C. Cinder," the song Brian refused to record with the Beach Boys.

Usher booked a session in early December with Chuck Britz at Western, where Usher, Borchetta, and Usher's musician friends, recorded "C.C. Cinder" and Usher's "The Chug-A-Lug," which, apart from its title, bore no resemblance to the song he had written with Brian. On December 12, they were back at Western to record "Barefoot Adventure," "R.P.M.," and "My Sting Ray," Usher's ode to the Corvette Dennis Wilson dreamed of owning. Usher sang lead on all three songs and enlisted Dennis to play drums on them. Borchetta recalled, "We told Brian he could come to the session, but couldn't sing on it. Of course, once you said that, Brian wanted to come in and sing. So, sure enough, we have Brian singing on 'My Sting Ray.' I paid Al Jardine five dollars to sing background vocals on 'R.P.M.' I have a copy of the record that Al signed 'Thanks Mike, Alan Jardine, the $5 singer.'"[28] It is, however, difficult to audibly discern Brian's or Al's background vocals.

Venet and Borchetta knew the owners of Challenge Records and arranged for the release of "C.C. Cinder" (b/w "The Chug-A-Lug," Challenge 9186) by the Sunsets and "R.P.M." (b/w "My Sting Ray," Challenge 9187) by the Four Speeds in February 1963. Both groups were essentially the same group of musicians. The surf-themed "Barefoot Adventure" was left in the can for the time being. The songs are weak and rather monotonous, in stark contrast to Usher's songwriting and production collaborations with Brian.

It may have been after these Western sessions that Usher reportedly helped himself to a microphone from the studio. Borchetta recalled, "Gary stole a microphone and Murry knew he stole it. That's why he threw Gary out of the fold. I talked Murry into letting Gary back in because he was a talented songwriter and Brian worked well with him."[29]

Jodi Gable recalled, "There was an incident and Brian was accused of stealing microphones and possibly some other equipment. Murry suspected it was Gary. After that, there were hard feelings with Murry and Audree about Gary, and they only tolerated him. When the name Gary Usher was mentioned in the Wilson house, I made tracks. I didn't want to hear it. But Gary wrote some good songs and was a really nice guy."[30] Usher began working less and less with Brian. Only two new Wilson-Usher compositions, "In My Room" and "We'll Run Away," would be released by the Beach Boys over the next two years.

With Christmas, and Dennis's and Carl's birthdays, December was a busy month in the Wilson home. Just a year earlier, the Yuletide excitement had been the debut of "Surfin'" at #33 on the KFWB chart out December 22. This year it was Brian's plan to propose to Judy. He asked Audree to accompany him to Zales Jewelry Store where they purchased a diamond engagement ring on a payment plan. The ring had a silver band with a round diamond in the center and diamond chips on each side. Audree thought it appropriate for a young girl.

"It was Christmas and we were in his red Impala outside my parent's house," Judy recalled. "He was mad that I knew I was getting it and it wasn't a surprise. He said 'You know you're getting this so here, here it is.' It wasn't especially romantic. It was like I received something and then felt guilty about it. It wasn't a big rock, but I was very happy with it. I thought I was the cat's meow. My mother asked me, 'Do you really want to marry Brian?' And I said, 'Yes, I do.'"[31] Brian and Judy made plans to marry in December 1963. Her mother suggested she attend summer school so she could graduate before getting married.

As 1962 drew to a close, Murry arranged a five-date tour for the group. This was the first time anyone made a coordinated effort to package a series of dates. Until now they'd been playing whenever an opportunity arose—dances, hotels, high schools, movie theaters, recreation centers, record stores, department stores, grand openings, and parking lots.

Murry recalled, "I held them down from the big time for nine months. Even after they had two major double-sided hits they were too green to go into the big time and New York and huge concerts. I held them down and took jobs at dances first, and then we went to different department stores, you know? One of their first dates was a dance in Inglewood and they played at Long Beach.[32] "I was told by a young man, a twenty-two-year-old man at William Morris, that the Beach Boys would never make more money than Ruby and the Romantics who were grossing $3,500 for seven days a week. This was after my son's first double-sided hit on Capitol. I got so mad. It was December 17. I called from my home to key places and we worked between Christmas Eve and New Year's Eve. We grossed $26,684 for five nights, five concerts. That was in 1962."[33]

The itinerary for this December 1962 tour is the subject of debate. Murry mentioned five concerts between December 24 and 31, but did not mention venues or cities. Author Keith Badman reported seven concerts in six cities, listing venues and specific dates between December 17 and 31.[34] Stebbins and Marks reported seven concerts in seven cities, but did not list venues or dates, and reported the tour concluded before Christmas with a show in Santa Cruz that Ron Swallow recalled vividly because of a post-concert altercation at a motel between Dennis and a young guy angry because his girlfriend fawned over the band.[35] Badman's venues and dates could not be corroborated. However, Eric Groves, who worked at the Roller Gardens in Wagon Wheel Junction, recalled seeing the Beach Boys at the Earl Warren Show Grounds in Santa Barbara "around Christmas time as it was cold and we wore heavy coats."[36]

Newspaper advertisements for this hastily arranged tour could not be found, but it seems likely Murry relied on radio, an effective but impermanent means of promoting the shows. Murry, the inveterate salesman, might have simply called disc jockeys in each city and asked them to promote the shows as public service announcements.

It seems likely the tour concluded before Christmas and the band celebrated the holiday in LA. They next appeared at Surf Fair at the Santa Monica Civic Auditorium on December 27 and 28. This surfing trade show was held during National Surf Week in conjunction with the First Annual Mid-Winter Surfing Championships at nearby South Beach. The Beach Boys appeared both days, although a 13" × 20" poster, considered the first concert poster to feature their photograph, noted only their December 28 appearance.

The band's accelerated touring schedule brought its own problems. Venet recalled, "If I had listened to the father back then, the Beach Boys would have fired Mike Love on their first tour. The father came roaring into my office one day and asked me to check out the legality and prepare papers. I just said, 'That's terrific. How shall we do this? That's just terrific, sir. Do you want me to call him on the phone or send him a telegram? Or do you want me to push him out a window? Which way do you want me to do this?' He got very serious and said, 'The boy used profanity backstage.' He had said 'fuck' twice, once before the show, once after the show, both times backstage. Biggest act in the country and he wants to break them up because he used the word 'fuck!'"[37]

Murry countered, "I probably *threatened* to do it. I was tough on obscenity. Mike swore under the microphone one time at a dance. I said, 'Don't you ever pull that again, Mike.'

He said, 'It slipped.' and I said, 'Well, don't let it slip again.' There was nothing vulgar. I even had their attire purchased so it wouldn't be vulgar. There wasn't any vulgarity on stage. I worried about things like that. I traveled around the country with my kids worrying about them. They had a clean-cut American image. Mike was twenty-one, so he was allowed to drink beer. If I caught anyone else drinking beer on tour, I said, 'No drinking. If I catch any of you guys you're going to be fined five hundred dollars. I was tough on them. I kept at them because I knew that fame and fortune might distort them.'[38]

Dennis later reflected on Murry's discipline. "It was a good thing dad travelled with us and managed us at first. He set the pace and the example to follow. He told us he expected a certain standard of conduct from us and warned us the public would expect it, too. Dad put us down the moment we got rude, flip, or offensive. And we valued him more than anything else."[39]

In *Billboard* out December 22, "Surfin' Safari" placed last in the Top 100 Singles of 1962. "The Loco-Motion" and "Sherry," each with the added distinction of being million sellers, placed #7 and #55, respectively. The award for Most Promising Vocal Group went to Peter, Paul and Mary.

In the final *Billboard* for the year, on newsstands December 29, "Ten Little Indians" peaked at #49, a respectable standing, but disappointing after the Top 20 "Surfin' Safari." It fared better in Chicago, reaching #28 on WLS, but Capitol omitted it from future hits compilations. "Ten Little Indians" and "County Fair" were included on an album produced by the Department of Defense for the Armed Forces Radio & Television Service (P-8114, SSL-14806) broadcast to American military personnel stationed overseas. In 1964, "Ten Little Indians" was an unusual choice to be covered by the Rackets, a German rock 'n' roll quartet.

In *Cash Box* out that day, Capitol placed a half-page ad in which the Beach Boys expressed appreciation for their first six months in the music business—"Thanks to Everyone for Making 1962 a Great Year for All of Us." It included a Ken Veeder photograph from the album sessions of them gathered around a microphone singing. It was the first music industry ad in which they didn't share the spotlight with other artists.

When Capitol Records finalized its quarterly royalty statement for October 1 through December 31, 1962, Hite Morgan's Guild Music received a check for $4,297.74 for the music publishing for "Surfin' Safari" and "Surfin'." The breakdown was: $2,869.42 for the sale of 143,471 copies of "Surfin' Safari" (b/w "409," Capitol 4777), $1,233 for the sale of 30,825 copies of *Surfin' Safari* (T 1808, monophonic), and $195.32 for the sale of 4,883 copies of *Surfin' Safari* (DT 1808, duophonic). To date, Capitol had sold 444,493 copies of the "Surfin' Safari" single.

As he looked back on the year, twenty-year-old Brian Wilson could be proud of all he had accomplished in the two and one-half years since graduating Hawthorne High School. After three semesters of college, he chose to concentrate on his music when his group scored a #3 hit in LA with their very first record. A demo tape of his songs landed the group a contract with Capitol Records and two more singles and a hit album followed. In addition to his work with the band, Brian began writing and producing songs for other artists. He owned his music publishing and made inroads in wresting from Capitol artistic control over how his music sounded. And, as the music industry would soon acknowledge, he was the creative leader of America's most exciting and promising new band.

On the personal front, life could not be better. He had moved out of his parents' home into an apartment he shared with a fellow musician and songwriter. He had all the young-guy essentials—new car, stereo, fiancée, sharp clothes, and the company of new and old friends. And his songs and music publishing were beginning to provide the financial freedom by which he could continue doing what he loved to do—write and produce music. He was finally settled in his romantic relationship. After a roller coaster seventeen-month courtship, his girlfriend Judy had accepted his marriage proposal and they planned to be married the following December.

Unlike the vast majority of his peers, Brian's path in life was focused. His talent for music and vocal harmony, which he had studied on his own for the past eight years, had finally emerged, bubbling up and spilling over from a wellspring that seemed as vast as the Pacific Ocean itself. Once he tapped into his muse there was no containing it. Brian understood the language of music. He got it. He could see and hear complex musical shapes and relationships in his mind. At first, he spun his talent into surf and car anthems that launched a rock 'n' roll renaissance. In less than four years, he would write, arrange, and produce *Pet Sounds*, raising the creative bar for albums to a height few artists would ever equal. It would elevate pop music, widely dismissed as inconsequential, into a serious art form—an unparalleled transformation with profound influence on generations of artists.

But, in 1962, Brian was just getting his feet wet.

20

A Sonic Tidal Wave
(January–March 1963)

January 1963

The Beach Boys were at a critical crossroad as they began work on their second album and third single for Capitol. After an impressive five-month run, during which it reached #14 in *Billboard* and #10 in *Cash Box*, "Surfin' Safari" left the charts in early December. Placing "409" on its B side made for an explosive debut, but left them with few choices for the crucial follow-up. "Ten Little Indians," a misguided effort inspired by the children's nursery rhyme, stalled at #49 and was gone by mid–January. But sales of *Surfin' Safari* were healthy and Capitol executives were already clamoring for another single and album. Thanks in part to "Surfin Safari," Capitol reported a thirty-one percent increase in singles sales between July and December 1962 compared to the same period the prior year. It was the most successful six-month period in the company's twenty-year history, welcome news after posting a $6.5 million loss for the fiscal year ending June 30, 1962.[1]

Their next recordings, written and rehearsed in the wake of *Surfin' Safari*, would determine if the Beach Boys were capable of charting their own creative course or be dismissed as just another music industry casualty. It was a situation not unlike that of a year earlier when "Surfin'" fell off the charts and Brian and Usher responded by recording three demos with Chuck Britz at Western and landing a Capitol contract. Now, under pressure to produce another album with only slightly more time than he had for *Surfin' Safari*, Brian would at first return to Britz and Western for an album dominated by surf instrumentals and named for the new single, a sweeping surf anthem he called "Surfin' U.S.A."

During the first six weeks of 1963, the Beach Boys recorded thirteen songs in seven sessions at two different studios. After a pair of sessions at Western in early January, Venet marshaled them back into the studio system and the album was completed, more or less, at the Capitol Tower. Six of the songs, nearly half their recorded output, were instrumentals—Brian's "Punchline" and "Stoked," Carl's "Surf Jam," and three surf band staples—Dick Dale's "Let's Go Trippin'" and "Misirlou," and Bill Doggett's "Honky Tonk." The other seven songs included Brian's and Roger Christian's "Shut Down" and "Ballad of Ole' Betsy," and five credited initially to Brian—"Surfin' U.S.A.," the ballads "Lana" and "Farmer's Daughter," and "Noble Surfer" and "Finders Keepers," a pair of two-minute surf tunes that would have been at home on *Surfin' Safari*. Mike was later awarded co-writing credit for the latter three.

At the first session at Western on January 2, Brian recorded "Punchline," a two-minute

259

surf instrumental that began with a brief drum intro followed by driving piano and then organ. Brian punctuates the track with intermittent vocal sound effects. We first hear a moaning bass voice on the verge of crying. It sounds over-the-top and a bit forced which, of course, it is. Later, there is general screaming and carrying-on with Brian's high-pitched laughter similar to what he would do on "Amusement Parks U.S.A." in July 1965.

Author Philip Lambert noted "Punchline" was a return to blues-based chord changes and a variation on the melody of "Church Key," a guitar and sax instrumental from summer 1960 by the Revels with Barbara Adkins on Impact Records.[2] In the days before pop-tops, "church key" was slang for a bottle opener, an indispensable item for late-night beach parties. The song is punctuated with Adkins's giddy laughter, the sound of a church key puncturing a beer can, and the song's title spoken deadpan. Emphasizing how songwriters build on their influences, Lambert commented, "Brian's latest surf instrumental is a study of a genre, but also an exploration of ways in which a prototype can be enriched and expanded."[3]

The *Cash Box* out January 5 featured a small article on the band drawn from their Capitol biography. As *Surfin' Safari* peaked at #32 in *Billboard*, the Beach Boys returned to Western and completed master takes for "Surfin' U.S.A." and "Shut Down," and began work on "Lana" and "Farmer's Daughter." Murry, with a touch of hyperbole regarding the work hours, recalled, "At Western Recorders, they stood and sang thirteen hours straight to get an album out—*Surfin' U.S.A.* Sometimes they were so exhausted I had to make them mad at me to get the best out of them. So I'd insult their musical integrity. I'd say, 'That's lousy, you guys can do better than that.' ... But they'd give that extra burst of energy and do it beautifully.... There's more than one way to give love to kids, you know, for their own good."[4]

The sessions for *Surfin' U.S.A.* marked a crucial step in Brian's development as a producer. All the songs were recorded on a three-track tape machine which later made a true stereo mix possible. It was the first time on a professional, commercial recording that Brian double-tracked the group's vocals, a technique which saturates a recording with a fuller, richer, and more sophisticated sound. Brian first experimented with overdubbing on the Wollensak tape deck he received on his sixteenth birthday in 1958. More recently, Brian and Norberg applied the technique more skillfully to their home demos.

"On 'Surfin' U.S.A.' we developed a stylish sound, the high sound became our sound," Brian recalled. "It was the first time we had ever sung our voices twice on one record. It strengthens the sound. Sing it once, then sing it again over that, so both sounds are perfectly synchronized. This makes it much brighter and gives it a rather shrill and magical sound without using echo chambers. It makes it sound spectacular, so much power."[5] "It gave the leads real punch and made our backgrounds sound like a choir."[6] Singer songwriter Jimmy Webb observed, "One of the secrets of how their voices blend is that they used very little vibrato. The voices lie down beside each other very easily. There's no bumping between the voices because the pitch is very precise."[7] Carl observed, "The close harmonies sounded fuller because all the voices were within the same octave. [Brian] used a lot of layered sound; it had a real depth to it."[8]

Carl recalled, "On 'Surfin' U.S.A.,' Brian wanted an opening lick and I just did this Duane Eddy riff. I was worried that it had been on another record, but what the hell. That was the first time we were aware we could make a really powerful record. For the first time, we thought the group sounded good enough to be played with anything on the radio. Instead of hokey California style music, Brian had moved into mainstream rock."[9] The riff Carl borrowed was from "Movin' N' Groovin'," Eddy's debut on Jamie Records (1101), which reached #78 in spring 1958, about seven months before Carl got his first guitar.

Brian recalled, "I started humming 'Sweet Little Sixteen.' And I got fascinated with the fact of doing it. And I thought to myself, 'God, what about trying to put surf lyrics to the "Sweet Little Sixteen" melody.' The concept was about 'They're doing this in this city, they're doing that in that city,' the Chubby Checker 'Twistin' U.S.A.' concept. So I thought of calling it 'Surfin' U.S.A.' I was going with a girl named Judy Bowles at the time and her brother, Jimmy, was a surfer and he knew all the surfing spots. I said to Jimmy, 'I want to do a song mentioning all the surf spots.' So he made a list and, by God, he didn't leave one out."[10] Brian also may have been inspired by "Kissin' Time," Bobby Rydell's #11 hit from 1959, which also borrowed heavily from "Sweet Little Sixteen."

Brian took the surfing travelogue provided by Jimmy Bowles and crafted a clever set of lyrics. A demo of Brian singing and playing "Surfin' U.S.A." on his upright piano was released on the *Good Vibrations* box set in 1993. The lyrics underwent very little revision, although waxing replaced sanding as the preferred way to prepare one's board for a day on the waves.

Others weighed in on the song's inspiration. Mike Borchetta recalled, "After 'Ten Little Indians,' Brian was shaken. He asked me, 'Mike, what are we going to do? Are we washed up?' I showed him a song I wrote with Kip Martin called 'Shakin' All Over' and suggested he change it to 'Surfin' All Over' and combine it with a Chuck Berry rhythm, something like 'Sweet Little Sixteen.'" Borchetta said Brian returned with a finished copy of "Surfin' U.S.A.," which he recorded at Capitol. "It sounded flat and had no punch. The Tower was all wrong for that type of song. I told him to go back to Western with Chuck Britz. When Voyle Gilmore found out, he was really pissed I had recommended a Capitol artist go elsewhere to record."[11] Although an AFM contract for a "Surfin' U.S.A." session at Capitol has yet to be discovered, Brian may have attempted a version of "Surfin' U.S.A." there, perhaps in late 1962.

Randy Nauert, the bassist in the Challengers, a surf band formed by Nauert, drummer Richard Delvy, and keyboard player Jim Roberts, after they left a later incarnation of the Belairs, recalled, "I had written surfing lyrics to 'Monster Mash' and 'Sweet Little Sixteen,' but they never got recorded. We did a gig with the Beach Boys at the Hermosa Biltmore Hotel where we did 'Sweet Little Sixteen' with the surfing lyrics."[12] The song was not recorded for *Surf Beat*, the Challengers' debut album engineered by Dino Lappas at World Pacific Studio in late 1962 and released on Vault Records in January 1963. But, they did cover a Beach Boys tune. Nauert recalled, "We recorded 'Surfin' Safari,' but when we heard our vocals we took them off and did it with a sax playing the melody."[13]

"Shut Down" was Brian's first recorded collaboration with Roger Christian, the midnight to 6:00 a.m. disc jockey on KFWB. Interestingly, Brian and Usher helped kick off the car song craze with "409" and, as Usher drifted from Brian's circle, Christian appeared to take his place. Like many guys his age, Brian liked cars, but not on the level of Usher or Christian. Christian became known as the "Poet of the Strip" for his notebooks of automotive-themed poems. "Shut Down" began life as a thirty-two line composition called "Last Drag" about a race between a Chevy Impala and an Oldsmobile 88 that ends at a treacherous patch of road called Dead Man's Curve. The song referred to the cars as "shorts," slang for a hot ride or cool set of wheels, and the relatively short wheel base of the cars.

For those in the know, the race was illegal because it happened on the strip where the road was wide.

The opening lines of the poem inspired the melody and, with judicious editing and a rewrite to fit song structure, Brian and Christian captured the drama and danger of a street race in a two-minute song. The cars changed to a Chevrolet Corvette Sting Ray and a 413 Super Stock Dodge Dart (try rhyming Impala or Oldsmobile), shortened to Sting Ray and 413. The song begins with the sound of revving engines and, as they peel down the road, a wall of double-tracked vocals throws down the gauntlet. The song takes off fast, mimicking a drag race as the listener is pulled along full throttle. The car jargon, most of it unfamiliar to the non-car enthusiast, added mystery and doom as we're propelled forward at break-neck speed dreading some horrible wreck. In fact, according to BMI, its alternate title was "Attention Accident." Mike's nasal tenor, double-tracked and drenched in treble, is young and vibrant, perfectly suited for the lead vocal. But Mike had trouble double-tracking his vocals and part of the third verse is muddy and difficult to understand. He also played a simple two-note sax solo over a guitar lead from Carl, both complementing the sheer exuberance of the track. As with *Surfin' Safari*, the AFM contracts for *Surfin' U.S.A.* all have the handwritten notation "bill for sax."

Christian later believed "Shut Down" shortened his writing partnership with Brian because he had released "Last Drag" in April 1963 as a dramatic reading for a label co-owned by Tony Butala of the Lettermen.[14] "When 'Shut Down' hit the charts, I heard from Tony. He was going to sue the Beach Boys because they stole his song. Murry Wilson was a little concerned that if Brian wrote with me there would be trouble. Brian and I wrote sixteen songs in the course of two years. Then the threat of this lawsuit popped up and we never really wrote together after that."[15]

Perhaps emboldened by Frankie Valli's unashamed falsetto in "Sherry" and "Big Girls Don't Cry," Brian showcased his own beautiful falsetto on two songs for which Carl and David laid down rhythm tracks inspired by Duane Eddy's blues-rooted guitar riffs in "Movin' N' Groovin'."

"Lana," a pretty ballad about a young couple contemplating their first romantic experience, had a catchy melody and a beautiful lead vocal from Brian who sang the first verse alone and was joined by a background choral for the second and third verses. Carl added a pleasant guitar break over a rhythm track on which Brian played a celeste, a keyboard instrument whose hammers strike metal plates for crisp bell-like sounds. It was a nontraditional rock 'n' roll instrument that portended Brian's experimentation with sound. He may have been familiar with its use on Buddy Holly's "Everyday," the B side to "Peggy Sue" in September 1957.

But "Lana" sounded thin and under-produced, and could have benefitted from a middle eight and another verse. Brian confided, "I had a song called 'Lana.' I would do that again."[16] Lambert noted, "The main verse of 'Lana' is based on chord changes unlike any he'd used before, an eight bar progression of the three primary triads resembling chord patterns in Eddie Cochran's 'C'mon Everybody' (1958) and the Drifters' 'Sweets for My Sweet' (1961)."[17] Brian contributed a version of "Sweets for My Sweet" to *Till the Night Is Gone: A Tribute to Doc Pomus* in 1995.

In "Farmer's Daughter" Brian's smooth falsetto and gorgeous production made for a classic early ballad and stand-out track on the second album. The cryptic lyrics explore teenage fantasy material as an itinerant handyman encounters a farmer's daughter with no farmer in sight. Marks believed his flirtatious encounter with a young girl after a show in northern California, perhaps in late December 1962, which he recounted to Brian and Mike, inspired the song.[18] The title may have come from an announcement in *Cash Box* out October 20, 1962, that Screen Gems had begun pre-production on *The Farmer's Daughter*, an ABC television series based on the 1947 film.[19]

Lambert described "Farmer's Daughter" and "Lana" as companion songs, but noted "Farmer's Daughter" is more musically reminiscent of "Number One," the song Brian and Usher demoed as "Visions" in April 1962 and re-recorded as "Number One" for the B side to Rachel and the Revolvers' "The Revo-Lution." Lambert noted, "It's yet another example of a songwriter revisiting earlier works to create something new, and with spectacular success."[20]

There exists a two-sided, seven-inch acetate with an early version of "Lana" on one side and "Farmer's Daughter" on the other.[21] The label on the disc identifies it as a master reference manufactured at Radio Recorders at 7000 Santa Monica Boulevard. Although the acetate was made there it doesn't necessarily mean the songs were recorded there.

On the "Lana" side of the acetate, the artist's name is typed "Johnny Dew," which Venet told McParland was an inside joke inspired by the frustration Brian felt over Murry constantly badgering him with "Brian do it." When Brian pleaded for suggestions on how to cope with Murry, a studio engineer jokingly suggested Brian could change his name to Johnny. Hence, "Johnny Dew."[22]

On the "Farmer's Daughter" side of the acetate, the client is listed as Wil-War Record Productions, the artist is the Beach Boys, and beneath the handwritten song title is written "Recorded Jan. 16, 1963."[23] Wil-War Record Productions was formed by Shane Wilder, who hosted Spotlight on Music, a daily four-hour syndicated radio show in LA, and Herb Warme, an LA businessman. Wilder told Domenic Priore he met Brian in a store in 1960, was associated with the Beach Boys from 1961 through 1963, and left because he got bogged down with other things and his business would not allow him to continue.[24] But many things Wilder told Priore have since been disproven. Although one would expect Wilder to be a wealth of information about the band's early days, little is known of him and he remains an enigmatic figure in the Beach Boys' history. However, because the acetate is inscribed "Wil-War Record Productions," it would appear Wilder's and Warme's production company was involved in recording these earlier versions of "Lana" and "Farmer's Daughter."

Around this time, amidst the *Surfin' U.S.A.* sessions, Dean Torrence recalled he and Jan Berry headlined a show near Hawthorne at which the Beach Boys, hometown favorites, were the opening act. Although Torrence recalled it was the first time they played with the Beach Boys, that distinction belongs to the Reseda Jubilee on August 25, 1962. Jo Ann Marks noted in her journal the Beach Boys played shows on January 2 and 9, but did not specify venues or cities. Perhaps one of these dates was a local appearance with Jan & Dean.

Because the duo was not a self-contained band, the Boys supported them instrumentally. They met in a classroom before the show (suggesting the show was at a school) and rehearsed a handful of Jan & Dean tunes, including their newly released single "Linda," a doo wop remake of the #1 hit for Buddy Clark with Ray Noble's Orchestra in 1947. The Beach Boys played their set and then backed them up. When the show ran a little short the promoter demanded they fill the remaining time. The duo invited the Boys to the front of the stage and together they reprised "Surfin'" and "Surfin' Safari." They enjoyed singing together and the enthusiastic audience response sparked an idea in Jan.

After five years in the music business, Jan & Dean hadn't had a hit record in nearly eighteen months. After moving from Doré to Challenge, they were now on Liberty Records where their first four singles failed to generate much chart excitement. Jan & Dean performed "Linda" on *American Bandstand* March 29, 1963, and it reached #26 in *Cash Box* that May. But the duo needed a new creative direction and Jan decided to get on board with surf and beach music.

Jan called Brian soon after the show and asked if he and Dean could record "Surfin'" and "Surfin' Safari" for their next album which, to capitalize on the trend, would be named *Jan & Dean Take Linda Surfin'*. Brian was thrilled as both songs had run their course with the Beach Boys and the duo's interpretations would give them new life. Although not a consideration, Hite Morgan benefited as he owned the mechanical royalty to both songs.

Brian visited Jan & Dean at the West Coast office of Aldon Music, Al Nevins's and Don Kirshner's music publishing company, whose LA office was headed by Lou Adler, who, along with Herb Alpert, produced the duo. They discussed the possibility of Brian writing songs and recording demos for Aldon to place with other artists. Although Brian did not sign as a contract songwriter, he did publish at least seven songs with Aldon, including "Your Summer Dream," "Keep an Eye on Summer," and "Gonna Hustle You" written with Norberg, "She Rides with Me" written with Christian, "Our Car Club" written with Mike, and his own "Hide Go Seek" and "The Summer Moon," a slight variant of "The Surfer Moon" to broaden its appeal to other artists. Although Brian relinquished the publishing to these songs, it was an opportunity to expand his creative outlets with an influential East Coast publisher. Murry later accused Brian of breaking contracts with him and Sea of Tunes by "giving songs to Kirschner's Alden [*sic*] group."[25]

During the course of his visit, Jan asked what songs Brian had in the pipeline and he played him "Surfin' U.S.A." When he finished, Jan asked if he and Dean could record it. Brian explained it was slated to be the Beach Boys next single, but that he had other songs. He played "Gonna Hustle You," a tune he wrote with Norberg about the frustrations the average high school guy felt over competing with jocks and upperclassmen for the attention of the popular girls. Jan liked that one, too.

Brian played him another song for which he had the melody, chorus, and some of the lyrics. Drummer Mark Groseclose, Carl's friend from Hawthorne High, told writer Bob Dalley the song began life as "Goody Connie Won't You Come Back Home," which Brian intended to produce for a group that included brothers Eddy and Albert Haddad.[26] For some reason, that plan fell through and Brian offered the song to Jan & Dean. Its new working title was the opening hook, "Two Girls for Every Boy," but evolved into the decidedly catchier "Surf City." Jan knew immediately it was a hit and asked, rather boldly, if he could have it. Brian, without giving it much thought, said yes. Most songwriters guard their creations, protecting them until they're ready to enter the world. Brian would later treat some of his compositions that way, but for now, his songs came so easily he thought nothing of tossing them off or giving them to friends. He gave little consideration to the financial rewards of a hit record. For Brian, it was about the music. It brought him joy to see something he wrote spring to life through collaboration with another artist.

Jan soon went over to Brian's apartment and, sitting side by side at his upright piano, they finished the song. Its authorship later came into question. In 1965, Dean Torrence said it was written by Jan, Brian, and Roger Christian.[27] Both Christian and Torrence later claimed to have made lyrical contributions. However, when the song was copyrighted May 13, 1963, it was credited only to Jan and Brian.

Torrence recalled, "Quite frankly, Brian had lost interest in 'Surf City.' He had a verse, maybe a verse and a half, part of the chorus written, and some minor arrangement parts. But since then he had started working on 'Surfin' U.S.A.,' about which he was a lot more excited. So he said, 'Well, you take this song. And if you want to finish it, it's yours.' He was writing a lot of tunes and almost no way he was going to get a chance to either finish all of them or execute all of them."[28]

In 2013, Torrence said he and Jan suggested Brian keep "Surf City" because he could publish its original melody with Sea of Tunes. They urged him to let them record "Surfin' U.S.A." because that melody belonged to Chuck Berry and, because they knew Berry, they could work out a co-writing credit. When they told Brian he could not use Berry's melody, he replied his father had assured him it was okay.[29]

After "Surf City," Jan began collaborating with Brian, Christian, and Usher, sparking a creative renaissance during which Jan & Dean scored eight Top 30 hits, six with Brian's involvement, including five Top 10 and a number one, and six charting albums, within just seventeen months.

On January 18, in the midst of recording the Beach Boys' new album, Brian held a session at Radio Recorders to produce "Ride Away," a two-minute upbeat boy-meets-girl love song he wrote with Bob Norberg. It first appeared, mistakenly titled "Runaway with You," on the unauthorized *In the Beginning* compact disc in 2007 and was released digitally on *The Big Beat* on December 17, 2013. The duet featured vocals by Cheryl (Sheri) Pomeroy and Brian, who adds a beautiful falsetto tag at the end. None of the other Beach Boys are on the recording. Ed "Sharky" Hall played drums, Steve Douglas a simple sax line, and Brian supplied guitar, bass, and keyboard. The AFM contract listed the employer as Wil-Don Record Productions and the authorizing signature as Shane Wilder. Although these are crossed out and changed to Radio Recorders, it raises the question whether the "Don" of "Wil-Don" was Don Kirschner and "Ride Away" was a demo for Aldon Music.

In late January, perhaps the 26th, the Beach Boys traveled 450 miles to play a fraternity party at the University of Arizona in Tucson.[30] Zeta Beta Tau, founded in 1898 as the nation's first Jewish fraternity, was open to all "men of good character." In a thinly veiled reference to the party atmosphere at the frat house at 1501 East Drachman Street, Mike told Stebbins, "We went there for one show and we stayed for three days." The *Arizona Wildcat*, the school newspaper, did not publish January 18 to February 3, 1963, in deference to final examinations. However, the February 4 issue reported the university had suspended ZBT because of rowdy behavior and alcohol use at a recent event. On January 30, the Beach Boys drove two hundred and sixty miles northeast from Tucson to Window Rock, Arizona, and played the Navajo Civic Center on the Navajo Nation Fairgrounds.

On January 31, the Beach Boys completed "Lana" and "Farmer's Daughter" at Capitol and recorded a new instrumental track for "Surfin' U.S.A." at a three-hour session in studio two at Western with thirty-three-year-old Frank DeVito, a jazz and session drummer who kept date books for his sessions.

Brian had not prepared a music chart for the session. DeVito recalled, "He said, 'Well, you play for a while and then you stop, and then you play for a while, and then you stop.' I asked, 'How many bars is a while?' He wasn't a schooled musician, but he knew exactly what he wanted. I play the boom-boom-boom-boom quarter notes on the bass drum. We played live and they put the vocals on later. Murry came out of the booth occasionally with suggestions like, 'Play harder on the kick drum, if you wouldn't mind' and he was very nice about it. He had strong opinions and I could tell he knew a little bit about music." Because "Surfin' U.S.A." was also recorded January 5 at Western, some have speculated the finished track may include both DeVito's and Dennis's drumming. DeVito refuted this emphatically. "He definitely did not play drums on it."[31]

February 1963

The Beach Boys and Jan & Dean shared the bill with headliner Dick Dale and the Del-Tones, and more than a dozen other artists, at the Fourth Annual March of Dimes Benefit Show and Dance sponsored by KFXM at the Swing Auditorium on the National Orange Show Fairgrounds in San Bernardino February 2. Dale was at the height of his popularity and "Peppermint Man" and "Surf Beat," its B side, shared the #1 spot on KMEN in San Bernardino. Surf music appealed largely to adolescent boys and young men. With several thousand guys packed shoulder-to-shoulder in frenzied anticipation, fights broke out before Dale took the stage. "We were really scared when people were climbing on the stage," recalled David Marks. "We couldn't play and ran out the back door."[32]

The fights and resultant chaos at some shows did little to endear Brian to live performances. Judy Bowles recalled, "He didn't like it. And Murry was always saying, 'Smile, smile!' It was a drag for him. He just wasn't the type of person who wanted to perform. Murry didn't want Brian to take me to their concerts. He wanted the group to go together and Brian didn't like that. Brian always wanted to stop and have something to eat, and was always late getting to the concert. It was like he didn't want to go. Once he stopped for an ice cream cone and some guy said, 'Hey, is that your car over there?' Do you want to go for a drag?' And Brian said, 'Oh gee, I'd like to, but I can't. I have to go to a concert.' The guy recognized him and knew who he was."[33]

On February 9 and 10, they played a 2:00 p.m. show at the Rod & Custom Car Show at the Great Western Exhibit Center in LA. The car show was part of the 1963 Winternationals Week festivities sponsored by the National Hot Rod Association and billed as "the car enthusiast's mid-winter Mecca." The thirty-six page event program contained a small black-and-white photo of the group without Dennis taken at the Bel-Air Bay Club in March 1962. Dennis's head was clipped from another picture and pasted crudely between Brian's and Mike's.

After the February 9 appearance at the car show, the Beach Boys went to Capitol and recorded the instrumental track for "Ballad of Ole' Betsy," a tender song as much about loss as it is about an aging roadster. Lambert noted, "Musically, it's a reworking of 'The Surfer Moon.' The melodies are different, but correspond in important places and exhibit the same general contours and interrelationships. The chord progressions also line up pretty closely."[34]

On February 11, they were back at Capitol to record "Noble Surfer," a tongue-in-cheek homage to a mythical Casanova surfer on which Brian played a celeste on the break, and three instrumental covers. They were the first surf band to cover "Honky Tonk," Bill Doggett's #1 R&B hit from summer 1956, and acknowledged the King of the Surf Guitar with able covers of "Let's Go Trippin'" and "Misirlou," which had been #1 on KFWB January 5.

The next day they recorded two original surf instrumentals—Brian's "Stoked" and Carl's "Surf Jam"—and "Finders Keepers," in which Mike turned a popular phrase into a slice of beach culture about a surfer who gets the last laugh on a ho-daddy who stole his 9'5" board. For the chorus, Brian nicked the melody of "Big Girls Don't Cry," the Four Seasons' follow-up to "Sherry" that hit #1 for five weeks in fall 1962.

"Surf Jam," Carl's first song on a Beach Boys album, kicks off with Dennis's pounding drums soon joined by David's and Carl's dueling Stratocasters. Carl delivered a blistering solo as the song hurtles forward at a frenzied pace. David recalled, "I was usually sitting down during those sessions, but on 'Surf Jam' we were all standing up, looking at Dennis most of the time because he was keeping the beat. You can hear Brian and Dennis yelling at each other and at me to keep up with them!"[35]

The AFM contracts list Mike and bear the notation "Bill for sax." In addition to "Shut Down," Mike played a few subtle sax notes mixed very low on "Let's Go Trippin'" and "Surf Jam." The original horn parts on "Honky Tonk," "Let's Go Trippin'," and "Misirlou" were perhaps beyond his skill, so Carl played them on guitar.

Sometime in mid–February, presumably after the twelfth, the date of the final session for the album for which he is listed on the AFM contract, Dennis crashed his Chevrolet Corvair into a cement wall. Although he wasn't seriously injured, he hurt his legs badly enough to be unable to play drums for a while. The group had some upcoming concert commitments and Carl asked Mark Groseclose to fill in for Dennis. Groseclose had recently begun playing with Carl and David at the Wilson home, jamming on R&B and rock 'n' roll songs the Beach Boys didn't typically perform. Brian gave Groseclose an acetate of "Surfin' U.S.A." so he could learn the band's forthcoming new single. Groseclose played drums for the Beach Boys on four dates beginning with "Cupid's Capers," a Valentine's Day Dance at Hawthorne High's boys' gymnasium on February 15 from 8:00 p.m. to midnight. The dance was presented by the Hawthorne Youth Canteen and sponsored by the Hawthorne Department of Parks and Recreation. Girls were advised to wear sweaters and skirts, or dresses, and boys to wear ties with Pendletons or sports coats.[36]

Beachboys to play at canteen dance

"Cupid's Capers" entitles the Hawthorne Youth Canteen's dance scheduled for Friday, February 15, 1963 in Hawthorne High boys' gym from 8-12 pm.

Entertainment stars the Beachboys for all attending students of the Centinela Valley High School District from ages 13-19. The fee for the event is 25 cents for members and 50¢ for non-members.

The dress for the occasion is school clothes and the attendants may come stag or in couples. The Canteen's dance is taking the place of the sophomore backwards dance because of the contract for the Canteen. Other backwards dances for the school year are being planned for a later date.

The Beach Boys played Cupid's Capers, a Valentine's Day dance sponsored by the Hawthorne Youth Canteen at the Hawthorne High School boys' gymnasium on Friday, February 15, 1963 (author's collection).

The next day, the Beach Boys, with Groseclose on drums, participated in a show at the LA Sports Arena sponsored by KFWB and benefitting eight charities. An ad in the *Los Angeles Times* listed the Beach Boys among twenty-one artists including Dick Dale and the Del-Tones, Annette, the Olympics, and the Rivingtons. Pop singers Fabian, Bobby Vinton, Paul Petersen, and Chris Montez also performed, and Jayne Mansfield and Ann-Margret brightened the stage. Tickets for the 8:00 p.m. event were only ninety-eight cents, KFWB's place on the dial, and included a free record with admission.

Groseclose recalled he also drummed for the Beach Boys at a show emceed by Roger Christian in Monterey Park.[37] Writer Domenic Priore recalled that show was at the Barnes Park Community Center across the street from his home and that the headliner was Dick Dale and the Del-Tones. Priore also recalled Dale and the Beach Boys played in the auditorium of Mark Keppel High School in nearby Alhambra.[38] It is likely Groseclose also filled in for Dennis at this show. The Rumblers, a surf quintet whose "Boss" hit #8 on KFWB that January, recalled playing with the Beach Boys at The Score, a teen dance club in Alhambra, in February.[39]

When Dennis returned to the performing line-up, he took a spill off the drum riser, landed awkwardly, and broke his ankle. Marks told Stebbins that by this time Dennis had already begun taking uppers and once passed out in the bathroom in the Wilsons' house, cracking his head on the toilet. Transported by ambulance to a local hospital, he was treated and released, but had transient damage that manifested as a stutter. "I remember Dennis developed a stutter all of a sudden," recalled Judy Bowles. "It was really strange. Everyone was worried about him."[40] The stutter eventually resolved.

By mid–February, the band had thirteen songs for their second album. Because Brian used part of its organ solo for "Surfin' U.S.A.," "Punchline" did not make the cut and remained unreleased until the *Good Vibrations* box set in 1993. As part of its marketing campaign to promote the set, Capitol paired "Punchline" with "409" as a jukebox only single. The vocals for "Ballad of Ole' Betsy" may not have been recorded yet and it was shelved for the time being. The instrumental track was released on *The Big Beat* in 2013. That left eleven songs. Venet recalled that during the *Surfin' U.S.A.* sessions Brian often visited him at Capitol and previewed as many as a dozen new songs on the piano. One of them was "Surfer Girl," which Brian suggested they could finish and release as a single. He offered to bring Venet the demo the group recorded with Hite Morgan at World Pacific. But with "Surfin' U.S.A." being readied as their next single, Venet recommended holding "Surfer Girl" for a future release.[41]

To bring the album up to the standard dozen tracks, Brian dusted off "Lonely Sea," co-written with Usher from the April 1962 demo session at Western. Although Usher co-wrote six songs on the first album, he didn't write one new song with Brian for the second effort, evidence of their drifting relationship. Brian created an unusual stereo mix of "Lonely Sea" by putting the demo, which had been mixed down to mono, onto the left channel of a new two-track recording. He then recorded new background vocals onto the right channel. That created an odd stereo track with the instrumental track and Brian's lead vocal on the left channel, and the newly recorded background vocals on the right channel.

For the "Lonely Sea" background vocals, Brian asked Al Jardine to lend his voice to the blend. Brian's vision had always been a vocal harmony group, not a guitar-based rock 'n' roll band. After Al quit, it was easy to find another rhythm guitarist, but finding a fourth singing voice that blended so seamlessly was not so simple. As Brian began to make more sophisticated records, he moved to again incorporate Al's vocals into the group's harmonic blend.

In early 1963, Al and Gary Winfrey moved from an apartment in Gardena to an apartment in Hermosa Beach. The rent was seventy-five dollars a month. "It was a two-story building and we lived in the back apartment close to the alley," recalled Winfrey. "It was small. We had another guy living with us who was going to El Camino at the time. When we rented it, you know guys don't look in the kitchen, we went in and it had one bedroom, a living room, and a bathroom for seventy-five dollars a month. We said, 'We'll take it.' We started moving in and found out there was no sink in the kitchen and no stove. There was a hot plate and a refrigerator and that was it. So we had to do all the dishes in the bathroom. But nobody was into making any food. We ate pizzas and hamburgers, that type of food."[42]

Al was in the second semester of his second year at El Camino, his third year of college overall. "Dennis and I were hanging out the twelve to thirteen months I was out of the band. I was also in touch with Brian. There would be times when Brian needed some more harmony and I would come in and sing."[43] Things were looking up for Al on the romantic front as he began dating Lynda Lee Sperry, a pretty brunette freshman he met in a political science course that semester. They married February 9, 1964.

On February 28, 1963, Al Jardine copyrighted an instrumental called "Pink Champagne," which Murry recorded as "Italia" for *The Many Moods of Murry Wilson* in 1967. Al recalled, "It reminded him of the type of music he enjoyed."[44] Brian produced it, but went uncredited.

March 1963

On March 2, after seventeen months on the midnight to 6:00 a.m. shift, Roger Christian moved to 9:00 p.m. to midnight on KFWB. Brian occasionally met him when he got off the air and they would go to Aldo's for a hot fudge sundae and talk for hours about music, radio, cars, girls, and songwriting.

"Surfin' U.S.A." (b/w "Shut Down," Capitol 4932), their second pairing of a surf and car song, was released March 4. That same day, Brian, Dennis, Carl, and Dave helped Jan & Dean record new versions of "Surfin'" and "Surfin' Safari" at Conway Recorders in Hollywood. They laid down the instrumental tracks and contributed guest vocals on both songs, which were included on *Jan & Dean Take Linda Surfin'* released that April and reaching #71 that summer.

Also on March 4, Frances Love filed for divorce from Mike in LA County Superior Court. According to court records reported by Timothy White, twenty-year-old Frances charged that Mike had struck her on the arm and ripped her clothes February 19, 1963, and threatened to injure her on other occasions. She added that she was in fear of severe bodily harm if Mike was not restrained from bothering her in any manner whatsoever. Frances was a college student earning ninety dollars a week working part-time at the UCLA library. She maintained Mike received a $1,400 royalty check from Capitol in January 1963 and was scheduled to receive another $4,000 at the end of March. The court awarded her custody of their two daughters and child support. Mike was ordered to pay $150 monthly

alimony, $250 monthly child support, $300 in attorney's fees, and $1,400 owed to Frances's family. The court ruled he could keep his 1961 Jaguar, bank accounts in his name, and his life insurance policies totaling $17,500.[45] After living with Dennis in Hermosa Beach in late 1962, Mike rented a two-bedroom home at 5642½ Aldama Street in the High-land Park section of Northeast LA, which he listed on the January 18 AFM contract.

"Mike really didn't want to be married," recalled Jodi Gable. "They had all this success and all the girls and it was so much candy for all of them."[46] Judy Bowles recalled a revelatory incident after an early Beach Boys concert. "We went to one of their concerts and while we were leaving these girls came running up to them saying, 'Oooh, the Beach Boys!' And then one young girl looked at Mike's wife and said, 'Oh my God, are *you* with him?' Mike grabbed my hand and said, 'Oh no, I'm with her,' and went off with me. Mike's wife was so upset she broke out in hives on the way home."[47]

With a new single and an album soon to follow, Murry arranged for Capitol to take new promotional photographs

The Beach Boys' third Capitol single, "Surfin' U.S.A." backed with "Shut Down," was released March 4, 1963. It took Capitol several pressings to get the label credits correct, removing Nick Venet as producer and crediting Roger Christian as co-writer of "Shut Down." Capitol credited the music publishing for "Surfin' U.S.A." to ARC Music Corp., the company owned by Chess Records on which Chuck Berry recorded, but failed to credit Berry as co-writer because the melody was Berry's "Sweet Little Sixteen" (author's collection).

of the group. Gone were the Pendleton shirts and khaki chinos as they raised the fashion bar a notch by dressing in identical black suits, white shirts, and black ties. From a variety of photos, Capitol chose an unconventional pose in which the Boys, each sitting higher than the next, appeared to be stacked vertically.

"Surfin' U.S.A." broke the group's career wide open. It exploded out of AM radios with a searing guitar intro, slicing rhythm guitars, a wave of crisp double-tracked vocals, and Brian's soaring falsetto. It revitalized rock 'n' roll with an electrifying burst of freedom and rebellion.

At its LA and Scranton, Pennsylvania, pressing plants, Capitol had difficulty with the label credits for "Surfin' U.S.A." as six variations appeared on singles released that spring and summer. The first pressing at both plants credited Brian alone with writing "Surfin' U.S.A." and "Shut Down," and Venet with producing both songs. For the second pressing, Scranton removed Venet from both sides, but LA retained him for "Surfin' U.S.A.," removing him later in the press run. The third pressing at both plants corrected the writing credit for

With a new Beach Boys' single and album to promote, Capitol took new photographs of the band in matching dark suits, white shirts, and ties. An 18" × 24" poster of this photograph was printed on heavy cardstock and sent to record stores to promote the group. (From top to bottom) Brian, Carl, Dennis, David, and Mike (author's collection).

"Shut Down" to Brian and Christian. But later in that press run, LA again credited Venet as producer of "Surfin' U.S.A.," perhaps applying labels from an earlier press run inadvertently. The fourth pressing at both plants credited "Surfin' U.S.A." to Chuck Berry alone, "Shut Down" to Brian and Christian, and did not list any producer. The band also suffered from a slight identity problem. The word "The," missing from "Surfin' Safari," but included on "Ten Little Indians," was once again absent. The matter was resolved on their next and all subsequent singles—they were, finally, "The Beach Boys."

The six label variations raise the question why the credits were so difficult to get right. Brian produced "Surfin' U.S.A." and "Shut Down" at Western, yet Venet received producer credit for both. Brian and Murry objected, and Capitol corrected and reprinted the labels. When Christian pointed out he was not credited with co-writing "Shut Down," Capitol again printed new labels. These mistakes were easily rectified, but assigning sole writing credit to Brian for "Surfin' U.S.A." would prove to be a costly mistake.

Al Jardine attended a "Surfin' U.S.A." session and brought an acetate home and played it for Gary Winfrey. "When I listened to the demo of 'Surfin' U.S.A.' I told Al, 'Well, that will never make it because it sounds too much like 'Sweet Little Sixteen.' That's the first thing I heard."[48] It's unclear whether Al ever relayed Winfrey's assessment to Brian.

Mike recalled, "'Surfin' U.S.A.' was patterned after Chuck Berry's record 'Sweet Little Sixteen.' We tailored the melody, Brian did the arrangement, and I wrote most of the words along with Brian. But I wasn't credited because we gave the credit to Chuck Berry because he was the originator of the song. We loved Chuck Berry's music. It wasn't like we were trying to steal his song. We just gave him credit."[49] Carl recalled, "'Sweet Little Sixteen' was just a great tune. Brian just did an arrangement of it and changed it around. Chuck Berry wasn't personally involved in that."[50] But it was a little more complicated than that.

Lambert noted, "'Surfin' U.S.A.' is basically the same tune as 'Sweet Little Sixteen' with different words, although Brian added a hook. It's an interesting early success because it's not Brian Wilson's music. It's Chuck Berry's music."[51] Brian was not being malicious. He was simply naive about copyright infringement.

The *Cash Box* out March 23 called "Surfin' U.S.A." a "pounding 'Sweet Little Sixteen'–flavored rocker." In its prescient review, the British music weekly *Melody Maker* noted, "Chuck Berry fans won't like it, but plenty of other people will."[52]

The *Long Beach Press-Telegram* enthused, "The Beach Boys bring back 'Sweet Little Sixteen' with their latest effort—only in a way that it has never been done before."[53] The *Syracuse Post Standard* noted, "The Beach Boys kick off their shoes and go 'Surfin' U.S.A.' A good new group that may make quite a splash for themselves."[54] The *Trenton Evening Times* was less kind, "Well, there is some comfort the Beach Boys at least changed the lyrics and the background arrangement a bit. Maybe they'll even come up with something original in their next platter."[55] But that didn't stop local teens from making "Surfin' U.S.A." #3 on that newspaper's Top Ten. Acknowledging this generational divide, the *Baton Rouge Advocate* called it "Sufferin' U.S.A." and wrote, "We were not overly impressed with this group the first time we heard them, but the public proved us wrong. The group make up with a solid knowledge of music what they may lack in style and originality. To us they sound like a good high school group, an attribute which no doubt is just what enhances their appeal to the young set."[56]

Why Berry went uncredited as co-writer was a puzzling error because Capitol printed

Arc Music Corp. on the record label. Gene and Harry Goodman, younger brothers of band-leader Benny Goodman, who affiliated their Regent Music Corporation with BMI in April 1942, landed the Chess Records' publishing contract in July 1953 and formed Arc Music, named by shuffling the letters in RCA. Arc Music was split four ways among Gene and Harry Goodman, and brothers Philip and Leonard Chess. When Leonard Chess saw the label on "Surfin' U.S.A.," he called Gene Goodman, who threatened legal action against Capitol, the Beach Boys, and Brian Wilson, for copyright infringement and songwriter's credit. Capitol settled out of court and Gene Goodman secured the entire copyright for Arc Music. On subsequent pressings of the single, Berry received sole writing credit despite not having written any of the lyrics. Ironically, Jimmy Bowles, the fifteen-year-old who provided the names of the surf locales, never griped about not receiving co-credit.

To capitalize on the success of "Surfin' U.S.A.," Chess rushed out *Chuck Berry on Stage* claiming it included "Surfin' U.S.A." But at the time Berry was incarcerated for violating the Mann Act by transporting a minor female across state lines for immoral purposes. *On Stage* was marketed as a live album, but it was a collection of studio recordings with over-dubbed audience response to make it sound live. The album did not include "Surfin' U.S.A.," but rather the studio version of "Sweet Little Sixteen."

In an interesting twist, on November 29, 2000, Johnnie Johnson, Berry's long-time pianist and collaborator, filed a lawsuit in St. Louis Federal District Court alleging co-authorship of fifty-seven of Berry's songs including "Sweet Little Sixteen." Johnson contacted Berry to resolve the issue without litigation, but Berry refused to discuss the matter. The case was later dismissed because too many years had elapsed since the songs were written. "Sweet Little Sixteen" was itself inspired by Frank "Franny" Beecher's guitar licks in "Blue Comet Blues," the flip to Bill Haley and His Comets' "Rudy's Rock" (Decca 30085, #34 Pop) in October 1956.

In 1974, "Surfin' U.S.A." was released as a single from *Endless Summer* and reached #36. To capitalize on the re-release, Arc Music printed sheet music with a photograph of Chuck Berry on the cover. In 1977, sixteen-year-old Leif Garrett scored a Top 20 hit with his pop rendition of "Surfin' U.S.A."

Usher chastised Brian for using Berry's melody instead of creating his own, but sensed Brian had not given it much thought. Usher recalled, "He never, at least at that stage, thought in business terms. I attempted to educate him to look out for his own interests, to be more aware of the business world, but at the same time trying not to put shackles on him."[57]

So, how did "Surfin' U.S.A." get released with the correct music publishing company on the label, but the incorrect songwriter's credit?

Venet offered an explanation. "I don't think at the time Brian really understood business. He was eighteen or nineteen years old. [*Note*: Brian was twenty]. Number one, he was very unsophisticated in the music business. Two, he came from a family that wasn't professional. I don't think he had any concept that you couldn't do that. It wasn't larceny in his heart. He was going for a good idea. He was naive about copyrights. I don't think Murry knew where the song came from. I don't think he ever heard it before. So he may have been ignorant of the fact that this was somebody else's song. And when I found out he did not know anything about it, he assumed they were in trouble. I said, 'You are not in trouble. We have to get permission to release it.' I told him I knew Leonard Chess and I would take care of it. I called Leonard and spoke with him on the phone in Chicago. I told him what

Brian had done with the record and he asked for an acetate. I sent him an acetate and called him several days later. He said he was not willing to split the publishing, but he was willing to give Brian fifty-percent of the writer's share. And that was agreed upon. And he stated we could use Brian's name on the label copy so it would say 'C. Berry—B. Wilson' as writers, in parentheses. And I told him that in press releases I would mention this was a collaboration with permission. It would never be misconstrued as just a lift of somebody else's melody. Several days later, I asked Murry to follow up on the contract because Brian would have to sign the contract with Chess. They controlled the copyright. They owned 'Sweet Little Sixteen,' so they would issue the writer's contract, not me. So that was out of my realm at Capitol. I had called the legal department and gotten permission for a license to release the song. There is a license on file. It was licensed under the new conditions. So we were granted our license. What I needed was for Murry to deal directly with Arc Music for the songwriter contract. After that it was out of my hands. And I didn't find out until recently, and I'm stunned, I really am, I just cannot believe that Brian Wilson never made a penny from that song. It was negotiated. It was approved. Capitol had a license. We had paid Chess a full two-cents, the full license fee based on the fact that Brian would be part of the writer's credit. And evidently, from what I've been told, Murry Wilson never followed up on it."[58]

While Venet maintained Murry didn't follow up on the songwriter's contract with Chess, this does not explain how the label copy got cleared for the single's release. Also, it does not appear Capitol ever issued a press release explaining "Surfin' U.S.A." was a collaborative effort between Brian and Berry. Although the incident cost Brian and the Beach Boys a considerable sum of money, "Surfin' U.S.A." was so wildly successful it didn't matter. The controversy never hurt the group and the matter was soon relegated to rock 'n' roll trivia. The Beach Boys apparently harbored no hard feelings and later recorded Berry's "Johnny B. Goode" (1964), "Rock and Roll Music" (1976), and "School Day (Ring! Ring! Goes the Bell)" (1980).

"Surfin' U.S.A." peaked at #3 in the May 18 and 25 *Cash Box*, and the May 25 *Billboard*. It topped the KFWB and KRLA charts for the week ending April 20. It made the Beach Boys America's number one vocal and instrumental group. That August, on the heels of the Beach Boys success, Chess Records re-released "Sweet Little Sixteen" (b/w "Memphis, Tennessee," Chess 1866), but it failed to chart.

For some reason Capitol did not produce a picture sleeve for "Surfin' U.S.A." in the United States. Color sleeves added about two cents to the production cost of each single and after the disappointing chart performance of "Ten Little Indians" Capitol may have reduced the marketing budget. But EMI/Capitol art directors in other countries designed some beautiful sleeves for "Surfin' U.S.A." 45s and EPs, including Brazil, Denmark, England, France, Italy, Japan, Mexico, New Zealand, Spain, and Sweden. By the mid–1960s, a source of constant irritation to Murry was the marketing dollars Capitol spent promoting the Beatles compared to the Beach Boys. It burned Murry to see his boys snubbed by the label they helped raise to prominence in the youth market. He might have had a point. It would have been inconceivable for Capitol to release a new Beatles' single without a picture sleeve.

"Surfin' U.S.A." was more than just a hit record. It had a profound impact on American popular music and the nation's consciousness. "Surfin' U.S.A." was the big picture, Brian creating on a sonic canvas as large as the country itself. Suddenly, both coasts and the vast landlocked heartland were swept up in the surfing phenomenon. Everyone wanted a bit of the idyllic lifestyle the Beach Boys sang about. It transformed surfing from a regional sport to a national pastime. A month after its release, Bill Cooper, executive secretary of the recently formed U.S. Surfing Association, predicted surfboard sales in the Southland would reach 20,000 and fifteen local manufacturers would capture the lion's share of sales approaching $300,000. Enthusiasts could spend upward of $135 for a custom board. For the gremmie, Sears offered an affordable production model in its national catalog.[59]

"They created this idea of California as a state of mind," writer Anthony DeCurtis noted. "The idea of 'Surfin' U.S.A.,' which connects surfing with America and with everything that song is putting forward as American, that was very much on people's minds, and almost in an unconscious way. It was well post-war by this point, the baby boom was in full swing, there were a lot of kids around, rock and roll had established itself, there was a lot of money, it was an affluent time. There seemed to be no place else but America. And the Beach Boys came along as representatives of this kind of California endpoint, the endpoint of the American dream, the Heaven, the Eden, the final delivery. And there it was—a perfect bundling of those ideas. 'Surfin' U.S.A.' just said it all."[60]

The day after "Surfin' U.S.A." was released Brian began work on an ambitious project outside the group. As he struggled with Venet over producer credits, he leveraged his position with Capitol to persuade the label to sign the vocal trio of sisters Marilyn and Diane Rovell, and their cousin Ginger Blake to a two-plus-two deal—two sides (a single) with the option for a follow-up single. Reportedly, Venet had only wanted to sign Ginger. Shortly after meeting the girls during the Beach Boys' week-long stand at Pandora's Box in late August 1962, Brian invited them over to the Wilsons' Hawthorne home. Marilyn and Diane soon reciprocated, and Brian became a frequent guest at Mae and Irving Rovell's home. "Brian made him laugh so much," recalled Marilyn. "I never saw my father laugh so much. And my mother loved him."[61]

Envisioning the girls as a female complement to the Beach Boys, Brian christened them the Honeys, the term for surfers' female companions, which he had used in the "Surfin' Safari" lyrics. Phil Spector wouldn't be the only producer of the girl group sound.

Brian and the Honeys entered the Capitol Tower to begin work on their first single on March 5. Brian had written surfing lyrics to Stephen Foster's "Old Folks At Home," better known by its first line "Way down upon the Swanee River," and called it "Surfin' Down the Swanee River." Written in 1851, Foster's melody was in the public domain. "Brian had us singing for him," recalled Marilyn, "and he goes, 'Oh my God! I have to produce you girls. So he started thinking, 'What would be a good song for you to record?' Brian always loved things that were old, nostalgic, and he loved 'Swanee River.' Then he goes, 'Oh my God! Surfin' Down the Swanee River, that's it! You could be girl surfers!"[62]

Although the title "Surfin' Down the Swanee River" may have struck some as a little weird or "out there," Brian saw how it could work and threw himself into the production. The song is all Brian—a quirky, lovable adaptation of a sweet melody he loved as a kid, with a vibrant sound full of heart. "Brian made it an exciting experience," the Honeys recalled. "When we made music together it was for the love and joy of what we were doing. Brian just takes the beauty and the person and makes it work. That's the beauty of him."[63]

Lambert noted "the production succeeded on many levels. The vocals, mixing unisons and harmonies and including a repetition of the bridge sung by Brian backed by the Honeys in half-dialogue, are infectiously conceived and executed." He further noted it was Brian's "first slow introduction. Before the main verse begins, he has the girls sing the bridge phrase in unison, out of rhythm, over a tremulous instrumental bed." "The best known precedent for the bridge-based down-tempo intro from Brian's sphere of influence is 'Over the Rainbow' by the Four Freshmen which is similar to the later version of the song recorded by the Mystics (1960)."[64]

Brian and Skip Taylor, Venet's friend and, later, manager of Canned Heat, sang the male vocals in the middle of the song. Gary Usher was on board for the fun and joined in on the hand claps on the fade. Judy Bowles was also at the session. "We were gathered around a microphone clapping. Brian leaned in to listen to me and said, 'Don't clap' because I couldn't keep time."[65]

"During the first year of Beach Boys recording sessions, Brian was already working on outside projects," recalled Venet. "At these sessions, I watched Brian work as I imagine Orson Welles must have looked when he directed his films. Brian would lean over the seated engineer's shoulders, mumbling mix instructions as if the tracks would never have a chance to be remixed again. He orchestrated and arranged sections of songs out of sequence, confounding the mixers, myself, and every musician in the studio. The engineers would look at me and I'd say, 'Just stay with him please.' I had no idea where he was going with the music, but I would plead with them to stay with him."[66]

Brian's sincerity and boyish enthusiasm were so genuine and charming that more than fifty years later "Surfin' Down the Swanee River" is still an utterly joyous record.

Brian did not enlist any of the Beach Boys on the Honeys session. This was his pet project and he wanted the freedom to experiment outside the confines of the band. He recruited LA's finest session musicians—Glen Campbell, Billy Strange, David Gates, Don Randi, Leon Russell, Earl Palmer, and Hal Blaine (real name, Harold Belski). It was a natural evolution of his growing mastery of the studio. Although he didn't write chord or melody charts for the session, Brian spoke the musicians' language by playing or singing each part and describing the overall feel or vibe he wanted. He appreciated how fast these seasoned pros got it, enabling him to work at an increasingly faster pace. He thrived in an atmosphere of spontaneity and collaboration. Initially unsure of a twenty-year-old kid without any musical training, the musicians learned to respect him as a songwriter and trust his instincts as a producer. While he maintained artistic control in the studio, Brian included them in the creative process, respecting their contributions and building on their ideas and suggestions. At a time when many studio musicians disdained rock 'n' roll, these studio musicians were laying down some of the most sophisticated instrumental tracks of the era. In time, the bond they shared with Brian brought his music to life and was crucial to his success later in the decade.

For the B side, the Honeys recorded "Shoot the Curl," the original surf tune Ginger and Diane had written. With a catchy chorus and a lively Brian Wilson production, the song delivered a good-natured challenge to male surfers that the Honeys were serious and here to stay.

On March 7, Brian was back at Conway Recorders to cut two new songs. "The Baker Man," inspired by "(Baby) Hully Gully," the 1959 Olympics' hit from which Brian had cribbed the melody for Carol Hess's campaign song, was also about a new dance. Brian experimented with his vocals, delivering an odd, gritty lead and a repetitive background chant that become tiresome and mask a wonderful instrumental track. Although it was not published by Aldon, it may have been intended as a demo and was released as a bonus track on the *Surfin' Safari* and *Surfin' U.S.A.* twofer compact disc in 1990. "Side Two" was a piano shuffle instrumental that may have been an early version of "Little Deuce Coupe." It was released on *The Big Beat* in 2013.

On March 10, the Beach Boys played the KMEN Party in San Bernardino to help celebrate the radio station's one-year anniversary. "Surfin' U.S.A." began a five-week reign at #1 on the KMEN chart out March 29.

Brian and Judy attended her junior prom at the Riviera Country Club in Pacific Palisades in the Malibu Hills March 15 from 8:00 p.m. to 11:00 p.m. A photograph of them dancing appeared in the Lennox High School's 1963 *Troubadour* yearbook. "While we were dancing, he leaned over and pretended to be giving me a hickey. The other guys on the dance floor saw this and imitated him. I had a photograph of the two of us that my mom took. My daughter took it to camp years later and lost it."[67]

On March 16, the group drove eighty miles east of Hawthorne to play the Armory in Hemet, California, on the grounds of the Farmer's Fair. On March 19, Brian recorded a demo of "Gonna Hustle You" at Conway Recorders and may have been joined by Norberg, Carl, and Dennis. Brian sang lead in a beautiful falsetto set against a doo-wop chorus of "papa doo run day run day" and a basic rhythm track. Dean Torrence loved the song and Brian agreed to give it to Jan & Dean to record.

On March 20, Jan & Dean and the Beach Boys went into Western where Jan Berry produced a track for "Gonna Hustle You." In an effort to tone down the sexual inference of "hustle," Berry penned the alternate title "That's All I Want from You," which was vetoed in favor of Mike's smoother "Get a Chance with You."

In a second session later that night, Berry arranged and produced tracks for "She's My Summer Girl," written with Don Altfeld and Brian, and "Surf City," the tune Brian had given him to complete. "'Surf City' was the first song Brian and I worked on together," recalled Berry. "Brian was such a joy to work with because he concentrated so hard when it came time to work and he was such a nice guy to be around."[68] Berry assembled LA's best musicians and produced a beautifully intricate track. The background vocals were sung by Berry, Brian, and the Matadors, a trio comprised of Tony Minichiello, Manuel Sanchez, and Vic Diaz. The lead vocal was sung by Berry, Brian, and Minichiello, standing at varying distances from the microphone, with Berry more prominent in the final mix. Minichiello sang the soaring background falsetto, while Brian and Berry added more subdued falsettos on the chorus.[69]

When Liberty Records rejected "Gonna Hustle You" and "Get a Chance with You" for being too suggestive, the song was shelved temporarily.[70] In early 1964, with new lyrics penned by Christian and background vocals by the Honeys, Jan & Dean recorded it as "The New Girl in School." It scored #26 in *Cash Box* and was overtaken by its flip side, "Dead Man's Curve," also co-written by Brian, which hit #9 in *Cash Box* and #8 in *Billboard*.

Surfin' U.S.A., the Beach Boys' sophomore effort, was released March 25 in monophonic (T-1890) and Full Dimensional Stereo (ST-1890). Before you even heard the twelve songs, the front cover, a brilliant piece of marketing, heightened your expectation of the danger and rebellion inside. Rather than photograph the Boys in another contrived surf-related scenario, art director Ed Thrasher chose a single image to communicate the power, danger, exhilaration, and majesty of surfing.

A lone surfer, balanced precariously on a nine-foot board, rides the crest of a monster wave hurtling toward shore. As the ocean swells above him, turbulent foam swirling about, a massive wall of water, unable to sustain its own weight, threatens to collapse in a thunderous roar, swallowing him whole and casting him to the murky depths of the ocean floor. One man against the terrible force of nature in a confrontation as old as the ocean itself. For the non-believers without an ocean, this image said it all—surfing was dangerously cool. And the album made it clear the Beach Boys were "The No. 1 Surfing Group in the Country." Cool by association.

On *Surfin' Safari*, the waves, if there were any, remained safely out of view. We got a hint of surfing and it seemed like a pleasant activity. On *Surfin' U.S.A.*, that killer wave was coming straight at you. It was impossible to turn away. And you knew, instinctively, the vicarious rush you got paled in comparison to what that dude on the board felt. And you wondered, could I do that? But the music inside that album jacket was something we could all experience, whether you lived in Malibu or Omaha. When you placed that twelve-inch platter on your turntable and that electrifying guitar riff of "Surfin' U.S.A." exploded out of your speakers, followed by those gorgeous layered vocals and otherworldly falsetto, you were closer to the feeling of riding that wave than you'd ever been before or ever would be again.

Capitol purchased the cover photograph from John Severson, a local artist, filmmaker, journalist, and surfer. Severson took the photo at Sunset Beach in January 1960. He intended to use it on the cover of his magazine, but one of the negatives was damaged during the four-color separation process and he shelved the image. Because Capitol was interested in purchasing it, Severson repaired the negative as best he could. The surfer immortalized in the photo is Leslie Williams, who first became aware of it when he spotted *Surfin' U.S.A.* while shopping in a discount appliance store. "You can see the flaw in the photograph by looking at my right knee and lower leg," Williams recalled. "Forty yards to my left were Ricky Grigg and some others, and even today he regrets not being in position to catch the set wave."[71]

The back album cover featured photographs taken for *Surfin' Safari*. The image of Brian is negative-reversed as his bass guitar strap is slung over his right shoulder. In a photo taken at Paradise Cove with the truck, the group mills around looking bored as Dennis checks under the hood.

Surfin' U.S.A. was an eclectic mix. It had the powerhouse double-sided hit ("Surfin' U.S.A." and "Shut Down"), beautiful ballads ("Lana," "Lonely Sea," "Farmer's Daughter"), two fun songs ("Finders Keepers," "Noble Surfer"), and five instrumentals. A local music reviewer wrote, "'Surfin' U.S.A.' may reach the envied number one spot again—only this time as an album by the same title. Some all instrumental numbers appear on their encore LP, but I feel their vocals take precedence over any of the instrumentals."[72] The instrumentals were solid and workmanlike—evidence the young musicians were intent on studying their craft. They were also relatively easy to record when Capitol pressured the band for a new album earlier in the year. While some found five instrumentals to be excessive, perhaps even padding necessitated by a lack of original material, they made *Surfin' U.S.A.* the band's truest guitar-based surf album. But not in time to secure an invitation to the three-day "Surf Battle" held the weekend before its release at the Deauville Castle near the Santa Monica pier. The Lively Ones, with whom the Boys had played the Diaper Derby in Oxnard when they were called the Surfmen, bested eighteen other instrumental surf bands in a hotly debated win.

With a new single and album to promote, the Beach Boys hit the road for a handful of West Coast dates. With blistering crowd pleasers like "Surfin' U.S.A." and "Shut Down," their live show was becoming more varied, entertaining, and original. Once "Surfin' U.S.A." joined the concert line-up, it never left. As one of their most recognizable songs, synonymous with the band and the waves of good memories they conjure, they have performed it thousands of times over the years.

In early 1963, Brian and Judy were still very much in love and happily engaged, but their lives were beginning to take markedly different paths. Brian was immersed in the ultra-competitive music industry with the pressure of writing and producing albums, and delivering that all-important next hit single. His parents, brothers, cousin, and friends were depending on him. Judy was a high school junior worried about homework. For a writing assignment, she once submitted a poem Brian wrote from a young girl's perspective. When she received it back, her teacher had written on it "Are you sure you wrote this?" Judy was often asked if she could arrange for the Beach Boys to perform at Lennox High. "I asked Brian and he said, 'No. Hawthorne High wanted them to perform, but they would not appear for free anymore.'"[73]

As "Surfin' U.S.A." entered the charts, Capitol began to put its marketing clout behind the group, placing two full-page ads in *Billboard* and a full-page ad in *Cash Box* on newsstands March 30. In appreciation for their support of "Surfin' Safari," they thanked Radio Sveriges, Sweden's national radio broadcaster and the "swingin' DJs in Australia."[74] Specially marked promotional copies of *Surfin' U.S.A.* were mailed to disc jockeys across the United States. For the first time, Capitol produced an in-store 2' × 3' poster on cardboard stock of the band's new promotional photograph for sales reps to distribute to record stores. "Surfin' U.S.A." sheet music was printed in the United

The Beach Boys played at the grand opening of Denno's Record Shop in the Orange County Plaza shopping center on Saturday, March 30, 1963. They played on a small riser in the parking lot and signed autographs after the show (author's collection with appreciation to the Garden Grove Historical Society).

States, Australia, and the United Kingdom, each featuring a different photograph of the band, and crediting lyrics to Brian, music to Chuck Berry, and publishing to Arc Music.

On March 30, the Boys played a 2:00 p.m. outdoor show at the grand opening of George Denno's Record Shop at 9709 Chapman Avenue in the Orange County Plaza shopping center in Garden Grove. They played on a low riser in the parking lot and fans recalled Mike arriving in his Jaguar and Dennis in his 1963 Corvette Stingray Coupe in Daytona Blue. After a forty-five minute show, the group signed copies of *Surfin' U.S.A.*

The new single created a demand for concert bookings and spoiled Jodi Gable's prom. "Denny was going to take me to my junior prom in 1963," she recalled. "But then they got a gig. Denny knew how much I was looking forward to it, but he was such a chicken he had Murry call me. I had the dress already and I was in tears. And Murry said, 'Jodi, you have to remember, they're stars now.'"[75]

Making Waves in
the Midwest
(April–June 1963)

April 1963

On April 5, the Beach Boys helped kick off the second annual Teen-Age Fair which, after its first year at P.O.P., had moved to the fifteen-acre Pickwick Recreation Center in Burbank. The ten-day fair was held while local schools were closed for Easter week. Teenagers made up the majority of the 300,000 people who enjoyed exhibits of hot rods, custom cars, boats, surfboards, Fender guitars, surf films, model slot car racing, and an Elvis film festival.

The Boys greeted fans at an autograph table and signed copies of "Surfin' U.S.A." and their new Capitol promotional photograph. Jodi Gable, president of their fan club and Burbank native, recalled that before their appearance the guys visited Jay Sebring's posh salon in West Hollywood to get their hair styled. After the autograph session, they took photographs with the Miss Teen USA pageant contestants, Wink Martindale, the fair's master of ceremonies, and actors Richard Kiel and William Engesser. Kiel later portrayed the villain Jaws in two James Bond films. A photograph of Jodi Gable and the Boys, sporting their new stage look with shirts, ties, and olive-brown cardigan sweaters, was published in *Cash Box* out April 27.

On April 6, the Beach Boys played in the parking lot at the grand opening of a new Build 'n Save building supply store at 9920 Westminster Avenue in Garden Grove. They played a thirty minute set and signed copies of *Surfin' U.S.A.*

The Honeys' debut single, "Surfin' Down the Swanee River" (b/w "Shoot the Curl," Capitol 4952), was released April 8. Two days earlier, *Billboard* noted, "Here's the latest surfing side and the first of substance by a girl group."[1] It was the first surf record by a female vocal group. Although the recording was conceived, arranged, and produced by Brian, Venet was credited as producer on the record label. The writing credit for "Swanee" went to Brian alone and the publishing to Sea of Tunes. Stephen Foster's music was long in the public domain. In the U.K., the writing credit was "Foster, arr. Brian Wilson" and, when the song was copyrighted April 11, the melody was noted as Foster's "Old Folks at Home."

Although Capitol did not place any ads in the music press, it did produce a full-color picture sleeve for the first few hundred copies of "Swanee" on the West Coast. The sleeve

The Beach Boys appeared at the second annual Teen-Age Fair at the Pickwick Recreation Center in Burbank, California, on April 5, 1963. Here they pose with Miss Teen U.S.A. contestants (author's collection).

is exceedingly rare today. The single received radio play, but never charted, not even locally. However, primed by "Surfin' Safari" and "Surfin' U.S.A.," the Honeys rode the top of the charts in Denmark and Sweden. Capitol's Danish art director designed an attractive sleeve with a photo of the girls holding an upright surfboard. The same photo was used in Sweden where four different colors of the sleeve were printed—red, orange, green, and blue. In the United States, Capitol sent select disc jockeys a Honey House with three small jars of honey to promote the single.

There is some thought Capitol and Murry chose not to promote the Honeys too vigorously, fearing outside productions would distract Brian and dilute the Beach Boys' sales. "Brian could never understand why we didn't have a hit record," recalled Marilyn. "He had more faith in us than anyone. The Beach Boys never supported the Honeys. The rest of the guys were jealous of Brian giving us any of Brian's time."[2]

When Capitol signed the Honeys it was a vote of confidence in Brian. It also signaled to other West Coast record companies that a major label was making a commitment to surf music. Suddenly, female surfer groups like the Surf Bunnies and the Beach Girls were the rage.

On April 12, Don Kirshner sold Aldon Music to Columbia Pictures-Screen Gems for $2 million. If Brian had contracted with Aldon earlier in the year, he would have been one

SURFIN' DOWN THE SWANEE RIVER
SHOOT THE CURL

4952

Brian leveraged his influence at Capitol to get the Honeys, from left, sisters Marilyn and Diane Rovell and their cousin Ginger Blake, a record deal. Brian penned "Surfin' Down the Swanee River," which he produced at Capitol on March 5, 1963. The single, backed with "Shoot the Curl," written by Ginger and Diane, was released April 8 (author's collection).

of a dozen songwriters included in the sale. The seven songs Brian published with Aldon are currently credited to Screen Gems-EMI Music, Incorporated.

That night, the Beach Boys played the Rendezvous Ballroom in Balboa as part of the annual Bal-Week celebration. According to Dennis Rose, lead guitarist of the Centurions, a surf septet from Costa Mesa, hardly anyone showed up at the Rendezvous. Perhaps frustrated by the low turnout, the Beach Boys drove to the nearby Newport Dunes, an aquatic park on a horseshoe-shaped inlet where kids swam, danced, and held picnics, and where the Centurions were playing to a large hometown crowd. "They asked if they could play a couple of songs," Rose recalled. "That was okay with us, but our fans started yelling 'We want the Centurions,' and started booing the Beach Boys. I felt really bad for them as it was really embarrassing."[3]

Centurion bassist Jeff Lear remembered a different scenario. He recalled the Beach

Boys left a poorly attended dance at Newport Harbor High and arrived at the Dunes while the Centurions were on break. They ambled on stage, picked up the Centurion's instruments, and began playing. The startled Centurions and their bouncer rushed back to the stage. Lear recalled, "Just as Mike Love kicks off the vocals to 'Johnny B. Goode,' up runs [the bouncer] flipping his finger in Mike's face yelling 'f-you.' [The bouncer] was going crazy and grabbed Mike's leg and ripped him off the stage." The Boys escaped to the parking lot with the bouncer "pounding on a few of them all the way."[4]

On the KFWB and KRLA surveys out the next day, "Surfin' U.S.A." was the #1 record in LA. Two weeks later it hit #8 in *Billboard*, becoming Capitol's first rock 'n' roll smash since Gene Vincent's "Be-Bop-a-Lula" reached #7 in summer 1956. Around this time, *Surfin' Safari* was finally released in the United Kingdom, but it failed to chart.

By early April, the William Morris Agency was booking venues for a Beach Boys tour of the Midwest later that month. While the demand for their personal appearances steadily increased, the group still found themselves doing one-off gigs like the one Mike recounted on Jim Ladd's radio program *Innerview* in 1978. "When the Beach Boys first started out we played on the rooftop of radio station KAFY in Bakersfield, California."[5] This show may have been April 15 while "Surfin' U.S.A." was #1 on the Radio-Active KAFY Fabulous 55 survey. Also that day, *Jan & Dean Take Linda Surfin'* was released featuring the duo's interpretations of "Surfin'" and "Surfin' Safari" on which the Beach Boys played and sang background vocals.

On April 19, the Beach Boys played the Aragon Ballroom at P.O.P. Complimentary passes, which could be exchanged for tickets at the box office, declared "The Fabulous Beach Boys." Although they were the number one teen group in the country, no one under eighteen was admitted. The next day, as the new *Billboard* favorably reviewed *Surfin' U.S.A.* in its Pop Spotlight column, the Boys played a dance sponsored by the Parent-Teacher Association for the sixth-, seventh-, and eighth-grade students of Felton Intermediate School in Lennox.

COMPLIMENTARY GUEST PASS
EXCHANGE AT BOX OFFICE FOR TICKET
(No one under 18 permitted)
GOOD ONLY ON FRIDAY, APRIL 19, 1963
★★★★★★★★★★★★★★★★★★★★★★★★★★
THE FABULOUS
BEACH BOYS
PLUS
DICK DELVY AND THE
CHALLENGERS
★★★★★★★★★★★★★★★★★★★★★★★★★★
Aragon Ballroom
PACIFIC OCEAN PARK
SANTA MONICA, CALIFORNIA

The Beach Boys played the Aragon Ballroom at Pacific Ocean Park (P.O.P.) on April 19, 1963. This 3.5" × 4.5" complimentary pass could be exchanged for a ticket at the box office (author's collection).

On April 21, the group taped an appearance on *The Red Skelton Hour* at CBS Television City in LA, performing "Surfin' U.S.A." and "The Things We Did Last Summer." Skelton was a jazz aficionado, but saw the appeal that rock 'n' roll performers held for a younger audience. This would be the Beach Boys' first appearance on national television, but it would not air until September 24, the season opener for Skelton's thirteenth year. It did little to promote "Surfin' U.S.A." which was long gone from the charts by then.

At a faux beach party setting without amplifiers or microphones, the guys lip synced their way through "Surfin' U.S.A." while a dozen older-looking "teens" in beach attire grooved to the music. Brian played his dark Fender Precision Bass, Marks his Sunburst Fender Stratocaster, and Carl his Olympic White Fender Jaguar.

The Beach Boys' national television debut is as memorable for the vintage performance as for the outfits the CBS wardrobe department selected for them. They were dressed identically in three-quarter length sleeved crew-neck shirts with dark, broad horizontal stripes, and three-quarter length white bell bottom pants known as clam diggers. "They looked like sailors," recalled Jodi Gable.

The Beach Boys played a dance sponsored by the Parent-Teacher Association for the sixth-, seventh-, and eighth-grade students of Felton Intermediate School in Lennox, California, on April 20, 1963 (courtesy Brian Stafford).

"I think somebody with the show made them wear those outfits. It wasn't fashionable even then and I think they felt a little silly at the time."[6]

They looked awkward and self-conscious, a situation exacerbated by the outfits. Their stage moves had not changed much since their appearance on *One Man's Challenge* at the Azusa Teen Club nine months earlier—a synchronized rocking back and forth inspired by The Stroll. Mike at least appeared like he was enjoying himself. But during the guitar solo, he stepped out in front to dance with a young woman, his moves resembling those of an injured rooster flailing about. For their second number, they gathered together without instruments, Brian and Mike sitting in front of the other three standing, and lip synced "The Things We Did Last Summer," a Top Ten hit for Jo Stafford in 1946 and covered that year by Frank Sinatra. The guys would have known Shelly Fabares's upbeat version from August 1962, which reached #46. The selection of songs was a shrewd move by Murry. "Surfin' U.S.A." hooked the kids while "The Things We Did Last Summer" showcased their beautiful vocals, appealing to an older demographic who remembered the Stafford and Sinatra versions.

"The Things We Did Last Summer" was recorded on the CBS soundstage with the house orchestra.[7] The show's detailed rehearsal schedule indicated Brian, Mike, and Dennis recorded their vocals 10:30 a.m. to 12:30 p.m. while Carl and David recorded their vocals 12:30 p.m. to 1:30 p.m.[8] However, David remembered only Brian, Mike, and Carl singing on it, while he and Dennis goofed off somewhere.[9] Sometime after the taping, an acetate was made at Hite Morgan's Stereo Masters.[10] Brian recalled they recorded the song for a movie soundtrack, but it was never used.[11] It was finally released on the *Good Vibrations* box set in 1993. As part of its marketing campaign to promote the set, Capitol paired "The Things We Did Last Summer" with "Be True to Your School" as a jukebox only single.

After *Surfin' U.S.A.* was released, demand for their personal appearances began pouring in from all over the country. If they wanted a viable career, they would have to venture from the Golden State to promote their music, and themselves, to the rest of America.

As the only two members of the band still in school, an extended tour outside of California would have a significant impact on Carl, a junior at Hawthorne High, and David, a freshman at Morningside High. Their local celebrity as the Beach Boys had begun to make them the recipient of unwelcome attention as some students, and even an occasional teacher, taunted them with snide remarks. When Carl was suspended for the petty infraction of not obtaining permission to use the rest room, Murry arranged to have him transferred to Hollywood Professional School, an accredited school in a two-story building on Hollywood Boulevard that offered a flexible curriculum to accommodate the erratic schedules of show business youngsters. David Marks and Marilyn and Diane Rovell soon followed suit. Founded in 1925, the school offered a standard academic curriculum through twelfth grade. Classes were held Monday through Friday from 8:30 a.m. to 12:30 p.m. With an abundance of talent, school assemblies, called "Aud Calls," were entertaining and memorable. In June 1963, as Carl completed his junior year, Brenda Lee wowed the student body, and scandalized the faculty, with her performance of Ray Charles's "What'd I Say."[12]

The William Morris Agency booked a nine-city tour of the Midwest that began April 24 and included nine shows in five states—Iowa, Illinois, Kansas, Minnesota, and South Dakota. Traveling some 5,000 miles in twelve days, the tour took them farther and longer from home than they had ever been. (See Appendix 11.) Murry again opted to stay home and asked Elmer Marks, David's father, to accompany the Boys as their tour manager.

Brian decided not to join the group on this tour. "I've always felt I was a behind-the-scenes man, rather than an entertainer," he recalled.[13] Also, the loud amplifiers caused pain and ringing in his ears and, because he already had significant hearing loss in his right ear, he needed to protect and preserve his remaining hearing. Of course, he may have not wanted to tour because he did not enjoy being away from home for long periods. By now, Brian was spending more and more time with Marilyn. Mae and Irving Rovell, her parents, accepted him warmly into a home filled with love, laughter, and a seemingly endless supply of comfort food. Although they had three daughters under the age of sixteen, the Rovells often permitted Brian to spend the night. If a romance was going to blossom, it would do so in the safety of their home. Of course, Brian's unusual living arrangement did not bode well for his engagement to Judy, which was on the rocks by that summer. As he began to work on a follow-up Honeys single, he found himself increasingly attracted to both Marilyn and Diane.

Brian decided not to go on the Midwest tour well before it began. But he knew the group's live show would sound thin without his bass and vocals, so he had to find a suitable replacement. Someone who could play bass, sing his high part, and was familiar with the group's live repertoire. Someone like Al Jardine. And by spring 1963, playing music on the road with the Beach Boys was a lot more appealing to Al than the academic rigors of his pre-dental curriculum at El Camino Community College.

Al was completing his third year of collegiate studies, working, and playing music with Gary and Don Winfrey as the Islanders. They had recently recorded "Lonely Islander" on the Wollensak in the Hermosa Beach apartment Al and Gary shared. The song had a loose calypso rhythm and was originally called "Banana Boat" when, as the Tikis, they worked on it with Bob Barrow in summer 1960. "Al rented a stand-up bass from Hogan's House of Music in Lawndale for the new recording," recalled Winfrey. "Al still likes that song and would like to record it again someday."[14]

When Brian called him, Al was glad to hear from his former classmate. "Brian sneaks in all these great songs after I leave the group," Al recalled. "I was listening to the radio like everybody else and I was starting to regret my decision. A year after I dropped out of the group, 'Surfin' U.S.A.' and 'Shut Down' had just come out."[15] "Just before summer 1963, Brian called and begged me to come back to the group. By then I was kind of fed up with school and Brian was feeling pressure from Murry to tour and support the album. He sent me a dub of the new single to help me prepare for the tour. I had already worked on 'Surfin' U.S.A.' from its inception so I knew that quite well, but I had to learn 'Shut Down.'"[16] "Brian started to get flustered because of the pressure of having to write, produce, and tour. It was just too much for him."[17] "He didn't enjoy going out there. And I think his weight had something to do with it even at that time. He was starting to get heavy, he didn't feel comfortable."[18]

Brian neglected to tell Murry that Al was filling in for him. Perhaps he wanted to avoid a confrontation until it was a done deal. Expecting a hero's welcome for pitching in to help the group, Al was greeted instead with Murry's wrath when he showed up at the airport unexpectedly. "I was so disappointed Murry was so hostile to me in particular," Al recalled. "I didn't understand it. I thought I was going to be the saving grace. So here I am like an interloper in my own band. I figured I started it, so why shouldn't I come back to it. The other guys were happy I was there because Brian wasn't coming."[19]

On April 24, this newly configured touring group—Mike, Dennis, Carl, David, and Al—flew from LA to Chicago. Rock 'n' roll tour itineraries had not changed much since the ill-fated 1959 Winter Dance Party that claimed the lives of Buddy Holly, Ritchie Valens, and J.P. "The Big Bopper" Richardson. They were still booked according to venue availability with little regard for the strain placed on the performers.

After arriving in Chicago, Elmer Marks rented a Chevrolet station wagon and a U-Haul trailer to transport their gear. "We got so crazy in that station wagon," Mike recalled. "There were five of us and a driver. And we all lugged our own instruments. And we'd drive sometimes five hundred miles to the next date because the routing wasn't that great."[20]

They drove 307 miles west for a show April 25 at the Val Air Ballroom in Des Moines, Iowa. They then drove 238 miles east to play the YWCA Teen Canteen April 26 in Rockford, Illinois, which they had passed on their way to Des Moines. On April 27, as they played the Danceland Ballroom in Cedar Rapids, Iowa, *Surfin' U.S.A.* debuted at #133 on the *Billboard* album chart. Meanwhile, "Shut Down," which had been bubbling under the *Billboard* Hot 100 for three weeks, sprinted twenty-seven places to #74. On KFWB it entered the starting gate at #32 and peaked at #5 three weeks later. "Shut Down" also jumpstarted the Four Speeds' "R.P.M.," which had stalled after its February release. Now it debuted at #40 and enjoyed a four-week ride, peaking at #28 May 18.

On April 28, the Beach Boys played the Terp Ballroom in Austin, Minnesota, and were off the next day. After playing the Arkota Ballroom in Sioux Falls, South Dakota, April 30, they drove 406 miles south to Wichita, Kansas, on May 1 to play a roller rink at a sports center known locally as Kiddieland.

May 1963

They spent the next day driving 535 miles north, passing Sioux Falls on their way, to play the 24th Annual Twin City High School Night at Excelsior Amusement Park and Big

Reggie's Danceland on the banks of Lake Minnetonka in Excelsior, Minnesota, on May 3. They headlined a free show on the outdoor stage of the amusement park from 6:30 p.m. to 7:00 p.m. and then moved indoors and across the street to Danceland, where they began playing at 8:30 p.m.[21] Danceland had one of the largest wooden dance floors in the Upper Midwest. The cavernous interior was all wood with arched columns, peaked ceiling, and huge beams from which light bulbs hung on wires from the rafters. The overall feeling was dark and cathedral-like. They played at the far end of the hall on a wide stage just slightly off the floor.

Mike remembered the Danceland show as the moment he realized the Beach Boys were successful. "We did four sets, forty-five minutes each. After the second set, we took a break and stepped outside and looked down the road. A line of cars went on for about a mile. I turned to Brian and said, 'This is what it must have been like when Elvis started.'"[22] However, unless Brian attended select dates on the tour, that comment must have been directed to another member of the band. And the line of cars may not have all been for the Beach Boys. Danceland and the amusement park shared Excelsior Boulevard as their only access road, and High School Night had drawn 8,000 teens to the amusement park the year before. However, Roy Colihan, the club manager known as "Big Reggie," told Elmer Marks the Beach Boys had attracted the largest crowd there since 1944 and that more than 1,000 fans had to be turned away. Elmer's tour journal noted 1,766 in attendance and a net of $1,974.50.[23]

On May 4, the Beach Boys played the Armory in Duluth, Minnesota, and a photograph from the show features Al on stage with the group. The next day, they finished their first Midwest tour at the Surf Ballroom in Clear Lake, Iowa, the venue at which Buddy Holly, Ritchie Valens, and J.P. "The Big Bopper" Richardson played their final show February 2, 1959. The Boys argued with ballroom manager Carroll Anderson when he refused to increase the volume of the club's PA system in an effort to control the loudness of their guitar amplifiers.[24]

While the guys toured the Midwest, Brian further extended himself by working on other projects outside the group. Despite the poor reception to Bob and Sheri's "The Surfer Moon," Brian was still interested in producing a boy-girl duo like Nino Tempo and April Stevens, Dick and Dee Dee, and Paul and Paula. Brian mentioned to Elizabeth Mackie, who had been a year ahead of him at Hawthorne High, that he was looking for a new female vocalist. Mackie recommended her sorority sister, Vickie Kocher, an eighteen-year-old freshman at El Camino Community College studying theatrical arts. At El Camino, Kocher was voted Grid Queen and Sigma Chi Sweetheart. In March 1963, she was busy rehearsing a song and dance for the Miss Los Angeles pageant televised March 19 on KCOP-TV, channel 13.

Kocher called Brian and soon met with him and Norberg at their Crenshaw apartment where they played her a few songs. When she expressed interest in recording "The Surfer Moon," Bob and Brian looked at each other kind of funny, which she later attributed to the song's history with Sheri. Kocher didn't think of herself as a surfer girl, so she suggested a name change to "The Summer Moon," prompting Brian and Bob to change the surfing references.

On May 9, Brian recorded the instrumental track for "The Summer Moon" at United Recorders in Hollywood. The musicians were Norberg (guitar), Brian (piano), Glen Campbell (guitar), Ray Pohlman (bass), and Hal Blaine (drums). The Sid Sharp Strings added lush orchestration of violins and cello. It was Brian's first recording with a string section and Jan Berry reportedly arranged the strings. The session was paid for by Nevins-Kirshner Productions as a demo for Aldon Music, which had recently been sold to Columbia Pictures-Screen Gems. The music publishing is currently owned by Screen Gems-EMI Music, Inc.

Norberg and Kocher rehearsed their vocals at the Crenshaw apartment before double-tracking them at the more intimate Western studio. Brian added his own vocals to the mix. Murry attended the session and coached Kocher by telling her to sing as if she was a young girl in love for the first time.[25] Brian made a rough dub from the three track recording and gave Kocher an acetate which she and Norberg autographed "Bob & Vickie" as a keepsake. The typewritten information on the label included "Nevins Kirshner," "Summer Moon," and beneath the song title, the credit "Bob Norman," the name he reportedly adopted when Murry suggested Norberg sounded too Jewish. The acetate contains two takes of the song with subtle vocal differences. Kocher put

Vickie Kocher (aka Victoria Hale) was a nineteen-year-old student at El Camino Community College when she recorded "The Summer Moon" with Brian and Bob Norberg at Western Recorders in May 1963 (courtesy Victoria Hale).

it on-line in fall 2010 for fans to enjoy. Brian played the demo for Lou Adler, but Adler declined to pursue it. Brian recorded a demo of "Teach Me to Surf," which he intended for Kocher and Norberg. Capitol surmised its title to be "Little Surfer Girl" when a snippet was released on the *Good Vibrations* box set in 1993.[26] "Rock and Roll Bash," written by Brian and Norberg with a lyrical assist from Kocher, was copyrighted December 18, but likely not recorded as it was not released on *The Big Beat*.

Another Brian and Norberg song that likely dates from spring 1963 is "The Big Beat." Inspired by Alan Freed's 1957 television show by that name, "The Big Beat" was a fast-paced mash up of iconic figures, some real and some mythical, digging the beat of the rock 'n' roll pioneers. The frenetic track features a driving piano and scorching guitar solo likely played by session musicians at Western or Gold Star. It was released on *The Big Beat* as by Bob and Sheri, and may have been recorded earlier in the year as Kocher recalled Sheri was out of the picture by May. Brian later rewrote it as "Do You Remember" in May 1964 for *All Summer Long* released that July. Brian's sole writing credit was later amended to reflect Mike's lyrical contribution.

In early May, former Candix A&R director Joe Saraceno released "Come and Get It" (b/w "Like Chop") by the Tri-Five on Damark 2400, his new label named for his sons Dana and Mark, and distributed by London Records. Both instrumentals, credited as written by Gary Usher and Mike Borchetta, were recorded earlier in the year in a garage studio in San Bernardino. The Tri-Five were Usher (rhythm guitar), Carl Wilson (lead guitar), Dennis Wilson (drums), Dick Burns (bass), and Randy Thomas (keyboards). Contrary to persistent speculation, Brian did not participate in the session. "Come and Get It" was inspired by the Czechoslovakian folk song "Stodola Pumpa," whose chorus was played by Good Humor ice cream trucks throughout Southern California in the early 1960s. The single failed to chart and was the only release on Damark. "Come and Get It" and "Like Chop" were included on *Surfin'* on Varèse Sarabande Records in 2000.[27]

In summer 1963, inspired by "Come and Get It," Brian wrote an instrumental on his Hammond organ called "Good Humor Man," which he shelved for the time being. Around this time, Brian and Jan Berry collaborated on an instrumental called "Chopsticks Boogie."

On May 16, the Honeys returned to Capitol with Nick Venet and recorded "From Jimmy with Tears" and "Raindrops." Marilyn recalled, "It was very different working with Nick because when you worked with Brian you were working with real talent. Nick was a producer! He hired people to do it all whereas Brian did it all himself."[28] While Brian sought to clarify Venet's role as the Honeys' producer, the follow-up single was shelved and the girls would not have another recording session for ten weeks.

Capitol had three Top Ten records in the May 18 *Billboard* ("Surfin' U.S.A.," the Kingston Trio's "Reverend Mr. Black," and Al Martino's "I Love You Because") and its singles sales, forty percent higher now than last year, were the highest in the company's twenty-year history. Capitol had to contract with an outside pressing plant to keep up with demand.[29]

On May 17, Liberty Records released "Surf City" by Jan & Dean. When Capitol's promotion men in the field heard it on the radio, some called the company asking why they hadn't received advance notice of the new Beach Boys single. With a surfing title, crisp production, youthful lead vocal, and soaring falsetto, they were surprised to learn "Surf City" was not the Beach Boys.

"Surf City" first charted four weeks after "Surfin' U.S.A." peaked. For radio program directors and the record buying public, it was essentially a follow-up to "Surfin' U.S.A." The Beach Boys had paved the way, whipping up a patriotic fervor and rallying the country around this exciting West Coast phenomenon. "Surfin' U.S.A." was a sweeping canvas on which "Surf City" painted a specific destination in our collective imaginations. An idyllic place where the sun was always shining, a party always growing, and girls outnumbered guys two to one.

By mid-summer, "Surf City" was #1 on the Hot 100 in *Billboard* out July 13 and 20. When they sang a gutsy live version on *The Steve Allen Playhouse*, filmed July 11 and broadcast July 23, Jan surprised Dean with a risqué lyrical substitution as "two girls" became "two furs." At the end of the performance, the camera cut to three elderly women clapping sedately in the studio audience. The following week, "Surf City" was #1 in *Cash Box* and Jan & Dean were on the cover. In LA, it spent two weeks at the top of the KFWB and KRLA surveys. In Chicago, where there was no surfing on Lake Michigan, WYNR disc jockey Dick Kemp took to riding around in a hearse, a popular alternate woodie, loaded with a surfboard. Record distributors were flooded with orders for a *Surf City* album that hadn't been released yet.

"Surf City" was Jan & Dean's first and only #1 record. Liberty rushed them into the studio and the album *Surf City (And Other Swingin' Cities)* was in stores by late July, accompanied by a full-page ad in *Billboard*. On the strength of "Surf City," Jan Berry signed a three-year songwriter's contract and a six-year producer's contract with Screen Gems.

Murry Wilson was furious Brian had given away a #1 record. Keep in mind how the Beach Boys singles had fared in *Billboard* so far—"Surfin'" (#75), "Surfin' Safari" (#14), "409" (#76), "Ten Little Indians" (#49), "Surfin' U.S.A." (#3), and "Shut Down" (#23). And "Surf City" would have put a considerable amount of money in the Wilson coffers. As it was, Brian only received co-writing credit. The arrangement and production was credited to Berry and the copyright to Screen Gems-Columbia Music, Inc. Two years later, it was still on Murry's mind when he wrote Brian. "You recorded on Jan & Dean's record, which was an absolutely treacherous act against not only your employers, but the welfare of your family financially; but more important, the combined integrity of the Beach Boys group itself."[30] Judy Bowles recalled, "Brian just threw 'Surf City' away. He was so thrilled about working with Jan & Dean. He told me Murry was really mad at him for giving it away. Brian thought it was funny, kind of like a little dig at his dad."[31]

A week after the Midwest tour, the Beach Boys played half a dozen shows around Southern California. On May 24, they played the Sacramento Memorial Auditorium. It was the band's first appearance in their home state's capital, where they met an entrepreneurial concert promoter who changed their approach to future personal appearances.

In late March 1963, eighteen-year-old Fred Vail was asked by the senior class of his alma mater, El Camino High School in affluent north Sacramento, to coordinate a fundraising event to raise money for their graduation party. As a senior the previous year, Vail organized a successful class fundraiser with top-name talent, including Jan & Dean, Smokey Robinson, and Bobby Freeman. Vail proposed a concert at the Sacramento Memorial Auditorium and, after considering surf bands like the Astronauts and the Chantays, decided on the Beach Boys.

Vail eventually got in touch with Marshall Berle, the junior talent agent at William Morris, and booked the Beach Boys for $750. The contract Vail received back from the group was signed by Audree Wilson and the commitment was for Carl Wilson and four musicians. Seven months shy of seventeen, Carl was already the de facto leader of the touring band.

"The entire bill for the concert was $1,000," Vail recalled. "I rented a hall for $150 and two policemen for security. We charged $1.75 for admission and I got free advertising from a local radio station because it was a high school. I went to Sacramento Municipal Airport and met six people including Murry. Brian had not shown and already there were rumors as to why. Carl asked who else was on the show and I told him they were the only ones. He said, 'You mean we're the headliners? Are you sure you're going to come out of this okay?' I said, 'I think so!'"[32] Vail loaded their gear into the back of his parents' 1954 Chevrolet station wagon, drove north past the venue, and got them settled into the Mansion Inn on 16th Street.

They played two forty-five minute sets for 3,000 wildly enthusiastic kids.[33] At dinner that evening, they figured they each made fifty dollars and asked Vail how he made out. He replied about four thousand dollars. "They could not believe they had that kind of earning potential in those days. What we set up that night became the format of American Productions, the Beach Boys' concert production firm. The next show we did together, they went from this $800 a night flat fee William Morris was booking them for to about $3,000 or better a night." After another show, Vail dumped about four thousand dollars on the hotel bed and the guys could not believe it was all for them. "The success Murry and I had with these shows opened the eyes of the agents at William Morris and promoters all over the country. People began to realize the potential impact of the Beach Boys and to give serious consideration to the Boys as a major attraction and not just a Southern California phenomenon."[34]

In the final days of May, as "Surf City" was on the brink of charting in LA, Jan & Dean joined the Beach Boys for a handful of shows that included two dates in San Francisco.

June 1963

The *Cash Box* out June 1 featured a collage on the cover of Capitol recording artists including three photographs of the Beach Boys. That day they played a show at the dance hall in Rio Nido, a resort community on the scenic Russian River in Sonoma County an hour north of San Francisco. During the show, Mike met and befriended Sharon Marie Esparza, a sixteen-year-old aspiring singer from Novato, California, and later helped her land a two-plus-two deal with Capitol, recording as Sharon Marie.

On June 7, the Beach Boys played a short set in the Hawthorne High cafeteria for the Senior Breakfast, an annual event for the school's graduating class. That evening they drove one hundred miles north to play three graduation parties for three Bakersfield high schools. The concerts were booked in October 1962 when a committee of teachers and parents began planning for graduation. Raymond "Duke" Hammett, whose son, Lee, was a senior at East Bakersfield High, was charged with hiring the entertainment. Hammett contacted the William Morris Agency and arranged for the Kern County school district to contract with the Beach Boys. The Cherry Creek Singers, a folk quartet that also did comedy routines, were booked separately. Over the next several months, a schedule was arranged by which both groups would travel from one party to another, appearing at each venue at different times. Local groups like the Titans II, the Illusions, and the Ivy Clansmen, filled in the remaining hours with music for dancing.

Lee Hammett was thrilled to have the Beach Boys perform at his school. Of course, in the time since his father booked them, they had become the hottest group in the country. With the success of "Surfin' U.S.A.," and with an early morning gig at Hawthorne High, the Boys were not too keen on playing three shows in one evening in what one organizer described as "a little cowtown like Bakersfield." As the date approached, the band reportedly tried to renege on its commitment and had to be reminded of their contractual obligation.[35]

After evening commencement ceremonies, two graduation parties got under way around 10:30 p.m. The band, with Al filling in for Brian, played a forty-five minute set at 12:30 a.m. for East Bakersfield High School's "Last Blast" at the Bakersfield College Campus Center. When a guitar string broke, the music came to a sudden halt and Mike joked, "Oh well, earn while you learn." After the show, they chatted with students and autographed a copy of *Surfin' U.S.A.* for Lee Hammett on which Dennis wrote his home address (1727 Hermosa Avenue) on the back cover.

Because they were unfamiliar with the Bakersfield area, fifteen-year-old Jeff Hammett, Lee's younger brother and a sophomore at East Bakersfield High, was tasked with escorting them to the Albert S. Goode Auditorium on the Kern County Fairgrounds for a 2:30 a.m. show for Bakersfield High's "Neptune's Whing Ding." Dennis had no idea where the next show was, so he asked Hammett to drive with him. Dennis had driven up in his Corvette, removing the spare tire to accommodate his bass drum. During the ride to the fairgrounds, he asked if there was a straightaway nearby and Hammett directed him to a deserted street. He stopped the car and took out his wallet. Hammett recalled, "He took out a five or a ten, maybe more, and told me I could have it if, when he hit the accelerator, I could reach it." Dennis floored it and the vette took off like a rocket, scorching the blacktop, exceeding 100 mph in seconds, and pinning Jeff to his seat. "Well, his money was safe. I never could reach the bill."[36]

The band played its third and final show that morning about 4:30 a.m. at Veterans Hall on West Norris Road, north of the Kern River and technically in Oildale, for North High's party. Because of a late evening commencement, this party did not get under way until nearly midnight.

Most alumni have fond memories of the Beach Boys playing at their graduation parties, but some thought the band resented being there. "I had the distinct impression they felt they were doing us a favor," recalled Neil Anson. "It was all in the attitude."[37] There was, however, a connection between the band and the community's workingman roots. In fall 1949, the Love Sheet Metal Service Company manufactured and installed two stainless steel range hoods in the East Bakersfield High School cafeteria and subsequently won a $36,379.81 contract in January 1955 for a custom-built kitchen in the new Bakersfield High School cafeteria.[38] In November 1955, the company was awarded the contract to manufacture and install cafeteria equipment at Bakersfield College.

According to the AFM Local 47 archives, the Beach Boys recorded "Surfer Girl" and "Little Deuce Coupe," their fourth Capitol single, at Western Recorders on June 12.[39] They played a show with Jan & Dean in Houston earlier that day and, unless the AFM contract information is incorrect, presumably went straight to the studio upon their return.

It had been more than sixteen months since the Beach Boys first recorded "Surfer Girl" with Hite Morgan at World Pacific Studio on February 8, 1962. The new recording went smoothly as the band had been playing the song in concert for several months. Brian's production was truer to his original vision, and the Morgan version remained unreleased until 1990. "I drove them crazy with 'Surfer Girl,'" recalled Jodi Gable. "I loved it so much, but they didn't want to put it out because it was a ballad. I told them, 'Trust me, it's going to be a smash, it's so good.' They gave me a demo of it and made me promise not to play it for anyone, which was hard to do, but I did it. I'd love to take credit for 'Surfer Girl,' but it was written about Judy Bowles."[40]

"Little Deuce Coupe," another automotive paean from the pen of Roger Christian, who once owned a 1932 Ford Coupe, may have been held off *Surfin' U.S.A.* because of its structural similarity to "Shut Down." Brian and Norberg recorded a medium tempo shuffle of "Little Deuce Coupe" in their apartment with Brian on piano and Norberg adding guitar licks. It was released on *Hawthorne, CA* in 2001.

Mike recalled, "Here's how impulsive Brian was. 'Little Deuce Coupe' was finished in the studio and we'd drive a couple of blocks down the street to the radio station and have them play it, much to the chagrin of the record company who would like to press it up and have it available for sale. But he wanted to hear it on the radio that night. So it played at like 1:00 a.m. for the first time on the radio."[41]

With their new single recorded, the group headed to Hawaii on June 13 as one of four acts for the week-long Summer Spectacular Show of Stars. Brian chose not to go and recruited Al, who had just completed his second year at El Camino on June 12. The tour was headlined by seventeen-year-old Dee Dee Sharp who had Top Ten hits with "Mashed Potato Time" and "Do the Bird." Also on the bill were the Treniers, an R&B octet, and Jackie DeShannon. Honolulu disc jockey Tom Moffat was the master of ceremonies.

Murry accompanied the guys to the airport, but remained in California. Audree took advantage of the opportunity to visit the Aloha State along with tour manager Elmer Marks. Between June 14 and 22, the Beach Boys played fifteen shows at eight different venues on the three largest Hawaiian Islands—Hawaii, Maui, and Oahu. Eight of the shows were played in Honolulu, the state capitol located on Oahu, at four different venues, including three U.S. military installations. Bruce Johnston, who would join the group in less than two years, was vacationing in Hawaii and went to one of the shows. He recalled, "I heard them back up Jackie DeShannon, who was doing very complicated songs at that time, and I thought, 'Whooaahh, not bad.'"[42]

On June 14, with the other guys in Hawaii, Brian held his first recording session at Gold Star, the studio where Phil Spector had produced "He's a Rebel" and was preparing to produce the Ronettes' "Be My Baby" in July and his Christmas album in August. Brian played piano on the session and hired many of the musicians Spector used including David Gates (bass), Carol Kaye (guitar), Steve Douglas and Jay Migliori (saxophones), and Hal Blaine (drums). It may have been around this time Lou Adler introduced Brian to Spector.

Paid for by David Gold for Gold Star Record Company, the session yielded two songs for Brian's projects outside the group. One was the instrumental track for a song that became the A side of Sharon Marie's first Capitol single, which Brian tentatively called "Black Wednesday." When Mike added lyrics it became "Run-Around Lover," which they copyrighted July 16. However, on the songwriter's contract dated November 1, Brian was listed as sole writer.[43]

Sharon traveled to LA with her mother later that summer to record her lead vocal. The background vocals were sung by the Blossoms, the vocal trio who sang on many of Spector's productions. Mike sang the line "Here she comes" in the first chorus and, according to Sharon, played the sax line. "I have read people didn't believe he played it, but he did. I saw and heard him. He might have been dubbed over later, but I didn't hear anything about that."[44] For the B side, Sharon suggested Gershwin's "Summertime" and they recorded it on a reel-to-reel tape deck in Brian's apartment, with Brian playing piano and bass, and Mike keeping the beat on a snare drum.[45]

The second song Brian recorded at Gold Star June 14 was "Back Home," a folksy shuffle written with Norberg about the pastoral pleasures of returning to the family farm and reconnecting with family and friends. Brian delivered earnest enthusiasm in a mid-range vocal over a sax-driven track. He also recorded all the background vocals. It is unclear what Brian intended to do with the song. He did not record a version with the Beach Boys and it sat on the shelf for six years. In December 1969, Al dusted it off and produced a rootsy, rollicking track the following month. He dropped the opening line about going back to Ohio, although it would have suited him as his grandfather still had a farm there, and penned new lyrics that transformed it into an ecological antidote to LA smog. But it didn't make the cut for *Sunflower* that August. Brian resurrected it for *15 Big Ones* in July 1976, recording a spirited track with only the original five Beach Boys and sparkling group harmonies. He dropped the song's original bridge and expanded the rousing chorus buried deep in the fade on Jardine's version. But Brian's jarring lead vocal, raspy and cracking in spots, sounded like a raw demo. During his renaissance as a solo artist, Brian recorded "Back Home" for *Live at the Roxy Theatre* in April 2000. The intervening quarter century, marked by achievement and struggle, matured Brian's voice with a confidence that transformed the song's wistful nostalgia into a poignant reflection on happier times. Brian's and Al's earlier versions were included on the *Made in California* box set in 2013.

Three songs Brian wrote and recorded with session musicians at Western or Gold Star, perhaps sometime that summer while the band was on tour, remained unreleased until *The Big Beat* in 2013. On "Marie" Brian sang a mid-range vocal over a soft boogie woogie piano, handclaps, and background vocals by the Honeys. The singer boasts about never seeing the same girl twice until he falls for Marie. "Mother May I," inspired by the children's game, is an uptempo song with a catchy melody and a beautiful falsetto lead by Brian as a young man asking his mother's permissison to pursue a young woman romantically. Twenty seconds into the song, Brian responds as the mother in a voice you'd expect from Norman Bates— an odd, menacing snarl that reduced the song to a novelty the band was likely too embarrassed to release. "First Rock and Roll Dance" was a raucous piano, sax, and guitar instrumental punctuated with thumping bass drum quarter notes.

The banner headline in *Billboard* on newsstands June 22 proclaimed "Surf Music Splashes Way Across U.S." Capitol kicked off a marketing campaign July 1 in which it provided record stores with free surfing dictionary brochures and surfboard display racks to promote *Surfin' Safari*, *Surfin' U.S.A.*, and its two albums by Dick Dale and the Deltones. *Billboard* asked none other than Murry Wilson to define surf music. "The basis of surfing music is a rock 'n' roll bass beat figuration coupled with a raunch-type, weird-sounding lead guitar, an electric guitar, plus wailing saxes. Surfing music has to sound untrained with a certain rough flavor to appeal to the teenagers. As in the case of true country and western, when the music gets too good and too polished, it isn't considered the real thing."[46] Capitol placed a half-page ad in the issue in which the Beach Boys thanked radio for their success. *Billboard* ran a news article announcing Brian and Murry had formed Sea of Tunes Production Company to produce songs for new artists, offering Capitol the first crack at releasing them.[47] Murry made it clear they would work with other labels' artists and material, but would stay out of the surfing field. "We don't want to build competition for ourselves or Capitol."[48]

After the band returned from Hawaii in late June, they had little time to rest as Brian had new songs to rehearse for their next album. After a few days of rehearsals, the group flew to Las Vegas to play the Convention Center June 29. They were greeted with good news in *Billboard* as *Surfin' U.S.A.* jumped to #2 on the album chart after being at #5 the previous two weeks. It remained #2 the following week and, although it never reached #1, would chart an impressive seventy-two weeks, becoming their first album certified gold for sales exceeding one million copies. After a three-month absence, *Surfin' Safari* re-entered the album chart at #146, charting another twenty weeks and reaching #47 in late August.

The Beach Boys finally cracked the British singles chart with "Surfin' U.S.A." (b/w "Shut Down," Capitol CL 15305), which reached #34. Meanwhile, Capitol Records' sales for the fiscal year ending June 30 reached the highest they had been since 1959 and the second highest in the company's history.[49]

About late June to mid–July, the Beach Boys played the Skate-O-Rama in Downey, with the Blazers, a surf quintet from Fullerton who had recently begun featuring thirteen-year-old Kathy Marshall on lead guitar. Marshall recalled, "Dennis Wilson kept giving me the eye and bugging me for my phone number. He was really trying to impress me. I finally got rid of him by giving him my girlfriend's number. He really got mad when he called only to get my girlfriend, but he asked her out instead and she turned him down, too!"[50] Also around this time, Dennis McLellend, rhythm guitarist with Speedy and the Reverbs, a surf quintet from Whittier, recalled opening for the Beach Boys at the Pasadena Civic Auditorium.[51] Other surf bands that recalled playing with the Beach Boys, most likely in fall/winter 1962 to spring 1963, were the Hustlers, the Nobles, the Nomads, the Sentinals, and the Vulcanes. Skip Hand, drummer in the Galaxies, a South Bay surf band, recalled a show at the Hermosa Biltmore with the Beach Boys and the Vibrants. "After our set, Carl Wilson came up to and started talking to me. I showed him a lick on the guitar and was real surprised to hear that same lick on a later Beach Boys album."[52]

After the phenomenal success of *Surfin' U.S.A.*, demand for the group's personal appearances skyrocketed, exposing a dilemma unique to artists who write their own songs—how to balance the twin goals of creating new music while promoting your current music. The untenable constraints that touring placed on Brian's time were eased occasionally when Al agreed to fill in for him on the road. But that was about to change.

The William Morris Agency booked a second Midwest tour beginning July 19 that would take them to thirty-six cities in fifteen states over forty-five days. It would also bring them to the East and Northeast for the first time, but senior agent Ira Okun recalled there was little interest in booking them in the Southeast. They broke attendance records in fourteen dance halls, including an eighteen-year-old mark held by Lawrence Welk at the Peony Park Ballroom in Omaha, Nebraska.[53] The tour would place an enormous amount of pressure on Brian as he struggled to balance writing, arranging, and producing songs for the group's next album with the relentless demands of personal appearances.

And, for the youngest member of the band, an impulsive, off-handed remark would mean the end of his career as a Beach Boy.

22

36 Cities in 45 Days
(July–August 1963)

The Beach Boys played two shows in Phoenix July 5 and 6 where Al once again filled in for Brian. On July 7, Brian completed a Popular Songwriter's Contract for a song tentatively called "Baa Baa Black Sheep" as its melody was based on that nursery rhyme. Two years later it became "And Your Dreams Come True," a stunning, sixty-two second a cappella meditation that closed *Summer Days (and Summer Nights!!)* in July 1965.

On July 11, the group played the Retail Clerks Union Hall, a landmark surf venue in Buena Park, California. Opening for the Boys were the Astronauts, a rock 'n' roll quintet transplanted from Colorado when RCA Victor hopped on the woody bandwagon and transformed them into a surf band. Guitarist Bob Demmon recalled, "After our set, we stayed to listen to the Beach Boys. They were so bad vocally and musically that we left. Brian Wilson later told me it was that gig that became the turning point in the Beach Boys' career because they realized they had to get it together for live appearances."[1]

The annual Orange County Fair was held July 9 to 14 in Costa Mesa, California. The Beach Boys, and Adrian and the Sunsets played the fair most likely on July 12.

On July 13, the Beach Boys played Veterans Memorial Stadium in Santa Maria with Usher's Four Speeds and the Honeys for "A Surfing Spectacular" sponsored by radio station KSEE. Dick Burns of the Four Speeds knew Santa Maria was largely Mexican-American and rehearsed songs like "Gaucho Rock," "Tequila," and other Chicano favorites. He also recruited a skilled lead guitarist for the gig. Burns maintained the Honeys asked if the Four Speeds, rather than the Beach Boys, could back them up during the show. Usher recalled the Boys were still not very good at performing live and the simple public address system did little to highlight their talent as a vocal group.[2]

The band resumed work on their third album, *Surfer Girl*, on July 16. In addition to "Surfer Girl" and "Little Deuce Coupe," recorded at Western June 12, they finished ten additional songs for the album. Capitol's liner notes for *Surfer Girl* in the 1990 twofer series stated all ten songs were recorded July 16. That, of course, is unlikely. However, because the AFM contracts are missing, the dates and studios for the sessions are unknown. The album was released two weeks after they returned from a six-week tour that started July 19. They recorded the songs rather quickly, a feat more readily achieved because the groundwork for four songs had already been done.

For "The Surfer Moon," Brian recycled the instrumental track of "The Summer Moon" that he produced for Norberg and Kocher that May. He recorded all the vocals himself, doubling his lead on the first verse and harmonizing with himself for the rest of the song.

With his soaring vocal and lush strings, the song was a highlight on an album that included some of his prettiest ballads. "South Bay Surfer" was another reimagined version of Stephen Foster's "Old Folks at Home." Brian reworked two instrumentals, the Tri-Five's "Come and Get It" and his own "Good Humor Man," into "The Rocking Surfer," which Marks recalled was recorded at Art Wenzel's studio in Downey. It was credited as a traditional melody arranged by Brian. "Boogie Woodie" was a rollicking, two-minute keyboard instrumental purportedly based on "The Flight of the Bumblebee" despite having no resemblance to that orchestral piece by Russian composer Nikolai Rimsky-Korsakov. It was inspired by "Boogie Woogie" by B. Bumble & the Stingers, a follow-up to "Bumble Boogie," a #21 hit in summer 1961 that remade the original, a jazzy send-up of "Flight of the Bumble Bee," a #7 hit for Freddy Martin and His Orchestra, with Jack Fina on piano, in 1946. "Boogie Woodie" owed a greater debt to "Pinetop's Boogie Woogie" by Clarence "Pinetop" Smith, which Audree taught her sons when they were young. "Boogie Woodie" was credited as Rimsky-Korsakov with an arrangement by Brian.

Of the remaining six new songs, four were written by Brian and Mike—"Surfer's Rule," "Our Car Club," "Hawaii," and "Catch a Wave." Mike received co-credit for the latter two in 1994. "Surfer's Rule" boasts the surfers' superiority over the ho-dads, the greasers or car guys. The misplaced apostrophe in the song title mistakenly indicated surfers had some kind of rule. It featured a lead vocal by Dennis, who moved easily between both groups, while Brian handled the choruses. In the vocal tag, they taunted the Four Seasons had "better believe it" over which Brian added a wailing falsetto lifted from the melody of "Walk Like a Man" as a good-natured jab at their East Coast rivals. The Seasons responded with "No Surfin' Today" on the B side of "Dawn (Go Away)" in January 1964. Twenty years later, Bob Crewe and Bob Gaudio wrote the nostalgic "East Meets West," which both groups recorded together, trading signature vocal licks about favorite places and memories of their respective coasts.

"Our Car Club" was a slice of California car culture, detailing the mechanics of starting a club with dues, initiation rites, a sponsor, and club jackets. Published by Aldon Music in early 1963, it began life as "Rabbit's Foot" and was inspired, in part, by Mongo Santamaria's "Watermelon Man," which reached #5 on KFWB for two weeks in late April as "Surfin' U.S.A." held the top spot. A rabbit's foot was a good luck talisman dragsters often attached to their key rings. It was a working title as embryonic songs were often named whatever popped into Brian's head. It may have been slated for the Honeys, but Brian reclaimed it for *Surfer Girl*. Mike helped transform it into "Our Car Club," celebrating the social aspects of car ownership over the technical specs Christian favored. Reportedly recorded at Gold Star, Brian produced a sophisticated instrumental track driven by Hal Blaine's masterful drumming, Steve Douglas's rumbling sax, and the Honeys exuberant background vocals. Mike and Brian traded lead vocals with group harmonies filling out the verses and choruses. The "Rabbit's Foot" instrumental track with snippets of the Honeys background vocals was released on *The Big Beat* in 2013.

"Hawaii," a fast-paced ode to the island paradise, was penned shortly after the group's return from there in June. It was recorded at Gold Star and Dennis's drumming was supplemented by Hal Blaine on timbales. Mike sang the lead and Brian's falsetto punctuated each chorus. The song paid homage to Hawaii's surfing heritage and helped promote the prestigious Makaha International Surfing Championship, then in its twelfth year, to be held for the first time in Hawaii that winter. "Hawaii" was released as a single or EP in Australia, Germany, Japan, and Sweden. Eight photographs of the band frolicking in the Hawaiian sand and surf graced the cover of "Surfer Girl" sheet music published that summer by Hite Morgan's Guild Music. A promotional photograph of Brian in suit and tie was included on the cover.

"Catch a Wave," copyrighted July 22 as "Sittin' on Top of the World," its imaginative hook, invited everyone to try the greatest sport around while putting the naysayers, dismissive of the sport as just a fad, squarely in their place. Despite battling a cold, Mike's lead vocal and delivery captured the sport's bravura and exhilaration. Maureen Love, Mike's twenty-year-old sister, sweetened the track with a harp glissando, evoking a rolling swell of water. An organ riff and guitar solo over rhythmic handclaps provided the instrumental break. Despite meeting all the earmarks of a hit record, "Catch a Wave" was not released as a single. A year later, Jan Berry asked Roger Christian to pen new lyrics to the music as Jan & Dean attempted a skateboard craze with "Sidewalk Surfin'." It appeared on the soundtrack to *Ride the Wild Surf* in August 1964 and the single reached #21 on KFWB that November. The film's title track was co-written by Berry, Christian, and Brian.

"Your Summer Dream" was a sparse, tranquil ballad about a summer romance written by Brian and Norberg. Over a simple rhythm track on which David strummed his original Silvertone guitar, Brian doubled his lead vocal, choosing not to add harmony vocals. A one-sided, seven-inch acetate of the song was made at MBS Recording Studios at 228 S. Wabash Avenue in Chicago, perhaps a day or two after the recording session when the band flew into the Windy City to embark on its second Midwest tour. It is unknown whether "Your Summer Dream" was considered as a potential single.

The new album's game changer was Brian's and Usher's "In My Room." Amidst fun-filled pop songs about surf and cars, came this serious, introspective ballad with a grown-up theme. A flawless union of music and words, "In My Room" helped teens better understand their world, exploring their feelings without condescension, trivialization, or melodrama. It gave voice to emotions most kids could not verbalize. Brian and Usher made it okay, daresay normal, to reveal that you felt safe and comforted in your room, even in the dark. This empathetic soul baring resonated with parents who heard "In My Room" and discovered those tender feelings transcended age. They knew, however subconsciously, that your room was your sanctuary, an impenetrable refuge where you left the world's troubles outside. It was your friend, confidante, and confessor. Great art is personal, resonating within us in some mysterious and permanent way. After "In My Room" was written, Brian remarked that he realized he was writing about himself.[3]

A demo of "In My Room," recorded shortly after its inception, was included on the fifth bonus disc in the *Good Vibrations* box set in 1993. It began with group vocals which Brian later changed in the finished recording. After a series of soothing arpeggios and Maureen Love's harp flourish, Brian layered the introductory vocals, starting alone before being joined by Carl, and then by Dennis. A musical moment tenderly evoking the many nights the brothers lay awake in the bedroom they shared, Brian teaching them intricate vocal harmonies. As Mike added his bass voice, "In My Room" crystallized the majesty of the group and why they have resonated with people for more than fifty years. Brian recalled, "The whole world could go away when we would sing around a microphone. The world could disappear."[4]

"He was the most highly regarded pop musician in America," said singer songwriter David Crosby. "Hands down. Everybody by that time had figured out who was writing it all and who was arranging it all. 'In My Room' was the defining point for me. I heard 'In My Room' and I went, 'Okay, I give up. I can't do that. I'll never be able to do that.'"[5]

Linda Ronstadt recalled, "What a heartrending song. When you think about, I won't be afraid. A place where I'll be safe. They were really deep, profound emotions that came out of a lot of pain. There was nothing shallow about it."[6]

Renowned as a vocal group, the Beach Boys were also capable musicians who played their own instruments on the majority of the songs on their first six albums. There were exceptions, of course, as demands of recording, touring, and more sophisticated productions eventually increased Brian's reliance on studio musicians.

Brian invited Al to some of the sessions and Al played bass on "Catch a Wave," "Boogie Woodie," and "Surfer's Rule," sang background vocals on "In My Room," and contributed lyrically to "South Bay Surfer."

Surfer Girl would be the first Beach Boys album to bear the credit "produced by Brian Wilson." That seemingly simple statement was the result of a hard-fought battle in which Brian challenged a studio system entrenched at Capitol for two decades by which every artist was assigned a company producer. Although *Surfin' Safari* and *Surfin' U.S.A.* were largely produced by Brian, with suggestions from Murry and Venet, Capitol's corporate policy prevailed and Venet received sole credit. Although he had good ears for a hit song, Venet contributed little to Brian's creative process or musical experimentation in the studio.

"I would help Brian choose which songs to record," Venet recalled. "I was an objective viewpoint. I would say to Brian, 'I don't think you need to do the record over.'"[7] Roger Christian recalled, "Brian could take it from start to finish. He'd create the idea, produce it, and perform on it. He knew what he could get out of his brothers and how to work with them because they'd been doing it at home for years. They didn't really feel they needed Nick. So those early records Brian produced and Nick executive-produced."[8]

In addition to the sole producer credits on the first two albums, Murry's and Brian's relationship with Venet had deteriorated over a number of things—the "Ten Little Indians" misstep; the initial pressing of "Surfin' U.S.A." and "Shut Down" on which Venet received producer credit; the loss of all the music publishing for "Surfin' U.S.A." to Arc Music; and the unresolved questions over who was actually producing the Honeys.

The most recent perceived offense was *Shut Down*, a hot rod compilation album Venet and Usher assembled, trading on the success of "409" and "Shut Down," and usurping an opportunity for the Beach Boys to use that title for their own automotive-themed album. Released in mid–June, *Shut Down* reissued six car-related songs Capitol had released over the last twelve years, the Beach Boys' two hits, and four new tunes written by Usher and Christian, and recorded as by the Super Stocks. Capitol distributed to radio stations a promotional album in its Balanced for Broadcast series that noted "Shut Down" was featured on the new *Shut Down* album, but failed to mention that it was on the Beach Boys' *Surfin' U.S.A.* The compilation album struck a chord with the public and it reached #7 on August 17, enjoying a forty-six week chart run. But it further alienated Venet and Usher from Murry and, hence, Brian and the Beach Boys.

There was also the issue of the physical space at the Tower. While many iconic recordings have been produced in Capitol's studios, Brian preferred the intimacy of the smaller room at Western. "When you're working on a harmony thing and you're in close quarters you can hear what the other guy's doing," recalled Christian. "But in a great big room Brian had a hard time getting the sound he wanted."[9] Carl, perhaps, said it best. "[Capitol] has a fabulous string sound, and it was great for those records that Nat King Cole made, but not for rock 'n' roll guitar."[10]

As he tired of Venet's influence on the Beach Boys sound, Brian asked Murry to help him break away from Capitol's studio system. Murry met with Capitol A&R vice president Voyle Gilmore and told him the Beach Boys did not want to work with Venet or record at the Tower. "Murry argued with the vice president of Capitol for five months," Audree recalled. "Murry and he would just be screaming at each other."[11] Murry recalled, "I told him right to his face, 'You folks don't know how to produce a rock and roll hit in your studios. ... Leave us alone and we'll make hits for you.'"[12]

In the early 1960s, record companies regarded pop and rock 'n' roll artists as if they came with built-in expiration dates. Their careers would be over in a few years and there was little need to invest in long-term development. The goal was to release as much product as possible before some new trend rendered them obsolete. No one at Capitol expected a long musical life for a bunch of teenagers singing about a fad like surfing. Certainly not fifty years.

At the time, 45 rpm records were not art. They were disposable, two-minute confections consumed by teenagers and AM radio. B sides were mere space fillers. No one wasted a good song on the flip side. Pop and rock 'n' roll albums were a commodity to be churned out for an unsophisticated teen market, sold on the strength of one or two hit singles, and filled out with largely forgettable songs. No one thought of albums as cohesive, creative statements to be nurtured over months or years. Artistic aspirations were a distant second to the financial realities of the corporate ledger.

Gilmore eventually relented, allowing the Beach Boys to record at studios of their own choice without oversight of Capitol's A&R department. But he insisted they shoulder the expense. In effect, the Beach Boys returned to what had brought them to Capitol in the first place—recording on their own, producing finished masters, and delivering ready-made hits.

At twenty-one, Brian accomplished something no other recording artist had ever done. He had wrested complete creative control of his music away from a major record company, its recording studios, engineers, and the watchful, but often intrusive, A&R man assigned to produce the group. That was unheard of in 1963. This simple yet revolutionary idea opened the doors for generations of new artists who could thank Brian for clearing the path by which they could retain creative control over their art.

Armed with this unprecedented artistic freedom, Brian began transforming popular music and, equally important, the industry's perception of it. Brian made 45 rpm singles special. Each new Beach Boys single was a work of art, a self-contained offering of two beautifully composed, arranged, and produced songs. Now the B side was celebrated. A list of Beach Boys B sides reads like a greatest hits album. Brian would also soon change how albums were perceived with creative milestones like *Beach Boys Today!* (1965), *Summer Days (and Summer Nights!!)* (1965), *Pet Sounds* (1966), and the legendarily unfinished *Smile* (1967).[13]

The nurturing environment at Western Recorders and Gold Star enabled Brian and the Beach Boys to produce some of their most beautiful and enduring music. "They felt free to do what they wanted," Chuck Britz recalled. "[At Capitol it was] easy for people to walk in and out, and destroy the process that gets you going. If you're in a groove, there's nothing worse than somebody coming in and asking a political or financial question."[14]

Brian's break from the studio system was emblematic of a generational struggle. "The Beach Boys were not accorded respect by Capitol because they were kids," recalled Christian. "It was hard to get the older people at Capitol to accept that the Beach Boys were keeping them alive at the record company. Everything the Beach Boys did at Capitol, they had to fight for."[15]

Years later, Venet acknowledged what Brian had achieved. "Brian was the first guy to do it until it was right. He damned everyone till it was right and then he gave them the record. A lot of us would get chicken after four hours and say 'We'd better get off that tune.' Brian would hang in there for nine hours no matter what the cost."[16]

By July 19, three days after a *Surfer Girl* session, the Beach Boys were in Chicago, where they rented a Chevy wagon and U-Haul, and drove two hours south to begin their second Midwest tour that evening at Indiana Beach Amusement Resort on Lake Shafer in Monticello, Indiana. The tour would take them to thirty-six cities in fifteen states over forty-five days. It included many Midwest ballrooms with large wooden dance floors and stages that once accommodated large orchestras. At a few dates, they performed two or three shows. Murry persuaded Brian to accompany the tour, reminding him that fans paid good money and would be disappointed not seeing him.

Murry replaced Elmer Marks as tour manager with thirty-six-year-old John Hamilton, recommended for the job by his twenty-one-year-old brother, Judd, who worked and toured with the Ventures since moving to LA from East Wenatchee, Washington, in spring 1961, to pursue a music career. Judd befriended Jack Chaplain, an actor Ginger Blake was dating, and later married, after her relationship with Gary Usher ended. Ginger introduced Judd to the Beach Boys and Murry at the Wilsons' home in Hawthorne. When Murrry mentioned he was looking for a new tour manager, Judd suggested his brother, John.

Unwilling to endure a repeat of the cramped traveling arrangements of the first tour, Mike drove out in his 1961 Jaguar. "I took out the right hand seat and made a bed in it," he recalled. "If there were three of us in the car, one guy would be able to sleep, one guy would be resting in the back, and one guy would be driving. It worked out really well."[17]

After shows in Cedar Rapids and Storm Lake, Iowa, the band was off July 22 as they drove west to their next show. That night on a hill overlooking West Okojobi Lake at Arnolds Park in northwest Iowa, they gathered around Dennis's transistor radio to hear Sonny Liston dispatch Floyd Patterson in two minutes and ten seconds to defend his world heavyweight boxing title.[18] Earlier that day, Capitol released the band's fourth single, "Surfer Girl" (b/w "Little Deuce Coupe," Capitol 5009).

The music publishing for "Surfer Girl" was incorrectly co-credited to Guild Music and Sea of Tunes rather than Guild Music alone. Hite Morgan wasted no time bringing the error to Capitol's attention and subsequent pressings noted Guild Music alone. Morgan sent Murry a letter on July 26, where, in exchange for Murry's efforts to promote the record, Morgan would pay him 33⅓ percent of Guild's share of the mechanical royalties. The offer, contingent on a songwriting royalty of one cent per record, was accepted by Murry and Brian.[19] On August 2, Capitol wrote Morgan advising him Murry relinquished Sea of Tunes' copyright claim to "Surfer Girl."

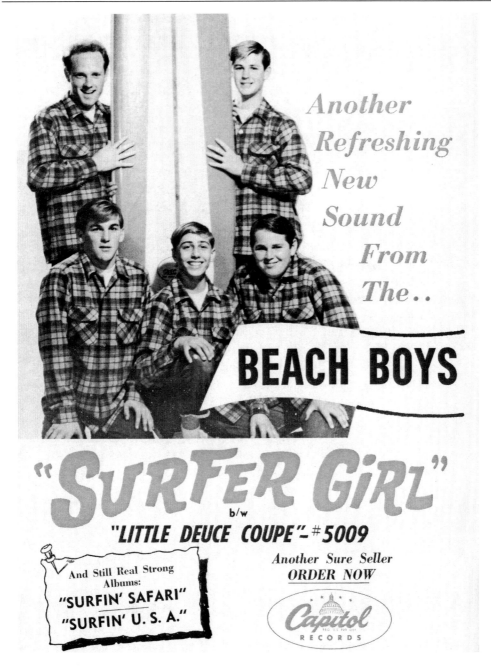

Capitol placed full-page advertisements in *Billboard* and *Cash Box* for "Surfer Girl" backed with "Little Deuce Coupe" released July 22, 1963. It was their third double-sided hit single to pair a surf song with a car song (author's collection).

According to an AFM contract dated July 24, Venet and Brian collaborated on a Honeys session at the Tower for Ginger's and Diane's "Pray for Surf," and Brian's "(Oly Oxen Free Free Free) Hide Go Seek." Venet was listed as producer and Brian as session leader and musician. Perhaps in a conciliatory gesture, Capitol credited Brian with arranging and conducting both songs when the single was released September 2 (Capitol 5034). In contradiction to the AFM contract, Marks recalled Brian was with the tour July 24 for the ninety-minute car ride to the Shore Acres Ballroom in Sioux City, Iowa. Marks remembered Brian repeatedly sang "Sioux City Sue," a #1 hit for Dick Thomas in fall 1945, doling out harmony parts for the others, and leading the group in an impromptu vocal session.[20]

According to an AFM contract dated August 5, Brian produced a session at Gold Star for the Survivors, a studio group comprised of Brian, Bob Norberg, and their neighbors at the Crenshaw Park Apartments, nineteen-year-old Dave Nowlen and eighteen-year-old Rich Peterson, who graduated that June from Lennox High School with Jimmy Bowles, Judy's older brother. In 1970, Peterson began using his original Armenian surname Alarian.

The Survivors recorded Brian's "Wich Stand"—an ode to the popular drive-in restaurant and teen hang-out—on which Nowlen, Peterson, and Steve Rusk, Nowlen's friend, shared credit. The musicians were Brian (piano and bass), Norberg and David Gates (guitars), Hal Blaine (session leader and drums), Maureen Love (harp), and saxmen Steve Douglas and Jay Migliori. Peterson recalled Phil Spector and Jack Nitzsche were also at Gold Star that day. Two other songs listed on the AFM contract, Brian's "Girlie" and "Hot Harp," presumably an instrumental featuring Maureen Love, have not been released and little is known of them.

Nowlen sang lead on "Wich Stand" and Brian, Norberg, and Peterson provided the oohs and aahhs for background vocals. Brian mixed and mastered it and cut an acetate the other guys brought to Capitol and played for Jim Economides, the label's new A&R producer. Although he liked it, Economides declined to release it because it sounded too much like the Beach Boys. When the others told Brian, he was furious, vowing to write a song that didn't sound anything like the Beach Boys. Within days he wrote "A Joyride Cruise," for which he, Norberg, and Peterson recorded a basic track at the Crenshaw apartment. Whether studio time was not immediately available or Brian had to return to the tour, the Survivors never finished it. In January 1965, its melody inspired Nowlen's "Beach Girl," recorded at Western and released that spring (b/w "Gypsy," Gold 1001) by the Nodaens, derived from Nowlen's first and last names.

A few days later, Brian wrote "Pamela Jean," a doo wop rocker reminiscent of Dion's "Runaround Sue." Peterson maintained he penned the lyrics about his girlfriend, Pamela Jean Adams, but did not receive credit because his agreement with Brian was that Brian paid for the recording sessions in exchange for sole credit.[21]

On August 8, the Beach Boys, with Al filling in for Brian, earned $1,700 for a four-hour show and dance at the Club Ponytail in Harbor Springs, a quaint resort town on Little Traverse Bay, an inlet of Lake Michigan. To their growing repertoire of hits and covers, the guys added their own take on "Surf City." They played a forty minute set each hour followed by a twenty minute break during which the teen audience filed into the Hippocrene Hide-Away, a smaller area downstairs with its own stage, to see the Kingtones, local favorites since beginning their six-night-a-week residency at Club Ponytail that May. Bruce Snoap, their keyboard player, recalled, "Stan Douglas, who owned Club Ponytail, had us play downstairs during the Beach Boys' breaks. Mike Love and another member, whom none of us can recall, surprised us by coming downstairs and playing sax with us. As a Top 40 cover band, we were in awe of the Beach Boys and thought they sounded very good. We later added 'Surfin' U.S.A.' to our show. They arrived around ten or eleven in the morning and we had lunch with them at the club. We watched them rehearse and, after 'Surfer Girl,' one of our members whispered to me, 'I don't have the heart to tell them, but that's a loser.' So much for that review!"[22]

The August 10 Petoskey, Michigan, *News-Review* noted, "At first the Beach Boys appeared to be the biggest disappointment of the season. They were lacking in organization and harmony all during the first performance. However, they did seem to improve with time and by the end of the evening were sounding more like everyone expected them to. There is one thing that cannot be taken away from the Beach Boys—they really packed the house."[23] The accompanying photo of David, Al, Mike, and Carl huddled close on the club's small stage, showed Mike holding his sax and Al playing bass.[24]

Without Brian, the Beach Boys had some difficulty recreating their records in concert. On ballads like "Surfer Girl," Dennis came forward from behind the drums to add his voice to the harmonies as they huddled around a microphone. The review heightened how detrimental Brian's absence could be to their reputation at a time when most people were getting their first glimpse of the band. Lukewarm reviews may have played a role in Murry's insistence that Brian return to touring.

The Beach Boys played Club Ponytail in Harbor Springs, Michigan, on August 8, 1963, with the Kingtones, a favorite local band (author's collection with appreciation to Bruce Snoap).

The morning after they played Chicago's Auditorium Theater on August 11, the Beach Boys drove 800 miles to Boston for Gilchrist Department Store's 5th Annual Back-to-School Fashion Hop and Surf-Sing Show in the Music Hall at 9:30 a.m. on August 13. For three hours, a crowd of 4,000, mostly adolescent girls, were entertained by headliners Jan & Dean, billed as "flying here from Surf City, California," two local bands, Mary Ann Mobley (Miss America 1959), and a beauty pageant and fashion show.

They then drove ninety minutes north to the Palace Ballroom in Old Orchard Beach, Maine (August 14), the Surf Auditorium in Hill, New Hampshire (August 15), and the Mount Tom Ballroom in Mountain Park in Holyoke, Massachusetts (August 16). The tour traveled west across Pennsylvania for the final day of the 101st Wayne County Fair in Honesdale (August 17), the Lakewood Ballroom in Lakewood Park in Barnesville (August 18), the Reimold Brothers Hall in Transfer (August 20), and Danceland in West View Park in

Pittsburgh (August 21). The following day they celebrated David's fifteenth birthday with a show at the Roller Rink in Wheeling Downs, West Virginia, and then worked their way back to the Midwest.

David kept a handwritten setlist from the Wayne County Fair. In addition to the new single ("Surfer Girl" and "Little Deuce Coupe"), their live repertoire consisted of six other originals ("Surfin' Safari," "409," "Surfin' U.S.A.," "Shut Down," "Farmer's Daughter," and "Blue City," a guitar instrumental by Carl and David that was never recorded), and ten covers ("Runaway," "Monster Mash," "Movin' N' Groovin'," "Silly Boy," "Papa-Oom-Mow-Mow," "Honky Tonk," "Louie, Louie," "Let's Go Trippin'," "Johnny B. Goode," and "What'd I Say" as an encore). While David drummed, Dennis stepped forward to sing "Silly Boy," a #81 hit for the Lettermen in fall 1962. David handled the lead vocal on "Louie, Louie."[25]

After the opening rush of "Surfin' Safari" and "409," Mike introduced each band member by demonstrating how the group went about recording. He introduced each instrument—drums, rhythm guitar, bass, and lead guitar—followed by each member playing a few bars of "Little Deuce Coupe." As each new instrument was introduced, the previous instruments were also played, giving listeners an appreciation of how the song was constructed. When Mike noted the vocals were added next, the group launched into the song. A refined version of his introduction can be heard on *Beach Boys Concert* released in October 1964.

While the Beach Boys played Boston for the first time August 13, Kyu Sakamoto, whose "Sukiyaki" (Capitol 4945) had been #1 for three weeks that June, arrived in LA from Tokyo for a three-day promotional tour. The twenty-one-year-old singer was the first Japanese artist to top the *Billboard* chart. Capitol Records held a cocktail party for him around the swimming pool on the Grand Veranda of the Beverly Wilshire Hotel on August 14. Roger Christian was invited with a guest. He and Brian were in the studio that afternoon when Christian suggested they take a break and attend the reception. "Brian and I had been writing for the last few days to get the last songs done for the *Little Deuce Coupe* album," Christian recalled.[26] "The Beach Boys had a couple of big records for Capitol, but they didn't have a party. We got there and Brian was talking to somebody, and he came over kind of discouraged. Voyle Gilmore had told him he had no business being there, he was upstaging Kyu. And I said, 'Just a minute, you're here as my guest, and we're writing some songs that are eventually going to make this company some money.' This is just one example of the typical things Capitol would do."[27] "They didn't treat Brian at the time with the respect he should have had. They didn't realize they had the most creative, young, talented producer in the country."[28]

An AFM contract for the mid–August session Christian referenced has not surfaced. He and Brian may have been working on "No-Go Showboat" about a custom dragster whose looks outdistanced its performance or "Spirit of America," a tribute to twenty-six-year-old Craig Breedlove who had just set a new land speed record August 5 on Utah's Bonneville Salt Flats in a vehicle christened Spirit of America. Breedlove's two runs averaged 407.45 miles per hour, breaking the previous record of 394 miles per hour set by Englishman John Cobb in 1947.

The success of the compilation album *Shut Down* compelled Capitol to push for a new Beach Boys album with an automotive theme built around "Little Deuce Coupe," which had just cracked the *Billboard* Top 40 and would reach #15 in three weeks. But *Surfer Girl* was in the process of being prepared for release and contained two songs, "Little Deuce Coupe" and "Our Car Club," that would have fit perfectly on a car concept album.

On August 27, Brian produced a Survivors session at Western for "Pamela Jean" on which he sang lead, arranged the background vocals, and employed many of the musicians that played on the group's August 5 session.

Around this time, Brian and Norberg wrote a hauntingly beautiful ballad called "Thank Him," which they recorded on a Wollensak in their apartment and cut an acetate at Gold Star, and on which Brian wrote "'Thank Him' / (cut in a living room) / B. Wilson." "There were so many things like that," recalled Rich Peterson. "It was like going down to the ocean and [listening to sea] shells. It was a love song, a beautiful love song."[29] In 2005, the acetate surfaced on an on-line auction site. It was soon withdrawn and reportedly returned to Brian. "Thank Him" was released on *The Big Beat* in 2013.

By August 29, Brian rejoined the Beach Boys on the road for the final two shows of the tour. How many dates Brian had performed since the tour began July 19 is the subject of some debate. To recap, Brian was in LA for a Honeys session July 24, a Survivors session in LA August 5, absent at Club Ponytail in Harbor Springs, Michigan, on August 8, with Christian in LA August 14, absent at Melody Mill in Sageville, Iowa, on August 25, as evidenced by a posed group photo on stage, and at a Survivors session in LA August 27. Furthermore, Nowlen and Peterson recalled that after "Wich Stand" was declined by Capitol shortly after August 5, Brian presented them with "A Joyride Cruise" and "Pamela Jean" in a matter of days.[30] Hence, it seems likely after he returned to LA for the Honeys session July 24 and summoned Al to replace him, Brian remained in LA writing, arranging, and producing new music, until he returned to the tour August 28 or 29.

Without parental oversight on the tour, the boys indulged in many of the temptations associated with rock 'n' roll musicians on the road. Marks told Stebbins that after a show at the Val Air Ballroom in West Des Moines, Iowa, July 25, John Hamilton arranged for the boys to visit prostitutes at a downtown hotel and that Brian did not indulge, preferring to remain at the hotel on a long-distance telephone call with Marilyn. If this is true and Brian was at a Honeys session in LA July 24, then Brian must have just returned to the tour. Meanwhile, Mike and Dennis egged on sixteen-year-old Carl and fourteen-year-old David, who were soon relieved of their virginity. There were other incidents of drinking and rowdy behavior. When an irate hotel manager called Murry to complain, the Wilson patriarch flew to Chicago to restore order.

"John just got fed up with the nonsense," recalled Judd Hamilton. "The guys were young and getting all this attention. Dennis had a pretty free spirit. John was constantly trying to keep him out of trouble and from doing silly stuff. They were in a hotel and Dennis decided to walk down the hall naked. That was the final straw. The guys were embarrassing him and he had never witnessed anything like that. He had a hard time keeping them corralled. He couldn't control them and it was getting to him. He just finally got fed up and said, 'They're nice kids, but they don't listen to a damn thing I say.' Then Murry came along and said, 'I've had enough.' And the one thing the guys didn't want was to be under Murry's thumb again."[31]

On August 29, the band played two shows sponsored by Pepsi-Cola at the Avalon Ballroom in La Crosse, Wisconsin. The tickets were likely the first to feature the band's photograph. After the show, they drove 224 miles southeast to Chicago to meet Murry at

O'Hare International Airport. Murry dismissed John Hamilton as tour manager and drove with the boys to New York for a show August 30 at the Fox Theatre in Brooklyn. There they shared the stage with a dozen acts including Stevie Wonder, the Shirelles, and the Drifters, for one night as special guests of the ten-day Labor Day holiday revue emceed by Murray the K (Murray Kaufman), the popular disc jockey who succeeded Alan Freed on WINS in New York.

During the grueling twelve-hour car ride to New York, David Marks, who had just turned fifteen August 22, got into an argument with Murry and, in a fit of anger, quit the band. "I was young and stupid," Marks recalled. "I was my own worst enemy. I was cocky and I thought I could make it alone. How many fifteen-year-olds would make a smart decision under those circumstances?"[32]

After announcing he quit, Marks remained a Beach Boy for thirty-six days, a nebulous period during which he performed with the band for about ten shows, including large, multiple-artist gigs in San Francisco, Seattle, and San Diego. He participated in recording sessions in early September for the band's fifth Capitol single, "Be True to Your School," and a few songs for their fourth album, *Little Deuce Coupe.*

After the Brooklyn show, the band flew back to LA on August 31. "Surfer Girl" was #1 for the second consecutive week on KFWB and #12 in the new *Billboard* which featured a full-page ad for "Surfer Girl" and "Little Deuce Coupe." That night they played the Show of Stars Spectacular featuring two dozen acts at the Memorial Sports Arena at 8:00 p.m. The twenty-four page program featured the band's photograph and an advertisement for *Surfin' U.S.A.*

Judy accompanied Brian to an evening concert where the Beach Boys shared the bill with many top-name acts that was most likely the Show of Stars. She was grounded that night, but Brian persuaded her parents to let her go. At the venue, an older girl approached Brian in a friendly manner and it was apparent he had invited her. During the car ride home that evening, Brian and Judy argued, and she asked him to stop the car. She got out, slammed the door, and walked the rest of the way home. "That was part of the breaking up cycle," she recalled. "We were growing apart and he was moving on. We started getting used to each other and not respecting each other. He was spending more time with musicians and in Los Angeles. I probably wouldn't have lasted much longer. He had his path in life and I had mine. It was very hard, very emotional, like a see-saw. He never asked for the diamond ring back. I pawned it two years later in Hollywood for fifty dollars."[33]

23

The Greatest Second
Chance in Rock 'n' Roll
(September–October 1963)

After the grueling six-week tour ended August 31, the Beach Boys were back at Western September 2, Labor Day, to work on songs for their fourth album, *Little Deuce Coupe*. Like *Surfer Girl*, the AFM contracts for *Little Deuce Coupe* are missing. The studios, musicians, and dates for all the sessions are unknown. Capitol's liner notes for *Little Deuce Coupe* in the 1990 twofer series stated eight of the songs were recorded September 2, but that seems unlikely. They were, however, recorded rather efficiently as the album was in record stores October 7, just three weeks after *Surfer Girl* was released September 16.

Let's examine how the band completed a new album in such little time.

Of the dozen songs on *Little Deuce Coupe*, four had been released previously ("409," "Shut Down," and "Little Deuce Coupe" as B sides on double-sided hits, and "Our Car Club" had just been released on *Surfer Girl*). Three featured recycled melodies. The Survivors' "Pamela Jean," which had not been released yet, became "Car Crazy Cutie," less raucous and stripped of its dueling saxes, and "Land Ahoy," the lone outtake from *Surfin' Safari*, became "Cherry, Cherry Coupe," after both songs received a lyrical overhaul from Christian. Mike pitched in by transforming Bobby Troup's "Their Hearts Were Full of Spring" into "A Young Man Is Gone," a moving a cappella tribute to James Dean who died September 30, 1955, in a horrific automobile accident.

Work on three new songs Brian wrote with Christian, "No-Go Showboat," "Spirit of America," and "Rockin' Roadster," had been started in August. "Rockin' Roadster" remains unreleased and may not have been committed to tape. Brian dusted off "Custom Machine," for which he had completed a Popular Songwriter's Contract with Sea of Tunes dated November 2, 1962.[1] Rich Peterson later maintained he provided uncredited lyrics to "Custom Machine" and "No-Go Showboat" in consideration for Brian's help with the Survivors.[2]

"Ballad of Ole' Betsy," whose instrumental track was recorded February 9 amidst the *Surfin' U.S.A.* sessions, was either dusted off or finished vocally. Lambert noted, "We hear the Four Freshmen connection right away in 'Betsy' in the rich choral harmony of the introduction. At the end, we hear Brian's first borrowing of a particular Four Freshmen cliché, the a cappella ending."[3]

During the *Little Deuce Coupe* sessions, David offered Brian a song he and Mark Groseclose wrote called "Kustom Kar Show," but Brian likely did not have time to develop the rudimentary tune into a full Beach Boys-style production. Also, after David quit the band in late August, there was little incentive, likely none from Murry's vantage, to include his song on the album and afford him songwriter royalties.

Completing the collection of car songs was a tune whose only automotive connection, like "Surfer Girl," was that its inspiration struck while Brian was driving. Dave Nowlen recalled Murry hired him and Bob Norberg to paint the stucco walls in the Wilsons' music room and do minor repair work around the house. It helped the struggling musicians earn some extra cash. While they were working, Brian stopped in and Murry tried to enlist him to help paint, but he was not interested. Words were exchanged, Brian left, hopped in his car, and drove off. Half an hour later, he raced back in, tore the drop cloth off the piano, taught Nowlen and Norberg some vocal parts, and played the introduction of "Be True to Your School." Nowlen recalled, "He had the basic idea and most of the words down already. He was really excited with what he had just come up with.[4] Brian finished "Be True to Your School" with a lyrical assist from Mike, who received a co-writing credit in 1994. The song was a romanticized look at Brian's Hawthorne High days, now three years in his rear view mirror. Brian borrowed four bars of "Onward Cougars," the football team's fight song, for the middle-eight bars of the song. Written in 1909 as "On, Wisconsin," for the University of Wisconsin's Badgers, the music was in the public domain.

Although there were no extended tours for the remainder of the year, the band kept busy with personal appearances at several back-to-school events. On September 4, they flew to Denver to sign autographs at the world's largest F.W. Woolworth in the Cherry Creek Shopping Center and that night played a Back-to-School Show at Lakeside Amusement Park.

On September 7, they played the Patio Gardens at the Lagoon, an amusement park in Farmington, Utah, just north of Salt Lake City. Bill "Daddy-O" Hesterman, a popular disc jockey on KNAK, Salt Lake City's top rock 'n' roll station, arranged for the appearance at the Lagoon where they attracted the largest crowd that summer. Later in the year, with the amusement park closed for the season, the Lagoon Corporation booked a December 27 show at the Terrace Ballroom, which it also owned. Tickets sold so fast a second show was added December 28. For the next three years, the Beach Boys played the Lagoon the weekend after Labor Day. In 1965, Brian and Mike poured their affection for the city into "Salt Lake City" on *Summer Days (and Summer Nights!!)* and Capitol pressed a limited promotional single (b/w "Amusement Parks U.S.A.," Capitol PRO 2936/2937) distributed courtesy of downtown Salt Lake City stores.

Before their September 7 appearance at the Lagoon, the guys made a promotional visit to KNAK where they overheard Shirley Johnson, the teenage daughter of station owner Howard Johnson, gripe about being grounded because of an incident the night before in which she borrowed her father's Ford Thunderbird. "I was going to the library and ended up at Shore's Drive-In, a hamburger shop," Shirley recalled. "I was complaining to the station staff that I was in trouble and the Beach Boys heard it."[5] Brian and Mike also heard a hit song and wrote "Fun, Fun, Fun" during a taxi drive back to the airport. It was recorded January 1 and 8, 1964, and released February 3.

On September 9, the band played Back-to-School-O-Rama at the Helix High School Stadium in La Mesa, seven miles east of San Diego. The event raised money for the local Junior Chamber of Commerce's youth fund drive. In mid–September, they performed their upcoming single "Be True to Your School" on one of seven episodes of *Back-to-School Ball*, a live thirty-minute television show on KHJ-TV channel 9 hosted by Bob Denver between

September 9 and 18 to kick-off the syndication of *The Many Loves of Dobie Gillis*, the popular TV show on which Denver co-starred as the beatnik Maynard G. Krebs. Before the taping, Brian visited Hawthorne High School and met with the varsity cheerleaders, requesting to loan their uniforms and pompoms for use on the show. The film does not survive so it is unclear if the uniforms were worn by actresses, the Honeys, or not used at all.

While the band played back-to-school shows, Dennis, Carl, and David were missing days at Hollywood Professional School, where, that fall, they befriended Rick Henn and Eddy Medora of the Renegades after seeing them perform at a school talent show. The Boys first met them July 3, 1962, when they played Dykstra Hall at UCLA where the Renegades were the house band for the summer concert series. In spring 1964, after the Beach Boys dismissed Murry as their manager, Carl suggested the Renegades audition for Murry. The Wilson patriarch had first offered to manage Jim Waller and the Deltas, a Fresno quintet who scored a minor hit with "Surfin' Wild" (Arvee 5072) in summer 1963, but they declined his offer.[6] Murry agreed to mentor the Renegades and, after a name change to the Sunrays, produced their debut single, "Car Party" and "Outta Gas," which Murry wrote and published with Sea of Tunes. It was the inaugural release on Tower Records (101), a subsidiary created by Capitol to avoid direct competition with the Beach Boys.

Around this time, Brian purchased his first new car. Dave Nowlen recalled being in the Crenshaw apartment when the local Pontiac dealership called to tell Brian the 1964 Grand Prix he ordered had been delivered. Nowlen recounted a one-sided telephone conversation in which Brian calmly repeated everything the dealer told him. The car was in, but apparently not equipped with several of the options Brian ordered including power windows and stereo system. At Nowlen's whispered suggestion, Brian dead-panned, "Hey, has it got doors?"[7] Brian referenced the car in "Wich Stand" as the guys cruise the strip in their metal flake blue Grand Prix. That fall, Carl also bought a 1964 Grand Prix, aquamarine with white leather seats, which he drove to school, picking up Marks and the Rovell sisters along the way.

In mid–September, Brian and Norberg moved one mile west from their apartment to a single-family home they rented on 108th Street just east of Prairie Avenue. On a handwritten note he left on Vickie Kocher's door, Brian drew a map of where the house was located and wrote, "Our phones were yanked out yesterday so you might as well not try to call." He added, "3 bedrooms, two bathrooms, 2 boys / $180 per month / <u>Sold</u> to the boy in the Grand Prix!!!!"[8]

As "Pamela Jean" was being readied for release, Brian assured Nowlen he would take care of the requisite B side, writing "After the Game," a wistful two-minute instrumental he recorded in Norberg's bedroom at the new house. The sparse instrumentation included Brian and Norberg on guitar, and Rich Peterson tapping a bedpost with a drum stick. Brian delivered the finished single later in September and, despite a Brian Wilson lead vocal and sounding remarkably like the Beach Boys, Jim Economides agreed to release it. When Capitol delayed its release, Brian tweaked it that December before "Pamela Jean" (b/w "After the Game," Capitol 5102) was finally released January 6, 1964. But the timing could not have been worse. It went unnoticed amidst the Beach Boys' "Fun, Fun, Fun" and "I Want to Hold Your Hand," the Beatles' American debut on Capitol.

As he worked to finish *Little Deuce Coupe*, Brian enlisted Al to play bass on "Be True to Your School" and fill in for him at shows requiring air travel and time away from home like the two sold-out gigs Fred Vail booked at the Sacramento Memorial Auditorium September 14. Some 2,000 pre-teens attended the matinee and 5,200 teens and adults attended the evening show. The group grossed $6,000, reinforcing Vail's prescient advice they could become the nation's top drawing band.

On September 17, the day after *Surfer Girl* was released, Brian took the Honeys into Gold Star and produced a song he wrote called "The One You Can't Have." After growing up with only brothers, Brian was fascinated by the Honeys' female perspective on issues of the heart, mining their conversations for his songwriting. The unrequited love inferred in the song's title remains unresolved as the girls name-drop the men in their lives, including Brian, Gary Leeds, the drummer in the Standells and future "Gary Walker" of the Walker Brothers, and Gold Star engineer Larry Levine, who helped Phil Spector craft the Crystals' "Then He Kissed Me" and the Ronettes' "Be My Baby," then #3 and #10, respectively, on KFWB. Brian loved those songs and hired many of the same musicians to produce his finest track with the Honeys, a shimmering, irresistible, danceable pop classic. "The One You Can't Have" (b/w "From Jimmy with Tears," Capitol 5093) was released December 2, but did not chart. "Brian always wanted our feedback in his writing sessions for the Honeys to make sure we were happy with the content of the songs," recalled Ginger Blake. "He loved our sound so much that he always sang a background part as the fourth Honey."[9]

After a show in Long Beach September 20, David McClellan, the band's ad hoc publicist, flew with the group the next day for a show at the Memorial Coliseum in Portland, Oregon. He witnessed an incident that did little to reverse Marks's departure from the group. "David was disrespectful toward his mother in front of a roomful of fans in Portland. Dennis blew up at him, berating him for being so nasty to his mom. Dennis was so angry he asked me, 'How fast can you learn rhythm guitar?' This, of course, was in jest, but it showed how disgusted he was at the moment."[10] Rich Peterson of the Survivors recalled a similar incident earlier that summer. "[David] was giving them trouble because he was a young kid. They wanted to dump him because Dennis never got along with him. Brian said, 'If you could only play the guitar, Rich, we'll make you a Beach Boy. If there's some way we can teach you to play the guitar in two weeks, you're gonna be a Beach Boy.'"[11]

On September 24, the Beach Boys appeared on national television for the first time when the segment they had filmed April 21 for *The Red Skelton Hour* aired on CBS-TV. They performed "Surfin' U.S.A." and "The Things We Did Last Summer," which illustrated beautifully how well Brian had learned vocal harmony from the Four Freshmen. Maybe a little too well. Mrs. Robert Piersall of Escondido, California, protested to the *San Diego Union*, "After watching the premiere of *The Red Skelton Show*, all I can say is you can't fool all of the people all of the time. Do they really believe people would think that lovely song 'The Things We Did Last Summer' was sung by that so-called vocal group the Beach Boys when in truth it was a recording by the Four Freshmen."[12] In a roundabout way, Mrs. Piersall had paid Brian and the Boys the ultimate compliment—the Four Freshmen never recorded "The Things We Did Last Summer."

Writer Timothy White reported Brian attended a September 26 session at Gold Star at which Phil Spector produced "Santa Claus Is Coming to Town" by the Crystals for *A Christmas Wish for You* released that November. Spector invited Brian to play piano on the track, but dismissed him after a few takes when he became dissatisfied with Brian's playing. A month later, Brian received a check for fifty-six dollars, union scale, for his efforts.[13]

On September 28, the Beach Boys played a show in San Francisco sponsored by radio station KYA at the Cow Palace called Surf Party with Jan & Dean, Little Stevie Wonder, the Ronettes, and many others. In her journal, Jo Ann Marks noted an appearance the following day in Fresno. It was likely a brief promotional stop as they had to catch a flight to Seattle for 3:00 p.m. and 7:00 p.m. shows in the '63 Hit Parade of Stars at the Opera House.

By late summer, Capitol was considering releasing a Honeys album that would have included their first two singles ("Surfin' Down the Swanee," "Shoot the Curl," "Pray for Surf, and "Hide Go Seek"). Other contenders were "From Jimmy with Tears" and "Raindrops," produced by Venet May 16, and covers of "In the Still of the Night," the 1956 doo-wop classic by the Five Satins, and "Make the Night a Little Longer," a 1961 album cut by the Shirelles, written by Gerry Goffin and Carole King, likely produced by Venet at Capitol. Brian may have also contributed three songs he wrote and produced—"The One You Can't Have," "You Brought It All on Yourself," and "Funny Boy," with a gritty lead vocal by Ginger. Two other songs, "Boys Will Be Boys" and "What'll I Wear to School?" were written around this time and likely intended for the Honeys.

The Honeys album was put on hold when Venet stunned the West Coast music world by resigning from Capitol. News of his sudden departure broke in *Billboard* on newsstands October 12, but he may have left much earlier. It also may be telling that when the Survivors brought "Wich Stand" to Capitol in early August, they played it for Jim Economides, who joined Capitol's A&R department that June, and not Venet. *Billboard* noted, "Venet asked to be relieved of his contract which had several years to go and Capitol agreed to this move. Internal differences between Venet and Capitol had developed during the past several months. Venet asked for his release before an article on pop music appeared in the October 5 issue of *The Saturday Evening Post* in which his salty comments about the Beach Boys drew the ire of the young group. *Billboard* learned that Venet was withdrawn as the Beach Boys' A&R man by the group itself."[14]

In the article Venet took a parting shot at the Beach Boys. "The record business is where you can take a group like the Beach Boys and in eighteen hours they become stars. When I found them, they had made one record on a one-shot label and all they got for it was a thousand dollars. Eighteen hours after I found them, we produced a record called 'Surfin' U.S.A.' and it was a smash. When I found them it was 'Mr. Venet this' and 'Mr. Venet that.' But eighteen hours later you can't even talk to them, you've got to talk to their manager. Their hats couldn't even fit on their heads. What they don't realize is that—well, take the Weavers, the Lettermen, and the Kingston Trio. They're like copper, bronze, and gold. The Beach Boys, they might turn out to be plastic. Copper, bronze, and gold, last a long time. Plastic, you keep it around for a while and then you throw it out."[15]

In 1971, Carl said, "Nick Venet is really full of shit regarding us. He did an interview with *The Saturday Evening Post* and he really lied his balls off in it. He hardly had anything to do with the group. He would be in the booth and he would call the take number and that was about it. Brian didn't want anything to do with Venet."[16]

Obviously, the Beach Boys and Venet had an acrimonious parting. Venet had been charged with increasing Capitol's share of the youth market. So when the hottest young group in the country refused to work with him, it placed him in an untenable situation. In October, Venet formed Ben-Ven Productions, a record production company, with Fred Benson, who had managed Nelson Riddle and the Four Freshmen, and contracted as an independent producer with MGM Records. One of their first releases was "Little Ford Ragtop" (b/w "Happy Ho-Daddy (with Ragtop Caddy)," MGM 13186) by the Vettes in mid–November. Produced by Steve Douglas and Venet, it featured a lead vocal on the A side by future Beach Boy Bruce Johnston.

When Venet left, Capitol reassigned Bobby Darin, Glen Campbell, Dick Dale, the Lettermen, Cindy Malone, and the Beach Boys to Jim Economides, and Lou Rawls to Dave Cavanaugh. Economides soon met with Murry and Brian in an effort to improve the company's relationship with the band. Murry held his ground—the Beach Boys would continue to produce their own material in studios of their own choosing. *Billboard* reported Economides would serve as a liaison between Capitol and the Beach Boys, helping to schedule their releases.[17] When that didn't work out, Karl Engemann, who had developed a personal relationship with Murry, Audree, and the guys, became Capitol's liaison with the band.[18] To shore up the company's relationship with the group, Engemann wrote Brian, "We are genuinely proud of The Beach Boys, and we know that with real effort on your part as well as the other boys, we can continue to have success with the recordings and each of you can build a fine career in the entertainment business."[19] Marilyn Wilson recalled, "Brian was always on the phone with Karl. We used to go over to their house and Brian loved it. Karl was a real nice family man. He was so gentle with him and Brian needed somebody like that."[20]

It may have been sometime in late September that seventeen-year-old guitarist Danny Hamilton, the younger brother of John Hamilton, the Beach Boys' former tour manager, was invited to fly from Wenatchee, Washington, to LA to audition with the Beach Boys and possibly replace Marks. For whatever reason, that never materialized. Before Marks actually left the band, while he continued to ride to school with Carl and hang out at the Rovells' home, he had begun playing with a local Hawthorne band called the Jaguars that included drummer Mark Groseclose. Marks continued to express his desire to leave the Beach Boys and his behavior was hardly conciliatory. "I started singing 'She's real fine, my sixty-nine' and 'Little Douche Kit' onstage," he recalled. "Murry would fine me for not smiling. Finally it ended. More or less a mutual agreement between Murry and me."[21]

On October 5, two days before *Little Deuce Coupe* was released, Marks played the final show of his original tenure with the Beach Boys at the Starlight Bowl on the grounds of Balboa Park in San Diego. "Surfin' at the Bowl" featured the Honeys, Eddie and the Showmen, and a surf film called *Once Upon a Wave*.

What seems to have precipitated Marks's actual departure was an argument between Murry, and Jo Ann and Elmer Marks over their interest in having a role in managing the band. When Murry refused, Jo Ann withdrew her son from the group, saying, "He's got his own group now anyway. You just watch us."[22] In November, apparently without consulting an attorney, Marks signed an amendment to the band's Capitol Records' contract acknowledging he ceased to be a member of the group on August 30, 1963. The agreement effectively deprived him of royalties for any songs recorded after that date.[23]

Murry believed David was too young to understand the group was also a business. In December 1965, writing to a fan who inquired about David, Murry wrote, "David became difficult and turned in his resignation which we accepted. From that time on, the Beach Boys went sky high in popularity because Al Jardine is a fantastic harmonizer as well as musician."[24]

Little Deuce Coupe pulled into record stores October 7 and raced to #4, charting forty-six weeks and leaving surf music in its wake as the band shifted gears into hot rod sounds. The album cover photo of the blue-pearl '32 Ford Coupe owned by Clarence "Chili" Catallo was an outtake from the photo session done for the cover of *Hot Rod* magazine in July 1961. Capitol's art department cropped out Catallo's head and shoulders, and he later quipped that he came within two inches of being famous. The back album cover showed the group with Marks conversing by Dennis's Corvette. As it had done for the surfing craze, Capitol produced a dictionary of hot rod terms and distributed it to record stores to be given free to customers.

Within days of Marks's departure, Al was once again a full-time Beach Boy. He began rehearsing with them and perfecting his vocal harmony parts. His pre-dental studies had come to an end, but his nineteen-month hiatus cost him dearly. Murry had not forgotten that Al walked away from the band as "Surfin'" peaked in LA at #3 and the group struggled to release a follow-up. Unlike Marks, Al was not afforded twenty-percent ownership in the Beach Boys. The last two years in the music industry made Murry a much shrewder businessman. The fifth member's twenty-percent share was rolled back into the family business. In effect, Al was a hired musician.

"Al talked with Brian and said the school thing wasn't for him and he wanted to come back," recalled Jodi Gable. "Of course, they all wanted him back. David was being a little difficult. He was very young and Jo Ann pumped his head with things like 'David, you're the band, without you there would be no band.' She always inflated his ego. A few years later, maybe 1966 or 1967, I ran into David at the Hullabaloo and we had a chance to chat. He said, 'You know what's really funny, Jodi, half of that stuff I never played on, but the Beach Boys gave me credit for it, so I just sit back and collect the money.' It was kind of hard on him and I felt really bad for him. He was there for a year and a half and then, boom, he's out. It was his decision to leave, but it was a bad decision. His mother had convinced him he was the band. And he locked horns with Murry. But I don't care what anybody says, Al was going to come back into the group."[25]

Capitol did not issue a press release to announce the personnel change, perhaps preferring not to call attention to it, hoping only the most astute observer would notice Marks was replaced with the smiling Al. The first hint of Al's return was in a three-page article and photo spread in the February 1964 *Teen Screen* on newsstands early that year.[26] That August, *New Musical Express* reported David left to return to school and that Al had initially left to become a dentist. Brian, misidentified as Mike Wilson, noted, "It's a bit like that game musical chairs. Al was with us when we first organized back in 1962. Then he dropped out to go to dental school—he knows all about teeth now—but when he finished there, he badly wanted to come back. So when David Marks decided he wanted to leave, the solution was easy. There were a lot of rumors going about at the time that we were fighting among ourselves. Actually, the feeling in the group now has never been better."[27]

With David gone and Al back full-time, Brian had no choice but to rejoin the touring band. They enjoyed having him back and his vocals added a key element to their live sound. But the unrelenting demands on Brian to compose, arrange, produce, sing, and perform new music, while maintaining an increasingly rigorous tour schedule, would soon prove overwhelming.

It had been nearly three months since the Beach Boys had released a new single, an eternity in the Sixties, and Capitol was anxious for a 45 to help drive sales of the new album. Despite several strong car songs ("No-Go Showboat" and "Spirit of America"), Brian chose "Be True to Your School." Rather than release the album version, he revisited the song, producing a more ambitious version at Western with studio musicians and, perhaps, his brother Carl. The new track was faster and in a lower key with marching band drums, a searing guitar solo, and cheerleader chants by the Honeys. Its infectious melody captured the spirited fun of a Friday night high school football game.

Although "No-Go Showboat" was overlooked by the band as a single, Usher saw its potential and enlisted Brian's help recording a version with the Timers, a group that included Chuck Girard and Joe Kelly of the Castells, at RCA Victor Studio in Hollywood October 11. Brian shared the lead vocal with Girard, but his arrangement and production ideas went uncredited when the single was released a month later (b/w "Competition Coupe," Reprise 231) and failed to chart. Petula Clark recorded a French version of "No-Go Showboat" ("J'ai Pas le Temps") in 1964.

Capitol placed a full-page ad for "Be True to Your School" in *Billboard* out October 19 featuring a May 1962 promotional photo of the band in which David knelt in the foreground between Dennis and Carl. The photo was cropped and modified to appear that Brian and Mike were holding an oversized record instead of a surfboard. Less than two weeks after its October 28 release, "Be True to Your School" (b/w "In My Room," Capitol 5069) was #1 on KFWB for the first of three consecutive weeks.

Perhaps driven by Marks's inclusion in the *Billboard* ad, Murry pressed Capitol for new promotional photos of the band with Al. In late October, Capitol photographed the group dressed collegiately at various locations on the UCLA campus. Murry soon printed sheet music for "Be True to Your School," the first for Sea of Tunes, and "In My Room" with a photo of the group on campus.

Al's first appearance back with the Beach Boys was October 19 at Y-Day at the Hollywood Bowl, an all-star concert hosted by Art Linkletter and sponsored by the Hollywood branch of the YMCA and KFWB, which broadcast the two-hour show. When Al filled in for Brian, he played bass. But now that he replaced David, he moved over to rhythm guitar. He may not yet have owned an electric guitar as he borrowed a white 1962 Gibson Les Paul SG Custom from Brett Brady of Eddie and the Showmen who played Y-Day earlier that morning.

The Y-Day concert began at 10:00 a.m. and featured eighteen artists, each singing a few songs. The Honeys joined Duane Eddy onstage and sang background vocals on his "Rebel Rouser" and "(Dance with) the Guitar Man."[28] Jan & Dean sang "Surf City" and "Honolulu Lulu," but they are difficult songs to sing live and their performance was flat and off-key.

The Beach Boys were the final performers at Y-Day. Linkletter introduced the Wilson brothers and Mike, curiously omitting Al, before handing the microphone over to Mike who launched into his introduction of the band before firing up "Little Deuce Coupe." He then told the crowd "In My Room" was the B side of their new single and invited the Honeys onstage to accompany "Be True to Your School" with a cheerleader routine complete with pompoms. Mike's introductory proclamation of school spirit was punctuated by Denny's thunderous, oddly discordant, drum riff. Mike delivered an energetic lead vocal and Carl played a blistering guitar solo before the song barreled headlong into a joyously raw ending. Because they were the final act, Mike suggested doing one more song. Carl called for "Surfin'

U.S.A.," but Brian began "Surfer Girl," catching Mike by surprise. Brian's sensitive lead vocal was occasionally overshadowed by the background harmony vocals. Brian closed with, "We'd like to sing a little tribute to the radio station that planned this whole afternoon" and they sang "KFWB channel ninety eight," an a cappella showcase of group harmony. Despite the rudimentary sound system and an outdoor venue, the band sounded good and their vocals strong. The entire concert was recorded and is available on-line.[29]

Inspired, in part, by Spector's plans for a Christmas album, Brian wrote "Little Saint Nick," a holiday hot rod song about Santa's sled. "I wrote the lyrics to it while I was out on a date and then I rushed home to finish the music," Brian recalled.[30] Mike was later awarded co-writing credit. At Western October 18, Brian produced a festive track on which the Beach Boys played piano, guitar, bass, and drums, and overdubbed celeste, sleigh bells, triangle, and glockenspiel. Brian also recorded tracks for two other songs. "Bobby Left Me" featured sax and castanets over a driving rhythm track intended for Sharon Marie, but vocals were never recorded. It was released on *The Big Beat* in 2013. "Drive-In" was shelved until April 1964 and appeared on *All Summer Long* that July. In June 1964, amidst sessions for a Christmas album, the Beach Boys recorded vocals for an alternate version of "Little Saint Nick" over the "Drive-In" instrumental track that also featured sleigh bells. It was included as a bonus track on *The Beach Boys' Christmas Album* compact disc in 1991.

On October 20, 1963, the group recorded vocals for "Little Saint Nick" and a stunning a cappella rendition of Albert Hay Malotte's musical adaptation of "The Lord's Prayer," perhaps the purest two minutes of vocal harmony ever recorded.[31] "Little Saint Nick" (b/w "The Lord's Prayer," Capitol 5096) was released December 9, reached #3 on the *Billboard* Christmas Single chart, and became a perennial seasonal favorite.

Sharon Marie's "Run-Around Lover" (b/w "Summertime," Capitol 5064) was released October 21. Two days earlier, *Billboard* ran a photo taken at Capitol of Sharon, Brian, Mike and Karl Engemann, recently promoted from A&R contract administrator to director of A&R Administration, reporting to vice president Voyle Gilmore. Outtakes from the photo session include Dennis and Carl, but neither David nor Al. The single made Sharon a celebrity at Novato High School where, when she lip synced the song at a fall talent show, it was rumored one of the Beach Boys (likely Mike) was in the audience. It was the first time Brian received credit as arranger and producer on a Capitol single by an artist other than the band. Capitol put very little marketing effort into the single and it failed to chart.

Within two months, Brian and Mike had written two songs for her follow-up single. Brian arranged and produced instrumental tracks for "Thinkin' 'Bout You Baby" and "The Story of My Life" at Western December 13 and coached her over the phone with them. Due to scheduling conflicts her vocals were not recorded until April 1964 at Gold Star with the Honeys singing background. When the single was released June 1 (Capitol 5195) and failed to chart, Capitol did not notify her that her contract would not be renewed, and her recording career came to a rather unceremonious end.

Also on October 21, Capitol released its first surf compilation, *Surfing's Greatest Hits* (Capitol ST-1995), featuring five songs by the Beach Boys ("Surfin'," "Surfin' Safari," "Surfin' U.S.A.," "Farmer's Daughter," and "Noble Surfer"), five by Dick Dale and the Del-Tones, and two surf novelties. A reviewer in a local newspaper noted it was the first time the instrumental force of Dick Dale had joined with the vocal force of the Beach Boys in one of surfing's greatest albums.[32]

On October 23, the Beach Boys played a show with the Honeys and Jan & Dean at the Santa Maria High School gymnasium. Al drove the two hours north in his new 1964 white Ford Thunderbird. Virginia Jardine recalled the group "persuaded" Al to sell his turquoise green Volkswagen Beetle to project a more upscale image. After the show, the group stayed at a local hotel, but Al and Dennis spent the night with Al's parents who had moved to Santa Maria because Don Jardine was now working at nearby Vandenberg Air Force Base.[33]

On October 31, they played 7:00 p.m. and 10:30 p.m. outdoor shows at Loyola Marymount University, just northwest of Hawthorne in Westchester. The concert was part of Loyola Carnival, celebrating the school's week-long homecoming festivities which the Four Freshmen kicked off four days earlier. Brian invited Bill Wagner, the Four Freshmen's manager, and his wife to attend the Beach Boys show. Wagner recalled, "After one song, Brian came over to me and said, 'Please go home.' I asked him why and he said, 'You know why. I'm embarrassed. We need to go home and practice more.' I told him, 'Don't be embarrassed, but don't do anything until you know for sure you can do it.'"[34]

On October 28, Brian formed Brian Wilson Productions, an independent record production company with offices at 6290 Sunset Boulevard near Vine Street, a few blocks south of Capitol Records. Brian, Mike, and Audree served on the board of directors and the articles of incorporation were endorsed by the California Secretary of State on December 2.

Around this time, Brian also formed his own music publishing company called Ocean Music, with which he completed Popular Songwriter's Contracts November 8 for songs for the Honeys ("The One You Can't Have," "You Brought It All on Yourself," "No Big Thing," and "What'll I Wear"), the Survivors ("Pamela Jean" and "After the Game"), Larry Denton ("If It Can't Be You"), and Sharon Marie ("Thinkin' 'Bout You Baby").

That October, as she turned seventeen, Judy worked as an usher at the Fox Theatre at 115 North Market Street in Inglewood. "Brian came in to see me and we talked. He asked, 'What's going on? How have you been?' My hair was frizzy from a bad home perm and he said, 'How could you do that to yourself after being with me?' I said, 'Well, at least I lost weight!' And he looked me up and down and said, 'Yes, you did. No more steak dinners and baked potatoes!' Then the manager of the theater told him 'You have to leave right now.' He was so mad at the manager for making him leave, he just walked out. That was the last time I saw him."[35]

"During the time we were breaking up, Brian once grabbed a pen and paper, and started writing furiously," Judy continued. "He wrote me a letter and read it back to me. I think he was looking into the future because he was flushed and exhausted when he finished. He said I would have several men in my life, but no one like Brian Wilson. It's funny, but that turned out to be true."[36]

24

"The Warmth of the Sun"
(November–December 1963)

November 1963

Brian returned to RCA Victor Studio at midnight on November 6 for a three-hour session with thirteen musicians to produce a track for "I Do," his and Roger Christian's tale of a young guy ready to settle down and get married. Brian recycled the melody of "County Fair" for the verses, which Mike sang while Brian countered with a soaring falsetto on the chorus. Single notes played on a triangle evoked wedding bells and a sampling of "Bridal Chorus," better known as "Here Comes the Bride," accompanied the fade. It would have made a great Beach Boys single but, perhaps intent on having a hit outside the group, Brian gave it to the Castells. In January 1964, he produced two vocal sessions with the Castells, first at Western and then Gold Star, and the single was released (b/w "Teardrops," Warner Bros. 5421) March 9, 1964, but failed to chart. The Beach Boys' version was released as a bonus track on the *Surfer Girl* and *Shut Down Volume 2* twofer compact disc in 1990. Their demo of "I Do," in a slower tempo, was released on *The Big Beat* in 2013.

On November 15, Wallichs Music City kicked off a ten-day celebration of the grand opening of its new store on the southeast corner of Artesia Boulevard and Hawthorne Boulevard in the South Bay. Several hundred people attended opening day festivities featuring music, dancing, autograph parties, prizes, and an album give-away every hour. Popular LA disc jockey Bob Crane, two years from starring in *Hogan's Heroes*, emceed a star-filled show at 7:00 p.m. with appearances by Kay Starr, the Beach Boys, Jack Jones, Jan & Dean, Dodie Stevens, and Rose Marie.

On a flat-bed truck in the parking lot, the Beach Boys played "Surfin' U.S.A.," "Surfer Girl," "In My Room," "Little Deuce Coupe," and "Be True to Your School," which moved from #2 to #1 on KFWB the next day. Capitol produced a limited pressing of a souvenir 45 rpm record of the Beach Boys' "Spirit of America" and "Boogie Woodie" on its Capitol Custom label. It was free while supplies lasted and came in an off-white, heavy paper sleeve proclaiming in red type "I Was There KFWB Day! Wallichs Music City, South Bay Store, Opening Nov. 16, 1963." KFWB began a twenty-four-hour live broadcast from Wallichs at midnight November 15. Hence, the record and sleeve noted that KFWB Day was November 16. The sleeve was actually a mailer with an adhesive flap used to send the record to local radio stations and newspapers to promote the event. Perhaps as few as one or two hundred sleeves were printed. The remaining copies of the record came in plain white sleeves. The "I Was There KFWB Day!" sleeve is one of the rarest pieces of Beach Boys memorabilia.

Across the street from the new Wallichs was the South Bay Shopping Center where, on November 1, 1960, Senator John F. Kennedy made one of his final campaign stops before being elected the thirty-fifth president of the United States. Now, three years into a term that would soon be romanticized as Camelot for its hope and promise, the Beach Boys played songs brimming with the youthful innocence of surfing, cars, falling in love, and school spirit. A week later, that innocence was shattered when President Kennedy was assassinated while riding in an open motorcade in Dallas, less than ninety minutes after Air Force One touched down on Love Field. It was such a national trauma, and everyone of a certain age would forever recall where they were when President Kennedy was killed. The Beach Boys were in Hawthorne preparing for an afternoon flight to Sacramento for a concert booked by Fred Vail at the Veterans Memorial Auditorium in Marysville. Vail telephoned Murry and told him he'd make some calls to determine whether the band should proceed with the concert. City officials gave Vail the green light and the concert went on as scheduled. Vail picked them up at the Sacramento Municipal Airport at 5:30 p.m. checked them into the El Dorado Hotel, and then drove them forty miles north to Marysville. Before the curtain rose on the Boys, Vail thanked the audience for coming and asked them to join him in a

Special MUSIC CITY -
KFWB Promotional Souvenier
Copy Celebrating Music City's
South Bay Store
Opening November 16, 1963

Sea of Tunes
Publishing Co.
BMI-2:40
(45-50438)

SPIRIT OF AMERICA
(Brian Wilson-Roger Christian)

THE BEACH BOYS

Top and above: The Beach Boys helped celebrate the opening of Wallichs Music City in the South Bay on November 16, 1963. Capitol gave away a custom 45 rpm single of "Spirit of America" backed with "Boogie Woodie" in a special heavy-paper "I Was There KFWB Day!" mailer sleeve. After a few hundred copies of the record with this sleeve were given away, the rest of the attendees received the record in a plain white sleeve. Today, the "I Was There KFWB Day!" mailer is the rarest Beach Boys' sleeve (author's collection).

moment of silence for the fallen president. The show broke the attendance record and the largely teen audience was appreciative the band had not cancelled.

Brian and Mike recalled "The Warmth of the Sun," their beautiful ballad about lost love, was inspired by the events in Dallas on November 22, 1963. However, over the years, they related conflicting stories as to where and when the song was written.

"The melody Brian came up with was very melancholy," Mike recalled. "I'd had this experience where this girl I liked decided she didn't want to reciprocate, so I wrote the lyrics from the perspective of, 'Yes, things have changed and love is no longer there, but the memory of it is like the warmth of the sun.'"[1] Vail recalled Brian and Mike began writing the song before the Marysville show and continued working on it at the hotel that evening and early morning.[2]

It is difficult to correlate the lyrics with the assassination. But the words seem especially poignant in light of Judy's recent break-up with Brian. Jodi Gable noted, "We wouldn't have had 'The Warmth of the Sun' if Judy hadn't broken up with Brian. She said she didn't love him anymore. Maybe she was just growing up or didn't want to be around a musician."[3]

Perhaps the song was inspired by personal relationships and the tragedy in Dallas. The instrumental track was recorded at Western January 1, 1964, and the vocals at Gold Star a week later. "The Warmth of the Sun" appeared on *Shut Down Volume 2* released March 2 and the B side of "Dance, Dance, Dance" that October. It remains one of Brian's and Mike's most personal and deeply moving songs. It is sad, but comforting. Desolate, yet hopeful. A reflection on love, once so beautiful, now lost forever. It transcends the gloom through its sheer beauty. And, as a meditation on that tragic time in our history, a musical salve for the wound inflicted on the American psyche by the death of a young president and the loss of so much promise.

December 1963

The back cover of *Billboard* out December 7 included a photo of Brian dressed as Santa sitting on the front of a roadster with Mike perched on his lap, as Carl, Al, and Dennis lined up to speak with him. It was Al's first appearance in a music industry publication. Capitol ran a full-page ad inside for a "Special Christmas Bonus from the Beach Boys" featuring "Little Saint Nick" in a paper Santa hat and beard.

On December 21, Carl's seventeenth birthday, Fred Vail presented the Beach Boys in a Gala Christmas Concert at Sacramento Memorial Auditorium, the band's third appearance there and first with Brian. Vail persuaded Murry that Capitol should record the concert for a proposed live album. Brian was dissatisfied with the resultant tapes and Capitol agreed to record two additional shows when the group returned to the venue August 1, 1964. *Beach Boys Concert* was released October 19 in a gatefold cover with four pages of Ken Veeder's concert photographs. A month later, it hit #1 for the first of four weeks, their first chart-topping album, and remained in the Top Ten for twenty of its sixty-two week run.

Cash Box out December 21 ran a full-page ad with a photo of the band at UCLA thanking the industry for another successful year and offering season's greetings to Radio Luxembourg, Sweden's Radio Sveriges, the British Isles, Australia, and New Zealand. A similar ad in *Music Reporter* ran a photo of the band with David from May 1962. A two-page spread in *Billboard* included a photo of the band at UCLA, promoted their four albums, and thanked the industry. They had much to be thankful for with three albums on the *Billboard* chart—*Little Deuce Coupe* (#13), *Surfer Girl* (#16), and *Surfin' U.S.A.* (#55).

The *Cash Box* out December 28 featured the band on the cover striking their best unsmiling tough guy pose dressed alike in white jeans, white button-down shirts, and blue collarless jackets, by Dennis's Corvette. The Top 100 hits for the year listed "Surfin' U.S.A." (#16), "Surf City" (#26), and "Surfer Girl" (#36). On the year-end album chart, *Surfin' U.S.A.* was #16 and *Shut Down*, credited as by the Beach Boys, was #34. They tied with the Four Seasons for Best Vocal Group, but the friendly bi-coastal rivalry would soon face a new challenge. On December 10, 1963, CBS Evening News aired a five minute segment on a new craze sweeping the United Kingdom. Something called Beatlemania.

⌖

Brian Wilson created and produced a staggering amount of music in 1963. The Beach Boys had released three albums in seven months—*Surfin' U.S.A.* (#2), *Surfer Girl* (#7), and *Little Deuce Coupe* (#4). They had seven consecutive hit songs on KFWB—"Surfin' U.S.A." (#1), "Shut Down" (#5), "Surfer Girl" (#1), "Little Deuce Coupe" (#16), "Be True to Your School" (#1), "In My Room" (#23), and "Little Saint Nick" (#15).

Brian helped revitalize Jan & Dean's career with "Surf City" (#1), "Drag City" (#5), and, recorded in November 1963 for release in February 1964, "Dead Man's Curve" (#11) and its B side, "The New Girl in School" (#37), which began life as Brian's and Bob Norberg's "Gonna' Hustle You."

Brian, Usher, and Christian copyrighted six songs November 21 ("Surfer's Holiday," "Muscle Bustle," "My First Love," "Surfin' Woodie," "Runnin' Wild," and "Muscle Beach Party") for the soundtrack of American International Pictures' *Muscle Beach Party* starring Annette, Frankie Avalon, and Dick Dale, which opened March 25, 1964.[4] A seventh tune by them, "Surf Route 101," was recorded by Jan & Dean for *Drag City* that November.

In addition to his work with the Beach Boys, Brian wrote, arranged, produced, or performed on some forty-two songs while working with the Honeys, Jan & Dean, the Survivors, Sharon Marie, the Timers, the Castells, Bob Norberg, Vickie Kocher, Gary Usher, Roger Christian, Paul Petersen, and Larry Denton. These range from demos to instrumental tracks to fully produced songs to unreleased gems. In late 1963, Brian copyrighted "No Big Thing," "Part of Me," and "Hello Operator." It is likely these songs remain unrecorded as they did not see release on *The Big Beat* in 2013.

As 1963 drew to a close, Brian had already written and rehearsed songs for the Beach Boys' fifth album, *Shut Down Volume 2*, recorded in seven sessions at Western and Gold Star over the first two months of the new year. During this time, he also produced sessions with the Castells (vocals for "I Do"), Paul Petersen ("She Rides with Me"), the Honeys ("Boys Will Be Boys," "What'll I Wear to School Today?," "He's a Doll," and "I Can See Right Through You"), and Larry Denton (a cover of "Endless Sleep"). In the midst of these sessions, the Beach Boys, including Brian, embarked on Surfside '64, a three-week tour of Australia and New Zealand with the Surfaris, Paul and Paula, the Joy Boys, and headliner Roy Orbison.

Between 1964 and 1966, the Beach Boys continued an astonishing creative output, releasing fifteen singles and eight albums, including *Pet Sounds* and "Good Vibrations," elevating, transforming, and revolutionizing popular music. Their run of hit songs reads like a page from the Great American Songbook—"Surfin' Safari," "409," "Surfin' U.S.A.," "Surfer Girl," "Little Deuce Coupe," "Be True to Your School," "In My Room," "Little Saint Nick," "Fun, Fun, Fun," "I Get Around," "Don't Worry Baby," "Do You Wanna Dance?," "Please Let Me Wonder," "When I Grow Up (To Be a Man)," "Dance, Dance, Dance," "Help Me, Rhonda," "Kiss Me Baby," "California Girls," "The Little Girl I Once Knew," "Barbara Ann," "Wouldn't It Be Nice," "God Only Knows," Sloop John B.," "Heroes and Villains," "Darlin'," "Wild Honey," "Friends," "Do It Again," "I Can Hear Music," "Add Some Music to Your Day," "Surf's Up," "Sail On, Sailor," "Rock and Roll Music," "It's O.K.," "Good Timin'," "Getcha Back," and "Kokomo."

In summer 2012, on the strength of *That's Why God Made the Radio*, their twenty-ninth studio album that reached #3 in *Billboard*, the Beach Boys embarked on a worldwide tour to celebrate their 50th anniversary. When the tour rolled into the Westchester County Center in White Plains, New York, my brother and I were in the audience. In that magical twilight before the concert began, Rich and I recalled all the times we had seen them in concert over the years—Carnegie Hall, Madison Square Garden, Kingsbridge Armory, Fordham University, Rockland Community College, Allentown Fair, Roosevelt Stadium, Nassau Coliseum, Aqueduct Raceway, Westbury Music Fair, Radio City Music Hall, Jones Beach, Giants Stadium, Six Flags, Brendan Byrne Arena, Garden State Arts Center, Capital Centre, Busch Gardens, DAR Constitution Hall, Warner Theatre, Kings Dominion, Merriweather Post Pavilion, George Mason University, Wolf Trap Farm, RFK Stadium, and the National Mall—musical touchstones that brought back waves of happy memories. Suddenly, the hall went dark.

"Ladies and gentlemen, from Southern California, please welcome ... the Beach Boys."

Over the cool introduction of that unmistakable drum riff of "Do It Again," the crowd leapt to its feet, applauding wildly with love and admiration for a band that, half a century ago, decided someone should write a song about surfing.

And I thought of that autumn day in October 1966 when "Good Vibrations" caught the attention of a sixteen-year-old kid playing basketball on a concrete court in the Bronx, who ran home and told his ten-year-old brother, "I don't know what I just heard on the radio, but I've never heard anything like it. We've got to find that record. We've got to find it right now."

Coda

The Hite Morgan Tapes—Discovery, Illumination and Litigation

In the span of six months—from October 1961 through March 1962—the Beach Boys recorded nine songs in four sessions for Hite and Dorinda Morgan, which were published through the Morgans' Guild Music. These nine songs, "Surfin'," "Luau," "Lavender," "Surfin' Safari," "Surfer Girl," "Judy," "Karate" (also known as "Beach Boy Stomp"), "Barbie," and "What Is a Young Girl Made Of?," are collectively known as the Hite Morgan recordings. They are the only recordings known to exist by the band before they signed a seven-year recording contract with Capitol Records on May 24, 1962. The original tapes, thought to be lost or missing for nearly thirty years, have been the subject of decades-long litigation. This chapter examines how the original tapes were rediscovered and remastered for commercial release and the litigation surrounding them.

I would be remiss not to acknowledge the assistance of Bruce Morgan, Paul Urbahns, and Steve Hoffman with the information in this chapter. Bruce's patience never wavered with my requests for answers to "just a few more questions." Paul sent me his files to better understand the project's genesis and progression. Steve answered countless questions from a non-audiophile with humor and grace. All three gentlemen have my sincere gratitude for sharing their unique perspective on the Hite Morgan recordings—the first steps of the Beach Boys' long and satisfying musical journey. I am proud to add my name to the long list of Beach Boys' fans and music lovers worldwide appreciative of their groundbreaking work in bringing these historic recordings to life and sharing them with the rest of us.

On March 31, 1969, Hite Morgan, doing business as Deck Records, leased duplicate master tapes of eight of the nine songs (Morgan held "Lavender" back) to Herb Newman's Era Records. Era released them in late 1969 on a vinyl album called *The Beach Boys Biggest Beach Hits*. It contained an alternate version of "Barbie" with one line which differed slightly from the single released in April 1962 on Randy 422. A single later paired "Surfer Girl" with "The Freeze" by Tony and Joe (Era 042).

At the time, Era was distributed by Happy Tiger Records, a short-lived label for Flying Tigers, the LA–based Air Freight Company, and the album bore a joint Happy Tiger/Era catalog number (HTE-805). Rather than feature a photograph or likeness of the Beach Boys, the album cover contained a cartoonish drawing of a suntanned blonde in a bikini standing on the shore holding a surfboard and gazing out at the ocean.

The album inexplicably included "Phantom Surfer" and "Bustin' Surfboards" by the

Tornadoes (misspelled as Tornados). "Phantom Surfer," written by Dorinda Morgan and Rue Barclay, but credited to Dorinda only, was published by Prestige Publishing Company, the Morgans' firm with ASCAP. "Bustin' Surfboards," published by Mate Music, BMI, was incorrectly credited to Prestige. The three Beach Boys songs previously credited as written by Bruce Morgan ("Luau," "Barbie," and "What Is a Young Girl Made Of?") were now credited to Dorinda and the publishing of the latter two changed from Guild Music to Prestige.

The contract granted Era the right to sell, and permit others to sell, tapes and/or records of the masters under any name they selected. In exchange, Morgan received ten percent of the wholesale price for which Newman sold the album. In the event a collection authorized by Newman included fewer than all eight recordings, Newman was to pay Morgan four cents per song used. Era continued to exploit the eight recordings throughout the 1970s and 1980s. K-Tel purchased Era in the 1980s and continued to exploit the recordings.

In 1970, the eight recordings appeared on Florence Greenberg's New York–based Wand Records (WDS 688) as *The Beach Boys' Greatest Hits (1961–1963)*, fleshed out with uninspired instrumental versions of "Little Deuce Coupe" and "409" reportedly performed by the Marketts masquerading as the Surfin' Six. Greenberg later released the same line-up on her Scepter Records as *The Best of the Beach Boys* (CTN 18004). They also appeared on Orbit Records (OR 688) as *The Beach Boys' Greatest Hits (1961–1963)*. These low-budget releases misspelled song titles as "Barbee" and "Little Deuce Coop."

The Happy Tiger/Era release sounded slightly sped up compared to the Scepter release. But the key difference was Carl's original guitar instrumental "Karate," alternately known as "Beach Boy Stomp." The Wand, Scepter, and Orbit releases included the song as "Karate" which clocked in at 1:26 and ended with the shout "Karate!" The Happy Tiger/Era release included the song as "Beach Boy Stomp," which was "Karate" with an additional forty-one seconds of instrumental taken from earlier in the song and spliced on after the "Karate! shout" to lengthen the song to a more respectable 2:07.

After Hite Morgan passed away October 4, 1974, Bruce guided the business concerns of Deck Records and Guild Music on behalf of his mother, Dorinda. In November 1974, the Wand line-up was released on Springboard (SPB 4021) as *The Beach Boys' Greatest Hits (1961–1963)* and by the end of the year, the Happy Tiger/Era line-up appeared on 8-track (Gambit G 507).

In early 1977, John Cevetello, owner of Gateway Records, approached Joseph Saraceno, the former A&R director for Candix Records, about licensing the Beach Boys' Hite Morgan recordings. Saraceno contacted Bruce Morgan and offered to act as an intermediary with Gateway Records.

On March 23, 1977, Morgan signed an agreement with Saraceno and delivered to him a tape of the recordings. Their agreement allowed for a one-time-only use of "Surfin'," "Surfer Girl," "Barbie," and "What Is a Young Girl Made Of?" by Cevetello on *Pop Anthology, Volume 3*, on Gateway Records. Saraceno delivered the tape to Cevetello, collected $2,490 pursuant to their separate agreement, paid Morgan $2,000 pursuant to their agreement, and retained the balance of $490. Saraceno also licensed a few recordings he owned by the Marketts to Cevetello for the same Gateway album. But Cevetello died and the record was never manufactured. Morgan later asserted the license ended with Cevetello's death.

In March 1977, the five-album set *The Encyclopedia of 100 Rock 'N' Roll Hits*, available only by mail order, contained "Surfin,'" "Surfin' Safari," "Surfer Girl," and "Barbie."

On May 12, 1977, Morgan licensed four of the recordings ("Surfin,'" "Surfer Girl," "Barbie," and "What Is a Young Girl Made Of?") to Saraceno's Dana Music.

In August 1977, the two-album set *Surfin' Roots* (Festival FR 1010) contained "Surfin,'" "Surfer Girl," "Barbie," and "What Is a Young Girl Made Of?" In January 1978, the double album *The Greatest Groups of Rock n' Roll* (Fairway TMC) contained "Surfin,'" "Surfin' Safari" and "Surfer Girl." In March 1978, the mail order album *Surf & Drag* (KBO Publishers/Columbia Special Products P 14439) contained the same three songs.

In January 1979, seven of the recordings (no "Judy" or "Lavender"), along with three cuts each by the Marketts and the Frogmen, appeared on *Surfing with the Beach Boys, Marketts and Frogmen* (Gateway Extra Play GSLP 10104).

Morgan later asserted that in 1981 Saraceno licensed the recordings to David Last and Jay Chernow, owners of San Juan Music Group, Brooklyn, New York. Morgan also asserted that on March 30, 1981, Saraceno, acting as agent for San Juan Music Group, licensed seven of the recordings (no "Judy" or "Lavender") to Jerry Wilson and Marshall Sehorn of El Dorado, Inc., in Nashville, for which they reportedly paid $10,000.

On December 27, 1982, Jay Chernow of San Juan Music Group licensed the recordings to Jefferson Jazz in Slidell, Louisiana, who in turn, on August 17, 1983, licensed them to Blackwood & Friends Music in Nashville.

On March 19, 1984, attorneys for Brother Records, Inc. (BRI) wrote to San Juan Records, Jefferson Jazz, and Blackwood Productions, demanding they cease and desist in the unauthorized use of the recordings. BRI received an April 2, 1984, response asserting the recordings had been licensed properly, but never acted to prevent continued unauthorized use of the recordings.

After Dorinda Morgan passed away February 23, 1986, Bruce arranged to have Art Laboe's Original Sound Record Company act as Deck Records' agent to license the recordings for use in motion pictures, television, and special promotions. Original Sound licensed "Surfer Girl" and "Surfin' Safari" for the second and third volume, respectively, in its *Oldies, But Goodies* series in 1986. From 1987 throughout the 1990s, Original Sound licensed the recordings, or snippets of them, to more than a dozen television shows and motion pictures. For instance, on May 21, 1990, Original Sound licensed the Deck Records' recording of "Surfin' Safari" to Buena Vista Pictures Distribution, Inc., for use in the motion picture *Green Card*. The contract stipulated the version of "Surfin' Safari" was "as originally recorded and released on Candix Records only, not the version on Capitol Records."[1] On December 3, 1990, Original Sound licensed eighteen seconds of the Deck Records' recording of "Surfin' Safari" to Paramount Pictures Corporation for use in episode number 006 in the television series *Ferris Bueller*.

On April 24, 1992, Original Sound contracted with the Chevrolet Motor Division to license the Beach Boys' Deck Records recording of "Surfer Girl" for *Sounds of the Sea*, a compact disc Chevrolet hired Carlson Marketing Group to manufacture as a premium item to promote Chevrolet's sponsorship of America's Cup. In May or June 1992, Paul Politi, vice president of Original Sound, received a telephone call from Elliott Lott, president of BRI, who advised that the Beach Boys 1992 Tour was sponsored by the Ford Motor Company and, hence, Original Sounds' contract with Chevrolet put the band in an awkward situation. Lott questioned Original Sounds' right to license the recordings. Politi explained to Lott the position held by Original Sound and Deck Records, and "never received another inquiry or concern."[2]

In February 2000, ABC aired the Emmy-nominated mini-series *The Beach Boys: An American Family*. Unlike the 1990 television movie *Summer Dreams: The Story of the Beach Boys*, which used sound-alike singers for the soundtrack, the creative team behind *An American Family* licensed the Beach Boys' original recordings. When a sound recording appears in a motion picture or television movie, the producer must obtain a Master Use License for the right to use the song and a Synchronization License for the right to use that song in a timed relation to visual pictures (i.e., synchronized to the actor's lips). Original Sound offered a license for the Deck Records' recording of "Surfin' Safari" to McFarlane Productions, Inc., on behalf of the film's production company, Columbia Tristar Television, a Sony Pictures Entertainment company, for the use of "Surfin' Safari" for $22,000 on a Most Favored Nation status with Capitol Records, which meant Original Sound was entitled to a higher fee than quoted if McFarlane had agreed to pay Capitol a higher fee for a similar use. The version of "Surfin' Safari" that appeared in the film was the version Capitol purchased in May 1962 which the Beach Boys recorded at Western in April 1962.

By the late 1980s, the recordings began appearing on unauthorized, low budget compact discs all over the world. Most of these were extremely poor sound quality. Some of the titles included *Surfin' Safari* (licensed by San Juan Music Group in 1985), *Greatest Hits* (Hollywood HCD 109/Deluxe CD1001 in 1986), *Surfin'* (Telstar TRCD 1001 in 1988), and *Super Hits* (Evergreen 2690842).

On May 22, 1991, Saraceno sent a letter to Chernow of San Juan Music Group reasserting his authority to license the recordings pursuant to his March 23, 1977, agreement with Bruce Morgan.

Paul Politi stated, "During the 1990s, it came to my attention and that of Deck Records, that there were unauthorized licenses, manufacture and sales of the Deck Records' Beach Boys recordings by a person by the name of Joseph Saraceno, located in Los Angeles, California, and by San Juan Music Group and Peter Pan Industries, Inc., both located in New Jersey."[3] Morgan later asserted Saraceno had made a low quality copy of the recordings and had licensed them repeatedly without authorization.

As compact discs of the recordings flooded the market, Beach Boys' fans and audiophiles began wondering why these historic recordings could not be released with better sound. It raised the question of whether the original tapes existed and, if they did, where were they? One guy took that challenge a little more seriously than others.

Discovery

Paul Urbahns is a historian with an aptitude for research and discovery. He is also a former disc jockey and Beach Boys fan. In 1990, this diverse background benefitted music fans worldwide. That year, Urbahns read an article by Neal Umphred in the June 1 *Goldmine* about the current Beach Boys catalog on compact disc. Referencing a low budget CD, Umphred wrote it was "one of several skimpy CDs regurgitating the Hite Morgan material, once again with no notes and no real sense of historical perspective. It's a shame Capitol

couldn't have gotten its hands on these masters and used them on a deluxe double-disc ret-
rospective of the group."[4] Urbahns had made the same observation. "The uniformity of
the irritating bad sound had given the public a general belief that the original tapes were
of extremely poor quality."[5] In Fayetteville, North Carolina, Gregory Orme read the same
article and wrote *Goldmine* detailing the various permutations of the Hite Morgan recordings on compact disc. Urbahns saw Orme's letter and got in touch with him. Orme suggested
perhaps all of the low budget albums and compact discs had been made from the same poor
quality dubs. Perhaps the original tapes had never been used and were somewhere just waiting to be found. It was an astute observation. And right on the money.

In July 1990, Urbahns wrote to Steve Hoffman, director of A&R and engineering at
Marshall Blonstein's DCC Compact Classics in Northridge, California, inquiring whether
the company would consider releasing a digitally remastered compact disc of the Beach
Boys' Hite Morgan recordings. Hoffman had garnered a reputation for breathing new life
into classic recordings and Urbahns was aware of his work for the label including a series
of remastered discs by Ray Charles. Hoffman fired back, "Of course I would like to release
a complete 'Morgan' Beach Boys compact disc. Who wouldn't? The only problem is where
are the master tapes? I have never been able to find them. Only fourth and fifth generation
dubs like everyone has used in the past."[6]

In September 1968, Bruce Morgan made a copy of the original tapes at Master
Recorders at 535 Fairfax Avenue in West Hollywood. He then made a copy of that copy
which he licensed to Era Record Sales October 2, 1968. "Era duplicated their tape countless
times for countless people overseas, each copy more dreadful than the first," Hoffman
explained. "When Bruce made tape copies in those days, they were done through a really
inferior console and the strained, distorted, and usually slightly off-speed sound, with compression from clipping, is a factor in the Era tape and the copy of 'Surfin'' made for Capitol
in 1962."[7]

Hoffman issued Urbahns a challenge. "I'll make a deal with you. If you can find the
masters, I'll let you produce our album and write the liner notes. What do you say?"[8] The
gauntlet had been thrown down. The search was on.

Urbahns reasoned if there was any way to find the original tapes it would be through
the music publishing. Record labels fold, recording studios go out of business, but the music
publishing lives on with the owner, his heirs, or, if the publishing company is sold, the new
owner. And the main clue was right there on the Candix record label for "Surfin'"—Guild
Music. Hite and Dorinda Morgan owned several music publishing companies over the years,
but all of the Beach Boys' recordings were published through their Guild Music and registered with BMI. Bruce Morgan had since arranged for Guild's publishing concerns to be
overseen by Original Sound, still owned by disc jockey and Morgan family friend Art Laboe.
Urbahns called Original Sound and obtained Bruce Morgan's contact information.

Urbahns called Bruce several times over the next few weeks, but he was out of the
country. Finally, on August 24, 1990, Urbahns called and Bruce answered. After a brief
introductory exchange, he told Bruce he was looking for the original master tapes of the
Beach Boys' Hite Morgan sessions. "I have them right here," Bruce replied. He explained
the tapes were second generation masters as the originals had been lost when his father
moved his studio twice and changed residences twice. They did, however, contain multiple
takes of all the songs, false starts, and studio chatter. Morgan cautioned, "These tapes have

not been played for years and some of the splices may have dried out and need re-splicing."[9] The good news? The recording tape used was one of the finest and most durable audio tapes ever made.

Urbahns and Morgan spoke about the tapes, what they contained, and their overall quality. Morgan was interested in the project, but a bit bemused there would be any interest or commercial demand in the recordings. He agreed to inventory the tapes and meet with Steve Hoffman. When he got off the phone with Morgan, Urbahns fired off a letter to Hoffman. "I took you up on your offer to locate the original Hite Morgan Beach Boys' tapes. And I did!"[10]

Illumination

Hoffman and his colleagues at DCC Compact Classics drew up a game plan for the tapes and in mid–September Hoffman met with Bruce Morgan and spent a few days with him in his home. Both men are laid-back and easy going, and they hit it off through a common connection of music. Bruce played him five ten-inch reels of the Beach Boys' recordings Hite Morgan had produced at World Pacific Studio and at his own Stereo Masters. During the visit, they came across a small box tucked away in a closet. Inside was a tape reel labeled "Pendeltones surfing song"—the group's first three demos Hite Morgan recorded in his living room studio at 2511 Mayberry Street in October 1961.

In the process of inventorying the tapes prior to Hoffman's arrival, Bruce discovered a short handwritten memoir in which his mother, Dorinda, reminisced about the Beach Boys. He loaned Steve the memoir for possible inclusion in the project's liner notes and signed a contract with DCC Compact Classics for the tapes.

Hoffman flew home to Burbank with the six reels of tape secured in his carry-on luggage. When the plane landed, he drove immediately to the DCC Compact Classic's office and secured the tapes in their vault.

Hoffman cleared his schedule to concentrate on the Morgan recordings. He went to Location Recording Service in Burbank, California, and listened to the tapes on an Ampex ATR-100 and Studer A-80 mastering deck with a full track mono head stack. Steve found the tapes to be in remarkable condition. They had not been played in years and being stored in a dark, dry closet helped with their preservation. They did not require any special handling or treatment. Hite Morgan had used 3M Scotch 111 tape, a very robust material lasting years without shedding (pieces of tape flaking off) or drop out (loss of audio signal). At the time, 3M used whale oil as a lubricant which, although no longer used, is far superior to any modern synthetics. Although Dino Lappas, the recording engineer at World Pacific Studios, recalled those sessions were recorded on three tracks, Hoffman assured me they were not. They were recorded in mono—all microphones being fed to the same channel for playback on one speaker.

"We didn't clean the tapes up," Hoffman recalled. "They didn't really need cleaning. They sounded fine. We just fixed the tonality so the vocals sounded more lifelike and less pinched. I did level matching so all the songs from four sessions sounded good together."[11]

DCC Compact Classics was justifiably proud of the fact they were the first company to ever use these masters. They had not even been used for the original Candix 45s which were made from EQ cutting dubs. Hoffman explained, "This means a tape copy was made of the Candix songs with added compression and equalization for cutting phonograph records. Those dubs were sent to the cutter (pressing plant) and stayed in their possession until they were eventually destroyed."[12]

For the demo recordings at his home, Morgan used an Ampex 400 tape deck. Hoffman believed the guys gathered around one microphone with the tape running at a speed of seven and one-half inches per second into the one track monophonic tape deck. This session yielded one take of "Surfin," three takes of "Luau," and four a cappella takes of "Lavender."

For the first session at World Pacific Studio, Hoffman believed the guys sang into German Neumann microphones plugged into an Ampex 351 tape deck. "This was done in a real studio and it sounds to me like four microphones were used. One on the bass amplifier, one on the guitar amplifier, one over the drum kit, and one on a stand or boom for the vocals. As in the home demo, the guys would have been grouped around the microphone and the vocal balance would have been achieved by that means."[13] This session yielded eight takes of "Surfin," twelve takes of "Luau," and four takes of "Lavender." It was from this session that their first single, "Surfin'" backed with "Luau," was released on Candix 331 on November 27, 1961.

The second session at World Pacific was held February 8, 1962. Hoffman recalled, "The second session was recorded in an underdub with just the rhythm guitar and an overdub which basically fed the first music back through the console while Carl added an overdubbed electric guitar."[14] This session yielded ten takes of "Surfin' Safari," six takes of "Surfer Girl," two takes of "Judy," and two takes of "Karate" (aka, "Beach Boy Stomp"). Although the session produced two future hits, a follow-up single on Candix, or any other indie label, was not forthcoming.

The World Pacific sessions were recorded in mono, but Hite Morgan did attempt a stereo overdub of "Surfin' Safari." Hoffman thought it was possible the stereo overdub could have been done at a studio other than World Pacific, perhaps Stereo Masters. "They played back one take of the finished mono overdub on one channel of a stereo tape machine while opening up a microphone for the second channel and new instruments were added. Why, I have no idea. But it was interesting to listen to."[15] In fall 1962, Hite Morgan leased this alternate stereo version to Ariola Records in West Germany where it was backed with "Luau" on Ariola 45 441.

The session at Stereo Masters, believed to have been held March 8, 1962, used state-of-the-art recording equipment similar to World Pacific and yielded seven takes of "Barbie" and six takes of "What Is a Young Girl Made Of?" Hoffman found these two songs the most difficult on which to work. "They needed a lot of work to sound good. The backing tracks were prerecorded without any involvement from the Beach Boys. The way the session worked for the vocals was the instrumental backing track was played back on a mono machine and that went to one track of a two-track machine. The microphone was open and, on the other channel, Brian, wearing headphones, did his lead vocals and the others did their background vocals at the same time. So, the final tape has all the music on one channel and all the vocals on the other. Later, the master take was selected and the two-track tape was redubbed to the mono machine with the vocal and music being combined on one channel for disc cutting. That mono mix does not survive. The stereo sessions still exist and that is the important part."[16]

On September 27, 1990, Hoffman wrote Urbahns and discussed ideas for the front cover artwork for the compact disc. Hoffman nixed the idea of using a photograph of the original Candix 45 rpm records. He asked Bruce Morgan for a photograph of Hite, but did not seem hopeful one would be forthcoming. Hoffman wanted to use a historically accurate photograph of the band circa 1961 with Al Jardine in the line-up and not David Marks.

Meanwhile, the sixteen-page booklet that would accompany the compact disc was beginning to take shape. It would consist of four components: Dorinda Morgan's reminiscences, Robert S. Levinson's "How I Came to Meet Brian Wilson and What Happened," Urbahns's original liner notes, and Brian Wilson's introduction from the spring 1964 *Song Hits Folio*.

By October, DCC Compact Classics had readied a twenty-one track collection called *The Lost Tapes (1961–1962)*. Hoffman's proposed line-up led off with home demos of "Surfin'," "Luau," and "Lavender," although Bruce Morgan had not yet given the green light to the latter.

On October 3, Hoffman responded to Urbahns's September 28 letter and advised that the stereo overdub of "Surfin' Safari," which had been released on Ariola Records in West Germany, would indeed be included in the collection. Hoffman also confirmed "Surfin'" had not been re-recorded for Capitol's *Surfin' Safari* album. Instead, Capitol leased the master from Hite Morgan and sped it up a semitone from the key of G to A flat which made the recording sound brighter and the Beach Boys sound even younger.

On October 19, Hoffman responded to Urbahns's October 15 letter and advised that the liner notes should detail the discovery process and how this was a "collector's dream come true for Beach Boys' fans."[17] Because no one had found an early photograph of the band with Jardine or one of Hite Morgan, Hoffman proposed a change in cover artwork. "The cover is going to be kind of like the Beatles *White Album*. The new name *The Beach Boys/Lost and Found* will be up in the top left in gold leaf on a white background."[18] Hoffman enclosed a transcription of Dorinda's memoir and advised typesetting on the CD booklet would begin soon. He urged Urbahns to write as much as he wanted for the liner notes, and to do it quickly.

On November 1, Hoffman wrote Urbahns thanking him for his liner notes, still hopeful the collection would include "Lavender."

But Urbahns didn't like the new cover idea and proposed a collage of objects evocative of the era and the music. He had gotten the idea from a release of Sun Records recordings by Elvis, Roy Orbison, Jerry Lee Lewis, Johnny Cash, and Carl Perkins that used iconic symbols of the artists. Hoffman agreed to the idea although it meant postponing the collection's release date a little further into 1991.

Hoffman and his colleagues at DCC Compact Classics began assembling a variety of eclectic items reminiscent of surf music and the early 1960s. The new cover showed a tape reel in an open tape box, a stack of tape boxes, a few vinyl 45s including the X and Candix releases of "Surfn'," a wicker picnic basket, a surfboard, and a plaid shirt suggestive of a Pendleton, on a desk in front of a lace-curtained window adjacent to a bookshelf in what looked like a teenager's bedroom in the early '60s. The actual location was Hoffman's office at DCC.

Marshall Blonstein asked his friend Jim Zuckerman, a photographer whose stock images graced many DCC Compact Classics covers, to shoot the image. Zuckerman shot the cover with black and white film, and then colored the final print.[19]

Meanwhile, as the collection neared release, Hoffman pulled "Lavender" and reversed the order of the first two songs, now leading off with "Luau" and then "Surfin." Urbahns suggested the in-studio chatter appear as separate tracks so that, upon future listening, one could program around them if so desired. When Bruce finally consented to the inclusion of the demo version of "Lavender," Hoffman added it as the twenty-first and final track.

The collection, renamed *The Beach Boys, Lost & Found, 1961–1962* (DCC Compact Classics DZS-054), was released February 21, 1991. Due to space constraints, Zuckerman's photo was cropped on the CD booklet, but the complete image appeared on the cardboard long box in which the collection was first released and in the advertisement in the February 16, 1991 *Billboard*. The March 30, 1991 *Billboard* called *Lost & Found* a "charming set, a vital reissue, and a gem for Beach Boys fans."

On March 28, 1991, five days after *Billboard* hit the newsstands, attorneys for BRI wrote Bruce Morgan. "Our clients, the Beach Boys, noticed an ad in *Billboard* magazine regarding the release of some Beach Boys' masters on DCC Compact Classics. I would appreciate any information you could provide to me regarding the rights to these masters."

The highlight of *Lost & Found* for many Beach Boys fans was the inclusion of the a cappella demo of "Lavender." It was a gift of a new Beach Boys song with a gorgeous Brian Wilson lead vocal discovered thirty years after its creation. It was sonic evidence of his devotion to the Four Freshmen and proof his gift for vocal arrangement was present right from the beginning. Hoffman recalled, "We needed to fix the demo of 'Lavender' by editing together a bunch of takes. We made a 15 inch per second mono tape copy and edited it to what we needed."[20] The studio version of "Lavender" recorded at World Pacific with just Al on bass remains unreleased. Hoffman explained, "The studio version of 'Lavender' wasn't released because Bruce didn't think it was very good and it distorted through the bass guitar amplifier. And Bruce wasn't sure the Beach Boys would like to hear it released all these years later."[21]

The tapes were returned to Bruce, but he recommended DCC Compact Classics retain the original tape boxes and legends for ten years. Hoffman explained, "Bruce was almost certain the Beach Boys would not be happy that this material was released officially. We needed to prove we didn't bootleg the material and that it came from the original owner. I was certain the second DCC released the compact disc it would be bootlegged all over the world. We had to prove we didn't bootleg any Beach Boys' music and that we licensed it officially from the proper owner."[22]

Ironically, despite Bruce Morgan's trepidation, the Beach Boys never threatened legal action against him or DCC Compact Classics. In fact, word filtered back to Hoffman that band members enjoyed hearing their earliest recordings in such fine form. "I remember thinking it was really remarkable that these were even out there," Al Jardine testified later in a deposition involving the tapes. "I was kind of proud of the fact that it was something we had recorded so early on."[23]

In late 1991, DCC Compact Classics licensed the collection to Sundazed Music, Inc., in Coxsackie, New York, for a twelve-inch album mastered and sequenced by Bob Irwin. The album was cut in Sony Studios in New York City and four separate pressings were produced on black, blue, yellow and green marble vinyl. There were eight tracks per side and the separate tracks of studio chatter were gone. The album used a photograph of the band with Honda Motor Scooters in 1964. The liner notes, now confined to the back album cover, underwent revision. Levinson's incongruous description of his 1966 encounter with Brian was replaced with an insightful essay by long-time fan and Smithereens' drummer Dennis Diken on the historical and musical significance of the recordings. Urbahns's notes and Dorinda's memoir followed, but gone was Brian's introduction from the spring 1964 *Song Hits Folio*. DCC Compact Classics reissued the collection on compact disc and, in an unusual turn, used the Sundazed cover.

On March 6, 2000, Original Sound licensed the recordings to Brad Elliott, author of the essential *Surf's Up! The Beach Boys on Record (1961–1981)*, who contracted with Varèse Sarabande Records of Studio City, California, for a collection called *Surfin'* released on compact disc later that spring (302 066 085 2). *Surfin'*, for which Elliott penned new liner notes, contained one take each of the nine recordings (including the "Lavender" demo), the alternate "Surfin' Safari" released on Ariola in West Germany, both sides of a 1963 single by the Four Speeds on which Dennis drummed, and both sides of a 1963 single by the Tri-Five on which Dennis drummed and Carl played lead guitar. At the end of his liner notes, Elliott promoted an even more ambitious collection he was planning. He wrote, "A more thorough examination of the Beach Boys' earliest recordings can be found on the two–CD set *First Wave: The Complete Hite Morgan Sessions* available from Surfs Up Records."[24] He provided a mailing address from which customers could presumably order the set.

Later in 2000, the *Lost & Found* line-up appeared on a compact disc titled *The Beach Boys, Studio Sessions, 1961–1962*, by Burning Airlines, a division of NMC Music Ltd. The liner notes in the sixteen-page CD booklet were rearranged—Dorinda's memoir, Diken's essay, Urbahns's notes, and Brian's introduction. Burning Airlines licensed their collection to Get Back, an Italian record company, which pressed it on a twelve-inch yellow vinyl album (Get 576). The liner notes from the Burning Airlines CD were printed on the inside of the album's gatefold cover. The album cover featured a mock-up of a tape box legend made to appear like a Hite Morgan session at World Pacific with three takes of "Luau" and two takes of "Surfin'." However, the mock-up was clearly the Power Plant recording studio in New York City and not World Pacific in LA. Both the CD and vinyl album featured a photograph of the group taken in Nick Venet's office at Capitol Records when the group signed with the label in May 1962. The photo was not historically accurate since it included David Marks instead of Al Jardine. But it was certainly closer to the Hite Morgan period than the 1964 photo used by Sundazed. On his on-line forum, Steve Hoffman indicated the Burning Airlines and Get Back releases appeared to be unauthorized and expressed regret Bruce Morgan would never see a dime from them.

Litigation

Since 1964, the Hite Morgan recordings have been the subject of numerous lawsuits. The following summary was compiled from documents obtained from the United States District Court, Southern District of California; United States District Court, Central District of California; Superior Court of California for the County of Los Angeles; United States Court of Appeals for the Ninth Circuit; and the attorney representing Bruce Morgan.

The Dispute Over the Copyright and Music Publishing of "Surfer Girl"

The first major dispute between Hite Morgan and the Beach Boys involved the initial pressing of "Surfer Girl" (b/w "Little Deuce Coupe," Capitol 5009) released July 22, 1963, on which the music publishing for "Surfer Girl" was co-credited betweeen Morgan's Guild Music and the Wilsons' Sea of Tunes. Nick Venet recalled that as he gathered label copy for the single, Murry told him "Surfer Girl" was published by Sea of Tunes. Murry called back later that day and said the publishing should be Sea of Tunes and Guild Music.

After "Surfer Girl" was released, Morgan contacted Capitol and advised he owned the publishing to "Surfer Girl" outright by virtue of the Standard Songwriter's Contract executed with Brian and Murry on January 29, 1962. Capitol conferred with Murry about Morgan's claim.

On August 23, 1963, Capitol advised Morgan that Murry relinquished any claim to the publishing for "Surfer Girl." All subsequent pressings of the "Surfer Girl" single noted Guild Music as the sole publisher. Murry had to resign himself that Sea of Tunes would not earn a penny from the publishing of one of Brian's most beloved ballads.

HITE B. MORGAN V. CAPITOL RECORDS, INC.
—AND—
CAPITOL RECORDS, INC. V. BRIAN D. WILSON,
DENNIS C. WILSON, CARL D. WILSON, DAVID L. MARKS AND
MICHAEL E. LOVE, INDIVIDUALLY, AND AS MEMBERS OF
THE GROUP PERFORMING AS THE BEACH BOYS

Civil Case No. 64–1044-FW, United States District Court, Southern District of California

In March 1964, Hite Morgan advised Capitol Records it was infringing on his copyright for "Surfin'," "Surfin' Safari," and "Surfer Girl" and had not paid mechanical royalties of two cents for every copy of each record sold to his Guild Music. When he was unable to reach an amicable settlement, Morgan sued Capitol for infringement and unfair competition on July 27, 1964.

On October 16, 1964, as Capitol prepared to release *Beach Boys Concert*, the company moved to dismiss Morgan's complaint. Capitol demanded Murry Wilson and the Beach Boys comply with the terms of paragraph eight of their July 16, 1962, recording contract which stipulated that for any original musical composition for which they were the author or composer they would grant or cause to be granted to Capitol a mechanical license fee for the use of that composition in the United States and Canada. In deposition, Nick Venet recalled first meeting with Murry, Brian, and Gary Usher in 1962. Murry had brought a box of tapes—the Morgan recordings and the April 1962 demo from Western Recorders—and Murry indicated he owned them all outright. Hence, Capitol asserted when Murry signed the interim recording contract with Capitol on May 24, 1962, on behalf of the Beach Boys, four of whom were still legally minors, he owned the copyright and therefore the mechanical royalty to "Surfin'," "Surfin' Safari," and "Surfer Girl." That carried over into the final recording contract with Capitol on July 16, 1962, which was ratified in LA Superior Court on November 8, 1962.

When Capitol did not receive a response from Murry, the company sued the Beach

Boys for indemnity from Morgan's lawsuit and demanded they comply with the terms of their contract. Capitol's position was that it was not responsible if Murry, intentionally or unintentionally, misrepresented his ownership of the recordings.

The court consolidated the two cases, making Capitol a defendant in the Morgan case and a third-party plaintiff against the Beach Boys. Following extensive discovery proceedings, the parties agreed it was in their best interests to resolve their differences amicably and avoid any further litigation. The case settled on June 21, 1966.

Morgan had registered the copyright for "Surfin'" on December 7, 1961, and granted Capitol a mechanical license November 6, 1962 (considered effective as of September 1, 1962). He had registered the copyright for "Surfin' Safari" on June 11, 1962, and granted Capitol a mechanical license November 30, 1962 (considered effective as of June 4, 1962). Although he had registered the copyright for "Surfer Girl" on July 26, 1962, Morgan had never granted Capitol a mechanical license for the song. Hence, Capitol agreed to pay Morgan two cents for every record containing "Surfer Girl" manufactured between July 15, 1963 (the day "Surfer Girl" was released as a single) and July 15, 1966. In turn, Morgan agreed to grant Capitol a license for "Surfer Girl" from July 15, 1966, thereafter.

HITE MORGAN V. CAPITOL RECORDS, INC.

Case No. 860296, Superior Court of the State of California for the County of Los Angeles

On March 14, 1965, Hite Morgan sued Capitol Records in LA Superior Court for $60,000 arising from breach of contract, conversion of his property, and punitive damages for Capitol's use of the song "Surfin'" other than on the *Surfin' Safari* album (Capitol T-1808). Specifically, Morgan cited *Surfing's Greatest Hits* (Capitol T-1995) released in September 1963.

Morgan asserted he made a gratuitous grant of "Surfin'" October 1, 1962, to Capitol for the use of "Surfin'" for three years on the *Surfin' Safari* album (T-1808) and for no other usage. On October 19, 1962, Morgan extended the grant for as long as Capitol cared to use "Surfin'" on the *Surfin' Safari* album. Morgan asserted Capitol's use of "Surfin'" on Capitol T-1995 violated the terms of their agreement.

On May 14, 1965, Morgan filed his formal complaint with the court. On August 19, 1965, Capitol Records denied the allegations.

On March 7, 1966, the day the case went to trial before Judge Frederick W. Mahl, Jr., in LA Superior Court, Capitol Records amended their response by asserting Morgan had not objected when he accepted substantial copyright royalty payments for the use of "Surfin'" on *Surfin' Safari* (T-1808) and *Surfing's Greatest Hits* (T-1995) through the second quarter of 1965. They asserted he had, therefore, waived any right for an accounting or claim for damages relative to Capitol T-1995.

On April 11, 1966, Judge Mahl ruled Capitol had used the recording of "Surfin'" consistent with the agreement and that Morgan suffered no loss or damage, and was not entitled to an accounting from Capitol. Judge Mahl also ruled Capitol was entitled to recover its court costs from Morgan. Morgan would later argue that, implicit in its findings, the court affirmed he owned the recording of "Surfin'."

During this case, Hite Morgan was deposed on March 8, 1965. Many of his statements in this deposition would be used against him posthumously in litigation thirty years later.

He acknowledged he never had any contract for services with the Beach Boys as recording artists; he had no written agreement with the Beach Boys directly other than the noted September 15, 1961, Standard Songwriter's Contract; he had no written agreement with Murry Wilson other than the March 29, 1962, Letter of Intent and Agreement; the March 29, 1962, document was not an agreement with the Beach Boys; he never talked to or asked Murry Wilson or any member of the Beach Boys whether Murry had authority to represent them; he never talked about having the March 29, 1962, document approved by a court; and when the Beach Boys signed a recording contract with Capitol Records July 16, 1962, it extinguished any agreement with him.

Bruce Morgan v. Joseph Saraceno

Case No. BC093327, Superior Court of the State of California for the County of Los Angeles

In 1993, Original Sound, the agent representing Bruce Morgan and Deck Records, asserted that many of the individuals and companies, domestic and international, responsible for unauthorized releases of the Hite Morgan recordings had received purported rights from Joseph Saraceno.

On November 17, 1993, Morgan brought suit against Saraceno and asserted breach of contract, unfair competition, conspiracy to commit fraud, and unlawfully exploiting, and providing the unlawful means and methods to allow others to unlawfully exploit Deck Records' eight Beach Boys' recordings. Saraceno filed a cross complaint for breach of implied warranty, fraud, and breach of the covenant of good faith and fair dealing. He asserted Hite Morgan never owned the rights to the recordings and that, in fact, the Beach Boys owned the recordings; any contract between Hite Morgan and the Beach Boys was void since four of the band members were minors at the time; and Bruce Morgan was not the successor in interest to Hite and Dorinda Morgan.

On June 22, 1995, while *Morgan v. Saraceno* was pending, Morgan wrote Raphael ("Ray") Tisdale, director of business affairs at Capitol Records, and requested the company's assistance because record pirates were not only pirating the Morgan masters, but were also representing certain recordings as being by the Beach Boys, which they were not. Neither Capitol Records nor BRI responded.

On July 20, 1998, the trial of *Morgan v. Saraceno* began in LA Superior Court before the Honorable Machlin Fleming. During the course of the trial, Elliott Lott, president of BRI, testified, "I didn't know which songs in particular, but I knew years ago there was a position by Hite Morgan's estate they owned some masters." BRI argued that ownership of the physical masters was of no significance and not in dispute. Ray Tisdale testified he was aware of Morgan's claim of ownership of the recordings and that Capitol never asserted a position contrary to Morgan's ownership. Al Schlesinger, Hite Morgan's attorney, via his September 27, 1996 deposition, testified that at no time during 1962 to 1966 when he represented the Beach Boys, or up to the present time, was he aware of any claim adverse to Hite Morgan's ownership of the recordings.

On September 2, 1998, Judge Fleming refuted all of Saraceno's claims and found Morgan owned the recordings from inception. Morgan estimated he spent $450,000 in legal fees obtaining judgments in his favor and injunctions to clear the market of infringers.

Morgan v. San Juan Record Company

Case No. 96–1916, United States District Court for the Central District of California

On May 28, 1996, while *Morgan v. Saraceno* was ongoing, Morgan and four other plaintiffs initiated legal action against San Juan Record Company and ten other defendants, including Jay Chernow, for copyright infringement for the unauthorized use of certain recordings including eight Hite Morgan recordings ("Lavender" was not included). The other four plaintiffs were Chancellor Records, Del-Fi Records, Post Records, and Original Sound Record Company, representing a total of twenty recordings by Fabian, Frankie Avalon, Ritchie Valens, the Skyliners, and the Crests.

In the course of the trial, Morgan discovered that Saraceno and his Dana Music, on behalf of the San Juan Music Group, had sued Charly Music International in Denmark on November 25, 1987, over its unauthorized use of the Hite Morgan recordings.

On January 28, 1999, after three years of litigation, the court issued a judgment and permanent injunction against San Juan Music Group and the other defendants. The court found Morgan was the owner of the recordings.

Bruce Morgan v. Brian Wilson, Brothers Records, Inc., Al Jardine, and Bradley S. Elliott

Case No. CV-00–13312, United States District Court for the Central District of California
Case No. 06–55825, United States Court of Appeals for the Ninth Circuit

Brother Records, Inc. v. Bradley S. Elliott and Bruce Morgan

Case No. CV-00–13314, United States District Court for the Central District of California
Case No. 06–56401, United States Court of Appeals for the Ninth Circuit

On March 6, 2000, Original Sound Record Company, the agent for Bruce Morgan and Deck Records, licensed the recordings to Brad Elliott and his Surfs Up! Records. Elliott planned to release a 2-CD set called *First Wave: The Complete Hite Morgan Sessions* that would deliver what its title promised—every take from the Morgan home demo session, both World Pacific Studio sessions, and the Stereo Masters session, nearly two hours of music and studio chatter. To raise the $10,000 licensing fee, Elliott solicited investments from several fans and collectors. He promised full restitution and a fair return on their investment. Having authored a discography of the band and penned the liner notes for several collections on Capitol Records, Elliott had considerable credibility in the Beach Boys fan community. Several people were eager to participate in the project and invested thousands of dollars. With the license secured, Elliott contacted audio engineer Steve Hoffman to assemble and remaster the recordings.

By July 2000, Elliott began promoting *First Wave* on his website and various on-line message boards. It would sell for thirty dollars and advanced orders would be numbered in a limited edition and, if requested, autographed by him. Later, the set would be sold and distributed by the LA–based Collector's Choice Music.

When *Lost & Found* was released a decade earlier, Bruce Morgan was concerned the
Beach Boys might take legal action against DCC Compact Classics or himself. Despite a
high-level marketing campaign and healthy sales, Brother Records, Inc., never objected to
Lost & Found. Ironically, this may have created an illusory sense of security for an enterprising fan like Elliott to license and release all of the Morgan recordings. When he marketed *First Wave*, something, perhaps the worrisome terms "outtakes" and "studio chatter,"
struck a nerve at Brother Records.

On August 18, 2000, Edwin F. McPherson of the LA law firm McPherson & Kalman-
sohn representing BRI advised Elliott that BRI intended to file suit to stop him from using
the trademark and tradename "The Beach Boys" and exploiting the group's early recordings.
McPherson demanded Elliott turn over any copies of the 2-CD set, financial documents
pertaining to its sale, and any documentation and licensing agreements by which he claimed
to have the right to exploit the recordings. McPherson further advised Elliott he would
have to make restitution once BRI had an opportunity to review the financial information.
Two days later, McPherson sent a similar letter to Bruce Morgan's attorney.

Each of the parties—Brother Records, Inc., Bruce Morgan, and Brad Elliott—communicated with one another through their attorneys. However, for ease of reference, I use
the names BRI, Morgan, and Elliott when referencing their correspondence. Over the next
four months, from August through December 2000, a legal chess game played out. We'll
examine the maneuvering, the lawsuits, the appeals, and the final resolution.

On August 22, 2000, Elliott advised BRI he had licensed the recordings from Morgan
and Morgan agreed to indemnify him from any lawsuits by the Beach Boys for the wrongful
exploitation of the recordings. That same day, BRI advised Morgan to cease and desist from
using the trademark and tradename "The Beach Boys" or any of the group's early recordings,
and advised Elliott that Morgan did not have the right to license the recordings.

On August 28, Elliott advised BRI that, pending legal resolution, he had temporarily
stopped advertising *First Wave* and had put its manufacturing on hold. On that same date,
BRI asked Elliott for documentation of his purported right to exploit the recordings.

On or about August 31, Morgan advised BRI that, in previous lawsuits, the court and
judges had always found he had a superior right to exploit certain recordings by the Beach
Boys. On September 5, BRI advised Morgan the current suit was not about the same recordings, and the Beach Boys had not been party to any of his previous lawsuits.

On November 21, BRI advised Elliott to confirm his agreement not to exploit the
recordings until the legal issues were resolved and to contact them if he was not going to
abide by the agreement.

On December 5, Morgan advised BRI he had the right to exploit the recordings and
had granted permission to Elliott to exploit the recordings. On or about December 6, Elliott
advised BRI it had not provided proof Morgan did not have the right to exploit the recordings. On December 6, BRI again wrote Morgan requesting documentation of his right to
license the recordings. On the same day, BRI again wrote Elliott requesting whether he
intended to abide by the agreement. BRI did not get a response from Elliott.

On December 17, BRI intercepted an email from Elliott indicating he intended to
commence sale of *First Wave* on December 20. On December 19, BRI filed in United States
District Court for a temporary restraining order against Bradley S. Elliott (Surfs Up!
Records) and Bruce Morgan (Deck Records) and requested an injunction to prevent the

release of any Hite Morgan recordings except those already released on *Lost & Found* in 1991.

On December 20, the District Court issued a temporary restraining order against Elliott and Morgan. That same day, in anticipation of BRI's lawsuit, Morgan filed a lawsuit against Brian Wilson, Mike Love, Alan Jardine, and BRI requesting (1) declaratory relief; and asserting (2) slander of title; (3) interference with contractual relations; and (4) unjust enrichment.

Within two hours, BRI filed a $340 million lawsuit against Elliott and Morgan claiming: (1) trademark infringement; (2) unfair competition; (3) violation of California Civil Code 980(a)(2); (4) violation of right of publicity; (5) misappropriation of name and likeness (Civil Code 3344) with punitive damages; (6) accounting; (7) preliminary and permanent injunction; and (8) requesting declaratory relief.

On January 8, 2001, the Honorable Harry L. Hupp granted BRI a preliminary injunction to prevent Elliott from publishing or licensing previously unpublished material, including outtakes, studio chatter, or other unpublished portions of the original recordings. Judge Hupp also granted BRI a preliminary injunction against Morgan from publishing or licensing the publication and sale of any musical performances of the Beach Boys except for certain recordings previously released or licensed by Deck Records. Judge Hupp wrote, "The issues on this motion require consideration at two levels. The first is whether Elliott has any rights whatever to publish any of the Beach Boys' material. A sub-issue is whether, if so, he has the right to publish previously unpublished material recorded by Hite Morgan at recording sessions but never released or intended to be released. The second level is whether Hite Morgan or Deck Records ever obtained rights to publish and sell certain early recordings of the Beach Boys, which he, and since his death, his son and heir has apparently been doing for thirty-eight years without challenge from plaintiff (BRI)."[25]

On March 12, Morgan and Elliott responded to BRI's complaint and demanded a jury trial. On April 30, the court consolidated the two cases. Elliott's position was simple—he asserted he had legally licensed the recordings from Morgan. BRI argued Morgan did not have the right to license the recordings to Elliott or, for that matter, anyone. Morgan asserted he did have the right to license the recordings and had done so numerous times over the last thirty-eight years without BRI ever objecting. During the course of the trial the court referred to the original nine Hite Morgan recordings released on *Lost & Found* as "The 1962 Recordings" and any alternate takes of these songs and unreleased studio chatter as "The 2000 Outtakes."

Over the next few years, the case chugged along as both sides presented their arguments and counter arguments. At the heart of the trial were exhaustive discussions of the documents pertaining to the recordings—the September 15, 1961, Standard Songwriter's Contract for "Surfin'" signed by Mike, Brian, and Murry as Brian's guardian; the December 5, 1961, purported lease of "Surfin'" and "Luau" from Hite Morgan to Bob Dix of Candix Enterprises, Inc.; the January 29, 1962, Standard Songwriter's Contract for "Surfin' Safari" signed by Mike, Brian, and Murry as Brian's guardian; the January 29, 1962, Standard Songwriter's Contract for "Surfer Girl" signed by Brian and Murry as Brian's guardian; the February 8, 1962, American Federation of Musicians contract for the second World Pacific Studio session; the March 29, 1962, Letter of Intent and Agreement from Murry Wilson to Hite Morgan; the April 17, 1962, letter from Averill Pasarow, the Beach Boys' attorney, to Alfred Schlesinger, Hite Morgan's attorney, disavowing the March 29, 1962, agreement because at the time the Beach Boys recorded the songs they were all minors and none of them formally conveyed any rights in and to their respective performances to Morgan; the May 24, 1962, interim recording contract Murry Wilson signed with Capitol Records on behalf of the Beach Boys; the June 18, 1962, letter from Alfred Schlesinger, Hite Morgan's attorney, to Averill Pasarow, the Beach Boys' attorney, in which Schlesinger opined it was doubtful the purported lease, dated December 5, 1961, was enforceable.

On February 6, 2002, BRI contacted Averill Pasarow and was told Pasarow had obtained an order from LA Superior Court disaffirming the March 29, 1962, agreement. Pasarow further told BRI that Alfred Schlesinger represented Morgan in connection with the disaffirmance and that Morgan and Schlesinger had met with Pasarow at the time and acknowledged the March 29, 1962, agreement was unenforceable. Bruce Morgan asserted that a search of the LA Superior Court records and archives and Averill Pasarow's files failed to produce any proof of the disaffirmance. Sometime after he helped negotiate the Beach Boys' July 16, 1962, recording contract with Capitol Records, Pasarow had a disagreement with Murry and Brian, and was fired. Murry then hired Schlesinger, Hite Morgan's former attorney.

On January 27, 2004, after taking the matter into consideration, but before making a final ruling, Judge Hupp suffered a massive stroke and passed away at home.

On May 27, 2004, the cases were reassigned to the Honorable Consuelo B. Marshall, who issued all of the subsequent summary judgment rulings.

On June 16, 2004, Judge Marshall ruled on three key issues:

The March 1962 Agreement. The court found the March 1962 agreement signed by Hite Morgan and Murry Wilson conveyed nothing to Hite and Dorinda Morgan. There was no grant of a trademark, copyright, license, or conveyance of any right in the recordings. The signing by the Beach Boys of a recording contract with Capitol Records July 16, 1962, later confirmed by the Superior Court, was a disaffirmance of the March 1962 Agreement. This was understood as such by Hite Morgan as shown by his sworn testimony in his separate suit against Capitol Records in 1965. Hite Morgan understood his contract ended with the signing of the Capitol contract and acted in accord with that understanding. He never again claimed to be the Beach Boys' producer, recorder, or promoter thereafter.

Hence, the court ruled the signing of the Capitol contract was a disaffirmance of any contract rights granted by the March 1962 Agreement.

The 1962 Recordings. The court found infringement because Morgan had no ownership interest or entitlement to the 1962 Recordings and the 2000 Outtakes. However, the court found BRI guilty of laches (the legal doctrine that a legal right or claim will not be enforced if a long delay in asserting that right or claim has hurt the opponent as a sort of legal ambush) in attempting to prevent the use of "The Beach Boys" trademark in connection with Deck Records' distribution of the 1962 recordings. The court found the Morgans could only acquire rights to the 1962 recordings by agreement from the Beach Boys for which there is no supporting evidence. However, since the 1960s, Deck Records had sold reproductions of the 1962 recordings and licensed others to do so without protest by the Beach Boys or Brother Records. The court also ruled that because Hite and Dorinda Morgan, and later Bruce Morgan, had invested so much time and money over the years that it would now be inequitable by reason of laches to enforce the trademark against their use in distributing the 1962 recordings.

Judge Marshall adopted the late Judge Hupp's position that the Pasarow letter was supportive of laches. Hupp wrote, "While the document does claim the right of the Beach Boys to disaffirm any contract created by the March 29, 1962, letter, it does not disaffirm. It merely says that the March 29, 1962, letter is voidable (which it was) but does not expressly say that it is disaffirmed! So the Pasarow letter is not a disaffirmance, but merely a claim of right to do so. But it is good evidence of laches. Here is the attorney for the Beach Boys expressing as early as April 1962, knowledge that Hite Morgan claims a right in the recordings which he claims he can license to others, and having this knowledge, nothing is done about it for 40 years!" Hence, the court denied BRI's trademark claim since the 2000 lawsuit was the first legal action BRI had taken against Morgan in the thirty-eight years since the recordings were made in 1962.

Hence, the court granted in favor of Morgan as to the 1962 Recordings.

The 2000 Outtakes. As for the 2000 Outtakes, the court ruled in favor of BRI and found that even if the Beach Boys expected their finished records to be played or marketed, there was no expectation their rehearsal sessions and studio chatter would ever be released. The court ruled that laches did not apply to the 2000 Outtakes since those recordings had never before been published and were never expected to be published. Thus, there was no "sitting on their rights" by the Beach Boys or BRI in not protesting earlier about the publication of this material and Morgan had no right to publish the 2000 Outtakes.

Hence, the court found in favor of BRI on the trademark infringement claim as to the 2000 Outtakes.

On December 7, 2005, the district court issued an Order to Show Cause, a procedure in which the court asked each of the parties what impact the June 16, 2004, motion for summary judgment had on their remaining claims. The parties filed their responses. On December 16, Morgan claimed the 2004 judgment was ambiguous and sought clarification or modification.

On January 3, 2006, Morgan filed a motion for judgment against BRI or, in the alternative, a trial on laches. On April 17, the district court ruled all other claims asserted by BRI were also barred by the laches defense and a final judgment was entered April 28.

On June 13, 2006, Morgan filed for BRI to pay $510,000 for his attorney's fees and costs which the court granted August 22 and BRI appealed September 22.

On July 25, 2007, BRI filed an appeal in the United States Court of Appeals for the Ninth Circuit claiming the district court erred in granting summary judgment in favor of Morgan and dismissing BRI's claims. Morgan requested the appellate court affirm the district court's dismissal of BRI's claims and find he was the owner of the recordings.

On May 1, 2008, the appellate court affirmed that: (1) BRI had standing to bring its claims; (2) the district court did not abuse its discretion in applying laches to bar BRI's claims for damages. In light of the royalty checks, public record sales and various lawsuits, the district court correctly concluded that BRI knew or should have known of Morgan's infringement long ago. Morgan has suffered significant evidentiary prejudice; several major witnesses have died and important documents have been lost during BRI's extremely long period of silence. In light of the public sales and royalty checks, Morgan did not fraudulently conceal his use of the recordings. In light of the ineffective March 29, 1962, agreement to transfer rights and Morgan's lawsuits against other infringers, Morgan was not a willful infringer; and (3) the district court did not err in holding that Morgan does not have the right to exploit the 2000 Outtakes. Laches works to equitably limit BRI's enforcement of it rights, not to transfer them. The March 29, 1962, letter was ineffective as a transfer of rights for the reasons given by the district court.

The appellate court reversed and remanded for further proceeding its finding that the district court abused its discretion by applying laches to bar BRI's request for injunctive relief. Morgan failed to demonstrate substantial investment made in reliance upon BRI's laxity that was not recovered through infringing sales.

On May 13, 2008, the appellate court granted Morgan's request for more time to file a petition for rehearing or modification of the May 1 decision. He filed that petition June 2 and the court denied it July 2. On July 10, the appellate court ruled the May 1 judgment took effect that date.

On March 16, 2009, the appellate court ruled that all pending motions were denied. BRI's motion for attorney fees on appeal was denied. BRI's motion to determine the prevailing party before the district court was denied. Morgan's motion for sanctions and fees was denied. Morgan's request to take judicial notice and motion to strike portions of BRI's briefs was also denied.

In a final message to both parties, one that hinted at more than a little judicial frustration, the court concluded, "This case is over. No further motions of any kind from any party will be entertained."[26]

On April 9, 2009, twenty-four days after the trial ended, Bruce Morgan sold the copyrights to the Beach Boys' Hite Morgan recordings to LA-based BUG Music, Inc., which was purchased in October 2011 by BMG Rights Management, the music publishing venture and now wholly owned subsidiary of Bertelsmann, the international media conglomerate headquartered in Gutersloh, Germany.

Bruce Morgan, however, still owns the actual tapes.

Appendix 1

The Beach Boys' Personal
Appearances, 1961–1963

Date	Venue	Details of Interest

December 23, 1961	Rendezvous Ballroom
	608 East Ocean Front
	between Palm and
	  Washington Streets
	Balboa Peninsula
	Newport Beach, CA
		Played two songs during intermission at Dick Dale and
		  the Del-Tones' final Rendezvous show.

December 30, 1961	*P.O.P. Dance Party* hosted by Bob Eubanks Aragon Ballroom (Pacific Ocean Park Pavilion) Santa Monica, CA	6:00 p.m. to 7:00 p.m. KTLA-TV channel 5. Their first appearance on local television.
December 31, 1961	Ritchie Valens Memorial Dance and Show Municipal Auditorium 270 East Seaside Boulevard Long Beach, CA	With the Ike and Tina Turner Revue, the Carlos Brothers, the Rivingtons, and possibly others.
January 6, 1962	*P.O.P. Dance Party* hosted by Bob Eubanks Municipal Auditorium 270 East Seaside Boulevard Long Beach, CA	8:00 p.m. to 11:00 p.m. Unconfirmed

This was the first of five *Dance Party* shows Bob Eubanks hosted at the Long Beach Municipal Auditorium. The first hour of each three-hour show was taped for broadcast the following Saturday. The January 6 *Long Beach Press-Telegram* noted the guests included the Four Cal-Quettes, Don Julian and the Meadow Larks, Vince Howard, Johnny Burnette, and the Bel Aires (a misspelling of Belairs). Paul Johnson of the Belairs recalled appearing on *Dance Party* with the Beach Boys, but does not recall the other artists listed who, perhaps, were among the artists who appeared following the taping.

January 21, 1962

The January 27, 1962, *San Bernardino County Sun*, had a column by Peggy Johnson entitled "Cruising Around" in which she discussed local teens' recent activities. Don Morgan of San Bernardino High School and Carole Baldwin of Pacific High School reported they spent Sunday, January 21, 1962, "listening to the Beach Boys." It is uncertain if they meant listening to them in person or listening to their record of "Surfin'."

January 25, 1962	Surf Nite Angeles Mesa Presbyterian	8:00 p.m. Their earliest known concert ticket is for this show.

Date	Venue	Details of Interest
	Church, 3751 West 54th Street at Mullen Avenue View Park-Windsor Hills, CA	
January 26, 1962	Black Friday Cafeteria Hawthorne High School 4859 W. El Segundo Boulevard Hawthorne, CA	7:00 a.m. breakfast Black Friday was the day report cards were sent home.
February 3, 1962	*P.O.P. Dance Party* hosted by Bob Eubanks Municipal Auditorium 270 East Seaside Boulevard Long Beach, CA	8:00 p.m. to 11:00 p.m. Unconfirmed Paul Johnson of the Belairs recalled appearing on *Dance Party* with the Beach Boys, Ketty Lester, and the Lettermen. During the car ride home, the Boys sang "Surfer Girl" a cappella and told Johnson it would be recorded the following week. "Surfer Girl" was recorded February 8, 1962.
February 10, 1962	*P.O.P. Dance Party* hosted by Bob Eubanks Municipal Auditorium 270 East Seaside Boulevard Long Beach, CA	8:00 p.m. to 11:00 p.m. Unconfirmed Ray Hunt of the Surfmen recalled appearing on *Dance Party* with the Beach Boys, James Darren, and others. This is likely the *Dance Party* held February 10 and advertised in the February 8 *Long Beach Press-Telegram*.
February 16, 1962	KRLA Friday Night Dance Rainbow Gardens 150 East Monterey Avenue Pomona, CA	Emceed by KRLA disc jockey Bob Eubanks with the Mixtures as the house band. Unconfirmed date.
February 19, 1962	Academy Fine Arts Theatre 3721 University Avenue San Diego, CA	During intermission of two showings of the film *Surf Crazy* at 7:00 p.m. and 9:00 p.m.
February 20, 1962	Academy Fine Arts Theatre 3721 University Avenue San Diego, CA	During intermission of two showings of the film *Surf Crazy* at 7:00 p.m. and 9:00 p.m.
c. January/February 1962	A record store owned by Shane Wilder. Thousand Oaks, CA	Wilder recalled they played shortly after "Surfin'" was released.
c. February/March 1962	Rainbow Gardens 150 East Monterey Avenue Pomona, CA	They may have played other Friday evenings there with the Mixtures.
c. February/March 1962	Lueders Park Community Center 1500 East Rosecrans Avenue Compton, CA	With the Mixtures.
March 2, 1962	Auditorium Millikan High School 2800 Snowden Avenue Long Beach, CA	During the 8:00 p.m. screening of the film *Surf's Up*

Date	Venue	Details of Interest
March 7, 1962	Auditorium Morningside High School 10500 South Yukon Avenue Inglewood, CA	They played two lunch period shows to fulfill a campaign pledge Steve Love, Mike's younger brother, made that January when he ran for freshman class president. He was elected and took office February 9.
March 10, 1962	Mardi Gras Costume Ball Bel-Air Bay Club 16800 Pacific Coast Highway Pacific Palisades, CA	8:00 p.m.
March 12–16, 1962	Prom Week Torrance High School 2200 West Carson Street Torrance, CA	They played a thirty minute show one day during this week-long fundraiser for the prom.
March 16, 1962	Monica Hotel 1725 Ocean Front Santa Monica, CA	8:00 p.m. to midnight with the Vibrants and the Belairs.
March 17, 1962	Monica Hotel 1725 Ocean Front Santa Monica, CA	8:00 p.m. to midnight with the Vibrants and the Belairs.
March 18, 1962	Monica Hotel 1725 Ocean Front Santa Monica, CA	1:00 p.m. to 5:00 p.m. with the Vibrants and the Belairs.
March 23, 1962	47th National Orange Show Orange Blossom Room of the Orange Show Restaurant National Orange Show Fairgrounds 689 South E Street at West Mill Street San Bernardino, CA	4:00 p.m. The "Citrus Centennial" ran March 15–25. The Beach Boys may have played March 23 at 4:00 p.m. as a local newspaper reported it was Kids Day and a teen hop was held. The fair inspired Brian and Gary Usher to write "County Fair."
March 23, 1962	The Giles Memorial Fund Variety Revue Auditorium Mira Costa High School 1401 Artesia Boulevard Manhattan Beach, CA	8:15 p.m. With Spencer and Allred, Twin Tones, and Tommy Terry. A fundraiser for Timothy J. Giles, a Manhattan Beach police officer killed in the line of duty.
March 24, 1962	Hi-Teen Easter Fashion Show The Harris Company 4th Floor Auditorium West 3rd and North E Streets San Bernardino, CA	1:30 p.m.

The Harris Company, an upscale department store, held teen fashion shows on March 24 and May 12, 1962. KMEN disc jockey William F. Williams recalled the station arranged a concert to accompany the fashion show. It is unclear whether the Beach Boys appeared March 24 or May 12 (see that entry). Williams recalled Murry Wilson begged him to let the Beach Boys be the opening act. March 24 seems more likely as securing an appearance then would have been more urgent.

Date	*Venue*	*Details of Interest*
March 24, 1962	Third Annual Surf-O-Rama Civic Auditorium Santa Monica, CA	1:00 p.m. to 10:30 p.m. This surfing industry trade show was held March 23 and 24.
March 24, 1962	Athletic Field Newport Harbor High School 600 Irvine Avenue Newport, CA	8:00 p.m. with the Vibrants. Murry got permission from Bill Meecham, the Vibrants' manager, for the Boys to appear at this sparsely attended show. Only Murry, Mike, Dennis, and Carl showed up. They borrowed the Vibrants' instruments and played a few songs.
March 31, 1962	National Guard Armory John Galvin Park 1001 North Grove Avenue Ontario, CA	8:00 p.m. to midnight with the Vibrants. Another show for which Murry asked Bill Meecham if the Beach Boys could play a few songs.
c. January–March, 1962	Venue unknown Riverside, CA	A possible venue is the Riverside Armory, 2501 Fairmount Boulevard.
April 18, 1962	Bal-Week Easter Show Auditorium Newport Harbor High School 600 Irvine Avenue Newport Beach, CA	7:00 p.m. with the Belairs, the Vibrants, Fabulous Biscaines, and Dodie and Dee Dee.
April 20, 1962	Easter Week Stomp Auditorium Redondo Union High School 1525 Aviation Boulevard Redondo Beach, CA	With the Belairs, the Vibrants, and Dodie and Dee Dee. Originally scheduled at Mira Costa High School.
April 21, 1962	Easter Week Stomp Auditorium Redondo Union High School 1525 Aviation Boulevard Redondo Beach, CA	With the Belairs, the Vibrants, and Dodie and Dee Dee. Originally scheduled at Mira Costa High School.
May 4, 1962	Inglewood Women's Club 325 North Hillcrest Boulevard Inglewood, CA	8:00 p.m. to midnight
May 11, 1962	Community Fair El Camino Community College 16007 Crenshaw Boulevard Torrance, CA	The fair was part of Camino Welfare Week.
May 12, 1962	"Fantasy in Fashion" Campus Deb Jamboree Time California Theater 562 West 4th Street San Bernardino, CA	A 9:00 a.m. debutante fashion show sponsored by the Harris Company. Although the Beach Boys are not listed, the May 12 *San Bernardino County Sun* promised "surprise guest stars with an autograph session afterwards in Harris' new Record Shop."
June 2, 1962	Azusa Teen Club Azusa Recreation Center	Their first appearance there.

Date	Venue	Details of Interest
	320 North Orange Avenue Azusa, CA	
June 9 or 16, 1962	Roller Gardens Buckaroo Road Wagon Wheel Junction Oxnard, CA	They played there on a Saturday shortly after "Surfin' Safari" was released June 4.
c. Spring/early Summer 1962	A function sponsored by the Sigma Chi fraternity at the University of Southern California (USC) Los Angeles, CA	The event at which Brian met Bob Norberg and Cheryl Pomeroy, a couple performing as Bob and Sheri.
July 3, 1962	Cafeteria Dykstra Hall University of California Los Angeles (UCLA) Los Angeles, CA	8:30 p.m. to midnight With Dante and the Evergreens, and Chris Montez. Emceed by KFWB disc jockey Roger Christian. The second of four concerts that summer sponsored by the Dykstra Hall Residents Association for which the Renegades were the house band. In 1964, the Renegades became the Sunrays and managed by Murry.

July 9, 1962

In a letter this date, Nick Venet told Murry to tell the group "they are doing a very good job at the record hops." Hence, it is likely there were additional personal appearances in June and early July 1962.

Date	Venue	Details of Interest
July 14, 1962	Diaper Derby Plaza Park 500 South C Street Sponsored by the Oxnard Downtown Merchants Association Oxnard, CA	With the Surfmen and an R&B vocal group. A live simulcast on KOXR from 10:30 a.m. to 2:30 p.m. from which a three-minute tape exists of Paul Johnson and the Beach Boys playing the final fifteen seconds of "Mr. Moto" followed by an interview with Brian.
July 14, 1962	Canteen Dance Hawthorne High School 4859 W. El Segundo Boulevard Hawthorne, CA	8:00 p.m.
July 18, 1962	Gable residence 416 Bethany Road Burbank, CA	Jodi Gable's sixteenth birthday party.
July 27, 1962	Azusa Teen Club Azusa Recreation Center 320 North Orange Avenue Azusa, CA	Filming for Dale Smallin's documentary *One Man's Challenge*.
July 28, 1962	Venue unknown San Bernardino, CA	This show was noted in a press release by David McClellan, the group's director of publicity.
July 29, 1962	The Dance Pavilion Lake Arrowhead, CA	With the Tornadoes, whose "Bustin' Surfboards" reached #2 on KFWB that October.

Date	Venue	Details of Interest
July 31, 1962	*Parade of Hits* KCOP-TV channel 13 915 North La Brea Avenue Los Angeles, CA	8:00 p.m. Hosted by KRLA disc jockey Dick Moreland, this half hour weekly music show featured the Mixtures as the house band with guest artists performing their Top 40 hits.
August 4, 1962	Azusa Teen Club Azusa Recreation Center 320 North Orange Avenue Azusa, CA	
August 19, 1962	The Palladium 6215 West Sunset Boulevard Hollywood, CA	8:00 p.m. to 1:00 a.m. Opened for Dick Dale and the Del-Tones.
August 20, 1962	Back-to-School Jam Teen Debutante Fashion Show The Broadway 401 South Broadway Los Angeles, CA	2:30 p.m. With Kathy Linden and the Genteels. They played in The Terrace, a rooftop restaurant in this chain of department stores. The shows were hosted by KFWB disc jockeys.
August 20, 1962	The Broadway Del Amo Mall Torrance, CA	7:30 p.m. With Bobby Rydell.
August 21, 1962	The Broadway West Covina Plaza West Covina, CA	2:30 p.m. This store opened August 6, 1962.
August 21, 1962	The Broadway Colorado Boulevard Pasadena, CA	7:30 p.m.
August 22, 1962	The Broadway Anaheim Plaza Orange County Anaheim, CA	2:30 p.m. David Marks's fourteenth birthday.
August 22, 1962	The Broadway Whittier Center Whittier, CA	7:30 p.m.
August 23, 1962	The Broadway Westchester Shopping Center 8739 Sepulveda Boulevard North Hills, CA	2:30 p.m.
August 23, 1962	The Broadway Crenshaw Plaza Baldwin Hills, CA	7:30 p.m.
August 24, 1962	The Broadway Los Altos Plaza Long Beach, CA	2:30 p.m. Emceed by KFWB disc jockey B. Mitchell Reed.

Date	Venue	Details of Interest
August 25, 1962	The Broadway 1645 Vine Street Hollywood, CA	10:30 a.m.
August 25, 1962	The Broadway Panorama Mall Panorama City, CA	3:30 p.m.
August 25, 1962	Reseda Jubilee Reseda, CA	1:00 p.m. to 10:00 p.m. With Jan & Dean. Emceed by KFWB disc jockey Gene Weed. "Surfin' Safari" hit #1 on KRLA and KFWB that weekend.
August 26, 1962	Pandora's Box 8118 Sunset Boulevard Los Angeles, CA	9:00 p.m., 10:30 p.m., and midnight.
August 27, 1962	Pandora's Box 8118 Sunset Boulevard Los Angeles, CA	9:00 p.m., 10:30 p.m., and midnight.
August 28, 1962	Pandora's Box 8118 Sunset Boulevard Los Angeles, CA	9:00 p.m., 10:30 p.m., and midnight.
August 29, 1962	Pandora's Box 8118 Sunset Boulevard Los Angeles, CA	9:00 p.m., 10:30 p.m., and midnight.
August 30, 1962	Pandora's Box 8118 Sunset Boulevard Los Angeles, CA	9:00 p.m., 10:30 p.m., and midnight.
c. Summer 1962	Private Party for Laurie Jean Loveton 440 South McCadden Place Hancock Park Los Angeles, CA	Radio and television producer John W. Loveton hired the Beach Boys to play a private party for his daughter who graduated from the Marlborough School on June 7, 1962.
c. Summer 1962	First Annual KMAK McKinley Avenue Festival of the Water KMAK radio station rooftop 2020 East McKinley Avenue Fresno, CA	KMAK staged this event after street construction disrupted the station's water supply.
c. Summer 1962	Cinnamon Cinder 11345 Ventura Boulevard Studio City, CA	KRLA disc jockey Bob Eubanks opened this teen club in July 1962.
September 2, 1962	Victoria Melanie Berle's 17th birthday party 1011 North Crescent Drive Beverly Hills, CA	Afternoon Victoria was the adopted daughter of Milton Berle and Joyce Mathews.

Date	*Venue*	*Details of Interest*
September 2, 1962	Pandora's Box 8118 Sunset Boulevard Los Angeles, CA	Evening
September 9, 1962	Pandora's Box 8118 Sunset Boulevard Los Angeles, CA	Evening

September 14, 1962	The Howdy Hop
	Cafeteria
	Hawthorne High School
	4859 W. El Segundo
	  Boulevard
	Hawthorne, CA
		An annual event at which students greeted incoming
		  freshmen with "Howdy!"

September 14, 1962	Surfers Ball Morgan Hall 835 Locust Avenue Long Beach, CA	8:00 p.m. to midnight $1.50 With the Bonnavills, Lonnie Belmore, Russ Starman, and Dean Long.
September 15, 1962	Helen Lee Stillman's 16th Birthday Dinner Dance 327 Delfern Drive Holmby Hills Los Angeles, CA	7:00 p.m. to 11:00 p.m.

Because the party was written up in the September 16, 1962, *Los Angeles Times*, and the band mentioned briefly, it is presumed the party was September 15. But Helen Lee Stillman advised her birthday is May 9 and does not believe her parents held her party four months later. However, Barret H. Collins, her guest at the party, recalled flying to San Francisco a few days after the party to begin his freshman year that September at Menlo College.

September 22, 1962	Roller Gardens Buckaroo Road Wagon Wheel Junction Oxnard, CA	A Battle of the Bands with the Casuals and probably one other band.

September 27, 1962	The Row
	West 28th Street
	University of Southern
	  California (USC)
	Los Angeles, CA
		7:00 p.m. to 10:00 p.m. with the Marketts.
		A street dance held between the Theta Sigma Phi and
		  Kappa Kappa Gamma houses on fraternity row and
		  sponsored by the Inter-Fraternity Council to celebrate
		  the re-opening of the International Student House.

c. Summer/Fall 1962	Spanish Castle Ballroom Midway Seattle-Tacoma Highway Des Moines, WA	A Friday night.
c. Summer/Fall 1962	Party Line Pioneer Square 707 1st Avenue Seattle, WA	The following night they appeared at the Party Line owned by KJR disc jockey Pat O'Day.
October 4, 1962	Glendale Community College 1500 North Verdugo Road Glendale, CA	A school assembly.

Date	Venue	Details of Interest
October 27, 1962	30th Annual Y-Day at the Hollywood Bowl 2301 North Highland Avenue Los Angeles, CA	9:00 a.m. to noon. Emceed by Art Linkletter and sponsored by the Hollywood chapter of the YMCA and the Hollywood Advertising Club.

With Annette, Walter Brennan, the Castells, Chaino, Chuck Connors, Shelley Fabares, Dean Jones, Wink Martindale, Gil Peterson, Paul Petersen, Jimmie Rodgers, the Rivingtons, Soupy Sales, Billy Vaughn, Bobby Vee, Doodles Weaver, the First Division Marine Band, the Western Stuntmen from Corrigansville, and Muzzy Marcellino and his band.

Date	Venue	Details of Interest
October 27, 1962	Parade of Stars Show National Cystic Fibrosis Research Foundation Benefit Fox Theatre 1350 Market Street San Francisco, CA	They took a noon flight for this evening show. With Annette, John Armond, Joey Bishop, Scott Brady, Peter Brown, Ed Byrnes, Glen Campbell, Gary Clark, Jan Clayton, Beryl Davis, Muriel Dow, Tony Dow, James Drury, and Chad Everett.
October 28, 1962	Pandora's Box 8118 Sunset Boulevard Los Angeles, CA	Evening.
November 1, 1962	Grand Opening, Leonard's Discount Department Store Pacific Coast Highway and Crenshaw Boulevard Torrance, CA	7:00 p.m.
November 3, 1962	Leonard's Discount Department Store 12891 Harbor Boulevard Garden Grove, CA	2:00 p.m.
November 3, 1962	Bob Eubanks's *Pickwick Dance Party* Pickwick Recreation Center 921–1001 Riverside Drive Burbank, CA	With Valjean and Maureen Arthur. The Beach Boys lip synced "Ten Little Indians" during the 5:30 p.m. to 10:30 p.m. taping, one hour of which aired November 10 on KTLA-TV.
November 4, 1962	Pandora's Box 8118 Sunset Boulevard Los Angeles, CA	John and Judy played November 2 and 3.
November 11, 1962	Pandora's Box 8118 Sunset Boulevard Los Angeles, CA	John and Judy played November 9 and 10.
November 21, 1962	Thanksgiving Day Eve Dance and Stomp Biltmore Ballroom Hermosa Biltmore Hotel 1402 The Strand Hermosa Beach, CA	8:00 p.m. to 1:00 a.m. With the Journeymen, a South Bay surf band. Sponsored by the Alpha Omega fraternity.
November 30, 1962	Albert S. Goode Auditorium Kern County Fairgrounds	8:00 p.m. Sponsored by KWAC, Schick Razors, and Mayfair

Date	Venue	Details of Interest
	1142 South P Street Bakersfield, CA	Markets. With the Revlons, Cindy Malone, and Kenny and the Ho-Daddies.
c. November 1962	Gymnasium William Howard Taft High School 5461 Winnetka Avenue Woodland Hills, CA	They played for the school's activity card holders.
December 1, 1962	Fifth Annual Fund Drive Pacific Lodge Boys Home Woodland Hills, CA At the Fox Van Nuys Theatre 6417 Van Nuys Boulevard Van Nuys, CA	With Dorsey Burnette, the Crystalettes, Dobie Gray, Jimmie Haskell, the Lively Ones, the Mixtures, the Pastel Six, Cindy Malone, and Dick Michals. Emceed by Sam Riddle and Arlen Saunders of KRLA. The show was sponsored by The House of Sight and Sound, a record store, and radio station KMPC broadcast live from outside the store.
December 3, 1962	Rose Bowl Gala Pep Rally for the USC Trojans Bovard Auditorium University of Southern California (USC) 3551 Trousdale Parkway Los Angeles, CA	3:00 p.m. to 5:00p.m. With Ernest Borgnine, the Countrymen, Joe Flynn, the Golden Horse Revue from Disneyland, and Doodles Weaver. The event was covered by local radio and television.
December 6, 1962	Grand Opening Cinnamon Cinder 4401 Pacific Coast Highway Long Beach, CA	Bob Eubanks's second Cinnamon Cinder. With the Challengers, Jan & Dean, and Sandy Nelson.

December 24–
December 31, 1962

Murry Wilson recalled booking five concerts between Christmas Eve and New Year's Eve that grossed $26,684. Although the dates and venues have not been documented, a fan recalled seeing the band at the Earl Warren Show Grounds in Santa Barbara, CA, "around Christmas as it was cold and we wore heavy coats."

| December 27, 1962 | Surf Fair Civic Auditorium 1855 Main Street Santa Monica, CA | 10:00 a.m. to 10:00 p.m. (poster) 11:00 a.m. to 11:00 p.m. (handbill) |
| December 28, 1962 | Surf Fair Civic Auditorium 1855 Main Street Santa Monica, CA | 10:00 a.m. to 10:00 p.m. (poster) 11:00 a.m. to 11:00 p.m. (handbill) |

The Mid-Winter Surfing Championships and the World's Fair of Surfing were held December 24–30, 1962, at South Beach in Santa Monica. Top U.S. surfers competed for national honors December 27 and 28. Surf Fair was held in conjunction with the competition and featured the Beach Boys, the Shenandoahs, the Surfaris, the Surf-Tones, and the Surf Side Four, whose "Surf Fair" on the Hollywood indie label Cloister Records (6202), was the fair's official theme song.

| Late December 1962 | Venue unknown Santa Cruz, CA | This show was recalled by Ron Swallow, Carl's friend from Hawthorne High who often traveled with the band. |

Date	Venue	Details of Interest
January 2, 1963	Venue unknown California	Listed in Jo Ann Marks's journal as cited in *The Beach Boys in Concert, the Ultimate History of America's Band on Tour and Onstage* by Ian Rusten and Jon Stebbins (hereinafter referred to as Jo Ann Marks's journal).
January 9, 1963	Venue unknown California	Jo Ann Marks's journal.
c. January 26, 1963	Zeta Beta Tau The University of Arizona Party at the fraternity house 1501 East Drachman Street Tucson, AZ	The February 4, 1963, *Arizona Wildcat*, the school newspaper, reported the university suspended Zeta Beta Tau because of rowdy behavior and alcohol use at a recent event.
January 30, 1963	Navajo Civic Center Navajo Nation Fairgrounds Highway 264 Window Rock, AZ	The *Navajo Times* had no mention of this show.
February 2, 1963	Fourth Annual March of Dimes Benefit Show and Dance, Swing Auditorium, National Orange Show Fairgrounds, 689 South E Street at West Mill Street San Bernardino, CA	8:00 p.m. to midnight $1 donation. Presented by KFXM. Attendees were asked to "dance for the life of a child."

Featuring Dick Dale and the Del-Tones with Eddie Hodges and Wink Martindale, and Nino Tempo and April Stevens. Special Guest Stars the Beach Boys, Jan & Dean, the Rivingtons, the Moments, the Rumblers, the Hollywood Tornadoes, Dobie Gray, the Chantays, the Ribbons, the Sa-Shays, the Furys, the Rollers, and the "Swingin' Seven" KFXM disc jockeys.

Date	Venue	Details of Interest
February 9, 1963	Winternationals Rod & Custom Car Show Great Western Exhibit Center Santa Ana Freeway and Atlantic Boulevard Los Angeles, CA	2:00 p.m. Presented by the National Hot Rod Association.
February 10, 1963	Winternationals Rod & Custom Car Show Great Western Exhibit Center Santa Ana Freeway and Atlantic Boulevard Los Angeles, CA	2:00 p.m. Presented by the National Hot Rod Association.
February 15, 1963	Cupid's Capers Valentine's Day Dance Boy's gymnasium Hawthorne High School 4859 W. El Segundo Boulevard Hawthorne, CA	8:00 p.m. to midnight Mark Groseclose filled in for Dennis who had injured his legs in a car accident.

Date	Venue	Details of Interest
February 16, 1963	KFWB Charity Show LA Memorial Sports Arena 3939 South Figueroa Street Los Angeles, CA	8:45 p.m. 98-cents; with Mark Groseclose on drums. With Annette, Molly Bee, Bob B. Sox & the Blue Jeans, Fabian, the Cascades, Bobby Crawford, Dick Dale and the Del-Tones, Mickey Hargitay, Henry Mancini, Jayne Mansfield, Chris Montez, the Olympics, the Penguins, Paul Petersen, the Rivingtons, the Routers, April Stevens, Nino Tempo, Billy Vaughn, Bobby Vinton. Supported eight charities including Community Chest, LA County Heart Association, YMCA, Crippled Children's Society, American Red Cross, City of Hope, American Cancer Society, and United Cerebral Palsy Association.
c. late February 1963	Barnes Park Community Center 350 South McPherrin Avenue Monterey Park, CA	With Dick Dale and the Del-Tones. Emceed by KFWB disc jockey Roger Christian. Mark Groseclose on drums.
c. late February 1963	Mark Keppel High School 501 East Hellman Avenue Alhambra, CA	With Dick Dale and the Del-Tones. Mark Groseclose on drums.
c. February 1963	The Score Alhambra, CA	With the Rumblers.
March 8, 1963	Venue unknown California	Jo Ann Marks's journal.
March 10,1963	KMEN Party One Year Anniversary Party San Bernardino, CA	"Surfin' U.S.A." was #1 on KMEN's best of 1963.
March 15, 1963	Junior-Senior Prom Lennox High School Riviera Country Club Pacific Palisades, CA	Brian accompanied Judy Bowles to her junior prom.
March 16, 1963	Hemet Armory West Acacia Avenue Hemet, CA	
March 18, 1963	Venue unknown California	Jo Ann Marks's journal.
March 30, 1963	Grand Opening Denno's Record Shop Orange County Plaza 9709 Chapman Avenue at Brookhurst Street Garden Grove, CA	2:00 p.m. They played on a small riser in the parking lot and later autographed copies of *Surfin' U.S.A.* which had been released March 25.
c. early 1963	Cinnamon Cinder 11345 Ventura Boulevard Studio City, CA	Bob Eubanks told writer David Leaf the Beach Boys played the Cinder in early 1963.

Date	Venue	Details of Interest
	4401 Pacific Coast Highway Long Beach, CA	
April 5, 1963	Second Annual Teen-Age Fair Pickwick Recreation Center 921–1001 Riverside Drive Burbank, CA	5:30 p.m.
April 6, 1963	Grand Opening Build 'n Save 9920 Westminster Avenue at Brookhurst Street Garden Grove, CA	They played in the parking lot and later autographed copies of *Surfin' U.S.A.*
April 12, 1963	Rendezvous Ballroom 608 East Ocean Front Balboa Peninsula Newport Beach, CA	Despite being Friday night of Bal-Week, when thousands of teens descended upon Balboa for Easter vacation, Dennis Rose, lead guitarist for the Centurions, a surf septet from Costa Mesa, recalled this show was sparsely attended.
April 12, 1963	Newport Dunes Aquatic Park 1131 Back Bay Drive Newport Beach, CA	Perhaps frustrated by the poor turnout at the Rendezvous, the Beach Boys drove to the Newport Dunes where the Centurions had drawn a large outdoor crowd. While the Centurions were on break, the Boys ambled onstage, picked up their instruments, and began "Johnny B. Goode." The Centurions and their bouncer were none too pleased. An altercation ensued and the Boys retreated to the parking lot and left.
April 15, 1963	Venue unknown Bakersfield, CA	Jo Ann Marks's journal. This may be the show Mike recalled playing on the roof of radio station KAFY in Bakersfield.
April 19, 1963	Aragon Ballroom Pacific Ocean Park Santa Monica, CA	With Dick Delvy and the Challengers.
April 20, 1963	Felton Intermediate School 10417 Felton Avenue (now Felton Elementary School) Lennox, CA	7:00 p.m. to 9:30 p.m. $1 Donation Sponsored by the Parent-TeacherAssociation.
April 21, 1963	*The Red Skelton Hour* Studio / Stage 33 CBS Television City 800 Beverly Boulevard Los Angeles, CA	They lip synced "Surfin' U.S.A." and "The Things They Did Last Summer" at a taping for their first national television appearance airing September 24, 1963.

April 24, 1963

Brian recruited Al to fill in for him on their first tour of the Midwest. The group flew from Los Angeles to Chicago, rented a Chevrolet station wagon and U-Haul, and drove 315 miles west to West Des Moines, Iowa. Allowing for the four-hour flight, two-hour time difference, and nearly five-hour drive, it's likely they travelled the day before the tour began.

Date	Venue	Details of Interest
April 25, 1963	Val Air Ballroom 301 Ashworth Road West Des Moines, IA	
April 26, 1963	YWCA Teen Canteen 4990 East State Street Rockford, IL	8:00 p.m. to midnight
April 27, 1963	Danceland Ballroom 124 Third Street, NE Cedar Rapids, IA	
April 28, 1963	Terp Ballroom River and Bridge Streets Austin, MN	8:00 p.m. to midnight $1.65
April 30, 1963	Arkota Ballroom 510 South Phillips Avenue Sioux Falls, SD	8:30 p.m. to 12:30 a.m.
May 1, 1963	Roller Skating Rink Sports Center/Kiddieland Amusement Park 3833 East Harry Street Wichita, KS	8:00 p.m. to midnight
May 3, 1963	Twin City High School Night at Excelsior Amusement Park and Big Reggie's Danceland Lake Minnetonka Excelsior, MN	6:30 p.m. to 7:00 p.m. on an outdoor stage 8:30 p.m. in Danceland
May 4, 1963	Duluth Armory 1607 London Road Duluth, MN	With Chet Orr and the Rumbles
May 5, 1963	Surf of the Four Seasons (also known as Surf Ballroom) 460 North Shore Drive Clear Lake, IA	9:00 p.m. to 1:00 a.m. $1.65 Newspaper ads billed them as "Beach Boys and Their Rock 'n' Band" and their hit "Surf In U.S.A."
May 13, 1963	Venue unknown California	Jo Ann Marks's journal.
May 17, 1963	Venue unknown Santa Fe Springs, CA	Jo Ann Marks's journal.
May 19, 1963	Venue unknown Long Beach, CA	Jo Ann Marks's journal.
May 24, 1963	Southern California Hot Rod Show Los Angeles, CA	

Date	Venue	Details of Interest
May 24, 1963	Memorial Auditorium 1515 J Street Presented by El Camino High School Alumni, Class of 1963 Sacramento, CA	8:00 p.m. $1.75 Al filled in for Brian at this first Beach Boys concert produced by Fred Vail.
May 26, 1963	Inglewood High School 231 South Grevillea Street Inglewood, CA	
May 29, 1963	Buc Gymnasium Bellflower High School 15301 McNab Avenue Bellflower, CA	A late morning assembly for the entire school. It has been reported Jan & Dean shared the bill, but articles in *The Blade*, the school newspaper, on May 24 and June 7 do not mention the duo.
May 29, 1963	Venue unknown San Bernardino, CA	Evening With Jan & Dean.
May 30, 1963	Venue unknown San Francisco, CA	With Jan & Dean.
May 31, 1963	Venue unknown San Francisco, CA	With Jan & Dean.
May 31, 1963	Venue unknown Oxnard, CA	With Jan & Dean.
June 1, 1963	Rio Nido Dance Hall (also known as The Barn) on the Russian River Rio Nido, CA	Mike befriended Sharon Marie Esparza here and Brian later produced two Capitol singles for her as Sharon Marie.

June 5, 1963

It has been reported they played the Municipal Auditorium in Modesto on this date. However, there was no Municipal Auditorium in Modesto, then or now. At the time, most local rock 'n' roll shows were held at Stockton or Fresno. A fan recalled getting their autographs on *Surfin' U.S.A.* after a show at the Fresno Memorial Auditorium, 2425 Fresno Street, but could not recall the date.

Date	Venue	Details of Interest
June 7, 1963	Senior Breakfast, Cafeteria Hawthorne High School 4859 W. El Segundo Boulevard Hawthorne, CA	8:00 a.m. An annual event for the graduating senior class.
June 7, 1963	"Last Blast" Graduation Night Party East Bakersfield High School Campus Center Bakersfield College 1801 Panorama Drive Bakersfield, CA	10:30 p.m. Titans II 12:30 a.m. The Beach Boys 2:00 a.m. Cherry Creek Singers
June 7, 1963	"Neptune's Whing Ding" Graduation Night Party	12:00 a.m. Cherry Creek Singers

Date	Venue	Details of Interest
	Bakersfield High School	2:30 a.m.
	Albert S. Goode Auditorium	The Beach Boys
	Kern County Fairgrounds	KAFY disc jockey Al Anthony emceed. The Illusions
	1142 South P Street	and the Ivy Clansmen also played.
	Bakersfield, CA	
June 7, 1963	Graduation Night Party	3:30 a.m. (approx.)
	North High School	Cherry Creek Singers
	NOR Veterans Hall	4:30 a.m. (approx.)
	400 West Norris Road	The Beach Boys
	(NOR = north of the Kern	
	River)	
	Oildale, CA	

The graduating seniors of three Bakersfield area high schools pooled their money to book the Beach Boys and the Cherry Creek Singers, a folk quartet that also did comedy, for their graduation night parties. The Beach Boys, with Al filling in for Brian, played forty-five minute sets at each venue and autographed copies of *Surfin' U.S.A.* to be raffled. It has been reported Jan & Dean, Sam Cooke, and Lou Rawls shared the bill, but programs for two of the parties and interviews with attendees do not support this. David Marks recalled the Beach Boys once backed up Cooke and Rawls, but that concert was likely another event.

Date	Venue	Details of Interest
June 8, 1963	Venue unknown	Jo Ann Marks's journal. KUTY disc jockey Chris
	Palmdale, CA	Charles recalled a four-hour show and the band
		earned $500. Most likely a multiple artist show.
June 12, 1963	Venue unknown	Jo Ann Marks's journal. With Jan & Dean, and Jimmy
	Houston, TX	Reed. The venue may have been the Cinnamon
		Cinder that opened in February 1963.
June 14, 1963	Show of Stars	8:00 p.m.
	Civic Auditorium	$1.25 Teenagers, $1.45 General
	1314 South King Street	$2.20 Reserved and 90¢ Under 12
	Honolulu, HI	With Dee Dee Sharp, the Treniers, and Jackie
	Island of Oahu	DeShannon. Al filled in for Brian.
June 15, 1963	Show of Stars	2:30 p.m. matinee
	Civic Auditorium	7:00 p.m.
	1314 South King Street	8:45 p.m.
	Honolulu, HI	
	Island of Oahu	
June 16, 1963	Show of Stars	2:30 p.m. matinee
	Civic Auditorium	
	1314 South King Street	
	Honolulu, HI	
	Island of Oahu	
June 16, 1963	Show of Stars	
	Schoefield Barracks	
	Honolulu, HI	
	Island of Oahu	
June 17, 1963	Show of Stars	7:00 p.m. and 9:00 p.m.
	Hickam Air Force Base	
	Memorial Theater	
	Honolulu, HI	
	Island of Oahu	

Date	Venue	Details of Interest
June 18, 1963	Show of Stars Barber's Point Beach Park Island of Oahu	
June 19, 1963	Show of Stars Marine Corps Air Station Kaneohe Bay Island of Oahu	6:30 p.m. and 8:30 p.m.
June 20, 1963	Show of Stars Henry Perrine Baldwin High School Auditorium Wailuku Island of Maui	7:00 p.m. and 8:45 p.m. Brian's twenty-first birthday.
June 21, 1963	Show of Stars Civic Auditorium 323 Manono Street Hilo, HI Island of Hawaii	2:30 p.m. and 7:30 p.m.
June 22, 1963	Show of Stars Bloch Arena at Pearl Harbor Honolulu, HI Island of Oahu	7:30 p.m.
June 29, 1963	Convention Center 3150 Paradise Road Las Vegas, NV	8:00 p.m. With the Teen Beats.
c. late June to mid–July 1963	Skate-O-Rama 12310 Woodruff Avenue Downey, CA	With the Blazers and Kathy Marshall.

c. early to mid–July
  1963
	Civic Auditorium
	300 East Green Street
	Pasadena, CA
		With Speedy and the Reverbs, a surf quintet from
		  Whittier, CA.

July 5, 1963	Venue unknown Phoenix, AZ	Jo Ann Marks's journal.
July 6, 1963	Venue unknown Phoenix, AZ	Jo Ann Marks's journal.
July 11, 1963	Retail Clerks Union Hall 8530 Stanton Avenue Buena Park, CA	With the Astronauts.
c. July 12, 1963	"Hawaiian Holidays" Orange County Fair Orange County Fairgrounds 88 Fair Drive Costa Mesa, CA	July 9 to 14 The Beach Boys, and Adrian and the Sunsets most likely played July 12.
July 13, 1963	A Surfing Spectacular	9:00 p.m. to 1:00 a.m.

Date	*Venue*	*Details of Interest*
	Veterans Memorial Hall 313 West Tunnel Street Santa Maria, CA	With the Honeys and the Four Speeds; sponsored by radio station KSEE.

July 19, 1963

They flew from Los Angeles to Chicago, rented a Chevrolet station wagon and U-Haul, and drove ninety miles southeast to Monticello, Indiana, to begin their second Midwest tour that evening. Brian accompanied them initially, but Al filled in for him on many later dates.

July 19, 1963	Indiana Beach Amusement Resort on Lake Shafer Monticello, IN	8:45 p.m. to 12:45 a.m.
July 20, 1963	Danceland Ballroom 124 Third Street, NE Cedar Rapids, IA	Second appearance here.
July 21, 1963	Cobblestone Ballroom on Storm Lake Storm Lake, IA	
July 22, 1963	Off / Travel Day	"Surfer Girl" (b/w "Little Deuce Coupe," Capitol 5009) released.
July 23, 1963	Roof Garden Ballroom overlooking West Okojobi Lake Arnolds Park, IA	8:00 p.m. to 11:00 p.m. $1.50
July 24, 1963	Shore Acres Ballroom 1401 Riverside Boulevard Sioux City, IA	8:00 p.m. to 11:00 p.m.

An AFM contract dated July 24 for a Honeys recording session at Capitol credited Brian with arranging and conducting. However, in *The Lost Beach Boy* Stebbins and Marks noted Brian was with the group on the drive from Arnolds Park to Sioux City, with Brian singing "Sioux City Sue," a #1 hit for Dick Thomas in fall 1945, and teaching harmony parts to the others.

July 25, 1963	Val Air Ballroom 301 Ashworth Road West Des Moines, IA	Second appearance here.

July 26 and 27, 1963

These Friday and Saturday dates were prime nights for a rock 'n' roll show, but it is unclear whether they played on either date. In *The Lost Beach Boy*, Stebbins and Marks recounted the band signed autographs July 26 at a record store in Rockford, IL. Rusten and Stebbins did not mention this appearance in *The Beach Boys In Concert*. On the morning of July 27 they likely began their 368 mile trek west to Omaha. It is unclear whether they had any commitments along the way.

There exists a 5" × 7" promotional photograph signed by Brian, Mike, Dennis, Carl, and David, obtained at an appearance at a record store in Kenosha, Wisconsin, 50 miles north of Chicago and 65 miles east of Rockford.

July 28, 1963	Peony Park Ballroom North 78th and Dodge Streets Omaha, NE	8:00 p.m. to 12:00 a.m. $1.50 advance; $1.75 night of the dance. They broke an eighteen year attendance record set by Lawrence Welk.

Date	*Venue*	*Details of Interest*
July 29, 1963		

Jo Ann Marks's journal listed a second, unadvertised show at the Peony Park Ballroom. It is uncertain if this is accurate or if the group used this day to drive 284 miles east to Davenport, Iowa.

July 30, 1963	Col Ballroom (The Coliseum Ballroom) 1012 West 4th Street Davenport, IA	8:00 p.m. to 11:00 p.m. $1.50
July 31, 1963	Indian Crossing Casino E1171 County Road Q Chain O' Lakes Waupaca, WI	
August 1, 1963	Surf of the Four Seasons (also known as Surf Ballroom) 460 North Shore Drive Clear Lake, IA	8:00 p.m. to midnight $1.50 Attendees had to be sixteen or older. Their second appearance here.
August 2, 1963	Prom Ballroom 1190 University Avenue St. Paul, MN	
August 3, 1963	Terp Ballroom River and Bridge Streets Austin, MN	Second appearance here.
August 4, 1963	Kato Ballroom 200 Chestnut Street Mankato, MN	
August 5, 1963		According to an AFM contract dated August 5, Brian produced a recording session for the Survivors at Gold Star in LA.
August 6, 1963	Electric Park Ballroom 310 West Conger Street Waterloo, IA	8:00 p.m. to 11:30 p.m. $1.75 Emceed by KXEL disc jockey Lou Wagner.
August 7, 1963	Venue unknown Ithaca, MI	
August 8, 1963	Club Ponytail Highway M-131 Harbor Springs, MI	8:30 p.m. to 1:30 a.m. The Kingtones, the club's house band, played downstairs in the Hippocrene Hide-Away during the Beach Boys' breaks. Al filled in for Brian as evidenced by a photograph in the August 10 *Petoskey News Review*.
August 9, 1963	Cold Springs Resort 260 Lane 120 Hamilton Lake Hamilton, IN	Approximately 3,000 people attended.

Date	Venue	Details of Interest
August 11, 1963	Auditorium Theatre 50 East Congress Parkway Chicago, IL	
August 13, 1963	Gilchrist's Fifth Annual Back-to-School Fashion Hop and Surf-Sing Show Music Hall (former Metropolitan Theatre) 252–272 Tremont Street Boston, MA	9:30 a.m. 90 cents 75 cents with three Coca-Cola bottle caps This teen fashion show and beauty pageant was scheduled for two hours, but stretched to three. It was sponsored by Gilchrist Department Store, radio station WMEX, Coty, Coca-Cola, and emceed by WMEX disc jockey Arnie "Woo Woo" Ginsburg. With Jan & Dean, Tony & the Del Fi's, Myles Connor & the Ravens. Mary Ann Mobley, Miss America 1959 and the first Mississippian to wear the crown, addressed the crowd of 4,000, mostly teenage girls.
August 14, 1963	Palace Ballroom West Grand Avenue and Staples Street Old Orchard Beach, ME	Billed as their only Maine appearance. $1.25 advance $1.50 at the door Roger Christian recalled he and Brian were in an LA recording studio working on songs for *Little Deuce Coupe* and that night attended a cocktail party at the Beverly Wilshire Hotel that Capitol Records hosted for Kyu Sakamoto.
August 15, 1963	Surf Auditorium Hill, NH	Near the Lakes Region.
August 16, 1963	Mount Tom Ballroom Mountain Park Route 5 Holyoke, MA	7:30 p.m. With Marcy Jo and Eddie Rambeau; Jan & Dean played a free show here the night before.
August 17, 1963	101st Wayne County Fair Route 191 North Honesdale, PA	Two shows. Closing day of this week-long fair.
August 18, 1963	Lakewood Ballroom (also known as the Dance Hall) Lakewood Park Barnesville, PA (five miles east of Mahanoy City)	8:30 p.m. to midnight With the Magics ("Chapel Bells") and the Bobby Mar Orchestra. An advertisement in the Mahanoy City *Record American* noted their hit songs included "Surf City." Lithuanian Day drew 20,000 people to the park that day.
August 20, 1963	Reimold Brothers Auction Hall Route 18, Sharon-Greenville Road, across from Reynolds Drive-In Transfer, PA	Dancing 8:00 p.m. to 11:00 p.m. Shows at 9:15 p.m. and 11:00 p.m. $1.25

Date	*Venue*	*Details of Interest*
August 21, 1963	Danceland West View Park Route 19 West View, PA	9:00 p.m. to 1:00 a.m. An amusement park northwest of Pittsburgh.
August 22, 1963	Wheeling Downs Roller Rink Wheeling Downs, WV	8:00 p.m. to 11:00 p.m. Presented by WKWK and International Artists. Emcee Bob Gampo gave copies of their new single, "Surfer Girl" backed with "Little Deuce Coupe," to the first 100 attendees. It was David Marks's fifteenth birthday.

August 23, 1963	LeSourdsville Lake
	  Amusement Park
	5757 Hamilton Middletown
	  Road
	Middletown, OH	

August 24, 1963	Midway Ballroom Route 41 South Cedar Lake Pier Cedar Lake, IN	7:30 p.m. to midnight With the Exports. Unaware there was a third set, Dennis left for a previous commitment, compelling Mike to find a volunteer drummer in the audience.
August 25, 1963	Melody Mill Highways 52 and 3 Sageville, IA (one mile north of Dubuque)	7:30 p.m. to 11:30 p.m. Al filled in for Brian as evidenced by a posed group photograph on stage.
August 26, 1963	Venue unknown	One of these dates may have been the Hammond Civic Center, 5825 Sohl Avenue, Hammond, Indiana. According to an AFM contract dated August 27, Brian produced a recording session for the Survivors at Western in LA.
August 27, 1963	Venue unknown	
August 29, 1963	Avalon Ballroom 206 Copeland Avenue La Crosse, WI	7:00 p.m. to 10:00 p.m. Brian rejoined the tour for two shows sponsored by Pepsi-Cola.

Emceed by WKBH disc jockey Lindy Shannon and WLCX disc jockey Pete Lakin. The band then drove 224 miles southeast to Chicago to meet Murry Wilson, who had flown in from LA to dismiss tour manager John Hamilton and accompany them to Brooklyn, New York. During the twelve hour drive, David and Murry argued and, in a rash moment, David quit the band. The last day of his first tenure with the band was October 5, 1963.

August 30, 1963	Murray the K's Holiday Revue Fox Theatre 20 Flatbush Avenue Brooklyn, NY	They played one night of this ten-day Labor Day Show. They may have played as a sextet. With the Angels, the Chiffons, the Dovells, the Drifters, Jay and the Americans, Ben E. King, the Miracles, Gene Pitney, Randy and the Rainbows, the Shirelles, the Tymes, and Little Stevie Wonder.
August 31, 1963	Show of Stars Spectacular LA Memorial Sports Arena 3939 South Figueroa Street Los Angeles, CA	8:00 p.m. Tickets $4, $3.50, $3, and $2.50

Date	*Venue*	*Details of Interest*

Masters of Ceremony were Wink Martindale, Roger Christian, and Gene Weed. With Steve Alaimo, Andrea Carroll, Mel Carter, the Challengers, the Cookies, the Cornells, Dick and Dee Dee, Jackie DeShannon, Tracy Dey, Little Eva, Johnny Fortune, Jan & Dean, Marvin Gaye, Rene Hall & Orchestra, Donna Loren, Darlene Love, Wayne Newton, the Olympics, the Orlons, Paul Petersen, the Righteous Brothers, Dee Dee Sharp, Ray Sharpe, and Soupy Sales.

Date	Venue	Details of Interest
September 4, 1963	Back-to-School Jamboree F.W. Woolworth The Symes Building Cherry Creek Shopping Center 16th and Champa Streets Denver, CO	4:30 p.m. to 5:30 p.m. The group, with Brian, autographed copies of *Surfin' Safari* and *Surfin' U.S.A.* in the world's largest F.W. Woolworth.

	Back-to-School Show and
	  Dance, Lakeside Ballroom
	Lakeside Amusement Park
	West 46th Avenue and
	  Sheridan Boulevard
	Denver, CO
		Evening

September 7, 1963	Patio Gardens
	The Lagoon
	375 Lagoon Drive
	(An amusement park north
	  of Salt Lake City)
	Farmington, UT
		$1.75; reservations taken
		When the Beach Boys returned to Utah that December,
		  the *Ogden Standard-Examiner* reported "the Beach
		  Boys produced the largest crowd to attend the
		  Lagoon this summer."

September 9, 1963	Back-to-School-O-Rama
	Helix High School Stadium
	7323 University Avenue
	La Mesa, CA
		7:30 p.m. to 10:00 p.m.
		$1.50
		They headlined a roster of twelve artists for a show
		  sponsored by La Mesa Junior Chamber of Commerce
		  for its youth fund drive.

September 9, 11, 12,
13, 16, 17, and 18,
1963
	Back-to-School Ball
	KHJ-TV channel 9
	Hosted by Bob Denver and
	  KHJ disc jockey Mort
	  Crowley
	Los Angeles, CA
		7:30 p.m. to 8:00 p.m.
		David Marks recalled playing one of these seven
		  live television shows hosted by Bob Denver to kick-
		  off the syndication of *The Many Loves of Dobie
		  Gillis* on September 19. Guests included Dodie
		  Stevens (9th), Dick Dale (11th), the Journeymen and
		  Jody Miller (13th). Others scheduled to perform were
		  Al Martino, the Lettermen, Trini Lopez, Steve
		  Franken, Rudy LaRusso, Albie Pearson, and Kenny
		  Hunt.

September 14, 1963	Memorial Auditorium 1515 J Street Sacramento, CA	2:15 p.m. matinee for teens and pre-teens, and parents admitted free. 8:00 p.m. Al filled in for Brian at both shows.
September 20, 1963	Venue unknown Long Beach, CA	Jo Ann Marks's journal.
September 21, 1963	Memorial Coliseum 300 North Winning Way Portland, OR	8:00 p.m. With Jan & Dean. Sponsored by radio station KISN.

Date	Venue	Details of Interest
September 24, 1963	*The Red Skelton Hour* CBS TV Los Angeles, CA	Their first appearance on national television which had been taped April 21, 1963.
September 28, 1963	The Surf Party The Cow Palace 2600 Geneva Avenue Daly City, CA (south of San Francisco)	8:30 p.m. Sponsored by radio station KYA and Tempo Productions.

With Freddie Cannon, the Coasters, Roberta Day, Jan & Dean, the Original Drifters, Bobby Freeman, Betty Harris, the Jaynettes, Jose Jimenez, Trini Lopez, Donna Loren, the Righteous Brothers, the Ronettes, Dee Dee Sharp, Ray Stevens, George & Teddy, April Stevens & Nino Tempo, Dionne Warwick, Little Stevie Wonder.

Date	Venue	Details of Interest
September 29, 1963	Unknown Fresno, CA	Jo Ann Marks's journal. This may have been just a promotional appearance as they played a 3:00 p.m. show in Seattle and the scheduling would have been tight.
September 29, 1963	'63 Hit Parade of Stars Seattle Opera House 321 Mercer Street Seattle, WA	3:00 p.m. and 7:00 p.m. Tickets $3, $4, and $5. Brian did not attend. With Freddie Cannon, Gail Harris, the Lancers, Billy Saint, Ray Stevens, Dee Dee Sharp, April Stevens & Nino Tempo, the Viceroys, the [Fabulous] Wailers, Little Stevie Wonder, and others.
October 5, 1963	Surfin' at the Bowl Balboa Park Bowl San Diego, CA	*Once Upon A Wave* surf film shown at 8:15 p.m. With the Honeys and Eddie and the Showmen. David's final show.
October 19, 1963	31st Annual Y Day at the Hollywood Bowl 2301 North Highland Avenue Los Angeles, CA	10:00 a.m. to noon Emceed by Art Linkletter and sponsored by the Hollywood chapter of the YMCA, the Hollywood Advertising Club, and KFWB.

With the Challengers, Mike Clifford, Keith Colley, the Cornells, Vic Dana, Jan & Dean, Duane Eddy, the Fleetwoods, the Honeys, the Mixtures, Paul Petersen, the Routers, Bobby Rydell, Eddie and the Showmen, Soupy Sales, Dodie Stevens, and the Surfaris. With Muzzy Marcellino and his band, and the United States Marine Corps Band.

Date	Venue	Details of Interest
October 23, 1963	Gymnasium Santa Maria High School 901 South Broadway Santa Maria, CA	With the Honeys and Jan & Dean.
October 31, 1963	Loyola Carnival Homecoming Week Westchester Campus Loyola Marymount University Westchester, CA	7:00 p.m. and 10:30 p.m. On October 27, the Four Freshmen helped kick off Homecoming Week.
November 15, 1963	Grand Opening Wallichs Music City South Bay Shopping Center Corner of Hawthorne and Artesia Boulevards Torrance, CA	7:00 p.m. This event launched a ten-day celebration and featured many Capitol recording artists. KFWB broadcast for twenty-four hours beginning at midnight.

Date	*Venue*	*Details of Interest*

Hosted by Bob Crane, morning disc jockey on KNX in LA and future star of *Hogan's Heroes*. Artists included Dick Dale, Vic Dana, Jan & Dean, Tony Jerome, Jack Jones & Jones Trio, the Lennon Sisters, Trini Lopez, Rose Marie, Gene McDaniels, Tim Morgan, Wayne Newton, Johnny Prophet, the Righteous Brothers, Kay Starr, Dodie Stevens, the Surfaris, Bud and Travis, and the Ventures.

November 16, 1963	*Dick Clark Celebrity Party* ABC-TV Hollywood Hills Los Angeles, CA	1:30 p.m. on the West Coast Filmed one evening in late October at Bob Marcucci's home on Sunset Plaza Drive in Hollywood. Marucci owned Chancellor Records and managed Frankie Avalon and Fabian. Newspaper listings for this one-hour special included the Beach Boys, but they do not appear on the kinescope available on-line.
November 22, 1963	Dance & Show Veterans Memorial 　Auditorium 824 E Street between 8th and 　9th Streets, Presented by 　Frederick Vail Productions Marysville, CA	8:30 p.m. $1.50 advance $2 at the door With Freddie and the Statics.
November 29, 1963	National Guard Armory 43–143 North Jackson Street Indio, CA	A handbill noted "their one and only Central Valley appearance"
November 30, 1963	The First Channel 18 　Saturday Night Bandstand 　Dance Municipal Auditorium 555 West 6th Street at North E Street San Bernardino, CA	8:30 p.m. to midnight. $4 per couple (advance); $4.50 (door) Hosted by Jay Michael of KCHU-TV channel 18, which telecast the 9:30 p.m. to 10:30 p.m. segment live.

The first of twenty-six planned Saturday Night Bandstand Dances was scheduled for November 23 with Dick Dale and the Del-Tones, the Elliott Brothers Band (Disneyland's Date Nite Band), the Torquays, and the Surfaris. In deference to the November 22 assassination of President Kennedy, organizers postponed the show and offered ticket holders a refund. On November 25, they announced the show would be held November 30, but only the Torquays could still keep the commitment. On November 26, organizers secured the Beach Boys and the Astronauts, and by November 30, the Dave Pell Octet. Tickets dated November 23 were honored. When Dick Dale rescheduled to December 14, with the Truants, stags were now welcome and the price had dropped to $1.50 per person.

c. Fall 1963	Stars of the Century Show Orange Show Stadium National Orange Show 　Fairgrounds, 689 South E. 　Street at West Mill Street San Bernardino, CA	Members of the Truants, a Redlands-based surf quartet, recalled playing the Stars of the Century Show at the National Orange Show Stadium in San Bernardino with the Beach Boys, Safaris, Tornadoes, and Coasters. Despite the Beach Boys national popularity at this time, there were no newspaper advertisements. However, the November 22 *San Bernardino County Sun* had an ad for a November 27 Dance and Show at the Swing Auditorium at the National Orange Show Fairgrounds featuring 15 Big Acts, but only listed Bobby Sox & the Blue Jeans, the Fabulous Coasters, and Don Julien Dance Band.

Date	Venue	Details of Interest
December 20, 1963	Civic Auditorium 525 North Center Street Stockton, CA	
December 21, 1963	A Christmas Gala Concert Memorial Auditorium 1515 J Street Presented by Frederick Vail Productions Sacramento, CA	8:00 p.m. $2 advance $2.25 at the door Recorded for *Beach Boys Concert*. Carl's 17th birthday.
December 27, 1963	The Terrace Ballroom 464 South Main Street Salt Lake City, UT	
December 28, 1963	The Terrace Ballroom 464 South Main Street Salt Lake City, UT	$2 advance and $2.50 at the door. Presented by radio station KNAK.

The Terrace Ballroom was operated by the Lagoon corporation who also owned the amusement park. A newspaper advertisement noted "due to the largest advance sale ever, the Beach Boys will play Friday and Saturday."

December 31, 1963	Opening Night The Cinnamon Cinder 1996 West Highland Avenue San Bernardino, CA	With multiple artists. Fred Vail drove home with Carl and when KFWB announced the #1 song for the year, it was "Surfin' U.S.A."

Appendix 2

Timeline of "Surfin'" Releases

Label, No.	Songs	Publisher (BMI)	Producer	Matrix Number	Delta Number	Pressing Plant	Release Date	Copies (approx.)
Candix 331	Surfin'	Drink-Guild Music	None listed	CD-TS-1	None	Unknown	Nov. 27, 1961	12,000
	Luau	Guild Music		CD-TS-2				
X 301	Surfin'	Drink-Guild Music	H. Morgan	CD-TS-1-R	Δ41389	Alco	Dec. 20, 1961	10,000
	Luau	Drink-Guild Music	H. Morgan	CD-TS-2-R	Δ41389x			
Candix 301	Surfin'	Guild Music	H. Morgan	CD-TS-1-R	Δ41389	Alco	Jan. 15, 1962	
	Luau	Guild Music	H. Morgan	CD-TS-2-R	Δ41389x			
Candix 301[1]	Surfin'	Guild Music	H. Morgan	CD-TS-1-R	Δ41389	Alco	Jan. 15, 1962	1,000
	Luau	Guild Music	H. Morgan	CD-TS-2-R	Δ41389x			
Candix 301[2]	Surfin'	Guild Music	H. Morgan	CD-TS-1-R	Δ41389	Alco	Jan. 15, 1962	At least 33,000
	Luau	Guild Music	H. Morgan	CD-TS-2-R	Δ41389x			
London M.1 7224[3]	Surfin'	Guild Music	H. Morgan	CD-TS-1-R	None	Made in Canada	Jan./Feb., 1962	Unknown
	Luau	Guild Music	H. Morgan	CD-TS-2-R				

1. Label notation: "AUDITION COPY; Dist. by ERA RECORD SALES INC."; 2. Label notation: "Dist. by ERA RECORD SALES INC."; 3. Label notation: "(Candix 301)"

Appendix 3

"Surfin'" Chart Position History

Billboard

Printing Date	Newsstand Date	Issue Date	Chart Position	Label & Number
January 3	January 6	January 13	118	Candix 331
January 10	January 13	January 20	112	Candix 331
January 17	January 20	January 27	—	
January 24	January 27	February 3	105	Candix 331
January 31	February 3	February 10	101	Candix 331
February 7	February 10	February 17	93	Candix 331
February 14	February 17	February 24	90	Candix 331
February 21	February 24	March 3	83	Candix 331
February 28	March 3	March 10	83	Candix 331
March 7	March 10	March 17	77	Candix 331
March 14	March 17	March 24	75	Candix 331

Cash Box

Printing Date	Newsstand Date	Issue Date	Chart Position	Label & Number
January 10	January 13	January 20	17 on Looking Ahead	Candix 331
January 17	January 20	January 27	14 on Looking Ahead	Candix 331
			Pick of the Week	Candix 301 Era
January 24	January 27	February 3	—	
January 31	February 3	February 10	96	Candix 331
February 7	February 10	February 17	94	Candix 331
February 14	February 17	February 24	95	Candix 331
February 21	February 24	March 3	86	Candix 301
February 28	March 3	March 10	85	Candix 301

KFWB and KRLA

Printing Date	In Stores Date	For the Week Ending	KFWB	KRLA	Label
December 20	December 22	December 29	33	—	Candix
December 27	December 29	January 5	19	32	Candix
January 3	January 5	January 12	11	29	Candix
January 10	January 12	January 19	6	6	Candix
January 17	January 19	January 26	6	4	Candix
January 24	January 26	February 2	4	3	Candix
January 31	February 2	February 9	4	4	Candix
February 7	February 9	February 16	3	8	Candix
February 14	February 16	February 23	9	11	Candix
February 21	February 23	March 2	9	15	Candix
February 28	March 2	March 9	19	25	Candix
March 7	March 9	March 16	25	—	Candix

Appendix 4

"Surfin'" Revenue and Expense Stream, and Production Flow

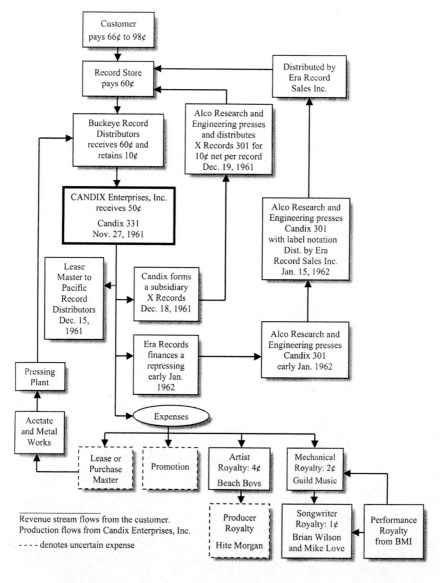

Customer
pays 66¢ to 98¢

Record Store
pays 60¢

Distributed by
Era Record
Sales Inc.

Buckeye Record
Distributors
receives 60¢ and
retains 10¢

Alco Research and
Engineering presses
and distributes
X Records 301 for
10¢ net per record
Dec. 19, 1961

CANDIX Enterprises, Inc.
receives 50¢

Candix 331
Nov. 27, 1961

Alco Research and
Engineering presses
Candix 301
with label notation
Dist. by Era
Record Sales Inc.
Jan. 15, 1962

Lease
Master to
Pacific
Record
Distributors
Dec. 15,
1961

Candix forms
a subsidiary
X Records
Dec. 18, 1961

Era Records
finances a
repressing
early Jan.
1962

Alco Research and
Engineering presses
Candix 301
early Jan. 1962

Pressing
Plant

Acetate
and Metal
Works

Expenses

Lease or
Purchase
Master

Promotion

Artist
Royalty: 4¢

Beach Boys

Mechanical
Royalty: 2¢
Guild Music

Producer
Royalty

Hite Morgan

Songwriter
Royalty: 1¢

Brian Wilson
and Mike Love

Performance
Royalty
from BMI

Revenue stream flows from the customer.
Production flows from Candix Enterprises, Inc.

- - - - denotes uncertain expense

Appendix 5

Standard Songwriter's Contract for "Surfin'" Dated September 15, 1961

Standard Songwriter's Contract

AGREEMENT entered into this *15th* day of *September* , 19*61*
by and between *Hite Music Co.* hereinafter designated as the PUBLISHER, and
author and/or composer, hereinafter jointly designated as the COMPOSER.

WITNESSETH:

The COMPOSER hereby sells, assigns, transfers and delivers to the PUBLISHER, its successors and assigns, the original
musical composition, written and composed by *Michael Love and Brian Wilson*
at present entitled *Surfin'*
Including Copyright No. E *EU# 698400 - 12/7/6*

which title may be changed by the Publisher; including the title, words and music thereof and all rights therein; and all
copyrights and the rights to secure copyrights and extensions and renewals of copyrights in the same and in any arrangements
and adaptations thereof, in the United States, Canada, and foreign countries, and all other rights that the COMPOSER now
has or may be entitled to or that he hereafter could or might secure with respect to this composition if these presents had not
been made, for all countries, including but not limited to the publishing rights, the performing rights, and the rights to use the
same for mechanical reproduction, and the right to make, publish and perform any arrangement or adaptation of the same,
and to license others to exercise in foreign countries any and all of the rights hereby conveyed, to have and to hold the same
absolutely unto the PUBLISHER, its successors and assigns forever.

And the COMPOSER hereby covenants, represents and warrants that the composition hereby sold is an original work
and that neither said work nor any part thereof infringes upon the title of or the literary or musical property or the copyright in any other work, and that he is the sole writer and composer and the sole owner thereof and of all the rights therein,
and has not sold, assigned, set over, transferred, hypothecated or mortgaged any right, title or interest in or to the said composition or any part thereof, or any of the rights herein conveyed, and that he has not made or entered into any contract or
contracts with any other person, firm or corporation whomsoever, affecting said composition or any right, title or interest
therein, or in the copyright thereof, and that no person, firm or corporation other than the COMPOSER has or has had, claims
or has claimed any right, title or interest in or to said work or any part thereof or any use thereof or any copyright therein, and
that said work has never been published, and that the COMPOSER has full right, power and authority to make this present
instrument, sale and transfer.

In consideration of this agreement, the Publisher agrees to pay the COMPOSER as follows:

(a) In respect to regular piano copies sold and paid for at wholesale in the United States of America, royalties per
copy, as follows:
Wholesale price *3.8* cents, royalty *6.3* cents per copy.

(b) A royalty of *50* % (in no case however less than 33-1/3% jointly) of all net sums received by the PUB-
LISHER in respect of regular piano copies and/or orchestrations thereof sold and paid for in any foreign
country.

(c) A royalty of *6* cents per copy of orchestrations thereof in any form sold and paid for in the United States
of America.

(d) For purposes of royalty statements, if a composition is printed and published in the United States of America,
as to copies and rights sold in the Dominion of Canada, revenue herefrom shall be considered as of domestic origin. If however, the composition is printed by a party other than the Publisher in the Dominion of Canada, revenue
from sales of copies and rights in Canada shall be considered as originated in a foreign country.

(e) As to "professional material"—not sold or resold, no royalty shall be paid.

(f) An amount equal to *50* % (in no case, however, less than 33-1/3% jointly) of:—

All receipts of the Publisher in respect of any license issued authorizing the manufacture of the parts of instruments
serving to mechanically reproduce the said composition, or to use the said composition in synchronization with sound motion
pictures, or to reproduce it upon so-called "electrical transcription" for broadcasting purposes; and of any and all receipts of
the Publisher from any other source or right now known or which may hereafter come into existence, all such sums to be
divided amongst the COMPOSER of the said composition.

It is specifically understood and agreed that the intention of this agreement is, not, and the COMPOSER shall not
be entitled to receive any part of the monies received by the PUBLISHER from the American Society of Composers, Authors
and Publishers, or any other collecting agency from which the PUBLISHER shall receive payments for the use of said musical
composition, except as above provided.

The COMPOSER hereby authorizes the PUBLISHER at its absolute discretion and at the COMPOSER'S sole expense
to employ attorneys and to institute or defend any action or proceeding and to take any other proper steps to protect the right,
title and interest of the PUBLISHER in and to the above entitled composition and every portion thereof acquired from the
COMPOSER pursuant to the terms hereof and in that connection to settle, compromise or in any other manner dispose of any
matter, claim, action, or proceeding and to satisfy any judgment that may be rendered and all of the expense so incurred and
other sums so paid by the PUBLISHER the COMPOSER hereby agrees to pay to the PUBLISHER on demand, further authorizing the PUBLISHER, whenever in its opinion its right, title or interest to any of the writer's compositions are questioned or
there is a breach of any of the covenants, warranties or representations contained in this contract or in any other similar contract hereafter entered into between the PUBLISHER and the COMPOSER, to withhold any and all royalties that may be or become
due to the COMPOSER pursuant to all such contracts until such question shall have been settled or such breach repaired,
and to apply such royalties to the repayment of all sums due to the publisher hereunder.

It is agreed that no royalties are to be paid for copies disposed of as new issues, or professional copies, for copies distributed for advertising purposes or printed in any folio, book, newspaper, or magazine or other periodical, or for copies of any
other arrangement except sheet music piano arrangements. It is also distinctly understood that no royalties are payable on con-
signed copies unless paid for and until such time as an accounting therefor can properly be made.

7

Appendix 6

Floor Plan of Hite and Dorinda Morgan's Home, 2511 Mayberry Street

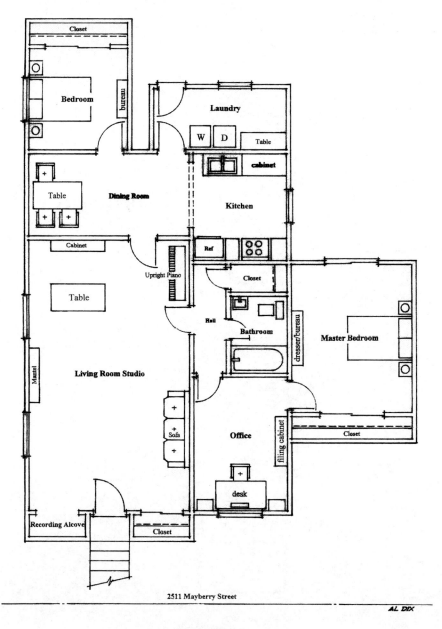

2511 Mayberry Street

AL DIX

Appendix 7

Floor Plan of CANDIX Enterprises, 6425 Hollywood Boulevard

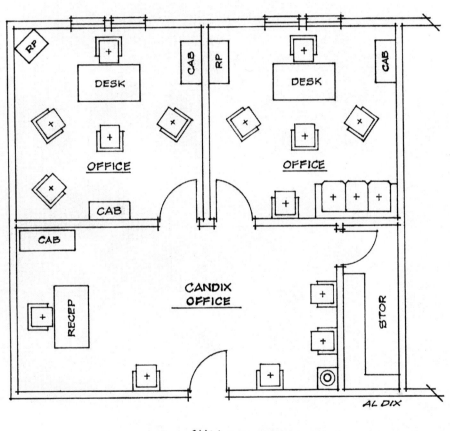

Appendix 8

American Federation of Musicians Contract Dated February 8, 1962

American Federation of Musicians Contract Dated February 8, 1962

Letter of Intent and Agreement from Murry Wilson to Hite B. Morgan Dated March 29, 1962

TEENAGE DANCES
RECORDING ARTISTS

TELEVISION, RADIO A
STAGE APPEARANC

The Beach Boys

3701 WEST 119TH STREET   •   OREGON 8-6054 — OSBORNE 5-6566   •   HAWTHORNE, CALIFORN

BRIAN WILSON. LEAC
M. WILSON, MI

*********** LETTER OF INTENT, AND Agreement***************

March 29, 1962

Hite Morgan, Producer
2512 Mayberry
Los Angeles, Calif.

Dear Sir,

This is to confirm our many conversations regarding the "BEACH BOYS", Singing, Playing, and Recording Artists:

(Morgan)

We do assign, and ask that you Hite Bowman Morgan, and or Mrs. Dorinda Mogan ac as, and perform the duties of Producing, Recording, and Promoting any and all reco and Songs Written, and or recorded by THE BEACH BOYS, for aperiod of One Year from the Above date, or for a longer period if agreeable to Mr. Hite Morgan, Dorinda Mo and THE BEACH BOYS.

We The Beach Boys, do appreciate the efforts made by the Morgans on the Song; "SURFIN" and the Recording of same, and hope that many such successfull recordings will follow as result of same.   It is asked that at all times will Mr. Hite Morga act in the best interests of The Beach Boys, in preventing other firms forcing the group to record songs that may not be beneficial to them, and to use his power of producer to refuse any contract which might conflict with the type of music or son; The Beach Boys do best.

It is hoped that through Mr. Hite & Dorinda Morgan that they obtain a major Rec Co. to Employ, or distribute all of the groups'record releases, and that as produce can make decisions pertaining to the Leasing of any of the "Beach Boys" tapes, mas1 and songs.   It is understood that Mr. Morgan , or the Morgans will protect the rig! of the Beach Boys in matters of Contracts, and that all contracts or Agreements wi1 any Record Company and/or Record Distributing firm will be in writing, and in favo1 of Hite & Dorinda Morgan and the "Beach Boys"

Should the Producers; Hite & Dorinda Morgan find a large Recording Company who would purchase the rights of Recording the "Beach Boys" on an exclusive basis, ther a contract will be made up in favor of Hite & Dorinda Mogan, inorder that they may legally execute said sale of Contract, and that Hite & Dorinda Morgan will equally share with the "Beazh Boys", One Half,of all proceeds of said Contract Sale, for th efforts in good faith, and for monies spent in promoting, and producing the "Beach Recordings, Songs, & Careers.

It is understood, that Brian Wilson, Leader,of the "Beach Boys" may hire or fire any one of the Beach Boys from time to time at his discretion, to keep the group together, or to improve same by adding a new member, or reducing the number of per known as the "Beach Boys!

Signed:

Appendix 10

Floor Plan of Stereo Masters, 5534–5538 Melrose Avenue

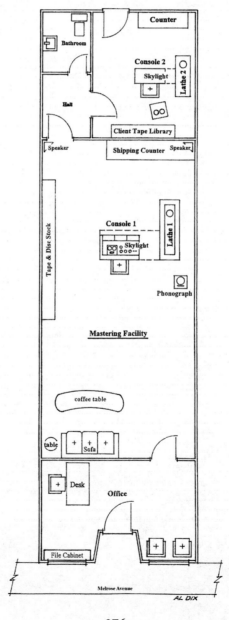

Appendix 11

The Beach Boys' Midwest Tour,
April 24–May 5, 1963

Appendix 12

"Dennis"
by Dorinda Morgan

"My mother was very fond of Dennis," recalled Bruce Morgan. "He was the genesis of the Beach Boys. This is a song she wrote for him after he passed away." The song was copyrighted on February 14, 1984. Lyrics reprinted with permission of Bruce Morgan.

Lost among the lotus eaters,
In the labyrinth of life.
Lead astray by easy greeters,
Till he couldn't find his way.

Say goodbye to youth forever,
Say goodbye to sweet romance,
In a world of hard ambition,
Dreamers never have a chance.

As I walk along the beach,
Your face comes back to me.
I know you'll be there forever,
Calling from the sea.

You were such an inspiration,
Lending me your strength and youth.
But you never found contentment,
For you couldn't find the truth.

On the sun-drenched beach of summer,
In the winter's bitter cold.
We will always feel you near us,
Singing of the tales untold.

Those who die young are remembered,
By their friends forevermore.
You are safe from all the peril,
That the living have in store.

Chapter Notes

Preface

1. Carl Wilson interview of June 11, 1996, *Hawthorne, CA*, track 4, Capitol CD 72435–31583–2–3, 2001, compact disc.

Chapter 1

1. *Early 60s Hawthorne California*, Feedback Page, comments by Hal Chauncey, February 7, 2005, http://cougartown.com.

2. John L. Scott, "Tony Martin Triumphs in Grove Show," *Los Angeles Times*, March 30, 1959, C9. Scott wrote, "In fine fettle and good voice, Tony Martin returned to the Cocoanut Grove Saturday night. The Ambassador Hotel's plush nightclub bulged at the seams as approximately 1,000 people crowded in to hear Martin." Tony Martin was backed up by Freddy Martin and His Orchestra, who were in their eighteenth year at the Cocoanut Grove.

3. "It's a Blue World" from *Music in My Heart* with Rita Hayworth was nominated for an Academy Award for Best Original Song in 1940, but lost to "When You Wish Upon a Star" from Walt Disney's *Pinocchio*.

4. Ken Sharp, "Christmas with Brian Wilson," *Record Collector*, January 2006, 75.

5. Irene Callahan, interview with author, October 30, 2008.

6. Ibid.

7. "More with Brian," *Endless Summer Quarterly*, Fall 2005 (aka the Hawthorne 1960 edition), 33.

8. Timothy White, "Still Waters Run Deep, a Child Is Father to the Band, the Return of Brian Wilson," *Crawdaddy*, June 1976, 41–42.

9. Corey Levitan, "Hood Vibrations—The Beach Boys Remember Hawthorne," *The Daily Breeze* (Torrance, CA), May 18, 2001.

10. Bob Barrow, interview by author, July 12, 2008.

11. Ibid.

12. John Hagethorn, interview by author, May 23, 2010.

13. Ibid. The record store Hagethorn referenced was Melody Music, 420 South Hawthorne Boulevard, Hawthorne, California.

14. *Early 60s Hawthorne California*, Feedback Page, comments by John Rout, March 1, 2000, http://cougartown.com.

15. *Early 60s Hawthorne California*, Feedback Page, comments by Hal Chauncey, June 22, 1999, http://cougartown.com.

16. *Early 60s Hawthorne California*, Feedback Page, comments by John Baker, April 9, 2001, http://cougartown.com. For the record, Al was 5'8" and 165 pounds.

17. Peter Ames Carlin, *Catch a Wave: The Rise, Fall & Redemption of the Beach Boys' Brian Wilson* (New York: Rodale, 2006), 15.

18. Ibid.

19. David Leaf, *The Beach Boys and the California Myth* (New York: Grosset & Dunlap, 1978), 20.

20. Hagethorn, interview.

21. Timothy White, "Back from the Bottom," *New York Times*, June 26, 1988, 32.

22. Ken Sharp, "Christmas with Brian Wilson," *Record Collector*, January 2006, 75.

23. Tom Nolan, "The Beach Boys: A California Saga. Part One: Mr. Everything," *Rolling Stone*, October 28, 1971, 34.

24. Brian Wilson, "My Philosophy," October 26, 1959, high school essay reprinted in *Made in California*, 6-CD set, Capitol UME, a Universal Music Company, B0018509–02, 2013.

25. "Brian Wilson: A Beach Boy's Tale," an interview with Rich Sloan, *A&E Biography*, written by Peter Jones and Morgan Neville, directed by Morgan Neville, DVD, 1999.

26. Warren Turnbull, *Inglewood Daily News*, December 5, 1959.

27. "Cougars Aim at C.I.F. Champions," *Cougar*, Hawthorne High School, December 11, 1959.

28. David Beard, "Al Jardine, Be True to Your School," *Endless Summer Quarterly*, Fall 2005 (aka the Hawthorne 1960 edition), 30.

29. Hagethorn, interview.

30. Carlin, *Catch a Wave: The Rise, Fall & Redemption of the Beach Boys' Brian Wilson*, 16.

31. Ibid., 16–17.

32. Vickie Amott, interview by author, May 5, 2010.

33. Marilyn Wilson, interview by David Leaf, "The Making of Pet Sounds," *The Pet Sounds Sessions*, 4-CD set, EMI-Capitol Records CDP 2 7243 8 37662 2 2, 1996, liner notes, 108.

34. "Censored!," *Cougar*, Hawthorne High School, December 11, 1959.

35. Carlin, *Catch a Wave: The Rise, Fall & Redemption of the Beach Boys' Brian Wilson*, 23.

36. Al Jardine, as interviewed in *The Beach Boys 50, Doin' It Again*, written by Frank Haney, directed by John Anderson and Joe Thomas, DVD BEM 10001 (David C. Levy Productions, 2012), DVD.

37. White, "Still Waters Run Deep, a Child Is Father to the Band, the Return of Brian Wilson," 32.

38. Roberta Burket, interview by author, December 21, 2007.

39. Roberta Burket, *El Molino* 1977 Yearbook, Hawthorne High School, Hawthorne, California, 8.

40. "Rich Sloan, Onward Cougars, Onward Cougars," *Endless Summer Quarterly*, Fall 2005 (aka the Hawthorne 1960 edition), 20.

41. Burket, interview.

42. Jerry Daquila, "Sports," *Cougar*, Hawthorne High School, March 11, 1960.

43. Barrow, interview.

44. *El Molino* 1960 Yearbook, Hawthorne High School, Hawthorne, California, 99.

45. Hagethorn, interview.

46. White, "Still Waters Run Deep, a Child Is Father to the Band, the Return of Brian Wilson," 32.

47. Fred Morgan, interview by Tom Quintana, *Hawthorne Today*, Hawthorne Cable Television, television broadcast, 1990s.

48. Leaf, *The Beach Boys and the California Myth*, 23.

49. Amott, interview.

50. Beard, "Al Jardine, Be True to Your School," 30.

Chapter 2

1. John Hagethorn, interview by author, May 23, 2010.

2. Ibid.

3. Terry Heyer, "Hawthorne, City of Good Neighbors, Is 40 Today," *Inglewood Daily News*, July 12, 1962.

4. Tom Nolan (with additional material by David Felton), "The Beach Boys: A California Saga. Part Two: Tales of Hawthorne," *Rolling Stone*, November 11, 1971, 50.

5. "Murry Wilson," *Song Hits*, October 1967, 32.

6. "Endless Harmony," directed by Alan Boyd, Brother Records under exclusive license to Capitol Records 72434–92353–9–7 (Delilah Films, 2000), DVD.

7. David Felton, "The Healing of Brother Bri," *Rolling Stone*, November 4, 1976, 39.

8. David Leaf, *The Beach Boys and the California Myth* (New York: Grosset & Dunlap, 1978), 17.

9. Felton, "The Healing of Brother Bri," 51.

10. *The Beach Boys: An American Band*, written and directed by Malcolm Leo (High Ridge Productions, 1985), DVD.

11. Dennis Wilson interview, *The Robert W. Morgan Special of the Week*, narrated by Robert W. Morgan, written and produced by Alan Daniel Goldblatt, Watermark, Incorporated, March 21, 1978.

12. Eunice Field, *IN (For the Girl of Today, the Woman of Tomorrow)*, "Beach Boys in Search of 5 Men," August 1966, 62.

13. Steven Gaines, *Heroes and Villains: The True Story of the Beach Boys* (New York: New American Library, 1986), 43.

14. Carl Wilson, interview, *Earth News*, radio broadcast, week of May 11, 1981.

15. "Rhythm & Blues Record Reviews," *Billboard*, December 15, 1951, 33.

16. Ken Sharp, "Surf's Up: An Interview, Brian Wilson," *Record Collector*, March 2001, 54. Neither BMI nor ASCAP currently list "His Little Darlin' and You."

17. Don Allen, personal communication, October 2008.

18. Ken Sharp, "Brian Wilson, Al Jardine, Mike Love Interview, Part 3," *Rock Cellar*, http://www.rockcellar magazine.com/2013/11/01/brian-wilson-al-jardine-mike-love-beach-boys-interview-part-3/#sthash.I0PH8OZ1.dpbs

19. Nolan, "The Beach Boys: A California Saga. Part Two: Tales of Hawthorne," 50.

20. "Mike Love of the Beach Boys," *Teen Set*, October 1966, 16.

21. Mike Love, as interviewed in *The Beach Boys 50, Doin' It Again*, written by Frank Haney, directed by John Anderson and Joe Thomas, DVD BEM 10001 (David C. Levy Productions, 2012), DVD.

22. "The Beach Boys' Temperamental Genius," *Teen Scoop*, September 1967, 40.

23. Undated letter from Emily Glee Love to Brian Wilson, reprinted in *Made in California*, 6-CD set, Capitol UME, a Universal Music Company, B0018509–02, 2013.

Chapter 3

1. Bruce Morgan (son of Hite and Dorinda Morgan), interview by author, June 26, 2007.

2. Ibid.

3. Ibid.

4. Ibid.

5. Ibid.

6. Ibid.

7. These are not the same Bachelors who recorded for Decca Records and London Records.

8. Alfred Schlesinger, interview by author, January 28, 2011.

9. "Welk Anniversaries at Aragon, in Tele," *Billboard*, August 1, 1953, 32.

10. Al Schlesinger did not recall a song called "Fiesta Day Polka," which some have credited as being written by Murry and recorded by Jimmie Haskell. Schlesinger pointed out, however, that in the early to mid–1950s, Haskell recorded as a member of the Bachelors and not as a solo artist. Neither BMI nor ASCAP currently list "Fiesta Day Polka."

11. "Reviews of This Week's New Records, Country & Western," *Billboard*, October 3, 1953, 28.

12. "Reviews of New Country & Western Records," *Billboard*, August 7, 1954, 38.

13. Dorinda Morgan's "Chapel of Love" is not the same song the Dixie Cups took to #1 in 1964.

14. Dorinda Morgan believed in the tenets of Christian Science and published her first article in the *Christian Science Sentinel* in August 1958. She later published articles in the *Christian Science Journal* in March 1961 and June 1962.

15. "Chapel of Love" was credited to Dorinda and Art Egnoian. It was backed with "Cool School," written by Dorinda and credited to Bruce, a rewrite of "Cool, Cool Christmas," the B side to "Always Forever" by the Sabers in November 1955.

16. Dorinda Morgan, *The Beach Boys, Lost & Found, 1961–1962*, produced by Hite and Dorinda Morgan, compiled and mastered by Steve Hoffman, DCC compact disc, DZS-054, 1991, liner notes.

17. Byron Preiss, *The Beach Boys* (New York: Ballantine, 1979), 8.

Chapter 4

1. John Grigsby, "Al Jardine's UT Connection," *The Toledo Blade*, August 12, 1990, 1.

2. Ibid.

3. Ibid.

4. Ibid.

5. Ibid., 2.

6. Ibid.

7. Eric Hirsimaki, "Super-Power Portraitist, Don Jardine: The Karsh of Lima," *Trains*, February 1977, 22–30.

8. Eric Hirsimaki, *Lima: The History* (Edmonds, WA: Hundman, 1985), 304.

9. Chuck Harter and Alan Boyd, "Virginia Jardine Interview," *Endless Summer Quarterly*, December 1995, 4.

10. Grigsby, "Al Jardine's UT Connection," 1.

11. Harter and Boyd, "Virginia Jardine Interview," 5.

12. Jeremy Roberts, "Persistence Pays Off—In Step with Al Jardine of the Beach Boys," www.examiner.com/article/persistence-pays-off-step-with-al-jardine-of-the-beach-boys, February 2, 2011.

13. Louis Thouvenin, interview by author, October 14, 2011.

14. Al Jardine, interview by Jocko Marcellino, Jocko's Jukebox, http://www.youtube.com/watch?v=IMsCAl0zT6k, uploaded February 16, 2012.

15. Thouvenin, interview.

16. "Industrial Photography Section Nears Completion with Darkroom," *RIT Reporter*, Rochester Institute of Technology, June 15, 1951, 8.

17. Thouvenin, interview.

18. "Al Jardine Rings Out Beach Boys' Folklore," *Endless Summer Quarterly*, Fall 2002, 6.

19. Al Jardine, spoken introduction to a live performance of "A Postcard from California," Roxy Theater, Los Angeles, October 19, 2008, http://www.youtube.com/watch?v=swG5OdaUVmk.

20. Al Jardine, interview by Peter Dixon and David Maclean, podcast audio, July 4, 2009, http://www.canstream.co.uk/radioteesdale/index.php?id=309.

21. Al Jardine, *A Postcard from California*, June 2010.

22. "Choo Choo Jardine Working in London," *RIT Reporter*, Rochester Institute of Technology, March 12, 1954, 4.

23. www.facebook.com/aljardine, December 4, 2014.

24. John Hagethorn, interview by author, May 23, 2010.

25. Harter and Boyd, "Virginia Jardine Interview," 4.

26. Ibid., 5.

27. Gary Winfrey, interview by author, August 2, 2008.

28. Ibid.

29. Ibid.

30. Bob Barrow, interview with author, July 12, 2008.

31. Ibid.

32. Winfrey, interview.

Chapter 5

1. Is Horowitz, "45 Disks Gain Edge Over 78 Pop Singles," *Billboard*, February 26, 1955, 27.

2. "Think Al Jardine of the Beach Boys," *Melody Maker*, December 31, 1966, 7.

3. "Brian Wilson," *Endless Summer Quarterly*, Fall 2005 (aka the Hawthorne 1960 edition), 33.

4. Brian Wilson, interview by Rob Hughes, "Brian Wilson," *Uncut*, September 2002, 6.

5. John Black, "Harmony's in My Head," *Mojo Collections*, Autumn 2001, 29.

6. David Leaf, *The Beach Boys and the California Myth* (New York: Grosset & Dunlap, 1978), 17.

7. Tom Nolan (with additional material by David Felton), "The Beach Boys: A California Saga. Part Two: Tales of Hawthorne," *Rolling Stone*, November 11, 1971, 53.

8. David Felton, "The Healing of Brother Bri," *Rolling Stone*, November 4, 1976, 39.

9. Leaf, *The Beach Boys and the California Myth*, 17.

10. Byron Preiss, *The Beach Boys* (New York: Ballantine, 1979), 8.

11. "Beach Boys: Riding New Waves of Success," *Teen Beat*, November 1976, 28.

12. Don Allen, personal communication, October 2008.

13. Paul Williams, "Brian Wilson," *Fi* 1, no. 2 (March 1996), 27.

14. "Brian Wilson: I Guess I Just Wasn't Made for These Times," directed by Don Was (Artisan Home Entertainment, 1995), DVD.

15. Williams, "Brian Wilson," 27.

16. Jerry Fink, "Founder Recaps Freshmen Years, Q&A with Bob Flanigan," *Las Vegas Sun*, January 3, 2008, http://69.89.25.185/~trexsoft/t-rexsoftware.com/fourfreshmen/freshnews/2q2008/pg15.pdf.

17. Jeff Bleiel, "Their Hearts Were Full of Spring: Four Freshmen and Five Beach Boys," in *Add Some Music to Your Day: Analyzing and Enjoying the Music of the Beach Boys*, ed. Don Cunningham and Jeff Bleiel, eds. (Cranberry Twp., PA: Tiny Ripple, 2000), 92–93.

18. Fink, "Founder Recaps Freshmen Years, Q&A with Bob Flanigan."

19. "Rhythm & Blues Record Reviews," *Billboard*, November 18, 1950, 30.

20. Fink, "Founder Recaps Freshmen Years, Q&A with Bob Flanigan."

21. Ross Barbour, interview by author, October 22, 2007.

22. Ken Sharp, "Surf's Up Again, an Interview with Brian Wilson," *Record Collector*, March 2001, 52.

23. "Brian Wilson: I Guess I Just Wasn't Made for These Times," DVD.

24. Sharp, "Surf's Up Again, an Interview with Brian Wilson," 52.

25. Bob Flanigan, interview by author, May 2, 2007.

26. "Endless Harmony," directed by Alan Boyd, Brother Records under exclusive license to Capitol Records 72434–92353–9–7 (Delilah Films, 2000), DVD.

27. Bleiel, "Their Hearts Were Full of Spring, Four Freshmen and Five Beach Boys," 92–93.

28. Barbour, interview.

29. John L. Scott, "Night Club Scene: Stars Will Spur Activity in Clubs," *Los Angeles Times*, May 17, 1958.

30. "The Beach Boys Story," presented by Bob Harris, written and researched by Jeff Griffin, BBC Radio 1, original radio broadcast 1974, rebroadcast in 1976 with updated ending.

31. Patrick Doyle, "Tributes," *Rolling Stone*, June 9, 2011, 22.

32. Ian Dove, "Al Rejoins Beach Boys," *New Musical Express*, August 14, 1964, 10.

33. Gary C.W. Chun, *Let's Swing*, Star Bulletin 11, no. 216, August 4, 2006.

34. Sharp, "Surf's Up Again, an Interview with Brian Wilson," 52.

35. Flanigan, interview.

36. Bill Wagner, interview by author, November 2007.

37. Felton, "The Healing of Brother Bri," 39.

38. Black, "Harmony's in My Head," 29.

39. Carl Wilson, interview by David Leaf, "The Making of Pet Sounds," *The Pet Sounds Sessions*, 4-CD set, EMI-Capitol CDP 7243 8 37662 2 2, 1996, liner notes, 21.

40. Geoffrey Himes, "The Beach Boys: High Times and Ebb Tides," *Musician*, September, 1983, 66.

41. Scott Cohen, "Mike Love and Carl Wilson Hang Ten on Surfin', Cruisin' and Harmonies," *Circus Raves*, April 1975, 26.

42. John Gilliland's Pop Chronicles, University of North Texas, "Forty Miles of Bad Road, Some of the Best from Rock and Roll's Dark Ages," show 20, radio broadcast (first aired KRLA, Pasadena, CA, February 1969), http://digital.library.unt.edu/search/?q=FORTY+MILES+OF+BAD+ROAD&t=fulltext.

43. Brian Wilson interview, *Best Summers of Our Lives*, six-hour radio special narrated by Charlie Van Dyke and Wolfman Jack, produced by Audio Stimulations, Summer 1976.

44. Timothy White, "Still Waters Run Deep, a Child Is Father to the Band, the Return of Brian Wilson," *Crawdaddy*, June 1976, 40–41.

45. Digby Diehl, "Hanging 10," *TV Guide*, July 31, 1976, 21.

46. Jane Ammeson, "Boys of Summer," *Northwest Airlines World Traveler*, December 1992, 34.

47. Peter Ames Carlin, *Catch a Wave: The Rise, Fall & Redemption of the Beach Boys' Brian Wilson* (New York: Rodale, 2006), 21.

48. Himes, "The Beach Boys: High Times and Ebb Tides," 67.

49. Mike Love interview, *The Beach Boys 50, Doin' It Again*, written by Frank Haney, directed by John Anderson and Joe Thomas, DVD BEM 10001 (David C. Levy Productions, 2012), DVD.

50. Mr. Bonzai, "Brian Wilson, American Innovator," *MIX*, March 1996, 42.

51. Black, "Harmony's in My Head," 29.

52. Billy Hinsche, "Good Vibrations, an Interview with Carl Wilson" (published posthumously), *Guitar One*, November 2001, 96.

53. Steve Caraway, "Carl Wilson, 14 Years a Beach Boy, *Guitar Player*, April 1976, 19.

54. Hinsche, "Good Vibrations, an Interview with Carl Wilson," 96.

55. Leaf, *The Beach Boys and the California Myth*, 18.

56. Caraway, "Carl Wilson, 14 Years a Beach Boy," 19.

57. David Marks gave a guitar clinic at Hawthorne High School on July 16, 2011. https://www.youtube.com/watch?v=gk-HhvXO7O4.

58. http://www.silvertoneworld.net/acoustic/0653/653_Kentucky_Blue.html.

59. Jon Stebbins with David Marks, *The Lost Beach Boy* (London: Virgin, 2007), 20.

60. Ibid.

61. *Let's Go to Hawthorne, CA! with David Marks*, Part 2, documentary produced by Chuck Kelley (uploaded July 11, 2011), http://www.youtube.com/watch?v=m_txZQz7AB0, 4:30.

62. Stebbins, *The Lost Beach Boy*, 22.

63. David Marks interview, *Brian Wilson, Songwriter, 1962–1969: Exploring Brian's Muse During a Decade of Dreams*, DVD documentary (Sexy Intellectual Production, www.chromedreams.co.uk), SIDVD 561, 2010.

64. Tony Norman, "It's Love That Keeps the Beach Boys Together," *Music Now*, November 28, 1970, page 2.

65. Ian Dove, "Beach Boys End an Emotional Struggle," *New Musical Express*, October 30, 1964, 14.

66. Robert DuPree, "David Marks on Being a Superstar at 13," *Two Louies*, September 1980, 3.

67. Vickie Amott, interview by author, May 5, 2010.

68. Ibid.

69. Ibid.

70. Ibid.

71. Ibid.

Chapter 6

1. John Hagethorn, interview by author, May 23, 2010. The book Al had read was *Poker According to Maverick: TV's Most Exciting Character Reveals the Secrets of the Most Exciting Game.*

2. Gary Winfrey, interview by author, July 28, 2008.

3. Bob Barrow, interview by author, July 12, 2008.

4. David Beard, "Al Jardine, Be True to Your School," *Endless Summer Quarterly*, Fall 2005 (aka the Hawthorne 1960 edition), 31.

5. Winfrey, interview.

6. Bruce Morgan, interview by author, June 26, 2007.

7. Winfrey, interview.

8. Byron Preiss, *The Beach Boys* (New York: Ballantine, 1979), 9.

9. Dorinda Morgan, *The Beach Boys, Lost & Found, 1961–1962*, produced by Hite and Dorinda Morgan, compiled and mastered by Steve Hoffman, DCC compact disc, DZS-054, 1991, liner notes.

10. Chuck Harter and Alan Boyd, "Virginia Jardine Interview," *Endless Summer Quarterly*, December 1995, 10.

11. Hagethorn, interview.

12. Scott Cohen, "Al Jardine's Beach Boyhood," *Circus*, May 26, 1977, 52.

13. Ren Grevatt, "Success Nearly Ruined Us!," *Teen Life*, October 1966, 18.

14. Jeremy Roberts, "Persistence Pays Off—In Step with Al Jardine," February 2, 2011, http://www.examiner.com/article/persistence-pays-off-step-with-al-jardine-of-the-beach-boys.

15. Ken Sharp, "Riding the Waves: My Life as a Beach Boy," *Record Collector*, August 2009, 59.

16. Roberts, "Persistence Pays Off—In Step with Al Jardine."

17. Registrar, Ferris State University, Big Rapids, Michigan.

18. *Hawthorne Today*, cable television show, Hawthorne, California, 1990.

19. Peter Ames Carlin, *Catch a Wave: The Rise, Fall & Redemption of the Beach Boys' Brian Wilson* (New York: Rodale, 2006), 25–26.

20. *The Collegian*, Los Angeles City College, May 5, 1959.

21. *The Collegian*, Los Angeles City College, May 19, 1959.

22. *The Collegian*, Los Angeles City College, December 11, 1959.

23. "The Stories of Success with Mike Love," Matt Weinberger, published May 1, 2013, www.youtube.com/watch?v=n2dJVX77KcY

24. "Be Casual," *Cougar*, Hawthorne High School, February 17, 1961.

25. "Surfin' Man" (b/w "Jailbreak," Dot 16068) by the Talismen was released in March 1960.

26. Mike Purpus, "Pier Avenue Junior High School," Hermosa Beach Historical Society Newsletter, March 2007.

27. Surfing Heritage & Cultural Center, "Mike Doyle, Champion Surfer & Paddler of the 1960s," Malcolm Gault-Williams, *Legendary Surfers, a Definitive History of Surfing's Culture and Heroes*, http://files.legendarysurfers.com/surf/legends/lsc220_doyle.html.

28. Paul Johnson, interview by author, June 6, 2008.

29. Ibid.

30. Ibid.

31. Stephen Curtin, interview by author, September 18, 2011.

32. Bob Levey, interview by author, September 21, 2011.

33. Judy Bowles, interview by author, January 22, 2011.

34. Ibid.

35. Curtin, interview.

36. Bowles, interview.

37. Ibid.

38. Ibid.

39. Beth Milligan, "Q&A with Beach Boys Guitarist Al Jardine," *The Ticker*, June 25, 2013, http://www.theticker.tc/story/q-a-with-beach-boys-guitarist-al-jardine.

40. Hagethorn, interview.

41. Winfrey, interview. In November 1959, during Al's senior year at Hawthorne High, a duo called the Islanders had a #15 hit with "The Enchanted Sea" (b/w "Pollyanna," Mayflower 16). In a quirky point of interest for Al, one of the Islanders, Randy Starr (real name Warren Nadal), was a dentist.

42. Steven P. Erie, *Globalizing L.A.: Trade, Infrastructure, and Regional Development* (Stanford: Stanford University Press, 2004), 97–102.

43. Winfrey, interview.

44. Bowles, interview.

45. Ibid.

46. Geoffrey Himes, "Fun, Fun, Fun: Carl Wilson's Life as a Beach Boy," guitar.com (original interview 1982).

47. Jon Stebbins with David Marks, *The Lost Beach Boy* (London: Virgin, 2007), 16–17.

48. David Leaf, *The Beach Boys and the California Myth* (New York: Grosset & Dunlap, 1978), 15.

49. Neal Gabler, "The Beach Boys: Riding a New Wave," *New Times*, April 2, 1976, 57.

50. Tom Nolan (with additional material by David Felton), "The Beach Boys: A California Saga. Part Two: Tales of Hawthorne," *Rolling Stone*, November 11, 1971, 52.

51. Gabler, "The Beach Boys: Riding a New Wave," 57.

52. Toby Mamis, "Beach Boys Hang Ten in Hotel Lobby," *Creem*, October, 1971, 76.

53. Ken Sharp, "Love Among the Ruins, the Controversial Beach Boy Speaks His Mind," *Goldmine*, September 18, 1992, 146.

54. Mike Love, interview by David Beard, *Endless Summer Quarterly*, Summer 2007, 11.

55. "Mike Love of the Beach Boys," *Teen Set*, October, 1966, 16.

56. Love, interview by David Beard, 11.

57. "The Beach Boys Story," presented by Bob Harris, written and researched by Jeff Griffin, BBC Radio 1, original radio broadcast 1974, rebroadcast in 1976 with updated ending.

58. Geoffrey Himes, "The Beach Boys: High Time and Ebb Tides," *Musician*, September 1983, 66.

59. Nikki Wine, "Brian Wilson Interview," *The Grapevine*, radio broadcast, KHTZ radio station, Los Angeles, October 4, 1980.

60. Jim Pewter, "Brian Wilson, a Unique Interview," *Who Put the Bomp*, Winter 1976/1977, 9.

Chapter 7

1. Bruce Morgan, interview by author, June 26, 2007.

2. Gary Winfrey, interview by author, August 2, 2008.

3. Ibid.

4. David Beard, "Al Jardine, Be True to Your School," *Endless Summer Quarterly*, Fall 2005 (aka the Hawthorne 1960 edition), 30–31.

5. Al Jardine, interview by David Beard, "Alan Jardine, Folk Music and Surfin,'" *Endless Summer Quarterly*, Summer 2007, 16.

6. Al Jardine interview, Sam Kogon, November 11, 2011, http://samkogen.bandcamp.com/track/al-jardine-interview.

7. Morgan, interview.

8. Deposition of Hite Morgan, *Hite Morgan v. Capitol Records, Inc.*, Case No. 860296 (Cal. Sup. Ct., Los Angeles Cnty.) (March 4, 1965). Hite Morgan was deposed by Frank G. Wells, an attorney for Capitol Records who later became president of the Walt Disney Company in 1984.

9. Dorinda Morgan's recollection that Brian mentioned that he liked "Duke of Earl" by Gene Chandler (Vee-Jay 416) does not help date their initial meeting. Although it did not appear in *Billboard* until November 27, 1961, "The Duke of Earl" may have played on LA radio much earlier as a record's release date does not always correlate with its chart entry.

10. Dorinda Morgan, *The Beach Boys, Lost & Found, 1961–1962*, produced by Hite and Dorinda Morgan, compiled and mastered by Steve Hoffman, DCC compact disc, DZS-054, 1991, liner notes.

11. Byron Preiss, *The Beach Boys* (New York: Ballantine, 1979), 9.

12. Mike Love, interview by Dr. Demento, *Dr. Demento Radio Show*, radio broadcast, July 1973, http://drdemento.com/online.html?c=e16&s=s.

13. Mike Love, interview by David Beard, *Endless Summer Quarterly*, Summer 2007, 11.

14. Morgan, interview.

15. Ibid.

16. Ibid.

17. Love, interview by David Beard, 11.

18. "The Beach Boys: Early Days & Family Life," *Life Story, The Beach Boys 50th Anniversary Tribute*, Bauer, 2012, 15.

19. Scott Cohen, "Al Jardine's Beach Boyhood," *Circus*, May 26, 1977, 52.

20. Ken Sharp, "Alan Jardine, a Beach Boy Still Riding the Waves," *Goldmine*, July 28, 2000, 16.

21. Deposition of Michael E. Love, *Morgan v. Wilson*, Case Nos. 00–13312, -13314 (C.D. Cal.).

22. "The Mad Happy Surfers, a Way of Life on the Wavetops," *Life*, September 1, 1961, 47–53.

23. *The Garage Tapes*, Sea of Tunes C 0760, 2007, unauthorized compact disc.

24. Jodi Gable (president of the Beach Boys first fan club), interview by author, March 19, 2012.

25. "The Beach Boys Story," presented by Bob Harris, written and researched by Jeff Griffin, BBC Radio 1, original radio broadcast 1974, rebroadcast in 1976 with updated ending.

26. *The Garage Tapes*.

27. Coach Jim Bunyard's personal remembrances, "Coach Bunyard vs Carl Wilson," Hawthorne High School alumni website, http://cougartown.com/rmbr when.html.

28. Standard Songwriter's Contract between Hite B. Morgan, Brian Wilson and Michael Love, dated September 15, 1961.

29. Morgan, interview.

30. "Al Jardine Rings Out Beach Boys' Folklore," *Endless Summer Quarterly*, Fall 2002, 9–10.

31. Ibid.

32. "The Beach Boys Story," radio broadcast.

33. Mike Love, interview, *Best Summers of Our Lives*, narrated by Charlie Van Dyke and Wolfman Jack, produced by Audio Stimulations, six-hour radio broadcast, Summer 1976.

34. Jardine, interview by David Beard, 16.

35. Al Jardine, interview by Jocko Marcellino, Jocko's Jukebox, http://www.youtube.com/watch?v=IMsCAl0zT6k, uploaded February 16, 2012.

36. Gable, interview.

37. Morgan, interview.

38. *The Garage Tapes*.

39. Bill Feinberg, "6'9" Stan Love's Last Chance to Stand Tall on the Basketball Court," *In the Know*, January 1976, 42.

40. "Lavender" was copyrighted March 21, 1955, and cannot help date the Beach Boys demo session at the Morgan home.

41. Dorinda Morgan, *The Beach Boys, Lost & Found, 1961–1962*, liner notes.

42. Stan Ross, interview by David Leaf, "The Making of Pet Sounds," *The Pet Sounds Sessions*, 4-CD set, EMI-Capitol Records CDP 7243 8 37662 2 2, 1996, liner notes, 57.

43. Stephen J. McParland, "The Richie Podolor and Bill Cooper Interview, Recorded in Woodland Hills, California, June 18, 1992," *Bull Sessions with the Big Daddy: Interviews with Those Who Helped Shape the California Sound* (New South Wales, Australia: CMusic, 2001), 62.

44. Morgan, interview.

45. Howard Kramer, interview by David Beard, *Endless Summer Quarterly*, Summer 2007, 9.

46. "Murry Wilson: Portrait of a Father-Manager," *Record World*, October 9, 1965, 12.

47. "Rock 'n' Roll Music, Beach Boys Rhythm Guitarist Al Jardine Explains the Band's Guitar Legacy," *Guitar One*, as told to Billy Hinsche, November 2001, 101.

48. Al Jardine, Landmark Dedication Ceremony, May 20, 2005, Hawthorne Cable Television, DVD.

49. Al Jardine, "Google Play: The Beach Boys Interview," June 6, 2012, http://www.youtube.com/watch?v=M9VY3zbCt24.

50. Sharp, "Alan Jardine, a Beach Boy Still Riding the Waves," 16.

51. Louis Thouvenin, interview by author, October 4, 2011.

52. Jardine, interview by David Beard, 16.

53. Al Jardine interview, The Archives of Music Preservation, December 16, 2011, http://archivesmp.com/videovault.htm.

54. Mike Love, interview by Joel Helmes, January 20, 2011, http://www.youtube.com/watch?v=c0WMaLV2TeI.

55. "Al Jardine Rings Out Beach Boys' Folklore," *Endless Summer Quarterly*, 11.

56. Jardine, interview by David Beard, 16.

57. Carl Wilson, interview, *Best Summers of Our Lives*, narrated by Charlie Van Dyke and Wolfman Jack, produced by Audio Stimulations, six-hour radio special, Summer 1976.

58. Robert DuPree, "David Marks on Being a Superstar at 13," *Two Louies*, September 1980, 3.

59. Billy Hinsche, "Good Vibrations, an Interview with Carl Wilson" (published posthumously), *Guitar One*, November 2001, 97.

60. Chuck Block, interview by author, May 13, 2008.

61. Ibid.

62. Jardine, interview by David Beard, 16.

63. Judy Bowles, interview by author, January 22, 2011.

64. David Felton, "The Healing of Brother Bri," *Rolling Stone*, November 4, 1976, 39.

65. Ian Whitcomb, *Rock Odyssey, a Chronicle of the Sixties* (New York: Hal Leonard, 1983), 40.

66. Tom Nolan (with additional material by David Felton), "The Beach Boys: A California Saga, Part Two: Tales of Hawthorne," *Rolling Stone*, November 11, 1971, 53.

67. Jardine, interview by Sam Kogon.

68. Deposition of Alan Jardine, *Bruce Morgan v. Brian Wilson*, Case No. 00–13312 (C.D. Cal.).

69. Theresa Kara Armijo (Hawthorne High School classmate of Al Jardine and Brian Wilson), interview by author, December 17, 2012.

70. Bowles, interview.

Chapter 8

1. Dino Lappas, interview by author, October 31, 2007.

2. Gordon Carmadelle, interview by author, March 28, 2007.

3. Lappas, interview.

4. Ibid.

5. Ibid.

6. Ibid.

7. Al Jardine interview, K-Earth 101, June 5, 2012, kearth101.cbslocal.com.

8. Al Jardine, interview by David Beard, "Alan Jardine, Folk Music and Surfin'," *Endless Summer Quarterly*, Summer 2007, 16.

9. Ken Sharp, "Alan Jardine, a Beach Boy Still Riding the Waves," *Goldmine*, July 28, 2000, 16.

10. Jardine, interview by David Beard, 17.

11. Geoffrey Himes, "The Beach Boys: High Times and Ebb Tides," *Musician*, September, 1983, 67.

12. Al Jardine interview, The Archives of Music Preservation, December 16, 2011, archivesmp.com.

13. Jardine, interview by David Beard, 16.

14. Ibid., 17.

15. Matt D'Arcy, "Birth of the Beach Boys," *Combo Musical Weekly*, January 1, 1965, 3.

16. Jeff Tamarkin, "Brian Wilson," *Goldmine*, November 18, 1988, 25.

17. "The Beach Boys, Still a Big Sound from Teenage Heaven, California," *Movie Teen Illustrated*, July 1966, 25.

18. Steven Gaines, *Heroes and Villains: The True Story of the Beach Boys* (New York: New American Library, 1986), 64.

19. Carl Wilson, interview by Tony Palmer, "All You Need to Know," seven-inch promotional record, EMI PSR 405, Los Angeles, California, May 1976.

20. John Stix, "Carl Wilson on Songwriting," *Guitar*, September 1989, 19.

21. John Hagethorn, interview by author, May 23, 2010.

22. http://www.laradio.com/wherea.htm.

23. Top 40 Radio Repository, Neil Ross Collection, http://reelradio.com/nr/index.html#nrkmpc83.

24. "Disc Jockeys Hold Meeting," *New Orleans Times-Picayune*, March 10, 1958, 54.

25. Chuck Blore, interview by author, April 2, 2007.

26. Joseph Saraceno, interview by author, June 30, 2007.

27. Gail Houseman Saraceno, interview by author, June 30, 2007.

28. Joseph Saraceno, interview.

29. Ibid.

30. Ibid.

31. BMI songwriters and ASCAP songwriters were not permitted to work with each other at the time, so Gordon used the last name of his friend Michael Daughtry. Hence, the writing credit was Saraceno—Daughtry.

32. Michael Z. Gordon, interview by author, May 4, 2010.

33. Paul Johnson, interview by author, June 6, 2008.

34. Albert Dix, interview by author, May 9, 2007.

35. Joseph Saraceno, interview.

36. Ibid.

37. Declaration of Richard K. Dix, May 10, 1995.

Chapter 9

1. Albert Dix (treasurer-secretary, Candix Enterprises, Inc.), interview by author, May 9, 2007.
2. Ibid.
3. Ibid.
4. Ibid.
5. Ibid.

Chapter 10

1. See Chapter 3, page 39.
2. Russ Regan, interview by Artie Wayne, 2006, http://www.spectropop.com/RussRegan/index.htm.
3. Claude Hall, "Strong Bond Between Disks and Radio: Regan," *Billboard*, February 16, 1974, 4.
4. Dorothy Freeman, interview by author, December 6, 2012.
5. Claude Hall, "Regan Recounts Hit Years," *Billboard*, February 9, 1974, 3.
6. Russ Regan, interview by author, May 17, 2007.
7. Brian Wilson interview, *The History of Rock and Roll*, fifty-two hour radio special written by Gary Theroux, produced by Bill Drake and Bill Chenault, and hosted by Bill Drake, 1978.
8. Judy Bowles, interview by author, January 22, 2011.
9. Mike Love interview, *Best Summers of Our Lives*, six-hour radio special, narrated by Charlie Van Dyke and Wolfman Jack, produced by Audio Stimulations, Summer 1976.
10. Byron Preiss, *The Beach Boys* (New York: Ballantine, 1979), 10.
11. Mike Love, interview by Joel Helmes, Part 1, January 20, 2011, http://www.youtube.com/watch?v=c0WMaLV2TeI.
12. John and Gary Walker, *The Walker Brothers, No Regrets, Our Story* London: John Blake 2009, page 37.
13. Bruce Morgan, interview by author, June 26, 2007.
14. Preiss, *The Beach Boys*, 10.
15. Dorinda Morgan, *The Beach Boys, Lost & Found, 1961–1962*, produced by Hite and Dorinda Morgan, compiled and mastered by Steve Hoffman, DCC compact disc, DZS-054, 1991, liner notes.
16. In correspondence, Richard Dix referred to the group alternately as the Pendletons and the Pendletones.
17. Declaration of Richard K. Dix, May 10, 1995.
18. Chuck Blore, interview by author, April 2, 2007.

Chapter 11

1. U.S. Department of Commerce, National Oceanic and Atmospheric Administration, National Environmental Satellite Data and Information Service, National Climactic Data Center, 151 Patton Avenue, Room 120, Asheville, North Carolina 28801–5001.
2. David Leaf, *The Beach Boys and the California Myth* (New York: Grosset & Dunlap, 1978), 29.

3. "Beach Boys Tour of Hawthorne," narrated by Paul Rogers, Hawthorne Cable Television, Hawthorne, California, 2005, http://www.youtube.com/watch?v=VSeS622wdQ8, 5:04.
4. "Al Jardine Rings Out Beach Boys' Folklore," *Endless Summer Quarterly*, Fall 2002, 12.
5. Virginia Jardine interview, *Endless Summer* television show, episode broadcast August 10, 1989.
6. Chuck Harter and Alan Boyd, "Virginia Jardine," *Endless Summer Quarterly*, December 1995, 4.
7. Geoffrey Himes, "The Beach Boys: High Times and Ebb Tides," *Musician*, September, 1983, 67.
8. United States Copyright Office, copyright.gov.
9. Tom Nolan (with additional material by David Felton), "The Beach Boys: A California Saga. Part Two: Tales of Hawthorne," *Rolling Stone*, November 11, 1971, 50.
10. Brian Wilson interview, *Best Summers of Our Lives*, six-hour radio special, narrated by Charlie Van Dyke and Wolfman Jack, produced by Audio Stimulations, Summer 1976.
11. Dennis Wilson interview, *Best Summers of Our Lives*, six-hour radio special, narrated by Charlie Van Dyke and Wolfman Jack, produced by Audio Stimulations, Summer 1976.
12. Audree Wilson interview, *Endless Summer* television show, episode broadcast, August 10, 1989.
13. Judy Bowles, interview by author, January 22, 2011.
14. Paul Johnson, interview by author, June 6, 2008.
15. "Brian Wilson: A Beach Boys' Tale," an interview with Greg Noll, *A&E Biography*, written by Peter Jones and Morgan Neville, directed by Morgan Neville, DVD, 1999.
16. Jim Roberts, interview by author, June 2008.
17. Michael Z. Gordon, interview by author, May 4, 2010.
18. *Record Exchanger* 2, no. 4, March, 1972, delta chart reprinted at http://www.anorakscorner.com/PressingPlantInfo.html.
19. Telegram from Bob Dix to Al Levine, December 19, 1961.
20. John Tefteller, telephone conversation with author, April 9, 2008.
21. Gerry Diez, interview by author, May 7, 2008.
22. The Beach Boys released a song called "Kokomo" in July 1988, which reached #1 that November.
23. Bowles, interview.
24. Timothy White, *The Nearest Faraway Place: Brian Wilson, the Beach Boys, and the Southern California Experience* (New York: Henry Holt, 1994), 147–48.
25. Byron Preiss, *The Beach Boys* (New York: Ballantine, 1979), 10–11.
26. Christopher H. Sterling and Cary O'Dell, eds., *The Concise Encyclopedia of American Radio* (London and New York: Routledge, 2010), 414.
27. Jodi Gable, interview by author, January 22, 2011.
28. "Mike Love Talks About the Beach Boy's Early Days," *Flip*, January 1967, 33.

29. The Beach Boys in Concert, tour program, 1964.

30. Brian Wilson with Todd Gold, *Wouldn't It Be Nice: My Own Story* (New York: HarperCollins, 1991), 53.

31. Timothy White, "Still Waters Run Deep, a Child Is Father to the Band, the Return of Brian Wilson," *Crawdaddy*, June 1976, 36.

32. Brian Wilson, interview by David Leaf, *Surfer Girl* and *Shut Down Volume 2* twofer CD, Capitol Records Compact Disc, Capitol CDP 7 93692 2, 1990, liner notes, 6.

33. *Endless Summer* television show, campfire sequence with Brian Wilson, episode broadcast June 22, 1989.

34. Bowles, interview.

35. Ian Dove, "Al Rejoins Beach Boys," *New Musical Express*, August 14, 1964.

36. Scott Cohen, "The Circus Raves Interview: Mike Love and Carl Wilson Hang Ten on Surfin', Cruisin' and Harmonies," *Circus Raves*, April 1975, 24.

37. *Endless Summer* television show, campfire sequence with Brian Wilson.

38. Leaf, *The Beach Boys and the California Myth*, 17.

39. Bowles, interview

Chapter 12

1. Ian Dove, "Beach Boys End an Emotional Struggle," *New Musical Express*, October 30, 1964, 14.

2. Paul Johnson, interview by author, June 6, 2008.

3. Jodi Gable, interview by author, January 22, 2011.

4. Chuck Harter and Alan Boyd, "Virginia Jardine Interview," *Endless Summer Quarterly*, December 1995, 9.

5. Western Union telegram from Murry Wilson to Soupy Sales, January 9, 1962.

6. "Record Ramblings," *Cash Box*, January 20, 1962, 18.

7. Albert Dix (treasurer-secretary, Candix Enterprises, Inc.), interview by author, May 9, 2007.

8. "Pick of the Week Newcomers," *Cash Box*, January 27, 1962, 12.

9. Alice Lillie, "Spotlight on Gary Usher," *Beach Boys Freaks United (BBFUN)*, May 1987.

10. David Leaf, *The Beach Boys and the California Myth* (New York: Grosset & Dunlap, 1978), 35.

11. Byron Preiss, *The Beach Boys* (New York: Ballantine, 1979), 11.

12. Bob Hughes, "Album by Album, Brian Wilson," *Uncut*, October 2006, 35.

13. Stephen J. McParland, *The California Sound: An Insider's Story, the Musical Biography of Gary Lee Usher* (New South Wales, Australia: CMusic, 2000), 39.

14. Ibid., 3.

15. John Blair and Stephen J. McParland, *The Illustrated Discography of Hot Rod Music, 1961–1965*, Ann Arbor, MI:, Popular Culture Ink, 1990.

16. Lauretta Cleaver, "Campus Rage," *Cougar*, January 19, 1962, 2.

17. Peggy Johnson, "Cruising Around," *San Bernardino County Sun*, January 27, 1962, 10.

18. Interview by author with Hawthorne High School alumnus, September 2, 2008.

19. McParland, *The California Sound: An Insider's Story, the Musical Biography of Gary Lee Usher*, 36.

20. "Chevy 409," *Car and Driver*, December 1964, 55.

21. "The Beach Years," interview with Gary Usher by Roger Christian, in *The Rock Shoppe*, six-hour radio broadcast, written and narrated by Roger Cristian and Jim Pewter, Custom Fidelity Records, 1975, 33⅓ rpm.

22. "David Marks, Mischief & Music," *Endless Summer Quarterly*, Fall 2005 (aka the Hawthorne 1960 edition), 35.

23. McParland, *The California Sound: An Insider's Story, the Musical Biography of Gary Lee Usher*, 46.

24. Ken Sharp, "Love Among the Ruins: The Controversial Beach Boy Speaks His Mind," *Goldmine*, September 18, 1992, 18.

25. McParland, *The California Sound: An Insider's Story, the Musical Biography of Gary Lee Usher*, 43.

26. Wink Martindale, interview by author, May 3, 2007.

27. Robert J. Dalley, *Surfin' Guitars, Instrumental Surf Bands of the Sixties* (Azusa, CA: Surf, 1988), 350.

28. Johnson, interview.

29. Ibid.

30. Ibid.

31. Vickie Amott, interview by author, May 5, 2010.

32. Ibid.

33. Matt Everitt, "Interview with Brian Wilson," *6 Music's The First Time*, BBC Radio, radio broadcast, October 23, 2011.

34. Two articles published in the late 1960s, "Meet the Beach Boys" by Joey Sasso in the August/September 1967 *Young Miss* and "The Beach Boys" in *Inside Pop, America's Top Ten Groups* published by Scholastic Books in 1968, mentioned it rained heavily on the day the Beach Boys recorded "Surfin'." In the greater LA area, there was no significant rainfall in August, September, or October 1961. It rained 0.58" on November 20, 1961, but "Surfin'" had already been recorded by then. Hence, it would appear the articles confused the "Surfin'" session with the "Surfin' Safari" session on Thursday, February 8, 1962, when it rained a torrential 3.91". The rainfall data was obtained from the U.S. Department of Commerce, National Oceanic and Atmospheric Administration, National Environmental Satellite Data and Information Service, National Climactic Data Center, 151 Patton Avenue, Room 120, Asheville, North Carolina 28801–5001.

35. Byron Preiss, *The Beach Boys*, 11.

36. Declaration of Valerio A. Poliuto, September 25, 1996, *Bruce Morgan v. Brian Wilson*, Nos. CV-00–13312, -13314 (C.D. Cal.).

37. Ken Sharp, "Brian Wilson, the Rhapsody of a Beach Boy," *Goldmine*, January 2011, 45.

38. Philip Lambert, *Inside the Music of Brian Wilson: The Songs, Sounds, and Influences of the Beach Boys' Founding Genius* (New York: Continuum, 2007), 25.

39. Legend on the original tape box of the Beach Boys recording session produced by Hite Morgan at World Pacific Studio, 8715 West Third Street, Los Angeles, California, February 8, 1962.

40. *The Beach Boys, Lost & Found, 1961–1962*, produced by Hite and Dorinda Morgan, compiled and mastered by Steve Hoffman, DCC compact disc, DZS-054, 1991.

41. Don Cunningham, "Surfer Girl," *Add Some Music*, December 1978.

42. Lambert, *Inside the Music of Brian Wilson: The Songs, Sounds, and Influences of the Beach Boys' Founding Genius*, 28.

43. Ibid., 31.

44. Paul Zollo, "Sleighbells in the Summer: Brian Wilson, the Song Talk Interview," *Song Talk*, published by the National Academy of Songwriters, Fall 1988, 6.

45. Lambert, *Inside the Music of Brian Wilson: The Songs, Sounds, and Influences of the Beach Boys' Founding Genius*, 30–31.

46. Ibid., 30.

47. Geoffrey Himes, "The Beach Boys: High Times and Ebb Tides," *Musician*, September 1983, 66.

48. David Felton, "The Healing of Brother Bri," *Rolling Stone*, November 4, 1976, 43.

49. Judy Bowles, interview by author, January 22, 2011.

50. Lambert, *Inside the Music of Brian Wilson: The Songs, Sounds, and Influences of the Beach Boys' Founding Genius*, 33.

51. Ibid.

52. Alfred Schlesinger, interview by author, January 28, 2011.

53. Gable, interview.

54. Ken Sharp, "Riding the Waves: My Life As a Beach Boy," *Record Collector*, August 2009, 60.

55. Jane Ammeson, "Boys of Summer," *Northwest Airlines World Traveler*, December 1992, 35.

56. "Al Jardine Rings Out Beach Boys' Folklore," *Endless Summer Quarterly*, Fall 2002, 13.

57. McParland, *The California Sound: An Insider's Story, the Musical Biography of Gary Lee Usher*, 43.

58. Andrew G. Doe, "Lookin' at Yesterday, Gary Winfrey 'Takes a Load Off' to Reflect on His Past with Al Jardine," *Endless Summer Quarterly*, Fall 2002, 39.

59. Memorandum from Harry Klusmeyer to Murry Wilson, dated February 11 [1962], reprinted in *Good Vibrations: Thirty Years of the Beach Boys*, 5-CD Capitol Records box set C2 0777 7 81294 2 4, 1993.

60. Leaf, *The Beach Boys and the California Myth*, 39.

61. Bob Eubanks with Matthew Scott Hansen, *It's in the Book, Bob!* (Dallas: BenBella, 2004), 48.

62. Sharp, "Love Among the Ruins, the Controversial Beach Boy Speaks His Mind," 18.

63. *Endless Summer* television show, campfire sequence with Al Jardine, episode broadcast June 22, 1989.

64. Faye Reis (Candix recording artist), interview with author, April 28, 2007.

65. Martin Grove, ed., "An Exclusive Interview with Roger Christian," *Music Favorites* 1, no. 2, 1976, 57.

66. Johnson, interview.

67. Robert Dupree, "David Marks on Being a Superstar at 13," *Two Louies*, September 1980, 3.

68. McParland, *The California Sound: An Insider's Story, the Musical Biography of Gary Lee Usher*, 44.

Chapter 13

1. Judy Bowles, interview by author, January 22, 2011.

2. Byron Preiss, *The Beach Boys* (New York: Ballantine, 1979), 11.

3. Jim Pewter, "The Flowering of Brian Wilson, a Unique Interview," *Who Put the Bomp*, Winter 1976/1977), 9.

4. Alice Lillie, "A Rap with Audree Wilson," *Beach Boys Freaks United (BBFUN)*, May 1978, 1.

5. *The Beach Boys, Lost & Found, 1961–1962*, produced by Hite and Dorinda Morgan, compiled and mastered by Steve Hoffman, DCC compact disc, DZS-054, 1991.

6. Hite Morgan misspelled "Barbie" as "Barbee" on the tape box legend.

7. Steve Hoffman, interview by author, November 1, 2011.

8. Billy Hinsche, "An Interview with Carl Wilson" *Guitar One*, November 2001, 97.

9. Donald Conder, interview by author, April 22, 2010.

10. "Hawthorne Rock and Roll Stars Ride Surf's Crest," newspaper clipping, unknown publication, undated.

11. Matt Everitt, "Interview with Brian Wilson," *6 Music's The First Time*, BBC Radio, radio broadcast, October 23, 2011.

12. Steve Love, interview by author, October 30, 2008.

13. "Rich Sloan, Onward Cougars, Onward Cougars," Hawthorne 1960, *Endless Summer Quarterly*, Fall 2005 (aka the Hawthorne 1960 edition), 21.

14. Andrew Hope, "Big Daddy of the Beach Boys," *Music Maker*, January 1968, 18.

15. "47th National Orange Show Opens Tomorrow with Big Program," *Redlands Daily Facts*, March 14, 1962, page 5.

16. Gary Usher, interview by David Leaf, *Surfin' Safari* and *Surfin' U.S.A.* twofer CD, Capitol Records Compact Disc, Capitol CDP 72435–31517–2–0, 2001, liner notes, 8.

17. David Leaf, *The Beach Boys and the California Myth* (New York: Grossett and Dunlap, 1978), 32.

18. Advertisement, *San Bernardino County Sun*, May 12, 1962, B7.

19. Memorandum from Harry Klusmeyer to Murry Wilson, dated February 11, [1962], reprinted in *Good Vibrations: Thirty Years of the Beach Boys*, 5-CD Capitol Records box set C2 0777 7 81294 2 4, 1993.

20. David Stadler, interview by author, February 10, 2009.

21. Steven Gaines, *Heroes and Villains: The True*

Story of the Beach Boys (New York: New American Library, 1986), 68.

22. Declaration of Russ Regan, *Bruce Morgan v. Brian Wilson*, Case No. 00–13312 (C.D. Cal.).

23. John Roberts, "Pop Singer Battles with Books, Cuts Hay–Making Discs on Side," *The Warwhoop*, El Camino Community College, March 30, 1962, 2.

24. Stadler, interview.

25. Richard Hoffman, interview by author, February 6, 2011.

26. Domenic Priore, "Shane Wilder, the Beach Boys First Manager," *Dumb Angel Gazette No. 1*, 1986, 62–68.

27. Bowles, interview.

28. David Felton, "The Healing of Brother Bri," *Rolling Stone*, November 4, 1976.

29. Lillie, "A Rap with Audree Wilson," 1.

30. Tom Nolan (with additional material by David Felton), "The Beach Boys: A California Saga. Part Two: Tales of Hawthorne," *Rolling Stone*, November 11, 1971, 51.

Chapter 14

1. Steven Gaines, *Heroes and Villains: The True Story of the Beach Boys* (New York: New American Library, 1986), 77–78.

2. Stephen J. McParland, *Our Favourite Recording Sessions* (New South Wales, Australia: CMusic, undated), 41.

3. Stephen J. McParland, *The California Sound: An Insider's Story, the Musical Biography of Gary Lee Usher* (New South Wales, Australia: CMusic, 2000), 46.

4. Ibid.

5. Chuck Britz, interview by David Leaf, "The Making of Pet Sounds," *The Pet Sounds Sessions*, 4-CD set, EMI-Capitol Records CDP 2 7243 8 37662 2 2, 1996, liner notes, 54.

6. *The Garage Tapes*, Sea of Tunes C 0760, 2007, unauthorized compact disc.

7. Ibid.

8. Ibid.

9. Ibid.

10. Jon Stebbins with David Marks, *The Lost Beach Boy* (London: Virgin, 2007), 42–43.

11. McParland, *The California Sound: An Insider's Story, the Musical Biography of Gary Lee Usher*, 46.

12. Chuck Britz interview, July 7, 2008, http://en.440tv.com/search.php?query=chuck+britz&cat=0.

13. Ibid.

14. Ibid.

15. Byron Preiss, *The Beach Boys* (New York: Ballantine, 1979), 11.

16. Tom Nolan (with additional material by David Felton), "The Beach Boys: A California Saga. Part Two: Tales of Hawthorne," *Rolling Stone*, November 11, 1971, 53.

17. Britz, interview.

18. David Leaf, *Surfin' Safari* and *Surfin' U.S.A.* twofer CD, Capitol Records, CDP 72435–31517–2–0, 2001, liner notes, 10.

19. Judy Bowles, interview by author, January 22, 2011.

20. Ibid.

21. Ibid.

22. McParland, *The California Sound: An Insider's Story, the Musical Biography of Gary Lee Usher*, 45.

23. Don Brann (Hawthorne High School classmate of Dennis Wilson), interview by author, October 29, 2008.

24. Stephen J. McParland, "The Russ Regan Interview, Recorded in Burbank, September 28, 1993," *Bull Sessions with the Big Daddy: Interviews with Those Who Helped Shape the California Sound* (New South Wales, Australia: CMusic Publishing, 2001), 70.

25. Stebbins, *The Lost Beach Boy*, 42.

26. Ibid., 42–43.

27. Nolan, "The Beach Boys: A California Saga. Part Two: Tales of Hawthorne," 53.

28. Bruce Morgan, interview by author, June 26, 2011.

29. Randy Wood sold Dot Records to Paramount Pictures for $3 million in 1957, but stayed on as the label's president.

30. Morgan, interview.

31. Andrew Hope, "Big Daddy of the Beach Boys," *Music Maker*, January 1968, 18.

32. Murry Wilson as told to Adam Walsh, "My Boys, the Beach Boys," *Melody Maker*, November 18, 1967.

33. Ken Nelson, *My First 90 Years Plus 3* (Pittsburgh: Dorrance, 2007), 187.

34. Ibid.

35. Ibid.

36. Rob Finnis, *Pet Projects: The Brian Wilson Productions*, Compact Disc, CDCHD 851, Ace Records, 2003, liner notes, 5, 6.

37. Gaines, *Heroes and Villains: The True Story of the Beach Boys*, 77–78.

38. "Music Meet to Analyze Legal Aspects," *Daily Trojan*, University of Southern California, April 6, 1962, page 1.

39. Declaration of Averill C. Pasarow, February 8, 2002, *Bruce Morgan v. Brian Wilson*, Case Nos. CV-00–13312, 13314 (C.D. Cal.).

40. Letter from Averill C. Pasarow to Bruce L. Wolfson, dated April 17, 1962.

41. Pasarow Declaration.

42. Gaines, *Heroes and Villains: The True Story of the Beach Boys*, 77.

43. Ken Sharp, "Alan Jardine, a Beach Boy Still Riding the Waves," *Goldmine*, July 28, 2000, 18.

44. Letter from Bruce L. Wolfson to Pacific Record Distributors and Era Record Distributors, dated February 13, 1962. Alfred Schlesinger, attorney for Hite Morgan, was copied on the letter.

45. Letter from Bruce L. Wolfson to Robert Field, dated June 12, 1962.

46. Paul Johnson, interview with author, June 6, 2008.

47. Affidavit of Nickolas Venet, February 1965, *Hite Morgan v. Capitol Records*, No. 860, 296 (Cal. Sup. Ct., Los Angeles Cnty.).

48. Declaration of Nik Venet, January 13, 1992.

49. Deposition of Nikolas Venet, March 5, 1992, *Brian Douglas Wilson v. Irving Music, Inc.*, Case No. C 737 675 (Cal. Sup. Ct., Los Angeles Cnty.).

50. Pat Twitty, "Music As Written, Nashville," *Billboard*, May 26, 1962, 12.

51. Nolan, "The Beach Boys: A California Saga. Part Two: Tales of Hawthorne," 50.

52. *Hawthorne, CA, the Birthplace of a Musical Legacy*, 2-CD set, "Mike on Brian's Harmonies," CD-1, track 4, March 20, 1998, Capitol Compact Disc 72435–31583–2–3, 2001.

53. Philip Lambert, *Inside the Music of Brian Wilson: The Songs, Sounds, and Influences of the Beach Boys' Founding Genius* (New York: Continuum, 2007), 40.

54. Deposition of Nikolas Venet.

55. Nick Venet, interview by Terry Gross, "Fresh Air," National Public Radio, radio broadcast, March 19, 1996.

56. Stephen J. McParland, "The Nick Venet Interview, Recorded at Farmers Market, Los Angeles, May 5, 1997," *Bull Sessions with the Big Daddy: Interviews with Those Who Helped Shape the California Sound* (New South Wales, Australia: CMusic, 2001), 81.

57. Wally George, "Strictly Off the Record, Wasted Wax," *Los Angeles Times*, February 8, 1958, B7.

58. Stephen J. McParland, "The Richie Podolor and Bill Cooper Interview, Recorded in Woodland Hills, California, June 16, 1992," *Bull Sessions with the Big Daddy: Interviews with Those Who Helped Shape the California Sound* (New South Wales, Australia: CMusic, 2001), 61.

59. Lee Zhito, "Music As Written, Hollywood," *Billboard*, October 12, 1959, 22.

60. Paul Vidal, "Derry Weaver," interview conducted in 2000 and 2001, May 2008, http://www.bigvjamboree.com/DerryWeaverStory.htm.

61. Martin Grove, ed., "An Exclusive Interview with Roger Christian," *Music Favorites* 1, no. 2, 1976, 57.

62. Barney Hoskyns, *Waiting for the Sun: A Rock 'n' Roll History of Los Angeles* (New York: Backbeat, 2009), 62.

Chapter 15

1. Gary Hallmark, "Neighborhood Pals," *Endless Summer Quarterly*, Fall 2005 (aka the Hawthorne 1960 edition), 37.

2. Stephen J. McParland, *The California Sound: An Insider's Story, the Musical Biography of Gary Lee Usher* (New South Wales, Australia: CMusic, 2000), 48.

3. Affidavit of Nickolas Venet, February 1965, *Hite Morgan v. Capitol Records*, No. 860, 296 (Cal. Sup. Ct., Los Angeles Cnty.).

4. Deposition of Nikolas Venet, March 5, 1992, *Brian Douglas Wilson v. Irving Music, Inc.*, Case No. C 737 675 (Cal. Sup. Ct., Los Angeles Cnty.).

5. Affidavit of Nickolas Venet, February 1965.

6. McParland, *The California Sound: An Insider's Story, the Musical Biography of Gary Lee Usher*, 48.

7. Ibid.

8. Stephen J. McParland, *Our Favourite Recording*

Sessions (New South Wales, Australia: CMusic, undated), 44.

9. "The Beach Boys Story," presented by Bob Harris, written and researched by Jeff Griffin, BBC Radio 1, original radio broadcast 1974, rebroadcast in 1976 with updated ending.

10. Affidavit of Nickolas Venet, February 1965.

11. Declaration of Nik Venet, October 20, 1997.

12. David Finkle, "Murry Wilson: Portrait of a Father-Manager," *Record World*, October 9, 1965, 12.

13. "Local Youths' First Record Called Hit," *Inglewood Daily News*, May 22, 1962.

14. Affidavit of Nickolas Venet, February 1965.

15. Declaration of Nik Venet, October 20, 1997.

16. McParland, *The California Sound: An Insider's Story, the Musical Biography of Gary Lee Usher*, 49.

17. Tom Nolan (with additional material by David Felton), "The Beach Boys: A California Saga. Part Two: Tales of Hawthorne," *Rolling Stone*, November 11, 1971, 51.

18. Ibid., 50.

19. McParland, *The California Sound: An Insider's Story, the Musical Biography of Gary Lee Usher*, 56.

20. Affidavit of Nickolas Venet, February 1965.

21. Undated note from Brian Wilson to Dave Marks, reprinted in *Good Vibrations: Thirty Years of the Beach Boys*, 5-CD Capitol Records box set C2 0777 7 81294 2 4, 1993.

22. Declaration of Nik Venet, October 20, 1997.

23. Fred Vail interview, *Open Sky Eight*, DVD, 2005.

24. Brian Gari, "The '76 Comeback & a Letter from Murry," letter from Murry G. Wilson to Brian Gari, dated December 11, 1965, reprinted in *Add Some Music* 7, no. 1, Winter, 1984, 48.

25. David McClellan, interview by author, January 4, 2012.

26. Ibid.

27. Nolan, "The Beach Boys: A California Saga. Part Two: Tales of Hawthorne," 51.

28. David Leaf, *The Beach Boys and the California Myth* (New York: Grosset and Dunlap, 1978), 37.

29. Declaration of Nik Venet, January 13, 1992.

30. "The Beach Boys Story," radio broadcast.

31. Ibid.

32. Lindsay Buckingham, "The Beach Boys, The 100 Greatest Artists of All Time," *Rolling Stone*, July 2011, 24.

33. Lydia Lee, interview by author, September 24, 2008.

34. Ibid.

35. McParland, *The California Sound: An Insider's Story, the Musical Biography of Gary Lee Usher*, 57.

36. Ibid.

37. Martin Grove, ed., "An Exclusive Interview with Roger Christian," *Music Favorites* 1, no. 2, 1976, 56.

38. "Capitol Pays at .76 a Share," *Billboard*, September 1, 1962, 6.

Chapter 16

1. Jimmy O'Neill (radio and television personality), interview by author, August 17, 2012.

2. Ibid.

3. Ibid.

4. Ibid.

5. Ibid.

6. Ibid.

7. Ibid.

8. *Cash Box*, October 27, 1962, 34.

9. O'Neill, interview.

10. Interview with Eddy Medora, *Part 1: The Renegades*, October 28, 2003. http://www.earcandymag.com/sunrays.htm.

11. Western Union telegram from Nick Venet to Murry Wilson, dated July 6, 1962.

12. Letter from Nick Venet to Murray [*sic*] Wilson, dated July 1962, reprinted in *Good Vibrations: Thirty Years of the Beach Boys*, 5-CD Capitol Records box set C2 0777 7 81294 2 4, 1993.

13. Gary Usher, interview by David Leaf, *Surfin' Safari* and *Surfin' U.S.A.* twofer CD, Capitol Records compact disc, Capitol CDP 72435–31517–2–0, 2001, liner notes, 5, 7.

14. Stephen J. McParland, *The California Sound: An Insider's Story, the Musical Biography of Gary Lee Usher* (New South Wales, Australia: CMusic, 2000), 62.

15. Judy Bowles, interview by author, January 24, 2011.

16. McParland, *The California Sound: An Insider's Story, the Musical Biography of Gary Lee Usher*, 50.

17. Paul Johnson, interview by author, June 6, 2008.

18. Richard Schneider, interview by author, March 5, 2013.

19. The interviewer has sometimes been mistakenly identified as Richard Laubacher, chairman of the Diaper Derby and owner of Laubacher Appliances, who advertised on KOXR.

20. Supplement, Capitol Contract Number 3374, July 16, 1962.

21. Steven Gaines, *Heroes and Villains: The True Story of the Beach Boys* (New York: New American Library, 1986), 81–82.

22. Jodi Gable, interview by author, March 19, 2012.

23. Fred Hopkins, "*Surf's Up! With David Marks*," *Psychotronic*, no. 28, 1998, 59.

24. Robert J. Dalley, *Surfin' Guitars: Instrumental Surf Bands of the Sixties* (Ann Arbor, MI: Popular Culture, Ink, 1996), 313.

25. Letter from Jo Ann Marks to Pendleton Mills, dated July 31, 1962.

26. David Marks, interviewed in *Dennis Wilson: The Real Beach Boy* television documentary, British Broadcast Corporation, 2010.

27. McParland, *The California Sound: An Insider's Story, the Musical Biography of Gary Lee Usher*, 55.

Chapter 17

1. Marc Savlov, "Cars and Speed and Flight, the Continuing Career of Director Monte Hellman," March 10, 2000, http://www.austinchronicle.com/screens/2000–03-10/cars-and-speed-and-flight/.

2. Paul Vidal, "Derry Weaver," interview conducted in 2000 and 2001, May 2008, http://www.bigvjamboree.com/DerryWeaverStory.htm.

3. Stephen J. McParland, *Our Favourite Recording Sessions* (New South Wales, Australia: CMusic, undated), 60.

4. Peter Reum, "Surfin' Safari Revisited," *Endless Summer Quarterly*, Fall 2012, 38.

5. Vidal, "Derry Weaver."

6. Jon Stebbins with David Marks, *The Lost Beach Boy* (London: Virgin, 2007), 48.

7. Stephen J. McParland, *The California Sound: An Insider's Story, the Musical Biography of Gary Lee Usher* (New South Wales, Australia: CMusic, 2000), 55.

8. Joe Osborn, interview by author, January 29, 2013.

9. Steve Douglas, *New Gandy Dancer*, ed. Dave Peckett, November 14, 1979.

10. American Federation of Musicians, Local 47, contract number 74654, dated August 8, 1962.

11. McParland, *The California Sound: An Insider's Story, the Musical Biography of Gary Lee Usher*, 56.

12. Robert DuPree, "David Marks on Being a Superstar at 13," *Two Louies*, September 1980, 3.

13. David Marks interview, *Brian Wilson, Songwriter, 1962–1969: Exploring Brian's Muse During a Decade of Dreams*, DVD documentary (Sexy Intellectual Production, www.chromedreams.co.uk), SIDVD561, 2010.

14. Reum, "Surfin' Safari Revisited," 36.

15. Stephen J. McParland, "The Nick Venet Interview, Recorded at Farmers Market, Los Angeles, May 5, 1993," *Bull Sessions with the Big Daddy: Interviews with Those Who Helped Shape the California Sound* (New South Wales, Australia: CMusic, 2001), 83.

16. McParland, *The California Sound: An Insider's Story, the Musical Biography of Gary Lee Usher*, 41.

17. Brian Wilson, Introduction, *Surfin' Safari* and *Surfin' U.S.A.* twofer CD, Capitol Records Compact Disc, Capitol CDP 72435–31417–2–0, liner notes.

18. Gary Usher, interview by David Leaf, *Surfin' Safari* and *Surfin' U.S.A.* twofer CD, Capitol Records Compact Disc, Capitol CDP 72435–31517–2–0, 2001, liner notes, 8.

19. Rich Miailovich, interview by author, September 16, 2013.

20. Jodi Gable, interview by author, March 19, 2012.

21. Judy Bowles, interview by author, January 24, 2011.

22. David Leaf, *The Beach Boys and the California Myth* (New York: Grosset & Dunlap, 1978), 49.

23. "Brian Wilson: A Beach Boys' Tale," an interview with Bob Norberg, *A&E Biography*, written by Peter Jones and Morgan Neville, directed by Morgan Neville, DVD, 1999.

24. Letter from Murry Wilson to Brian Wilson, dated May 8, 1965.

25. Jerry Osborne, "Dave Nowlen: A Survivor," *DISCoveries*, October 1989, 137.

26. "Brian Wilson: A Beach Boys Tale," an interview with Dave Nowlen, *A&E Biography*, written by Peter Jones and Morgan Neville, directed by Morgan Neville, DVD, 1999.

27. Steve Gaines, *Heroes and Villains: The True Story of the Beach Boys* (New York: New American Library, 1986), 264 (referencing *Record World* magazine).

28. Osborne, "Dave Nowlen: A Survivor," 137.

29. Alan Boyd, *Hawthorne, CA, Birthplace of a Musical Legacy*, Capitol Compact Disc 72435-31583-2-3, 2001, liner notes.

30. "Brian Wilson," *Uncut*, September 2002, 6.

31. Johnny Black, "Harmony's in My Head," *Mojo Collection*, Autumn 2001, 28.

32. Brian Wilson, interview by David Leaf, "The Making of Pet Sounds," *The Pet Sounds Sessions*, 4-CD set, EMI-Capitol Records CPD 2 7243 8 37662 2 2, 1996, liner notes, 10–11.

33. McParland, *The California Sound: An Insider's Story, the Musical Biography of Gary Lee Usher*, 53.

34. Andrew G. Doe, "Lookin' at Yesterday: Gary Winfrey 'Takes a Load Off' to Reflect on His Past with Al Jardine," *Endless Summer Quarterly*, Fall 2002, 39–40.

35. Advertisement, *Los Angeles Times*, August 16, 1962, 8.

36. *(Let's Go) to Hawthorne, CA, with David Marks!*, Part 1, documentary produced by Chuck Kelley (uploaded July 11, 2011), http://www.youtube.com./watch?v=q3zqUU73riY.

37. "The Note Book," *The Hollywood Reporter*, August 23, 1962, 8.

38. *One Man's Challenge* was first available on VHS in 2000.

39. Dale Smallin recorded the famous cackle that opens "Wipe Out" by the Sufaris.

40. McParland, *The California Sound: An Insider's Story, the Musical Biography of Gary Lee Usher*, 50.

41. Jon Stebbins with David Marks, *The Lost Beach Boy* (London: Virgin, 2007), 46.

42. Gable, interview.

43. Leaf, *The Beach Boys and the California Myth*, 35–36.

44. Gable, interview.

45. "The Beach Boys Story," presented by Bob Harris, written and researched by Jeff Griffin, BBC Radio 1, original radio broadcast 1974, rebroadcast in 1976 with updated ending.

46. Gaines, *Heroes and Villains: The True Story of the Beach Boys*, 95–96.

47. David Felton, "The Healing of Brother Bri," *Rolling Stone*, November 4, 1976. 41.

48. Victoria Balfour, *Rock Wives: The Hard Lives and Good Times of the Wives, Girlfriends, and Groupies of Rock and Roll* (New York: HarperCollins, 1986), 100, 107.

49. "Brian Wilson: A Beach Boys' Tale," an interview with Ginger Blake, *A&E Biography*, written by Peter Jones and Morgan Neville, directed by Morgan Neville, DVD, 1999.

50. Bowles, interview.

51. http://www.ronjacobshawaii.com/2008/05/got-on-my-knees-pretended-to-pray.html.

52. The program for the band's January 30, 1965, concert at the Seattle Center Coliseum noted their Spanish Castle appearance was in summer 1962 shortly after "Surfin' Safari" was released.

53. Peter Blecha, *Sonic Boom, The History of Northwest Rock, from "Louie, Louie" to "Smells Like Teen Spirit"* (Milwaukee: Backbeat, 2009), 159–60.

54. Pat O'Day, interview by author, August 8, 2013.

55. Martha Chabin, "Social Whirl: Looks Like Teenagers Play Sweet, Slow Music," *Hutchinson, Kansas News*, October 21, 1962, 11.

Chapter 18

1. Michael Borchetta, interview by the author, March 19, 2013.

2. In 1963, after the Beach Boys proved themselves a touring powerhouse, they were assigned to senior agent Ira Okun.

3. Milton Berle with Haskel Frankel, *An Autobiography* (New York: Delacorte, 1974), 248.

4. Jon Stebbins with David Marks, *The Lost Beach Boy* (London: Virgin, 2007), 51.

5. Letter from Murry Wilson to Brian Wilson, dated May 8, 1965.

6. Stephen J. McParland, *The California Sound: An Insider's Story, the Musical Biography of Gary Lee Usher* (New South Wales, Australia: CMusic, 2000), 52.

7. Ibid., 50.

8. Philip Lambert, *Inside the Music of Brian Wilson: The Songs, Sounds, and Influences of the Beach Boys' Founding Genius* (New York: Continuum, 2007), 56.

9. Writer Stephen J. McParland noted that in 1964 Gary Usher recycled "Number One" into "Lori," which he intended for singer Rod Lauren. Glen Campbell also recorded demos of "Lori," "Human" (aka, "My Only Alibi"), and "The Beginning of the End."

10. McParland, *The California Sound: An Insider's Story, the Musical Biography of Gary Lee Usher*, 52.

11. Stephen J. McParland, *The Wilson Project* (Sydney, Australia: PTB), 1991, 74–75.

12. "The 500 Greatest Songs of All Time," Number 73, "Summertime Blues" by Eddie Cochran, *Rolling Stone*, December 9, 2004, 106.

13. "20 Visionary Musicians at 20," *Mojo*, December 2013, 66–67.

14. The Beach Boys, *The Smile Sessions*, "Our Prayer" session, compact disc 2, track 2 (recorded October 4, 1966), Capitol Records 509990 27658 22, 2011.

15. Jodi Gable, interview by author, March 19, 2012.

16. McParland, *The California Sound: An Insider's Story, the Musical Biography of Gary Lee Usher*, 54.

17. Ron Maynard, "Brian Wilson, The Wild Wacky World of a Beach Boy," magazine clipping, unknown publication, circa 1965, 56.

18. Gary Usher, interview by David Leaf, *Surfin' Safari* and *Surfin' U.S.A.* twofer CD, Capitol Records Compact Disc, Capitol CDP 72435-31517-2-0, 2001, liner notes, 9.

19. Don Cunningham, "Song Scrutiny: 'County Fair' and 'I Do,'" *Add Some Music*, fanzine.

20. Press release, *bi-og'ra-phy, The Beach Boys*, Capitol Records, September 1962, 2.

21. Jane Veeder, interview by author, September 18, 2012.

22. Letter from Evelyn Klein of the law office of Walter Hofer, 150 West 55th Street, New York, New York, to Hite Morgan dated September 7, 1962.

23. Lambert, *Inside the Music of Brian Wilson: The Songs, Sounds, and Influences of the Beach Boys' Founding Genius*, 56.

24. Interview with Brian Wilson and Dennis Wilson by Daryl Dry for "Rocketing Rhythms," a thirty-minute music and interview program produced by the Department of Defense for its Armed Forces Radio & Television Service. It was recorded mid–September 1962, a twelve-inch 33⅓ rpm album was pressed September 25, and the show was programmed for broadcast October 6.

25. Wanda Henderson, "A Chaperone Learns Ropes," *Los Angeles Times*, September 16, 1962, H3.

26. Helen Lee Stillman, interview by author, August 5, 2013.

27. Barret H. Collins, interview by author, August 2, 2013.

28. "Casuals Dance Combo to Get Record into National Sales," *Oxnard Press-Courier*, September 6, 1962.

29. Randy Ray, interview by author, March 22, 2011.

30. Ibid.

31. Bob Clark, interview by author, December 9, 2009.

32. Tom Capra, ed., "Pledges Stage Clean Up of International House," *Daily Trojan*, University of Southern California, 1.

33. Affidavit of Nickolas Venet, February 1965, *Hite Morgan v. Capitol Records*, Case No. 860296 (Cal. Sup. Ct., Los Angeles Cnty.).

34. Judy Bowles, interview by author, January 24, 2011.

35. Ibid.

36. Gable, interview.

Chapter 19

1. "Late Pop Spotlights," *Billboard*, October 20, 1962, 6.

2. Dave Wagner, Youth Editor, "Slightly Off Beat: 'Ten Great Bands' Set Now Available at Special Price," *Daily Northwestern*, Oshkosh, Wisconsin, November 1, 1962, 44.

3. Rob Finnis, *Pet Projects: The Brian Wilson Productions*, Compact Disc, CDCHD 851, Ace Records, 2003, liner notes, 8.

4. Nick Wise, *The Beach Boys, in Their Own Words* (New York: Omnibus, 1994), 21.

5. Robert DuPree, "David Marks on Being a Superstar at 13," *Two Louies*, September 1980, 3.

6. "Dennis Wilson: We Just Want to Be a Good Group," *Hit Parader*, June 1967, 16.

7. Bob Hughes, "Album by Album, Brian Wilson," *Uncut*, October 2006, 85.

8. "Beachboys Appear—Not Appreciated," Fred Radloff, Staff Writer, *El Vaquero*, Glendale Community College, Glendale, California, October 12, 1962.

9. Stephen J. McParland, *The California Sound: An Insider's Story, the Musical Biography of Gary Lee Usher* (New South Wales, Australia: CMusic, 2000), 63.

10. Philip Lambert, *Inside the Music of Brian Wilson: The Songs, Sounds, and Influences of the Beach Boys' Founding Genius* (New York: Continuum, 2007), 57.

11. "Capitol Sales up 39% in 1st. Qtr." *Cash Box*, October 27, 1962, 7.

12. Al Schlesinger, interview by the author, January 28, 2011.

13. Ian Rusten and Jon Stebbins, *The Beach Boys in Concert: The Ultimate History of America's Band on Tour and Onstage* (Milwaukee: Backbeat, 2013), 14.

14. *Torrance Press*, Torrance, California, October 31, 1962

15. *Torrance Herald*, Torrance, California, November 1, 1962.

16. Patricia Valdivia, interview by author, March 24, 2011.

17. McParland, *The California Sound: An Insider's Story, the Musical Biography of Gary Lee Usher*, 65.

18. "Reviews of New Singles," *Billboard*, November 10, 1962, 48.

19. Update to the listing for "Here's to Veterans" found on page 346 of Brad Elliott's *Surf's Up!*: It is program 866, and Brian introduced five songs.

20. Fred Hopkins, "Surf's Up with David Marks," *Psychotronic Video Magazine* #28, 1998, 59.

21. "Pick of the Week, Newcomers," *Cash Box*, November 17, 1962, 12.

22. Email from Gary Steelberg to author, January 21, 2014.

23. "Fund Drive at Van Nuys," *Teen Post*, December 9, 1962, 13.

24. Tedd Thomey, "In Person: Morgue Come Back to Life," *Long Beach Press-Telegram*, December 13, 1962, C3.

25. Ibid.

26. David Beard, Editor, "Shut Down Volume 2," *Endless Summer Quarterly*, Spring 2014, 23. After he crashed his Chevrolet Corvair in mid–February 1963, Dennis purchased a 1963 Corvette Stingray Coupe. Mike's recollection of Dennis racing home from the Cinnamon Cinder in Long Beach in his Corvette may indicate an undocumented show there in spring 1963.

27. Deposition of Nikolas Venet, March 5, 1992, *Brian Douglas Wilson v. Irving Music, Inc.*, Case No. C 737 675 (Cal. Sup. Ct., Los Angeles Cnty.).

28. Mike Borchetta, interview by author, March 19, 2013.

29. Mike Borchetta, interview by author, July 7, 2007.

30. Jodi Gable, interview by author, March 19, 2012.

31. Judy Bowles, interview by the author, January 24, 2011.

32. Tom Nolan, "The Beach Boys: A California

Saga. Part Two: Tales of Hawthorne," *Rolling Stone*, November 11, 1971, 52.

33. Ibid.

34. Keith Badman, *The Beach Boys, The Definitive Diary of America's Greatest Band: On Stage and in the Studio* (San Francisco: Backbeat, 2004), 29.

35. Jon Stebbins with David Marks, *The Lost Beach Boy* (London: Virgin, 2007), 53.

36. Email from Eric Groves to author, August 2, 2013.

37. Nolan, "The Beach Boys: A California Saga. Part Two: Tales of Hawthorne," 52.

38. Ibid.

39. Eunice Field, *IN (For the Girl of Today, the Woman of Tomorrow)*, "Beach Boys in Search of 5 Men," August 1966, 62.

Chapter 20

1. "Capitol Chalks Up Hottest Half-Year," *Billboard*, February 2, 1963, 4.

2. Philip Lambert, *Inside the Music of Brian Wilson: The Songs, Sounds, and Influences of the Beach Boys' Founding Genius* (New York: Continuum, 2007), 61–62.

3. Ibid., 63.

4. Tom Nolan (with additional material by David Felton), "The Beach Boys: A California Saga. Part Two: Tales of Hawthorne," *Rolling Stone*, November 11, 1971, 52.

5. David Leaf, *Surfin' Safari* and *Surfin' U.S.A.* twofer CD, Capitol Records, CDP 72435–31517–2–0, 2001, liner notes, 11.

6. Richard Buskin, *Inside Tracks: A First-Hand History of Popular Music from the World's Greatest Record Producers and Engineers* (New York: HarperCollins, 1999), foreword by Brian Wilson.

7. David Leaf, *Little Deuce Coupe* and *All Summer Long* CD, Capitol Records, CDP 93693 2, 1990, liner notes, 8.

8. Geoffrey Himes, "Carl Wilson," in *Back to the Beach: A Brian Wilson and the Beach Boys Reader*, Kingsley Abbott, ed. (London: Helter Skelter, 2003), 244.

9. Geoffrey Himes, "Fun, Fun, Fun: Carl Wilson's Life as a Beach Boy," Guitar.com, 1982, interview, http://www.guitar.com/articles/fun-fun-fun-carl-wilsons-life-beach-boy.

10. Leaf, *Surfin' Safari* and *Surfin' U.S.A.* twofer CD, liner notes.

11. Mike Borchetta, interview by author, July 10, 2007.

12. Robert J. Dalley, *Surfin' Guitars: Instrumental Surf Bands of the Sixties* (Ann Arbor, MI: Popular Culture, Ink, 1996), 57.

13. Randy Nauert (Challengers' bassist), interview by author, February 5, 2013.

14. "Last Drag" (b/w "Big Bad HoDad," NBI Records 100) was released by Roger Christian in April 1963. "Last Drag" was credited as co-written by Tony

Butala and Christian, co-produced by Butalla and Bob Todd, and co-published by Butala's and Todd's Tonto Music. In 1964, Butala and Todd produced "Love Those Beach Boys," a tribute record co-written by former Candix recording artist Lanny Duncan that incorporated snippets of new recordings of several Beach Boys' songs. It was recorded by the Sea Shells, a female surf group, for Butala's and Todd's Goliath Records.

15. Martin Grove, ed., "An Exclusive Interview with Roger Christian," *Music Favorites* 1, no. 2, 1976, 60–61.

16. Brian Wilson Q&A, Smiley Smile Message Board, January 26, 2015, http://smileysmile.net/board/index.php/topic,19756.0.html.

17. Philip Lambert, *Inside the Music of Brian Wilson: The Songs, Sounds, and Influences of the Beach Boys' Founding Genius* (New York: Continuum, 2007), 66.

18. Jon Stebbins with David Marks, *The Lost Beach Boy* (London: Virgin, 2007), 58–59.

19. *Cash Box*, October 27, 1962, 22.

20. Lambert, *Inside the Music of Brian Wilson: The Songs, Sounds, and Influences of the Beach Boys' Founding Genius*, 67.

21. Stephen J. McParland, *Inception & Conception* (New South Wales, Australia: CMusic, 2011), 70.

22. Stephen J. McParland, "The Nick Venet Interview, Recorded at Farmers Market, Los Angeles, May 5, 1997," *Bull Sessions with the Big Daddy: Interviews with Those Who Helped Shape the California Sound* (New South Wales, Australia: CMusic, 2001), 82.

23. McParland, *Inception & Conception*, 104.

24. Domenic Priore, "Shane Wilder, the Beach Boys First Manager," *Dumb Angel Gazette* No. 1, 1986, 62–68.

25. Letter from Murry Wilson to Brian Wilson, dated May 8, 1965.

26. Dalley, *Surfin' Guitars, Instrumental Surf Bands of the Sixties*, 174–75. Eddy and Albert Haddad later formed Kenny and the Fiends, who later became the Band Without a Name, a quintet that included Mark Groseclose and David Marks. They were managed by the Haddad's cousin, disc jockey Casey Kasem, who left KEWB in San Francisco and joined KRLA in Los Angeles in May 1963.

27. Dean Torrence, *Jan & Dean Golden Hits Volume 2*, Liberty Records LRP-3417, August 1965, liner notes.

28. Dean Torrence interview, "The Beach Boys," The United Stations Programming Network, Arlington, Virginia, July 3–5, 1987.

29. David Beard, "Surf City, the First #1 Pop Surf Song," *Endless Summer Quarterly*, Fall 2013, 27.

30. "Al Jardine Rings Out Beach Boys Folklore," *Endless Summer Quarterly*, Fall 2002, 13–14. Al recalled that Brian first asked him to fill in for him at a show in Arizona. When Al arrived at the LA airport for the flight, Murry was angry to learn Brian had arranged for Al to take his place. This would seem to place the show in late January 1963 for a show at the University of Arizona in Tucson. There are, however, some inconsistencies in Al's recollection. He recalled it was a flight to Phoenix, not Tucson, for a show at Big Surf, a waterpark in nearby Tempe that did not open until 1969. The Beach Boys' first appearance in Phoenix was July 5 and

6, 1963. By then, Al had filled in for Brian many times and it is unlikely Murry would have been surprised to see him.

31. Frank DeVito, interview by author, February 25, 2013.

32. Stebbins, *The Lost Beach Boy*, 49.

33. Judy Bowles, interview by author, January 22, 2011.

34. Lambert, *Inside the Music of Brian Wilson: The Songs, Sounds, and Influences of the Beach Boys' Founding Genius*, 109.

35. Dennis Diken, "Surfin' U.S.A., the Album that Changed Everything," *Endless Summer Quarterly*, Fall 2013, 19.

36. "Beachboys to Play at Canteen Dance," *Cougar*, Hawthorne High School, February 15, 1963.

37. Dalley, *Surfin' Guitars: Instrumental Surf Bands of the Sixties*, 174.

38. Domenic Priore, "Dick Dale & His Del-Tones Rule L.A. 1961–'63!," *Dumb Angel Gazette* No. 4, 2005, 22.

39. Dalley, *Surfin' Guitars: Instrumental Surf Bands of the Sixties*, 251–52.

40. Bowles, interview.

41. Affidavit of Nickolas Venet, February 1965, *Hite Morgan v. Capitol Records*, No. 860, 296, (Cal. Sup. Ct., Los Angeles Cnty.).

42. Gary Winfrey, interview by author, August 2, 2008.

43. "Al Jardine, Band Mate and High School Chum," *Endless Summer Quarterly*, Summer 2005, 13.

44. "Al Jardine Rings Out Beach Boys' Folklore," *Endless Summer Quarterly*, 34.

45. Timothy White, *The Nearest Faraway Place: Brian Wilson, the Beach Boys, and the Southern California Experience* (New York: Henry Holt, 1994), 177–78.

46. Jodi Gable, interview by author, March 19, 2012.

47. Bowles, interview.

48. Winfrey, interview.

49. Mike Love interview, "The Beach Boys Story," narrated by Ron Lundy, Unistar Radio Programming, Colorado Springs, Colorado, June 29–July 4, 1990.

50. "The Beach Boys Story," presented by Bob Harris, written and researched by Jeff Griffin, BBC Radio 1, original radio broadcast 1974, rebroadcast in 1976 with updated ending.

51. Philip Lambert interview, *Brian Wilson, Songwriter, 1962–1969: Exploring Brian's Muse During a Decade of Dreams*, DVD documentary (Sexy Intellectual Production, www.chromedreams.co.uk), SIDVD 561, 2010.

52. Geoffrey Himes, "Carl Wilson," in *Back to the Beach: A Brian Wilson and the Beach Boys Reader*, Kingsley Abbott, ed. (London: Helter Skelter, 2003), 21.

53. Ted Plonas, "DISC-ussion," *Long Beach Press-Telegram*, March 14, 1963, A23.

54. Dick Van Patten, "Pop—Jazz—Broadway," *Post Standard*, Syracuse, New York, April 21, 1963, 17.

55. Pat Colonna, "Teen Times: Same Songs, New Names," *The Trenton Evening Times*, May 24, 1963, 34.

56. Charles J. Schreiber, "Top Pop Recordings," *Baton Rouge Advocate*, March 31, 1963, 87.

57. Stephen J. McParland, *The California Sound: An Insider's Story, the Musical Biography of Gary Lee Usher* (New South Wales, Australia: CMusic, 2000), 80.

58. Deposition of Nikolas Venet, March 5, 1992, *Brian Douglas Wilson v. Irving Music, Inc.*, Case No. C 737 675 (Cal. Sup. Ct., Los Angeles Cnty.).

59. Larry Allison, "Surfboard Making Forges into Southland Industrial Limelight," *Long Beach Press-Telegram*, April 14, 1963, R-1.

60. Anthony DeCurtis interview, *Brian Wilson, Songwriter, 1962–1969: Exploring Brian's Muse During a Decade of Dreams*, DVD documentary (Sexy Intellectual Production, chromedreams.co.uk), SIDVD561, 2010.

61. Steven Gaines, *Heroes and Villains: The True Story of the Beach Boys* (New York: New American Library, 1986), 96.

62. Marilyn Wilson interview by Steve Kolanjian, *The Honeys Capitol Collectors Series*, Capitol Records Compact Disc, CDP 7 931932, 1992, liner notes, 3.

63. Ibid., 4.

64. Lambert, *Inside the Music of Brian Wilson: The Songs, Sounds, and Influences of the Beach Boys' Founding Genius*, 77.

65. Bowles, interview.

66. Nick Venet, interview by David Leaf, "The Making of Pet Sounds," *The Pet Sounds Sessions*, 4-CD set, EMI-Capitol Records CDP 2 7243 8 37662 2 2, 1996, liner notes, 48.

67. Bowles, interview.

68. David Beard, "Head to 'Drag City' 45 Years Later With Jan & Dean," *Goldmine*, April 13, 2010.

69. Mark A. Moore, *"A Righteous Trip": In the Studio with Jan Berry, 1963–1966*, ©2001–2011.

70. Brian's demo of "Gonna Hustle You" was released on the third of six EPs in the unauthorized "California Collectors Series" in 1982 and digitally on *The Big Beat* in December 2013. Jan & Dean's recording of "Get a Chance with You" appeared on the second EP in the "California Collectors Series."

71. Leslie Williams, interview by Malcolm Searles, January–February, 2003, http://www.pipeline-opera glass.moonfruit.com.

72. Ted Plonas, "DISC-ussion," *Long Beach Independent*, May 3, 1963, 19.

73. Bowles, interview.

74. *Billboard*, April 6, 1963, 11, 42.

75. Gable, interview.

Chapter 21

1. "Singles Reviews," *Billboard*, April 13, 1963, 34.

2. Victoria Balfour, *Rock Wives: The Hard Lives and Good Times of the Wives, Girlfriends, and Groupies of Rock and Roll* (New York: HarperCollins, 1986), 101–02.

3. Robert J. Dalley, *Surfin' Guitars: Instrumental Surf Bands of the Sixties* (Ann Arbor, MI: Popular Culture, Ink, 1996), 51–2.

4. Kent Crowley, *Surf Beat, Rock and Roll's Forgotten Revolution* (New York: Backbeat, 2011), 104–05.

5. Mike Love interview, *Innerview* radio show hosted by Jim Ladd, series 10, show number 13, June 1978.

6. Jodi Gable, interview by author, March 19, 2012.

7. Jon Stebbins, Smiley Smile Message Board, May 13, 2006, http://www.smileysmile.net/board/index.php/topic,277.msg37508.html.#msg37508.

8. Ian Rusten, "The Beach Boys, Television and Film," *Endless Summer Quarterly*, Spring 2009, 16.

9. Stebbins, Smiley Smile Message Board, May 13, 2006.

10. Stephen J. McParland, *Inception & Conception* (New South Wales, Australia: CMusic, 2011), 104.

11. David Leaf, *Good Vibrations: Thirty Years of the Beach Boys*, 5-CD Capitol Records box set C2 0777 7 81294 2 4, 1993, liner notes.

12. Tom Nolan, "Fame Los Angeles Style," *Los Angeles Magazine*, October 1980.

13. Eunice Field, *IN (For the Girl of Today, the Woman of Tomorrow)*, "Beach Boys in Search of 5 Men," August 1966, 62.

14. Gary Winfrey, interview by author, August 2, 2008. The music store in Lawndale referenced by Winfrey was Hogan's House of Music.

15. Jane Ammeson, "Boys of Summer," *Northwest Airlines World Traveler*, December 1992, 35.

16. Ken Sharp, "Alan Jardine, a Beach Boy Still Riding the Waves," *Goldmine*, July 28, 2000, 16.

17. Ammeson, "Boys of Summer," 35.

18. David Felton, "The Healing of Brother Bri," *Rolling Stone*, November 4, 1976, 50.

19. "Al Jardine Rings Out Beach Boys' Folklore," *Endless Summer Quarterly*, Fall 2002, 14.

20. "The Beach Boys Story," presented by Bob Harris, written and researched by Jeff Griffin, BBC Radio 1, original radio broadcast 1974, rebroadcast in 1976 with updated ending.

21. "Excelsior Park Hosts Hi School Night Friday," *The Minnetonka Record*, May 2, 1963.

22. Richard Duckett, "Good Vibrations," *Worcester Telegram & Gazette*, November 30, 2008.

23. Jon Stebbins with David Marks, *The Lost Beach Boy* (London: Virgin, 2007), 70.

24. Ibid., 71.

25. Lee Dempsey, "The Summer Moon, the Victoria Hale Interview," *Endless Summer Quarterly*, Spring 2011, 18.

26. Ibid., 20.

27. *Surfin'*, Varèse Sarabande Records, compact disc 302 066 085 2, 2000.

28. Stephen J. McParland, *The Honeys Collection*, Collector's Choice Music Compact Disc 72435–29850–2–9, EMI-Capitol Music Special Markets, 2001, liner notes.

29. Lee Zhito, "Capitol Come Back on Singles Front: Three in Top 10," *Billboard*, May 18, 1963, 1.

30. Letter from Murry Wilson to Brian Wilson, dated May 8, 1965.

31. Judy Bowles, interview by author, January 24, 2011.

32. Fred Vail, interview, *Open Sky Eight*, DVD, 2005.

33. "The Beach Boys' Story," radio broadcast.

34. Ibid.

35. Raymond M. "Duke" Hammett, interview by author, October 14, 2013.

36. Email from Jeffrey Hammett to author, October 16, 2013.

37. Email from Neil Anson to author, October 17, 2013.

38. "Bakersfield High School Cafeteria Contract Let," *Bakersfield Californian*, January 26, 1955, 24.

39. American Federation of Musicians, Local 47, Contract Number 75991, June 12, 1963.

40. Gable, interview.

41. Mike Love, "Google Play, the Beach Boys Interview," June 6, 2012, http://www.youtube.com/watch?v=M9VY3zbCt24.

42. Ralph M. Newman and Jeff Tamarkin, "The Beach Boys, from the Beginning: An Interview," *Time Barrier Express*, April–May 1979, 33.

43. Brian listed the Wilsons' Hawthorne address on his songwriter's contracts and certificates of copyright because Murry was administering Sea of Tunes music publishing.

44. Andrew G. Doe, "The One That Got Away, the Sharon Marie Interview," *Endless Summer Quarterly*, Spring 2011, 27.

45. Ibid., 30.

46. "The Beat, Beat of Surf Music," *Billboard*, June 29, 1963, 26.

47. "Surfer Sets Own Firm," *Billboard*, June 29, 1963, 6.

48. "New Firm Not in Surf Field," *Billboard*, July 13, 1963, 6.

49. "Capitol Sales Hit Highest Since '59," *Billboard*, August 31, 1963, 1.

50. Dalley, *Surfin' Guitars, Instrumental Surf Bands of the Sixties*, 183.

51. Dalley, *Surfin' Guitars, Instrumental Surf Bands of the Sixties*, 239.

52. Ibid., 124.

53. "The Beach Boys," *Keen Teen*, September 1964, 27.

Chapter 22

1. Robert J. Dalley, *Surfin' Guitars: Instrumental Surf Bands of the Sixties* (Ann Arbor, MI: Popular Culture, Ink, 1996), 5.

2. Stephen J. McParland, *The California Sound: An Insider's Story, the Musical Biography of Gary Lee Usher* (New South Wales, Australia: CMusic, 2000), 85.

3. Brian Wilson interview, *Nashville Sounds, The Making of Stars and Stripes*, Brother Records Inc., 1996, DVD

4. "Brian Wilson: A Beach Boys' Tale," an interview with Bob Norberg, *A&E Biography*, written by Peter Jones and Morgan Neville, directed by Morgan Neville, DVD, 1999.

5. David Crosby, as interviewed in *Brian Wilson: I Guess I Just Wasn't Made for These Times*. Directed by Don Was (Artisan Home Entertainment, 1995), DVD.

6. Linda Ronstadt as interviewed in *Brian Wilson: I Guess I Just Wasn't Made for These Times*. Directed by Don Was (Artisan Home Entertainment, 1995), DVD.

7. David Leaf, *The Beach Boys and the California Myth* (New York: Grosset & Dunlap, 1978), 38.

8. Ibid., 37.

9. Martin Grove, ed., "An Exclusive Interview with Roger Christian," *Music Favorites* 1, no. 2, 1976, 57.

10. Geoffrey Himes, "Carl Wilson," in *Back to the Beach: A Brian Wilson and the Beach Boys Reader*, Kingsley Abbott, ed. (London: Helter Skelter Publishing, 2003), 244.

11. "The Beach Boys' Story," presented by Bob Harris, written and researched by Jeff Griffin, BBC Radio 1, original radio broadcast 1974, rebroadcast in 1976 with updated ending.

12. Tom Nolan (with additional material by David Felton), "The Beach Boys: A California Saga. Part Two: Tales of Hawthorne," *Rolling Stone*, November 11, 1971, 51.

13. Brian Wilson completed *Smile* thirty-seven years later. He released *Brian Wilson Presents Smile* in 2004. In 2012, Capitol Records released *The Smile Sessions*, garnering the Best Historical Album award at the 55th Annual Grammy Awards in 2013.

14. Leaf, *The Beach Boys and the California Myth*, 37.

15. Ibid.

16. Tom Nolan, "The Beach Boys: A California Saga. Part One: Mr. Everything," *Rolling Stone*, October 28, 1971, 32.

17. "The Beach Boys' Story," radio broadcast.

18. Jon Stebbins with David Marks, *The Lost Beach Boy* (London: Virgin, 2007), 86.

19. Letter from Hite B. Morgan to Murry Gage Wilson, dated July 26, 1963.

20. Stebbins, *The Lost Beach Boy*, 86–87.

21. Brad Elliott, "Interview: The Survivors," *Add Some Music*, Summer 1983, 28–29.

22. Bruce Snoap, interview with the author, September 10, 2013.

23. Bob Shephard, "Platter Patter," *Petoskey News Review*, August 10, 1963, 6.

24. Ibid., 6.

25. Stebbins, *The Lost Beach Boy*, 90.

26. Grove, ed., "An Exclusive Interview with Roger Christian," 60.

27. Leaf, *The Beach Boys and the California Myth*, 52.

28. Grove, ed., "An Exclusive Interview with Roger Christian," 59–60.

29. Elliott, "Interview: The Survivors," 39.

30. Ibid., 28.

31. Judd Hamilton, interview by author, December 15, 2013.

32. Stebbins, *The Lost Beach Boy*, 7.

33. Judy Bowles, interview by author, January 22, 2011.

Chapter 23

1. Popular Songwriter's Contract for "Custom Machine" between Brian Wilson and Sea of Tunes Publishing Company, dated November 1, 1962.

2. Brad Elliott, "Interview: The Survivors," *Add Some Music*, Summer 1983, 22.

3. Philip Lambert, *Inside the Music of Brian Wilson: The Songs, Sounds, and Influences of the Beach Boys' Founding Genius* (New York: Continuum, 2007), 109.

4. Elliott, "Interview: The Survivors," 21–22.

5. Keith McCord, "Beach Boys' Hit Inspired by a Utah Gal Having All the Fun," February 11, 2007, ksl.com/index.php?nid=481&sid=886044.

6. Robert J. Dalley, *Surfin' Guitars: Instrumental Surf Bands of the Sixties* (Ann Arbor, MI: Popular Culture, Ink, 1996), 94.

7. Elliott, "Interview: The Survivors," 39.

8. Vickie Kocher, interview by author, August 5, 2013.

9. Liner notes for compact disc two written by Sheila Burgel, *One Kiss Can Lead to Another: Girl Group Sounds, Lost & Found*, 4-CD set, Rhino Entertainment Company, 2005, liner notes, 108.

10. David McClellan, interview by author, January 16, 2013.

11. Elliott, "Interview: The Survivors," 18.

12. "On the Skelton Show," *San Diego Union*, September 30, 1963, 12.

13. Timothy White, *The Nearest Faraway Place: Brian Wilson, the Beach Boys, and the Southern California Experience* (New York: Henry Holt, 1994), 186.

14. "Nick Venet Quits Capitol Over 'Internal Differences,'" *Billboard*, October 19, 1963, 4.

15. Alfred G. Aronowitz, "The Dumb Sound," *Saturday Evening Post*, October 5, 1963, 93–94.

16. Tom Nolan (with additional material by David Felton), "The Beach Boys: A California Saga. Part Two: Tales of Hawthorne," *Rolling Stone*, November 11, 1971, 50.

17. "Venet People Assigned to Economidas [*sic*]," *Billboard*, November 9, 1963, 38.

18. Karl Engemann, interview by David Leaf, "The Making of Pet Sounds," *The Pet Sounds Sessions*, 4-CD set, EMI-Capitol Records CDP 2 7243 8 37662 2 2, 1996, liner notes, 109.

19. Letter from Karl Engemann to Brian D. Wilson dated October 25, 1962, reprinted in *Made in California*, 6-CD set, Capitol UME, a Universal Music Company, B0018509–02, 2013.

20. Marilyn Wilson, interview by David Leaf, "The Making of Pet Sounds," *The Pet Sounds Sessions*, 4-CD set, EMI-Capitol Records CDP 2 7243 8 37662 2 2, 1996, liner notes.

21. Robert DuPree, "A Beach Boy Looks Back: Good, Clean Boyish Fun," *Trouser Press*, January/February 1981, 2.

22. Stebbins, *The Lost Beach Boy*, 102–103.

23. Ibid., 106–07.

24. Letter from Murry G. Wilson to Brian Gari, dated December 11, 1965.

25. Jodi Gable, interview by author, March 19, 2012.

26. "The Story Behind the Success of the Beach Boys, *Teen Life*, February 1964, 16–18.

27. Ian Dove, "Al Rejoins Beach Boys," *New Musical Express*, August 14, 1964, 10.

28. "(Dance with) the Guitar Man" (b/w "Stretchin' Out," RCA Victor 8087) by Duane Eddy and the Rebelettes was released in October 1962. Once thought to be the Honeys incognito, the Rebelettes were actually the Blossoms. The same holds true for the K-C Ettes who backed up Al Casey on "Surfin' Hootenanny" (b/w "Easy Pickin'," Stacy 962) and "Surfin' Blues" (b/w "Guitars, Guitars, Guitars," Stacy 964) in June and July 1963, respectively.

29. Y-Day at the Bowl–1963, http://pastdaily.com/2012/07/07/y-day-at-the-bowl-1963-the-beach-boys-surfaris-the-routers-the-challengers-past-daily-pop-chronicles/.

30. "The Story Behind the Success of the Beach Boys, *Teen Life*, 18.

31. "The Lord's Prayer" holds special significance for me. In high school, my friend and classmate Bob Noguera, who put his encyclopedic knowledge of music to good use every weekend working at a record store in the Village, asked if I ever heard "The Lord's Prayer" by the Beach Boys. My brother and I then had every Beach Boys' album ever made, so I told Bob I thought he was mistaken. The Beach Boys had never recorded "The Lord's Prayer." The following Monday, Bob presented me with a 45 rpm record of "Little Saint Nick," egging me on, "Go ahead, turn it over." Well, sure enough, "The Lord's Prayer." Whoever heard of releasing a song on a B side and never using it on an album? My brother and I rejoiced that afternoon at a nearly ten-year-old new-to-us Beach Boys song. And that sent me on a quest. A quest to find every Beach Boys single, B side, rare recording, tape, well, the list goes on and on. For more than thirty years, Bob owned the much-beloved Strider Records on Jones Street in the Village. Whenever I see Bob, I remind him he's responsible for me collecting the Beach Boys. He responds, with a laugh and a smile, "Well, don't hate me for that." Of course, we both know nothing could be further from the truth.

32. Craig Dougherty, "DISC-ussion: Dick Dale in Surfing Classic," *Long Beach Independent*, October 25, 1963, 24.

33. Chuck Harter and Alan Boyd, "Virginia Jardine Interview," *Endless Summer Quarterly*, December 1995, 10.

34. Bill Wagner, interview by author, November 2007.

35. Judy Bowles, interview by author, January 22, 2011.

36. Ibid.

Chapter 24

1. Barney Hoskyns, "Mister Optimism," *Uncut*, March 2008, 64.

2. "The True Story Behind the Beach Boys' Classic Song 'Warmth of the Sun,'" *Forgotten Hits*, http://forgottenhits.com/the_story_behind_the_warmth_of_the_sun.

3. Jodi Gable, interview by author, March 19, 2012.

4. "Muscle Beach Party" was similar in structure and harmonies to "Car Crazy Cutie" and "Pamela Jean." "Surfer's Holiday" was a rewrite of "Ride Away," which Brian produced with Bob and Sheri at Radio Recorders on January 18, 1963, perhaps as a demo for Aldon Music. A one-sided, three and one-half minute *Muscle Beach Party* EP (American International, A01), pressed at Alco as a Special Lobby and Intermission Record, was mailed to radio stations to promote the film, which opened March 25, 1964.

Coda

1. Letter from E. Shain, manager, music licensing, Buena Vista Pictures Distribution, Inc., to Paul Politi, Original Sound Entertainment, dated May 21, 1990.

2. Declaration of Paul Politi, January 8, 2001, Submitted in Opposition to the OSC Re: Preliminary Injunction, *Brother Records, Inc. v. Bradley S. Elliott*, Case No. CV-00–13314 (C.D. Cal.).

3. Ibid.

4. Neil Umphred, "The Beach Boys on Compact Discs, Still Cruisin' After All These Years," *Goldmine*, June 1, 1980, 28.

5. Paul Urbahns, *The Beach Boys, Lost & Found, 1961–1962* DCC compact disc, DZS-054, 1991, liner notes.

6. Letter from Steve Hoffman to Paul Urbahns, undated.

7. Steve Hoffman, Music Corner, Steve Hoffman Music Forum, November 19, 2012, http://forums.stevehoffman.tv/threads/what-were-the-first-issues-of-the-beach-boys-morgan-candix-tapes.301773/#post-8257738.

8. Letter from Steve Hoffman to Paul Urbahns, undated.

9. Paul Urbahns's notes of telephone conversation with Bruce Morgan, August 24, 1990.

10. Letter from Paul Urbahns to Steve Hoffman, dated August 24, 1990.

11. Steve Hoffman, interview by author, December 7, 2011.

12. Ibid.

13. Ibid.

14. Ibid.

15. Ibid.

16. Ibid.

17. Letter from Steve Hoffman to Paul Urbahns, dated October 19, 1990.

18. Ibid.

19. Jim Zuckerman, interview by author, July 9, 2012.

20. Hoffman, interview.

21. Ibid.

22. Ibid.

23. Deposition of Alan Jardine, *Bruce Morgan v. Brian Wilson*, Case No. 00–13312 (C.D. Cal.).

24. Brad Elliott, *Surfin',* Varèse Sarabande Records, Compact Disc 302 066 085 2, 2000, liner notes.

25. Temporary Restraining Order; Order to Show Cause Re Preliminary Injunction, *Brother Records, Inc. v. Bradley S. Elliott*, Case No. CV00–13314 (C.D. Cal. January 8, 2001).

26. Order, *Bruce Morgan v. Brian Wilson*, Case No. 06–55825 (9th Cir. March 16, 2009).

Bibliography

Books

Abbot, Kingsley, ed. *Back to the Beach: A Brian Wilson and the Beach Boys Reader*. London: Helter Skelter, 2003.

_____. *The Beach Boys Pet Sounds: The Greatest Album of the Twentieth Century*. London: Helter Skelter, 2001.

Anthony, Dean. *The Beach Boys*. London: Crescent, 1985.

Badman, Keith. *The Beach Boys: The Definitive Diary of America's Greatest Band on Stage and in the Studio*. London: Outline, 2004.

Barbour, Ross. *Now You Know: The Story of the Four Freshmen*. Lake Geneva, WI: Balboa, 1995.

Barnes, Ken. *The Beach Boys: A Biography in Words and Pictures*. New York: Sire Books–Chappell Music, 1976.

Berle, Milton, with Haskel Frankel. *An Autobiography*. New York: Delacorte, 1974.

Blair, John. *The Illustrated Discography of Surf Music, 1961–1965*. Ann Arbor, MI: Pierian, 1985.

Blecha, Peter. *Sonic Boom: The History of Northwest Rock, from "Louie, Louie" to "Smells Like Teen Spirit."* Milwaukee: Backbeat, 2009.

Broven, John. *Record Makers and Breakers, Voices of the Independent Rock 'n' Roll Pioneers*. Chicago: University of Illinois Press, 2009.

Buskin, Richard. *Inside Tracks: A First-Hand History of Popular Music from the World's Greatest Record Producers and Engineers*, Foreword by Brian Wilson. New York: HarperCollins, 1999.

Carlin, Peter Ames. *Catch a Wave: The Rise, Fall & Redemption of the Beach Boys' Brian Wilson*. New York: Rodale, 2006.

Chidester, Brian, and Domenic Priore. *Pop Surf Culture: Music, Design, Film, and Fashion from the Bohemian Surf Boom*. Santa Monica, CA: Santa Monica, 2008.

Clark, Alan. *The Beach Boys: The Early Years*. National Rock and Roll Archives, 1993.

Coleman, Rick. *Blue Monday, Fats Domino and the Lost Dawn of Rock 'n' Roll*. Cambridge: Da Capo, 2006.

Cosar, Neil. *This Day in Music*. London: Collins and Brown, 2005.

Crowley, Kent. *Surf Beat: Rock and Roll's Forgotten Revolution*. New York: Backbeat, 2011.

Cunningham, Don, ed. *Add Some Music to Your Day: Analyzing and Enjoying the Music of the Beach Boys*. Cranberry Township, PA: Tiny Ripple Books, 2000.

Dachs, David. *Inside Pop, America's Top Ten Groups*. New York: Scholastic, 1968.

Dalley, Richard J. *Surfin' Guitars: Instrumental Surf Bands of the Sixties*, 2d ed. Ann Arbor, MI: Popular Culture, Ink, 1996.

Dawson, Jim, and Ian Whitcomb. *Rock Around the Clock: The Record That Started the Rock Revolution!* San Francisco: Backbeat, 2005.

Dawson, Jim, and Steve Propes. *45 RPM: The History, Heroes & Villains of a Pop Music Revolution*. San Francisco: Backbeat, 2003.

Dean, Anthony. *The Beach Boys*. New York: Crescent, 1985.

DeForest, G.A. *Beach Boys vs Beatlemania: Rediscovering Sixties Music*. United States: Booklocker.com, Inc., 2007.

Dixon, Walt, and Jerry Roberts. *Hawthorne*. Charleston, SC: Arcadia, 2005.

Doe, Andrew G., and John Tobler. *The Complete Guide to the Music of the Beach Boys*. London: Omnibus, 1997.

Elliott, Brad. *Surf's Up! The Beach Boys on Record, 1961–1981*. Ann Arbor, MI: Pierian Press, 1982.

Eubanks, Bob, with Matthew Scott Hansen. *It's in the Book, Bob!* Dallas: Benbella, 2004.

Gaines, Steven. *Heroes and Villains: The True Story of the Beach Boys*. New York: New American Library, 1986.

Gioia, Ted. *West Coast Jazz: Modern Jazz in California, 1945–1960*. Berkeley: University of California Press, 1992.

Guralnick, Peter. *Dream Boogie: The Triumph of Sam Cooke*. New York: Little, Brown, 2005.

_____. *Feel Like Going Home: Portraits in Blues and Rock 'n' Roll*. New York: Back Bay/Little, Brown, 1971.

Halberstam, David. *The Fifties*. New York: Villard, 1993.

Hall, Claude, and Barbara Hall. *This Business of Radio Programming*. New York: Billboard, 1977.

Hirsimaki, Eric. *Lima: The History*. Edmonds, WA: Hundman, 1985.

Hoffman, Frank, comp. *The Cash Box Singles Charts, 1950–1981*. Metuchen, NJ: Scarecrow, 1983.

Hoskyns, Barney. *Waiting for the Sun: A Rock 'n' Roll History of Los Angeles*. New York: Backbeat, 2009.

Hull, Geoffrey P. *The Recording Industry*. New York: Routledge, 2004.

Jackson, John A. *American Bandstand: Dick Clark and the Making of a Rock 'n' Roll Empire*. New York: Oxford University Press, 1997.

_____. *Big Beat Heat: Alan Freed and the Early Years of Rock & Roll*. New York: Schirmer, 1991.

Keane, Bob. *The Oracle of Del-Fi*. Los Angeles: Del-Fi International, 2006.

King, Carole. *A Natural Woman: A Memoir*. New York: Grand Central, 2012.

Lambert, Philip. *Inside the Music of Brian Wilson: The Songs, Sounds, and Influences of the Beach Boys' Founding Genius*. New York: Continuum, 2007.

Leaf, David. *The Beach Boys and the California Myth*. New York: Grosset & Dunlap, 1978.

Lees, Gene. *Portrait of Johnny: The Life of John Herndon Mercer*. New York: Pantheon, 2004.

_____. *You Can't Steal a Gift: Dizzy, Clark, Mel, and Nat*. New Haven: Yale University Press, 2001.

Lehmer, Larry. *The Day the Music Died*. New York: Schirmer, 1997.

Lhamon, Jr., W. T. *Deliberate Speed: The Origins of a Cultural Style in the American 1950s*. Washington: Smithsonian Institution, 1990.

Marsh, Dave, and Kevin Stein. *The Book of Rock Lists*. New York: Dell, 1984.

Martindale, Wink. *Winking at Life*. n.p.: Century Hill Books, 2000.

McParland, Stephen J. *Bull Sessions with the Big Daddy, Interviews with Those Who Helped Shape the California Sound*. New South Wales, Australia: CMusic, 2001.

_____. *The California Sound: An Insider's Story, the Musical Biography of Gary Lee Usher, Volume One*. New South Wales, Australia: CMusic, 2000.

_____. *Inception and Conception: From Hite Morgan to Nick Venet*. New South Wales, Australia: CMusic, 2011.

_____. *Our Favourite Recording Sessions: In the Studio with Brian Wilson and the Beach Boys*. New South Wales, Australia: CMusic Publishing, undated.

_____. *The Wilson Project*. Sydney, Australia: PTB Productions, 1991.

Merritt, Christopher, and Domenic Priore. *The Rise and Fall of Los Angeles' Space-Age Nautical Pleasure Pier*. Port Townsend, WA: Process, 2014.

Milward, John. *The Beach Boys Silver Anniversary*. Garden City, NY: Dolphin/Doubleday, 1985.

Nelson, Ken. *My First 90 Years Plus 3*. Pittsburgh: Dorrance, 2007.

Olesker, Michael. *Journeys to the Heart of Baltimore*. Baltimore: Johns Hopkins University Press, 2001.

Oppenheimer, Jerry. *Toy Monster: The Big, Bad World of Mattel*. Hoboken, NJ: John Wiley, 2009.

Osborne, James. *Lawndale*. Charleston, SC: Arcadia, 2006.

Passmore, Mark Thomas. *Dead Man's Curve and Back: The Jan and Dean Story*. n.p.: 1st Books Library, 2003.

Pegg, Bruce. *Brown Eyed Handsome Man: The Life and Hard Times of Chuck Berry*. New York: Routledge, 2002.

Preiss, Byron. *The Beach Boys: The Authorized Biography of America's Greatest Rock and Roll Band*. New York: Ballantine, 1979.

Ribowsky, Mark. *He's a Rebel: Phil Spector, Rock and Roll's Legendary Producer*. New York: Cooper Square, 2000.

Rodriguez, Aimee. *The Harris Company*. Mount Pleasant, SC: Arcadia, 2008.

Rusten, Ian, and Jon Stebbins. *The Beach Boys in Concert: The Ultimate History of America's Band on Tour and Onstage*. Milwaukee: Backbeat, 2013.

Schock, Harriet. *Becoming Remarkable: For Songwriters and Those Who Love Songs*. Nevada City, CA: Blue Dolphin, 1999.

Starr, Michael Seth. *Bobby Darin: A Life*. Lanham, MD: Taylor, 2004.

Stebbins, Jon. *The Beach Boys FAQ*. Milwaukee: Backbeat, 2011.

_____. *Dennis Wilson: The Real Beach Boy*. Toronto: ECW, 2000.

_____. *The Lost Beach Boy*. London: Virgin, 2007.

Stewart, Dick. *Eleven Unsung Heroes of Early Rock and Roll*. Sandia Park, NM: Lance Monthly, 2010.

Tobler, John. *The Beach Boys*. London: Hamlyn, 1977.

Whitcomb, Ian. *Rock Odyssey: A Chronicle of the Sixties*. New York: Limelight, 1994.

White, Timothy. *The Nearest Faraway Place, Brian Wilson, the Beach Boys, and the Southern California Experience*. New York: Henry Holt, 1994.

Whiting, Cecile. *Pop L.A.: Art and the City in the 1960s*. Berkeley: University of California Press, 2006.

Williams, Paul. *Brian Wilson & The Beach Boys: How Deep Is The Ocean? Essays and Conversations*. London: Omnibus, 1997.

Wilson, Brian, with Todd Gold. *Wouldn't It Be Nice: My Own Story*. New York: HarperCollins, 1991.

Wincentsen, Edward. *Denny Remembered: Dennis Wilson in Words and Pictures*. El Paso: Vergin, 1991.

Wise, Nick, ed. *The Beach Boys: In Their Own Words*. London: Omnibus, 1994.

Wright, Michael. *Guitar Stories, Volume 2*. Bismarck, ND: Vintage Guitar, 2000.

Selected Newspaper and Periodical Articles

Aronowitz, Alfred G. "The Dumb Sound." *Saturday Evening Post*, October 5, 1963

Dove, Ian. "Al Rejoins Beach Boys." *New Musical Express*, August 14, 1964.

Felton, David. "The Healing of Brother Bri." *Rolling Stone*, November 4, 1976.

Grigsby, John. "Al Jardine's UT Connection." *The Toledo Blade*, August 12, 1990.

Hirsimaki, Eric. "Super-Power Portraitist, Don Jardine: The Karsh of Lima." *Trains*, February 1977.

Nolan, Tom. "The Beach Boys: A California Saga. Part One: Mr. Everything." *Rolling Stone*, October 28, 1971.

_____. "The Beach Boys: A California Saga. Part Two: Tales of Hawthorne." *Rolling Stone*, November 11, 1971.

Sharp, Ken. "Rhapsody of Brian." *Record Collector*, November 2010.

Smucker, Tom. "The Critics Kept a Knockin but the Stars Kept a Rockin' (and the Choppin' Didn't Get Very Far)." *Creem*, July 1972.

White, Timothy. "Back from the Bottom." *New York Times*, June 26, 1988.

_____. "Still Waters Run Deep: A Child Is Father to the Band, the Return of Brian Wilson." *Crawdaddy*, June 1976.

_____. "Still Waters Run Deep, Part Two: A Child Is Father to the Band, the Return of Brian Wilson." *Crawdaddy*, July 1976.

U.S. Music Publications

Billboard
Cash Box
Cheetah
Crawdaddy
Creem
DISCoveries
Goldmine
Hit Parader
Music Vendor
Record World
Rolling Stone
Trouser Press
Variety

UK Music Publications

Disc and Music Echo
Melody Maker
Mojo
Music Now
New Gandy Dancer
New Musical Express
Record Collector
Record Mail
Record Mirror
Sounds
Uncut

Fanzines

Add Some Music (Editor, Don Cunningham).

BBFUN (Beach Boys Freaks United; Editor, Alice Lillie).

Endless Summer Quarterly (Editors, Lee Dempsey and David Beard).

Newsletters

The Collegian, Los Angeles City College, 1958–1959.

Cougar, Hawthorne High School, Hawthorne, California, 1958–1963.

Lion's Roar, Morningside High School, Inglewood, California, March 16, 1962.

Surface Noise, National Academy of Recordings Arts and Sciences, 1962–1964.

El Vaquero, Glendale Community College, 1962–1963.

The Warwhoop, El Camino Community College, Torrance, California, 1960–1966.

School Yearbooks

The Atinian, William Howard Taft High School, Woodland Hills, California, 1963.

Circle, Susan Miller Dorsey High School, Los Angeles, California, 1956–1959

El Molino, Hawthorne High School, Hawthorne, California, 1957–1962.

Torch, Torrance High School, Torrance, California, 1962.

Warrior, El Camino Community College, Torrance, California, 1961–1963.

Court Proceedings and Documents

Brother Records, Inc. v. Bradley S. Elliott and Bruce Morgan, Case No. CV-00–13314, United States District Court for the Central District of California; Case No. 06–56401, United States Court of Appeals for the Ninth Circuit.

Bruce Morgan v. Brian Wilson, Brothers Records, Inc., Al Jardine, and Bradley S. Elliott, Case No. CV-00–13312, United States District Court for the Central District of California; Case No. 06–55825, United States Court of Appeals for the Ninth Circuit.

Bruce Morgan v. Joseph Saraceno, Case No. BC093327, Superior Court of the State of California for the County of Los Angeles.

Declaration and Deposition Valerio Poliuto

Declaration, Deposition, and Affidavit of Nick Venet
Declaration of Averill C. Pasarow
Declaration of Paul Politi
Declaration of Richard K. Dix
Declaration of Russ Regan
Deposition of Alan Jardine
Deposition of Hite Morgan
Deposition of Mike Love
Hite B. Morgan v. Capitol Records, Inc. and Capitol Records, Inc. v. Brian D. Wilson, Dennis C. Wilson, Carl D. Wilson, David L. Marks and Michael E. Love, individually, and as members of the group performing as the Beach Boys, Civil Case No. 64–1044, United States District Court for the Southern District of California.
Hite Morgan v. Capitol Records, Inc., Case No. 860296, Superior Court of the State of California for the County of Los Angeles.
Morgan v. San Juan Record Company, Case No. 96–1916, United States District Court for the Central District of California.

Audio Recordings—The Beach Boys

The Alternate Surfin' Safari Album. Unsurpassed Masters Volume 1 (1962), Sea of Tunes, compact disc, C 9703, 1997 [unauthorized release].
The Alternate Surfin' U.S.A. Album. Unsurpassed Masters Volume 2 (1963), Sea of Tunes, compact disc, C 9703, 1997 [unauthorized release].
Christmas with the Beach Boys. Capitol Records, Inc. 72435 79765–2–7, 2004, compact disc.
Concert and *Live in London.* Capitol Records, 72435–31861–2–8, 2001, compact disc. Originally released 1990.
Endless Harmony Soundtrack. Compilation, Capitol Records 72434–96391–2–6, 1998.
Get the Boot, 2-CD set [unauthorized release].
Good Vibrations: Thirty Years of the Beach Boys. Compilation produced by Mark Linett, David Leaf, and Andy Paley. 5-CD set, Capitol Records CDP 0777 7 81295 2 3, 1993.
Hawthorne, CA, Birthplace of a Musical Legacy. Compilation by Mark Linett and Alan Boyd, 2-CD set, Capitol Records, CDP 72435–31583–2–3, 2001.
In the Beginning: The Garage Tapes. Sea of Tunes, 2-CD set, C 0759, 2007 [unauthorized release].
Jardine, Al. *A Postcard from California.* Robo Records, RRAJ0001, 2012, compact disc.
Lost & Found, 1961–1962. DCC Compact Classics DZS-054, 1991. Original recordings produced by Hite and Dorinda Morgan. Compiled and mastered for compact disc by Steve Hoffman.
Made in California, Capitol UME, a Universal Music Company, 6-CD box set, B0018509–02, released August 27, 2013.
Pet Projects: The Brian Wilson Productions. Compilation and annotation by Rob Finnis, Ace CDCHD 851, 2003, compact disc.

The Pet Sounds Sessions, EMI-Capitol Records, 4-CD box set, CDP 2 7243 8 37662 2 2, 1996.
The Smile Sessions, Capitol Records, 5-CD box set, 509990 27658 22, 2011.
Still I Dream of You. Rare Works of Brian Wilson. M&M Enterprise MMCD-409, 1993, compact disc.
Surfer Girl and *Shut Down Volume 2.* Capitol Records, CDP 7 93692 2, 1990, compact disc.
Surfin', Varèse Sarabande Records, 302 066 085 2, 2000, compact disc.
Surfin' Safari and *Surfin' U.S.A.* Capitol Records, CDP 7 93691 2, 1990, compact disc.
Ultimate Christmas. Capitol Records, Inc. 72434 95734 2 0, 1998, compact disc.

Audio Recordings—Other Artists

Cowabunga! The Surf Box Set. Compilation produced by John Blair and James Austin, 4-CD box set, Rhino Records, R272418, 1996.
The Four Freshmen. *The Four Freshmen.* Capitol Collectors Series. Capitol Records CDP 7 93197 2, compact disc, 1991.
The Four Preps. *The Four Preps: The Best of the Four Preps.* Collectables Records Corp., compact disc, COL-5673, CEMA S21–18991, 1996.
Hey, Beach Girls! Female Surf 'n' Drag 1961–1966. Compilation compact disc, Ace Records Ltd. CDCHD 1282, 2010.
The Honeys. *The Honeys Collectors Series.* Compilation produced and researched by Ron Furmanek. Liner notes by Steve Kolanjian. Capitol Records CDP 7 93193 2, compact disc, 1992.
The Honeys. *The Honeys Collection.* Executive Producer Gordon Anderson. Liner notes by Stephen J. McParland. Collectors' Choice Music 72435–29850–2–9, compact disc, 2001.
Jan & Dean. *The Complete Early Years.* Sparkletone, SP 99004, CCM-949, compact disc, 1995.
Jan & Dean. *The Complete Liberty Singles*, Collector's Choice Music, 2-CD set, 509992–26253–2–8, 2008.
The Lettermen. *The Lettermen.* Capitol Collectors Series, Capitol Records CDP 7 98537 2, compact disc, 1992.
Muscle Bustle: Classic Tracks from the Surf 'N' Drag Era. Compilation compact disc, Ace Records Ltd. CDCHD 533, 1994.

Radio Programs

Armed Forces Radio & Television Service, Department of Defense, Program P-8114, SSL-14806, Fall 1962.
"The Beach Boys." The Robert W. Morgan Special of the Week, Series III, Watermark, Inc., Hollywood, California, LP, March 21, 1978.
"Beach Boys." Solid Gold Scrapbook, The United

Stations Programming Network, LP, November 26–December 2, 1988.

"Beach Boys." The United Stations Programming Network, 3-LP, July 3, 1987.

"The Beach Boys, A California Saga." Produced by the PH Factor in Hollywood, Executive Producer Jim Hampton, Special Writing and Research by Jim Pewter and Scott Paton, Custom Music by Jodie Lyons, Announcer Don Bleu, ABC Radio Network, American Broadcasting Companies, 1980.

"The Beach Boys Story." Presented by Bob Harris, written and researched by Jeff Griffin, BBC Radio 1, original radio broadcast 1974, rebroadcast in 1976 with updated ending.

"The Beach Boys Story." Unistar Radio Programming, 4-LP, June 29–July 4, 1990.

"The Beach Boys Story." The United Stations Programming Network, 4-LP, June 30–July 4, 1989.

"Best Summers of Our Lives." Six-hour radio special narrated by Charlie Van Dyke and Wolfman Jack, produced by Audio Stimulations, Summer 1976.

"Carl Wilson Interview." Innerview, Show No. 6, 2-LP, 1976.

"Dick Clark Presents the Beach Boys." A Memorial Day Special Presented by the Mutual Broadcasting System, 3-LP, 1983.

"Mike Love Interview." Innerview, Series No. 4, Show No. 9, LP, 1978.

"Rocketing Rhythms." Armed Forces Radio & Television Service, Department of Defense, October 6, 1962.

"The Veterans Administration Presents Here's to Veterans." Program 866, LP, Winter 1962.

"The Veterans Administration Presents Soundtrack Five." Program 10, LP, Winter 1962.

"The Warmth of the Sun." One-hour radio special, Broadcast Window: May 19–29. Capitol Records promotional compact disc, 2007.

Video Programs

The Beach Boys: An American Band. Written and directed by Malcolm Leo. High Ridge Productions, 1985.

The Beach Boys 50, Doin' It Again. Written by Frank Haney, directed by John Anderson and Joe Thomas, DVD BEM 10001, David C. Levy Productions, 2012.

The Beach Boys Landmark Dedication Ceremony. Hawthorne Cable Television, 2005.

The Beach Boys Tour of Hawthorne. Hawthorne Cable Television, 2005.

Brian Wilson: A Beach Boys Tale. A&E Biography, 1999.

Brian Wilson, Songwriter, 1962–1969: Exploring Brian's Muse During a Decade of Dreams. Sexy Intellectual Production, 2010.

Endless Harmony: The Beach Boys Story, a Documentary. Directed by Alan Boyd. Delilah Films, 2000.

I Guess I Just Wasn't Made for These Times. Directed by Don Was. Artisan Entertainment, 1995.

Open Sky, Eight, Open Sky, 2005.

Selected Websites

bigvjamboree.com

bsnpubs.com

cougartown.com

esquarterly.com/bellagio/ (Andrew G. Doe and Ian Rusten)

jananddean.com

legendarysurfers.com

popculturefanboy.com

recordresearch.com (Joel Whitburn, Record Research)

reverbcentral.com (Phil Dirt)

silvertoneworld.net (Randy Holmes)

uncamarvy.com (Marv Goldberg Notebooks)

Index